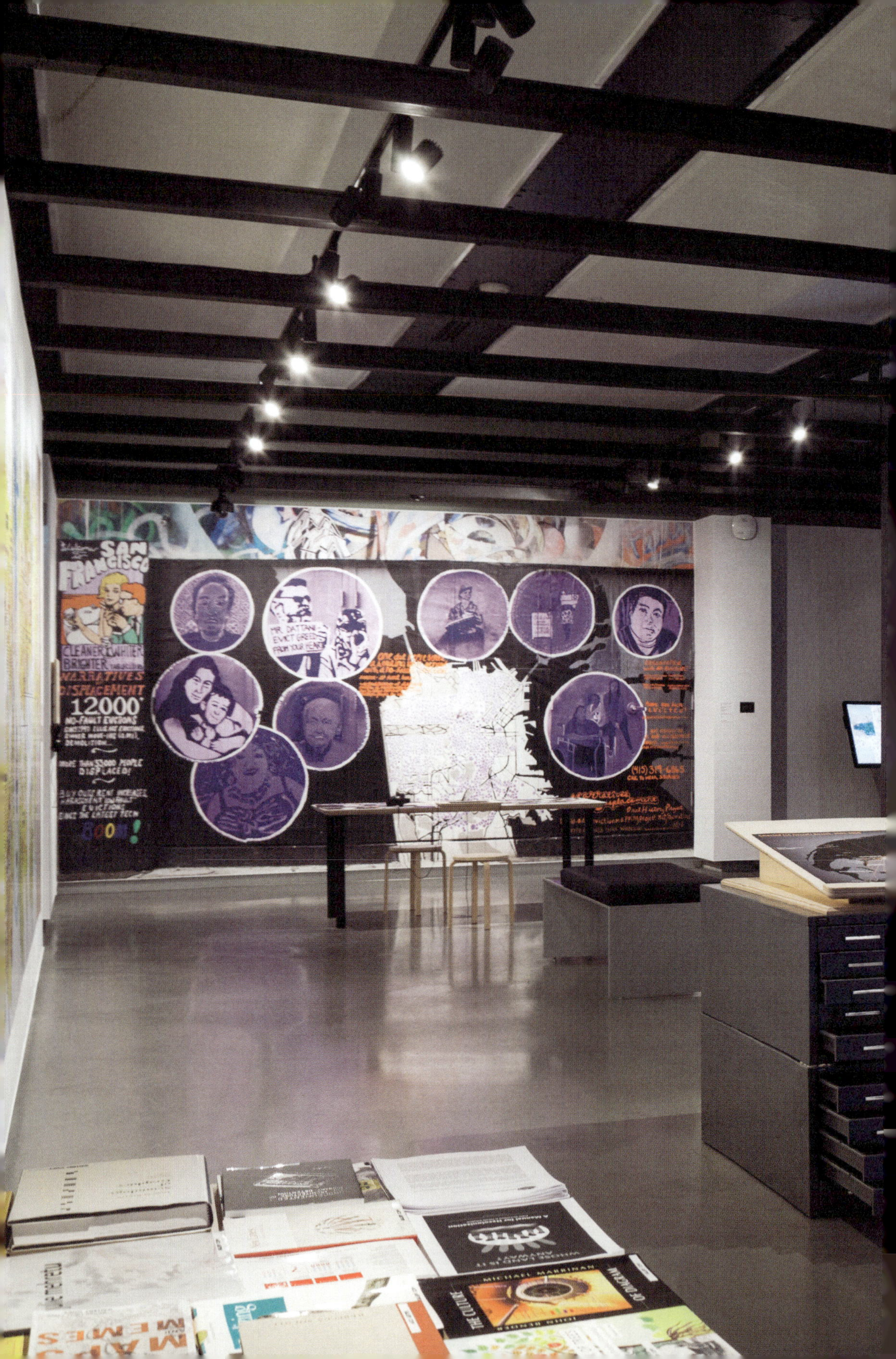

SAN FRANCISCO
CLEANER & WHITER & BRIGHTER
NARRATIVES of DISPLACEMENT
12000
NO-FAULT EVICTIONS
MR. DATTANI EVICT GREED FROM YOUR HEART
(415) 314-6863
MICHAEL MARRINAN
THE CULTURE

DIAGRAMS OF POWER

Visualizing, mapping, and performing resistance

Edited by Patricio Dávila

Contents

The earliest version of this essay was produced for the original *Diagrams of Power* (2018) at Onsite Gallery at OCAD University, Toronto.

Visualizing, Mapping, and Performing Resistance
by Patricio Dávila

When I draw with pencil and paper—an idea, a bicycle, a family tree, or a park—I draw a diagram that floats between my concept of a thing and the actual thing. I draw it for myself to help me think and to help me communicate to others. My diagram represents what I know and/or what I want to be true. It uses lines, colour, text and information that I have gathered to put forth a vision of what I think is important. The word diagram comes from the Greek—to write through. A diagram is not just a collection of gestures on a plane. It is not a static object. Since it

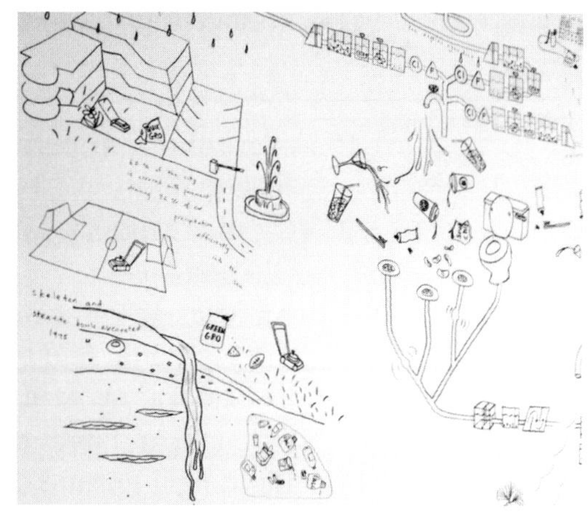

Detail. Jane Tsong, *Los Angeles River Ecology*, 2007. Courtesy of Lize Mogel and Alexis Bhagat.

works to organize thoughts and facts about the world, a diagram creates an effect—when I write across a page or a screen, I also inscribe a line through a landscape or between members of a group.

This may be counterintuitive, but a diagram also describes a non-visual thing. It describes an arrangement of things that are felt. For example, I am situated in a map of relations that include an employer, students, regulations, physical buildings, etc. This can be thought of as an abstract machine where different and interchangeable parts may operate directly or indirectly with one another. What is important to note is that these are structures that are flexible and mutable, and that reproduce in different instances with slightly different parts. Visualization involves several processes like gathering data from people and things, sorting and analyzing and re-analyzing data, representing data in a tangible form such as a map or graph and, most importantly, circulating this artifact among different people, experts, or organizations. Thus, as a process, visualization arranges people and things.

It is through these two meanings of diagram that I come to the idea of a diagram of power. It is both a visual work that represents and communicates ideas or data as well as a process that arranges bodies and things. In both of these dimensions, I note the way in which power can be depicted and exercised. In other words, a diagram can be used to show how power is distributed and it can also be the actual way in which power is distributed.

Maps do this kind of work. They are used to understand the features of a landscape and its inhabitants. From the beginning, maps were used to communicate the understanding of an inhabited territory as well as to transport knowledge of a remote, newly discovered place to a central governing place. In this way, maps have often been used to control a space and dominate a people.

Visualizations and maps are often viewed as depictions of truths produced by scientific inquiry or statistical analysis conducted by experts in universities or governments—this is how they draw some of their power. We forget they can never be fully objective. I am reminded of how theorist Donna Haraway warns us of the god trick that maps (and visualizations) can perform. They have a tendency to make us think that they are beyond human and therefore beyond reproach. Yet, we must ask who is doing the representing? Are they made by an objective and omniscient being that only sees truth and therefore cannot lie? Or are they situated in a specific place with a specific knowledge and experience, and

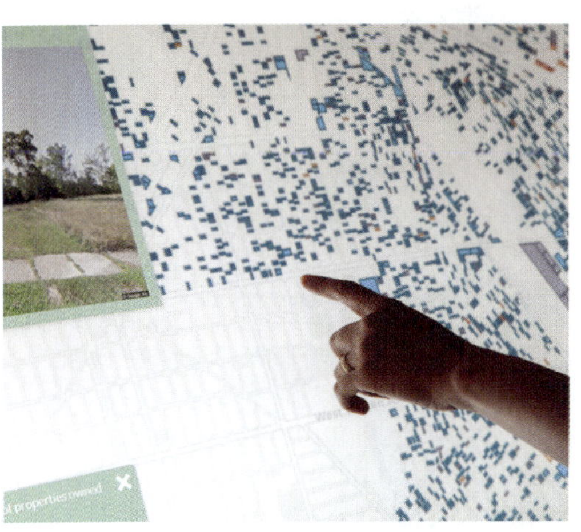

Installation View. Joshua Akers, *Property Praxis*, 2016/2018. Courtesy of Onsite Gallery. Photography by Yuula Benivolski.

committed to a specific agenda—all of which guides the gathering of data, the premise of the analysis and the style of the visualization?

Rather than perform a god trick, diagrams of power speak from a position—they are situated and they work against representations that hide other stories and other realities. They take extra care of what and who is represented, and who does the representing.

Margaret Pearce's work, *Coming Home*, does precisely this. Margaret has designed a map of Indigenous place names in Canada. A radical project in the sense that it performs the root work of grounding us live within an Indigenous territory and knowledge. The radical work is also performed through the

respect given to the traditional Indigenous knowledge keepers of place names. Margaret's map decentres the dominant idea of Canada as English and French coded territory by reinscribing the names that existed before settler colonization and continue to exist today. She assembles knowledge and thereby forms relations between herself as a cartographer and the many Indigenous communities throughout Turtle Island.

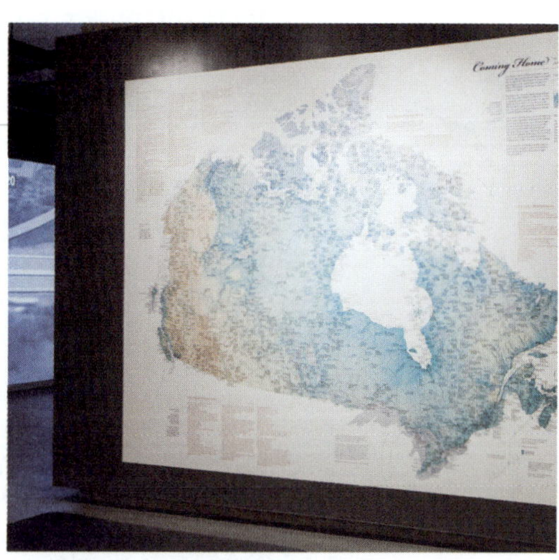

Installation View. Margaret Pearce, *Coming Home to Indigenous Place Names in Canada*, 2017. Courtesy of Onsite Gallery. Photography by Yuula Benivolski.

Laura Poitras' *O'Say Can You See* is another diagram performed. It sets up a relation between those who witnessed the rubble of the World Trade Towers after 9/11 and those captured in the War on Terror. Laura helps us see and perhaps feel part of the power relation that is performed—the implication of passive witnesses of a very public event in covert military action. Through this work I view mapping and visualization as a media practice that acts critically and not just affirmatively. All the designers and artists in this exhibition either challenge a dominant idea or unearth hidden knowledge. They present evidence by assembling data, images and/or personal accounts into cohesive wholes to be explored. The arrangement of evidence is a particular task that diagrams, as visualizations, are particular adept at doing. *The Ayotzinapa Case*, a work by Forensic Architecture, functions in this way as it assembles eyewitness accounts, social media posts, police reports and many other sources that relate to the disappearance and murder of 43 university students in Iguala, Mexico in 2014.

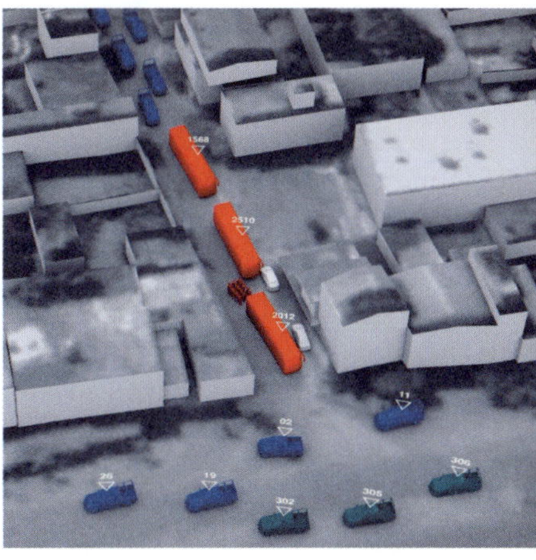

Still. Forensic Architecture, *El Caso De Ayotzinapa (The Ayotzinapa Case)*, 2017. Courtesy of the artist.

Part of acting critically involves resisting narratives used to displace, control, or forget. For example, the Argentine collective Iconoclasistas, formed by Julia Risler and Pablo Ares, uses a mappa mundi (a medieval world map) to reverse a dominant understanding of ownership. In their work *¿A quién pertenece la tierra? / Who owns the land?* they have made two strategic choices to resist deep-seated assumptions. First, they flip the North Pole and the South Pole in their map in order to challenge the intuition that north is up and south down—more precisely that the Global South is at the bottom of the Global North, a technique famously used by artist and theorist, Joaquín Torres-García. Second, Iconoclasistas use what is commonly referred to as the Gall-Peters projection which includes the characteristic elongated look of land masses—an attempt to accurately represent countries of the Third World which are often depicted erroneously as equal in size to European countries. These strategies make sense to me as tools for radical pedagogy informed by their practice which revolves around the use of mapping in popular education, collaboration and community-led research. Their critical mappa mundi performs this function, it works as an educational tool to engage viewers and challenge unquestioned assumptions—in *¿A quién pertenece la tierra?/Who owns the land?*, they ask who really owns what.

Ownership and relationships that form networks of power are complex and notoriously difficult things to make visible. Power through governmental or corporate entities, or through capital flow or military force, are largely felt when they intersect our everyday life but hard to see as lines of direct relations—especially at their global scale. Bureau D'Études is not daunted by this scale or complexity and aims to make these connections through their *World Government* maps. Through successive iterations, they create more comprehensive documents of global finance and governmental control.

Visualizations of global scale dynamics can be complex and demand an analytical approach yet when I look at Julie Mehretu's work I find instead the aesthetic and expressive dimension of global movement, history and flows. I read her large-scale paintings and prints as both diagrams and as landscapes. They incorporate image as data to influence the structure and feeling of her works. Her marks on the canvas work as vectors and as trails of movement. Her drawings often evoke rudimentary maps of ambiguous entities in a territory either migrating or gathering. In contrast to these modes for which she is very well known, one of her works, *Minneapolis and Saint Paul are East African Cities*, is particularly interesting due to its digital, interactive and participatory nature. Working in collaboration with Ethiopian and Eritrean youth living in the USA, Julie mapped their stories onto the city's territory. While I find that there are visual similarities between this

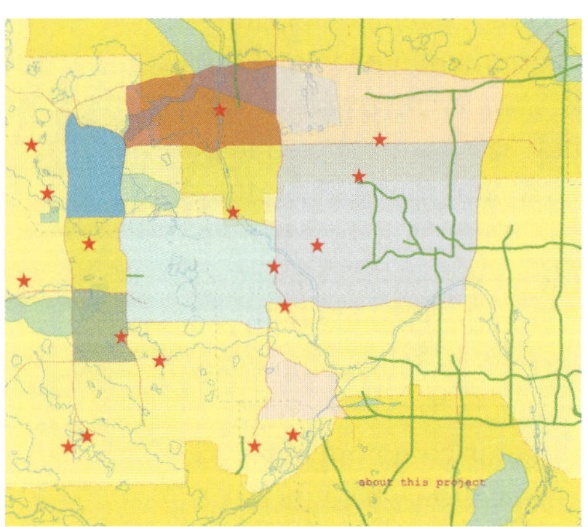

Still. *Minneapolis and St. Paul are East African Cities* website for Julie Mehretu residency, designed by entropy8zuper!, 2003. Courtesy www.walkerart.org

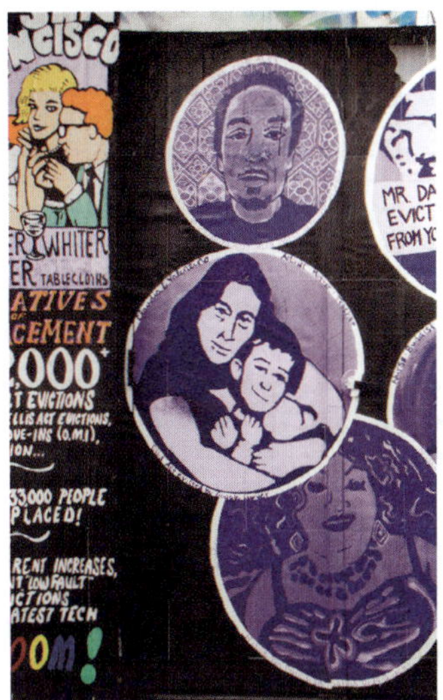

Detail. *Mural in Clarion Alley*, 2015
Courtesy of the artist. Photography
by Carla Wojczuk.

work and some of her more well-known works, there is also a conceptual bridge here that links her use of the diagram and map to evoke a feeling and insert a narrative. Participation in the mapping and telling of stories situated in a specific space also constitutes a diagram. In Julie's project, the diagram involved the represented, in this case the youth, in a process of representing, in this case the digital interactive map. This is an attempt to distribute power amongst the participants via their choices of what to tell and how to tell it.

Maps are often good vehicles to engage community members and visualize their lived experience. Groups like the Anti-Eviction Mapping Project, take a similar approach with their maps that tell the story of resisting displacement through geo-located data and survivor stories. In fact, they make participation even more meaningful by conducting other activities such as interviews, events, creating murals and zines. While the premise is a mapping project, this group, sponsored by the San Francisco Tenants Union, amplifies the positive effects of mapping and visualizing through activities directly aimed at representing and supporting residents.

Maps, diagrams and visualizations are both artifacts and processes. They are tools that tell a story, and create ways of bringing people and things together in the telling of that story. The outcomes are often visualized so that they can be viewed and inspected, but also performed so that they can be heard and felt. Evidence that other realities exist is presented through compelling forms. An exhibition like *Diagrams of Power* shows the wide variety of ways in which different people engage in this type of practice. Each designer, artist, cartographer, geographer, researcher and activist demonstrates a commitment to using this mode to tell inconvenient stories that upset and resist the status quo.

Dialogues One— Intersections in Indigenous Mapping, Feminist Visualization, and Community-Building

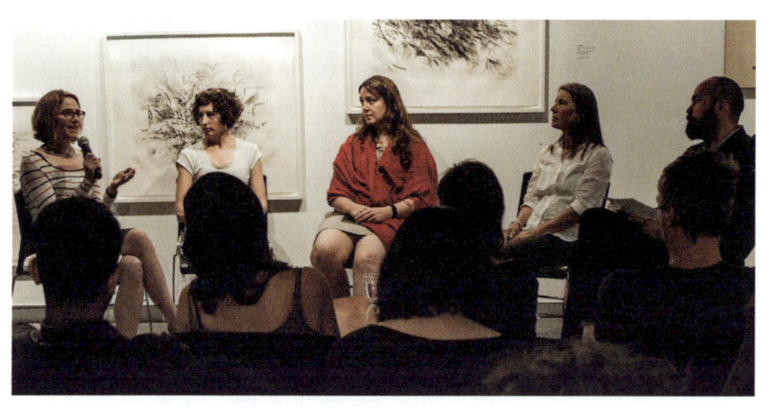

(Left to Right) Catherine D'Ignazio, Lize Mogel, Eliana Macdonald, Margaret Pearce, Patricio Dávila.

Catherine D'Ignazio, Eliana Macdonald, Lize Mogel, Margaret Pearce

<u>Friday, July 13, 2018 at 11 AM</u>
<u>OCAD University, Toronto, Canada</u>
<u>Onsite Gallery, 199 Richmond St. W.</u>

We will talk about a mistrust of maps since they have often been used as a tool of colonialism, surveillance and control. Data, maps and visualizations are too often the tools for extracting knowledge in order to be used in spite or against a community. We will explore ways in which mapping as a process, alternatively, can be a generative act that can help represent and build community. This leads to questions like: how do we make sure we are accountable to the people and territories we visually represent?; and can maps even help us heal?

Lisa Smith

OCAD University acknowledges the ancestral and traditional territories of the Mississaugas of the New Credit, the Haudenosaunee, the Anishinaabek and the Huron-Wendat, who are the original owners and custodians of the land on which we stand and create.

Patricio Davila

Do you have a recent project you can tell us about that uses space: that incorporates space, community and representation in how it was articulated, and how it was created?

Catherine D'Ignazio

I'll talk about an old project from 10 years ago that I believe fits here. I was a part of a small art performance collective called the Institute for Infinitely Small Things. We had this idea that the city should be open source. So what would it mean for the city to be read-write? Meaning, specifically, why are places named the way that they are, and who did they represent, and whose history do they represent, and whose history do they leave out? So we started in our own hometown at that time of Cambridge, Massachusetts, which if you know Cambridge, Massachusetts, that's where Harvard University is. It's where MIT is. So, who might you imagine all the streets are named after? Anyone want to guess?

Yeah. White men, mostly affiliated with Harvard, actually. MIT representation isn't there. We said, "Well, actually the contemporary social reality of Cambridge is super different now, and there are many people's stories and social uses of space that aren't reflected there." So we had a two-year re-naming campaign, where we staged these re-naming parties and asked anybody who wanted to come re-name any part of Cambridge that they wanted to. Collectively, we collected over 300 new names for the city of Cambridge, and then we published a map called *The City Formerly Known as Cambridge*, and then distributed that to everybody who participated. If the city were like Wikipedia, and we could all be authors of the landscape, this is what it would've look like in 2008. If we did it again now, it would probably look quite different.

I see resonance with a lot of the works in this show in terms of how does one use the mode of mapping to challenge what are sometimes the hegemonic structures that are inscribed in the landscape. Whose voices do we see in the landscape and how do we challenge those?

Lize Mogel
One important aspect of this project for me was it both embraced and critiqued the socio-economic structure of naming. You had to pay to play, to add a placename to the map. The pricing started out at, what, five cents?

Catherine D'Ignazio
25 cents.

Lize Mogel
That's not very expensive, but it's an acknowledgement of how many places get named. Which is about power and money. If you give $5 million to an institution, they will name something significant after you. So that's why there's a museum named for David Geffen and there's a public plaza named for the Koch brothers. So, the Mapping Cambridge project had a nice twist on the role of money. Catherine, is it correct that you could outbid somebody?

Catherine D'Ignazio
Yep.

Lize Mogel
So you could pay 25 cents to name a street after your aunt, but then somebody else could pay 30 cents to re-name the street. What was the highest amount someone paid?

Catherine D'Ignazio
The highest was $5.25. (Laughter) People would get mad about this project, because they'd be angry at us for doing a community art project that made them pay, and then we would tell them, collectively, we made $24 doing the project. So it's not like we're in it to make the big bucks of money, but yeah, there was somebody who paid $5 flat out to reserve a street—she re-named Harvard Street to Radcliffe Street, because she felt like Ann Radcliffe really got the short end of the stick. She donated most of the money to found Harvard University, but has only one or two things named after her.

Margaret Pearce
You also had project expenses. So it's not like the $24 was right into your pocket.

Catherine D'Ignazio
We used it to buy beer. (Laughter)

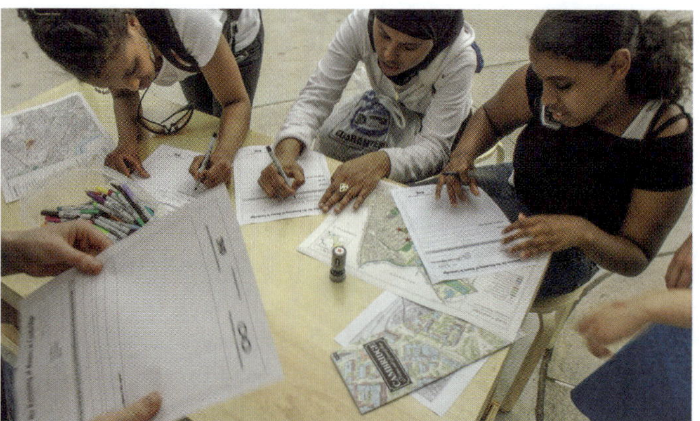

Youth Renaming Cambridge. Image courtesy of Catherine D'Ignazio. Photography by Lino Ribeiro.

<u>Margaret Pearce</u>

Catherine, I used your map to inspire my students because it was such an early example, and no one was doing this with as much joy and embracing the idea of addressing the politics of place naming directly with maps. I bought a copy from you and brought it right into the classroom, put it on the wall, and the students loved it.

<u>Margaret Pearce</u>

About the *Coming Home* map being shown in *Diagrams of Power*: I would love to have a conversation with anyone in the audience about the map, since it is about Canada and, except for one fortuitous trip to Vancouver Island, I created it entirely from home in Maine, USA.

<u>Margaret Pearce</u>

Coming Home to Indigenous Place Names in Canada was a commission in 2016 to mark Canada's 150th birthday at the Canadian-American Center at the University of Maine. The director there was very excited. He said "You just finished collaborating on place names with Penobscot Nation. We really want to do a place names map for Canada's 150."

And I said, "No, no way. I don't have the knowledge or the expertise. I don't have the right to do that and work on those names." So I tried to find other topics to work on, while talking with people and reading about the critique around this problematic celebration of Canadian sovereignty. Over time, I began to think I could do something if I just went really slow and paid attention. However, I still didn't feel that working

with place names would be appropriate—when I spoke about it to a long-time friend and collaborator on place names, and she gave me this completely disappointed look, and said, "When are place names never the topic? They are the topic. They are central." That was the first of many hundreds or thousands of little moments where someone guided me and re-directed me in small steps towards this map.

Coming Home is about scale: listening to what people are saying about what's important to them, and the scale at which those values and issues reside. Paying attention to scale resists this ongoing notion that maps are inventories, which is a totally colonial cartographic tradition. "Maps as inventories" is a very effective tool of erasure, by creating narratives that imply that everything is in the map, and nothing else exists. This construct makes us forget that story and narrative, whether visual or written or otherwise embodied, resides at different scales for different reasons, at different temporal scales and at different spatial scales. Paying attention to scale was a main process in making this map, and it's something we're constantly working on.

<u>Eliana Macdonald</u>

The type of mapping I would like to talk about is related to Margaret's work. It's use and occupancy mapping, or what is sometimes called traditional use studies. It's where people go in and decide what questions they want to ask their community members about how they use the land. It can be everything from place names to habitat for different types of animals that are valuable, along with spiritual places, cultural practices, birth sites, death sites. I've participated in a few of these, both from just the cartographic side as well as doing the actual studies. It's a powerful, interesting process.

It's also expensive—you're sitting down with elders who have a lot of knowledge of the land, along with hiring people who have a social science background to formulate the questions. So it's often paid for by industry or potentially government, but they also form the basis for resistance. "The master's tools will not tear down the master's house", has been percolating in my brain since Patricio mentioned that. Occupancy maps are really wonderful to represent people's experiences of the land and to have the honour to make that visible.

Lize Mogel
I just want to mention that this is the first time any of us have been on an all-female panel about maps.

Margaret Pearce
And women at the last minute.

Catherine D'Ignazio
Right. Sometimes, token women, sometimes included at the last minute, but sometimes included really specifically to have a critical voice, because all of us do work that's very different from conventional cartography. So we're really excited to be here together, with Patricio, of course.

Lize Mogel
The project I've got in Diagrams of Power is called Performing Infrastructure (New York City Water Supply). It's part of a larger project which explores the politics of the relationship between New York City and the place where most of its water comes from: a rural community 240 km north called the Catskills. It's a 125-year-old relationship, and extraordinarily complicated, with a lot of history that was sometimes traumatic for the Catskills. The Catskills lives this relationship every day, but it is absolutely invisible to New York City residents.

Lize Mogel
The relationship over time has become more collaborative and more about compromise, but there's still a lot of generational bitterness towards the city. The city also has quite heavy-handed policy around what you can do in the Catskills, how you can develop and use the land. It has to do with keeping the water supply for New York City very, very clean and avoiding having to build a filtration plant that would cost billions of dollars. So there is this very specific and complex relationship that's absolutely invisible to people who live in New York City. Part of what I'm trying

to do is make that more visible.

For the first two-plus years of this project, I did research and worked on building relationships in the Catskills, gaining trust in a place where I'm an outsider. Because I live in NYC and drink Catskills water, I do have a connection. But I don't necessarily belong.

So this is the preliminary work for a long-term engagement that will probably last at least another five years. The first project I've completed is the *Performing Infrastructure* workshop, which introduces people to the physical and social geography of the water system. The City of New York is the public face of the water supply. They publish a single map to represent the water system. This map is limited—it only shows geography and scale.

I am using more embodied strategies to break into this map, and put the relationship between the two ends of the water system at the center of the representation. So participants in the workshop/performance use their bodies to make a "human map" of the water supply. They each play a part in the system, with a little help from some water system cos-play. They literally connect with each other by holding hands and vocalizing the water flowing through the system.

Patricio Davila

So far, a few ideas have come up around how these projects think about its participants. My next question, which has been on my mind for several years and gave fruit to many choices I made in this exhibition, is how do we make sure that we're accountable to the people and territories that we're visually representing? Are there conditions, protocol or practical approaches around ensuring respect? These diagrams work against de-territorialization, or moving and shifting around globally without any further connection to what they are purporting to represent. How do we maintain these vital connections to the people and places we represent?

Eliana Macdonald

It's not ice cream. A lot of my work is private. It doesn't actually make it into the public sphere. So working with communities, it is produced for them, with them. I feel more like a tool that they use to make their experiences visible. A tool that's sometimes used is creating a data sharing agreement. In general I love getting feedback from the community, when people tell me what they like to see. I love hearing people's experiences of what I create, because everybody has different viewpoints. When I do get to publish people's work, or the work that I produce for people, it's always with feedback first.

Catherine D'Ignazio

To add onto that, how do we avoid an extractive model of production. It speaks to what Margaret mentioned about how problematic it is when maps are seen as inventory. Even in a fun, silly project like re-naming Cambridge, there was the responsibility of being accountable to the people who were contributing information. Even though inputs were often, "Oh, I'm going to name this street after my dog", people were still contributing a name, their creative effort, and a personal narrative.

At the back of the map, everyone's story for why they re-named the place is included... in very small print, because there were a lot of stories. We also collected folks' addresses so we could share the map back with them. This speaks to how the artifact or the output of this process circulate and to whom, and who does it create value for? Certainly, it has circulated for me and for the other members of the Institute for Infinitely Small Things, in that we get to talk about it at events like this and show it on our websites. But if it were only to serve that purpose, that would be a bummer. Recently, we wrote everybody and asked them if they remembered the project and what they thought about it, and we got some really interesting responses back. So, even though it's a very lightweight, loose conception of community, there were ways that we shared back and touched back and tried to keep listening and keep the dialogue open.

A criteria for me going forward is thinking about relationships. How does the collection process, the production process, and the design process facilitate the meaningful, authentic, ongoing production of relationships? For me, that is at the forefront of my mind as I think about data projects and data visualization. If it's not bridging relationships and deepening meaningful relationships, then maybe it's not doing anything.

<u>Eliana Macdonald</u>
That's a good point. After we finish a use and occupancy study, we create map biographies. Participants not only get summary maps of all of the berry picking places and all of the hunting sites we explore, but also a map biography of everything that people created. Everyone gets copies at the end.

<u>Lize Mogel</u>
We all practice participatory action research in some way, formally or informally, by involving people in creating the thing that then is used by them in one way or another. For me, a project that speaks to this is the *Sharjah Info Cart/City Map*, a participatory mapping project that I did with Alexis Bhagat in the United Arab Emirates, for the Sharjah Biennial. We asked about 500 people living in Sharjah to tell us about the place in which they live. We made a map based on their responses, and then distributed it back to them.

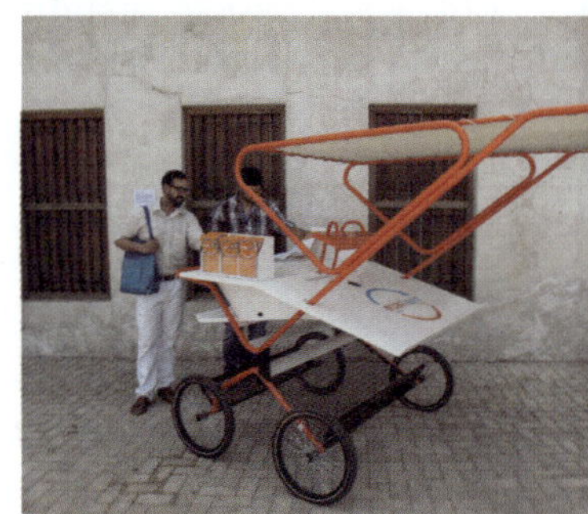

However, there were barriers to facilitating deeper conversations with participants. One of them was a monarchic government which stifles free speech. Another was that we were outsiders, and there for only a short time—this is one of the drawbacks of working within an art institutional framework, that your time is

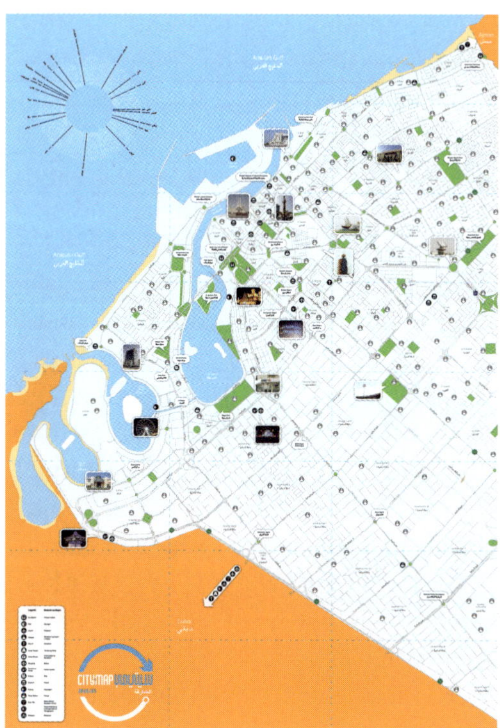

Sharjah Info Cart/City Map, 2011, Lize Mogel and Alexis
Bhagat. Images courtesy of the artists.

limited by the length of, for example,
the exhibition.

The feedback we did get from
people we showed the map to was that
they were really thrilled to see their experiences represented in this new way.
So that has a certain amount of value.

Lize Mogel

Catherine, what you said about making
your process an ongoing relationship
resonates with me. It leads me to a
question for Margaret around the static
nature of the paper map, and how you
negotiate that. I think of maps as temporal–you have to continually remake
them to represent how places and politics are in flux.

Margaret Pearce

I would love to explore that. Would you
say that a painting is somehow problematic because it's fixed on canvas?

Lize Mogel

Yes and no. Paintings, or maps, can
become reinvigorated by context, right?
You can re-insert them into the present
moment, so that they look backwards
and forwards at the same time. So they
can be both static, and not. For example, many of the maps in *An Atlas
of Radical Cartography* were made in
response to G.W. Bush era policies– the
increasing use of extraordinary rendition and widespread surveillance, for
example. These practices gained a lot
of traction right after 9/11, but they are
still happening today and it's important
to keeping talking about them.

Margaret Pearce

I agree we need to always be looking
and re-looking and remaking maps as
cartographic theorists. It's really important to make them the same way we
write a book. The same way we make
a painting. The same way we make any
kind of narrative and give it closure,
for the next person to pick it up from
there and move it forward. I came to
cartography from writing, and I see
cartography as just writing in a different
form. Many of the names on *Coming
Home* are already changing– people are
always working on the names. Many
others didn't share names because they
continue to work on the names and do
not want anything in print.

Some other names I came by through websites. When I asked for permission for those names, sometimes the request would be rejected, and people would tell me the names have changed since they were posted.

In terms of accountability, I feel that asking permission before anything happens is really important. Also communicating intentions right from the beginning as clearly as possible, as there so many ways that miscommunication will inevitably arise down the road, because we're discussing their names long-distance.

It's also important to be clear about what happens afterwards. I've signed contracts that stated the need to destroy the excel file of place names from my work computer after the work was done. It's not mine to keep—the things we're mapping are not ours. That can be a hard lesson, because you are proud of the things you work on and want the work to stay. I'm constantly relearning that it doesn't belong to me.

In Indigenous protocols, reciprocity, responsibility, respect, and relationality are important values to foreground. They are also much a part of feminists' protocols. Accountability is knowing when and where to make those conditions happen, and it changes with each context.

<u>Catherine D'Ignazio</u>
That's super interesting, I'd love to talk

more about Indigenous values and protocol. Another accountability structure that came to my mind is from a participatory design project we organized called *Make the Breast Pump Not Suck Hackathon*. We had 300 people redesign the breast pump with us, and also redesign ideas around access to and choice around, breastfeeding, breastfeeding information, education, and support in a US context. We had a year-long lead-up process to foreground and center the voices of those who are most marginalized by the current US model of the healthcare system in relation to breastfeeding, being women of colour, LGBTQ parents and low wage workers. Factors include healthcare policy and family leave policy.

Being cognizant that the team leading the project was primarily white, we installed an advisory board and got amazing leaders in the space including community organizers, folks in nonprofits and so on who could hold us accountable as the leadership team. We scheduled regular check-in points where we were able to run things by them and catch many of our own blind spots in trying to produce something for people who we are not. That was highly useful for us to not screw up internally, and avoiding screwing up as much publicly. This might be a useful strategy if a map maker is not part of the community you're working with to make that map.

<u>Lize Mogel</u>

I'll add one more thing to the account-ability checklist. Discussion is time, so as an artist, one thing that's always been frustrating to me is the lack of time and resources in general. It is difficult to do this kind of socially or community-engaged artistic practice in a US context, where there is much more focus on the market. A lot of my work has been in the context of commissions or exhibitions—I'll get a really nice invitation to visit and interpret something in two weeks. The Sharjah project was six months, and that still wasn't enough to do that project really well. We would have needed to live there a year or more, to really build relationships with people.

Walking the Watershed is independent and has the most minor funding; I simply began the project after thinking about it for a couple of years. So far, it's been two years of talking to people, finding out how life is in the Catskills, how the water supply affects it. It's also been building relationships on all sides, not only with organizations in the Catskills, but also with the city agency. Especially when you're working from the outside, this takes an extraordinary amount of time. Especially as an outsider, how can you actually contribute something that's of value?

<u>Eliana Macdonald</u>

I wanted to follow up on one thing Margaret mentioned. Destroying data is one part of the process; the other is the keeping of data for communities and giving it back. At our small organiza-tion, we now have over three terabytes of data stored on our servers. It's also about ensuring you're returning it to the right people.

<u>Patricio Davila</u>

Just to build on this last point—this idea of raw data being a construct. All data is cooked in a sense, in that it's situated. It comes from a place, and it has frames around how it was created. If we can agree on data as not being neutral or necessarily objective, should we strive for more neutrality and objectivity, or should we strive for something else? I'm setting it up as a dichotomy as a starting point—if you have other ways of thinking about it, please share. How do we deal with the promise of data as truth?

<u>Margaret Pearce</u>

I'll start with the data part. I'm already feeling shame for using the word 'data' because I try to not to ever use it unless I'm truly working on numbers. Not everything should be counted. Sometimes it's disrespectful to count, because counting is a cultural value that's not always present. So to speak of people as data is a problem—it's problematic language that relates to extraction, data, mining...

<u>Patricio Davila</u>

Warehousing.

<u>Catherine D'Ignazio</u>

Cleaning.

Eliana Macdonald
Yes. What was your question about data?

Patricio Davila
Can we think of data in ways other than striving for more objectivity, more neutrality? I think your reminder that not everything should be counted is really valuable, because it sets up another paradigm of how we think about reality and representing things.

Margaret Pearce
Yeah. I think we need a feminist critique of visualization for that answer. Catherine?

Catherine D'Ignazio
My response to this question is yes. Because what passes for objectivity in our society is not actually objective at all. This is a familiar feminist critique of science in the Western context– the scientific studies, the so-called facts and the things that we count, number, and measure–these things are produced by a particular subset of our population, mostly white, mostly men. This is the subset that's determining what matters as data.

There's a famous cardiologist named Dr. Nieca Goldberg who wrote a book called *Women Are Not Small Men*. It talks about how in science women's bodies have been looked at this way— first, men's heart health will be studied, and then results will just be multiplied by 0.7, because women are apparently 70% percent the size of men. Dr. Goldberg's argument is that if we actually study women's bodies, we'll find that cardiovascular disease takes on a different epidemiology. So, in this way, we actually do need more objectivity. We need more representation in what passes for objectivity of all the people who are being left out of current objectivity.

If we were able to equalize who is at the helm of making, counting, and measuring decisions, then I think we would be counting and measuring different things, and in different ways. So, on the one hand, we really do need more objectivity. On the other hand, we need to think about how a society that counted and measured everything would not be the perfect society either.

So, there always needs to be some mechanisms of escape or re-imagination or resistance, because we will never arrive at the perfect socially-just power structure. There will always be inequality around who is wielding the tools of knowledge and against whom. So, we have to have ways of escaping and resisting and positing alternate worlds. And those often are not done with the language of objectivity.

I've been reading a lot of Patricia Hill Collins, a Black feminist scholar from the US. Her case is that in knowledge production, we need to value reason and emotion and ethics at the same time, and equally. Striving for pure objectivity and achieving totalizing information excludes these other ways of knowing that are emotional, care-based, ethical, grounded in duty and obligation, whether to people, land, or otherwise. These things that can't be captured if we're fetishizing objectivity and facts.

<u>Lize Mogel</u>

Catherine co-wrote a great essay about feminist data visualization. One idea she posits is about making visible the labor that goes into collecting and visualizing data.

There's also the myth of totality around data. So how do you visualize the gaps in the dataset, the missing data, the blank spots on the map? In an earlier version of the Bureau d'Études *World Government* project which is in the exhibition, they included lines of inquiry that would end with question marks, to say "we don't actually know."

I also want to point to the Anti-Eviction Mapping Project's mural on evictions in San Francisco, also in the exhibition. This project is both quantitative and qualitative. They collect data and produce maps and data visualizations about evictions; and they collect and publicize oral histories, people's stories about evictions. And use both of these for advocacy and organizing. The mural, which features hand-painted portraits of San Francisco residents, is reproduced full-scale in the exhibition, and the data graphics are displayed on a very small screen to the side. This curatorial choice emphasizes the importance of people, of personal narrative which is often dismissed as subjective, not "data." And that's a problem.

<u>Margaret Pearce</u>

Something that really interests me is dialogue. Thinking of mapping as dialogical is really central to my work. Now, all I want to do is work on climate. A piece that I don't see being addressed at all is moving through climate action together in a dialogical way. For example, the same units of time do not apply culturally across the globe. Visualizations can make all these unspoken assumptions visible. So, I'm curious if, in any of your projects, you have been thinking about data as multivocal narratives.

<u>Catherine D'Ignazio</u>

One of the principles that we have in the data feminism paper is embracing pluralism. I think that is adjacent to this polyvocality that you're talking about. I just saw an amazing keynote talk at a gathering about climate change, where the speaker talked about how narratives around climate change need to change. Based on his work from community organizing, he found most people found dominant narratives around climate change to be very alienating. These science-based narratives around how in the somewhat-distant future, gasses are going to be at a certain level, thus we should all care. What he was advocating for instead was narratives around why it matters for us to mobilize, grounded in a politics of solidarity, and immediate repercussions for wellbeing in the here and now for specific communities. There is a difference between the language of science and the language of care or solidarity or tradition.

<u>Eliana Macdonald</u>

Around the question of objectivity, we need more context for everything. Metadata is a word that we don't appreciate enough. I don't appreciate it enough…

Margaret Pearce

What's metadata?

Eliana Macdonald

Data about data—it describes a dataset. When you download spatial data, it will tell you it was produced at this scale, by this person, for these dates. But it could go further. It could say this was produced by a man, for this reason. Or it could say, this is all the data we couldn't collect. These perspectives are never acknowledged. I want metadata that says: here's what and who is not here, so when you're using this data, think about that. The presentation of a data set, even as raw data already erases many things, and there's no mechanism to question it.

Margaret Pearce

Missing metadata is a theme that runs through, I think, every project in this realm. In *Diagrams of Power*, it's alluded to through the surveillance imagery throughout.

Catherine D'Ignazio

We are writing about this in our book— what happens with the metadata, or the lack of. It doesn't provide a way of challenging the veracity of the data. In particular, when it comes to women or marginalized people, their bodies are literally not represented in that data accurately because often the collection environment is flawed. For example, there was an article from Wired Mag-

azine 10 years ago that made the argument, which is now still I think the reigning ideology, that data will speak for itself—meaning, just get the data and whatever the numbers show, that's the truth, right?

If you download data from the US department of Education about sexual violence on college campuses and visualize those numbers, the data implies the exact opposite of the truth. What the data implies is the places that seem to have high rates of sexual violence and rape are instead places with better policies and resources in place to create environments for survivors to come forward. If you don't have the context of how that data was collected, and its limitations, or if you don't understand the institutional and individual incentives to either report or not report, then you would tell an absolutely false story.

This is why metadata is just so important. I have my students write data biographies when they download a data set, then they do some due diligence and begin asking questions like, where is this from? Why do people collect it? What's it for? How is it used? Who is not there? What would be ideal, is that the collecting institution would express limitations and ethical considerations of the datasets. There are examples of where people have done this well, but in general metadata is underinvested in.

Patricio Davila

It strikes me that there is another decision to be made: should something be represented in the first place? Should something be collected? Should something be parsed and put up again? There is this notion that data and the collection of it is inherently a social good or an ethical imperative: the more you have, the more 'transparent' of a worldview we have. But sometimes, we don't want to be seen.

Margaret Pearce

To speak to the common ground between Indigeneity and feminism, no means no.

Eliana Macdonald

At Ecotrust Canada we support a lot of small boat fishermen to help coastal communities survive. On the Federal government side, Fisheries and Oceans Canada is committed to increasing marine protected areas on the west coast, however this affects the livelihood of these fishermen. Now there is a push to collect information from them: where are you fishing, when and how? There is a looming imperative to report this data: otherwise, marine-protected areas will be made to cut off your entire livelihoods, unless you give us your data to tell us where we can't. How can fishermen self-advocate in this time of electronic monitoring for fishermen, on behalf of fishermen?

Lize Mogel

We have to put a huge amount of trust in the mechanisms and the institutions that collect our data, whether we want it to be collected or not. It seems like the fishermen did not have a say in determining what data should be collected, how it should be collected, and how it was going to be used. What would that look like if this process was done in collaboration with fishermen? When an institution with power invites participation, it can change what data and data collection means, and the outcomes change.

There's a map in *An Atlas of Radical Cartography* made by Unnayan, an NGO of radical planners and architects working in Kolkata, India in the 1980s and 90s. They worked with informal communities who lived on the literal margins of the cities. Unnayan mapped these settlements in detail: on the map there are about a hundred little squares representing dwellings situated between a factory, an industrial canal, and railroad tracks. They then took this map to the planning department to say: there are people living here, so you should recognize them, provide services to them. In India at that time, if you had an address, you could receive ration cards, you could vote, you could have an official identity. And it was very important for the settlers Unnayan worked with to be visible in this way. On the other hand, there are many situations in which informal communities, for example refugee communities, don't want to be mapped, it would be dangerous for them to be "on the radar."

Catherine D'Ignazio

Another example of when and when not to map, although it has an unhappy ending. I was collaborating with Ofelia Rivas, an elder on the Tohono O'odham reservation on the southwest U.S. Mexico border. She told me about how the traditional lands of the O'odham straddle the U.S. Mexican border; although the reservation is formally only on the US side, people still live on both sides. In the Bush era, the US government erected a 700 mile fence which runs right through the O'odham's native land, cutting off access for those on the Mexican side off to services like healthcare. In Ofelia's backyard is the fence. When the government came to put up the fence, the O'odham organized to stop it from being built.

One of their arguments was, "you're putting this fence through all of these areas where the remains of our ancestors are here, and you can't dig these up". The U.S. Government replied, "Just give us the exact locations of all of these ancestor remains, and we'll just make sure that the fence doesn't go on top of them." However, this information is sacred information, and never under any circumstances can they divulge this information outside of their own community. They decided not to breach their traditions and customs; ultimately the fence was built, and it did dig up an overturn of ancestor remains, and the O'odham had to wage a legal battle for several years to get them returned.

It is an example of navigating the politics of visibility versus invisibility, and also the tremendous power of institutions who wield these mapping practices over other communities. How long had the O'odham been there, versus how long has this particular border been there? The power differential becomes so visible at those moments of decision making and who gets to wield that technology of geo-location.

Audience 1

Thank you everyone, it was really amazing to listen. Margaret, I understand there are groups that interpret territory and names in different ways, and there can be multiple claims to one territory. How did you put all information together in a way that respected all of these groups?

Margaret Pearce

If I found that people were giving me multiple names for a place, I included as many as I could fit in that space; there were only a couple I had to leave out. I tried to state very clearly in the introduction that the map is not an inventory. These are the names and there are thousands beyond that are not here. You may have also noticed I drew no lines for territories; I wouldn't presume as an American to engage in that, it's not my business.

I began from published website sources and quickly found that I couldn't use them. Once I included a name given from someone south of the Canada/U.S. border, not the international first nation border. When people questioned the name, I pointed to a source, to which they responded "that's not what we call that place". It's a lesson

I had to keep relearning, to my shame, to really pay attention to how a place is being described and named locally, because that's who's taking care of that name and whose rights are there. There are going to be multiple names, which represent multiple rights to territories, which are different kinds of rights. Also, sometimes when people shared their names, they would say "there is no meaning because we don't want to give you the meanings".

Audience 2
Margaret, I'm a Cree person from Saskatchewan, and I'm thinking about yesterday's Ogimaa Mikana walk with Hayden, and thinking through visualizations of clan governance as being a map in itself. I'm thinking about the responsibilities that we have to be reciprocal and make sure that we are granted consent, to be on certain territories and even to do the walk itself. What happens if consent also integrates sacred knowledges that some are not willing or able to give freely, as visitors in another territory? What happens if the layers of consent making are so multitudinous and so sacred that, even as Indigenous peoples we aren't able to access those consensual practices? For example, if the consent comes from a clan or comes from a rock. We have to be willing to not get it. We have to be willing to acknowledge that this might be incommensurable for us as Indigenous people. I'm also thinking of furtive and fugitive codes, what if this was created by those knowledge holders themselves? They might be able to give us an

abstraction of the actual sacred knowledge to use in our mapping practices.

Margaret Pearce
Thank you. Your point about abstraction is really important. The name-meanings depend on the context in which they have been articulated; they've been vetted in a certain way. There's a place on that map where there are three names that come together, and together they make a statement of, "You have no business knowing our names," though they are obstensibly names with translated meanings. I feel our job is to pay attention to what those terms of consent are and to do our best to represent if we are in the role of re-representing those terms.

Audience 2
My work explores place-name as gesture or choreography. What are the choreographies of futurity through map-making. Our people had sign languages for a place and for relationality and for consent. I'm wondering if as Indigenous feminist practitioners, maybe we should be open to place names as gesture, as movement.

Margaret Pearce
Yes, that encodes that traditional engagement of place names as visiting and standing in the place of our ancestors, and seeing what they saw, and hearing the sound of their voices when we speak their names. One of the place-names on the map, which is I'm guess-

ing is near your territory, that describes something that was stolen. It's not physically there, but it's supposed to be there. So that's a kind of a gesture citing it where it's supposed to be.

<u>Audience 2</u>
Thank you.

<u>Audience 3</u>
I wanted to go back to the discussion of metadata and whether the goal is to make data objective. Those in the data science community working in data criticality such as Lynn Bartram or Sheila Carpendale talk about the

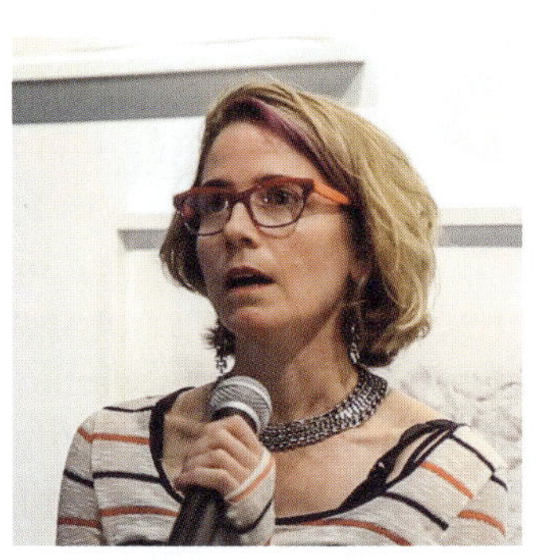

margins of datasets as being incredibly important to consider in machine learning and visualization. I would propose that the job is not to step away from data, but rather how can you have multiple datasets be aware of their provenance in the ways that you've described. I don't think it's about fake news versus objectivity. It's about knowing that even the instruments of collection are not neutral: technologies are designed with certain kinds of users in mind and certain kinds of outcomes. But to always begin to think about mitigating that.

<u>Catherine D'Ignazio</u>
Thank you, I agree and I think there are some interesting things happening. I just spoke with a woman named Margaret Mitchell at Google, who's doing natural language processing with machine learning, but looking at the

ways in which things that are unreported are actually implicit in a lot of these models.

When you computationally analyze a lot of human language, you would see that 'doctor' tends to be associated with male, which illustrates bias. When we say bananas, the implicit assumption is that those bananas are yellow; if there's a modifier before the banana, like green, it's because the bananas are in a different state. So, Mitchell is making a model that can detect that when we say 'doctor' in language, often what we mean is male doctor. Data doesn't represent reality. It represents how a certain set of people have been talking about things. Whereas, I think in a more modernist data-science, there's a naive assumption of a 'real reality'. I think there's a lot of productive encounters that can be had across these disciplines for exactly that reason.

<u>Audience 4</u>
I just want to thank (Audience 2), I really loved what you were saying and I wanted to think how as soon as you say something can't be done or can't be shared, then there's this flocking of curiosity and theft that occurs, which goes beyond appropriation. It's the urge to know, and maybe one uses respect as a way to prohibit the curiosity.

<u>Audience 2</u>
Sometimes the knowledge itself comes

from a place of extreme heartbreak.
We don't have a right to a compulsion
to know about other people's extreme
heartbreak. This is a big problem in
western Eurocentric knowledge practice, extractive extracting. Right now, if
we look at what happened with Colten
Boushie, Tina Fontaine, why would we
want to extract this knowledge?

Audience 5

I was wondering if in a collaborative
community project, when they share
their knowledge and their experience
with you, do you think they get something back from it? In the end of the
project, who does the story get told to,
strangers or people in the community
as well?

Lize Mogel

These last two comments are both
things that I'm grappling with. First,
the early history of the New York City
water supply's impact on the Catskills
is a traumatic history of community
displacement and erasure. It's also
a sensational history, of towns sub-
merged under reservoirs, and because
of that, it's sometimes the only history that the public knows. So I want to
honor this history but focus more on the
contemporary relationship between the
City and the Catskills, how it's changed
because of advocacy by local folks and
a willingness to compromise on the part
of the City.

I think a lot about what the mutual benefit might be for this project.
What can I, as an outsider, offer to the
communities in the Catskills that would
be useful? Government regulation
to protect the water supply keeps the
Catskills economy small, and reliant on
tourism dollars from New York City. So
one thing I am trying to do is to create
"water supply tourism" and maybe some
economic good out of this situation.
I also want to complicate the sense
of place of what's normally seen as a
recreational landscape, by pointing to
economic struggle, and producing new
visibility for under-recognized histories.

Audience 6

Going back to the dichotomy of objectivity, I don't think it is adequate. I
think one of the problems is we're using
scientific methods only. In this conversation, the answers were focused on
arts and humanities—the issues around
metadata or context or interpretations.
Perhaps we can do better with humanist
methods more so than with scientific
methods. In arts and design and humanities in general, we take for granted
what is actually not part of who we are
and what we do, and we actually need to
rethink. As humanists it's important for
us to start questioning those scientific
methods that are perhaps not appropriate for what we're trying to do.

Margaret Pearce

I agree. The scientific method is not
always appropriate. I come to cartography from writing, and I taught cartography like a language. When I started
teaching I made a point to tell them it's
language from the first day, so we can

move forward and decide what kind of language that's going to be.

Catherine D'Ignazio

I guess I wouldn't throw away the scientific method, it's more a question of when is it the right method and who is it for.

Audience 6

The issue for the humanist is the context, so eventually it can be the relationship or the context or the interpretation, rather than the data point.

Catherine D'Ignazio

The thing I am most excited by is the emerging critical conversation about data, algorithms and bias and so on. ProPublica for example reports on algorithmic bias and risk assessment algorithms. These studies are undertaken using very empirical methods of data science or data analysis and so on, statistical modelling, but in the service of different values.

In terms of methods, I think that we should use multiple, and think carefully about the values. It also goes back to that question of who's benefiting from this? Most of the time when we're talking about data science, who's benefiting are tech and finance companies, or surveillance machines of governments. And there's a very narrow set of values that drives a lot of those questions. We need to pay attention to which values each of those methods fosters and which ones they limit.

Audience 7

If you look closely at practices of objectivity in the sciences, you'll see they look far more like forms of accountability, and that a situated objectivity can be practiced. We have to decenter and push back against the sciences because there are norms and pedagogies at work in the sciences that will continue to do the extractive work, that will continue to reduce, and continue to produce really violent abstractions. I want to advocate for people working in the arts and the humanities to imagine that we can build robust enough modes of knowing that can push back up against the sciences and actually force the sciences to ask better questions and to change the value system. One way is by experimenting with data forms that look nothing like the legibility and extractability of being laid out on a grid. I'm interested in art practices that detune our desires for legibility, quantification, extraction and exploitation. If you look really closely at inquiry more broadly and recognize inquiry means metadata has to take on much richer, deeper sense of meaning. Can we invent data forms, maybe what we could call kind of alter data, that refuses to let go of context, that refuses to let go of the thickness of the live visceral relations that make up what we end up calling data. There's a lot of responsibility for artists to take up these other modalities that say, no, actually rigour means falling in love and building relations with the phenomena you're interested in. That the effective entanglements of inquiry are that which will give us deeper, more situated, more partial and limited knowledge rather than be able to make giant claims. If we're not attentive to all of the ways that the sciences force us not to know, then we're screwed.

Eliana Macdonald

Coming back to the value that fisheries brings to small communities. When you talk about value and fish, it means pounds, it means dollars. So we designed a project to talk to fishermen about the other values, the spiritual values, the cultural values, the intergenerational values, the community values when you trade fish. But how do you actually represent that in data? It turned out to a ball of yarn.

Audience 7

I work across art and geography, and I'm trying to imagine this same conversation in a room of geographers. It probably wouldn't be happening in this way. For geography, because of its history of its violence and domination, the discipline is very slow and I'm finding it very difficult to get that discipline to consider different forms of visualization, of knowledge. There's a hierarchy of knowledge, and it's hard and slow work to get geographers to understand or accept, on any kind of a level playing field, the kind of variety or difference of knowledges that we're talking about here.

Audience 8

In a lot of the work that I do around data, we talked about legibility and assumptions that are in it. So there is a process of producing it. What does that mean? What does that look like in the data too? What the data captures, particularly when you look at property for example, is race and class structure in society. What's interesting about data to me are the absences and the errors, because it moves away from that idea of an all-knowing kind of government entity or agency, and you begin to see the limits of their vision and legibility.

What is captured indicates the priority and hierarchy. If you're looking at what's captured in that way, we often try to bring in other data and information that subverts that direction or that power structure, and makes exploitive relationships more legible. So in some ways, treating the data itself as an object of study and understanding can show us a lot and can build strategies for resistance. I'm giving a shout out to a historical Detroit project called the *Detroit Geographic Expedition and Institution*, which did that.

Patricio Davila

I want to thank our round table participants for their contribution and for everyone in the audience for their attention and their very thoughtful comments and contributions to the discussion.

Coming Home

To honor the names and their caretakers.
To protect sovereignty.
To foreground Indigenous protocols.
To get it right, for once.

To make something beautiful.
To contribute something useful.
To specify.
To provoke questions.

To be quiet and listen.

To structure projection, size, and fold in dialogue
    with maps by Natural Resources Canada.
To represent borders with place names, as they
    are experienced.
To indicate that place names participate at
    all time scales.
To let meaning come from an accumulation of feeling.

To be wary of my assumptions as they continue
    to come up.
To be okay with not knowing what's next.
To remember it's none of my business.
To trust the design process to show the way.

To work against complacency, condescension,
    and dystopia.
To shift societal expectations for what a map
    can do or be.
To call it cartography, not counter-cartography.
To remind people that print is not broken.

Margaret Pearce

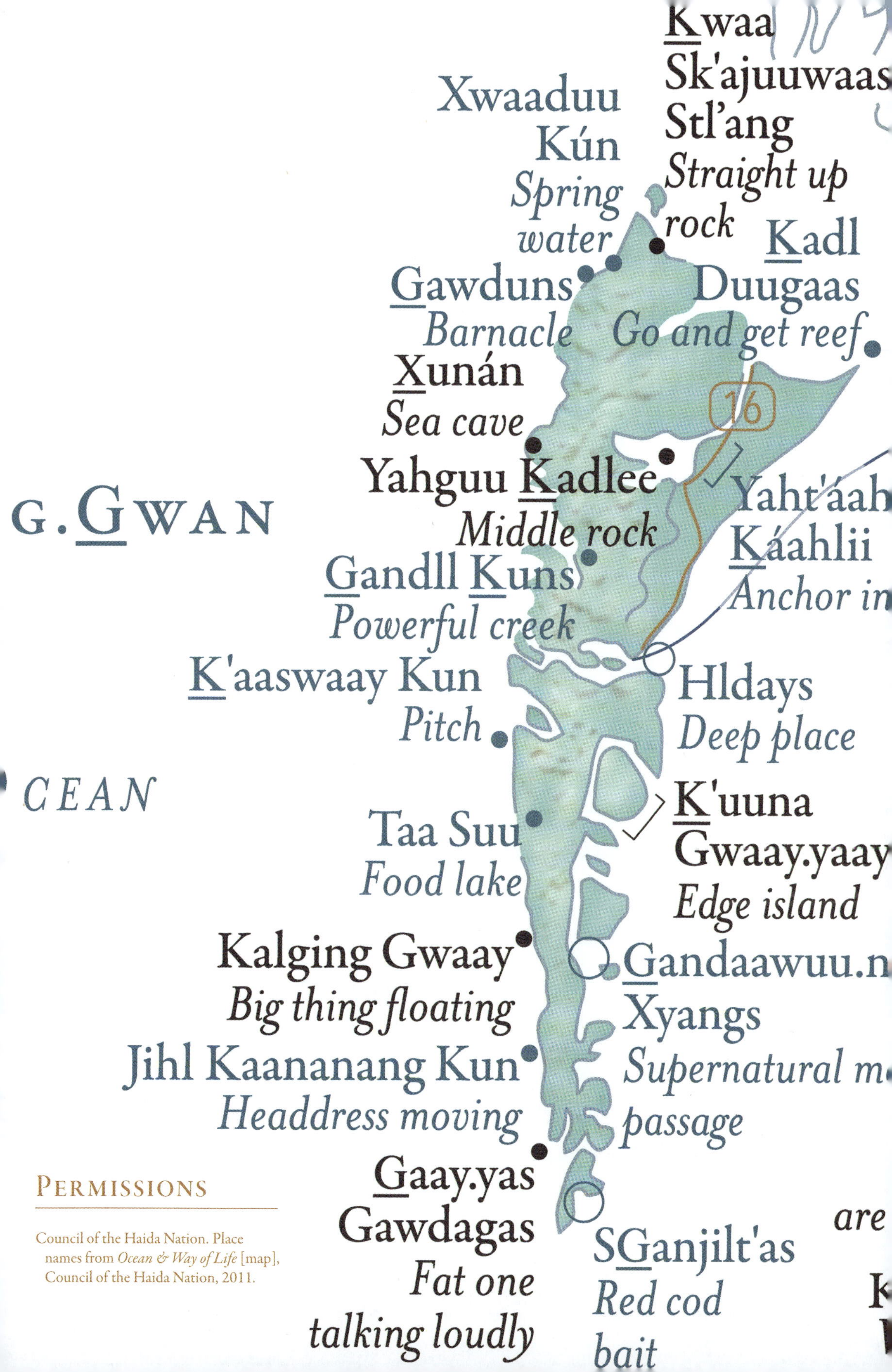

Kwaa
Sk'ajuuwaas
Stl'ang
Straight up
rock

Xwaaduu
Kún
Spring
water

Kadl
Duugaas
Go and get reef

Gawduns
Barnacle

Xunán
Sea cave

16

Yahguu Kadlee
Middle rock

Yaht'aah
Káahlii
Anchor in

G.Gwan

Gandll Kuns
Powerful creek

K'aaswaay Kun
Pitch

Hldays
Deep place

CEAN

K'uuna
Gwaay.yaay
Edge island

Taa Suu
Food lake

Kalging Gwaay
Big thing floating

Gandaawuu.n

Xyangs
Supernatural m
passage

Jihl Kaananang Kun
Headdress moving

Gaay.yas
Gawdagas
Fat one
talking loudly

SGanjilt'as
Red cod
bait

are

Permissions

Inuvialuit Cultural Centre, Inuvialuit Regional Corporation

NWT Cultural Places Program / Prince of Wales Northern Heritage Centre / Department of Education, Culture and Employment / Government of Northwest Territories, Canada

ʔehdzo Gotʼınę Gotsʼę́ Nákedı (Sahtú Renewable Resources Board) www.srrb.nt.ca, including assistance from Camilla Rabisca (Kʼáhsho Gotʼınę), Leon Andrew (Shúhtaotʼınę) and Deborah Simmons. Further assistance from Morris Modeste (Délı̨nę Gotʼınę). Place names from *Sahtú Atlas* and *Rakekee Gokʼe Godi: Places We Take Care Of.* Contact info@srrb.nt.ca for more information.

Inuit Heritage Trust. Place names at www.ihti.ca/eng/iht-proj-plac.html and ᐃᓄᕕᐅᑦ ᐊᐅᓪᓛᕐᕕᕗᓪᓗᑦ *Inuuvivut Aullaarvivullu/ Nunavut: Where We Live and Travel* (IHT 2015).

Kitikmeot Heritage Society. Place names at inuitplaces.org

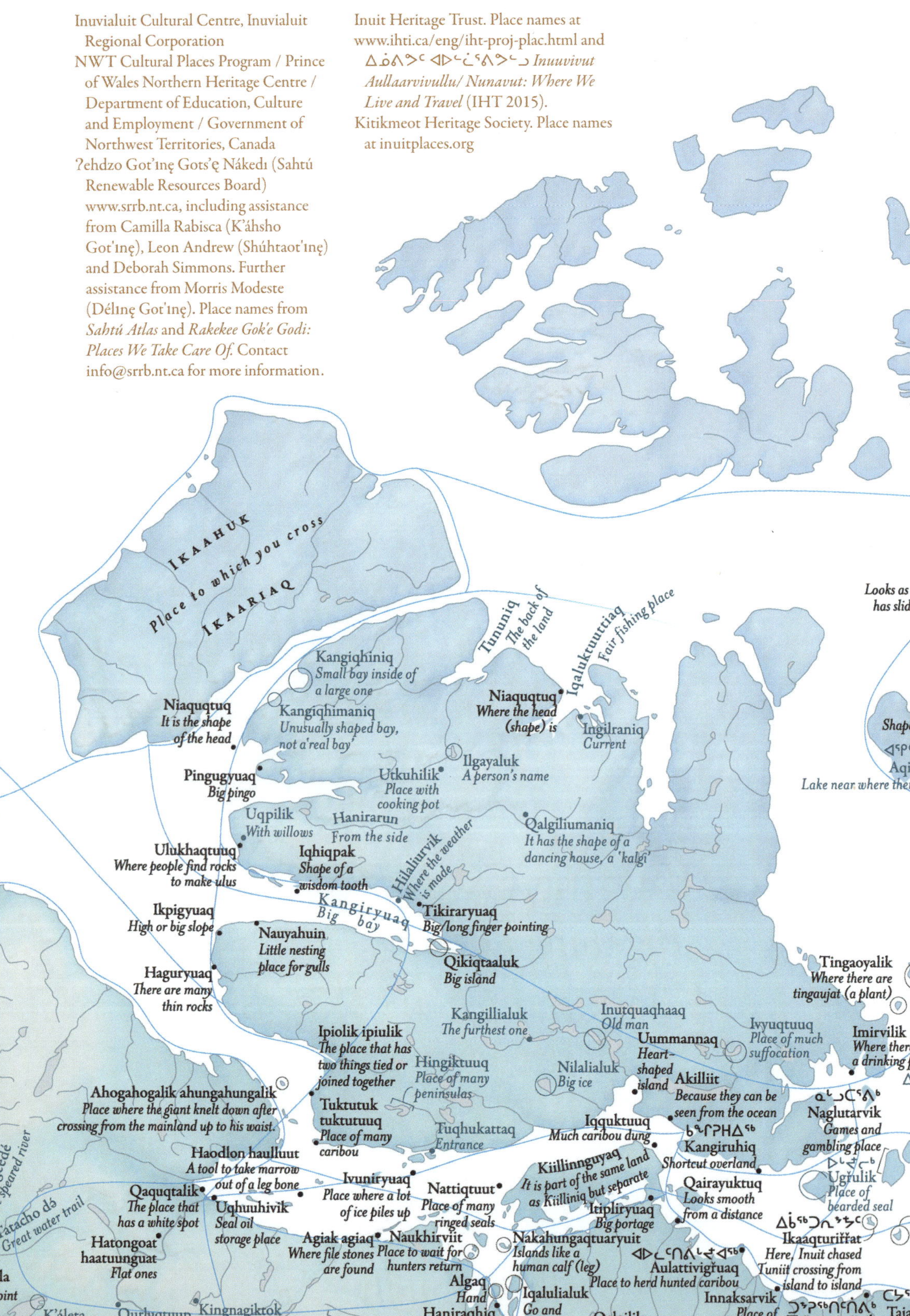

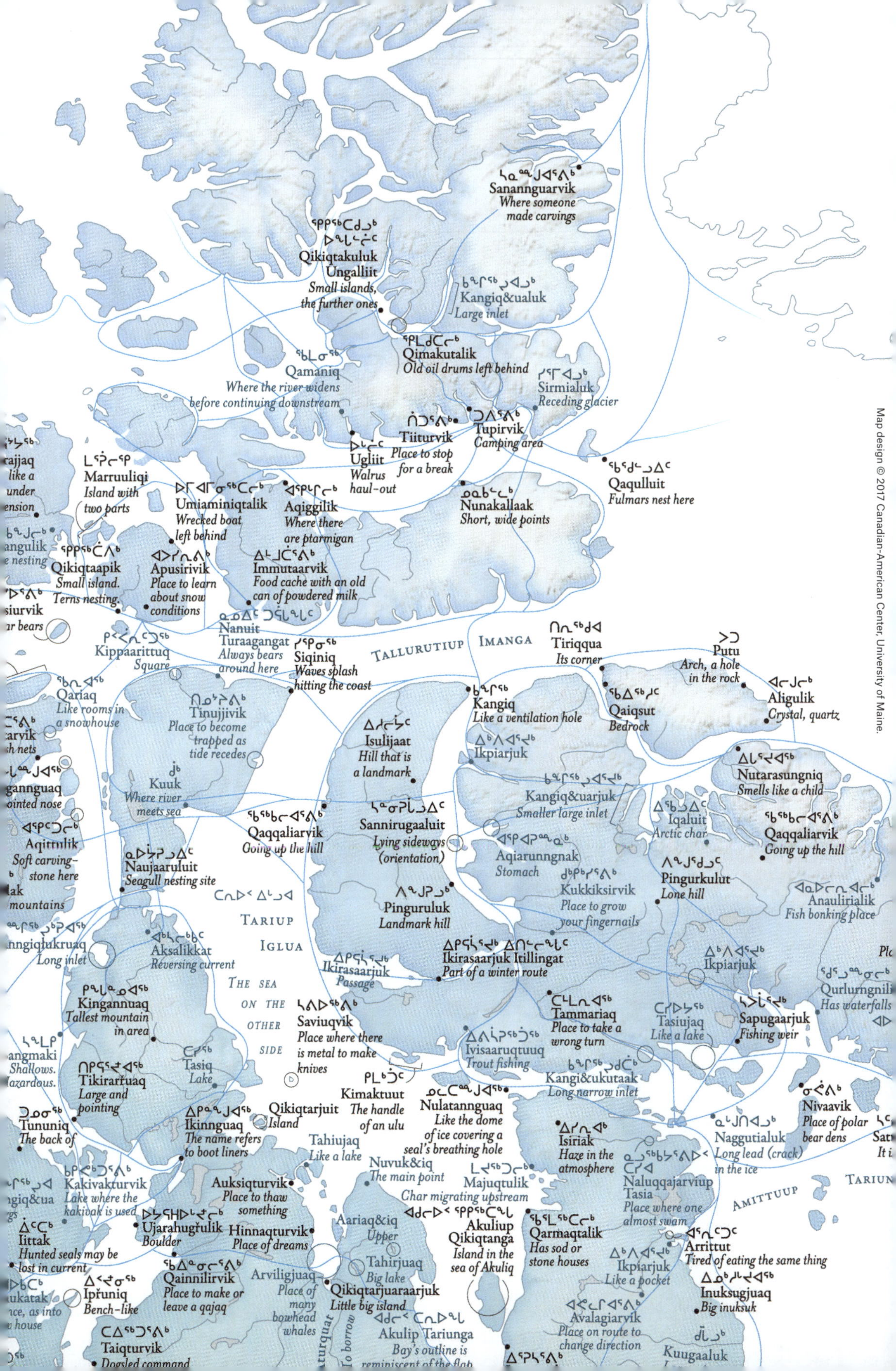

Sanannguarvik
Where someone made carvings

Qikiqtakuluk Ungalliit
Small islands, the further ones

Kangiq&ualuk
Large inlet

Qamaniq
Where the river widens before continuing downstream

Qimakutalik
Old oil drums left behind

Sirmialuk
Receding glacier

Tiiturvik
Place to stop for a break

Tupirvik
Camping area

Ugliit
Walrus haul-out

Qaqulluit
Fulmars nest here

Marruuliqi
Island with two parts

Umiaminiqtalik
Wrecked boat left behind

Aqiggilik
Where there are ptarmigan

Nunakallaak
Short, wide points

Qikiqtaapik
Small island. Terns nesting.

Apusirivik
Place to learn about snow conditions

Immutaarvik
Food cache with an old can of powdered milk

Nanuit Turaagangat
Always bears around here

Siqiniq
Waves splash hitting the coast

TALLURUTIUP IMANGA

Tiriqqua
Its corner

Putu
Arch, a hole in the rock

Aligulik
Crystal, quartz

Kippaarittuq
Square

Qariaq
Like rooms in a snowhouse

Tinujjivik
Place to become trapped as tide recedes

Isulijaat
Hill that is a landmark

Kangiq
Like a ventilation hole

Ikpiarjuk

Qaiqsut
Bedrock

Nutarasungniq
Smells like a child

Kuuk
Where river meets sea

Qaqqaliarvik
Going up the hill

Sannirugaaluit
Lying sideways (orientation)

Kangiq&uarjuk
Smaller large inlet

Aqiarunngnak
Stomach

Iqaluit
Arctic char

Qaqqaliarvik
Going up the hill

Aqittulik
Soft carving-stone here

Naujaaruluit
Seagull nesting site

Kukkiksirvik
Place to grow your fingernails

Pingurkulut
Lone hill

Pinguruluk
Landmark hill

Anaulirialik
Fish bonking place

TARIUP IGLUA

Aksalikkat
Reversing current

Ikirasaarjuk
Passage

Ikirasaarjuk Itillingat
Part of a winter route

Ikpiarjuk

Qurlurngnili
Has waterfalls

Kingannuaq
Tallest mountain in area

Saviuqvik
Place where there is metal to make knives

Tammariaq
Place to take a wrong turn

Tasiujaq
Like a lake

Sapugaarjuk
Fishing weir

THE SEA ON THE OTHER SIDE

Ivisaaruqtuuq
Trout fishing

Tasiq
Lake

Kimaktuut
The handle of an ulu

Kangi&ukutaak
Long narrow inlet

Nivaavik
Place of polar bear dens

Tikirarruaq
Large and pointing

Tununiq
The back of

Ikinnguaq
The name refers to boot liners

Qikiqtarjuit
Island

Tahiujaq
Like a lake

Nulatannguaq
Like the dome of ice covering a seal's breathing hole

Isiriak
Haze in the atmosphere

Naggutialuk
Long lead (crack) in the ice

Naluqqajarviup Tasia
Place where one almost swam

Kakivakturvik
Lake where the kakivak is used

Nuvuk&iq
The main point

Majuqtulik
Char migrating upstream

Arrittut
Tired of eating the same thing

Iittak
Hunted seals may be lost in current

Ujarahugrulik
Boulder

Hinnaqturvik
Place of dreams

Auksiqturvik
Place to thaw something

Aariaq&iq
Upper

Akuliup Qikiqtanga
Island in the sea of Akuliq

Qarmaqtalik
Has sod or stone houses

Ikpiarjuk
Like a pocket

Inuksugjuaq
Big inuksuk

Iprruniq
Bench-like

Qainnilirvik
Place to make or leave a qajaq

Arviligjuaq
Place of many bowhead whales

Tahirjuaq
Big lake

Qikiqtarjuaraarjuk
Little big island

Avalagiarvik
Place on route to change direction

Taiqturvik
Dogsled command

Akulip Tariunga
Bay's outline is reminiscent of the flap

Kuugaaluk

AMITTUUP

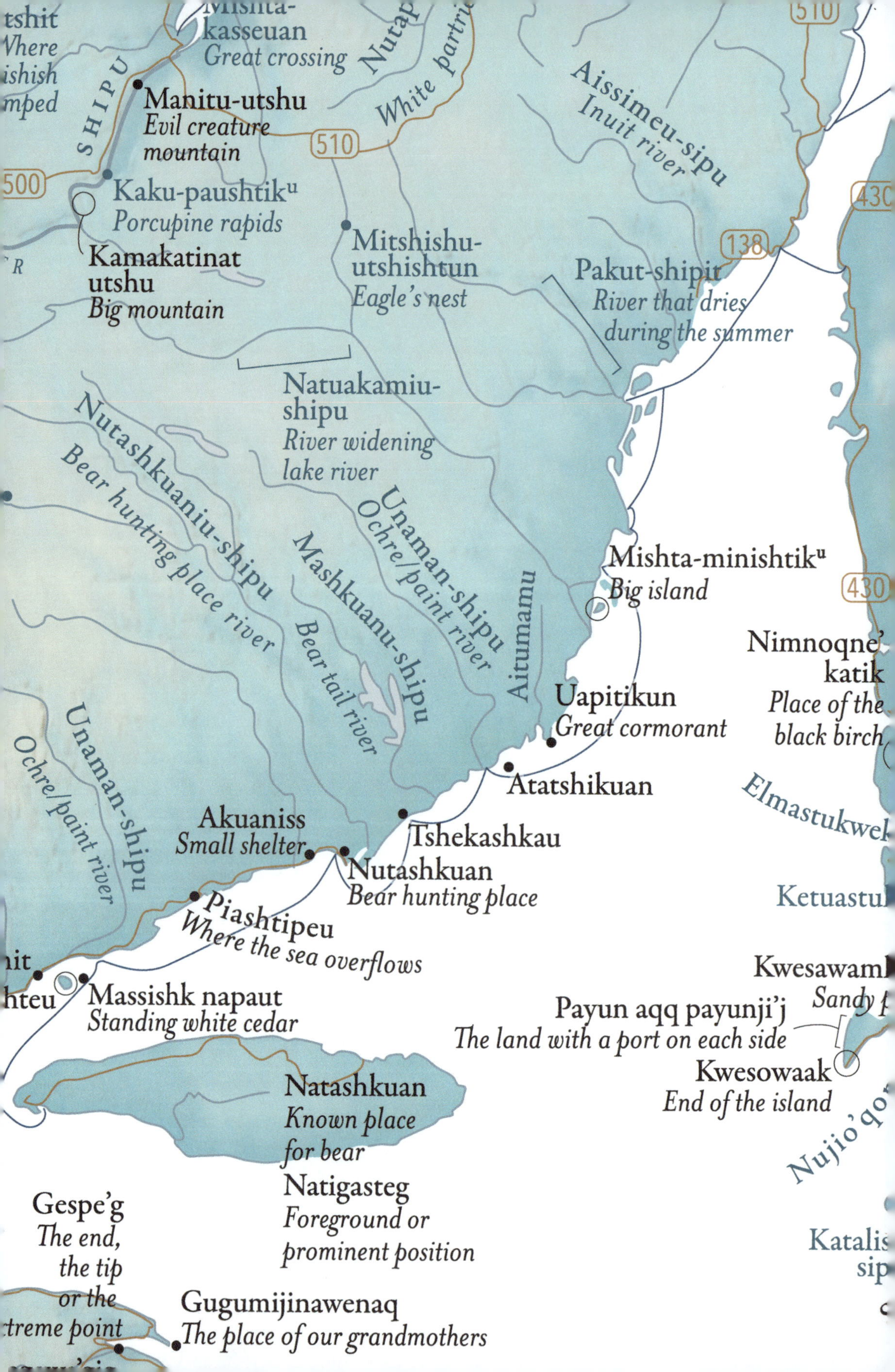

...tshit
*Where
...ishish
...mped*

Mishta-kasseuan
Great crossing

Manitu-utshu
Evil creature mountain

White part...

Nutap...

Aissimeu-sipu
Inuit river

510

510

Kaku-paushtik^u
Porcupine rapids

500

Kamakatinat utshu
Big mountain

R

Mitshishu-utshishtun
Eagle's nest

Pakut-shipit
River that dries during the summer

430

138

Natuakamiu-shipu
River widening lake river

Nutashkuaniu-shipu
Bear hunting place river

Mashkuanu-shipu
Bear tail river

Unaman-shipu
Ochre/paint river

Aitumamu

Mishta-minishtik^u
Big island

430

Nimnoqne' katik
Place of the black birch

Uapitikun
Great cormorant

Elmastukwel...

Atatshikuan

Unaman-shipu
Ochre/paint river

Akuaniss
Small shelter

Tshekashkau

Nutashkuan
Bear hunting place

Ketuastu...

Piashtipeu
Where the sea overflows

Kwesawaml...

...nit
...hteu

Massishk napaut
Standing white cedar

Payun aqq payunji'j
The land with a port on each side

Sandy f...

Kwesowaak
End of the island

Natashkuan
Known place for bear

Natigasteg
Foreground or prominent position

Nujio'qo...

Gespe'g
The end, the tip or the ...treme point

Gugumijinawenaq
The place of our grandmothers

Katalis... sip...

Permissions

Benoit First Nation Mi'kmaq Band
Flat Bay First Nation
Innu Nation. Place names from
Pepamuteiati Nitassinat at
www.innuplaces.ca. © Innu Nation and
Sheshatshiu Innu First Nation, 2008.
By permission of Innu Nation.
Institut Tshakapesh
Miawpukek First Nation
Mi'gmawei Mawiomi Secretariat
St. George's Indian Band

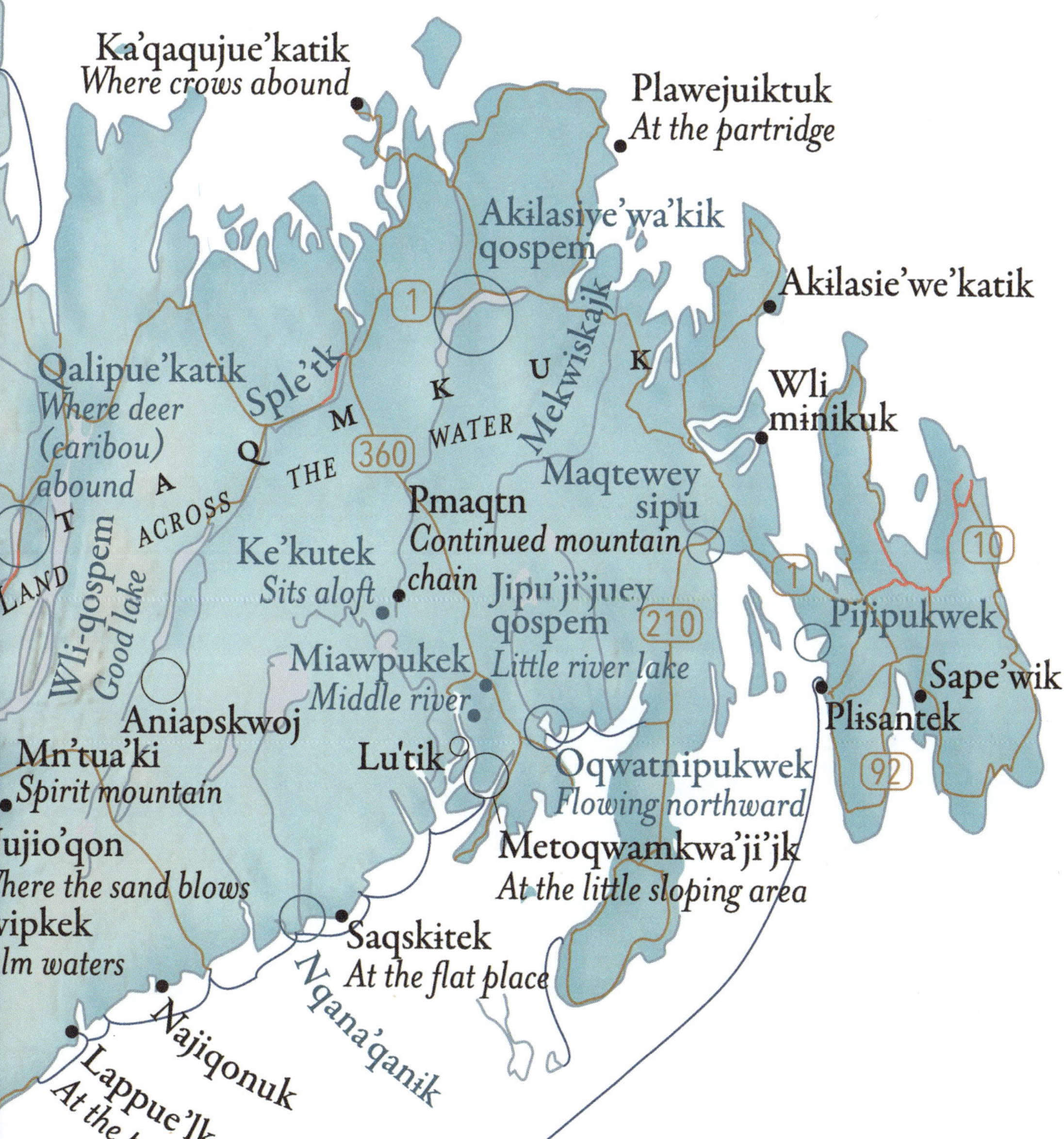

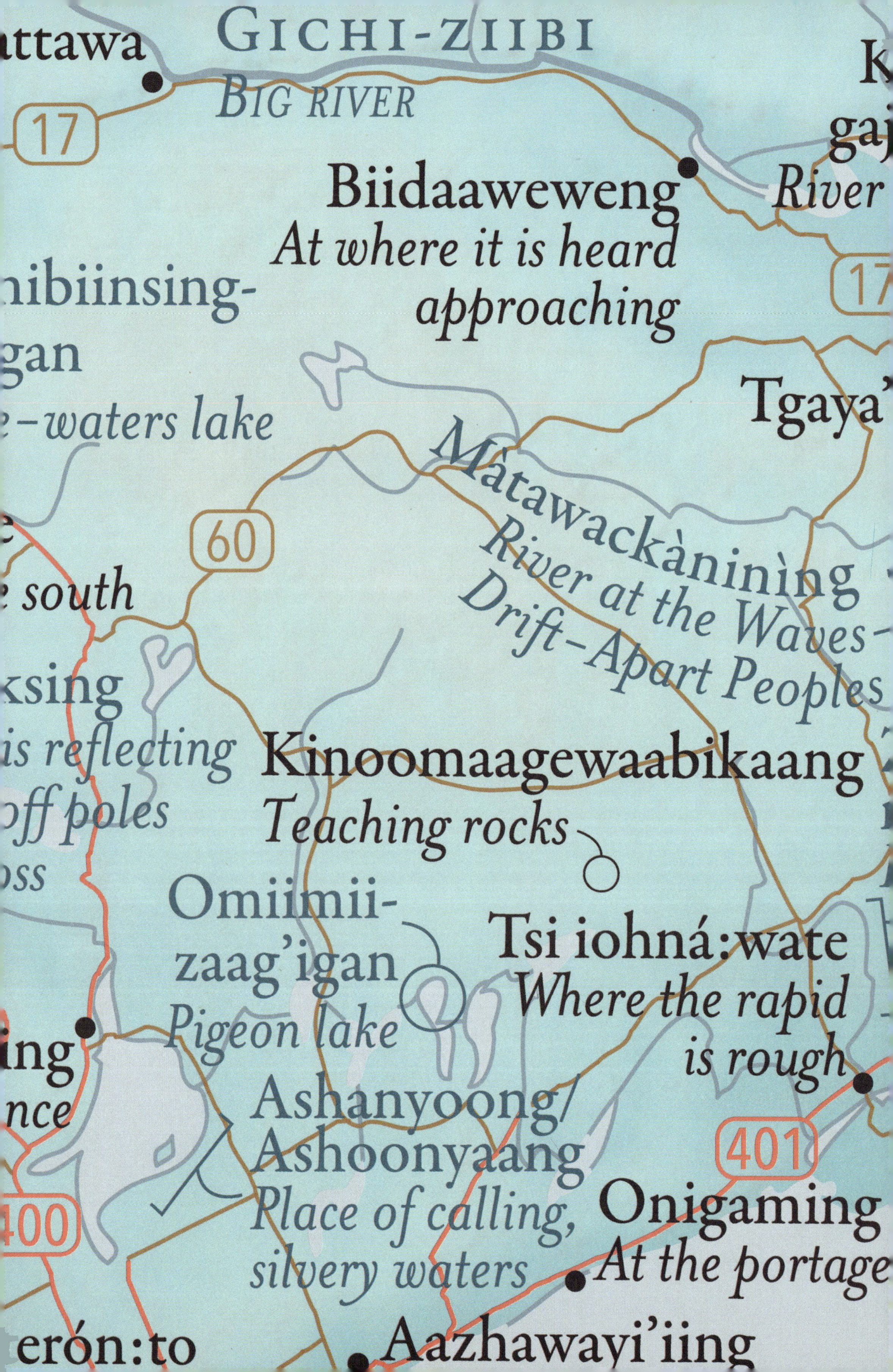

ttawa
GICHI-ZIIBI
BIG RIVER
17
K
gaj
River
Biidaaweweng
At where it is heard
approaching
17
nibiinsing-
gan
Tgaya'
e-waters lake
Màtawackàninìng
River at the Waves-
Drift-Apart Peoples
60
e south
ksing
Kinoomaagewaabikaang
is reflecting
off poles
Teaching rocks
oss
Omiimii-
zaag'igan
Tsi iohná:wate
Where the rapid
is rough
Pigeon lake
ing
Ashanyoong/
Ashoonyaang
nce
401
Place of calling,
silvery waters
Onigaming
At the portage
400
erón:to
Aazhawayi'iing

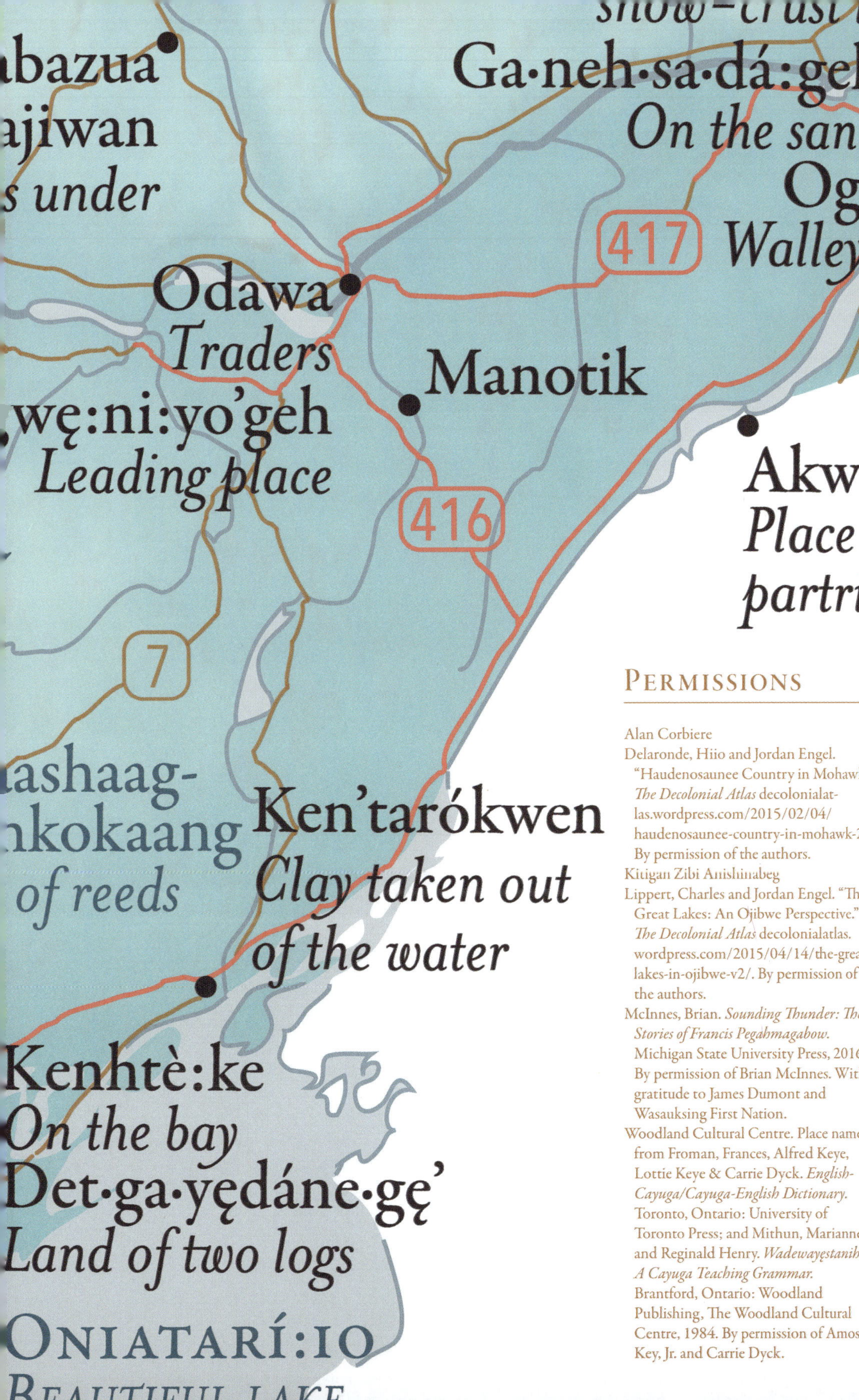

PERMISSIONS

Alan Corbiere
Delaronde, Hiio and Jordan Engel. "Haudenosaunee Country in Mohawk." *The Decolonial Atlas* decolonialatlas.wordpress.com/2015/02/04/haudenosaunee-country-in-mohawk-2/. By permission of the authors.
Kitigan Zibi Anishinabeg
Lippert, Charles and Jordan Engel. "The Great Lakes: An Ojibwe Perspective." *The Decolonial Atlas* decolonialatlas.wordpress.com/2015/04/14/the-great-lakes-in-ojibwe-v2/. By permission of the authors.
McInnes, Brian. *Sounding Thunder: The Stories of Francis Pegahmagabow.* Michigan State University Press, 2016. By permission of Brian McInnes. With gratitude to James Dumont and Wasauksing First Nation.
Woodland Cultural Centre. Place names from Froman, Frances, Alfred Keye, Lottie Keye & Carrie Dyck. *English-Cayuga/Cayuga-English Dictionary.* Toronto, Ontario: University of Toronto Press; and Mithun, Marianne and Reginald Henry. *Wadewayęstanih. A Cayuga Teaching Grammar.* Brantford, Ontario: Woodland Publishing, The Woodland Cultural Centre, 1984. By permission of Amos Key, Jr. and Carrie Dyck.

Western Permissions

Acho Dene Koe First Nations
Aseniwuche Winewak Nation
Vince Ahonakew
Beaver First Nation
Blackfoot Digital Library
Chipewyan Prairie Dene First Nation
Council of the Haida Nation. Place names from *Ocean & Way of Life* [map], Council of the Haida Nation, 2011.
Shirlee Crow Shoe
Bruce Cutknife. Place names from Bruce Cutknife, the Late Louis Sunchild, and the Late Jackson Roan.
Doig River First Nation
Elliott, Dave. *Saltwater people*. Ed. Janet Poth. School District 63 (Saanich), 1983. By permission of John Elliott.
Otto Fietz, Prince Albert Grand Council
Fort McKay Sustainability Department
Fort Nelson First Nation
The Gift of Language and Culture Project
Gitwangak Education Society
Gitxaala Nation
Gwich'in Place Names Atlas (atlas.gwichin.ca/index.html?module=gwichin.module.main) Gwich'in Tribal Council, Department of Cultural Heritage (formerly Gwich'in Social & Cultural Institute).
Inuit Heritage Trust. Place names at www.ihti.ca/eng/dteproj-plac.html and ᐃᓄᐃᑦ ᓄᓇᖏᑦ *Inuusirini Aullaaruinullu/ Nunavut: Where We Live and Travel* (IHT 2015).
Inuvialuit Cultural Centre, Inuvialuit Regional Corporation
James Smith Cree Nation
Kapawe'no First Nation. By permission of the Chief of the Nation.
Kaska Dena Council
Kitasoo/Xai'xais Integrated Resource Authority
Kitkxot Heritage Society. Place names at lootplaces.org
Kitselas Administration
Kitsumu Nation Council
Kwadacha Nation
Líllwat?ul Cultural Centre
McLeod, Neal. *100 Days of Cree*. University of Regina Press, 2016. Place names reprinted by permission of University of Regina Press.
McLeod, Neal. *Cree Narrative Memory*. Purich Publishing, 2007. Place names reprinted with permission of the Publisher. All rights reserved by the Publisher.
M'Lot, Maria. *Kâ êmâhcâak Askîy: Using Cree knowledge to perceive and describe the landscape of the Wapusk National Park Area*. Masters thesis, University of Manitoba, 2002. By permission of Maria M'Lot. With gratitude to the Elders and people from York Factory First Nation and Fox Lake Cree Nation residing in Churchill, York Landing, Bird and Gillam who graciously shared their knowledge.
Mosakahiken Cree Nation
Musqueam First Nation

Nadleh Whut'en First Nation, Chief Larry Nooski. And we wish to recognize the people who gathered the information through interviews with Nadleh Elders: Beverly Ketlo, Lands Manager; Michelle Lockheed, CSTC Mapper; Sue Ketlo, Education Coordinator, and current contributor Language & Culture Program Eleanor Nooski.
Nahanni Butte First Nation
'Namgis First Nation
Nekaneet First Nation
Nisga'a Lisims Government
Northwest Territories Cree Language Program
NWT Cultural Places Program / Prince of Wales Northern Heritage Centre / Department of Education, Culture and Employment / Government of Northwest Territories, Canada
Pehdzeh Ki First Nation
Sambaa Dene First Nation
Sahtú Research and Resource Management Centre at Sahtú Nation
Syilx (Okanagan Nation Alliance)
Jessie Sylvester
Tahltan Central Government. Place names from Thomas McIlwraith, *'84: Are Still Didene: Stories of Hunting and History from Northern British Columbia*. University of Toronto Press, 2012. By permission of Tahltan Central Government and Thomas McIlwraith.
Taku River Tlingit First Nation, trtfn.com. Place names from *Taku River Tlingit Place Names* at trt.geolive.ca.
Tl'azt'en First Nation
Tlin-ts-qut-aht First Nation
Tlicho Government. Place names from Allice Legat, Georgina Chocolate, Madelaine Chocolate, and Sally Anne Zoe, *Habitat of Dagëts Territory: Place Names as Indicators of Biogeographical Knowledge*; and John B. Zoe, *Trails of Our Ancestors: Building a Nation*. By permission of Tlicho Government.

Toquaht Nation, Tyee ha'wilth Chief Anne Mack. Thanks also to Gale Johnson, Toquaht Language Coordinator.
Tr'ondëk Hwëch'in Government
Tsilhqot'in National Government. Thanks to the Tsilhqot'in Communities and its members for their input over the years on various projects.
T'Sou-ke First Nation
Wet First Nation
Chris Wilson, Haida Nation
Woodland Cree First Nation
Yellow Quill First Nation
Yukeka Dëné Language Institute
Yukon Geographical Place Names Board. Place names from *Gazetteer of the Yukon 2016*.
Yukon Native Language Centre. Place names from "Dákeyi (Our Country)"
Pehdzo Got'ınę Got'ınę Nákedı (Sahtú Renewable Resources Board) www.srrb.nt.ca, including assistance from Camilla Rabisca (K'áhsho Got'ınę), Leon Andrew (Shúhtaot'ınę) and Deborah Simmons. Further assistance from Morris Modeste (Délı̨ne Got'ınę). Place names from *Sahtú Atlas* and *Rakekee Gok'e Godı: Places We Take Care Of*. Contact info@srrb.nt.ca for more information.

Western place names also from:

Manitoba First Nations Education Resource Centre. *Traditional First Nations Community Names* [map]. MFNERC, 2009. mfnerc.org/community-map.

Southern Permissions

Aanischaaukamikw (Cree Cultural Institute)
Anishnaabeg Zaagi'igan Anishinaabek
Aroland First Nation
Bigwigagog Nishnaabeg
Biinjitiwaabik Zaaging Anishinaabek
Louis Bird. Place names in Louis Bird, *Telling Our Stories: Omushkego Legends and Histories from Hudson Bay*. Ed. Jennifer S. H. Brown and Paul Warren DePasquale. Toronto: University of Toronto Press. By permission of Louis Bird and Jennifer S. H. Brown.
Biigtigong First Nation
Buffalo Point First Nation
Caribou Lake First Nation
The Chippewas of Nawash Unceded First Nation / Neyaashiinigmiing Band Council
Alan Corbiere
Dakota Tipi First Nation
Fisher River Cree Nation
Fort Albany First Nation
Fort William First Nation
God's Lake First Nation
Iskatewizaagegan First Nation
Jones, Nancy, Gordon Jourdain, and Rose Tainter. *Eedahigaayang: Ojibwe Word List*. Eds. Anton Treuer and Keller Paap. Waaswaaganning Ojibwe Immersion Charter School, 2011. By permission of Anton Treuer.
Kitigan Zibi Anishinabeg

Lippert, Charles and Jordan Engel. "The Great Lakes: An Ojibwe Perspective." *The Decolonial Atlas* decolonialatlas.wordpress.com/2015/04/14/the-great-lakes-in-ojibwe-v2/. By permission of the authors.
Long Plain First Nation
Long Point First Nation
Matachewan First Nation
McInnes, Brian. *Sounding Thunder: The Stories of Francis Pegahmagabow*. Michigan State University Press, 2016. By permission of Brian McInnes. With gratitude to James Dumont and Wasauksing First Nation.
McLeod, Neal. *Cree Narrative Memory*. Purich Publishing, 2007. Place names reprinted with permission of the Publisher. All rights reserved by the Publisher.
Michipicoten First Nation
Mistpawitik Cree Nation
M'Lot, Maria. *Kâ êmâhcâak Askîy: Using Cree knowledge to perceive and describe the landscape of the Wapusk National Park Area*. Masters thesis, University of Manitoba, 2002. By permission of Maria M'Lot. With gratitude to the Elders and people from York Factory First Nation and Fox Lake Cree Nation residing in Churchill, York Landing, Bird and Gillam who graciously shared their knowledge.
Mosakahiken Cree Nation
Nation Huronne-Wendat Archives et Centre de Documentation, Nation Huronne-Wendat
Neskantaga First Nation
Nibinamik First Nation

Ocean Man First Nation
O-Chi-Chak-Ko-Sipi First Nation
Pheasant Rump Nakota First Nation
Pimachiowin Aki Corporation
Pimicikamak
Poplar River First Nation
Sachigo Lake First Nation
Sagkeeng Anicinábe
St. Theresa Point First Nation
Sapotaweyak Cree Nation
Taykwa Tagamou Nation
Temagami First Nation. Place names in Macdonald, Craig K. *Historical Map of Temagami*. Ontario Geographic Names Board, 1985. By permission of Temagami First Nation.
Tootinaowaziibeeng First Nation
Wahnapitae First Nation
War Lake First Nation
Webiquie First Nation
White Bear First Nations
Woodland Cultural Centre. Place names from Froman, Frances, Alfred Keye, Lottie Keye & Carrie Dyck. *English-Cayuga/Cayuga-English Dictionary*. Toronto, Ontario: University of Toronto Press, and Mithun, Marianne and Reginald Henry. *Wadewayestanih: A Cayuga Teaching Grammar*. Brantford, Ontario: Woodland Publishing, The Woodland Cultural Centre, 1994. By permission of Amos Key, Jr. and Carrie Dyck.
Waskwi Sipihk First Nation

Southern place names also from:

Johnston, Basil H. *By Canoe & Moccasin: Some Native Place Names of the Great Lakes*. Lakefield: Waapoone Publishing, 1986.

Manitoba First Nations Education Resource Centre. *Traditional First Nations Community Names* [map]. MFNERC, 2009. mfnerc.org/community-map.

Coming Home
TO INDIGENOUS PLACE NAMES IN CANADA

First Nations, Métis, and Inuit place names express territorial rights and describe the shapes and sounds of sovereign lands. They mark the locations of the gathering places, the communities, the places of danger and of beauty, and the places where the treaties were signed.

Place names are instructive signage along land and water routes. They tell how to walk on the ice there, or which direction is wrong, or where the eggs and berries are. They connect to each other in stories. They are ancient and recent, both in and outside of time. They express and assert Indigenous authority across the Canadian landscape.

These are not all of the names, nor are all Indigenous Nations and communities represented here. Beyond these names are thousands, upon thousands, upon thousands more, an ever growing and expanding atlas of intimate geographical knowledge and experience. These are some of the names, generously shared for the purpose of this map. They are written as they were shared, with translated meanings or standing alone to affirm themselves in the language.

To be coming home to Indigenous place names is to find a place among these names from which to listen, reorient, and remember, and to imagine future possibilities.

> *Coming home is "a return to Indigenous memories and narratives [that] serve as a map for people to find their way through life."*
>
> — Neal McLeod, *Cree Narrative Memory*

Legend

Permissions

The place names in this map are the intellectual and cultural property of the First Nation, Métis, and Inuit people on whose territories they are located. The names may not be mapped, copied, or reproduced in any way without the permission of the Nations, communities, and organizations who are their caretakers. Permissions credits are listed according to the four directions.

NORTHERN PERMISSIONS

WESTERN PERMISSIONS · EASTERN PERMISSIONS

SOUTHERN PERMISSIONS

Northern Permissions

Inuit Heritage Trust. Place names at www.ihti.ca/eng/iht-proj-plac.html, and *Inuusivut Aallasivvialu/ Nunavut: Where We Live and Travel* (IHT 2015)
Inuvialuit Cultural Centre; Inuvialuit Regional Corporation

Kitikmeot Heritage Society. Place names at inuitplaces.org
NWT Cultural Places Program / Prince of Wales Northern Heritage Centre / Department of Education, Culture and Employment / Government of Northwest Territories, Canada.

Eastern Permissions

Aanischaaukamikw (Cree Cultural Institute)
The Abenaki Language Committee with the support of the Abenaki Council of Odanak and the Abenaki Council of Wôlinak
Andrea Bear Nicholas
Bersin First Nation Mi'kmaq Band
Bird, Louis. *Telling Our Stories: Omushkego Legends and Histories from Hudson Bay.* Ed. Jennifer S. H. Brown and Paul Warren DePasquale. Toronto: University of Toronto Press, 2005. By permission of Louis Bird and Jennifer S.H. Brown.
Delaronde, Hilo and Jordan Engle. "Haudenosaunee Country in Mohawk." *The Decolonial Atlas* decolonialatlas.wordpress.com/2015/02/04/haudenosaunee-country-in-mohawk-2/. By permission of the authors.
Eel Ground First Nation
Eqpenobpeoitij First Nation
Flat Bay First Nation
Fort Folly First Nation
Bernie Francis

Innu Nation. Place names from *Pepamuteiati Nitassinat* at www.innuplaces.ca. © Innu Nation and Sheshatshiu Innu First Nation, 2008. By permission of Innu Nation.
Institut Tshakapesh
Inuit Heritage Trust. Place names at www.ihti.ca/eng/iht-proj-plac.html, and *Inuusivut Aallasivvialu/ Nunavut: Where We Live and Travel* (IHT 2015).
Kitigan Zibi Anishinabeg
Lippert, Charles and Jordan Engel. "The Great Lakes: An Ojibwe Perspective." *The Decolonial Atlas* decolonialatlas.wordpress.com/2015/04/16/the-great-lakes-in-ojibwe-v2/. By permission of the authors.
Misaquek First Nation
Mi'gmawei Mawiomi Secretariat
Naskapi Development Corporation
Nation Huronne-Wendat Archives et Centre de Documentation, Nation Huronne-Wendat
Nunatop Project, Avataq Cultural Institute
PEI Mi'kmaq Place Names remembered by the Mi'kmaq Confederacy of PEI
Pekuakamiulnuatsh Takuhikan
Qalipu First Nation
Sable, Trudy and Bernie Francis. *The Language of This Land, Mi'kma'ki.* Cape Breton University Press, 2012. By permission of the authors.
St. George's Indian Band
Ta'n Weji-Sqalia'tiek: Mi'kmaw Place Names Digital Atlas and Web Site (mikmawplacenames.ca)

Produced by the Canadian-American Center, a National Resource Center on Canada at the University of Maine.

Stephen J. Hornsby, Director

UNIVERSITY OF MAINE

Map by Margaret Wickens Pearce. Concept by Stephen J. Hornsby.

No portion of the place name content of this map may be reproduced or used for other purposes without permission from the Nations, people, and communities that are their caretakers.

Map design © 2017 Canadian-American Center, University of Maine.

O'Say Can You See

Laura Poitras

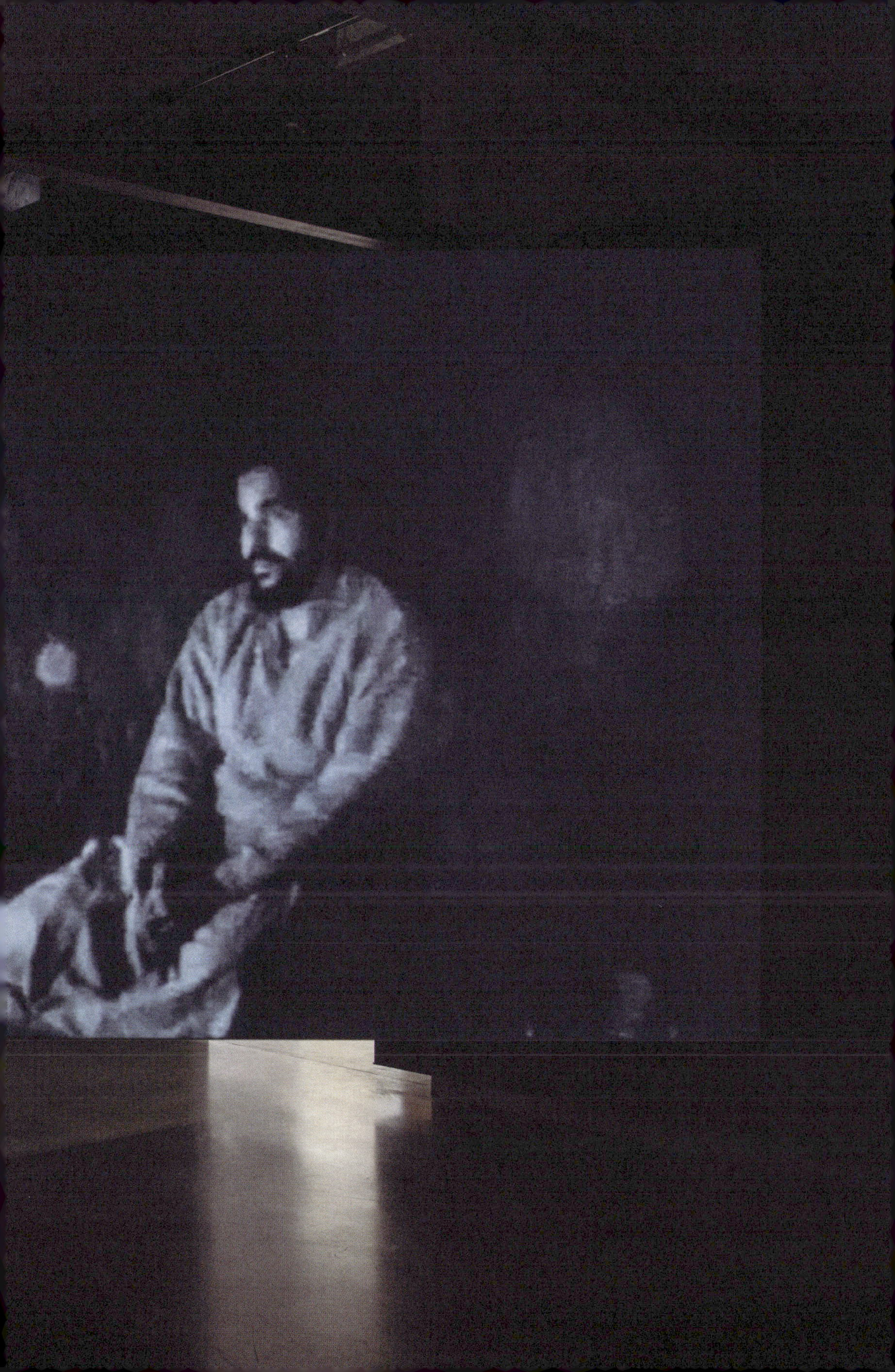

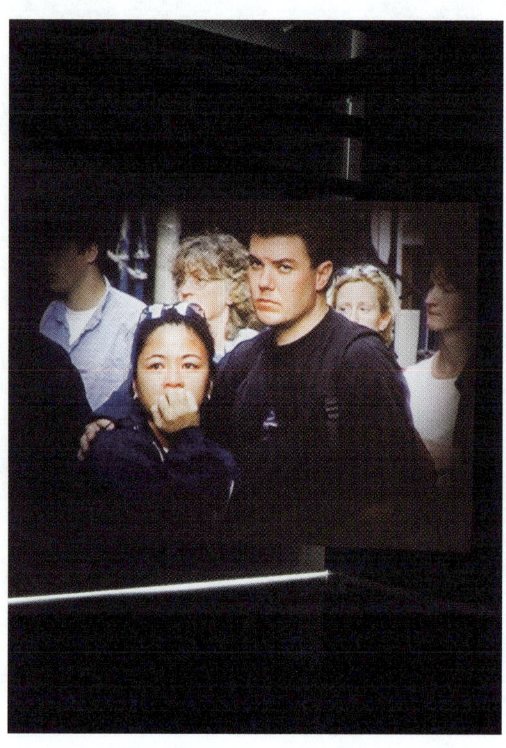

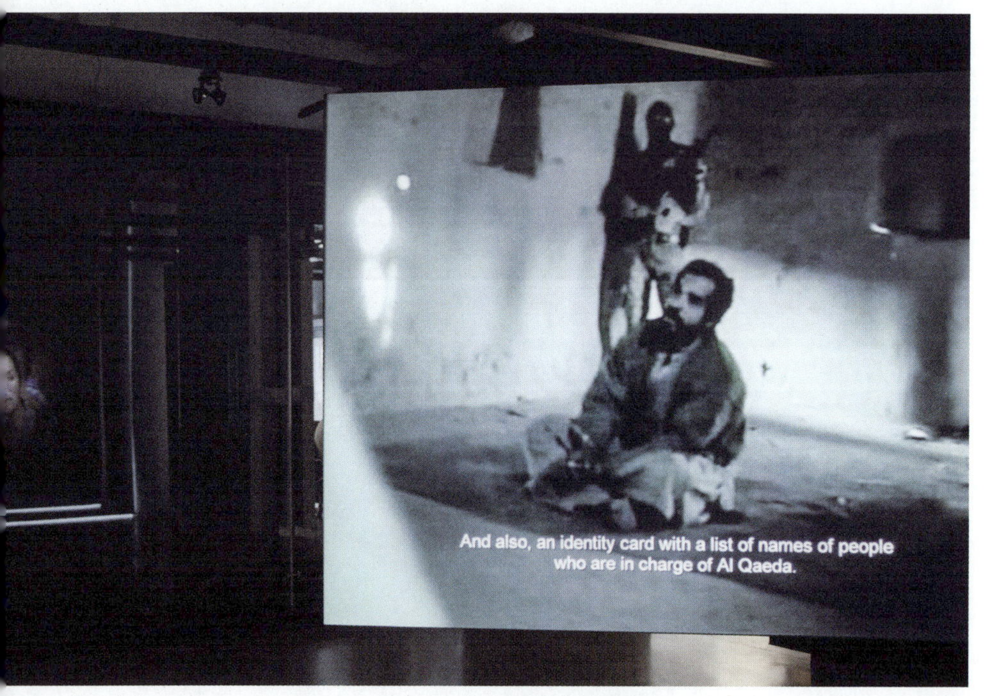

And also, an identity card with a list of names of people
who are in charge of Al Qaeda.

O'Say Can You See
Laura Poitras

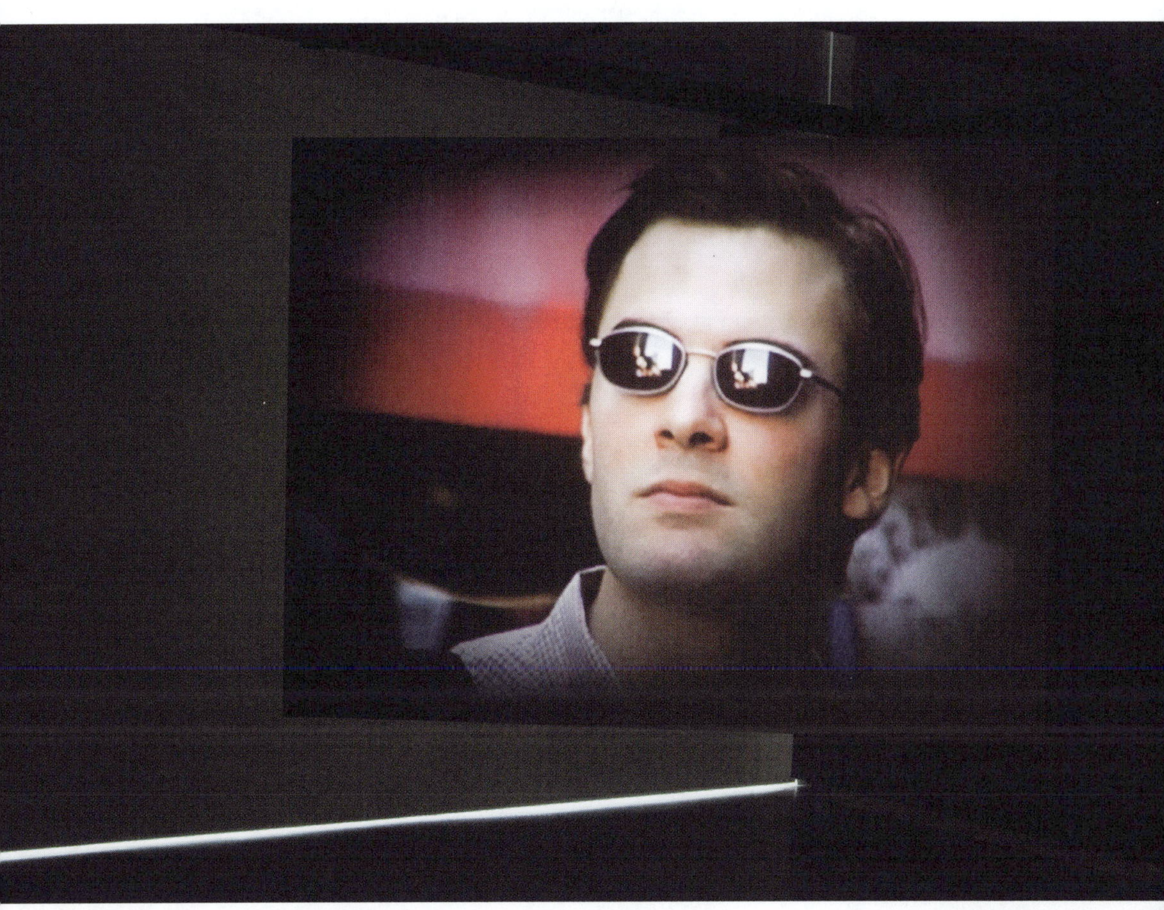

Installation views (this page and previous
page). Laura Poitras, *O'Say Can You See*,
2001/2016. Two-channel digital video,
color, sound. Courtesy of Onsite Gallery.
Photography by Yuula Benivolski.

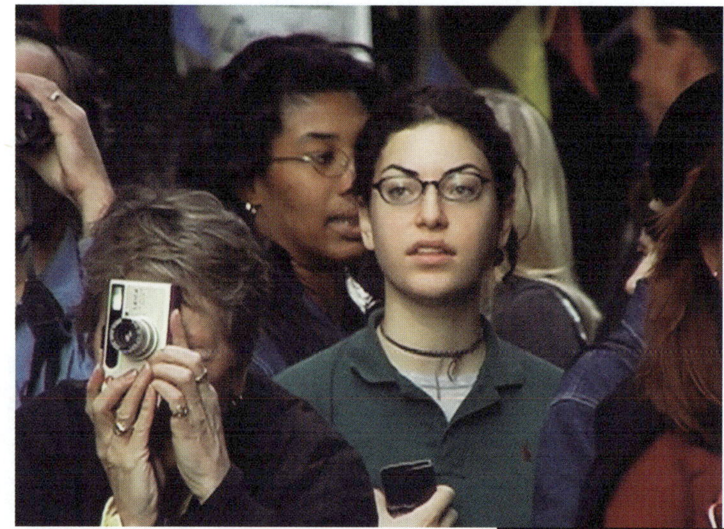

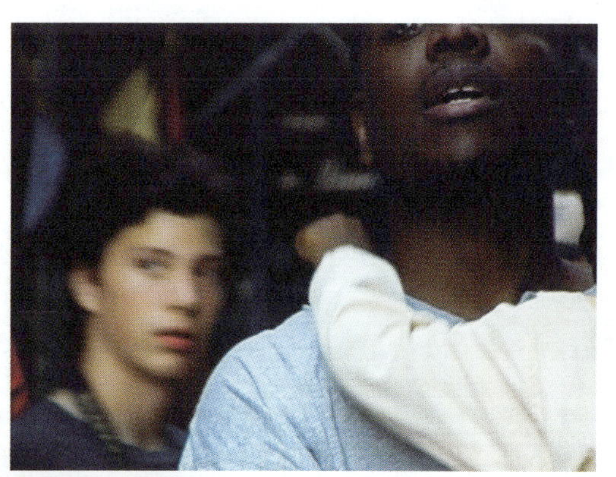

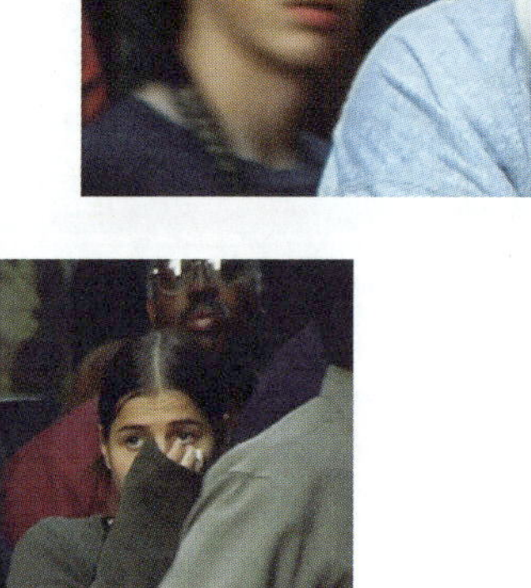

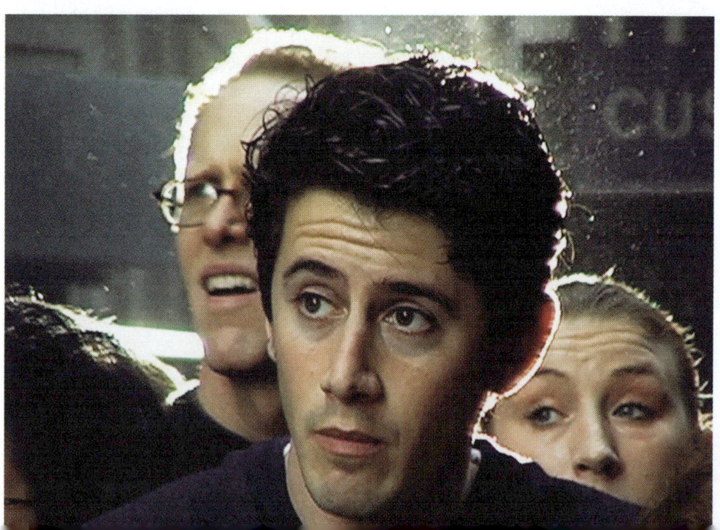

O'Say Can You See
Laura Poitras

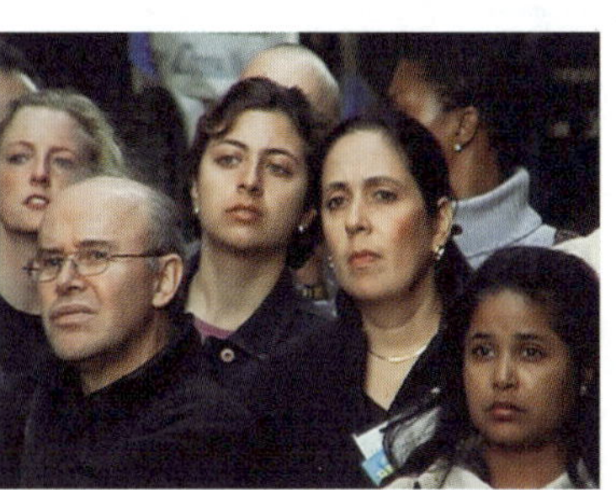

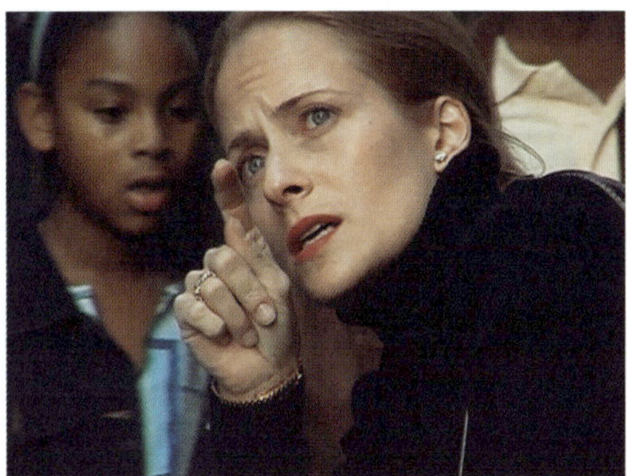

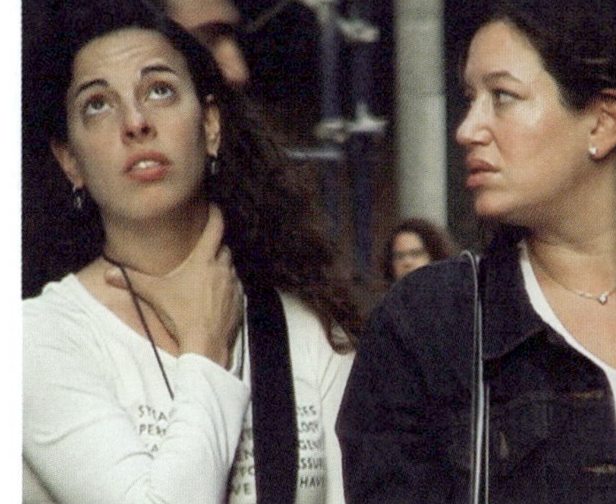

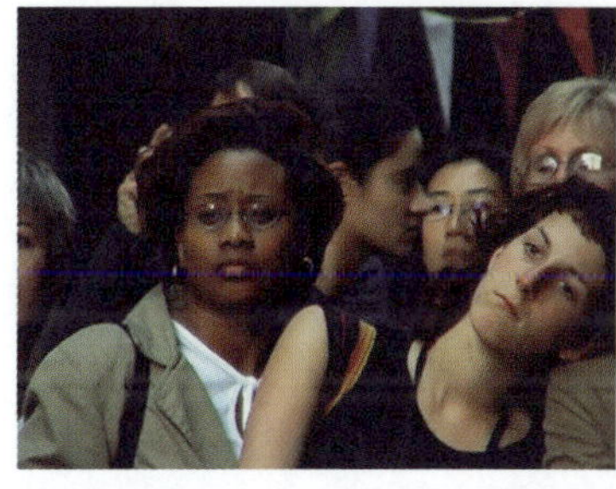

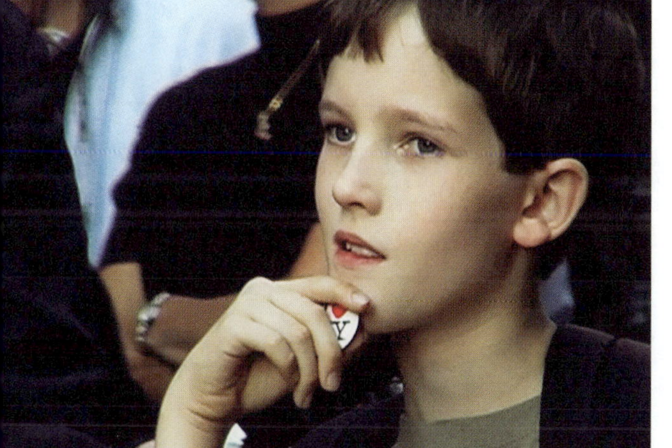

Stills. Laura Poitras, *O'Say Can You See*, 2001/2016. Two-channel digital video, color, sound. Courtesy of the artist.

From Far Away and Up Close: Visualization and Documentary Modes

Laura Poitras and Josh Begley with Patricio Dávila

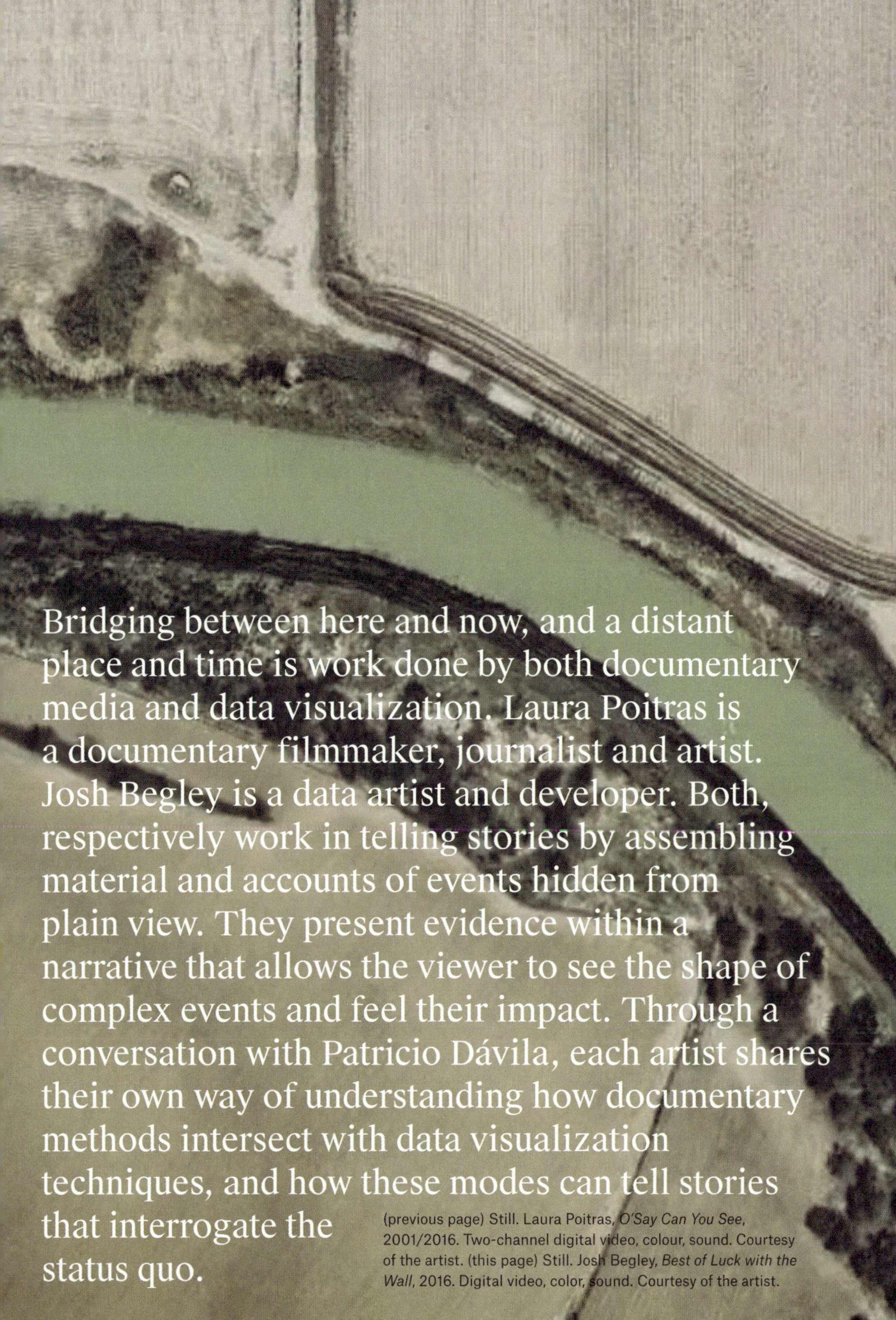

Bridging between here and now, and a distant place and time is work done by both documentary media and data visualization. Laura Poitras is a documentary filmmaker, journalist and artist. Josh Begley is a data artist and developer. Both, respectively work in telling stories by assembling material and accounts of events hidden from plain view. They present evidence within a narrative that allows the viewer to see the shape of complex events and feel their impact. Through a conversation with Patricio Dávila, each artist shares their own way of understanding how documentary methods intersect with data visualization techniques, and how these modes can tell stories that interrogate the status quo.

(previous page) Still. Laura Poitras, *O'Say Can You See*, 2001/2016. Two-channel digital video, colour, sound. Courtesy of the artist. (this page) Still. Josh Begley, *Best of Luck with the Wall*, 2016. Digital video, color, sound. Courtesy of the artist.

Patricio Dávila

The title of the exhibition, *Diagrams of Power*, works on two levels. The first part is visually manifest, which you can take in as a plan or as a representation of something. Maps can work like this, charts can work like this. All forms of data that are transformed into these visual forms. On the other side, for me, is a diagram that is invisible. This idea of power relations, specifically. Associations, how we're hooked up to technologies and spaces that frame our performance, our attitudes, our reality. In the exhibition, I wanted to play with that productive and generative notion of diagram, and that's why it's incredible to be able to exhibit both of your works. It was very much a work of data art from Josh, and Laura's work had this idea of mapping and creating the diagram—making visible through the two-sided nature of the installation, the unsuspecting or tacit approvers of a foreign policy on one side, and the veiled activities on the other.

Laura Poitras

I'm going to throw in another starting-off point that grounds my work: how do you interrogate or expose power relations, and what are the different modes where these relations can be communicated in a way that connects with people in unexpected ways? And hopefully, by doing so, how can it shift consciousness in some way? In 2012, Josh created an app where any time there was a U.S. drone assassination anywhere in the world, he would send a text message to you. Usually when you pick up your phone, you get a text message, it's your friend who wants to get together for dinner or something. It's not usually, "At 11 PM in Pakistan, four people were killed by US drone assassination." So this app he created, one could call it a data project. You could call it a diagram. I would say it's also a mode of expression to expose power relationships in a way that communicates to people about a contemporary political reality. That ability to use other methodologies to communicate those power relationships is what draws me to the work that Josh does, both for its capacity to reach people, but also because it's different than the way that I work. I enjoy being in dialogue with people who work in different modes. In this case, there's no protagonist who's being followed over a long period of time. It's a different relationship to exposing power.

Josh Begley

It's such a treat to be in conversation with Laura for a few reasons. Right now, I'm realizing there's a conversation between us that started in 2012. At the end of that summer, there was a film that debuted on the New York Times website called *The Program*, and it was the first time I'd encountered Laura's work. It was a short film about NSA whistleblower Bill Binney that painted this picture about power relations in the United States and what it means to listen to every phone call, potentially. And it gave me a frame to understand something that was very difficult for me to see. I didn't know how to think about what it meant—that phone calls across this country and across this world are being recorded and stored in a database or a set of databases, or perhaps just a giant building in Utah. Seeing the visual geography of how power maps out in this particular way actually changed how I wanted to engage data visualization. I was very interested in these phones that we all have in our pockets, these phones where we open a map and it puts us at the center. It changes our relation to what a map is. And more and more I actually think that narrative is the frame through which one has to enter any of these experiences, particularly these phone experiences. I also think about something that Toni Morrison said in 2016. "You know the formula. There's data, which becomes information, which becomes knowledge. But the step after that is wisdom. Neither one of those first three is sufficient." She goes on to say that this is why she writes literature: because it's indeterminate and it's provocative, and it can be beautiful.

Patricio Dávila

I'm taken by the similarity between documentary where you're working with found footage, and data visualization where, especially with you, Josh, a lot of work has been reframing existing datasets. I think of the work of Theaster Gates and Fred Wilson, who both work in these ways of found objects and putting them in collections in order for a narrative, loosely speaking, to emerge. Or Fred Wilson, where he took a collection of the Baltimore Heritage Museum and unveiled the systems of racism that buttressed that society. And so you're taking historical artifacts or data and then reframing them through that narrative. I'm wondering, how do you both negotiate that narrative? There's an article by Tess Takahashi where she posits that data visualisation is a documentary genre. And that one of the things to think about is documentary voice. There's a voice of God, the bodiless voice, that comes in and sutures everything together so it's nice and tight. But there's also this other voice of collecting. Who collected this data? Who made these causal or narrative links within a story or within a dataset that might not say anything?

Laura Poitras

That's super interesting. I would begin by saying that I don't consider documentary as a genre, per se. I think it's a mode of communication that's based on some set of primary documents that have some relationship with what we could call empirical reality. And not in any positivist sense that there's any singular truth, but it's in dialogue with something not in the realm of fiction. For W.E.B. DuBois, he is examining and commenting on race, and the history of race and America. And his mode of expression are these diagrams *The Georgia Negro: A Social Study*. Another example is Josh's *Best of Luck with the Wall*, which is stitching together Google satellite images to tell a story. These objects don't necessarily speak for themselves. But the way in which he then connects them is the message, right? It's what's being communicated. So I do think data visualization is a form of documentary practice.

Josh Begley

I'm more and more convinced that data visualization is most effective as a methodology—as a way of engaging any sort of empirical evidence or raw data or information. But the step that comes after data visualization is perhaps the most under-theorized one. A lot of times we'll get the data, we'll throw it on a map, we'll say, "Okay cool. That's beautiful, it's done." And I'm much more interested in what the data says and what we can mobilize in terms of narrative from that data. I think of questions like the one that the scholar Mimi Onuoha is asking, which is, "What are missing datasets?" It implies a whole set of questions about how we construct what data is, and I think a lot of folks think of it as this objective truth when in fact it is highly subjective at every point. So yeah, I think what Laura is saying is something that I have come to learn only recently, that data visualization is often a snapshot of the research process that can then end with something more powerful, a bit more theoretically grounded in some senses, and maybe a bit more emotional. And ultimately, how do we make data visualizations that have emotional content that aren't just activating your intellectual sense of seeing something, but in fact making you feel something?

Laura Poitras

In terms of this question of activation, what is exciting about the work that Josh is doing—and I would also put Forensic Architecture in this category—is how to not rely on the sort of standard tropes of narrative. The single individual narrative has drawbacks, right? I mean, I do that kind of work so I'm very aware of its drawbacks. For instance, my film *Citizenfour* has a central protagonist, he's a hero, and he becomes a sort of elevated iconic figure. But in the process of making a documentary narrative, because of the focus on the individual, it then fails to recognize how many hundreds of thousands of contractors are also employed by intelligence agencies who might also have issues or concerns with what's happening. You lose the sense of scale. And what I think is very exciting about data visualization is that it doesn't rely on those tested, tried and true methods of the individual protagonist, right? Or, as a method of understanding the world through this individual lens. What are the other methodologies to open up so you can actually understand scale in a different way? With that all said, yes, there will always be questions of what counts as data. And there are acts of exclusion in any kind of narrative storytelling, and we need to ask why.

Patricio Dávila

For my PhD, my dissertation was on assemblages that are created around visualization projects. So, precisely to the point being made, there is this artifact; but how do we think before and beyond that artifact? It might be a snapshot, it might be a film. However, who gets enlisted into this production? Under what circumstances? How do we create these associations and how do we become accountable to people who are being represented through the artifact? And then, how does the artifact itself circulate? For me, those are really important questions. And they push through a lot of the choices made in the exhibition in terms of how things circulate. There is this dominant notion of visualization as having the data speak for itself; as being highly technocratic. As being a simple representation of reality and that we can draw a direct connection to where the data was generated with the visualization. The projects both of you engage in are urgent. They're trying to create a space where people can experience something, or see a representation of something, that they have experienced themselves. Have you seen *La Hora de Los Hornos* (*The Hour of the Furnaces*)? It's an Argentinian agit-prop film from the 1960s by Fernando Solanas and Octavio Getino, an aggressive, formally very inventive film. It could only be shown in clandestine meetings, moving around constantly. They did this in order to mobilize resistance, to mobilize communities, and to survive. And so I'm reminded now, that we are experiencing the fact-resistant moment, in which there's a particular urgency. And I was wondering how you might see that distribution of the work that you do in order to mobilize. In order to interpret and experience the work. We have Field of Vision films. We have

apps. We have installation. So those are all different sort of contexts and spaces for seeing the work.

Laura Poitras

As a filmmaker, there is something wonderful about working in a medium that has the potential to connect outside of a small, rarefied audience, be that an academic audience or an art world context. I think that there are lots of things that are at odds between documentary filmmaking and what we would call more commercial filmmaking, but I have an aspiration to reach as many people as possible without compromising anything. With that said, there are also amazing possibilities to be explored in other contexts. Like the gallery or museum space–I did an exhibition at the Whitney Museum in New York and created the piece *O'Say Can You See*, which you exhibited again in *Diagrams of Power*. It is a double-screen installation where you walk into the room and you're encountered with one set of images with one emotional relationship to you; and then you turn a corner and there's another image which is of an interrogation. The audience then has to navigate that juxtaposition in space. That's not something I can do in single channel cinema. The closest I could get to that would just function as an edit. It's a different thing than having what you'd call a reveal, in a spatial way. For me, to work in both feels both organic and important. Because despite the spatial limitations, there is also something amazing about making something that people will buy popcorn for and watch, and it'll be kind of political. *Citizenfour* was an exposé of the US government's mass surveillance of the entire planet. So that obviously has political meaning. It's also a story about a young person who risks everything to expose the powerful's secrets—it hits all the points of a narrative. I couldn't *not* make a film about this person. We are drawn to certain things. I'm actually curious about what turns Josh on about data? What's the turn-on?

Josh Begley

First I would say that this actually one of the biggest things I've learned from Laura, that it's possible to make work that can cross disciplinary lines and audience lines, and exist both on the internet or in a gallery or on a bigger screen. This is someone who won a Pulitzer Prize for journalism and an Academy Award for filmmaking in essentially the same year. So, to be able to work in multiple formats, and then also have this Whitney solo show is just unparalleled. For me, I think, there's a question that has run through a lot of conversations we've had both at Field of Vision and with the fellows that Field of Vision supports—we had a couple of retreats last year. Thinking about moving image and video artwork that exists primarily in a gallery space alongside the more industry standard short films or longer-form films that exist online or in theaters. For a lot of people, they're going to make work wherever they can continue to make work. So, if that means editioning video artworks,

because it's going to be collected by major museums, which will allow them to make their next work—that's one reason they would do that. Or, signing a deal with Netflix so they can continue to make work in a more public way. I think that for me, what turns me on about data, to answer your question Laura, is that it's really a chance to do research. It's a chance to sit with an archive and really think with an archive, and see what there is to be said by that archive, or with that archive. So I think that in some ways the word, "data," at least as it was circulating four or five years ago, was a chance to buy time to do more research. It returns an artistic practice to a process of research, and not just thinking you know the story before you've done the rigorous work of examining the minutia. The practice of data visualization is attractive to me because it allows me to think in very small ways about the data that make up whatever the larger story is.

Patricio Dávila

Laura, I'm still thinking about how, when you're bringing data together, and you're creating these experiences in art galleries, there's still this tendency for the authority of that image. The authority of: this is a reality. It's increasingly hard to say it's a reality, and maybe it's within that artistic ability to express that you mentioned Laura, where there is latitude. But this is my question to both of you. Is there value in pointing to the incompleteness of the project? And if you do, how do you do it?

<u>Laura Poitras</u>

I do think there's a question of what the voice is, right? If you look at data visualization, I totally agree it can have a very techno-authoritarian voice of "this is the truth", as can documentary if you have a voice-over that's telling you what to believe. And both of these forms are trafficking with a certain kind of authorial knowledge that's not questioning itself. Obviously the public must be critical around engaging with anything calling itself "empirical data" or even "based on the real world". I also think there are kind of tried and true tactics where you break the fourth wall, so to speak. You expose that there is an author here, and that author is a singular perspective. I think you can do that by not trying to adopt an authorial knowledge-base but rather to be something that either directly exposes the methodology and/or the circumstances in which something is made. For instance, I made a film and at some point we decided to include my voice off-camera more often, just because we wanted to tell the audience, "we know you know there's a camera here, and there's a person behind it." And that's all it did, it just helped the audience understand that there's a person there, which then shifts the audience's perspective. It's how you articulate that. And I think the same can be said of Josh's works. If you look at *Best of Luck with the Wall*, after the first 40 seconds or so, there's a joke. And everybody gets the joke. I think once you throw in a joke with a data visualization project before it gets wildly abstract, you kind of know you're in a different terrain, right? You know that you're working with somebody who thinks that the audience is smart, and they are going to go along for the ride. Because of the title, *Best of Luck with the Wall*, which comes in kind of late, everybody gets it. It's basically a wink and a nod to the audience, to know this is why you're on the ride. And then it goes into this psychedelic, wild experience, which would be something we'd expect more to see in avant-garde cinema with two people in the audience, and not be seen by probably the five million people who have watched it on the internet.

<u>Josh Begley</u>

This is one of the reasons that I love Kirsten Johnson's film, *Cameraperson*. One of the scenes I'm thinking of as you're speaking right now Laura, is the scene in Sanaa, Yemen, when it sounds like you are in the car with Johnson driving to this secretive prison where the Al Qaeda suspects are kept. And so much of that film operates because of the voice behind the camera and because the subject of the film is, in many cases, the person holding the camera and what can happen when that voice is present. It's something that draws me to that form a whole lot. And I think this question of voice is really core to what feels dissatisfying to me about so much data visualization, in that many of the tools that we have to visualize data are tools that have a military lens. They're satellite mapping tools, or a map-making tool with coordinate systems. Things that are looking at the ground from above but rarely visualizing the above, or the whole pie from below. So it makes me want to think about things like Google Street View. How do you reverse the gaze, so that instead of looking down at the earth, you're looking up from the earth. How do you speak back to the military lens much data visualization takes for granted? And I think in some sense, that's where the idea for the iPhone app came from, how do you take this technology that is using people's telephones to target drone strikes and speak back, or close that feedback loop a little and allow you to experience on your phone information about this news from far away? I saw an article yesterday or the day before, by John Herrman in the Times, it was a profile of this new app called *Citizen* that is trying to innovate on the 911 system. So you download it and it's a map of all of these major incidents that have occured near you. You can see where there was a robbery three blocks away, or there was some sort of fire, and it optimizes for you because you're at the center of the map. What would it mean to create an app that optimizes for all of the events that are the furthest away from you, and what kinds of questions can we ask of the data that's not just

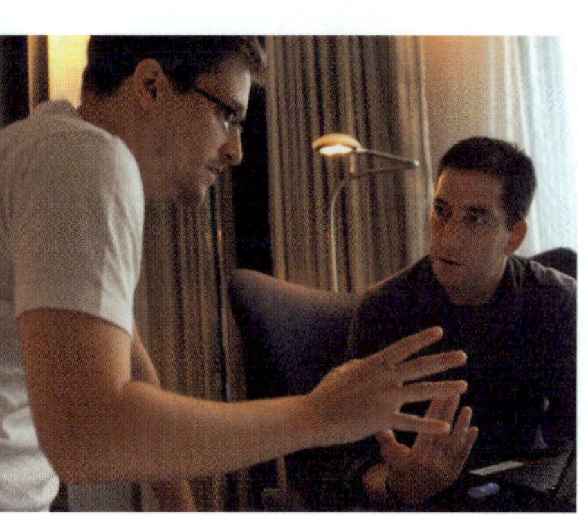

Still. *CITIZENFOUR*, (Poitras, 2014), Courtesy of Praxis Films.

'give me the nearest incidents by where I am'? I think so many things are possible when you can ask questions of a dataset. But it feels like we ask such basic, half-baked questions.

Patricio Dávila
This makes me think of this notion of cognitive mapping. Where you have your own lived experience, and it is situated within something very remote or highly complex. The functioning of capital, let's say—how am I imbricated within capitalism? Well, I have my purchases: my ethical purchases, my non-ethical purchases. This is how I negotiate my day-to-day, within something that's so large, so complex, that it outstrips human scale. How do I act? Resist? So I'm thinking back to Josh's drone app, where, as Laura had described it, a reality that is happening very far away interrupts your daily state related to you. Are there other modes, is it the personal that is most useful in order to make that cognitive map stick, rather than just a rational mapping?

Josh Begley
I think there has to be some kind of intimacy that is developed. I think the best data visualizations are the ones that make you feel something, that make you feel tied to or implicated by or connected to or repelled by whatever is being displayed. I think Saidiya Hartman recently said something about the charts that W.E.B. Du Bois made with his students, these amazing data visualizations that were made a hundred years ago and are profoundly

creative. And she was wondering why he never returned to that form, and why we're putting so much weight on these maps if he never returned to that form? I wonder what would've happened had there been more visual work that Du Bois made—and maybe he did and I'm just not aware of it. I wonder about the choice to focus in different mediums.

Laura Poitras

Yeah. I think it's how do you expose institutional structures that promote and perpetuate inequality, injustice, violence, wars, capitalism, structural racism. Data visualization has the potential to do that kind of scaling. Like, how do you wrap your arms around something so massive? And how do you translate concerns that are oftentimes hidden into something that can be communicated and that will reach people? Going back to what Josh's quote of Morrison, how do you translate knowledge or information to wisdom that shifts consciousness? I think that's our challenge as artists, as journalists, as citizens: to expose institutional forms of injustice, inequality, violence.

Patricio Dávila

I'm thinking of a more recent collaboration you guys did, titled *Concussion Protocol*, where you're basically taking something that, over a long period of time, is harder to perceive. But when they're jammed up right against each other it becomes a typology. One concussion, two concussions… this is what they all look like, so that we can start comparing them across. And what

is really striking about that is the move you make to undo the normative way of experiencing this on TV by playing footage backwards.

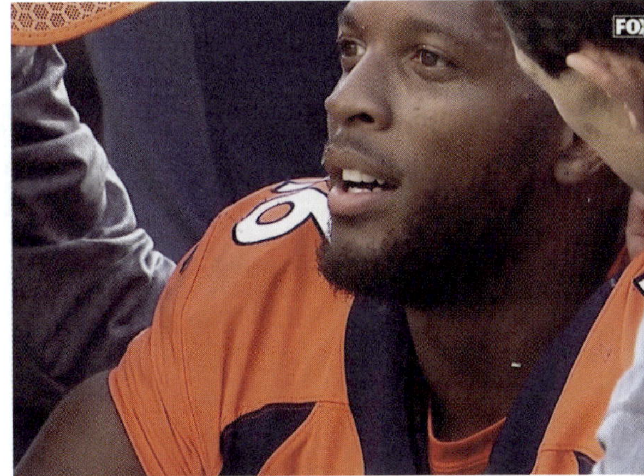

Still. Josh Begley, *Concussion Protocol*, 2018. Video. Courtesy of the artist and Field of Vision.

Laura Poitras

I think what you just described is how do you translate the normalcy of the fact that Americans every Sunday sit down and watch football players participate in a sport that is injuring their brains? How can you shift that pleasure into a reflection of risks and spectacle that we're engaged in, right? Josh approached me at the beginning of the football season with the idea of a prospective project that collects all the concussions as they happen. He wrote a computer script that it would alert him when there were reported injuries.He was able to create a proof of concept from the first week of the season, with the plan to release it right before the Super Bowl. So this was not looking at past data, but rather turning the lens to the future. Millions of people have

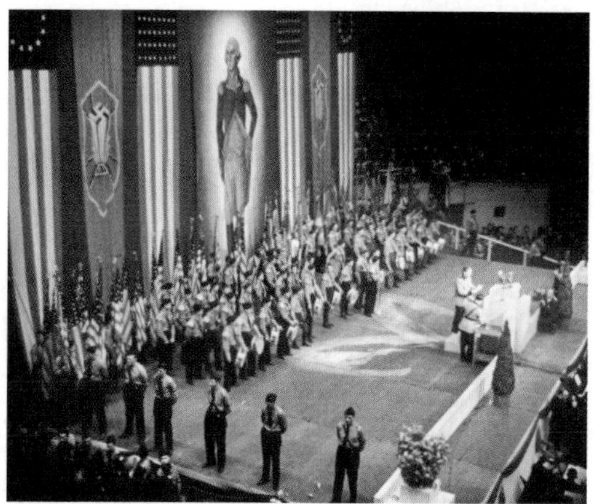

Still. Marshall Curry, *A Night at the Garden*, 2017. Video. Courtesy of Field of Vision and Marshall Curry Productions.

watched it. It is a powerful work of cinema, that not only shows in a compressed form all the concussions and brain injuries that happened in the season, but also celebrates the athleticism of the sport. It's not only a condemnation or critique.

Josh Begley

The only thing I would add is that in some ways the unwinding, or the reversing, of some of that footage comes from something that Saidiya Hartman has written—about defamiliarizing the familiar. American football is so normative. It's on in every bar you walk into, it's difficult to get out of the mode of watching that can settle in when you just see football scenes in forward motion. So what does it mean to unwind or rewind those particular moments of violence and moments of trauma?

Laura Poitras

Yes, I agree. We need to be brainstorming around how you take something that we've normalized, if that's structural racism, or if that's capitalism, or if that's police violence, and what are the strategies, prospectively looking forward, to denormalize? How can you de-normalize torture, or Guantanamo Bay prison?

Patricio Dávila

I think it's probably not just more information that's needed, it's the way of putting it together. And what I note in that particular video is the very data-like nature of it—it has a Josh Begley feel. It's the difficulty in unraveling what is exactly happening, first. And then there's a reveal at the end, where we go back to what we see all the time, but now in forward motion with fresh eyes. We see these things all the time, so how do we use our inventive powers to actually make it new again?

Josh Begley

You're making me think of the John Berger quote that is the core of so much for me: "The relation between what we see and what we know is never settled." I have that written on a little piece of paper on my wall somewhere. For me, that's an argument for continuing to make visual work, because it does have the power to unsettle these normative understandings of the historical moment in which we live and the world in which we live. That so much of what changes what I think I know is something that I see.

Laura Poitras

I want to reference another film that Field of Vision also supported, called *A Night at the Garden*. It does what Josh is referring to. It's a short film, seven minutes long, that goes back to this footage of twenty-thousand people gathering in Madison Square Garden in the heart of New York City, for a Nazi rally in 1939 several months before Hitler's invasion of Poland. So, before the official beginning of the Second World War, but certainly after Kristallnacht, after a lot of the building of the concentration camps. This is a history that Americans are not told. They literally don't know it exists, save for a few exceptions. So when they are presented with this documentary evidence of twenty-thousand people in the middle of New York City saluting Hitler, their first response is anger. They don't believe it. How is it that they don't know? And it does create an actual rewiring of their understanding of American history. The narrative that the US has told about the Second World War is that we were on the right side of history—it's not, we could've been on either side of history. We could've been on the wrong side.

What other ways can we continue to do this work? Is there material documentary, primary documents where you can create those sorts of rewiring of how we understand ourselves historically and in the present tense, and in our relationship to power. I want to return to this idea of diagrams and methodologies. Diagramming is one of many methodologies and it has a lot of potential benefits. It can scale. It tries to take a bigger picture than we as individuals are able to experience and that's a really powerful thing. It has potential risks of being like the voice of God, an authorial position. What are they capable of telling us, and what are their blind spots?

Patricio Dávila

One of the projects that I've written about, and is in the exhibition, is the Anti-Eviction Mapping Project, and I find it to be one of the most successful, amazing projects, because of precisely what you're talking about in terms of multiple modalities. As part of the San Francisco Tenants Union, they organize. They use a mutual benefit framework. If someone is going to be evicted, they show up at the courthouse. They're going to know the people that they represent in maps, in the oral storytelling project. They created a mural which is right in Clarion Alley in the Mission District. And so, through and through, they represent the community in the ways that are necessary. They create a zine, they make a mural, they organize events, they also had small GIFs that got circulated through AJ+ on social media networks. So they're thoughtful with the particular modes because of how they're meaningful for particular communities.

Laura Poitras

Right, and I imagine that they have a legal support structure as well. Something we don't probably do enough in our work is building multidisciplinary teams that can take on issues with different, multifaceted methodologies to impact change. The multifaceted approached of the Anti-Eviction Mapping Project is exciting. We need more of that.

Best of Luck with the Wall

Josh Begley

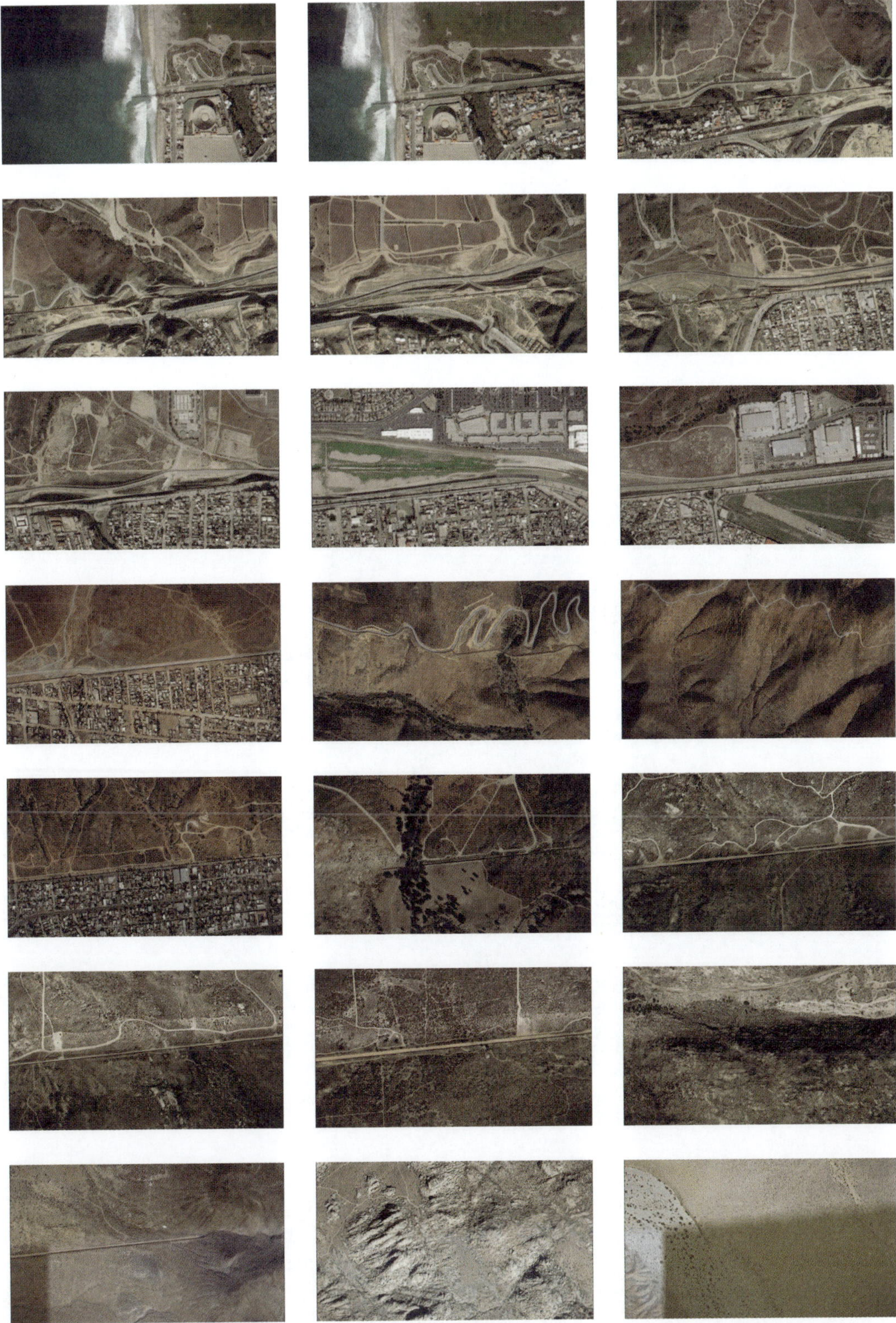

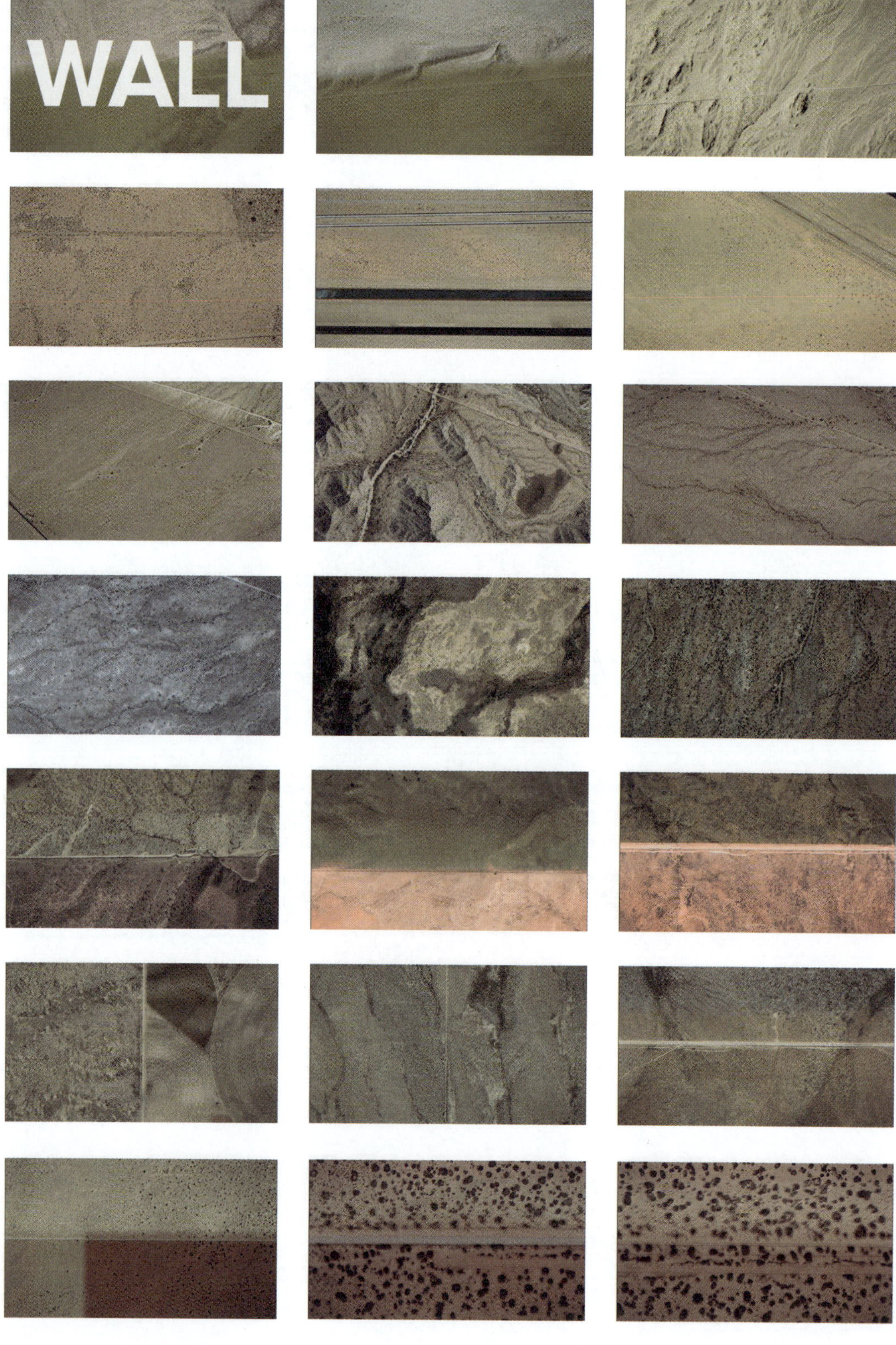
WALL

Best of Luck with the Wall
Josh Begley

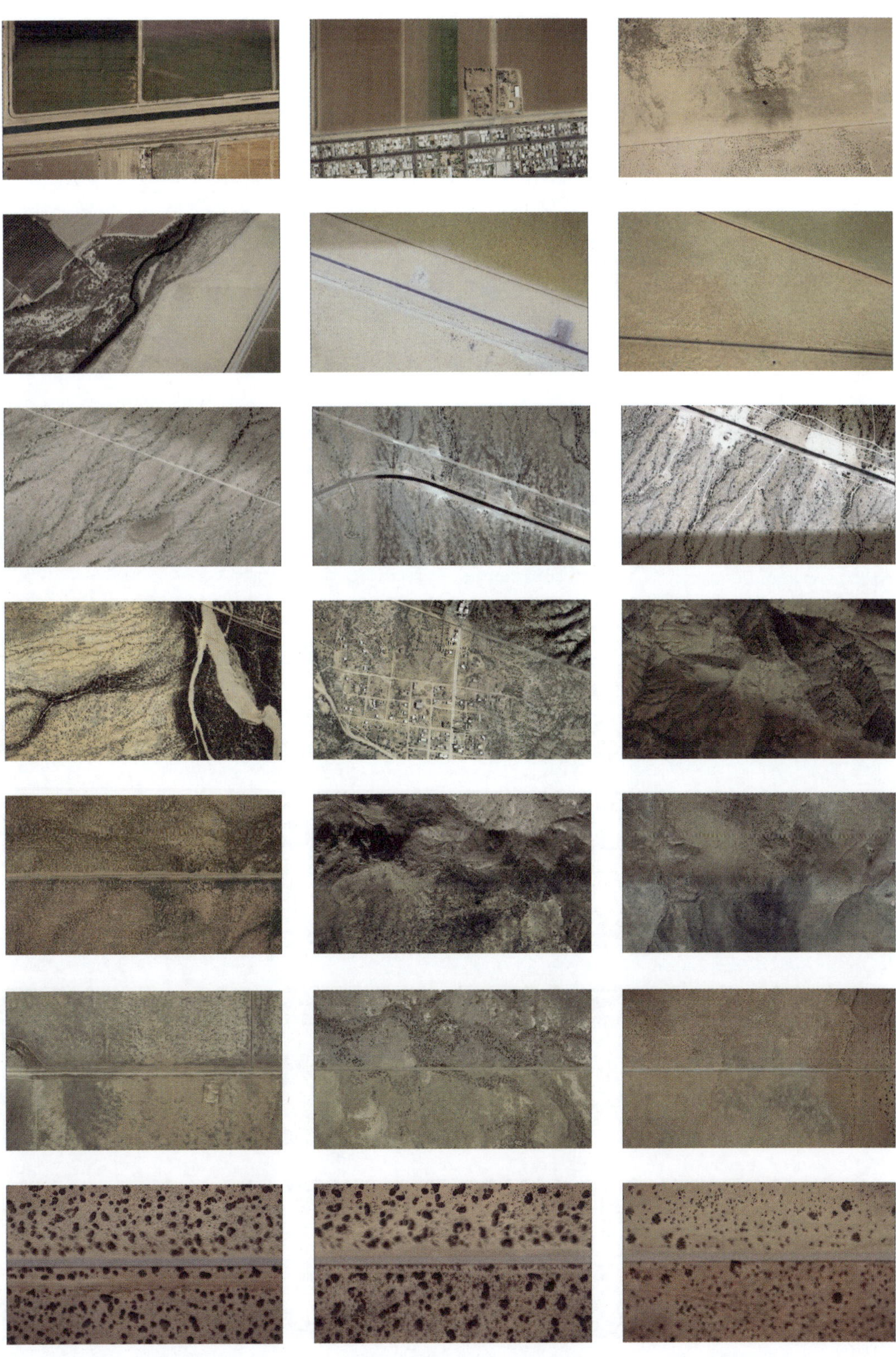

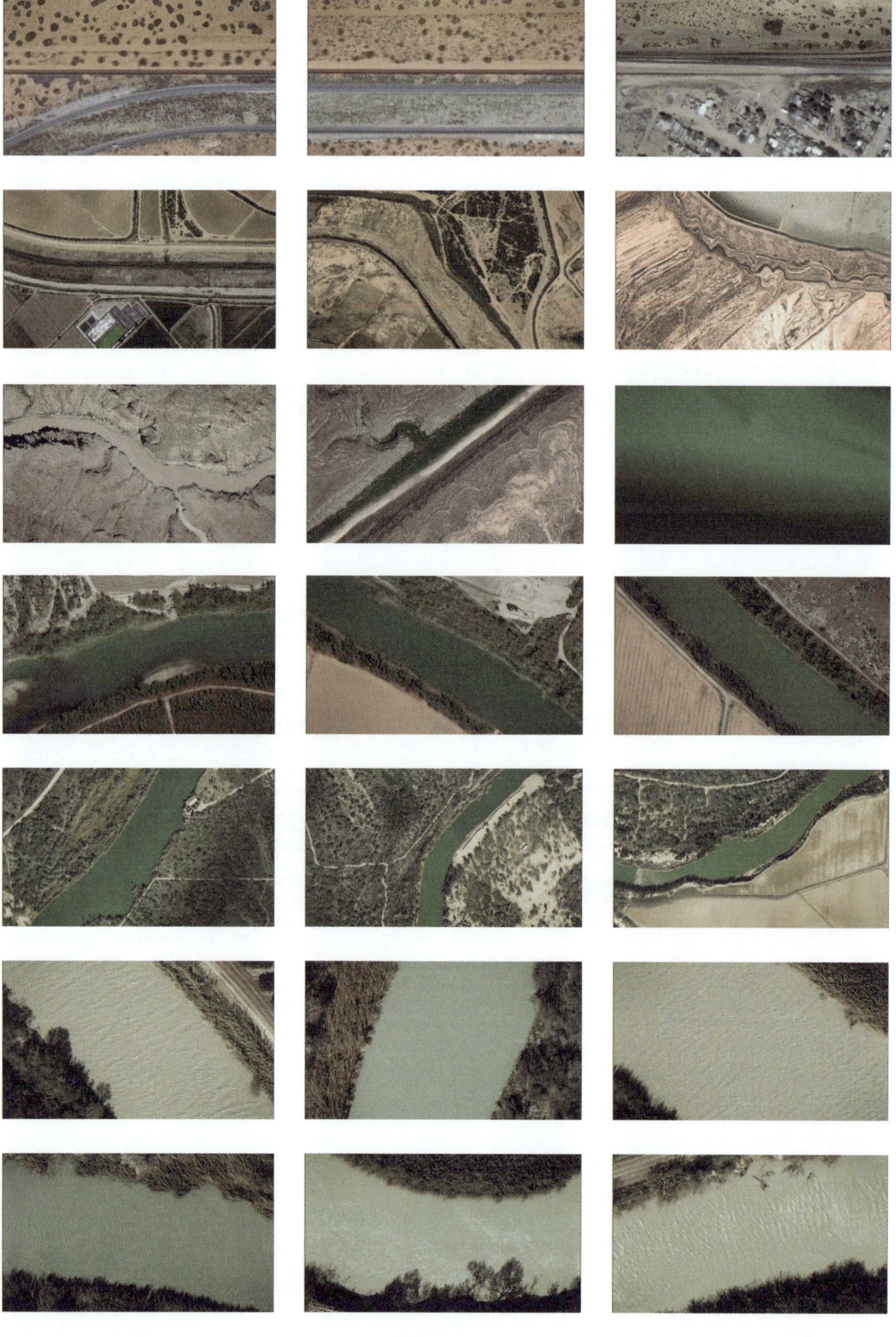

Best of Luck with the Wall
Josh Begley

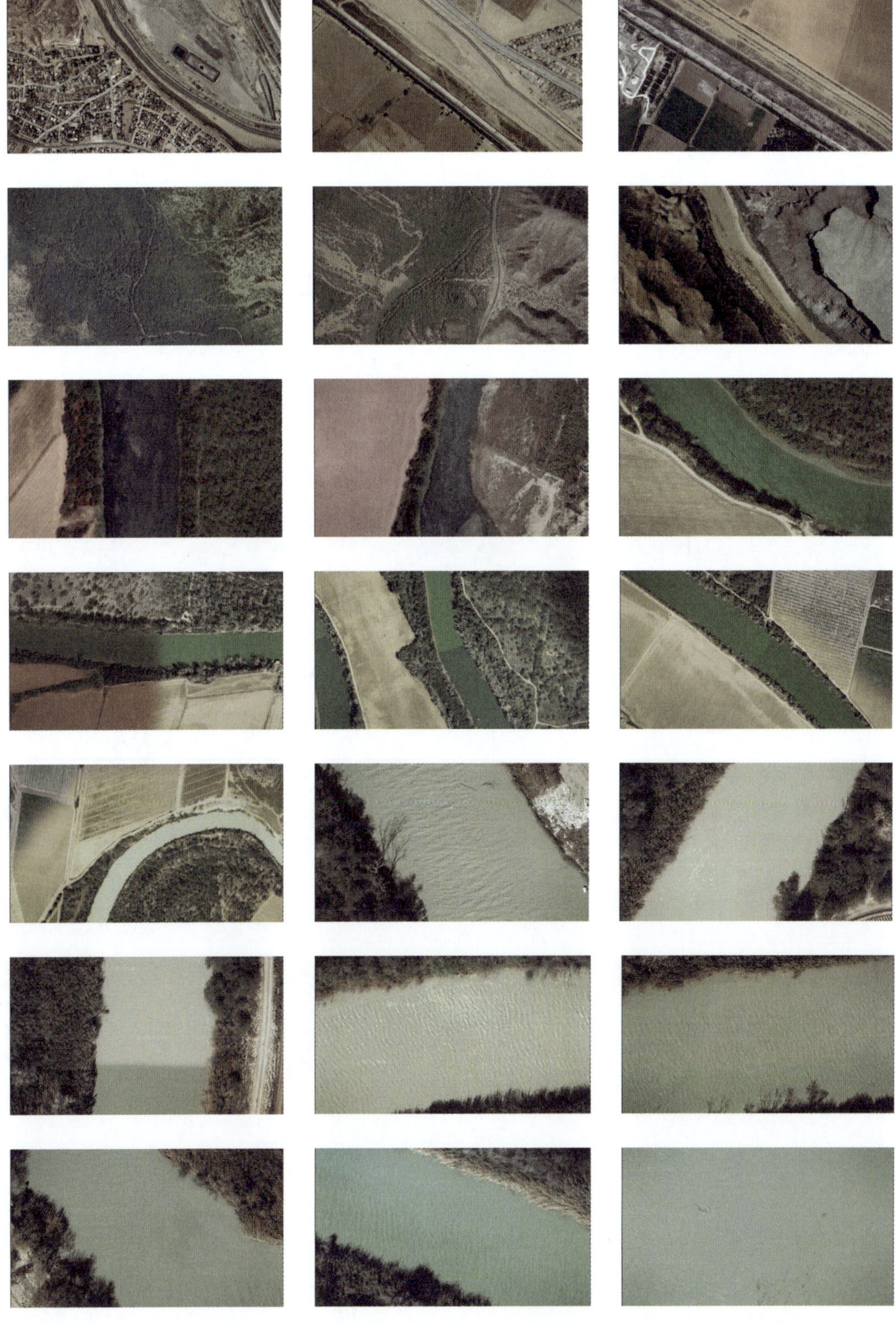

DIAGRAMS OF POWER

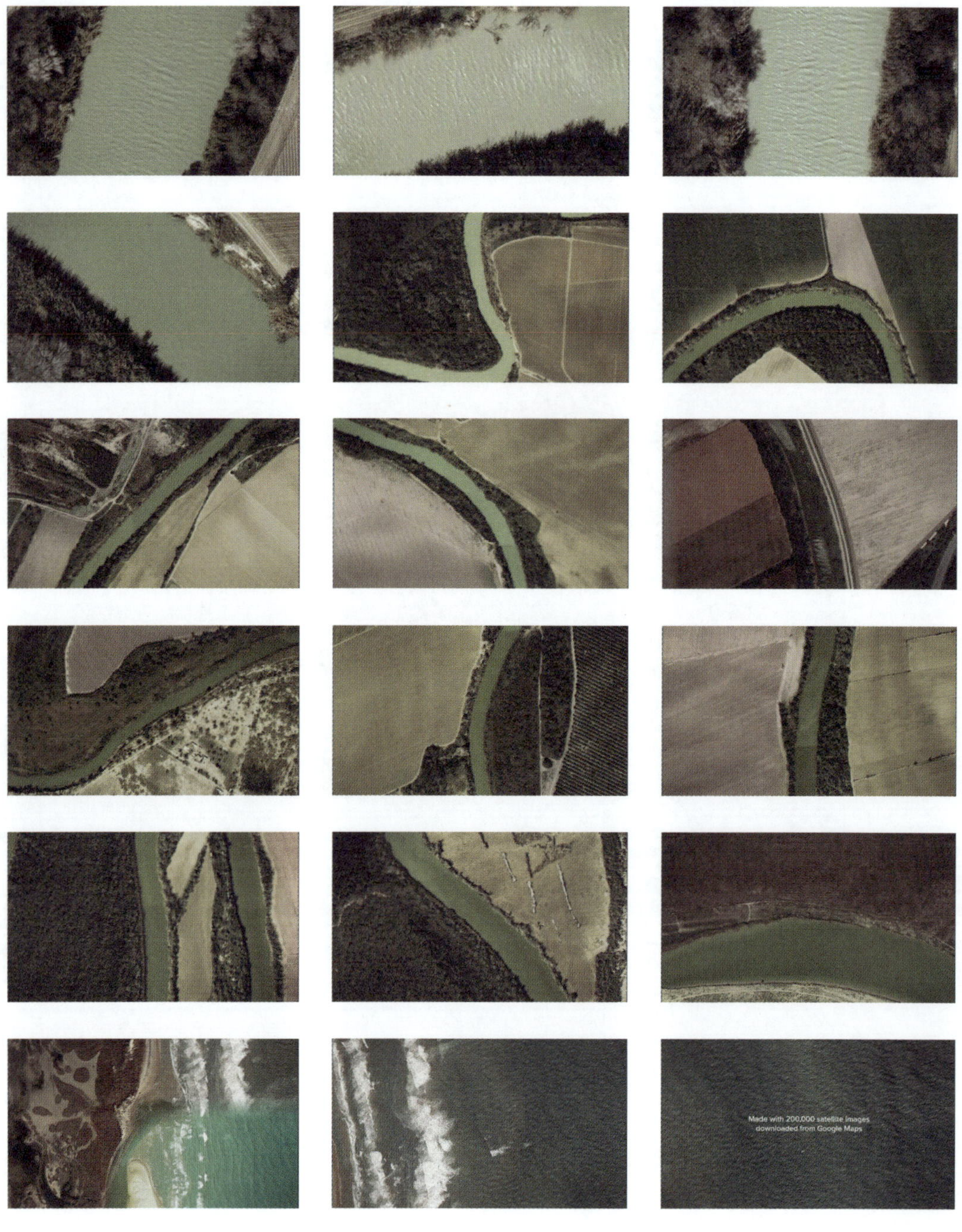

Stills. Josh Begley, *Best of Luck with the Wall*, 2016. Video. Courtesy of the artist and Field of Vision.

The Anti-Eviction Mapping Project

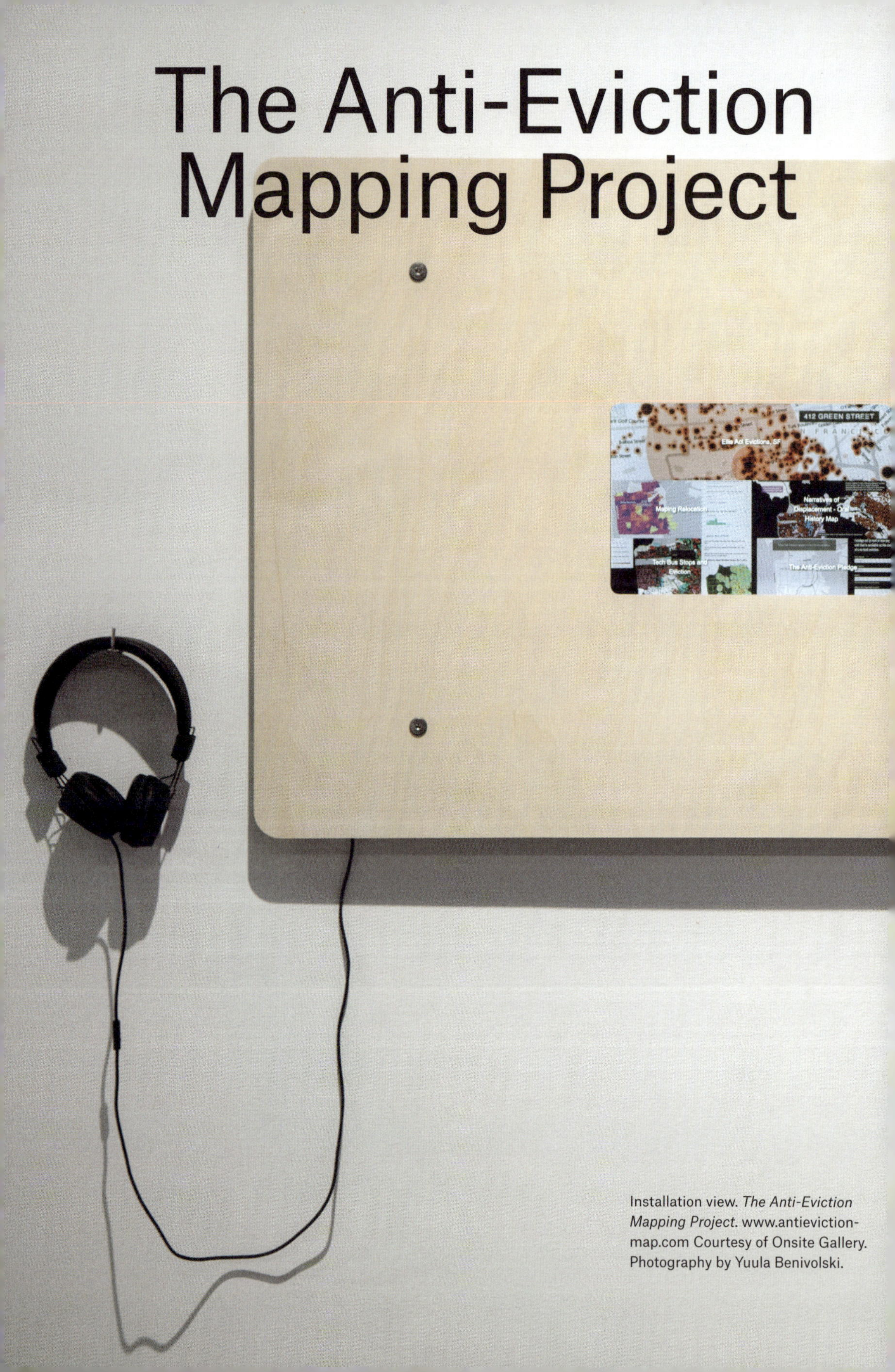

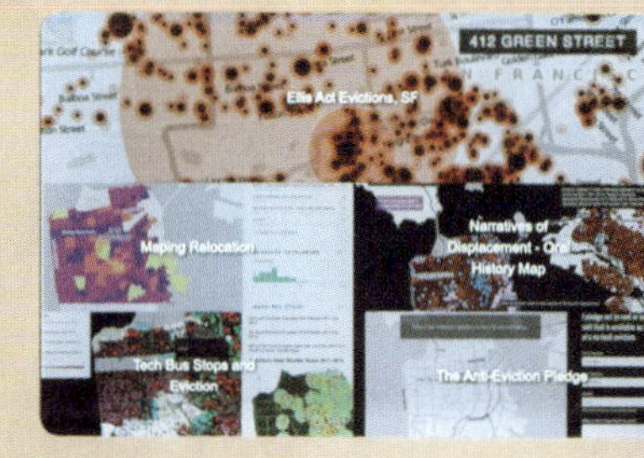

Installation view. *The Anti-Eviction Mapping Project*. www.antieviction-map.com Courtesy of Onsite Gallery. Photography by Yuula Benivolski.

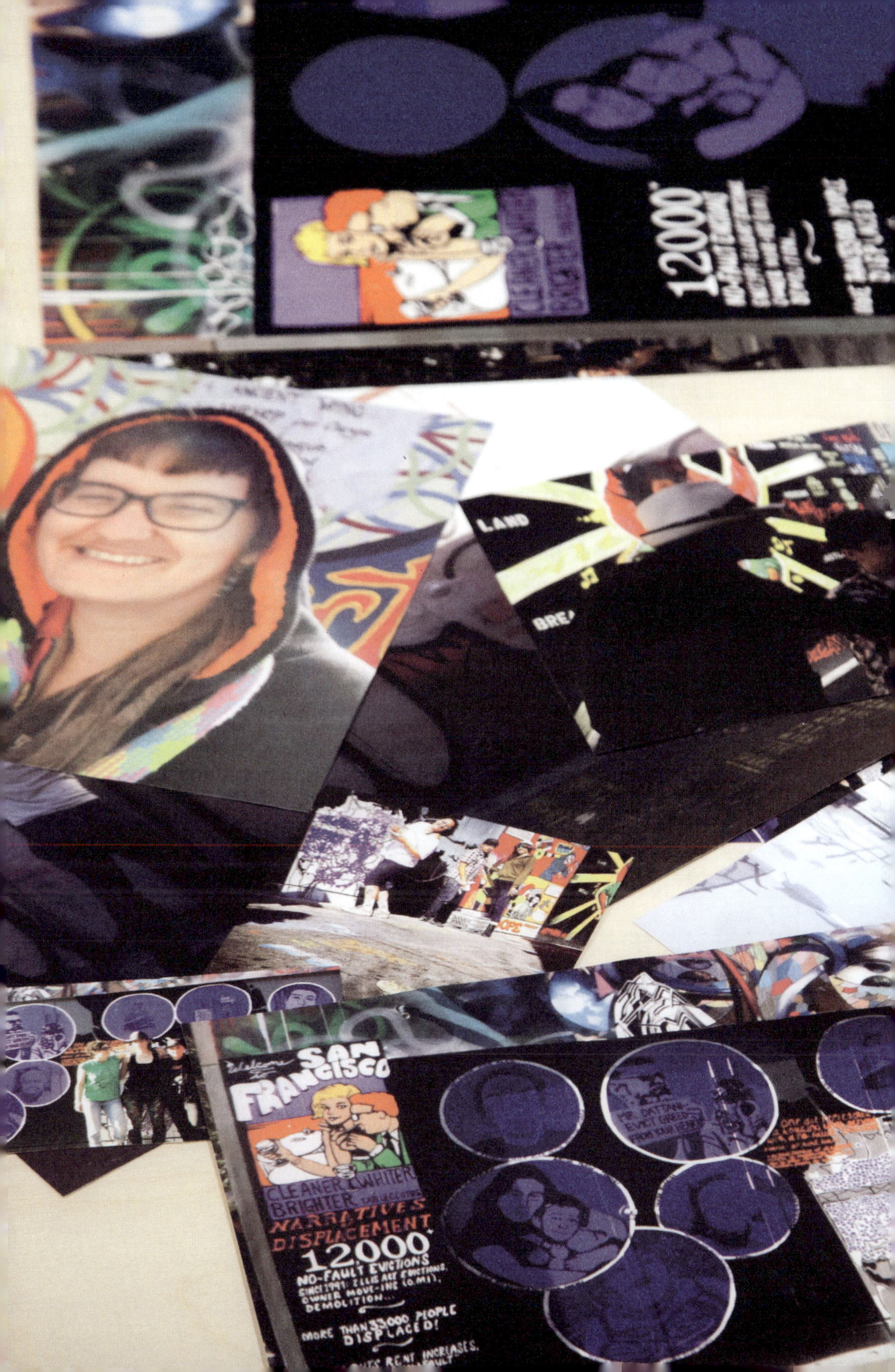

12000
LAND
BREA
Welcome to
SAN FRANCISCO
CLEANER WHITER
BRIGHTER
NARRATIVES
DISPLACEMENT
12000
NO-FAULT EVICTIONS
SINCE 1997. ELLIS ACT EVICTIONS,
OWNER MOVE-INS (O.M.I),
DEMOLITION...
MORE THAN 33000 PEOPLE
DISPLACED!
MR. DATTANI,
EVICT GREED
FROM YOUR HEART

The Anti-Eviction Mapping Project is a data-visualization, data analysis, and storytelling collective
documenting the dispossession and resistance upon
gentrifying landscapes.
Primarily working in the
San Francisco Bay Area,
Los Angeles, and New York
City, we are all volunteers
producing digital maps,
oral history work, film,
murals, and community
events. Working with a
number of community
partners and in solidarity
with numerous housing
movements, we study
and visualize new entanglements of global capital,
real estate, technocapitalism, and political economy.
Our narrative oral history and video work centers the
displacement of people and complex social worlds, but
also modes of resistance.

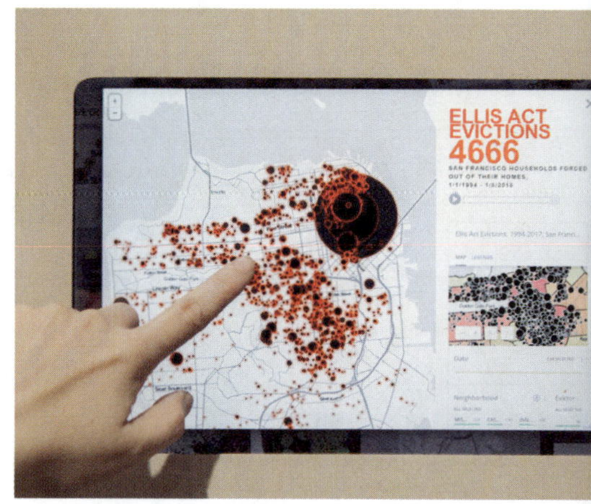

The Anti-Eviction Mapping Project.
www.antievictionmap.com Courtesy of
The Anti-Eviction Mapping Project.

Artists with the Anti-Eviction Mapping Project teamed up with the Clarion Alley Mural Project
to paint a 20 foot mural in Clarion Alley at Valencia
Street. The mural depicts a rendering of the online
map of no-fault evictions since 1997 and highlights

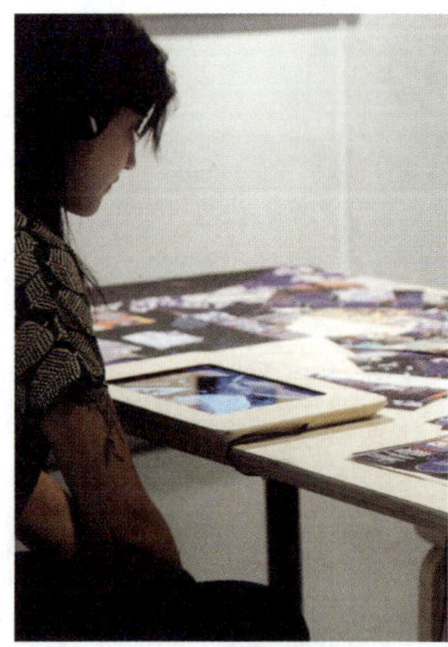

the portraits of eight San Franciscans
fighting their evictions. Viewers can call
a phone number 415-319-6865 to hear
stories of the people whose portraits are
depicted on the mural. The mural includes a portrait of Alex Nieto, killed by
SFPD in 2014 on Bernal Hill, to make
the connection between gentrification
and the criminalization of people of
color. The left panel of the mural, facing Valencia Street, "welcomes" visitors
to the alley with a remixed design of a
poster developed by the SF Print Col-
lective and pasted around the Mission in the 1990's in
response to the dot com boom.

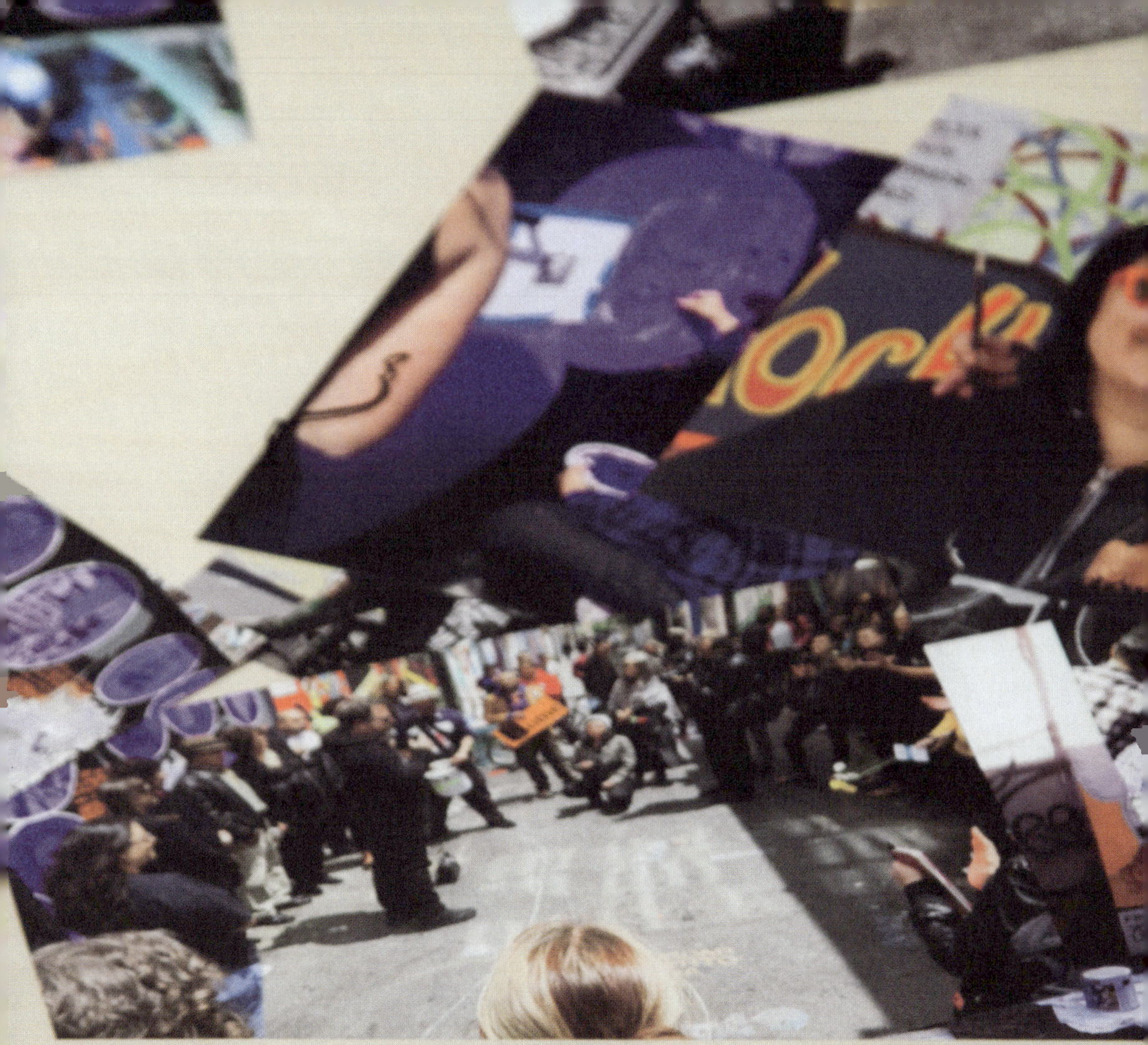

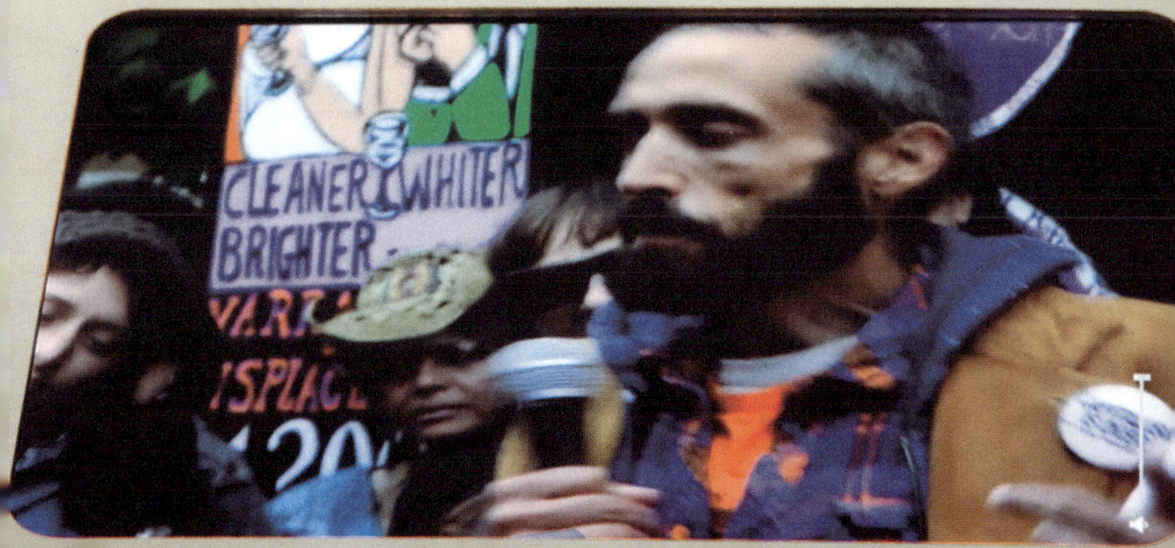
CLEANER WHITER
BRIGHTER

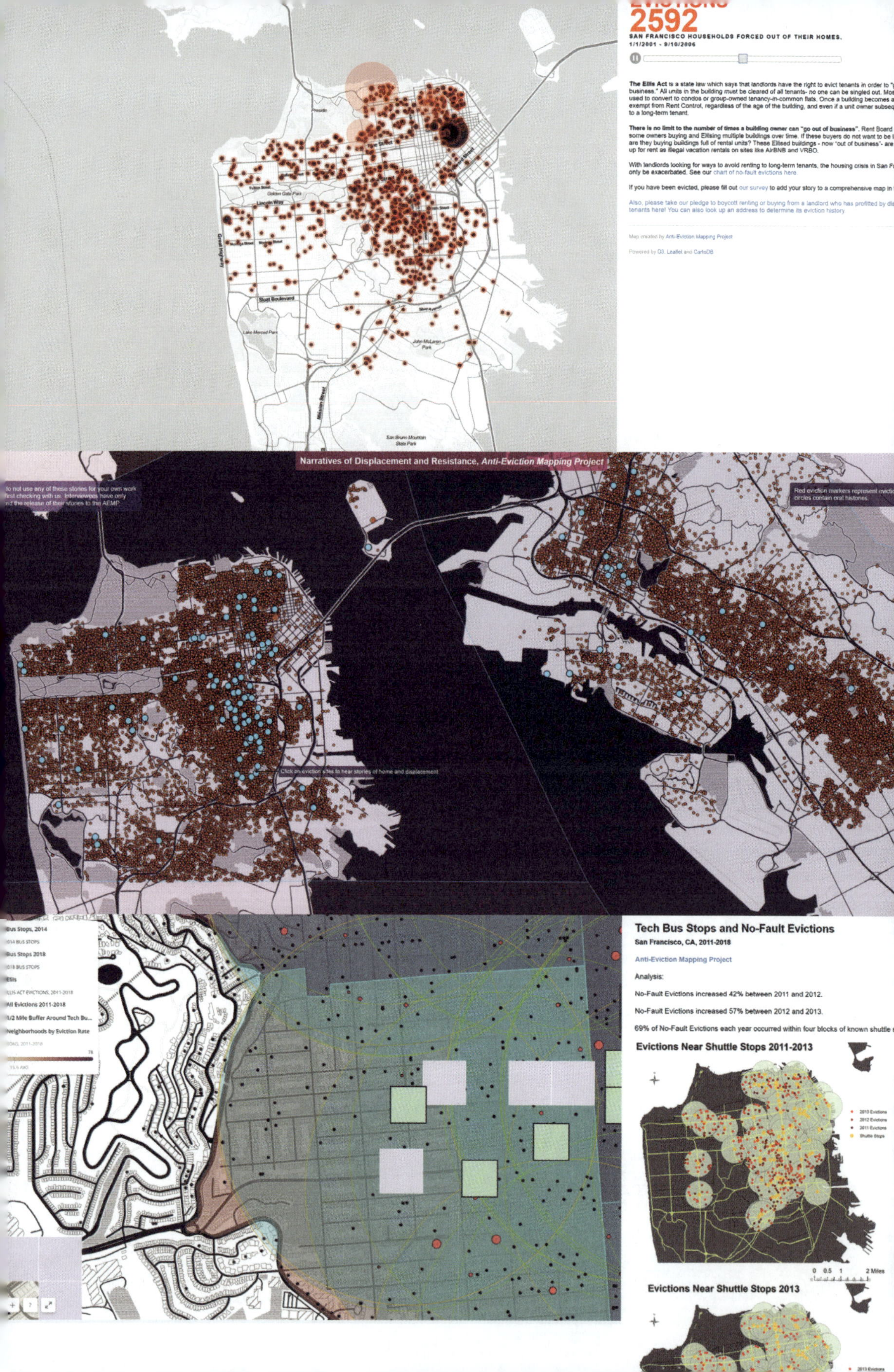
EVICTIONS
2592
SAN FRANCISCO HOUSEHOLDS FORCED OUT OF THEIR HOMES.
1/1/2001 - 9/10/2006

The Ellis Act is a state law which says that landlords have the right to evict tenants in order to "go out of business." All units in the building must be cleared of all tenants- no one can be singled out. Most used to convert to condos or group-owned tenancy-in-common flats. Once a building becomes a exempt from Rent Control, regardless of the age of the building, and even if a unit owner subseq to a long-term tenant.

There is no limit to the number of times a building owner can "go out of business". Rent Board some owners buying and Ellising multiple buildings over time. If these buyers do not want to be l are they buying buildings full of rental units? These Ellised buildings - now 'out of business'- are up for rent as illegal vacation rentals on sites like AirBNB and VRBO.

With landlords looking for ways to avoid renting to long-term tenants, the housing crisis in San Fr only be exacerbated. See our chart of no-fault evictions here.

If you have been evicted, please fill out our survey to add your story to a comprehensive map in

Also, please take our pledge to boycott renting or buying from a landlord who has profited by dis tenants here! You can also look up an address to determine its eviction history.

Map created by Anti-Eviction Mapping Project

Powered by D3, Leaflet and CartoDB

Narratives of Displacement and Resistance, Anti-Eviction Mapping Project

to not use any of these stories for your own work
first checking with us. Interviewees have only
ed the release of their stories to the AEMP.

Red eviction markers represent evicti
circles contain oral histories.

Click on eviction sites to hear stories of home and displacement

Bus Stops, 2014
014 BUS STOPS
Bus Stops 2018
018 BUS STOPS
Ellis
LLIS ACT EVICTIONS, 2011-2018
All Evictions 2011-2018
1/2 Mile Buffer Around Tech Bu...
Neighborhoods by Eviction Rate
ONS, 2011-2018

Tech Bus Stops and No-Fault Evictions
San Francisco, CA, 2011-2018
Anti-Eviction Mapping Project
Analysis:
No-Fault Evictions increased 42% between 2011 and 2012.
No-Fault Evictions increased 57% between 2012 and 2013.
69% of No-Fault Evictions each year occurred within four blocks of known shuttle st

Evictions Near Shuttle Stops 2011-2013

2013 Evictions
2012 Evictions
2011 Evictions
Shuttle Stops

0 0.5 1   2 Miles

Evictions Near Shuttle Stops 2013

2013 Evictions

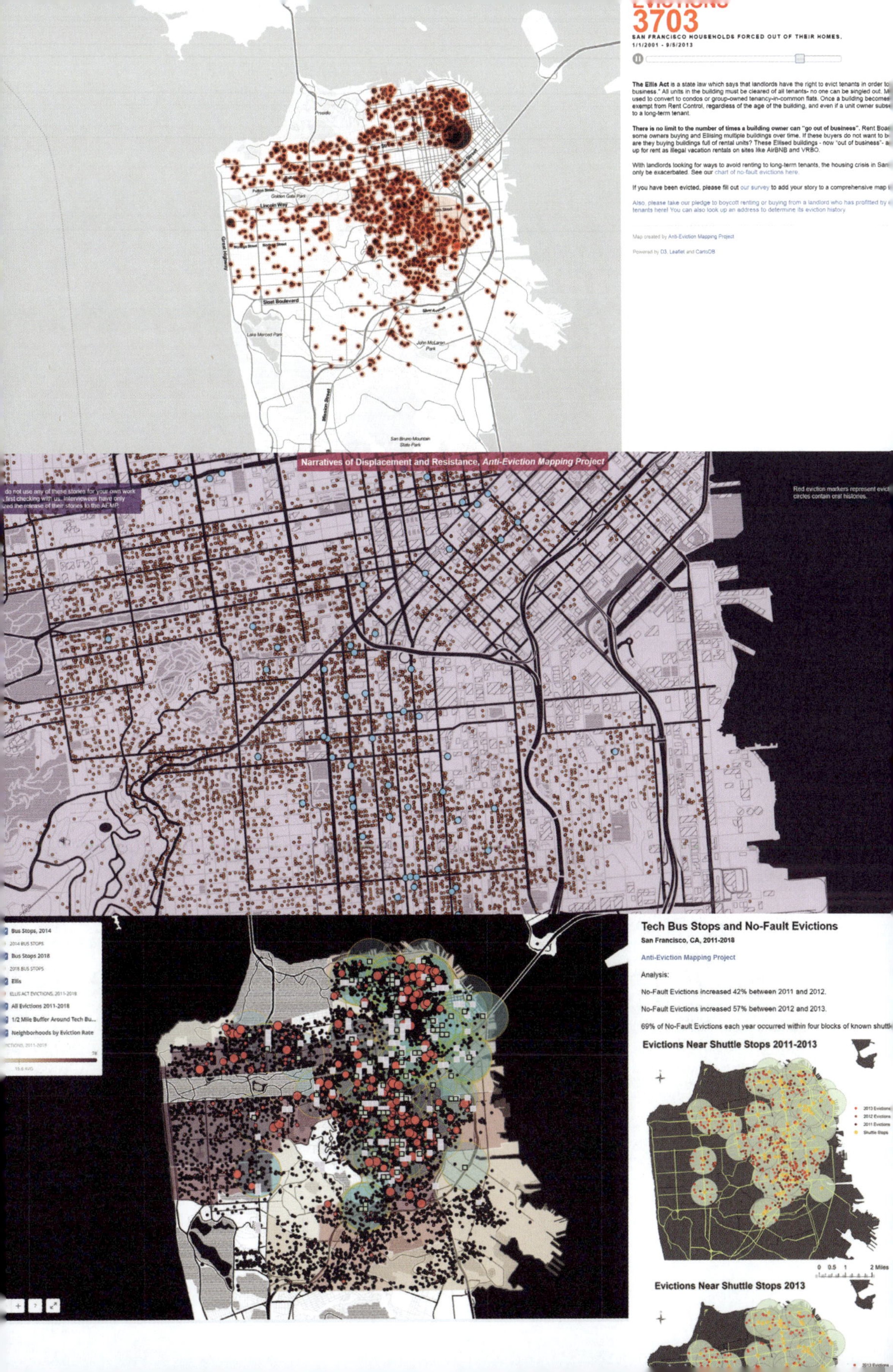
EVICTIONS
3703
SAN FRANCISCO HOUSEHOLDS FORCED OUT OF THEIR HOMES.
1/1/2001 - 9/5/2013

The Ellis Act is a state law which says that landlords have the right to evict tenants in order to
business." All units in the building must be cleared of all tenants- no one can be singled out. M
used to convert to condos or group-owned tenancy-in-common flats. Once a building becomes
exempt from Rent Control, regardless of the age of the building, and even if a unit owner subse
to a long-term tenant.

There is no limit to the number of times a building owner can "go out of business". Rent Boar
some owners buying and Ellising multiple buildings over time. If these buyers do not want to b
are they buying buildings full of rental units? These Ellised buildings - now "out of business"- a
up for rent as illegal vacation rentals on sites like AirBNB and VRBO.

With landlords looking for ways to avoid renting to long-term tenants, the housing crisis in San
only be exacerbated. See our chart of no-fault evictions here.

If you have been evicted, please fill out our survey to add your story to a comprehensive map i

Also, please take our pledge to boycott renting or buying from a landlord who has profitted by
tenants here! You can also look up an address to determine its eviction history.

Map created by Anti-Eviction Mapping Project

Powered by D3, Leaflet and CartoDB

Narratives of Displacement and Resistance, Anti-Eviction Mapping Project

do not use any of these stories for your own work
first checking with us. Interviews have only
ved the release of their stories to the AEMP

Red eviction markers represent evict
circles contain oral histories.

Bus Stops, 2014
2014 BUS STOPS
Bus Stops 2018
2018 BUS STOPS
Ellis
ELLIS ACT EVICTIONS, 2011-2018
All Evictions 2011-2018
1/2 Mile Buffer Around Tech Bu...
Neighborhoods by Eviction Rate

Tech Bus Stops and No-Fault Evictions
San Francisco, CA, 2011-2018

Anti-Eviction Mapping Project

Analysis:

No-Fault Evictions increased 42% between 2011 and 2012.

No-Fault Evictions increased 57% between 2012 and 2013.

69% of No-Fault Evictions each year occurred within four blocks of known shuttle

Evictions Near Shuttle Stops 2011-2013

2013 Evictions
2012 Evictions
2011 Evictions
Shuttle Stops

0 0.5 1   2 Miles

Evictions Near Shuttle Stops 2013

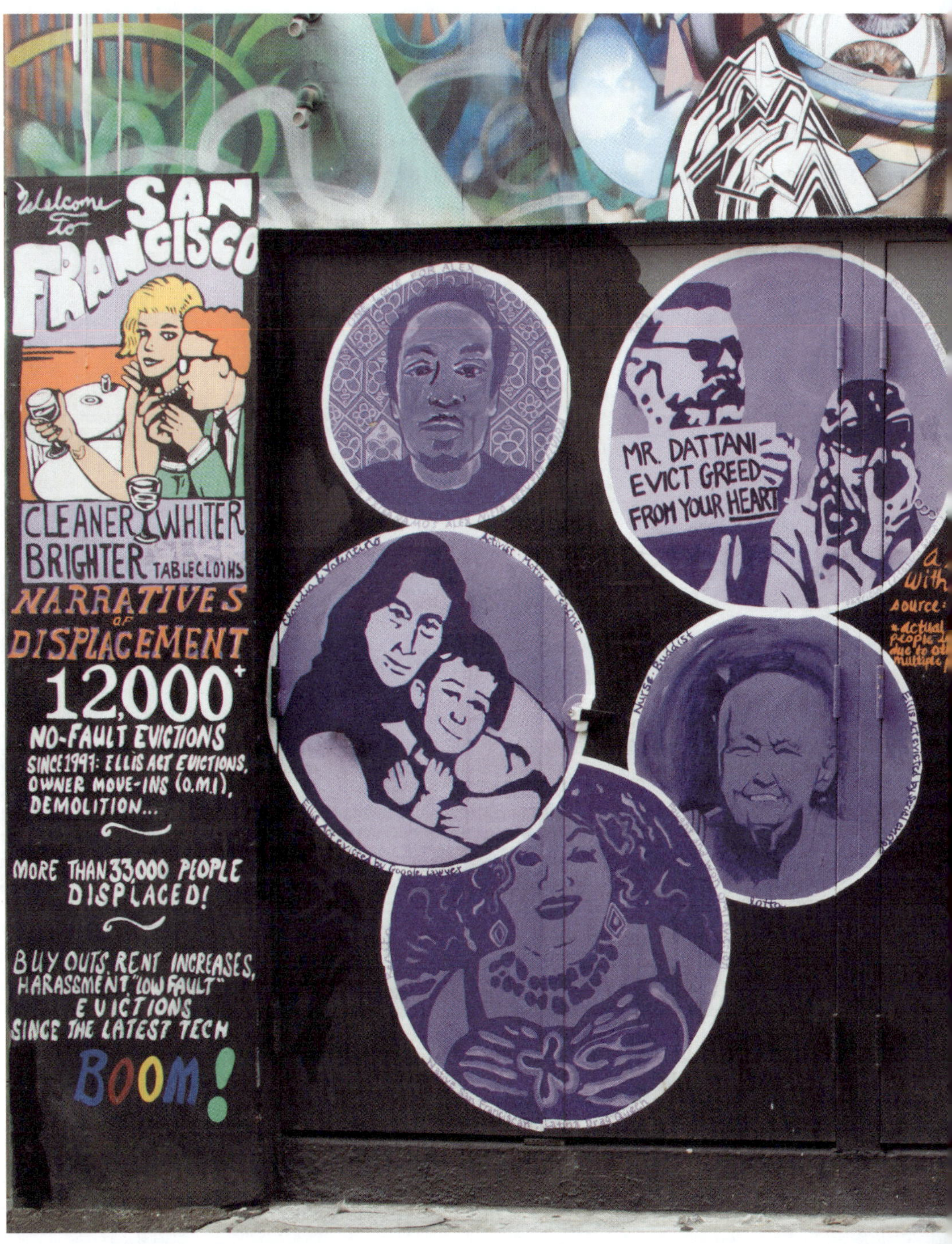
Welcome to SAN FRANCISCO
CLEANER WHITER BRIGHTER TABLECLOTHS
NARRATIVES of DISPLACEMENT
12,000+
NO-FAULT EVICTIONS
SINCE 1997: ELLIS ACT EVICTIONS, OWNER MOVE-INS (O.M.I.), DEMOLITION...
MORE THAN 33,000 PEOPLE DISPLACED!
BUY OUTS, RENT INCREASES, HARASSMENT "LOW FAULT" EVICTIONS SINCE THE LATEST TECH BOOM!
MR. DATTANI - EVICT GREED FROM YOUR HEART

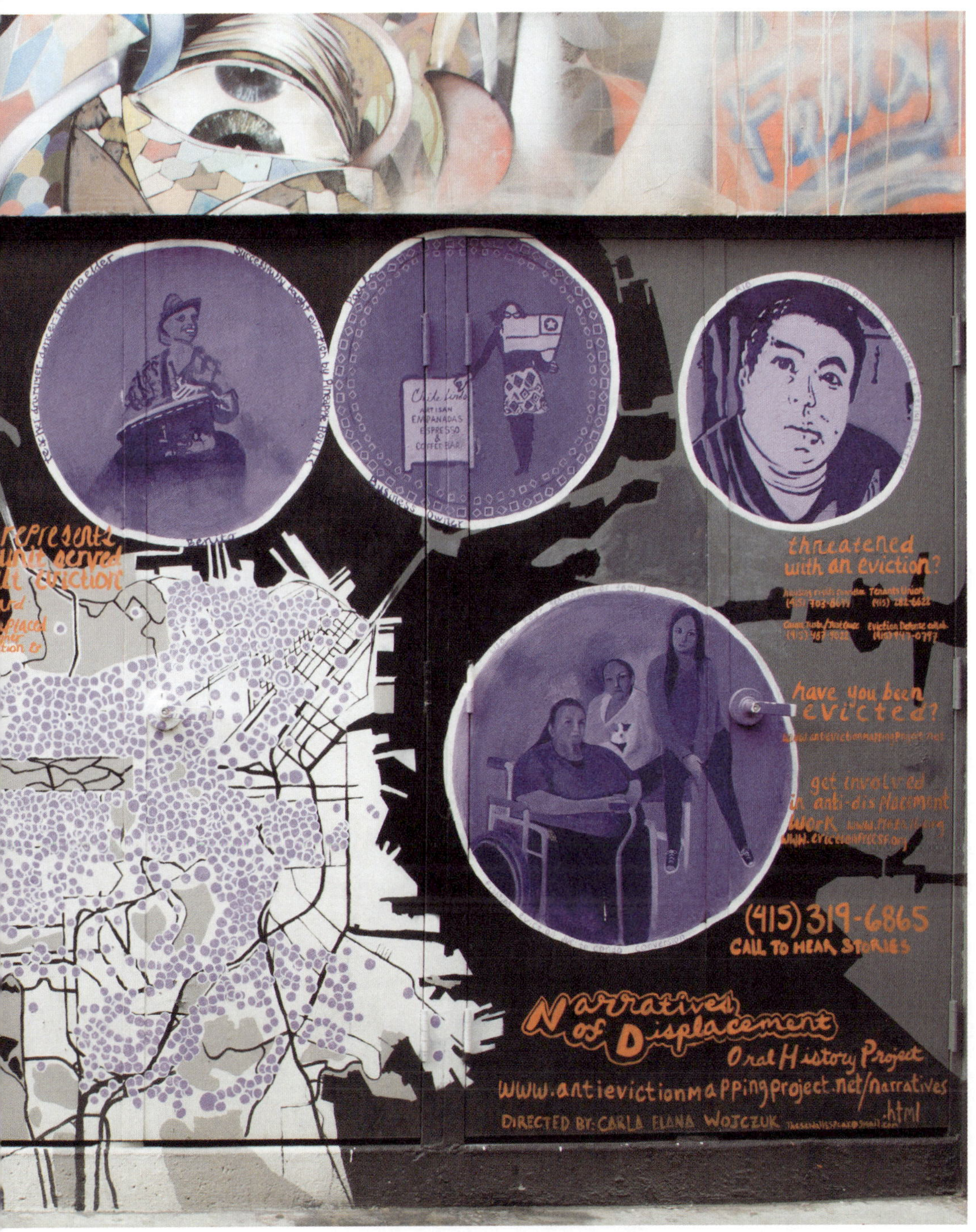

Mural in Clarion Alley, 2015. Courtesy of The Anti-Eviction
Mapping Project. Photography by Carla Wojczuk.

How the Dictatorship of the Parties Can Be Overcome

Joseph Beuys

EIN VERGLEICH ZWEIER GESELLSCHAFTSFORMEN

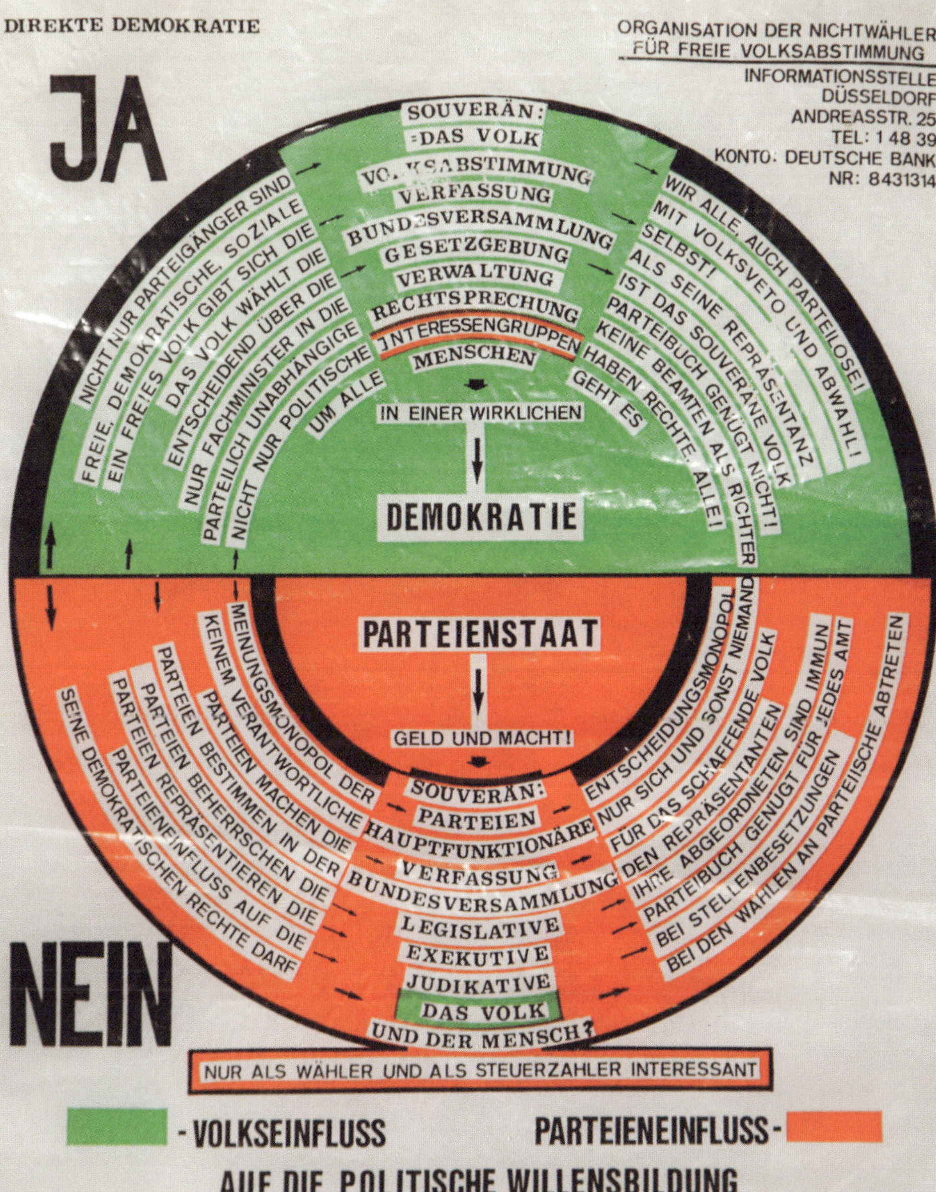

Joseph Beuys, art intermedia EDITION, Tragetasche aus Polyäthylen mit Filzplastik, 1. Auflage 10000 Exemplare, 1971

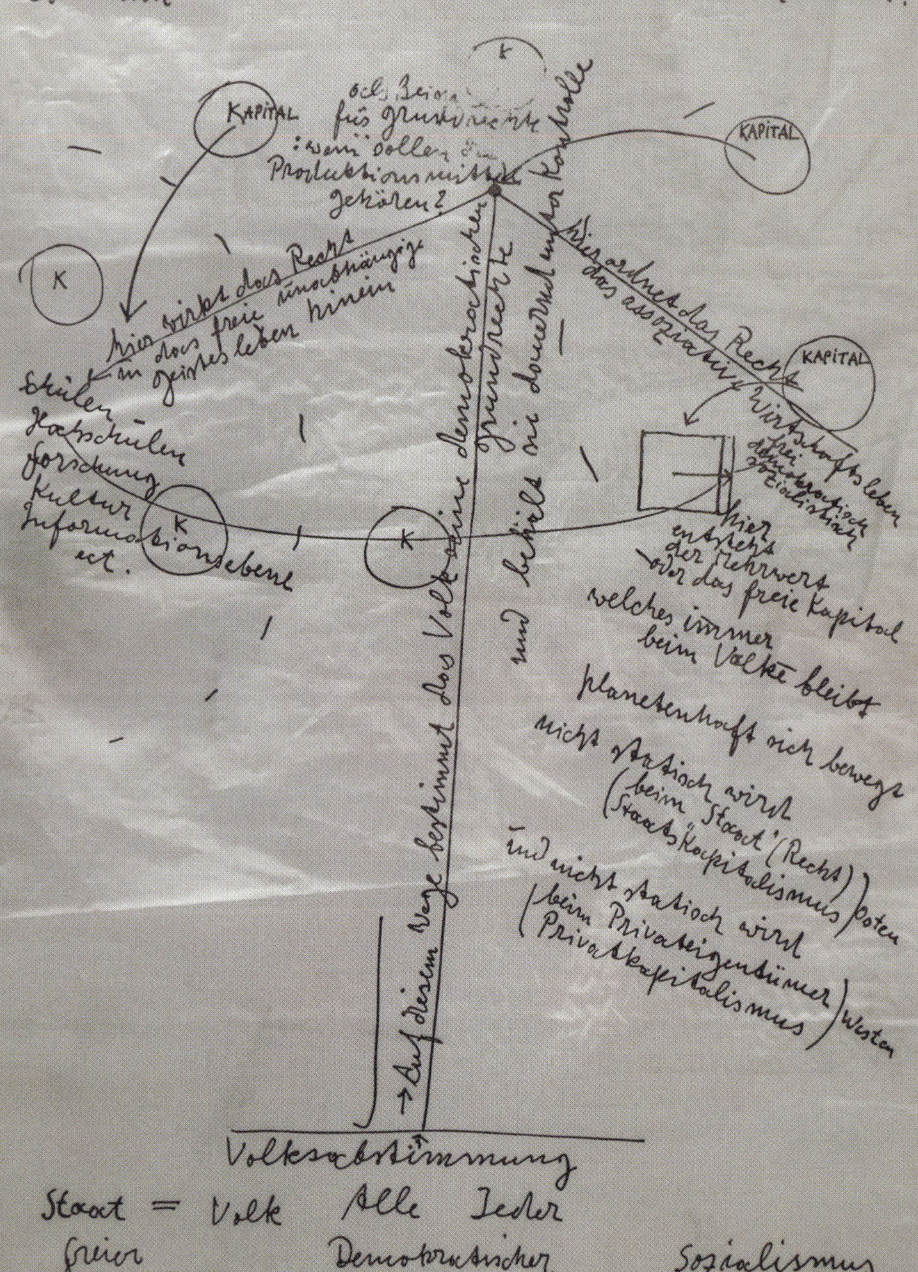

So kann die Parteiend [?] überwunden werden!
KAPITAL
K
als Beispiel fürs Grundrecht: wem sollen die Produktionsmittel gehören?
KAPITAL
hier wirbt das Recht das freie unabhängige in das Geistesleben hinein
hierordnet das Recht das assoziativ Wirtschaftsleben
KAPITAL
Schüler
Hochschulen
Forschung
Kultur
Informationsebene
ect.
K
K
demokratischen Grundrechte
und behält sie dauernd unter Kontrolle
hier entsteht der Mehrwert für das freie Kapital welches immer beim Volke bleibt
planetenhaft sich bewegt
nicht statisch wird (beim Staat) (Recht) (Staatskapitalismus) Osten
und nicht statisch wird (beim Privateigentümer) (Privatkapitalismus) Westen
Auf diesem Wege bestimmt das Volk ohne demokratische Grundrechte
Volksabstimmung
Staat = Volk frei   Alle Jeder Demokratischer   Sozialismus

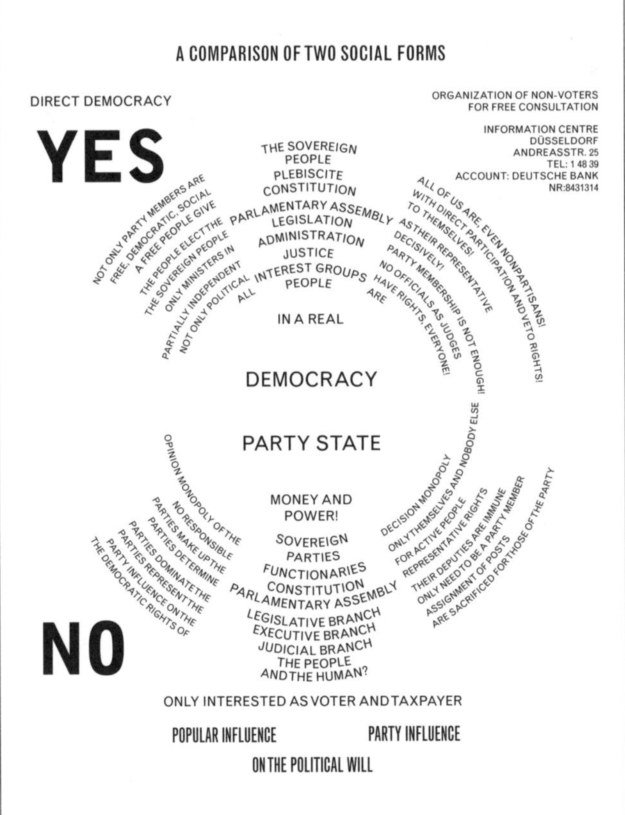

Joseph Beuys' diagrams show both critique and possibilty. First, how a party structure concentrates power in members of the government rather than the possibilities for true democracy with full participation from everyday people. Second, an outline of the advantages of direct referendum-style democratic governance. While one diagram is highly structured with a formal visual language that looks intent on being comprehensive and educational, the other is scrawled quickly as if done during a heated discussion. Both illustrations were screenprinted onto plastic shopping bags that contained literature on Beuys' *Organisation for Direct Democracy through Referendum*. The work was also part of several performances or social sculptures that took place in the early 1970s. The bag and its contents were sold first at Documenta 5 in Kassel, Germany in 1972.

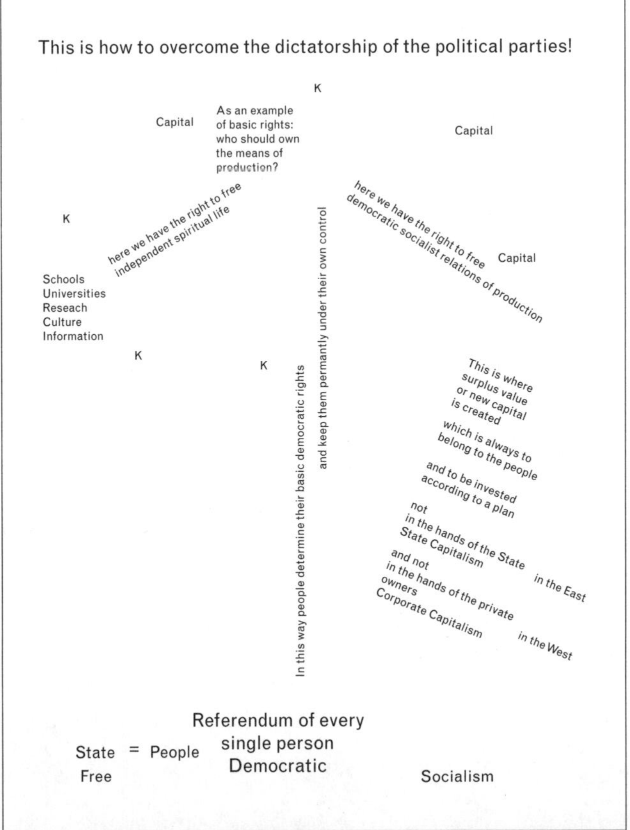

Installation view (previous page and left page). Joseph Beuys, *How the Dictatorship of the Parties Can Be Overcome*, 1971. Courtesy of Onsite Gallery. Photography by Yuula Benivolski. © Joseph Beuys, c/o Pictoright Amsterdam 2019.

La voix autoritaire (voir totalitaire) d'une système invisible

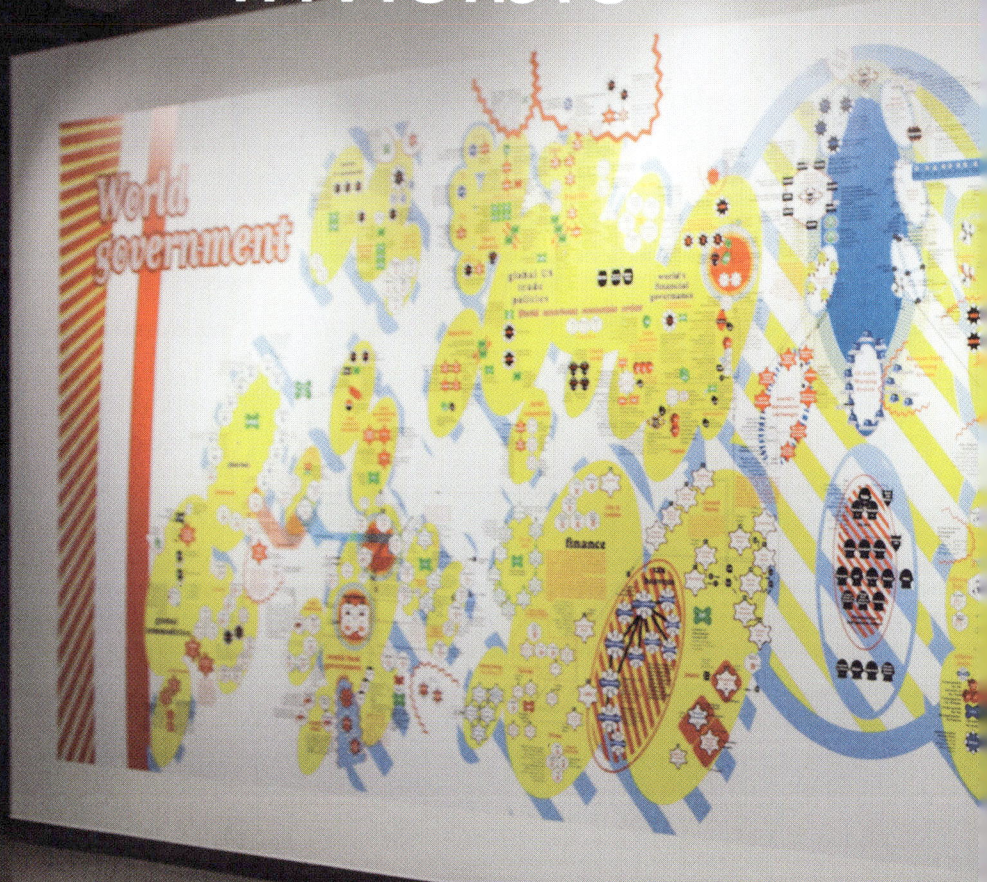

Bureau d'Études & Philippe Rekacewicz

The authoritative voice (totalitarian view) of an invisible system

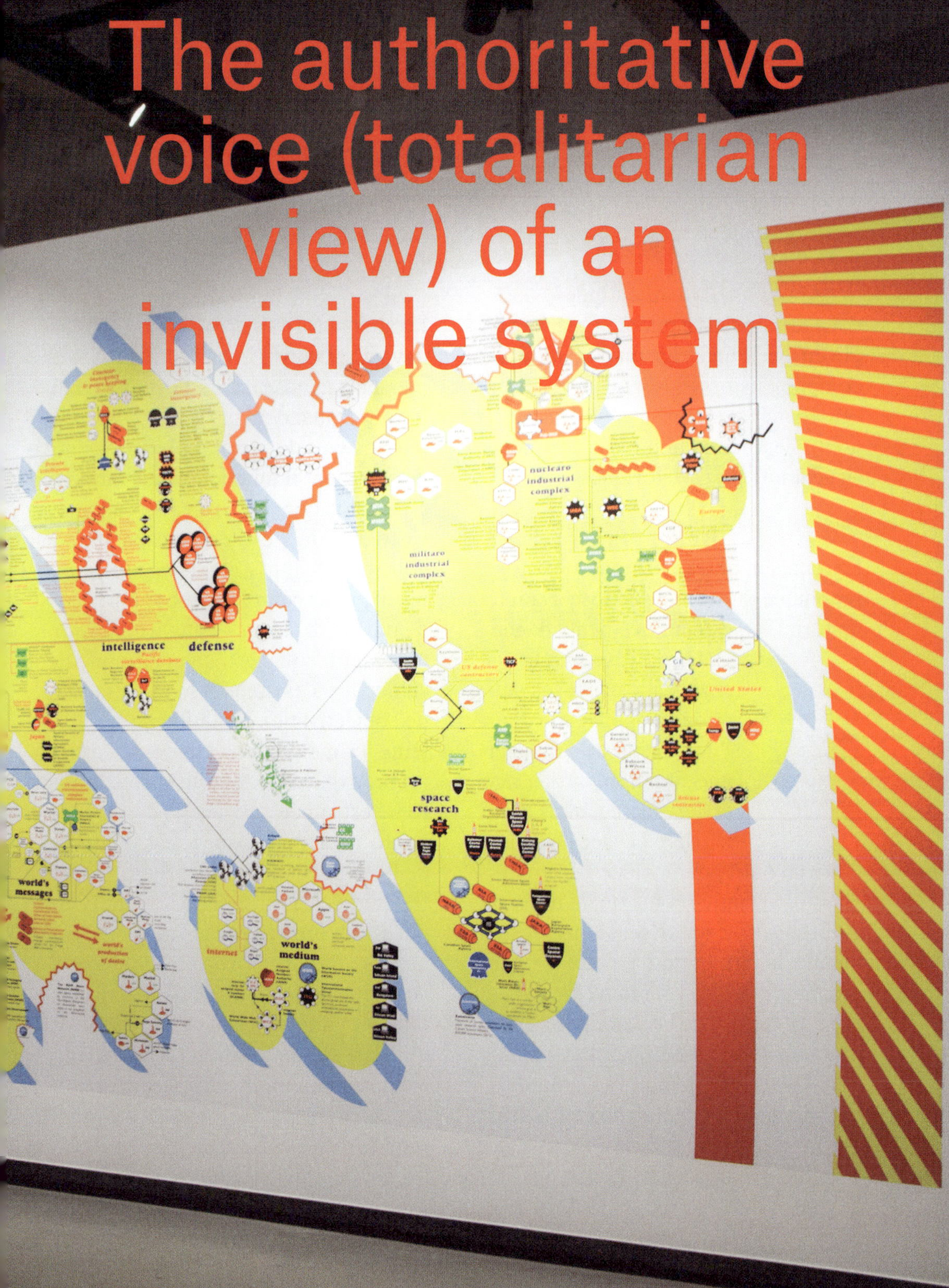

Patricio Dávila

Comment gérez-vous l'informalité, le sérieux et l'esprit enjoué face à la représentation de la violence et de l'oppression systémiques?

Bureau d'Études

C'est une question téléologique (stratégie en vue d'un usage ou d'un mode de compréhension) plutôt qu'une question esthétique (question de style ou de goût). Le ton ou l'humour n'y sont pas structurant mais rhétoriques.

Philippe Rekacewicz

La représentation « critique » (carto) graphique du monde suppose avant tout un formidable acquiescement à la vie et donc à l'espoir. On ne représente pas le les situations d'oppression dans l'unique but de dénoncer une situation particulière et désespérée, mais avec l'arrière pensée de produire un outil pour « aider » à l'émancipation. Dans ce contexte, la dérision et l'ironie bien maitrisées sont traitées comme la terminologie, la sémiologie graphique (formes et mouvements), mise au service de la clarté pour les destinataires des cartes. L'humour est dans ce cas un tremplin pour une attitude constructive. La démarche de la cartographie critique ou radicale, ce n'est pas seulement dénoncer mais c'est aussi agir sur le terrain.

Previous and next pages: Installation view, Bureau d'Études, *World Government*, 2013. Courtesy of Onsite Gallery. Photography by Yuula Benivolski.

Patricio Dávila

La tentative de tout contenir et d'être complet peut souvent communiquer une voix autoritaire d'un œil qui voit tout. En revanche, une esquisse est une tentative qui reconnaît l'incomplétude et la subjectivité de son auteur. Comment travaillez-vous entre ces deux dimensions?

Bureau d'Études

La voix autoritaire (voir totalitaire) est davantage dans l'invisibilité du système que dans la mise en visibilisation d'une totalité. Quand on parle de l'État, ne pas en avoir de cartographie descriptive de comment il fonctionne, est davantage autoritaire que d'en avoir une cartographie. Réstituer la capacité de voir tout—ce tout n'étant pas univoque, unifié, mais complexe et appréhendable de plusieurs façons—est une condition nécessaire non pas d'un positionnement subjectif ou existentiel mais de la saisie de l'objectivation produite par le système lui-même. Il faut simplement comprendre que cette totalité et cette objectivité est située : c'est celle d'un système s'auto-décrivant. Dans le cas d'une carte de l'État, c'est une carte produite depuis les données, les rapports, les analyses que l'État produit sur lui-même. N'étant jamais dans une position ou on peut voir tout, cette tentative d'objectivation d'une totalité du système par un citoyen qui n'est pas en position d'omniscience, est nécessairement partielle, c'est nécessairement une esquisse puisque le monde n'est pas transparent, qu'il y a du secret, de l'invisibilité, etc.

Philippe Rekacewicz

La carte n'est jamais une représentation fidèle de la réalité, mais au plus une représentation tronqué du réel;

Même si les cartographes et géographes prétendent le contraire, la carte n'est qu'un pâle représentation de la manière dont nous percevons le monde et est à cet égard un dialogue un peu fouillis entre l'imaginaire et le réel. Et ce qu'on y représente n'est qu'une partie de ce qui existe. Il n'est pas question de tout mettre dans une représentation cartographique, ce qui fait qu'on échappe à la tentation totalitaire. Par contre, ce qui est intéressant et qui représente un véritable défi, c'est de faire apparaître concrètement graphiquement, faire littéralement apparaître aux yeux du monde les aspects oppressifs invisible qui font intrinsèquement partis des systèmes politiques, économiques et sociaux. Dans ma recherche en cartographie expérimentale, je n'ai jamais envie d'ambitions englobantes ou exhaustives car je sais que c'est totalement vain. J'ai privilégié le travaille d'esquisse qui laisse infiniment plus de liberté dans la création des formes, et parce qu'elle symbolise aussi, non maps l'incomplétude des sujets sur lesquels on travaille (qui peut prétendre vouloir tout couvrir sur un sujet ?) mais plutôt le caractère mouvant, dynamique systémique pourrait-on dire, des phénomènes que nous représentons. Le défi cartographique est de trouver un moyen de représenter de manière appropriée des phénomènes en constante évolution. Quand à la subjectivité, elle est complètement assumée et revendiquée, puisque la carte est une « manière de voir » qui suppose comme prérequis de livrer un message politique, orienté en fonction du système de valeurs (fonda-mentales) qui nous constituent (pour ma par justice sociale, justice spatiale, droits humains fondamentaux, constructions de systèmes politiques basés sur l'établissement du droit en général et des droits que les citoyen·nes élaborent ensemble). La carte est une vision qui fait référence à des valeurs ou des idéologies, qui reposent sur des critères subtilement choisis et pesés. En ce sens elle est beaucoup plus une construction intellectuelle qu'une représentation « fidèle » du monde.

<u>Patricio Dávila</u>
Comment donnez-vous un sens aux différents types de cartographie? Contre, critique, radical, expérimental?

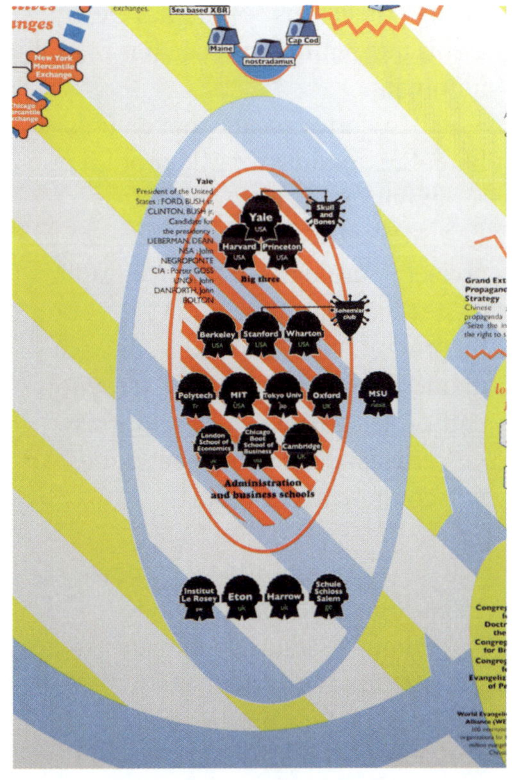

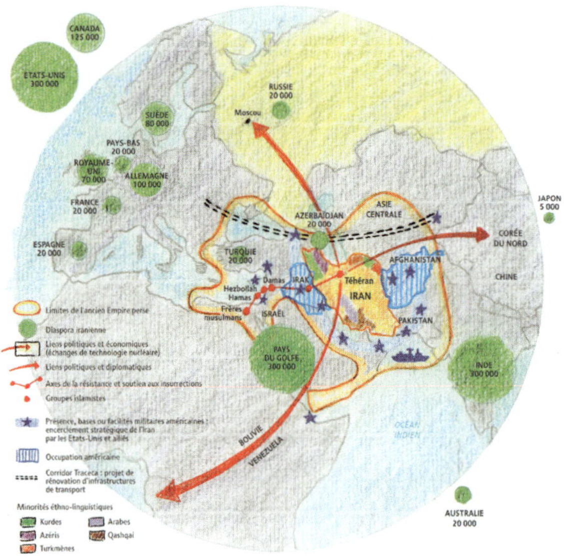

Philippe Rekacewicz, *Cartes en colère*, 2008-2018. Courtesy of the artist.

Bureau d'Études

La contre-cartographie produit une autre réalité que celle imposée par la norme, ou le sens commun. Elle amène a voir une réalité masquée par la réalité dominante.

La carte critique met en tension la réalité dominante. Elle produit une réflexivité sur cette réalité.

La carte expérimentale peut réviser l'ontologie de la cartographie, c'est-à-dire travailler sur la façon dont on produit, ou déplace la réalité par la manière dont on symbolise (l'espace, les entités, les positions, les relations). La carte expérimentale peut donc être une contre-cartographie.

Philippe Rekacewicz

La cartographie traditionnelle revendique le statut de science exacte s'appuyant sur des données fiables. Elle se targue de fournir une image neutre et fidèle de la réalité. Mais une telle approche fait l'impasse sur l'utilisation politique et sociale de la carte, et sur son rôle tant de propagande que de contestation. Depuis le début des années 2000, l'émergence de la cartographie radicale ou critique, dans un désordre jubilatoire et pétillant (ce qui montre son côté contestataire et émancipé) a montré l'exercice d'une riche combinaison revendiquée d'art, de sciences, de géographie, de politique et de militantisme social. Les cartographes orthodoxes ont vu naître avec beaucoup de méfiance les premiers projets exploratoires qui bousculaient, voire cassaient, les codes. Cette cartographie engagée a trouvé la voie d'une forme de contestation au service de la justice sociale, dénonçant des pratiques politiques et économiques douteuses. Elle est un exercice libre de déconstruction de l'espace et des phénomènes sociaux, pour lequel les protagonistes se permettent de pervertir les conventions les plus classiques. Les premiers à s'en emparer furent des artistes, mais aussi des architectes, des urbanistes et des militants, rejoints plus tard par des géographes. Les projets, individuels ou collectifs, se sont multipliés, couvrant un champ thématique assez large (finance, surveillance et sécurité, marketing, environnement, organisation des territoires, pour ne donner que quelques exemples), et profitant largement de la puissance des outils de la cartographie participative et des réseaux sociaux. Déchiffrer pour dénoncer, mettre en images des processus peu visibles qui concourent à confisquer l'espace public (voire des biens publics), à compromettre les libertés individuelles, à détourner des lois, tels sont les principaux objectifs des promoteurs de cette cartographie. Dans cet esprit, informer n'est qu'un début. L'étape suivante de la démarche reste l'action pour le changement sur le terrain. Largement informelle, cette initiative se reconnaît quelques affinités avec les mouvements de résistance soutenus aujourd'hui par les forums sociaux.

Patricio Dávila

Quel rôle l'émotion joue-t-elle dans les cartes? Devrions-nous croire une carte plus parce qu'elle est «émotionnelle» ou devrions-nous la croire moins?

Bureau d'Études

Pour nous, la question passe par les différentes manières dont on produit du réel par des effets d'objectivation ou de subjectivation. Et toutes les formes d'objectivation produisent une forme d'émotion : oppression dans le cas de la carte sublime, qui a un effet de sidération. Participation, capacité de se lier, de se situer, d'être en accord dans le cas d'une carte située produite à partir de l'action des parties prenantes elles-même. La croyance dans la carte tient plutôt aux structures symboliques implicites par lesquelles on reconnaît une carte comme une carte.

Philippe Rekacewicz

Une partie de mon travail est de réintroduire les gens dans la carte. Cela suppose de se questionner sur la manière d'appréhender, de capter, de représenter les émotions. Il faut d'abord interroger le processus de création de l'image car-

tographique. La carte porte la marque de son auteur, cette marque est une référence parce qu'elle relève d'une « intention cartographique » initiale, une vision de l'auteur. Cela suppose de la subjectivité (à ne pas confondre avec l'objectivité ou la neutralité, ce sont trois concepts différents). On voit là le paradoxe de la cartographie actuelle : elle se dédouble entre ce qui est une discipline encadrée, avec des méthodologies, voire des dogmes d'une part, et la création spontanée, la cartographie qui repose sur la spontanéité et l'expérimentation d'autre part. Est-il possible de résister à cette tendance de vouloir classer les choses dans des petites cases logiques, systématiquement regrouper ce qui semble se ressembler ? Au musée Léopold de Vienne, par exemple, un panneau indique que toutes les œuvres ont été mélangées ! Il n'y avait plus de catégories (en termes de styles, périodes ou écoles) pour « ranger » les peintures. Les œuvres ont été réorganisées pour montrer autre chose : les liens entre les formes, les couleurs, les mouvements. Ce choix muséographique original et inédit, est l'expression de ce qu'on aimerait faire en « cartographie expérimentale ». La cartographie émotionnelle et la cartographie sensible, dont les champs se recouvrent, permettent de réintroduire dans la carte une certaine forme de sentimentalité dont elle a été dépouillée. Dans ce contexte l'esquisse manuelle permet cette transition. Présentée dans un musée, une esquisse cartographique a pu faire dire à un visiteur, il y a quelques années

« quand on voit cette carte, on comprends bien que le cartographe devait être très en colère ».

Patricio Dávila

Les cartes sont aussi bonnes que leur volume de circulation. Une carte que personne ne voit est à peine une carte. Comment l'accessibilité et la distribution font-elles partie de la cartographie?

Bureau d'Études

Cela varie beaucoup selon les contextes. Certaines cartes activent des situations précises avec des enjeux situés qui sont intelligibles par certains acteurs impliqués. Ces cartes peuvent avoir des enjeux stratégiques importants parce qu'elles peuvent déterminer des plans d'action, de coordination, d'organisation entre un ensemble d'acteurs. Dans ce cas, la circulation doit être bien maîtrisée, pendant tout le temps de la mise en opération de la carte ou des cartes.

D'autres cartes peuvent être des coups, ou la diffusion massive est déstinée à amplifier un contenu, à le rendre public, à lancer une alerte, etc. D'autres cartes encore prennent sens dans une micro-situation, une mise au travail et n'ont pas vocation à être reproduites. La diffusion ou la mise en action (ce qui n'est pas la même chose) sont en elles-mêmes des régimes cartographiques.

Philippe Rekacewicz

Je pense sincèrement c'est un faux problème. Dans la société du spectacle, très prédominante en ce moment, exacerbée par les possibilités de visibilité offertes par les réseaux sociaux, presque tout le monde est obsédé par le buzz, la présence et l'apparence la plus large possible quelque soit le public en face. Cette dimension narcissique pervertit la création cartographique dans le sens où la recherche du résultat final risque de répondre plus aux attentes supposés d'un public qu'on souhaite captif qu'aux intentions cartographiques profondes initiale du producteur de la carte. On ne produit pas les cartes pour qu'elles soient nécessairement visibles, mais pour exprimer un point de vue, pour dénoncer des situations, représenter des phénomènes systémiques. En d'autres termes pour-qu'elles existent sur le long terme et qu'elles existent dans l'histoire comme témoins d'une période ou d'un événement. Cela ne me dérange pas du tout qu'une production soit invisible pendant un certain laps de temps jusqu'au jour où, à l'occasion d'un événement particulier, elle apparaissent au grand jour…ou pas. Même si elle n'est pas « grand public », il y a toujours un petit public à qui cette production de savoir sous forme visuelle permet de progresser dans leur propre recherche ou questionnement.

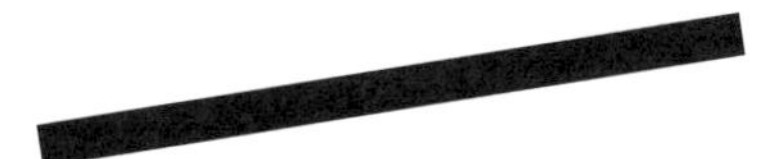

Patricio Dávila

How do you manage informality, seriousness and playfulness in the face of representing systemic violence and oppression?

Bureau d'Études

It is a teleological question (strategy for

a use or a mode of understanding) rather than an aesthetic question (question of style or taste). The tone or the humour are not structural but rhetorical.

Philippe Rekacewicz

The "critical" (carto) graphic representation of the world presupposes above all a tremendous acquiescence to life and therefore to hope. Cases of oppression are not represented for the sole purpose of denouncing a particular and desperate situation, but with the ulterior motive of producing a tool to "aid" emancipation. In this context, well-mastered derision and irony are treated as terminology, graphic semiology (forms and movements), in the service of clarity for the recipients of the maps. Humour is in this case a stepping stone for a constructive attitude. The critical or radical mapping approach is not only to denounce but also to act on the ground.

Patricio Dávila

The attempt to contain it all and be comprehensive can often communicate an authoritative voice from an all-seeing eye. On the other hand a sketch is an attempt that admits its incompleteness and subjectivity of its author. How do you work between these two dimensions?

Bureau d'Études

The authoritarian voice (totalitarian view) is more in the invisibility of the system than in the visibility of a totality. When we talk about the state, not having a descriptive cartography of how it works, is more authoritarian than having a map. To resituate the capacity to see everything–this whole being not univocal, unified, but complex and apprehendable in many ways–is a necessary condition not of a subjective or existential positioning but of the grasping of the objectivation produced by the system itself. One must simply understand that this totality and this objectivity are situated: it is that of a self-describing system. In the case of a map of the state, it is a map produced from data, reports, analyses that the state produces on itself. Never being in a position where we can see everything, this attempt to objectify a totality of the system by a citizen who is not in a position of omniscience, is necessarily partial, it is necessarily a sketch since the world is not transparent, there is secrecy, invisibility, etc.

Philippe Rekacewicz

The map is never a faithful representation of reality, but at most a truncated representation of reality. Even if cartographers and geographers claim the opposite, the map is only a pale representation of the way we perceive the world and in this respect it is a somewhat messy dialogue between the imaginary and the real. And what we represent is only part of what exists. It is not a question of putting everything in a cartographic representation, which makes one escape the totalitarian temptation. On the other hand, what is interesting and which represents a real challenge is to make appear concretely graphically,

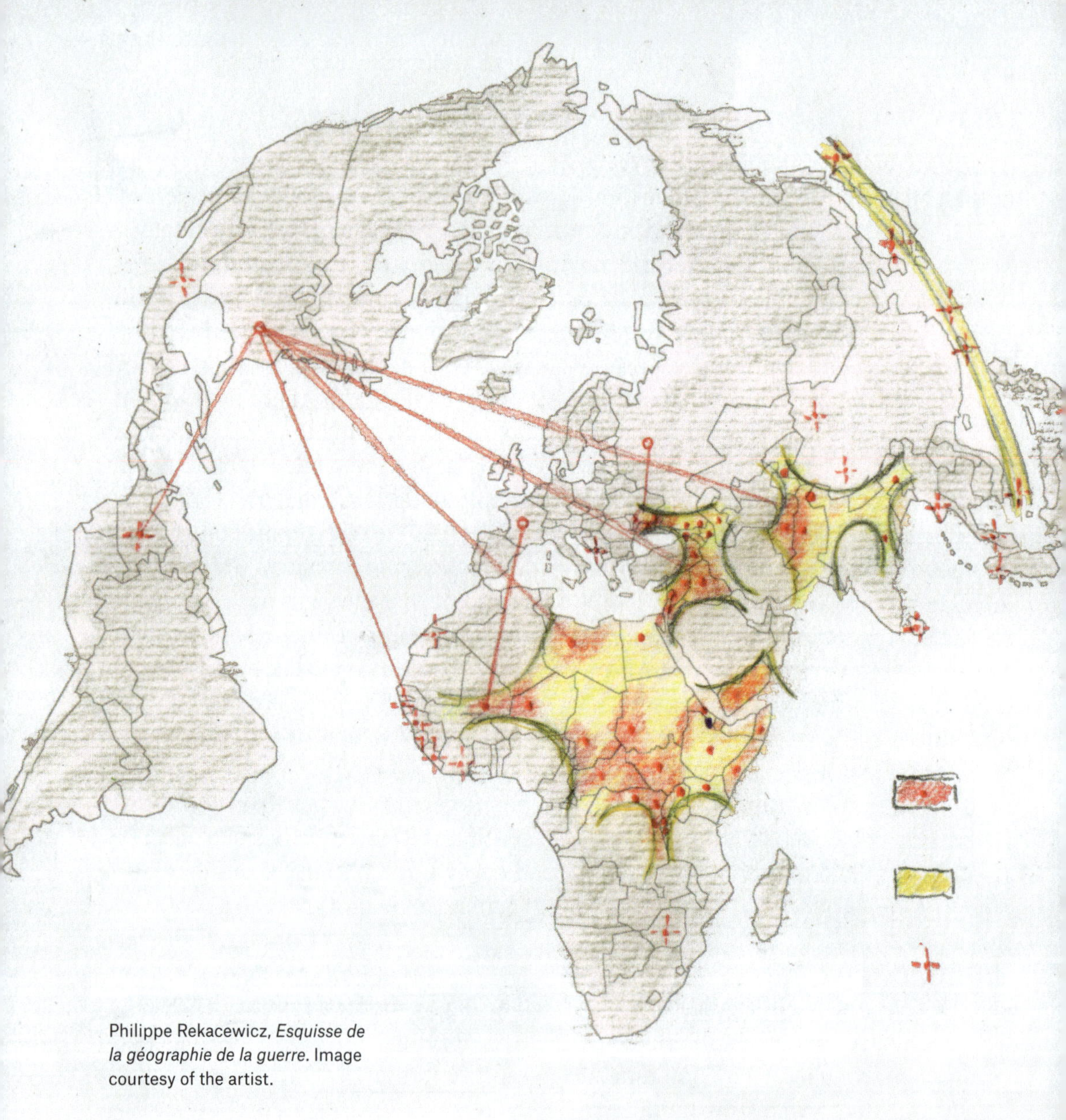

Philippe Rekacewicz, *Esquisse de la géographie de la guerre*. Image courtesy of the artist.

to make literally appear in the eyes of the world the invisible oppressive aspects which are intrinsically part of the political, economic and social systems. In my research in experimental cartography, I never have ambitions of encompassing or being exhaustive because I know it's totally futile. I privileged the work of sketching which leaves infinitely more freedom in the creation of the forms, and because it also symboliz-

es, not map the incompleteness of the subjects on which one works (who can pretend to want to cover everything on a subject?) but rather the shifting character, systemic dynamics one might say, of the phenomena we represent. The challenge is to find a way to appropriately represent evolving phenomena. When it comes to subjectivity, it is completely assumed and claimed, since the map is a "way of seeing" that assumes

La voix autoritaire (voir totalitaire)
d'une système
Bureau d'Études & Philippe Rekacewicz

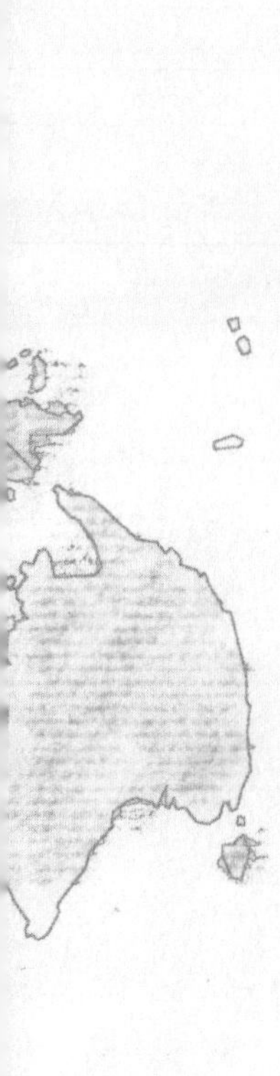

as a prerequisite to deliver a political message, oriented according to the system of (fundamental) values that constitute us (for my own sake social, spatial justice, fundamental human rights, building political systems based on the establishment of law in general and the rights that citizens develop together). The map is a vision that refers to values or ideologies based on subtly chosen and weighed criteria. In this sense, it is much more an intellectual construction than a "faithful" representation of the world.

Patricio Dávila
How do you make sense of the different kinds of mapping? Counter, critical, radical, experimental?

Bureau d'Études
Counter-mapping produces another reality than that imposed by the norm, or common sense. It brings to view a reality masked by the dominant reality.

The critical map puts in tension the dominant reality. It produces a reflexivity on this reality.

The experimental map can rethink the ontology of cartography, that is to say, work on the way we produce, or move reality by the way we symbolize (space, entities, positions, relations). The experimental map can therefore be a counter-mapping.

Philippe Rekacewicz
Traditional cartography claims the status of exact science based on reliable data. It prides itself on providing a neutral and faithful image of reality. But such an approach ignores the political and social use of the map, and its role as both propaganda and contestation. Since the early 2000s, the emergence of radical or critical cartography, in a jubilant and effervescent disruption (which shows its contesting and emancipated side) has shown the application of a rich combination of art, science, geography, politics and social activism. The orthodox cartographers witnessed with great suspicion the birth of the first exploratory projects that trampled or broke codes. This committed mapping has found the way to a form of protest at the service of social justice, denouncing dubious political and economic practices. It is a free act of deconstruction of space and social phenomena, for which the protagonists allow themselves to pervert the most classic conventions. The first to seize it were artists, but also architects, planners and activists, later joined by geographers. Projects, individual or collective, have multiplied, covering a fairly broad thematic field (finance, surveillance and security, marketing, environment, organization of territories, to give only a few examples), and taking advantage of the pow-

er of the tools of the participatory mapping and social networks. Deciphering to denounce, to put in images the not very visible processes that conspire to confiscate public space (even public goods), to compromise the individual liberties, to avert laws, such are the principal objectives of the promoters of this cartography. In this spirit, informing is only a beginning. The next step in the process is action for change on the ground. Largely informal, this initiative recognizes some affinities with the resistance movements supported today by the social forums.

Patricio Dávila

What role does emotion play in maps? Should we believe a map more because it is "emotional" or should we believe it less?

Bureau d'Études

For us, the question goes through the different ways in which reality is produced by effects of objectification or subjectivation. And all forms of objectification produce a form of emotion—oppression, in the case of the sublime map, has a stifling effect. Participation, the ability to bond, to situate oneself, to be in agreement in the case of a situated map produced by stakeholders themselves. The belief in the map is held primarily through the symbolic structures by which we recognize a map as a map.

Philippe Rekacewicz

Part of my job is to reintroduce people into the map. This involves questioning how to apprehend, capture, represent

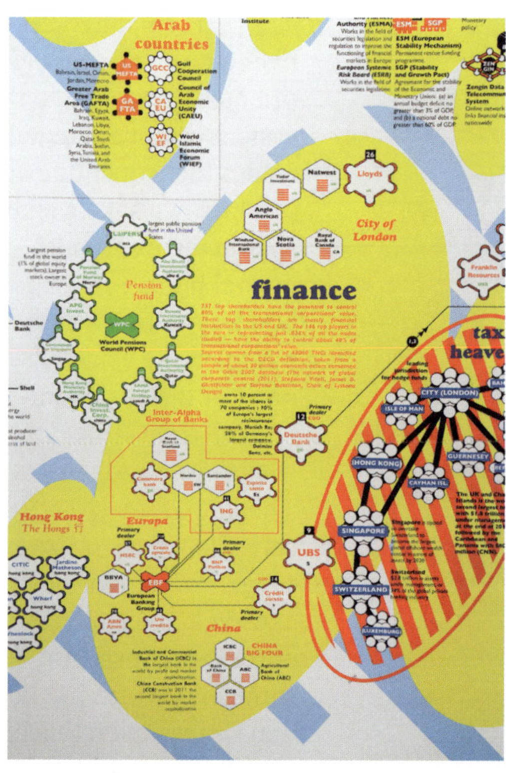

emotions. We must first examine the process of creating the cartographic image. The map bears the mark of its author, this mark is a reference because it is part of an initial "cartographic intention", an author's vision. This presupposes subjectivity (not to be confused with objectivity or neutrality, these are three different concepts). We see here the paradox of the current cartography: it is split between what is a framed discipline, with methodologies, even dogmas on the one hand, and spontaneous creation, cartography based on spontaneity and experimentation on the other. Is it possible to resist this tendency to want to classify things in small logical boxes, systematically group what seems to be similar? At the Leopold Museum in Vienna, for example, a sign indicates that all the works have been mixed! There were no more categories (in terms of styles, periods or schools) to "tidy up" the paintings. The works have been reorganized to show something else: the links between forms, colors, movements. This novel and original museographic choice is the expression of what we would like to do in "experimental cartography". Emotional cartography and sensitive cartography, whose fields overlap, allow us to reintroduce into the map a certain form of sentimentality from which it has been stripped. In this context the hand-drawn sketch allows this transition. Presented in a museum, a cartographic sketch was able to tell a visitor a few years ago "when we see this map, we understand that the cartographer must have been very angry".

Patricio Dávila
Maps are as good as how much they circulate. A map that no one sees is barely a map. How is accessibility and distribution part of mapping?

Bureau d'Études
It varies a lot depending on the context. Some maps activate specific situations with situated issues that are intelligible to certain actors involved. These maps can support important strategic issues because they can determine action plans, coordination, organization among a set of actors. In this case, the circulation must be well-controlled during the whole time of putting into action the map or maps.

Other maps can be salvos, or the mass broadcasts intended to amplify content, to make it public, to launch an alert, etc. Other maps still make sense in a micro-situation, a work-setting and are not intended to be reproduced. Broadcasting or putting into action (which is not the same thing) are in themselves cartographic regimes.

Philippe Rekacewicz
I honestly think it's a false problem. In the society of the spectacle, very predominant at the moment, exacerbated by the visibility potential offered by social networks, almost everyone is obsessed by the buzz, the presence and the widest possible appearance to whatever public is present. This narcissistic dimension perverts cartographic creation in the sense that the search for the final result risks responding more to the supposed expectations of a captive audience than to the initial cartographic intentions of the map producer. Maps are not produced to be necessarily visible, but to express a point of view, to denounce situations, to represent systemic phenomena. In other words, that they exist in the long term and that they exist in history as witnesses to a period or an event. It does not bother me at all that a production is invisible for a certain period of time until, on the occasion of a particular event, it appears in the open...or not. Even if it is not "general public", there is always a small public for whom this production of knowledge in visual form makes it possible to progress in their own research or questioning.

Astropolitique

Bureau d'Études

Astropolitique, déplétion des ressources terrestres et devenir cosmique du capitalisme : une cartographie

Le *Traité de l'espace* (1967) définissant l'espace comme le bien commun de tous les hommes n'a pas résisté aux enjeux stratégiques, industriels et commerciaux du ciel. Désormais, l'astropolitique veut établir un «principe de souveraineté du marché libre dans l'espace» en instaurant l'espace comme nouvelle Terra Nullius ouverte à la colonisation et à l'extraction. La loi américaine dite "Competitiveness Act" du 25 novembre 2015 autorise les citoyens américains à récupérer à titre commercial les ressources se trouvant sur un astéroïde ou une planète, pour les détenir, les posséder, les transporter, les utiliser et les vendre. L'Inde, la Russie, la Chine planifient de leur côté la mise en place de complexes d'exploitation des ressources minières lunaires. Parallèlement, les films de science-fiction ont relancé la conquète imaginaire de l'espace.

C'est par le ciel désormais, que se décide le devenir de la Terre et des terriens. Car le contrôle

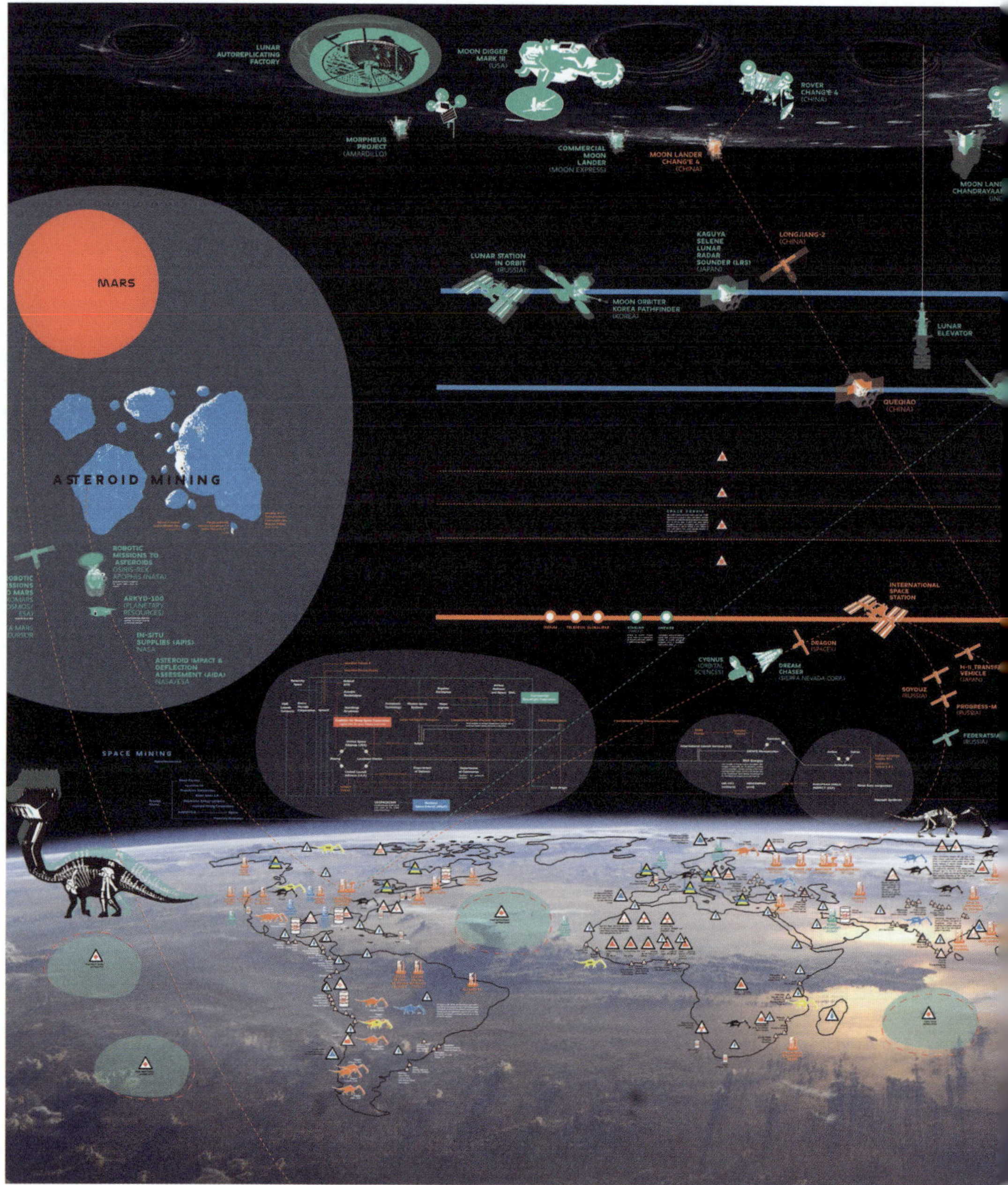

Bureau d'Études, *Astropolitique*, 2018. Image courtesy of the artist (this page), Installation view, Courtesy of Onomatopee. Photography by Blickfanger. (previous page).

de l'espace garantit non seulement un contrôle à long terme des confins de l'espace cosmique, mais offre également un avantage à court terme sur le champ de bataille terrestre. En d'autres termes, qui contrôle l'orbite terrestre basse contrôle l'espace proche de la Terre. Qui contrôle l'espace proche de

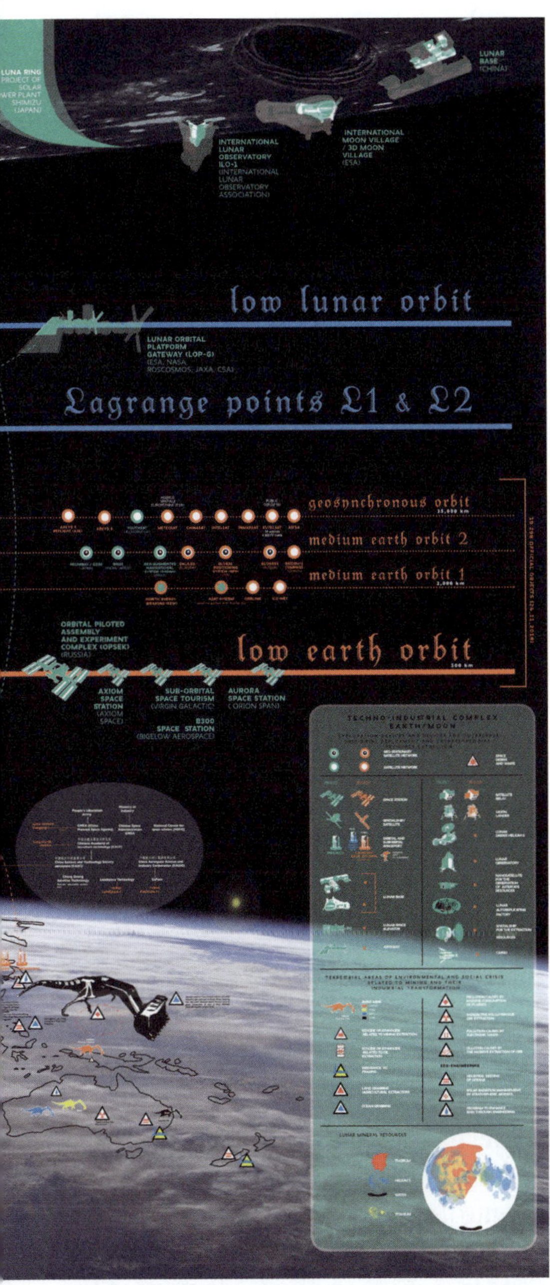

la Terre domine la Terre. Qui domine la Terre détermine le destin de l'humanité.

L'espace circumterrestre, est défini par Everett C.Dolman comme la région qui s'étend de l'orbite la plus basse de la Terre aux orbites géostationnaires.

On y trouve les satellites de télécommunication, de contrôle ou de surveillance de la Terre. On y trouve aussi les armes anti-satellites, les missiles de défense, les lasers et les armes à énergie dirigée pouvant agir sur n'importe quel point de la surface terrestre. On y trouve enfin, tournant autour de la planète en myriades de fragments, une aura de déchets et débris. Cet espace technologique et militaire autant que civile et commercial constitue le premier palier dans une échelle d'appareils permettant d'aller et venir entre la Terre et la Lune.

L'enjeu premier selon cette vision subjonctive, qui fait advenir un futur comme si on le connaissait déjà et qu'on pouvait le prévoir à l'avance, est d'y extraire des matières premières. Car la croissance de la démographie mondiale augmente vertigineusement la demande.

En 1969, alors que le premier homme marchait sur la Lune, Aurélio Peccei créait le club de Rome qui débouchera sur le rapport *The Limits to Growth* (1972) soulignant la trajectoire insoutenable dans laquelle s'engage l'époque et annonçant la possibilité d'un effondrement de la société thermo-industrielle et de son écosystème planétaire. La Lune sera-t-elle le moyen de sortir de cette impasse ou ne serait-t-elle qu'une nouvelle étape dans l'asservissement général des hommes, transformant les oppresseurs autant que les opprimés en jouets des instruments de domination qu'ils ont fabriqués eux-mêmes et ravalant ainsi l'humanité vivante à être la chose de choses inertes ?

À l'horizon 2050 il faudrait extraire, pour satisfaire les besoins, plus de métaux du sous-sol que l'humanité n'en a extrait depuis son origine. Les terres rares, parmi d'autres matières premières, sont indispensables pour des applications comme les batteries de véhicules électriques, les panneaux solaires, les éoliennes. Elles sont produites à 90% par la Chine et s'épuisent rapidement quoiqu'une réserve de près de 100 milliards de tonnes estimées ait été détectée dans le fond du pacifique. Et il en va de même de nombreuses autres ressources dont on trouve certaines sur la Lune.

Des milliards de tonnes de glace ont été trouvés près des pôles de la Lune constituant une ressource indispensable pour installer des équipements lunaires. Des piles à combustible peuvent utiliser l'hydrogène lunaire extrait à partir de la glace. On peut extraire du régolithe lunaire du silicium, de l'aluminium, du magnésium, et d'autres éléments indispensables à la fabrication locale de cellules photovoltaïques. La Lune a également entre un et cinq millions de tonnes d'hélium-3, pouvant être utilisé dans les centrales à fusion thermonucléaire, cette quantité étant suffisante pour couvrir les besoins en énergie de la Terre pendant 10 000 ans (100 tonnes d'Helium 3 couvrent les besoins actuels de la Terre pour un an). La Chine et la société russe RSC Energia ont annoncé leur intention d'exploiter ces réserves. Ainsi se projettent les désirs humains infinis dans le gouffre sans fin du cosmos.

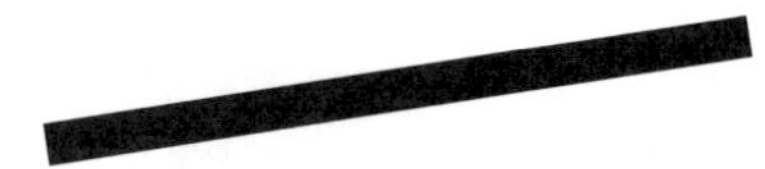

Astropolitics, depletion of earth's resources and cosmic becoming of capitalism: a cartography

The Outer Space Treaty (1967) defining space as the common good of all men did not resist the strategic, industrial and commercial stakes of the sky. From now on, astropolitics wants to establish a "principle of free market sovereignty in space" by creating space as a new terra nullius open to colonization and extraction. The US Competitiveness Act of 25 November 2015 allows US citizens to commercially recover resources on an asteroid or planet, to hold, possess, transport, use and sell them. India, Russia and China are planning to set up complexes to exploit the lunar mineral resources. At the same time, science fiction films have revived the imaginary conquest of space.

It is by the sky henceforth that the future of the Earth and the earthlings is determined. Because space control not only guarantees long-term control of the outer reaches of cosmic space, but also offers a short-term advantage over the Earth's battlefield. In other words, who controls the low Earth orbit controls space close to the Earth. Who controls space close to the Earth dominates the Earth. Whoever dominates the Earth determines the destiny of humanity.

Near-Earth space is defined by Everett C.Dolman as the region extending from the Earth's lowest orbit to geostationary orbits. There are satellites for telecommunication, control or surveillance of the Earth. There are also anti-satellite weapons, defense missiles, lasers and directed energy weapons that can act on any point on the Earth's surface. There is finally, orbiting around the planet in myriad fragments, an aura of waste and debris. This technological and military, as well as civilian and commercial space constitutes the first stage in a scale of apparatuses allowing travel between the Earth and the Moon.

The primary issue according to this subjunctive vision, which makes a future come into existence as if we already knew it and could be foreseen in advance, is to extract raw materials from it. Because the growth of the world's population is increasing demand tremendously.

In 1969, while the first man was walking on the Moon, Aurélio Peccei created the Rome club which would culminate in the report The Limits to Growth (1972) highlighting the unsustainable trajectory in which the era is immersed and announcing the potential of a collapse of thermo-industrial society and the global ecosystem. Will the Moon be the way out of this impasse or would it be only a new stage in the general enslavement of men, transforming the oppressors as much as the oppressed into toys of the instruments of domination they have they made themselves and thus swallowing living humanity to be the thing of inert things?

By 2050, more metals from the subsoil would have to be extracted to meet the needs than mankind has extracted from its own beginning. Rare earths, among other raw materials, are essential for applications such as electric vehicle batteries, solar panels, wind turbines. Ninety percent is produced by China and they are quickly running out even though a reserve of nearly 100 billion tonnes has been detected in the Pacific. And so are many other resources, some of which are found on the Moon.

Billions of tons of ice have been found near the Moon's poles as an indispensable resource for installing lunar equipment. Fuel cells can use lunar hydrogen extracted from ice. The lunar regolith can be extracted from silicon, aluminum, magnesium, and other elements essential for the local manufacture of photovoltaic cells. The Moon also has between one and five million tons of helium-3, which can be used in thermonuclear fusion power plants, enough to cover the earth's energy needs for 10,000 years (100 tons of Helium 3 cover the current needs of the Earth for one year). China and Russia's RSC Energia have announced plans to exploit these reserves. Thus infinite human desires are projected into the endless chasm of the cosmos.

Cartes en colère
Angry Maps

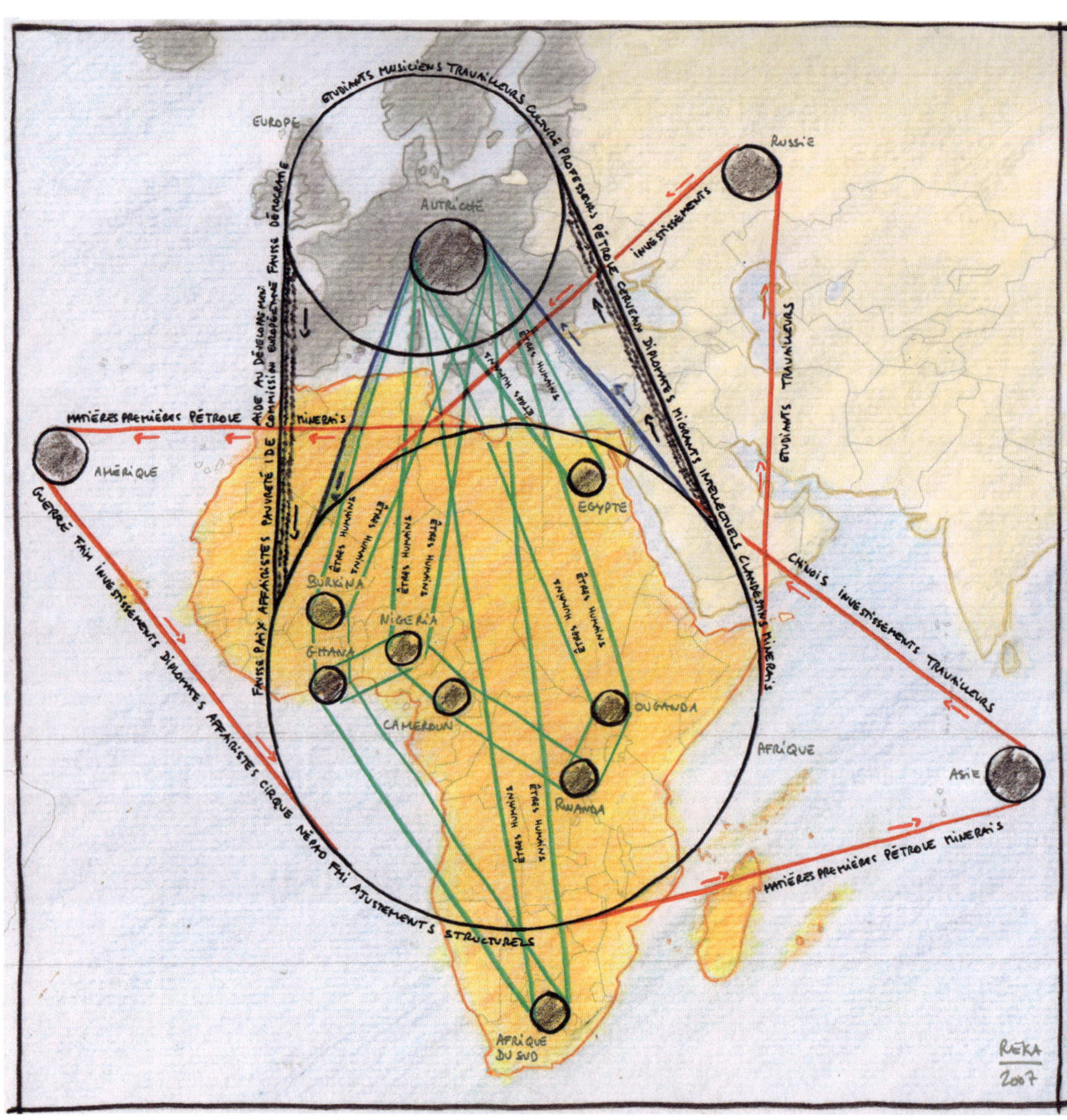

Philippe Rekacewicz

<u>La grande roue africaine : l'histoire d'un pillage en règle, 2007</u>
Echanges euro-africains : l'Afrique sauve l'Europe qui appauvrit l'Afrique qui nourrit l'Europe qui asservit l'Afrique qui paye l'Europe.

Qui continue de détrousser l'Afrique...

Mali, 2006 : une radio organise le procès pastiche de la Banque mondiale et du Fonds monétaire international (FMI), lequel devint le film très émouvant, "Bamako", imaginé et mis en scène par Abderrahmane Sissako.

Des instances financières internationales ridiculisées, mais trop tard. Les ajustements structurels qu'elles ont imposé pour « assainir » les économies ont brisé l'Afrique.

Au début des années 2000, la Banque mondiale a reconnu s'être trompée et a publié un communiqué de presse d'environ dix lignes qui annonçait l'abandon de ces plans, en soulignait « les effets négatifs » et s'excusait « des désagréments provoqués auprès des populations ». Désagréments qui ont tué, dépouillé les populations, détruit des économies, anéanti des pans entiers du secteur public.

L'Europe feint l'aide au développement : dans les faits, et à de très rares exceptions près, n'exportons « chez les pauvres » que des modèles inapplicables. l'Afrique, par exemple, offre aussi de la culture, de la musique et du théâtre. Des diplomates, des professeurs. Des étudiants, des travailleurs. Des écrivains. Autant d'êtres humains

que l'Europe renvoie souvent par charters entiers de là où nous pensons qu'ils viennent, quand ce n'est pas dans des linceuls, lorsqu'ils ont échoué à obtenir un visa, un titre de séjour ou simplement un droit d'entrée.

Eva Joly, longtemps juge spécialisée dans la criminalité financière, le dit autrement : *« Qui contestera les contrats conclu par Areva pour l'uranium au Niger ou Elf-Total au Gabon pour le pétrole ? La France a contracté une dette. Notre prospérité est nourrie de richesses que nous volons. A ces migrants clandestins qui risquent leur vie pour gagner l'Europe, il pourrait être versé une rente au lieu d'un avis d'expulsion. »*

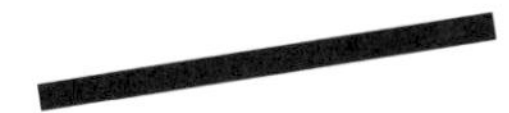

<u>The Big African Wheel: the general History of a looting, 2007</u>
Euro-African trade: Africa saves Europe, which impoverishes Africa, which feeds Europe, which enslaves Africa, which pays Europe.

They continue to rob Africa...

Mali, 2006: a radio station is organizing the pastiche trial of the World Bank and the International Monetary Fund (IMF), which became the very moving film, "Bamako", directed and produced by Abderrahmane Sissako.

International financial bodies were ridiculed, but it was too late. The structural adjustments they imposed to "clean up" economies had shattered Africa.

In the early 2000s, the World Bank admitted to having made a mistake and issued a press release of about ten lines announcing the abandonment of these plans, underlining "the negative effects" and apologized "for inconveniences caused to populations". Disappointments that killed and robbed people, destroyed economies, and wiped out entire sections of the public sector.

Europe feigns development aid: in fact, and with very few exceptions, we are exporting inapplicable models "to the poor". Africa, for example, also offers culture, music and theater. Diplomats, teachers. Students, workers. Writers. As many human beings as Europe often return by whole charters from where we think they come, when not in shrouds, when they have failed to obtain a visa, a residence permit or simply an entrance fee.

Eva Joly, a long time judge specializing in financial crime, says it differently: "Who will dispute Areva's contracts for uranium in Nigeria or Elf-Total in Gabon for oil? France has incurred a debt. Our prosperity is nourished by riches that were stolen. To those illegal immigrants who risk their lives to reach Europe, rent could be paid instead of a deportation notice."

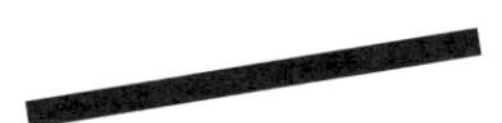

L'œuf asiatique : l'inversion du regard, 2012

Les bouleversements qui transforment aujourd'hui la Chine en particulier, et par extension l'Asie du Sud-Est, sont d'une intensité exceptionnelle, à l'image des projets pharamineux de développement d'infrastructures ou d'extension urbaines. Aucun pays, aucune région n'a connu une croissance de cette ampleur depuis deux ou trois décennies, ce qui nous incite à revoir nos visions du monde et proposer d'autres interprétations géographiques.

Considérés à travers le prisme du concept très classique du couple « centre-périphérie », les dynamismes socio-économiques en Asie nous conduisent à inverser notre regard.

Le géographe Christian Grataloup explique : « *La métaphore géométrique du centre et de la périphérie est souvent utilisée pour décrire l'opposition entre les deux types fondamentaux de lieux dans un système : celui qui le commande et en bénéficie, le centre, et ceux qui le subissent, en position périphérique.* »

Les pays autrefois classés la catégorie « en voie de développement » étaient considérées comme des périphéries dépendant des centres développés, puissants et riches, autour desquels se structurait l'activité économique mondiale.

Mais il semble que depuis deux décennies, le monde se recentre, ou plutôt se « décentre » vers une Asie ultra-dynamique principalement emmenée par la Chine, désormais au centre des processus socio-économiques importants, rejetant sur la périphérie les grandes puissances traditionnelles en voie d'essoufflement…

« *Les excédents sont chinois, les déficits sont américains* » : cette formule illustre bien les tendances que sont en train de suivre l'économie et le commerce dans le contexte de la mondialisation. La Chine, qui est partie à la chasse aux matières premières tous azimut, s'interconnecte aussi très étroitement avec des pays qui furent, et restent parfois, de grands rivaux, comme les États-Unis ou le Japon.

Deux citations évoquent joliment et historiquement cette situation : *« En 1492, comme un vol de gerfauts hors du charnier natal, Christophe Colomb, ses routiers et ses capitaines, partirent à la recherche de l'or que l'Asie mûrissait en ses mines lointaine. Ils ne se doutaient pas qu'ils allaient découvrir un Nouveau monde, bouleverser la géopolitique de la planète, ouvrir la voie à la conquête de l'Amérique du Nord par l'Europe. Et l'avenir paraissait flou à ces marins, aux bords mystérieux du monde occidental. »* (Jose Maria de Heredia)

« Cinq siècles plus tard, il ne reste plus d'îles à découvrir, plus d'océans inconnus à affronter, plus de peuples à soumettre. Et pourtant, le paysage qui émerge est toujours aussi déroutant, sinon que l'Asie y reprend sa place du milieu. Et, en pleine crise économique, sociale, écologique, les peurs millénaires resurgissent : qui pourrait démêler ces lointaines clameurs, est-ce un monde qui naît ou l'avenir qui meurt ? Car tout être de chair jette indistinctement le même cri pour la mort et pour l'enfantement. » (Louis Aragon)

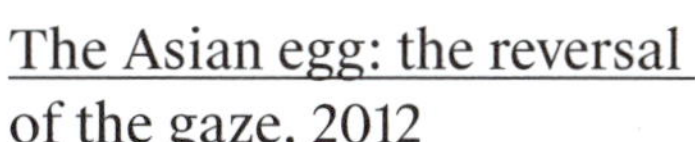

The Asian egg: the reversal of the gaze, 2012

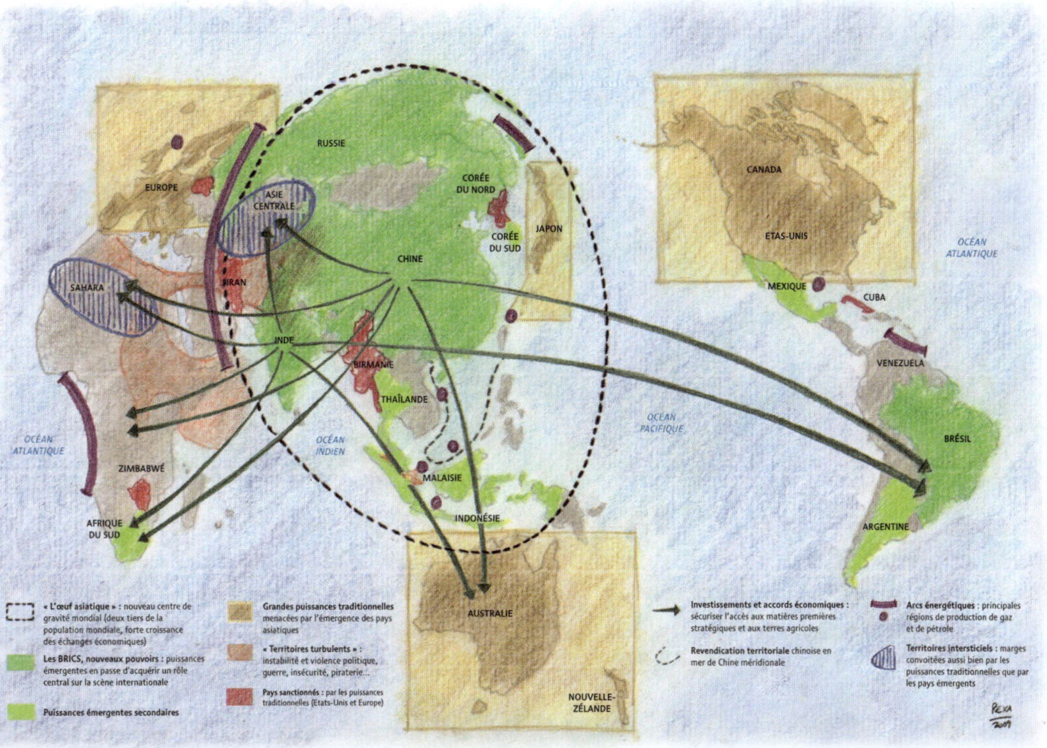

The upheavals today that are transforming China in particular, and by extension Southeast Asia, are exceptionally intense, as with the development of enormous infrastructure projects or urban expansion. No country, no region has witnessed growth of this magnitude in the past two or three decades, which prompts us to revisit our worldviews and propose other geographical interpretations.

Considered through the prism of the very classic concept of the couple "center-periphery, the socio-economic dynamisms in Asia lead us to reverse our eyes.

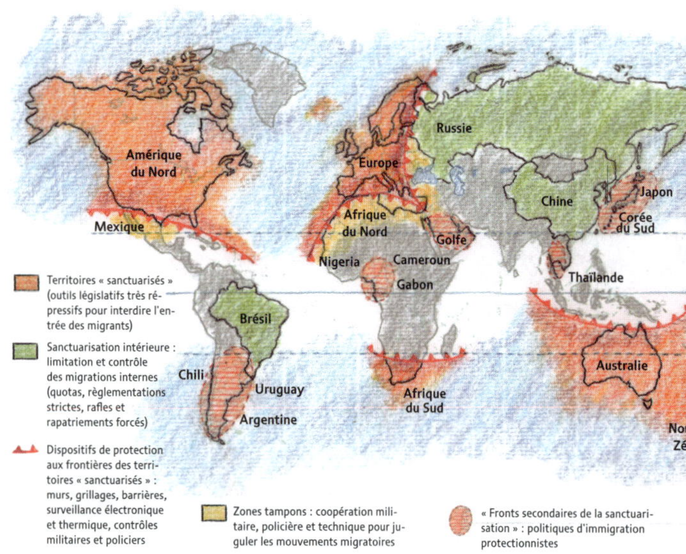

Geographer Christian Grataloup explains: "The geometric metaphor of the center and the periphery is often used to describe the opposition between the two fundamental positions in a system: one that commands and benefits, the center, and those who suffer, in the periphery."

Countries formerly classified as "developing" were considered peripheries of the developed, powerful and rich centers, around which world economic activity was structured.

But it seems that for two decades, the world has refocused, or rather "decentered" towards an ultra-dynamic Asia led mainly by China, now at the center of important socio-economic processes, rejecting on the periphery the great traditional powers in shortness of breath…

"The surpluses are Chinese, the deficits are American": this formula is a good illustration of the trends that are taking place in trade in the globalizing economy. China, which has gone all-out in the hunt for commodities, is also interconnecting very closely with countries that were, and still are, big rivals, like the United States or Japan.

Two quotes nicely and historically evoke this situation: "In 1492, like a flight of giants out of the mass grave, Christopher Columbus, his truckers and captains, set off in search of the gold that Asia was ripening in its distant mines. They had no idea they were going to discover a New World, upset the geopolitics of the planet, open the way to the conquest of North America by Europe. And the future seemed vague to these sailors, to the mysterious edges of the western world." (Jose Maria of Heredia)

"Five centuries later, there are no more islands to discover, no more unknown oceans to face, no more peoples to submit. And yet, the landscape that emerges is still as confusing, except that Asia takes it's place in the middle. And, in the midst of an economic, social, ecological crisis, millennial fears reemerge: who could unravel these distant clamors, is it a world that is born or the future that dies? Every being indiscriminately throws the same cry for death and for childbirth." (Louis Aragon)

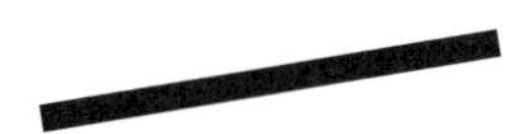

La sanctuarisation du monde :
Quand les riches s'enferment, 2011
C'est étrange, cette peur paranoïaque de l'invasion, cette idée de se « protéger » coûte que coûte d'êtres humains en détresse qui, chaque année, prennent le chemin de l'exil vers les territoires en recherche de paix et de sécurité. Pour tous ceux là, nous sommes terre d'espérance.

Mais les riches ont décidé que cette humanité-là était indésirable. Ils renforcent leurs frontières, dressent des barrières, construisent des murs toujours plus hauts. Une véritable stratégie de guerre mise en œuvre pour contenir l'envahisseur.

Par un effet d'entraînement, d'autres grands pays comme la Chine ou la Russie mettent aussi en place une « sanctuarisation intérieure » pour limiter les migrations économiques des régions pauvres vers les zones de forte croissance.

Ces obstacles physiques accompagnent tout un arsenal de lois, de dispositions juridiques et de directives qui permettent de criminaliser l'immigration. Et rendre acceptable l'emploi d'expressions inacceptables : « immigrant illégal » ou « clandestin ». On arrive à nous faire croire qu'ils transgressent la loi alors que ce sont nos lois qui violent nos constitutions, nos engagements internationaux et—ce n'est pas la moindre des violences—la déclaration universelle des droits humains qui spécifie en son article 13 que « toute personne a le droit de circuler librement et de choisir sa résidence à l'intérieur d'un Etat, de quitter tout pays, y compris le sien, et de revenir dans son pays. »

C'est étrange, ce paradoxe : comment concevoir que les pays supposés parmi les meilleures gouvernances mondiales trahissent à ce point les valeurs fondamentales les plus universelles ?

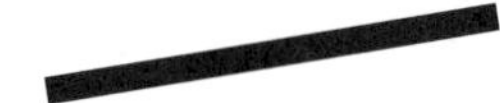

The sanctuarization of the world:
When the rich shut themselves up, 2011
It is strange, this paranoid fear of invasion, this idea of "protecting" at all costs from human beings in distress, who every year take the path of exile to the territories in search of peace and security. For all those, we are a land of hope.

But the rich decided that this humanity was undesirable. They strengthen their boundaries, build barriers, build walls ever higher. A real strategy for war, implemented to contain the invaders.

By a ripple effect, other large countries such as China or Russia are also setting up an "internal sanctuary" to limit economic migration from poor regions to areas of high growth.

These physical barriers are accompanied by an arsenal of laws, legal provisions and guidelines that criminalize immigration. They make acceptable use of unacceptable expressions:

"illegal immigrant" or "illegal". We are led to believe that they transgress the law when it is our laws that violate our constitutions, our international commitments and—this is not the least of the violence—the universal declaration of human rights which specifies in its article 13 that "everyone has the right to move freely and to choose his residence within a State, to leave any country, including his own, and to return to his country."

This paradox is strange: how to conceive that countries amongst the best world governments betray the most universal fundamental values to this extent?

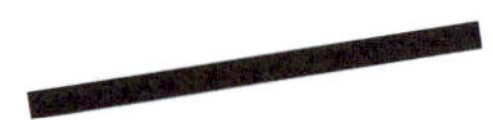

<u>Mourir aux portes de l'Europe : L'Europe des trois frontières, 2003, mise-à-jour en 2006, 2009, 2011, 2014 et 2017</u>
Cette carte, nous l'avons dressée pour la première fois en 2003 grâce au méticuleux travail d'Olivier Clochard, membre du réseau européen *Migreurop*. Nous mettons régulièrement à jour ce document et hélas, à chaque fois, nous devons rajouter des points noirs, grossir toujours plus les cercles rouges, changer les chiffres pour les remplacer par d'autres, hélas toujours plus élevés.

Le 1er janvier 1993, Gerry Johnson, un citoyen du Liberia—pays alors dévasté par une guerre civile meurtrière—est découvert mort étouffé dans un wagon de marchandises à Feldkirch, en Autriche. Le 8 décembre 2015, les autorités turques ont repêché, à mi-chemin entre la côte et l'île grecque de Chi-

os, les corps sans vie de six jeunes enfants d'origine afghane. Entre ces deux dates et ces deux lieux, un peu plus de 33 000 autres migrants—estimation a minima d'une hécatombe ignorée—ont perdu la vie en tentant de rejoindre l'Europe, terre de la liberté et des droits de l'homme.

On meurt aussi en repartant, comme Marcus Omofuma, citoyen nigerian assassiné (ficelé comme un saucisson, le visage entièrement bandé) sous les yeux horrifiés des autres passagers de l'avion, le 1er mai 1999, par trois policiers autrichiens sadiques (qui n'ont jamais été condamnés) dans un avion de la Balkan Air lors de son rapatriement forcé.

Ces chiffres effrayants sont fourni par l'organisation non gouvernementale « United for Intercultural Action », « Forteresse Europe » de Gabriel del Grande et l'initiative « Migrant files (http://www.themigrantsfiles.com) » qui se fondent sur des rapports de presse et des signalements effectués par des réseaux d'organisations locales et régionales. Seuls les décès connus figurent sur la carte, qui n'est donc qu'une représentation a minima d'une hécatombe longtemps restée ignorée.

Cette boucherie, c'est la conséquence des choix de l'Europe. De Nouakchott à Tripoli en passant par Niamey et Agadir, consciencieusement, et déjà loin, très loin de son propre territoire, l'Europe se dote d'une « préfrontière » : au cœur du désert, contrôles policiers, refoulements, regroupements

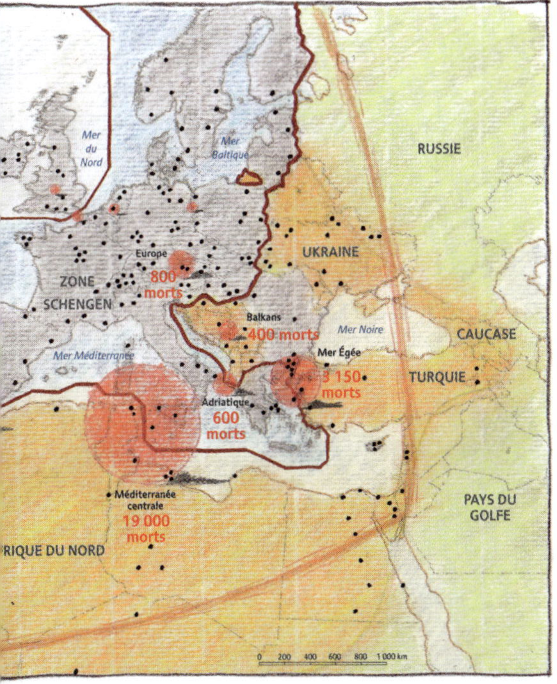

informels et premiers camps. Pour qui passe les mailles de ce premier filet, la vraie « frontière » est de loin la plus mortelle. Et ceux qui passent la ligne rouge seront attendus aux points noirs, dans les camps de rétention, prison ou zones d'attente d'aéroports, c'est-à-dire à la « postfrontière ».

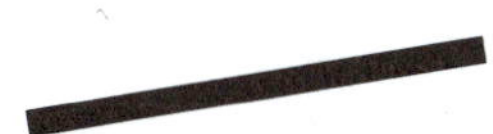

Dying at the gates of Europe: the three borders of Europe, 2003, updated in 2006, 2009, 2011, 2014 and 2017
This map was first compiled in 2003 thanks to the meticulous work of Olivier Clochard, member of the European network Migreurop. We regularly update this document and unfortunately, each time, we have to add black dots, expand more red circles, and change the numbers to replace them with, alas, ever climbing numbers.

On January 1, 1993, Gerry Johnson, a citizen of Liberia–a country devastated by a deadly civil war–was found dead in a freight car in Feldkirch, Austria. On December 8, 2015, the Turkish authorities drew the dead bodies of six young children of Afghan origin midway between the coast and the Greek island of Chios. Between these two dates and these two places, a little more than 33,000 migrants–a minimum estimate for a bloodbath ignored–lost their lives trying to reach Europe, land of freedom and human rights.

We also die by leaving, like Marcus Omofuma, murdered Nigerian citizen (tied like a sausage, his face completely bandaged) under the horrified watch of the other passengers of the plane, on May 1, 1999, by three sadistic Austrian policemen (who have not been convicted) on a Balkan Air plane during his forced repatriation.

These scary figures are provided by the non-governmental organization "United for Intercultural Action", "Fortress Europe" by Gabriel del Grande and the "Migrant files (http://www.themigrantsfiles.com)" initiative, which are based on press reports and reports by networks of local and regional organizations. Only known deaths appear on the map, which is therefore only a minimal representation of a slaughter that has long been ignored.

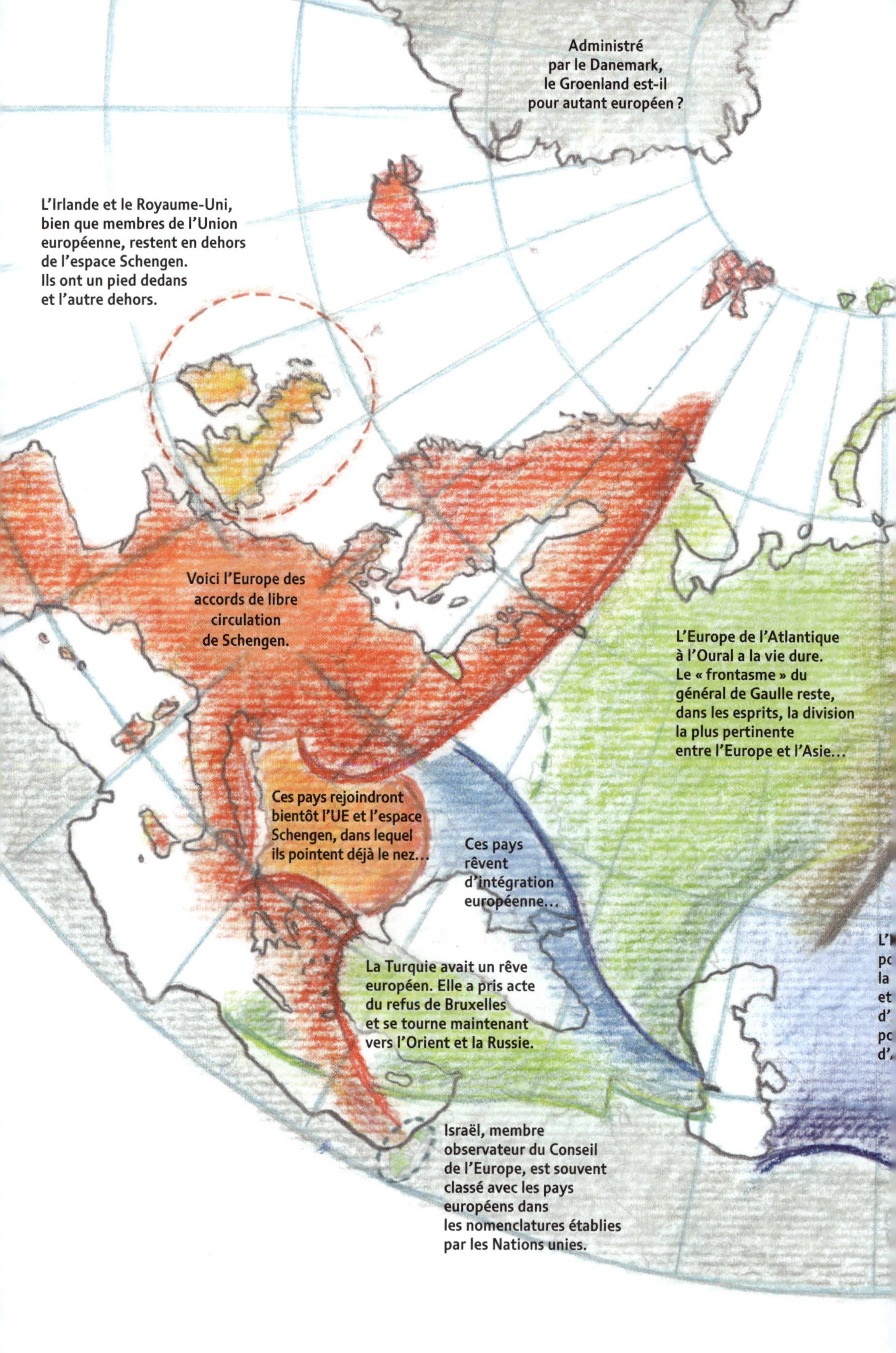

Administré par le Danemark, le Groenland est-il pour autant européen ?
L'Irlande et le Royaume-Uni, bien que membres de l'Union européenne, restent en dehors de l'espace Schengen. Ils ont un pied dedans et l'autre dehors.
Voici l'Europe des accords de libre circulation de Schengen.
L'Europe de l'Atlantique à l'Oural a la vie dure. Le « frontasme » du général de Gaulle reste, dans les esprits, la division la plus pertinente entre l'Europe et l'Asie…
Ces pays rejoindront bientôt l'UE et l'espace Schengen, dans lequel ils pointent déjà le nez…
Ces pays rêvent d'intégration européenne…
La Turquie avait un rêve européen. Elle a pris acte du refus de Bruxelles et se tourne maintenant vers l'Orient et la Russie.
Israël, membre observateur du Conseil de l'Europe, est souvent classé avec les pays européens dans les nomenclatures établies par les Nations unies.

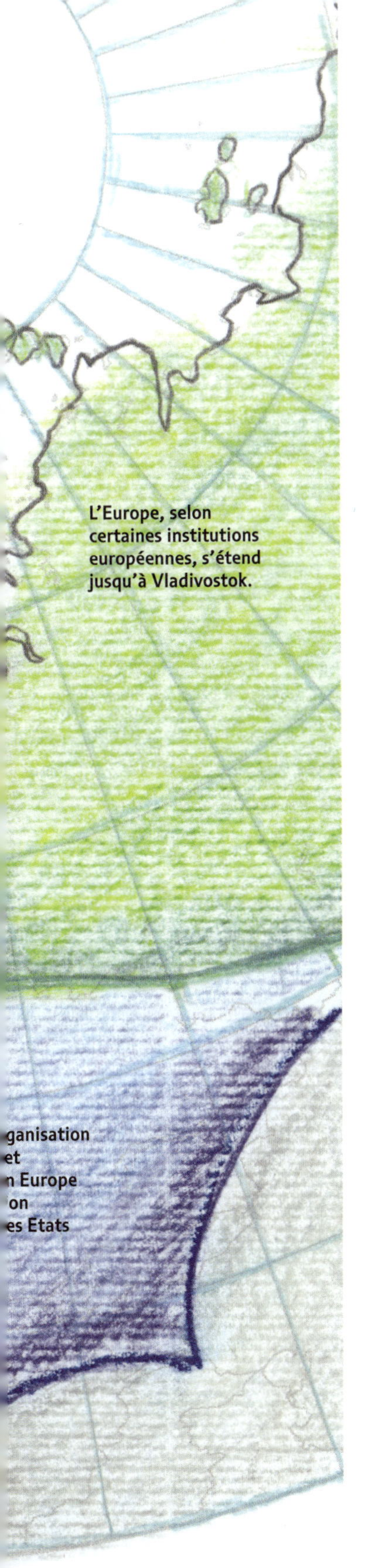

Cartes en colère (Angry Maps)
Philippe Rekacewicz

This slaughter is the consequence of decisions made by Europe. From Nouakchott to Tripoli via Niamey and Agadir, conscientiously, and already far, far from its own territory, Europe is endowed with a "prefrontier": in the heart of the desert, police checks, repressions, informal groupings and first camps. For those who pass the meshes of this first net, the true "border" is by far the most deadly. And for those who cross the red line, they will be expected at the black dots, in detention camps, jails or airport waiting areas, that is to say at the "postfrontière".

______

<u>La longue étreinte des frontières orientales de l'Europe : L'Europe, l'Europe, l'Europe !!, 2012</u>
« Où donc finit l'Europe à l'est ? » A l'ouest, c'est clair, il y a de l'eau. Mais à l'est ? Des « experts » définissent des lignes de partage qui n'existent pas : l'Europe et son « identité chrétienne » (?), l'Europe continentale, l'Europe « blanche » (?), l'Europe culturelle (?), l'Europe géographique (?), l'Europe et son « ventre mou » (?), l'Europe et sa banane bleue (?), l'Europe et sa « frontière naturelle »…

L'Europe ! l'Europe ! l'Europe !
« Ceux qui se disent européens trouvent que l'Europe des patries (?), ce n'est pas assez, et que l'Europe de l'Atlantique à l'Oural, c'est trop. Et vous, vous sentez-vous européen ? », demande le journaliste Michel Droit à Charles de Gaulle en décembre 1965… *« Alors, répond le président, on ne fait pas de politique autrement que sur des réalités : bien entendu, on peut sauter sur sa chaise comme un cabri en disant "l'Europe ! l'Europe ! l'Europe !" Mais ça ne signifie rien ! »* De Gaulle affirmait que l'Europe allait *« de l'Atlantique à l'Oural »*. Cette définition mythique ne reposait en effet sur rien d'autre que sa propre vision européenne : la « belle et bonne alliance » avec Moscou contre l'Allemagne.

Les limites de l'Europe sont multiples : avec ou sans la Turquie, avec ou sans Israël, avec ou sans l'Arménie…

Il y a ceux qui attendent derrière les portes de Schengen, comme la Roumanie ; ceux qui en rêvent la nuit, comme la Géorgie ; ceux qui, comme les Grecs, s'interrogent sur une Europe qui les a trahis. Puis, il y a nos lointains voisins d'Asie centrale, membres d'institutions européennes. De tous ceux-là, qui sont les plus européens ? Et si, simplement, l'Europe à l'est était sans fin ?

Et si l'Europe venait juste se fondre dans l'Asie en une immense étreinte ?

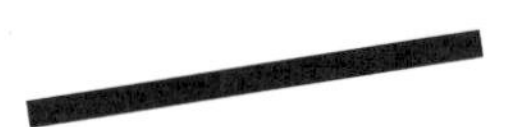

<u>The long embrace of the eastern borders of Europe: Europe, Europe, Europe!!, 2012</u>
"Where does Europe end in the east? To the west, it's clear, there is water. But in the east? "Experts" define dividing lines that do not exist: Europe and its "Christian identity" (?), Continental Europe, "White" Europe (?), Cultural Europe (?), geographical Europe (?), Europe and its "soft underbelly" (?), Europe and its blue banana (?), Europe and its "natural border" …

Europe! Europe! Europe!

"Those who call themselves Europeans find that the Europe of their homelands (?) is not enough, and that Europe from the Atlantic to the Urals is too much. And you, do you feel European?" Asks journalist Michel Droit to Charles de Gaulle in December 1965 … "So, says the president, we do not make politics outside of realities: of course, we can jump on chairs like a goat saying Europe! Europe! Europe! But that does not mean anything!" De Gaulle said that

Europe goes "from the Atlantic to the Urals". This mythical definition was based on nothing but its own European vision: the "beautiful and good alliance" with Moscow against Germany.

The limits of Europe are many: with or without Turkey, with or without Israel, with or without Armenia…

There are those who wait behind the gates of Schengen, like Romania; those who dream of it at night, like Georgia; those who, like the Greeks, wonder about a Europe that betrayed them. Then there are our distant neighbors of Central Asia, members of European institutions. Of all those who are the most European? And if, simply, Europe to the east was endless?

And if Europe had just melted into Asia in an immense embrace?

<u>Géographie d'une humanité indésirable : la politique européenne des visas, 2011</u>
A l'Ouest : les copains, bienvenus chez nous, le portefeuille garni. À l'Est et au Sud : les indésirables, les gueux, le petit peuple du monde trop pauvre pour être utile.

Dans une symétrie presque parfaite, on trouve des îlots de pauvres à l'Ouest, et des des îlots de riches à l'Est.

Cette analyse peut sembler simpliste et manichéenne, mais cette géographie politique des visas montre avec une certaine cruauté la vision européenne du monde : égoïste et opportuniste. Il faudra que l'on m'explique ce qu'il y a de logique quand l'UE exige des ressortissants du Kosovo—Etat le plus pauvre de toute l'Europe—un visa hors de prix pour circuler dans l'Espace Schengen.

Il y a de multiples façons de partager le monde, les territoires, les régions. Que ce soit selon le principe des Nations, du regroupement de Nations en fédérations ou en espaces intégrés, d'indicateurs socio-économiques ou politiques. Cette image pourtant simple nous renvoie cyniquement à nos paradoxes et notre brutalité. Cette image est choquante parce que nous nous percevons démocrates et généreux alors que

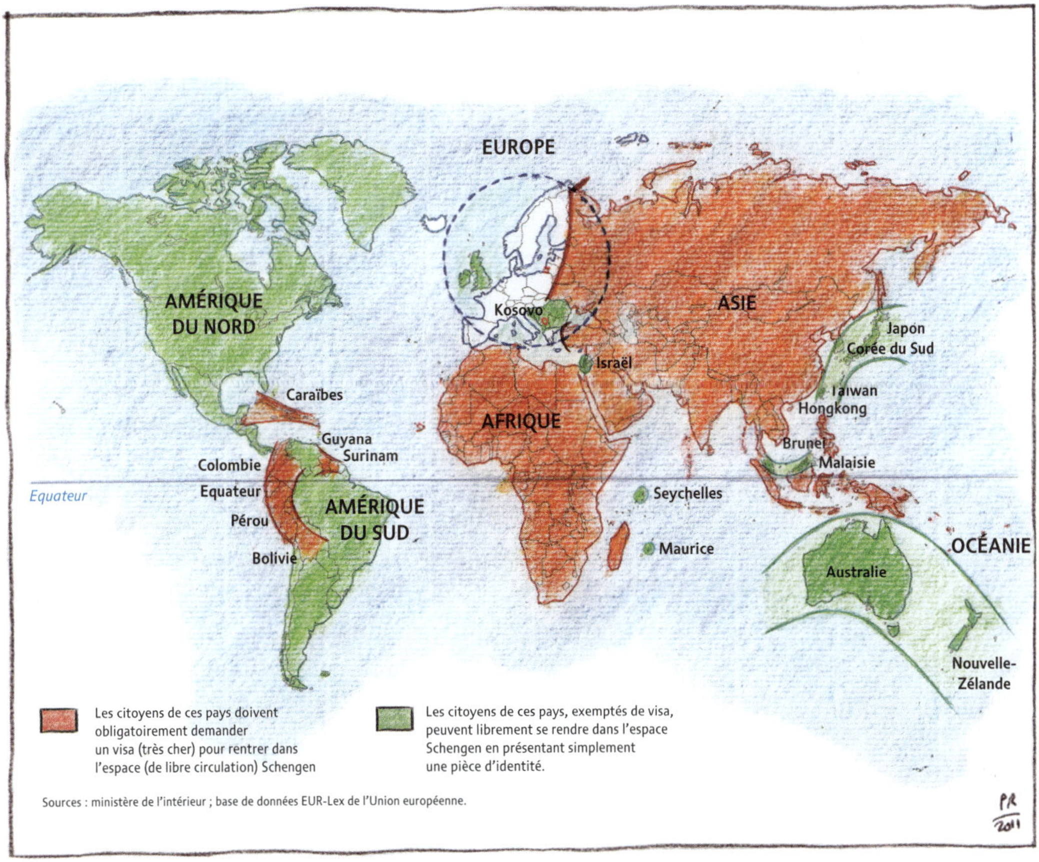

sociale que ces deux-tiers pourraient partager avec nous.

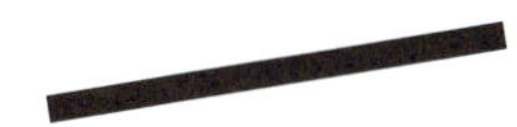

Geography of an unwanted humanity: European visa policy, 2011

In the West: friends, welcome to our home, the overflowing wallet. In the East and in the South: the undesirables, the beggars, the little people of the world too poor to be useful.

In almost perfect symmetry, there are pockets of the poor in the west, and

nous nous fermons aux deux-tiers de l'humanité et à la richesse culturelle et

pockets of wealth in the east.

This analysis may seem simplistic and dualistic, but this political geography of visas shows with some cruelty the European vision of the world: selfish and opportunistic. It will be necessary to explain to me what is logical when the EU requires citizens of Kosovo—the poorest state in all of Europe—an expensive visa to travel in the Schengen Area.

There are many ways to share the world, the territories, and the regions. Whether according to the principle of Nations, the grouping of Nations into federations or integrated spaces, or into socio-economic or political indicators. This simple image cynically returns us to our paradoxes and our brutality. This image is shocking because we see ourselves as democrats and generous as we close ourselves from two-thirds of humanity, and the cultural and social wealth that these two-thirds could share with us.

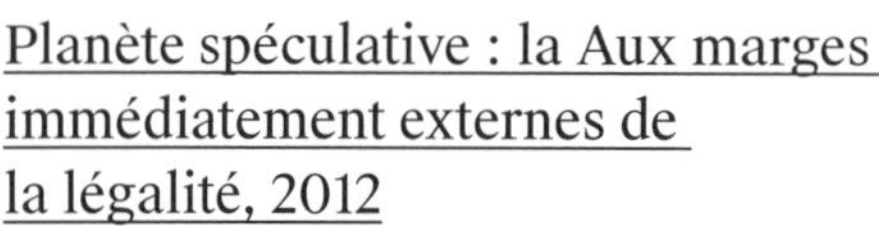

Planète spéculative : la Aux marges immédiatement externes de la légalité, 2012

Rien n'est plus opaque que la grande finance spéculative. Mais, grâce au travail de fourmi des organisations non gouvernementales et de certains magistrats, on sait qu'elle représente des volumes de transaction et d'argent qui dépassent complètement l'imagination. Selon des estimations concordantes, les sommes transférées dans le cadre de ventes et d'achats de produits financiers spéculatifs représentent 200 000 fois le produit intérieur brut du continent afric-

ain, ou l'équivalent de 1 920 000 Airbus A380 au prix catalogue… Et, dans ce contexte, les gouvernants sont toujours incapables de trouver des miettes de fonds financiers pour parer aux plus grandes urgences humanitaires. Cette dérégulation économique et financière qui date du début des années 1980 a fait entrer le monde dans une ère surréaliste. Michel Camdessus, l'ancien patron du Fonds monétaire international (FMI) et père des ajustements structurels qui ont dévasté l'Afrique et l'Asie, avait estimé que 100 milliards de dollars par an pendant dix ou quinze ans seraient suffisants pour régler définitivement les problèmes d'accès à l'eau potable et fournir des sanitaires corrects à l'ensemble de la population de la planète.

Le calcul est simple : avec une année de spéculation financière, on aurait pu régler le problème de l'eau 7 200 fois. Mais je suis sûr que même ce chiffre, personne n'est vraiment capable d'en appréhender l'importance…

Speculative Planet: At the immediate external margins of legality, 2012

Nothing is more opaque than big speculative finance. But thanks to the hard work of non-governmental organizations and certain magistrates, we know that it represents transaction and money volumes that completely exceed the imagination. According to concordant estimates, the sums transferred as part of sales and purchases of speculative financial products represent 200,000 times the gross domestic product of the

African continent, or the equivalent of 1,920,000 Airbus A380s at list price… And, in this context, the rulers are still unable to find pockets of financial funds to ward off the greatest humanitarian emergencies. This economic and financial deregulation that dates back to the early 1980s brought the world into a surrealistic era. Michel Camdessus, the former head of the International Monetary Fund (IMF) and father of the structural adjustments that devastated Africa and Asia, estimated that 100 billion dollars a year for ten or fifteen years would be enough to definitively settle the problems related to accessible drinking water, and provide adequate sanitation for the entire population of the planet.

The calculation is simple: with a year of financial speculation, we could have solved the water problem 7,200 times. But I'm sure that even with this figure, no one is really able to grasp the importance…

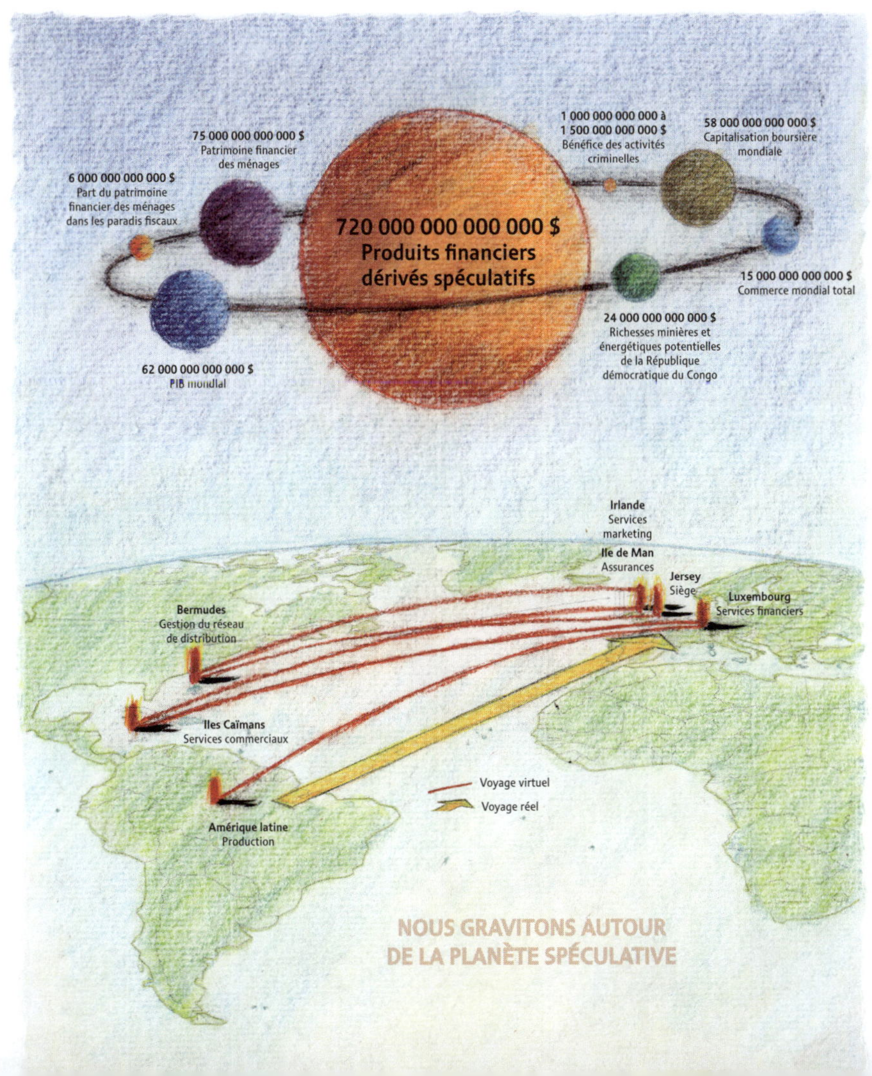

Performing Infrastructure

Lize Mogel

The installation *Performing Infrastructure (New York City Water Supply)* documents a workshop in which people make a "human diagram" of New York City's drinking water system. This counter-mapping is based on the official map of the water system, produced by the City agency that manages it.

The human diagram visualizes and embodies the connections between the parts of the water system. Each participant wears a costume or holds a prop so that they can become an element in the system: reservoir, aqueduct, forested mountain, water treatment plant, water tunnel, or faucet. They form the connections between the parts of the system with their arms and hands. After the diagram is in place, participants create an infrastructure orchestra in which they vocalize the water flowing through the system. The workshop viscerally illustrates how water is a social connector, and that there are human relationships embodied in this infrastructural landscape.

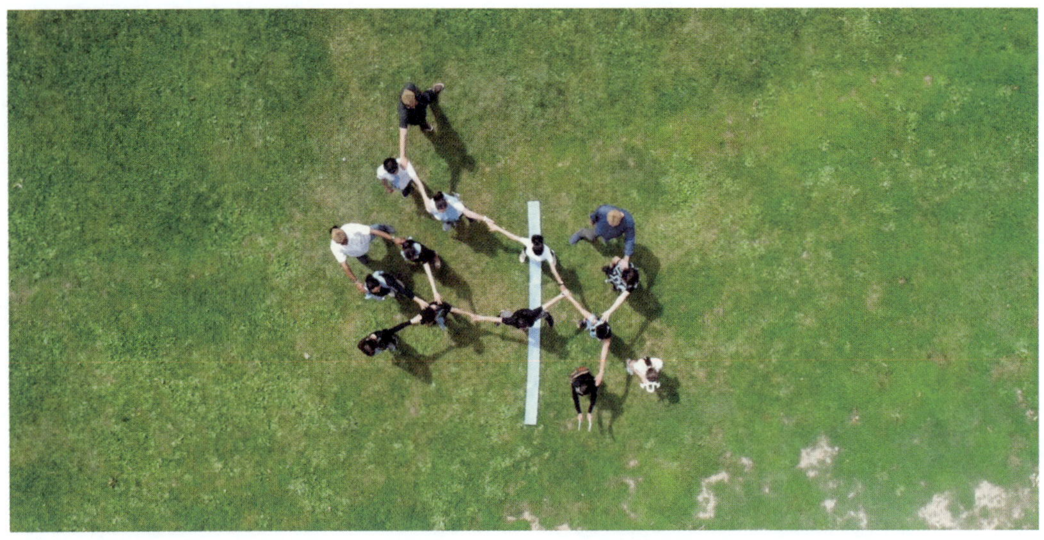

Performing Infrastructure is part of a larger project, *Walking the Watershed*, which critically explores the relationship between New York City and the distant places that supply the City's water. Much of the physical and policy infrastructure of the water system is invisible to City residents. However, it has major impacts on the local communities in which the drinking water originates and is managed—it's an extractive relationship. *Walking the Watershed* brings the social, economic, political and ethical questions around this infrastructure to the surface.

The project centers on the Catskills, a rural, mountainous region about 150 miles from NYC, where 90% of the City's water comes from. Since 2016, I've been re-searching the relationship between the communities at both ends of the water system, and building my own relationships with people and organizations in the Catskills.

The relationship between New York City and the Catskills is complicated and contradictory—it's both symbiotic and parasitic. The history of the water system reveals its politics as both a hegemonic system and a commons. As New York City grew, city leaders looked increasingly farther away for water. They first tapped the Croton River watershed in Westchester, at that time rural farmland just north of the city. When another expansion was needed, they considered several schemes before deciding on two watersheds within the Catskills. Beginning in 1907 and over the next

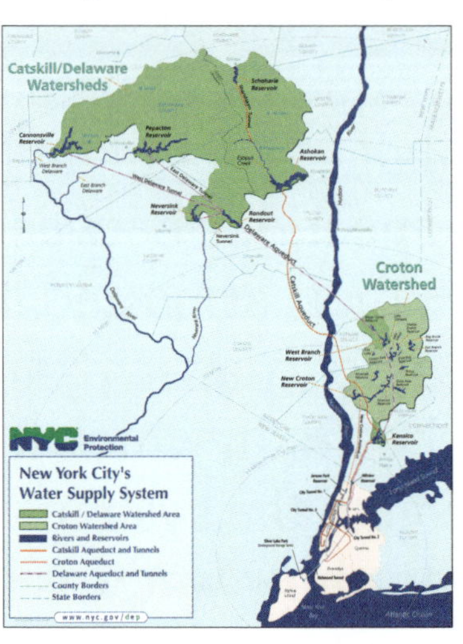

Map of New York City Water Supply System; Source: New York City Department of Environmental Protection.

60 years, the City built six large reservoirs there. They offered buy-outs and used eminent domain to depopulate several small towns that occupied the valleys in which the reservoirs now sit. The towns were demolished, and families, farms, buildings, possessions, and even cemeteries were displaced to higher ground, or elsewhere entirely. More than one hundred years later, there is residual bitterness towards the City for their actions.

The federal Clean Water Act of the 1980s created new mandates for drinking water quality. The City wanted to avoid building a prohibitively expensive water treatment plant for the Catskills system, so they proposed strict land and water management policies to regulate potential sources of pollution, including dairy farming, development, and waste treatment.

Local resistance to some of these policy ideas resulted in several years of heated negotiation between the Catskills and the City. In 1997 these and other stakeholders forged an agreement that would set the relationship for years to come. It laid out "payment for eco-system services," in which the Catskills would live by NYC's regulations, and NYC would fund farm modernization, wastewater treatment, economic development, and flood planning. The City would acquire massive amounts of land, but open much of it up for limited public use like hiking, hunting, and fishing. These policies are partly why the City's water is called "the champagne of drinking water." Still, it's an imperfect union, and one that many Catskills residents still feel is uneven.

NYC's current land use policies restrict density, manufacturing, dairying and farming, which in turn constricts economic development. While these regulations protect the water supply, they also keep the local economy very small scale and reliant on tourism, the success of which varies between towns and counties. (NYC residents make up the largest group of Catskills visitors.)

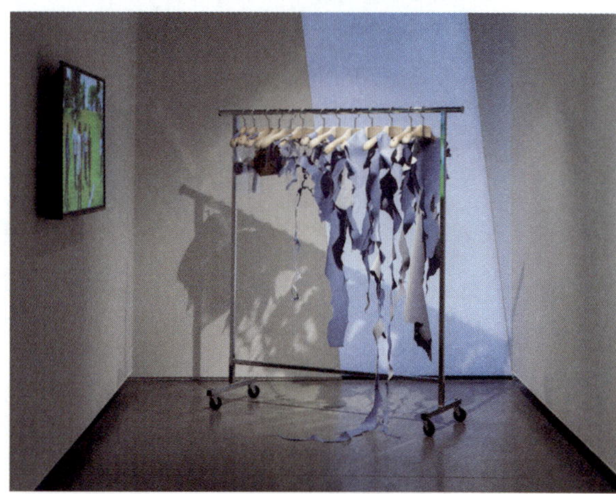

Lize Mogel, *Performing Infrastructure (NYC Watershed)*, 2018. Installation views courtesy of Onsite Gallery. Photography by Yuula Benivolski. Video stills courtesy of the artist.

Walking The Watershed is a long-term project meant to create "water supply tourism" of the Catskills as both a cultural intervention and potential economic catalyst.

The project will draw attention to the social and political conditions under which NYC's water gets to residents. It will complicate visitors' idea of the landscape as a merely recreational one, producing a different collective imaginary that elevates local voices along with the more dominant institutional ones.

DIAGRAMS OF POWER

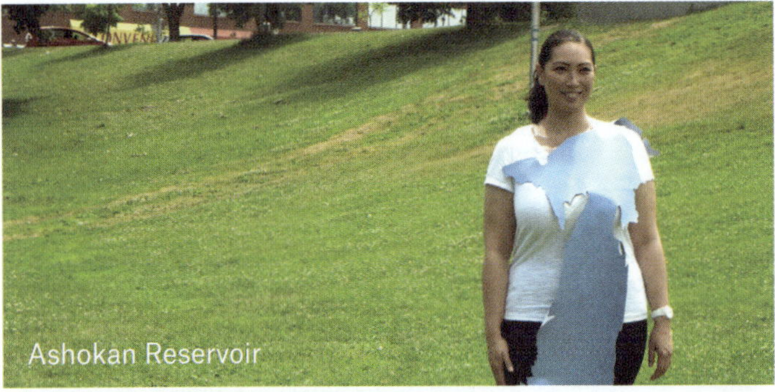

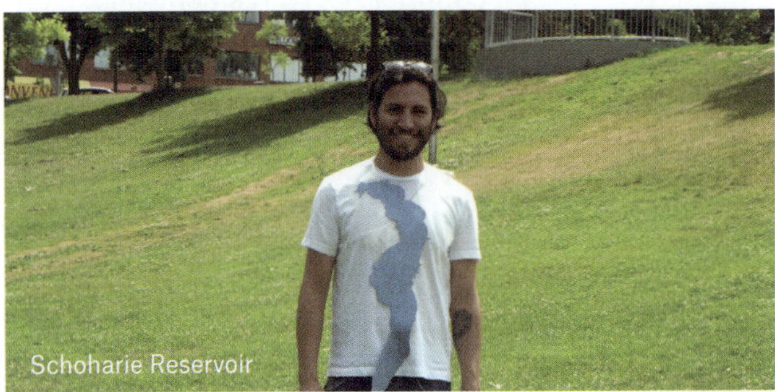

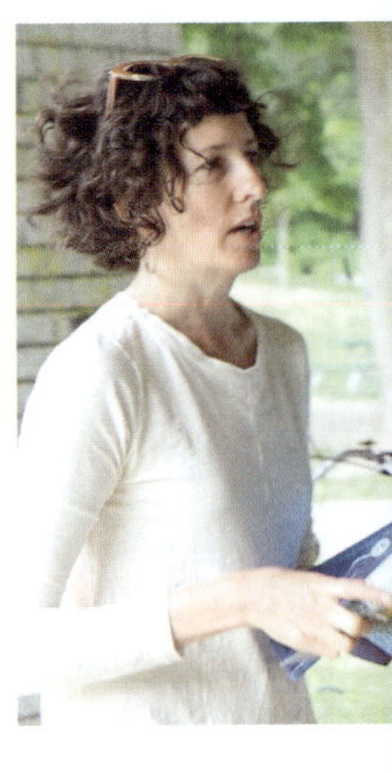

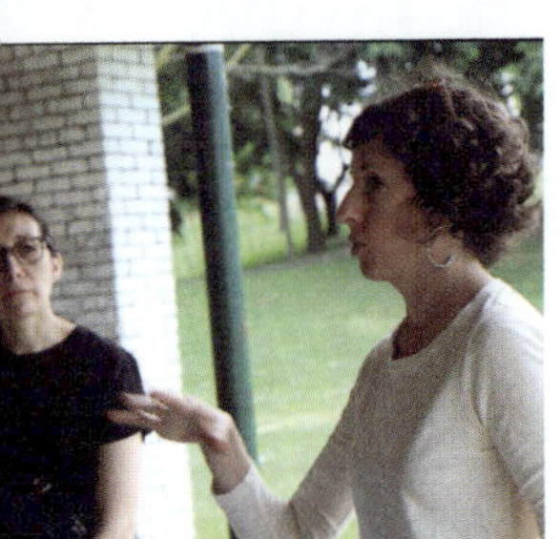

Workshop photography by
Preethi Jagadeesh.

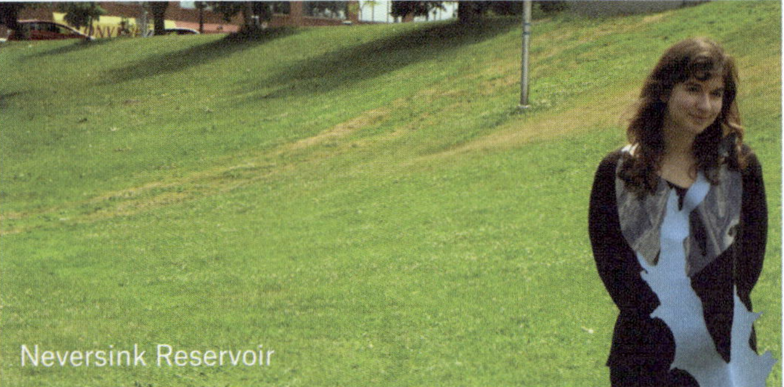

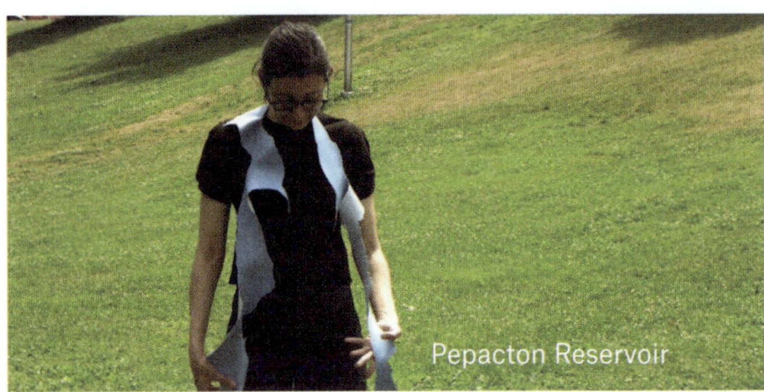

Performing Infrastructure
Lize Mogel

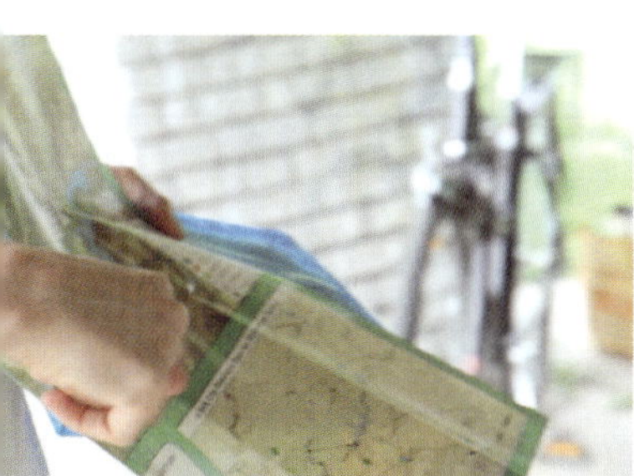

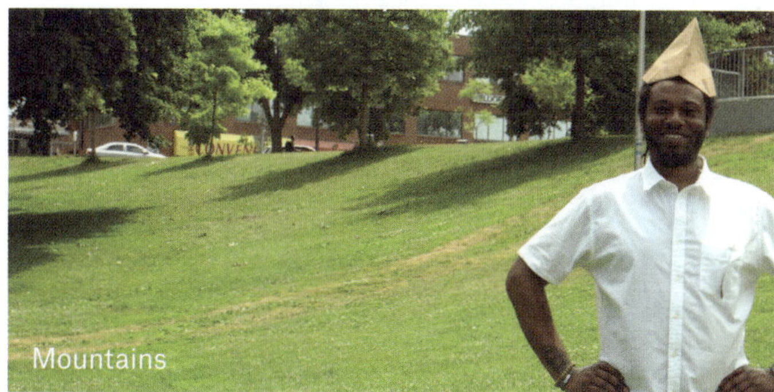

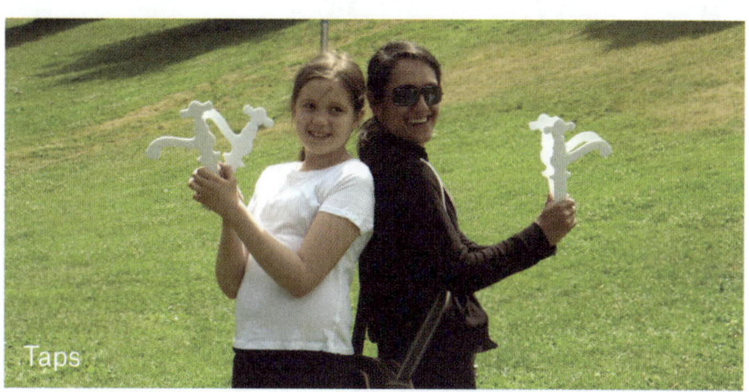

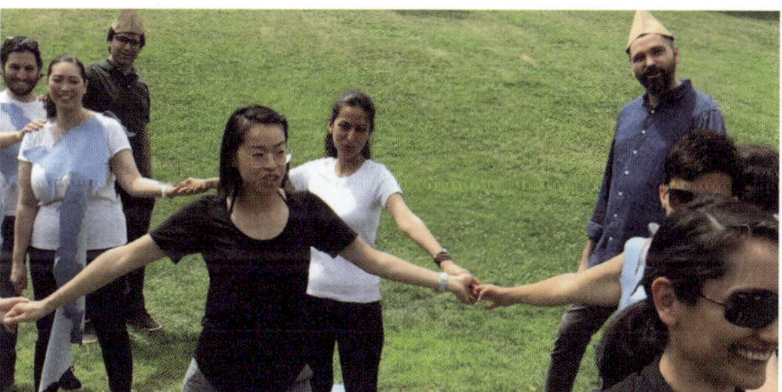

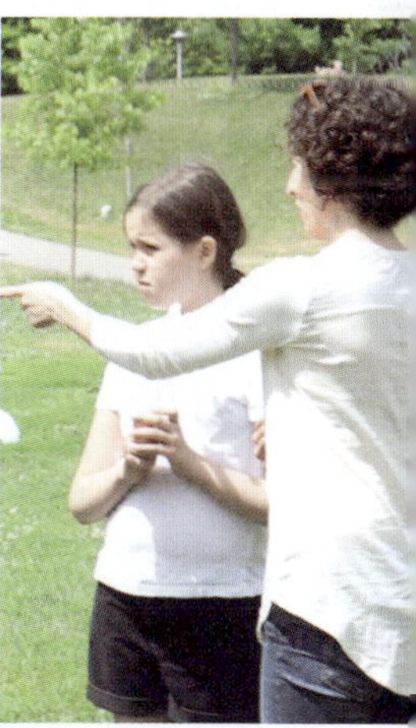

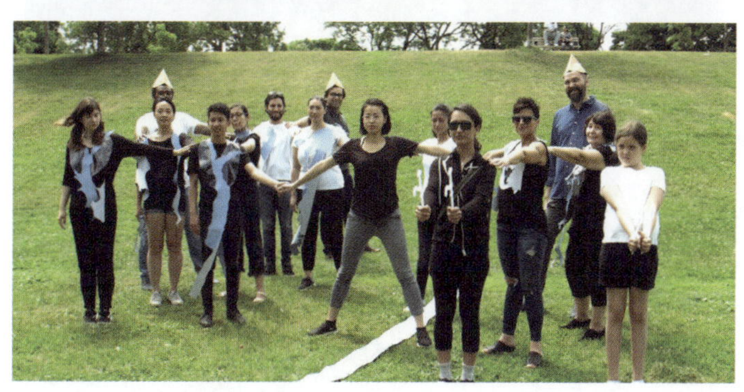

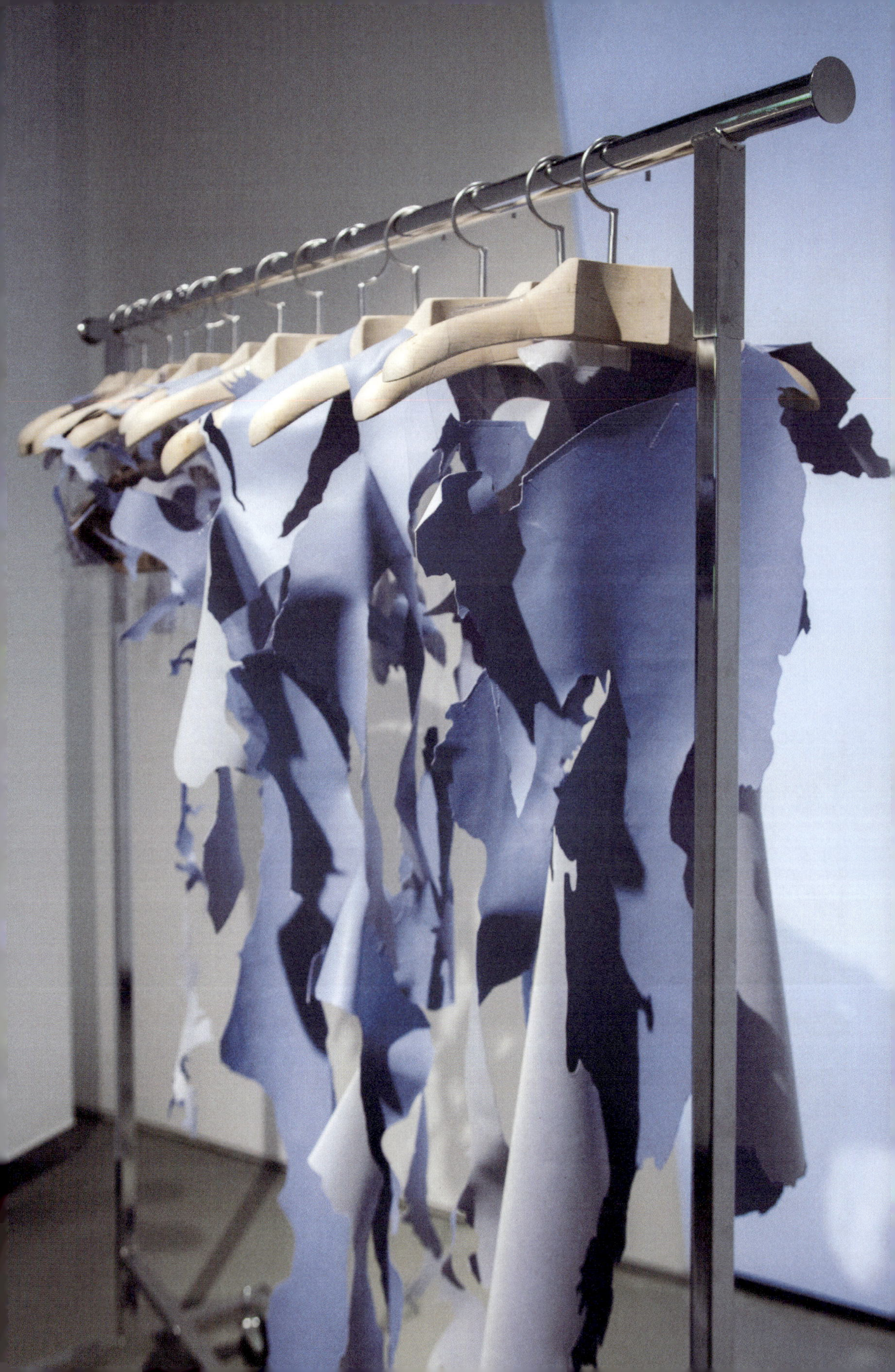

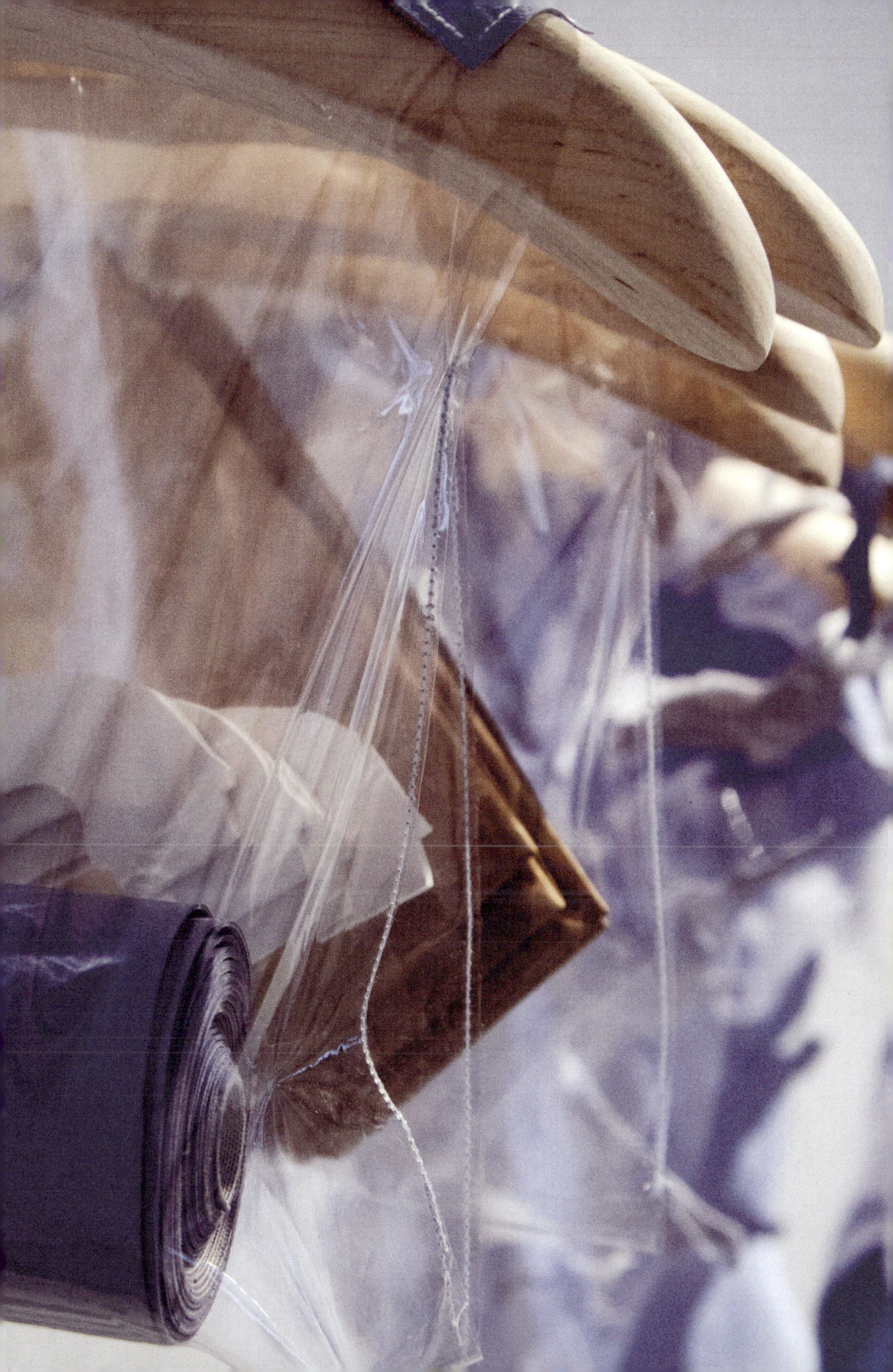

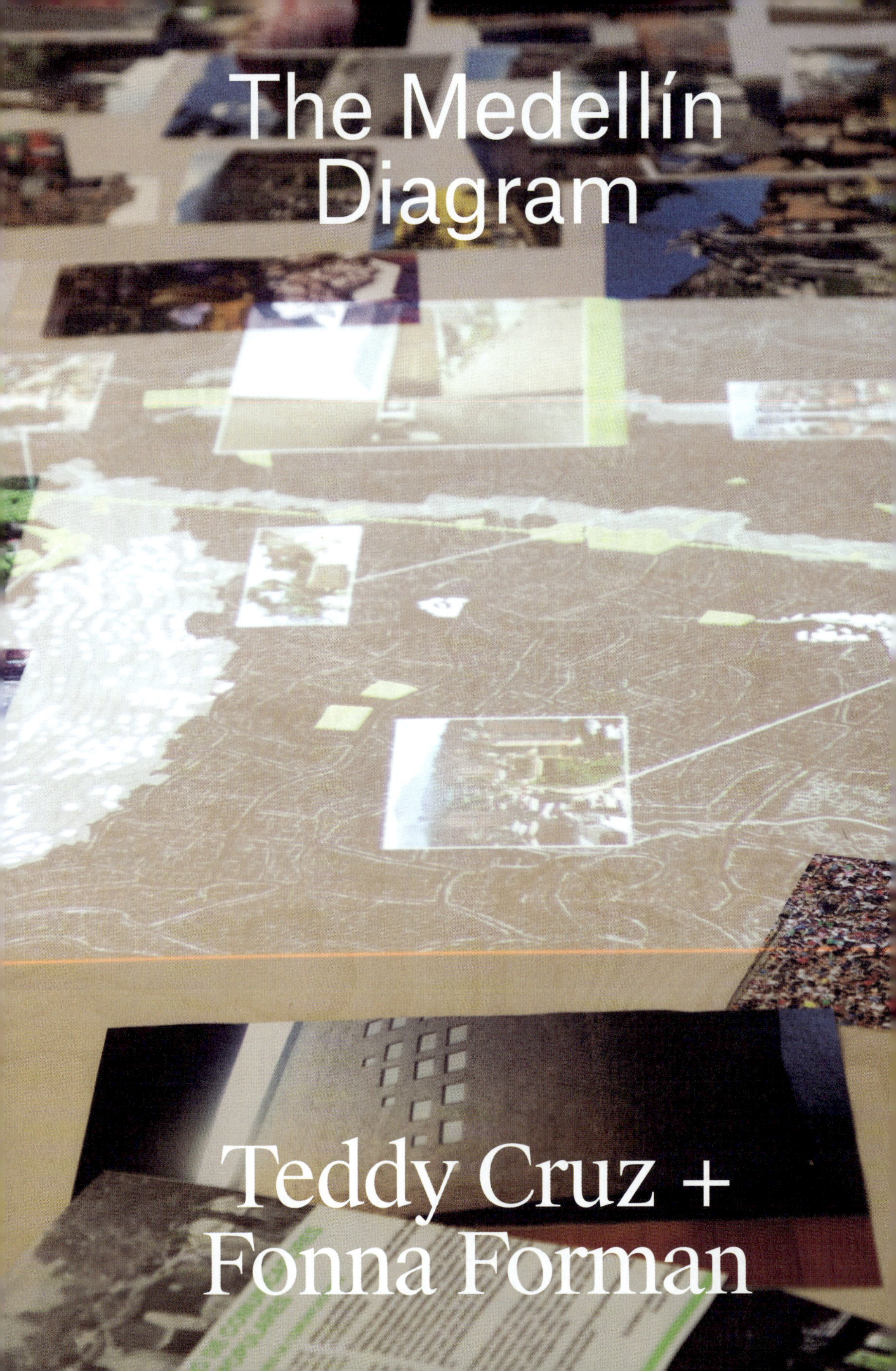

The Medellín
Diagram

Teddy Cruz +
Fonna Forman

Our current period of urban crisis calls into question traditional methods of artistic and architectural intervention in the city. Not only is there a renewed attention to the multiple urban dynamics at play—socio-cultural, political and economic, but this paradigm shift has also instigated a re-definition of the role of artists and architects in conceptualizing new institutional protocols, new systems of representation and collaboration, and a fundamental re-organization of socio-economic and political relations necessary for a more democratic urbanization.

We believe that one of the most pressing urban problems today pertains to a crisis of knowledge-transfer between institutions, fields of specialization and publics. Our intervention in *Diagrams of Power* advances an urban-pedagogical research project that presents a new model of knowledge-exchange, whose point of departure is the visualization of political process: How to translate and visualize the complexity of political and civic processes that characterize the most progressive projects in the city, so that they may be translated and re-deployed in other contexts to cultivate a renewed civic imagination. This re-activation of public agency is the most radical project we can think of, at a time when the survival of the welfare state paradigm is under attack worldwide.

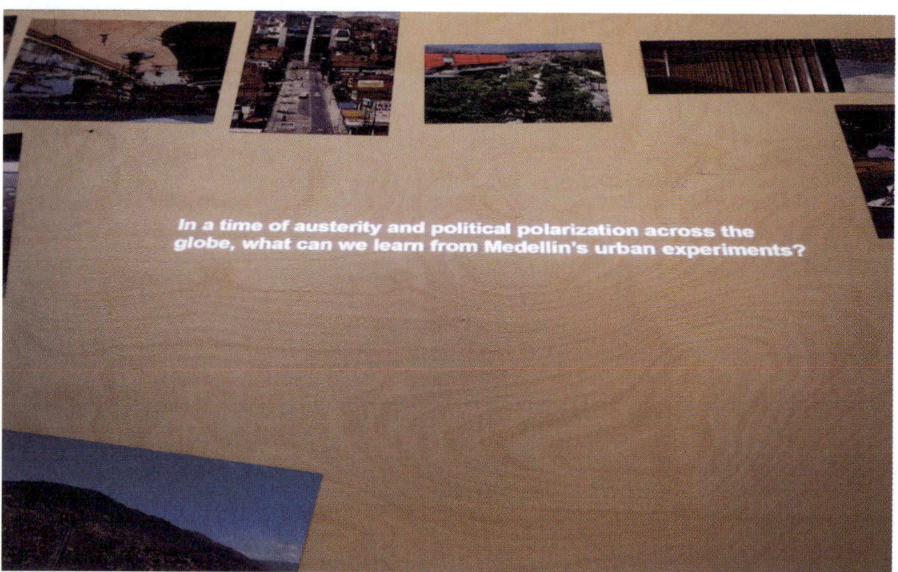

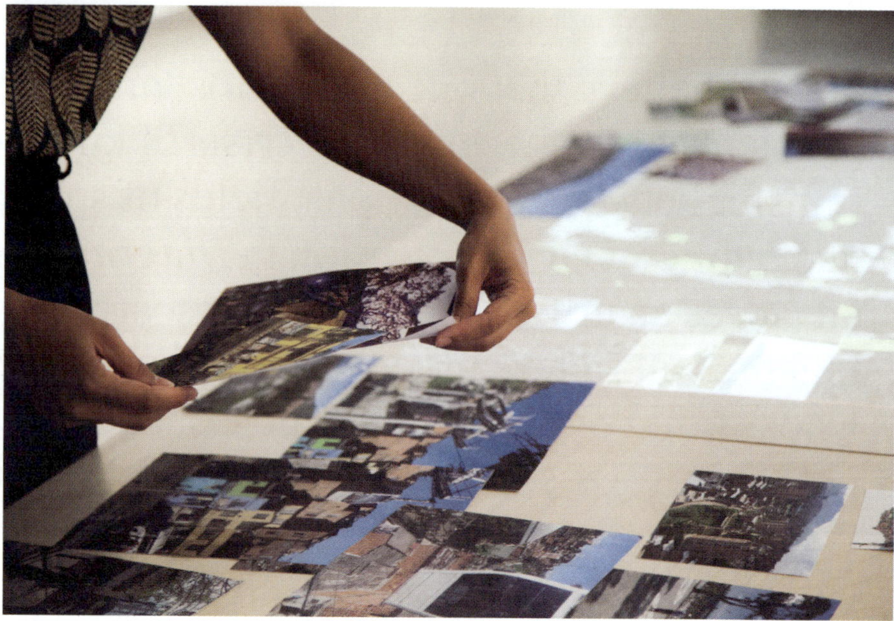

Latin America has long been one of the global epicentres of social injustice, marked by oppressive military dictatorships, deeply-rooted oligarchy and United States cold-war interventionism. But in the last decades, many countries and subnational governments have resisted the neoliberal path and have experimented with progressive politi-

Teddy Cruz and Fonna Forman. *The Medellín Diagram*, 2016. Installation views courtesy of Onsite Gallery. Photography by Yuula Benivolski.

cal, economic and social agendas that prioritize public investment, participatory governance and equality. Challenging private logics of urban development, homogeneity and exclusion, visionary mayors in cities like Porto Alegre and Curitiba, Brazil, and Bogotá and Medellín, Colombia reimagined municipal institutions as engines of social justice, and developed new methods of engaging the public and collaborating across sectors to confront poverty and rethink public infrastructure, pubic space, housing and social service. What makes these Latin American cases distinctive in contemporary urbanization is not only that they were driven by egalitarian commitments and produced significant though sometimes uneven improvements in quality of life for the urban poor, but that their top-down public investments were coupled with a commitment to renewing civic life and activating participatory democratic practices from the bottom-up.

No other continental region in the world has produced so vibrant a set of collective efforts, led by municipal governments seeking urbanizations of social justice and economic inclusion. These experimental political projects were not marked by the protagonism of stand-alone buildings but by the reconfiguration of social and economic relations and the re-thinking of public management.

Latin America has produced dozens of experimental urban projects in recent years, marked not only by top-down municipal redistribution of resources through massive capital invest-ment in public infrastructure and social service—conventional tactics of social justice—but also by a redistribution of knowledges, rethinking the role of the public in co-producing the city from the bottom-up. While left and right everywhere today seem to be joining forces in their rejection of public governance, what emerged in Latin America was a radically progressive form of collaborative government oriented around public goods.

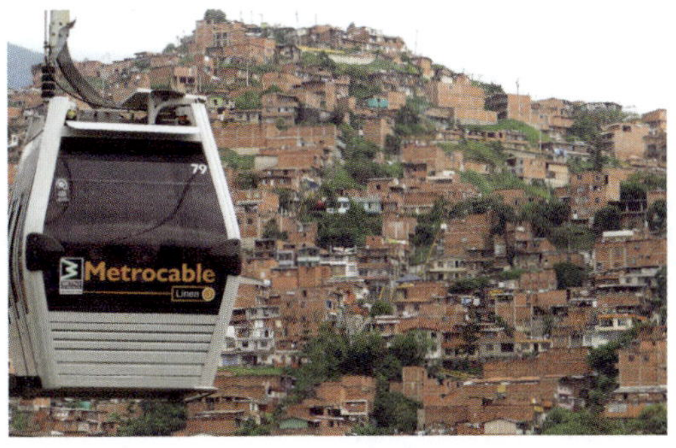

Photographs courtesy of the artists.

We have written at length about these projects elsewhere—from Sao Paulo's SESCs (1977), to Porto Alegre's 'Participatory Budgets' (1989), to Curitiba's urban acupunctural interventions, to Bogota's citizenship-culture interventions (1995). While these Latin American cases occurred across diverse political contexts, and have had spotty successes over the long term, there was a significant and well-documented learning curve that established a late twentieth-century continental tradition of mobilizing of the citizenry to shape the future of the city. In each case, municipalities were essential top-down catalysts to activating bottom-up sensibilities that were typically squashed

PRIORITIES

1.
Putting inequality first

Medellín constructed a new political agenda

1.A
Committing to zones of poverty

1.B
Mediating urban conflict

1.C
Cultivating a new civic imagination

1.A.1 Medellín was first and foremost a political project, not an architectural one

1.A.2 Medellín chose a new political leadership committed to confronting inequality

1.A.3 Medellín declared that violence is rooted in poverty

1.A.4 Medellín sought to narrow the gap between wealth and poverty

1.A.5 Medellín re-imagined the city from its periphery

1.A.6 Medellín identified sites of urgency, and invested in the poorest zones of the city

1.A.7 Medellín built immediate public trust with small-scale neighborhood interventions while planning a long-term urban vision

1.B.1 Medellín visualized urban conflict as point of departure

1.B.2 Medellín pursued social order not through police repression but through community processes

1.B.3 Medellín embraced empathy as a pathway to inclusive urbanization

1.B.4 Medellín created spaces for mediation and conflict resolution

1.B.5 Medellín mediated divergent perspectives and challenged polarization with constructive dialogue and debate

1.B.6 Medellín facilitated understanding between marginalized communities and institutions

1.B.7 Medellín constructed a new social contract to guarantee peace and democracy

1.B.8 Medellín summoned artists to resuscitate urban memory

1.C.1 Medellín cultivated respect for human dignity

1.C.2 Medellín prioritized public thinking

1.C.3 Medellín learned from examples of participatory urbanization across Latin America

1.C.4 Medellín imagined a new era of civic participation

1.C.5 Medellín developed strategies to restore collective agency

1.C.6 Medellín facilitated community forums to discuss the future of the city

1.C.7 Medellín summoned diverse civic actors to collaborate

1.C.8 Medellín designed new platforms for public communication

1.C.9 Medellín awakened its own institutional memory

1.C.10 Medellín recovered its own lineages of civic commitment

1.C.11 Medellín resuscitated a history of collaboration between labor and industry

PROCESSES

2.
Designing Gove[rnment]

Medellín transformed munici[pal]

2.A
Assembling transparent and inclusive public management

2.B
Integ[rating] redis[tributive] know[ledge] reso[urces]

2.A.1 For Medellín urban equality demanded a transformation of government bureaucracy

2.A.2 Medellín studied the best models of municipal governance from across Latin America

2.A.3 Medellín tackled institutional corruption

2.A.4 Medellín prioritized bureaucratic efficien[cy] agility

2.A.10 Medellín invested public utility dividends into public infrastructure

2.A.11 Medellín created new public institutions tasked with social and economic inclusion

2.B.1 Medellín committed to collaborative municipal governance

2.B.2 Medellín reconceived public management [as] a transversal curato[rial] project

2.B.8 Medellín encouraged public input into municipal resource allocation

2.C.1 Medellín did not 'outsource' urban design

2.C.2 Medellín summoned the design professionals to collaborate 'in house'

2.C.3 Medellín engaged loc[al] universities to rethi[nk] urban policy

2.C.9 Medellín conceptualized infrastructure as a platform for social density

Teddy Cruz and Fonna Forman. *The Medellín Diagram*, 2016.
Diagram courtesy of the artists.

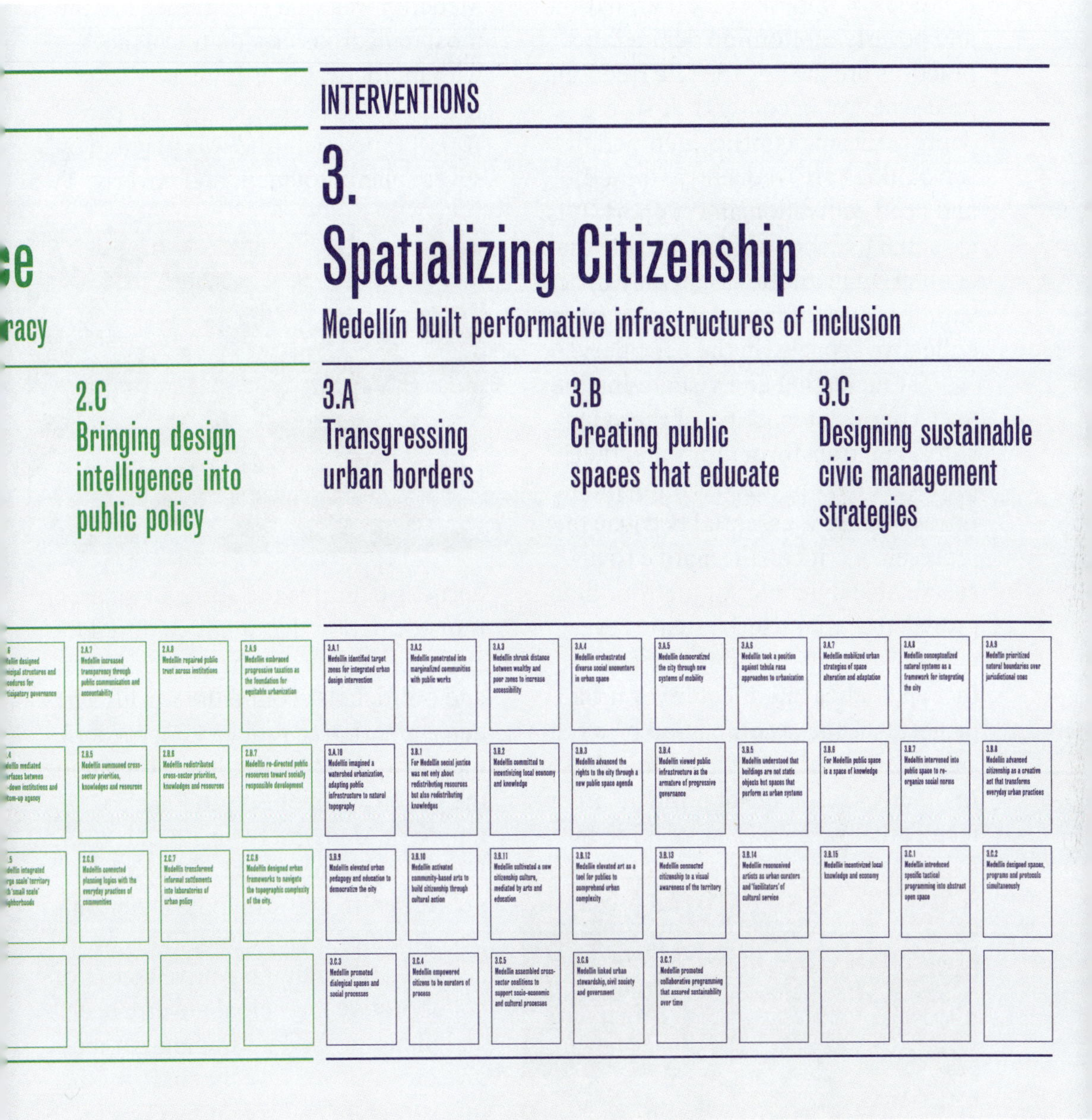

INTERVENTIONS

3.
Spatializing Citizenship

Medellín built performative infrastructures of inclusion

2.C
Bringing design intelligence into public policy

3.A
Transgressing urban borders

3.B
Creating public spaces that educate

3.C
Designing sustainable civic management strategies

racy

2.A.6
...ellín designed ...ncipal structures and ...cedures for ...ticipatory governance

2.A.7
Medellín increased transparency through public communication and accountability

2.A.8
Medellín repaired public trust across institutions

2.A.9
Medellín embraced progressive taxation as the foundation for equitable urbanization

3.A.1
Medellín identified target zones for integrated urban design intervention

3.A.2
Medellín penetrated into marginalized communities with public works

3.A.3
Medellín shrunk distance between wealthy and poor zones to increase accessibility

3.A.4
Medellín orchestrated diverse social encounters in urban space

3.A.5
Medellín democratized the city through new systems of mobility

3.A.6
Medellín took a position against tabula rasa approaches to urbanization

3.A.7
Medellín mobilized urban strategies of space alteration and adaptation

3.A.8
Medellín conceptualized natural systems as a framework for integrating the city

3.A.9
Medellín prioritized natural boundaries over jurisdictional ones

2.B.4
...ellín mediated ...rfaces between ...-down institutions and ...tom-up agency

2.B.5
Medellín summoned cross-sector priorities, knowledges and resources

2.B.6
Medellín redistributed cross-sector priorities, knowledges and resources

2.B.7
Medellín re-directed public resources toward socially responsible development

3.A.10
Medellín imagined a watershed urbanization, adapting public infrastructure to natural topography

3.B.1
For Medellín social justice was not only about redistributing resources but also redistributing knowledges

3.B.2
Medellín committed to incentivizing local economy and knowledge

3.B.3
Medellín advanced the rights to the city through a new public space agenda

3.B.4
Medellín viewed public infrastructure as the armature of progressive governance

3.B.5
Medellín understood that buildings are not static objects but spaces that perform as urban systems

3.B.6
For Medellín public space is a space of knowledge

3.B.7
Medellín intervened into public space to re-organize social norms

3.B.8
Medellín advanced citizenship as a creative act that transforms everyday urban practices

2.C.5
...ellín integrated ...rge scale' territory ...h 'small scale' ...ighborhoods

2.C.6
Medellín connected planning logics with the everyday practices of communities

2.C.7
Medellín transformed informal settlements into laboratories of urban policy

2.C.8
Medellín designed urban frameworks to navigate the topographic complexity of the city.

3.B.9
Medellín elevated urban pedagogy and education to democratize the city

3.B.10
Medellín activated community-based arts to build citizenship through cultural action

3.B.11
Medellín cultivated a new citizenship culture, mediated by arts and education

3.B.12
Medellín elevated art as a tool for publics to comprehend urban complexity

3.B.13
Medellín connected citizenship to a visual awareness of the territory

3.B.14
Medellín reconceived artists as urban curators and 'facilitators' of cultural service

3.B.15
Medellín incentivized local knowledge and economy

3.C.1
Medellín introduced specific tactical programming into abstract open space

3.C.2
Medellín designed spaces, programs and protocols simultaneously

3.C.3
Medellín promoted dialogical spaces and social processes

3.C.4
Medellín empowered citizens to be curators of process

3.C.5
Medellín assembled cross-sector coalitions to support socio-economic and cultural processes

3.C.6
Medellín linked urban stewardship, civil society and government

3.C.7
Medellín promoted collaborative programming that assured sustainability over time

into habits of acquiescence through centuries of imperialism, domination and poverty. Bottom-up democratic practices are the key to civic freedom, no doubt. But in contexts of severe deprivation and conflict, democratic sensibilities are frequently stunted, and need cultivation and support. It is essential to acknowledge the role that egalitarian institutions can play in activating a sense of injustice, urgency and collective capacity in the periphery.

Elucidating and visualizing the 'procedural complexity' of these institutional transformations and their physical effect in transforming public infrastructure is essential because they represent a critical alternative to unsustainable dynamics of metropolitan growth that characterizes cities everywhere. They give us important clues that any radical architecture or urban project must be accompanied by a radical transformation of the political itself. In other words, it is not political architecture that we should be seeking but

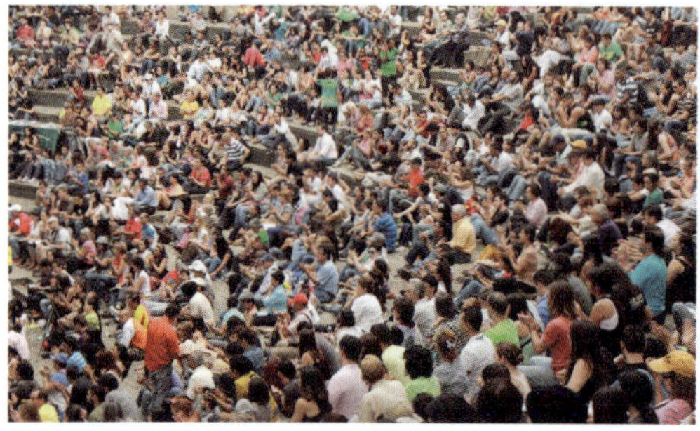

the construction of the political itself: a radical institutional transformation that prioritizes public as opposed to private interests, in the formation of the future city. Medellín is the most comprehensive of these stories.

During the 1980s and 1990s, Medellín was widely regarded as "the most dangerous city on the planet"– with murder rates as high as 6,300 in 1991 alone (a staggering 380 per 100,000 people)–and was plagued by severe unemployment and poverty. Two

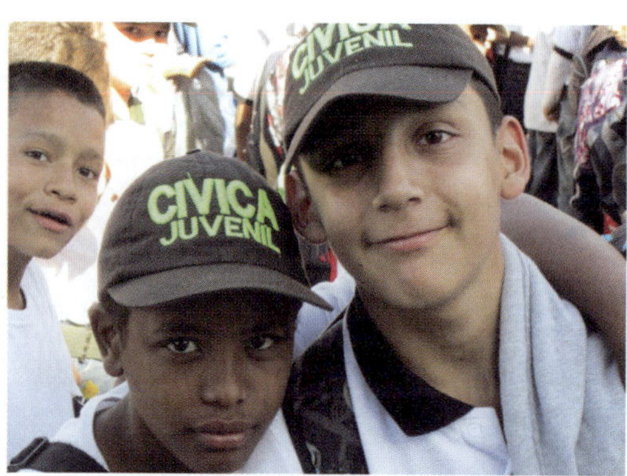

decades later it is the scene of an urban transformation that it has captured the attention of city planners, architects, and politicians around the world. The determination to reduce violence and inequality in Medellín intensified under the government of Sergio Fajardo, mayor of Medellín from 2003 to 2007. His government sought to improve public health and stimulate a vibrant, participatory civic culture. This was activated through innovative tactics of collaborative municipal governance and planning, and a campaign of massive cross-sector investment in public infrastructure and social services in the poorest and most violent neighborhoods in the city.

There is no other project of this magnitude in the world where a city decided to confront urban inequality and conflict by investing in the most challenged and marginalized zones of

The Medellín Diagram
Teddy Cruz + Fonna Forman

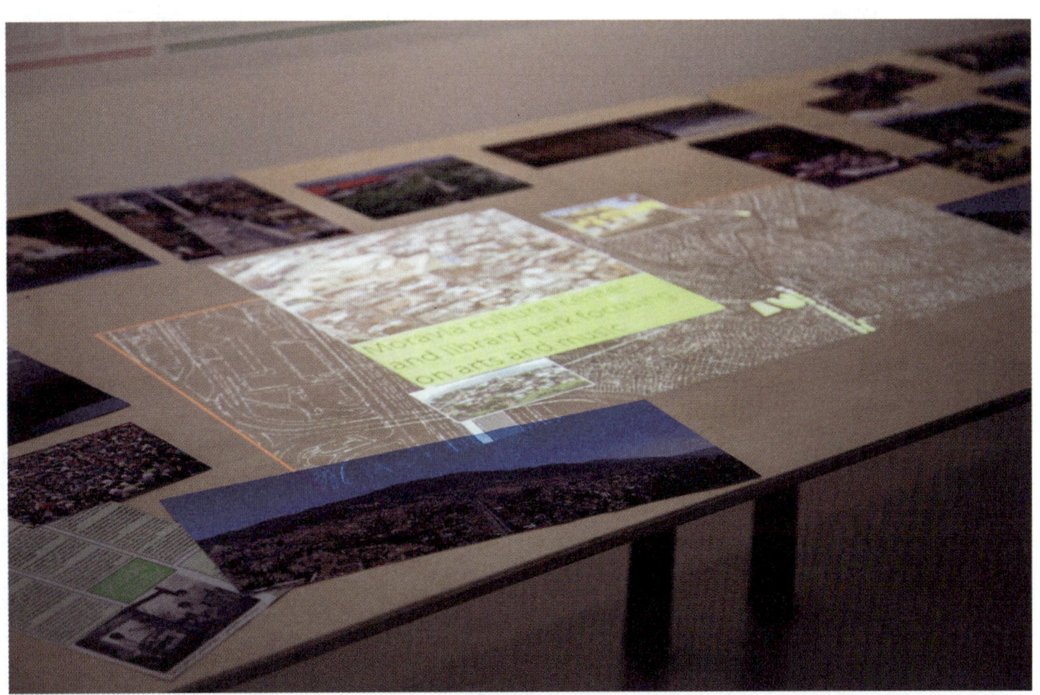

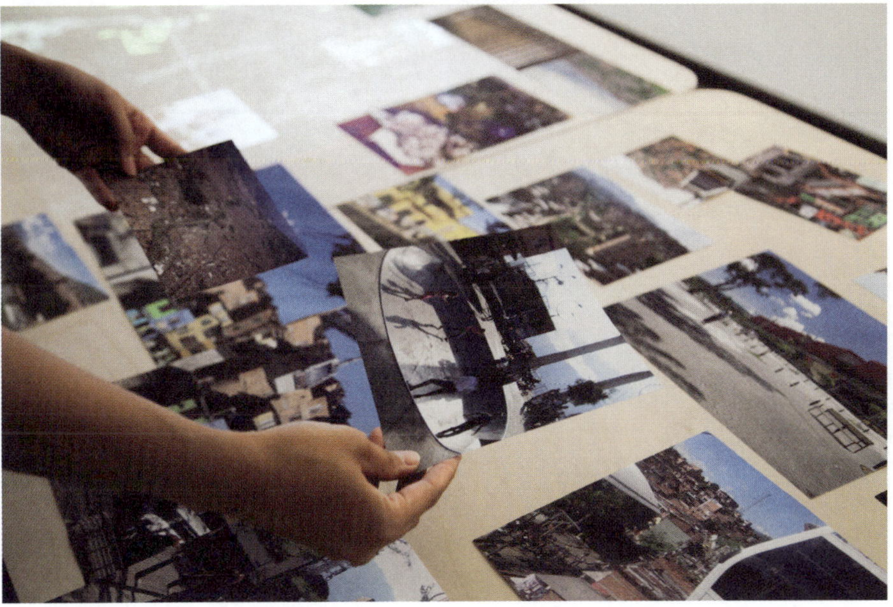

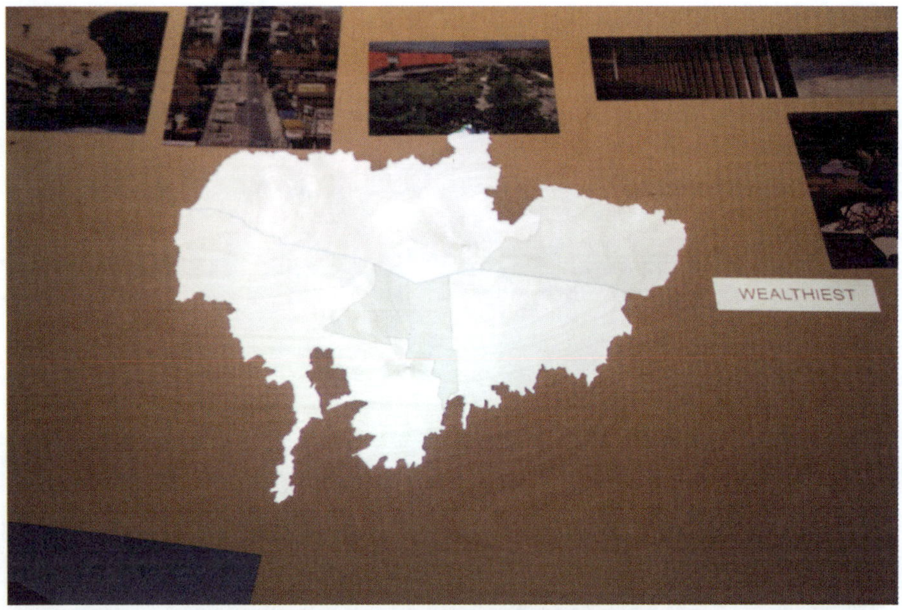
WEALTHIEST

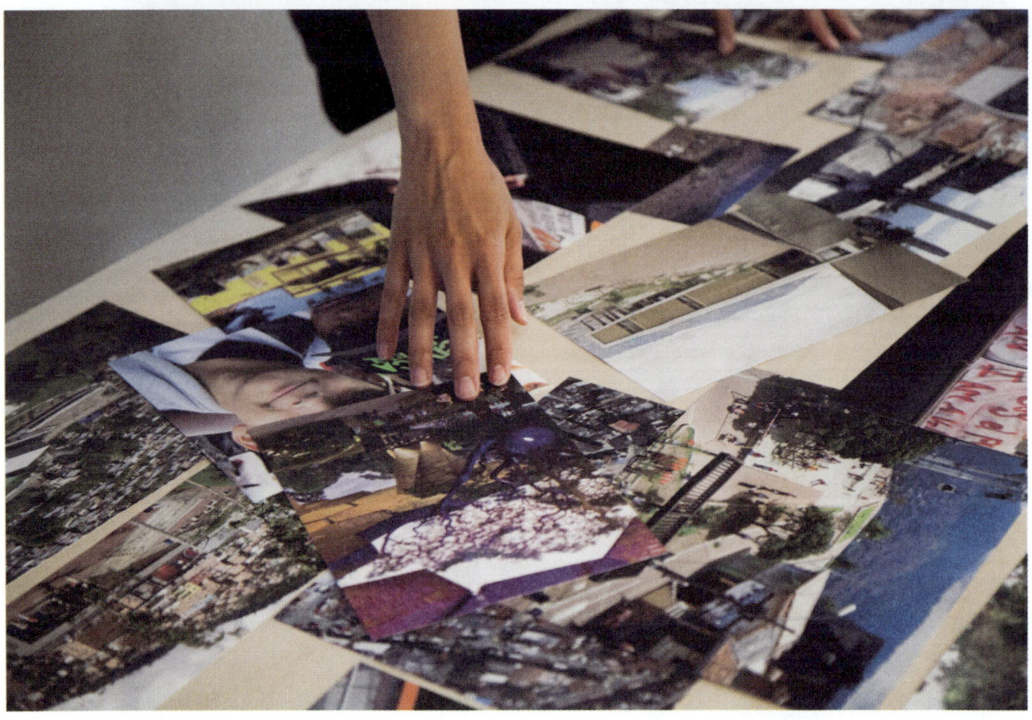

the city, re-imagining public space and infrastructure as mediating systems for social and economic inclusion.

The Medellin Diagram is an urban pedagogical project that visualizes the political and civic processes that enabled Medellín's now-legendary urban transformation. Developed by urban designer Teddy Cruz and political theorist Fonna Forman, in collaboration with architect and urbanist Alejandro Echeverri, and graphic designer Matthias Goerlich, the diagram is designed as a tool for municipalities and publics eager to learn from Medellín's achievements. We demonstrate that it is not by emulating buildings and transport systems that cities across the globe can begin to

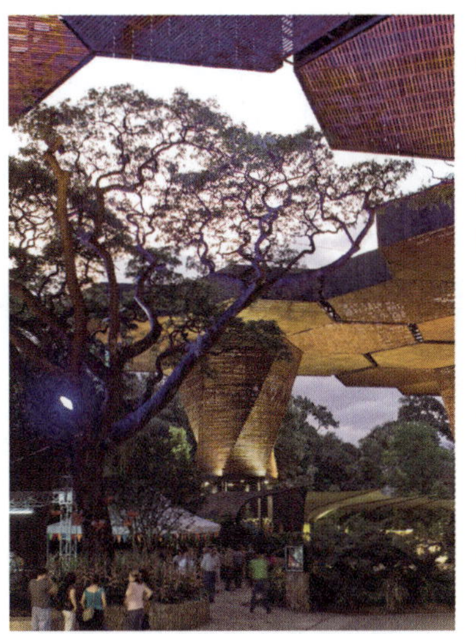

approximate the inclusive urbanization that transformed this city. The key is to understand the complex processes through which institutions reimagined themselves, and cross-sector collaborations facilitated new interfaces between top-down and bottom-bottom knowledges and resources.

So, while Medellín has rightfully captured global attention for the excellence of its public architecture and infrastructure; *the Medellín Diagram* reveals that it was first a political project, through which institutions reimagined themselves, and cross-sector collaborations facilitated new interfaces between

top-down and bottom-bottom knowledges and resources. It is this reorganization of the political and the civic that enabled Medellin's urban projects to be conceived, designed, funded, built, programmed and maintained. From the perspective of participatory democracy and social justice, Medellín is a story about how a public restored urban dignity, activated collective agency, and reclaimed the future of its own city.

The Medellín Diagram is an iterative research project. It was launched in April 2013 as a periodic table at the Medellin Museum of Modern Art on the occasion of the World Urban Forum. The second phase was exhibited as a multimedia scaffold at the Museum of Modern Art in Los Angeles in 2014, as part of the exhibition "Citizen Culture: Artists and Architects Shape Policy." Soon after, *the Medellín Diagram* was presented in 2015 at the Shenzhen Biennial's Radical Urbanism exhibit as a multi-media installation, comprising a series of dynamic process diagrams through video and other visualization tools. In Spring 2017, in "Visualizing Citizenship,' a solo exhibition of our work at the Yerba Buena Center of the Arts in San Francisco, *The Medellín Diagram* functioned as a table that subdivided areas of government intervention that were animated by specific examples of infrastructural change and process diagrams.

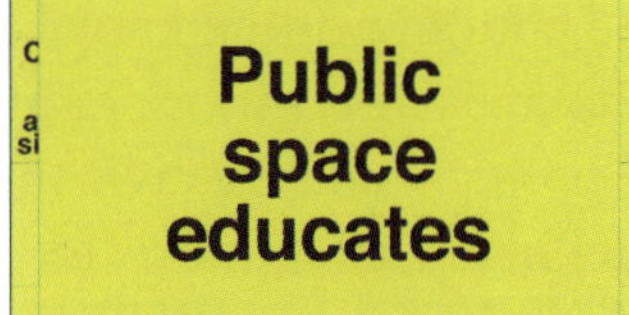

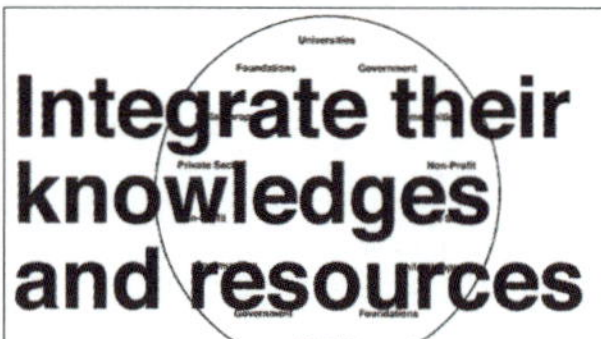

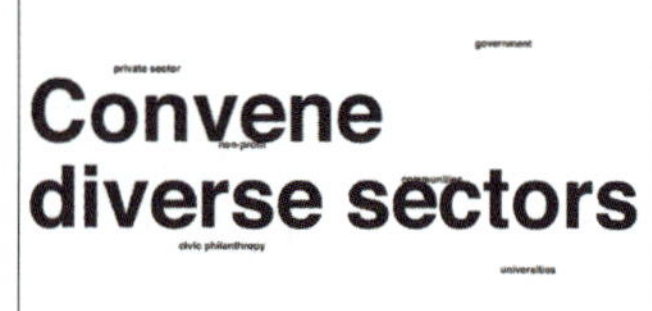

Redistribute knowledges and resources	Public space educates	Don't privatize!
Mediate top-down and bottom-up	Transgress urban borders	Redesign governance

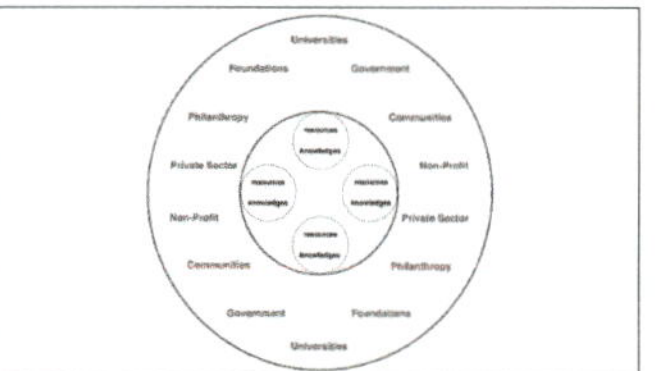

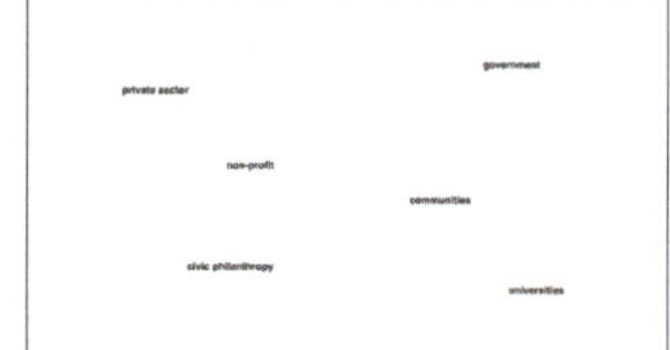

Redistribute knowledges and resources

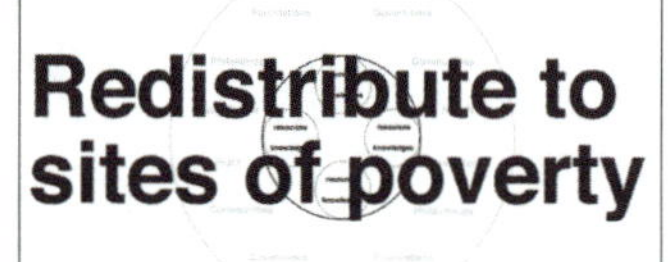

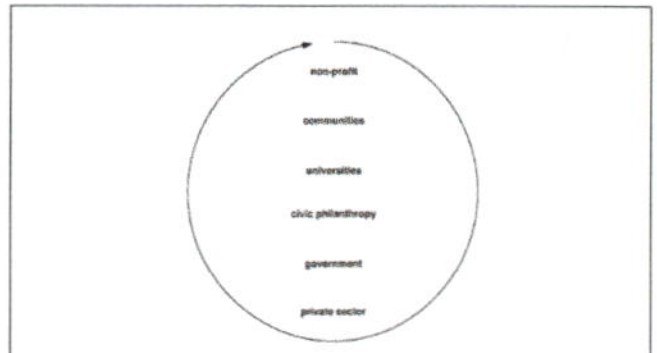

Fragmented institutions fragment the city

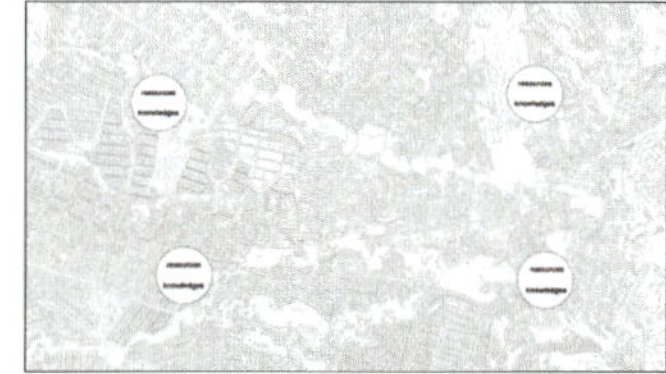

Share responsibility for public works

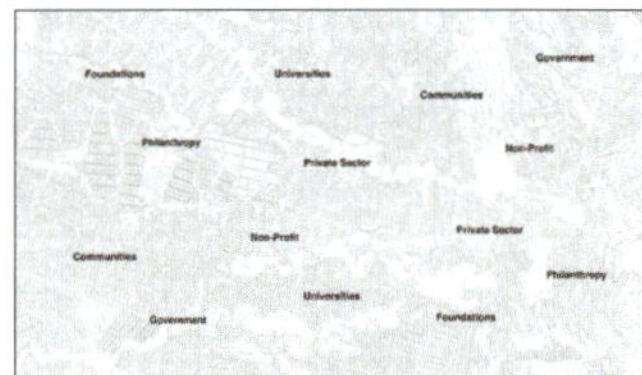

Centralize and decentralize knowledges and resources simultaneously

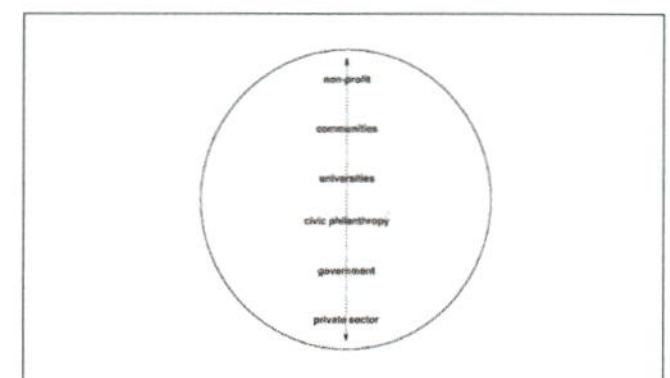

Summon institutions to collaborate

Public space educates

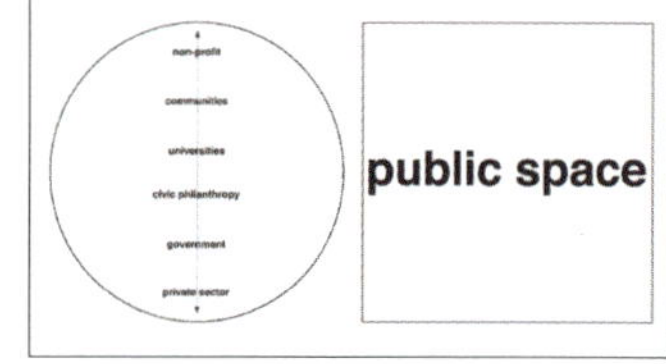

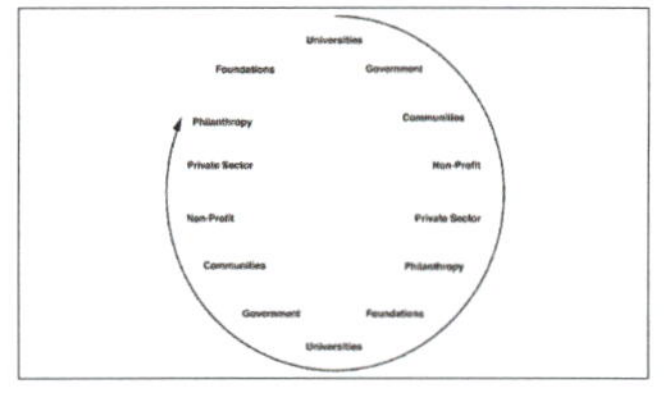

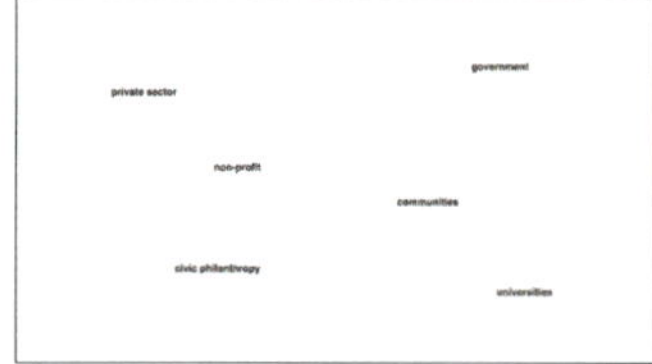

Co-produce cultural progamming

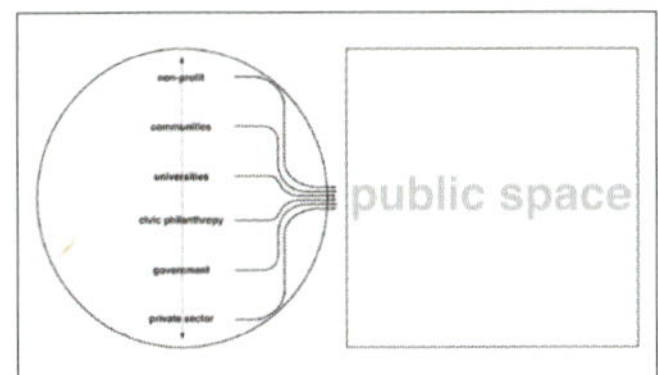

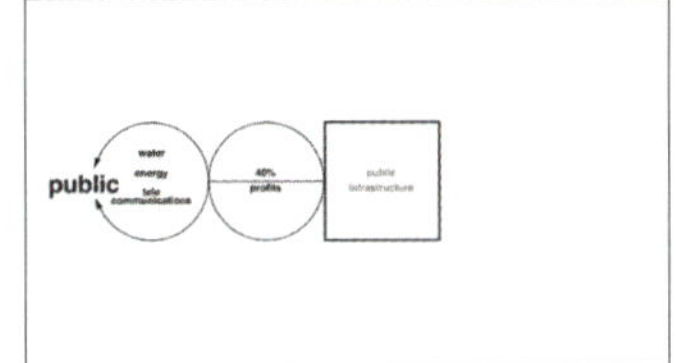

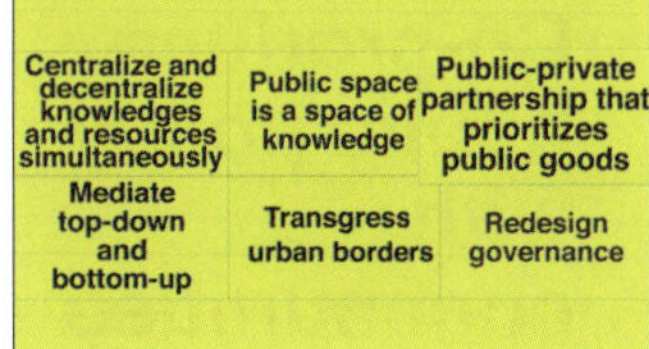

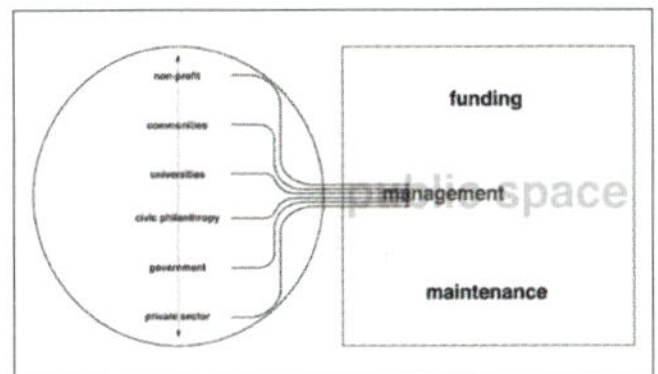

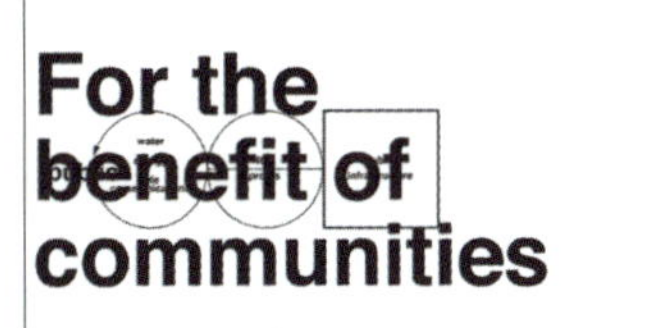

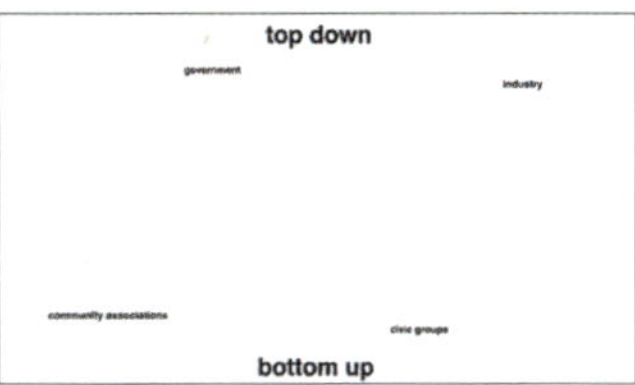

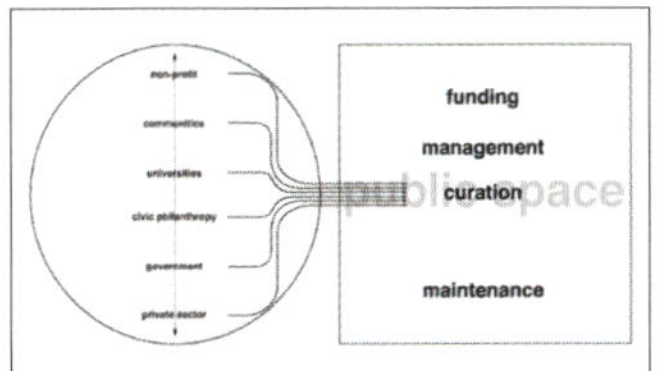

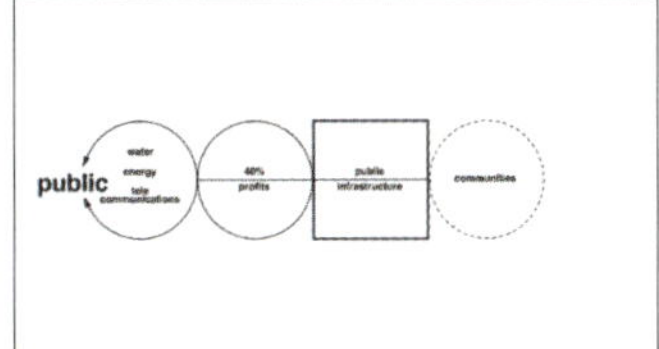

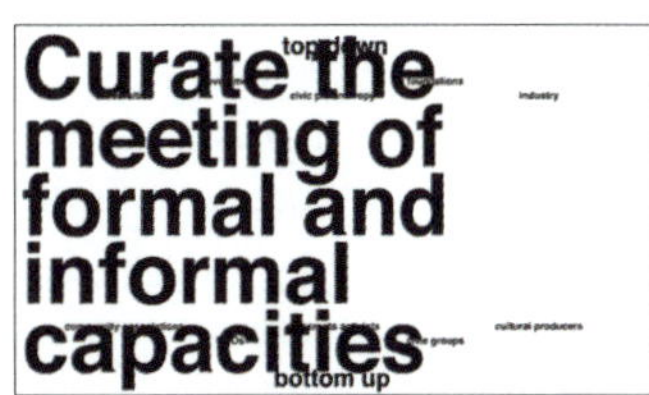

Design public spaces and programs simultaneously

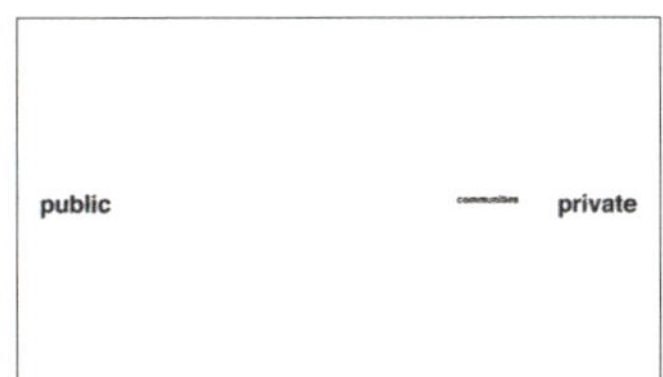

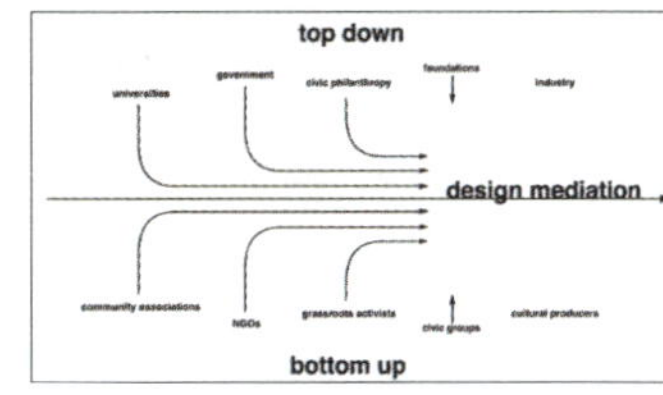

public   utilities   private

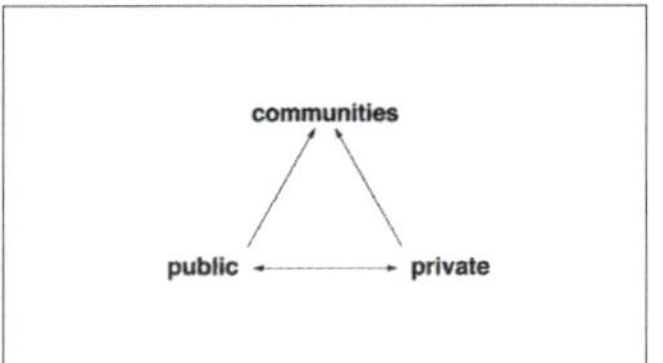

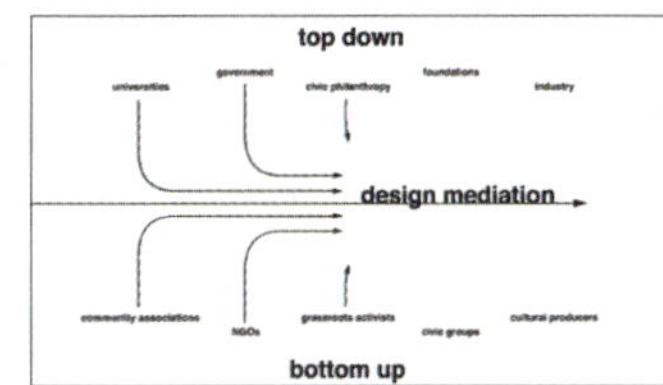

The city owns water, energy and tele-communications
public utilities

Public-private partnership that prioritizes public goods
communities
public
private

Profits are invested in public infrastructure
public
energy

Mediate top-down and bottom-up

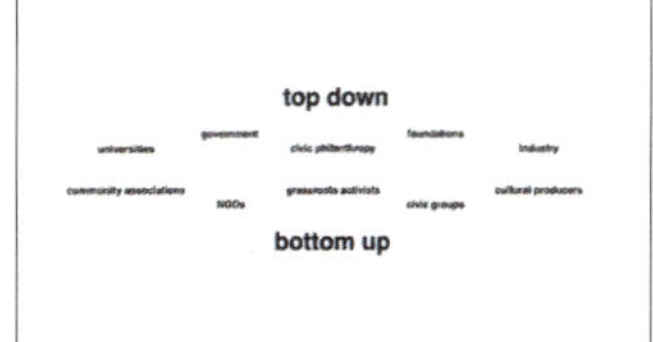

Co-produce public policy with communities

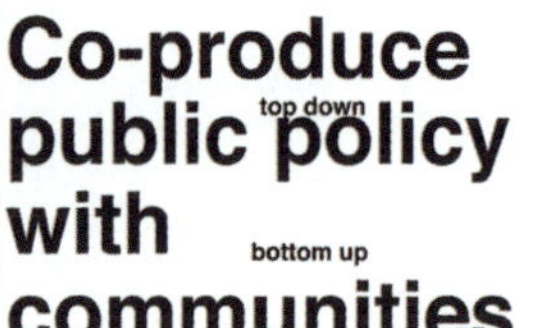

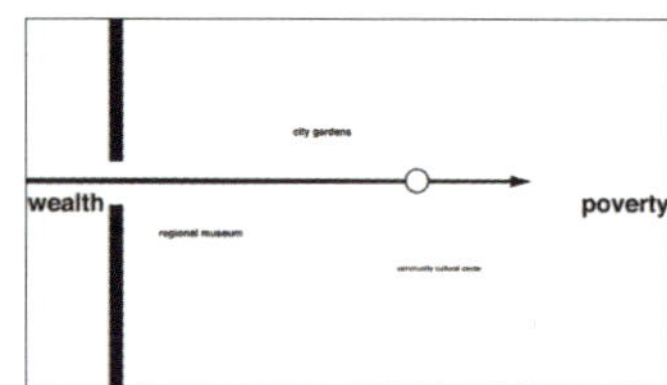

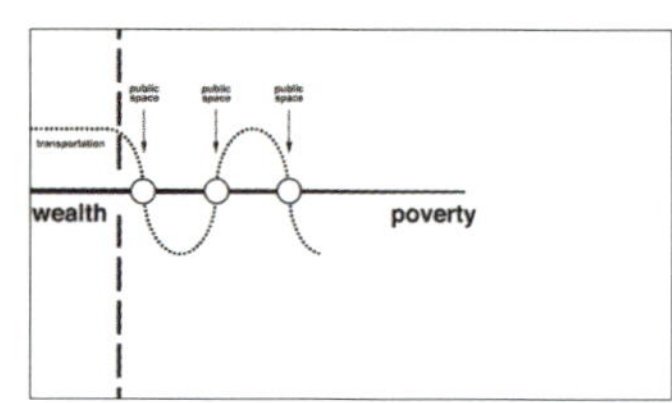

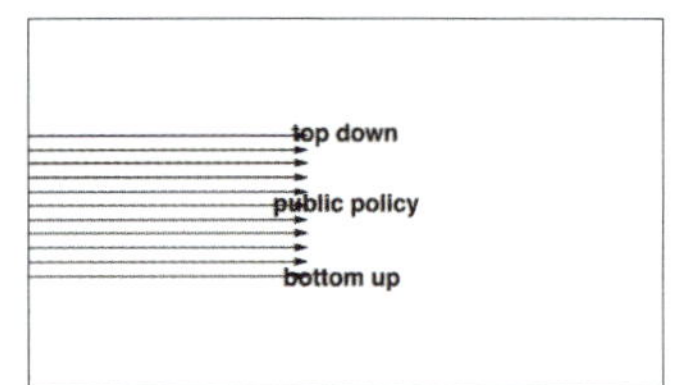

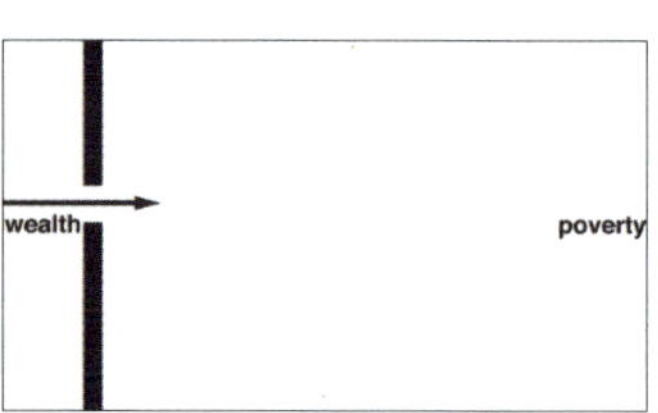

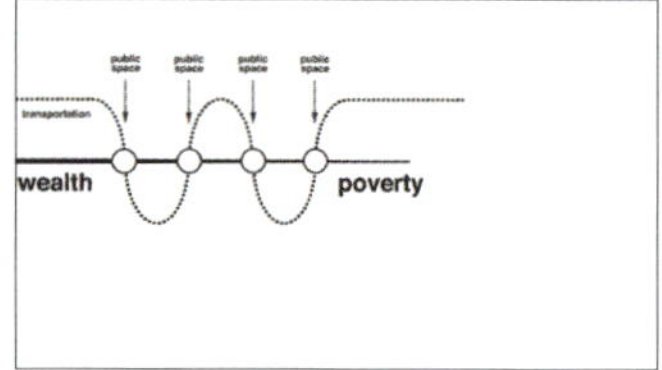

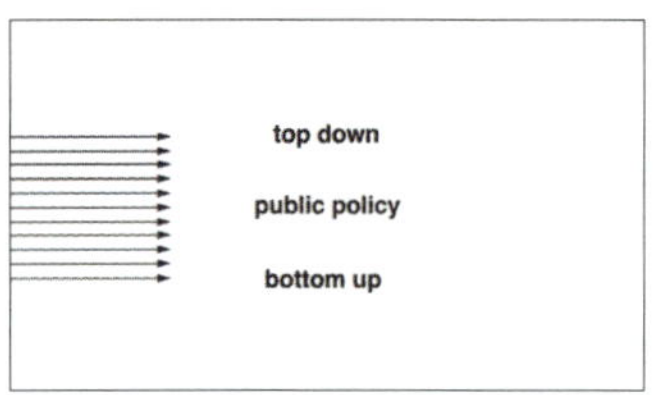

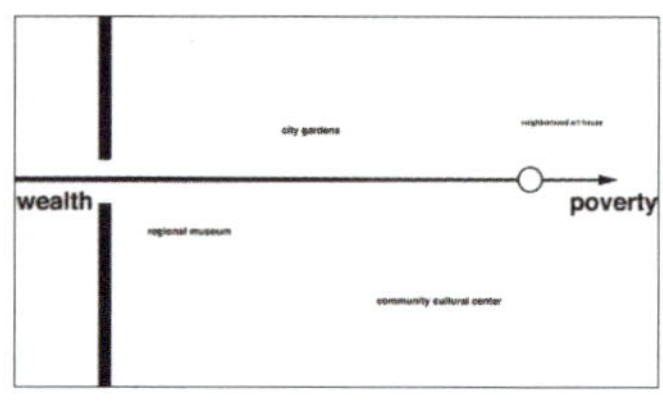

Shrink distance, expand access

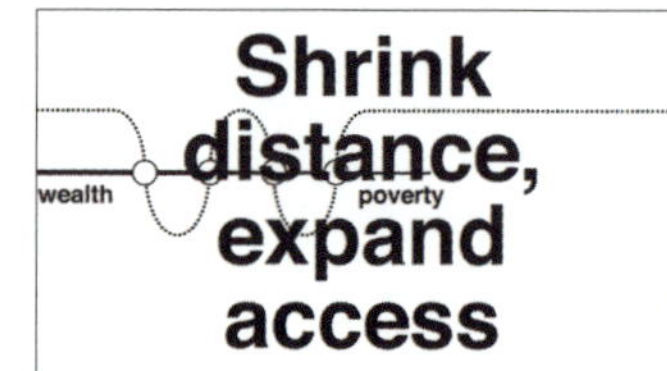

Facilitate the interface between institutions and civil society

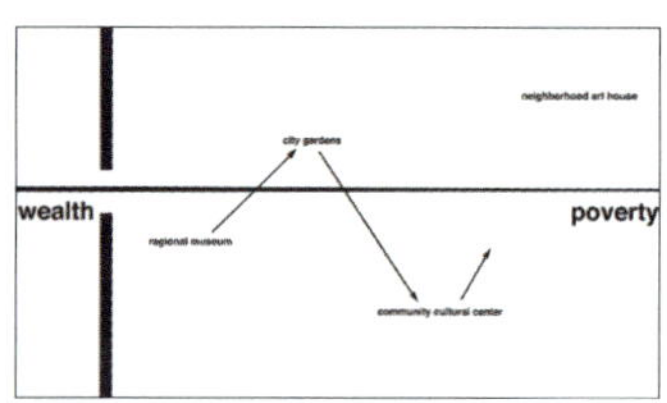

Shrink distance, expand access

Transgress urban borders

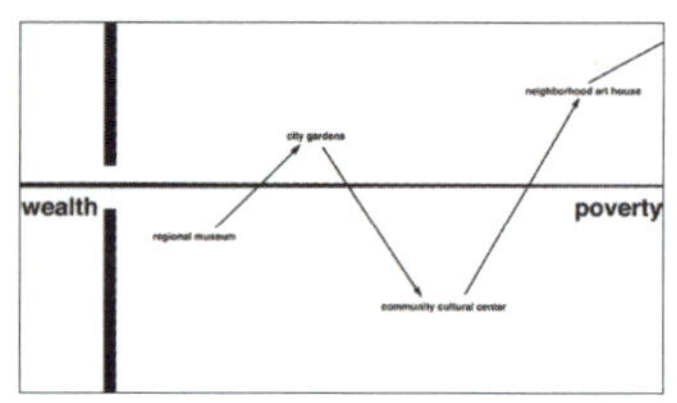

Redesign governance

Inclusive public spaces demand new accessibility and mobility

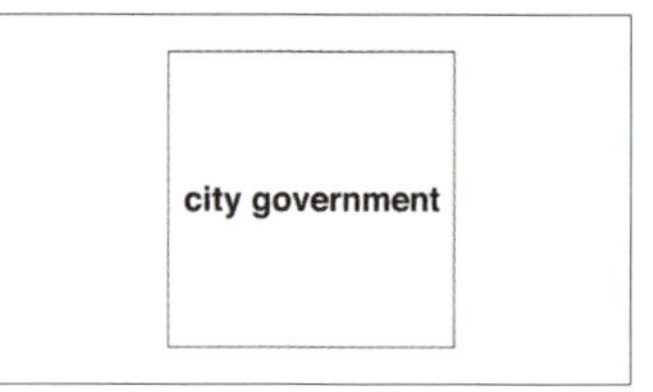

Penetrate marginalized communities with public works

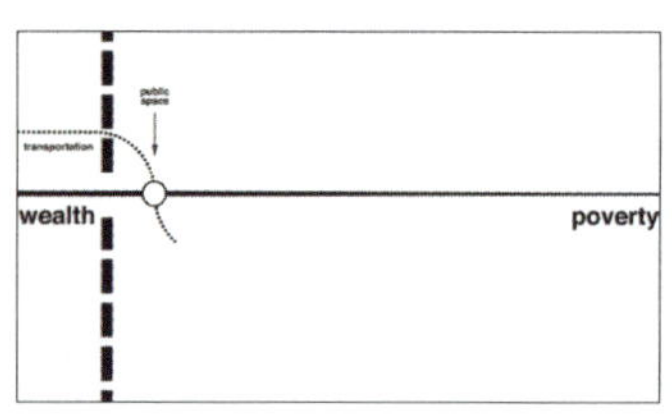

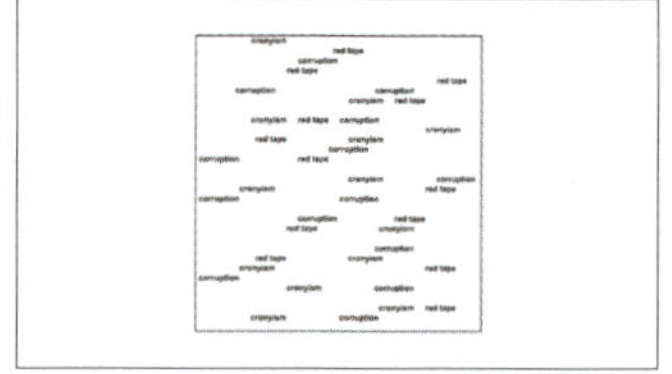

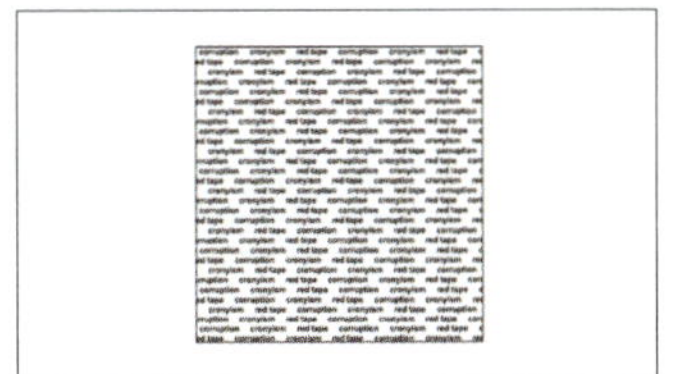

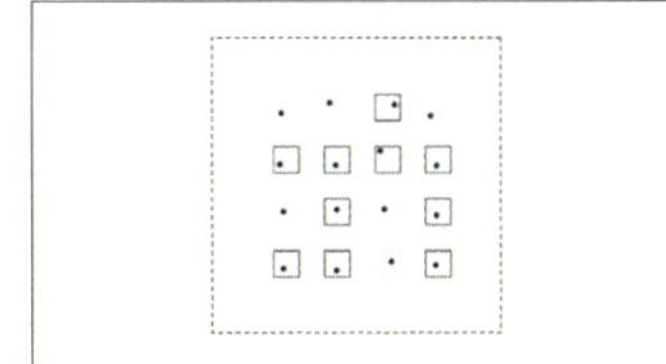

Transform the mayor's office into a cross-sector urban laboratory

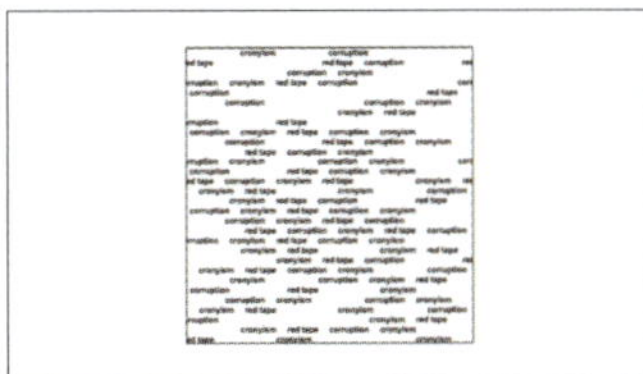

Commit to collaborative municipal governance

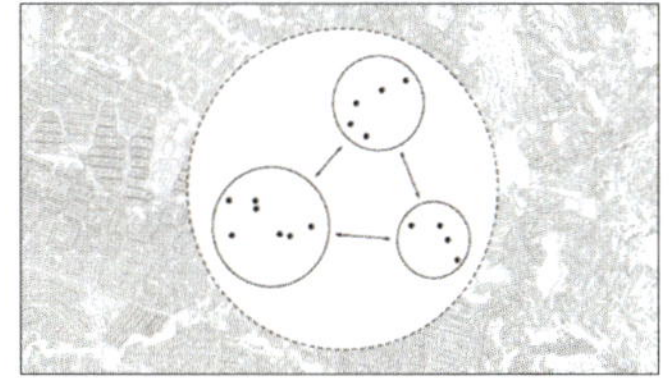

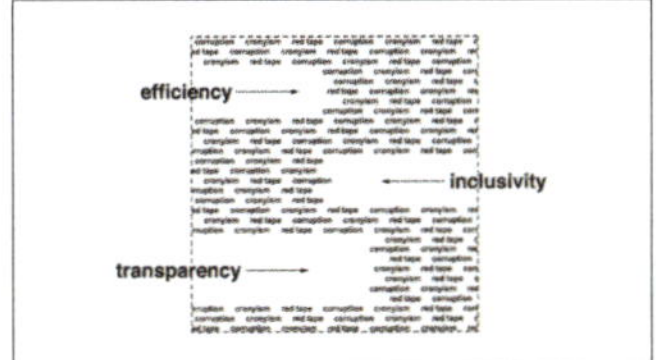

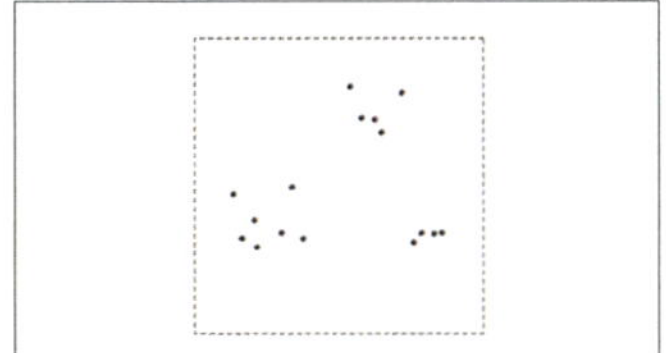

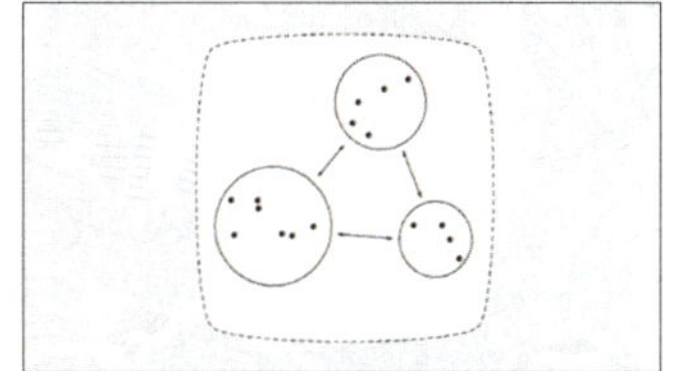

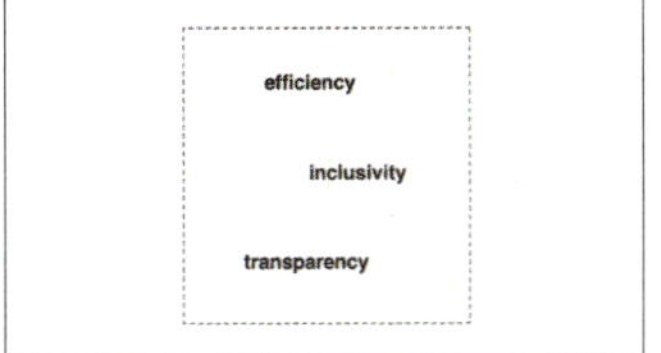

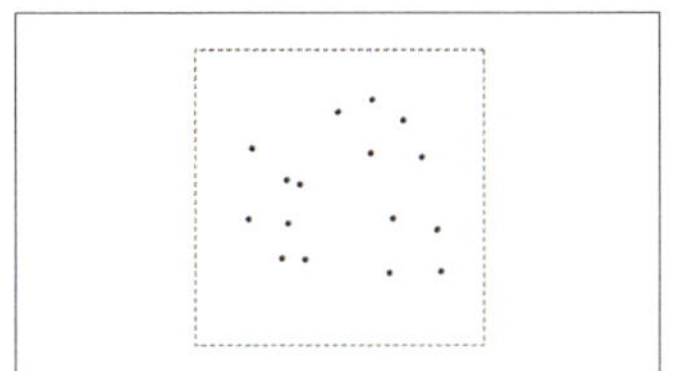

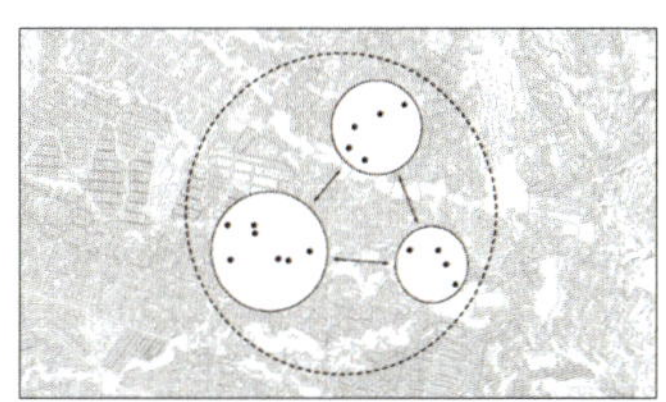

Inequality demands a transformation of government bureaucracy

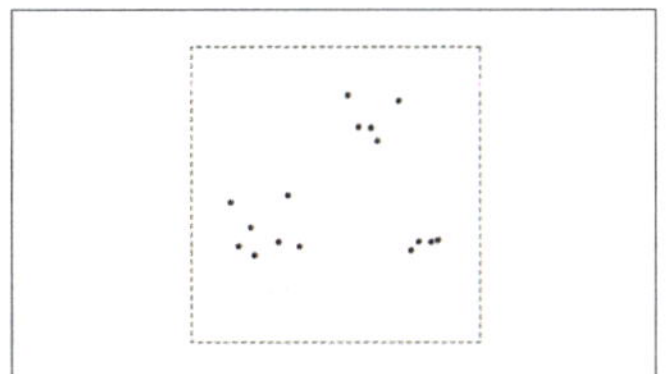

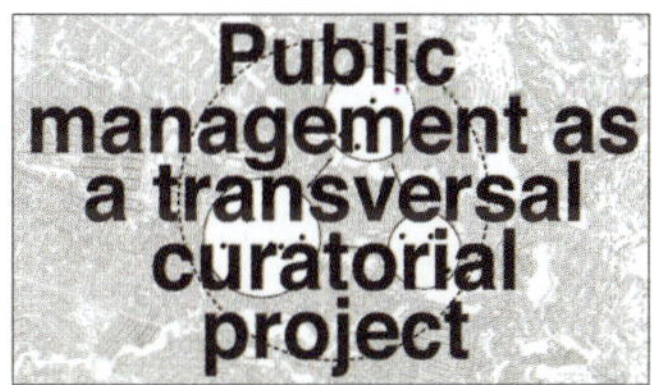

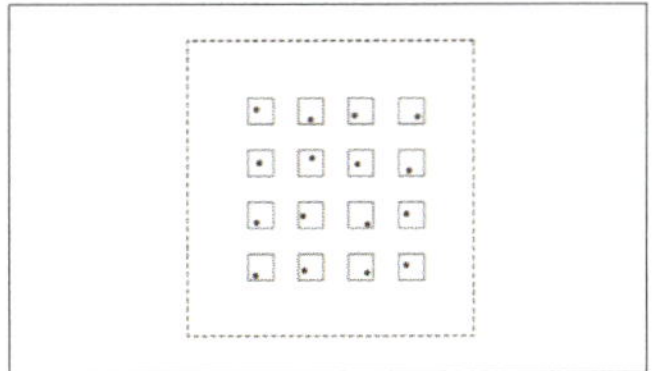

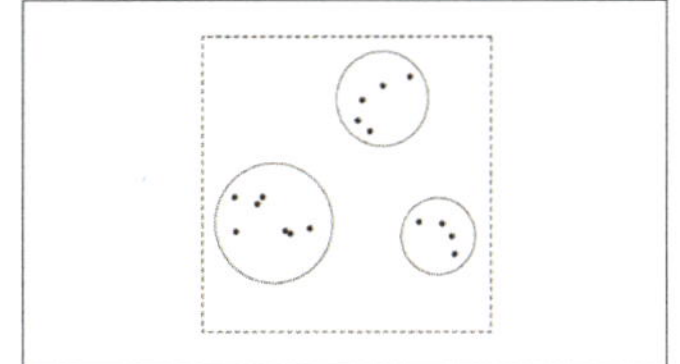

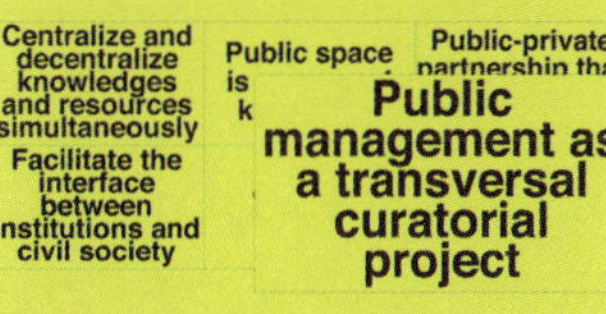

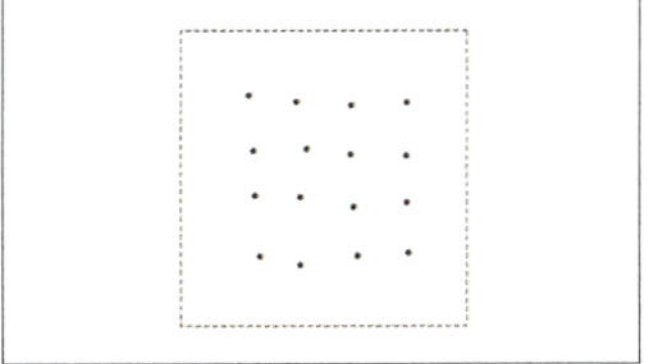

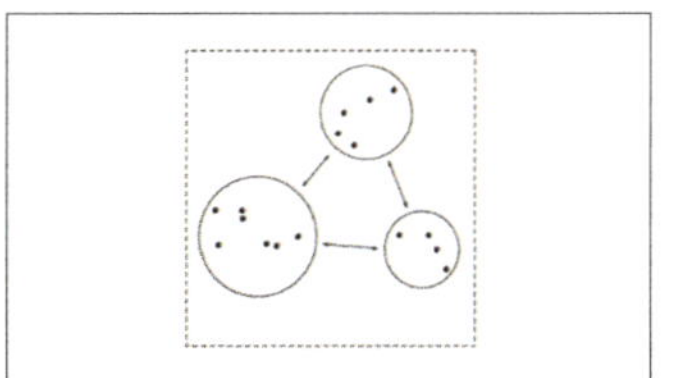

The Georgia Negro: A Social Study

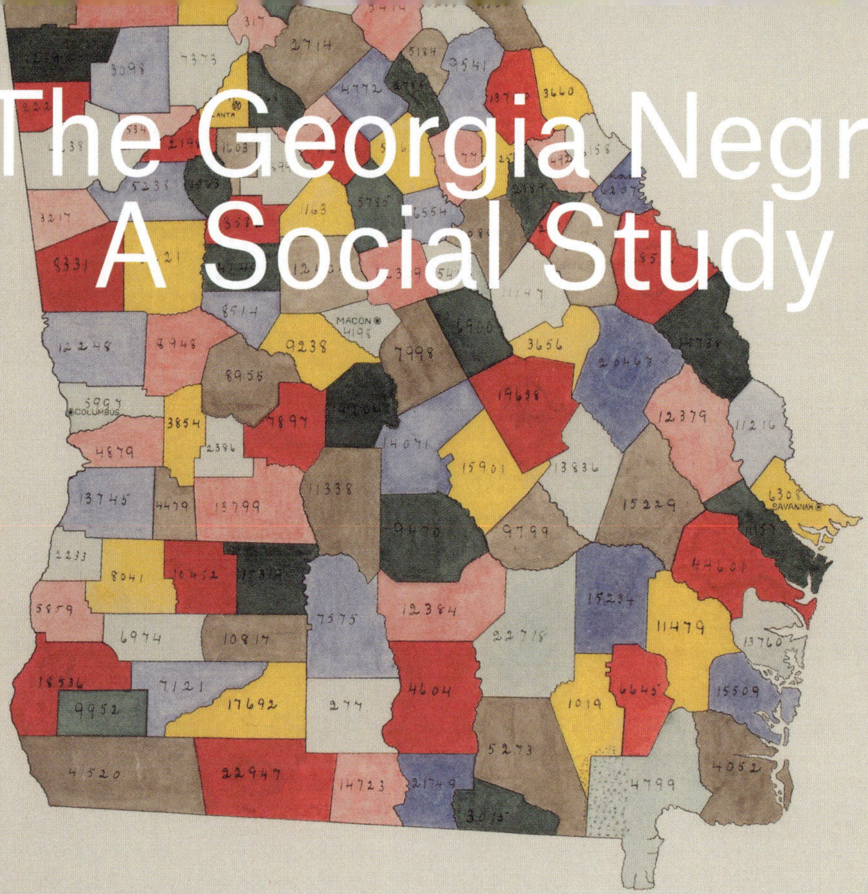

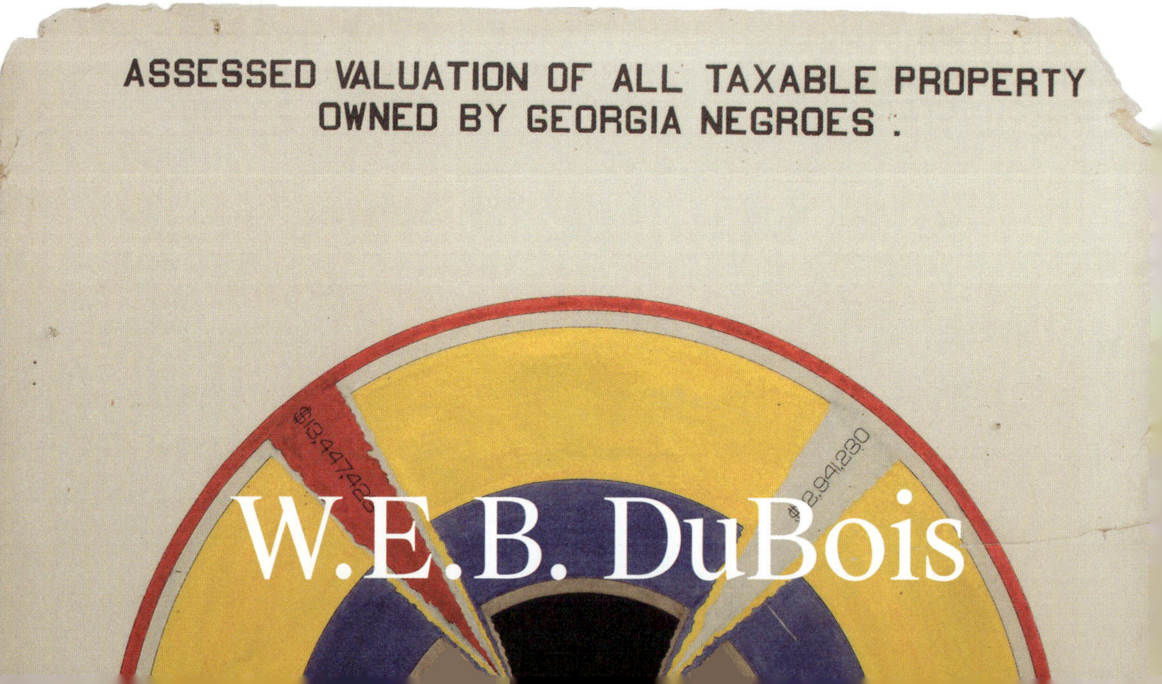

W.E.B. DuBois

ASSESSED VALUATION OF ALL TAXABLE PROPERTY OWNED BY GEORGIA NEGROES.

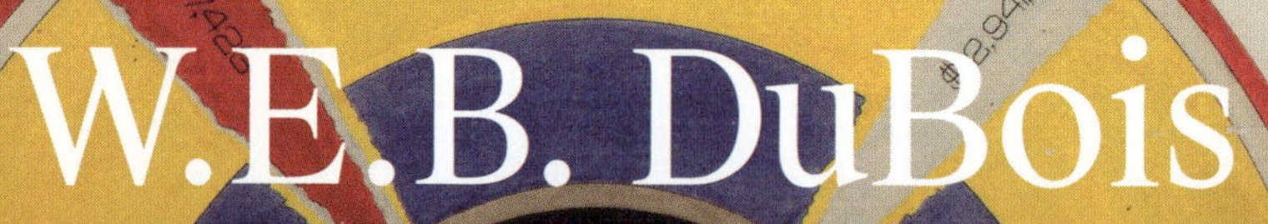

The American Negro at Paris

On the banks of the Seine, opposite the Rue des Nations, stands a large, plain white building, where the promoters of the Paris Exposition have housed the world's ideas of sociology. As a matter of fact, any one who takes his sociology from theoretical treatises would be rather disappointed at the exhibit; for there is little here of the "science of society." On the other hand, those who have followed historically the development, out of the old Political Economy, of a miscellaneous body of knowing chiefly connected with the larger aspects of human benevolence, will here find much of interest: the building and mutual-aid societies of France; the working-man's circles of Belgium; the city governments of Sweden; the Red Cross Society; the state insurance of Germany,—are all here strikingly exhibited by charts, statistics, models, and photographs.

The United States section of this building is small, and not, at first glance, particularly striking. There are, in the center, well-made tenement-house models; in one corner a small exhibit of the American Library Association, and elsewhere sets of interesting maps and photographs showing the work of factory inspectors and typical industrial plants. All these exhibits, are, unfortunately, rather fragmentary, and do scant justice to the wonderful social and economic development of America.

In the right-hand corner, however, as one enters, is an exhibit which, more than most others in the building, is sociological in the larger sense of the term—that is, is an attempt to give, in as systematic and compact a form as possible , the history and present condition of a large group of human beings. This is the exhibit of American Negroes, planned and executed by Negroes, and collected and installed under the direction of a Negro special agent, Mr. Thomas J. Calloway.

In this exhibit there are, of course, the usual paraphernalia for catching the eye, photographs, models, industrial work, and pictures. But it does not stop here; beneath all this is a carefully thought-out plan, according to which the exhibitors have tried to show:

W.E.B. Du Bois, "The American Negro at Paris", *American Monthly Review of Reviews*. vol. XXII, no.5 (November): pp. 575-577.

(a) The history of the American Negro.
(b) His present condition.
(c) His education.
(d) His literature.

The history of the Negro is illustrated by charts and photographs; there is, for instance, a series of striking models of the progress of the colored people, beginning with the homeless freedman and ending with the modern brick schoolhouse and its teachers. There are charts of the increase of Negro population, the routes of the African slave-trade, the progress of emancipation, and the decreasing illiteracy.

There are pictures of the old cabins, and, in three great manuscript volumes, the complete black code of Georgia, from colonial times to the end of the nineteenth century. Not the least interesting contribution to history is the case given to Negro medal-of-honor men in the army and navy from the man who "seized the colors after two color-bearers had been shot down and bore them noblv through the fight" to the black men in the Spanish War who "voluntarily went ashore in the face of the enemy and aided in the rescue of their wounded comrades." It was a Massachusetts lawyer who replied to the Patent Office inquiry, "I never knew a negro to invent anything but lies;" and yet here is a record of 350 patents granted to black men since 1834.

The bulk of the exhibit, is naturally an attempt to picture present conditions. Thirty-two charts, 500 photographs, and numerous maps and plans form the basis of this exhibit. The charts are in two sets, one illustrating conditions in the entire United States and the other conditions in the typical State of Georgia. At a glance one can see the successive steps by which the 220,000 negroes of 1750 had increased to 7,500,000 in 1890; their distribution throughout the different States; a comparison of the size of the Negro population with European countries bringing out the striking fact that there are nearly half as many Negroes in the United States as Spaniards in Spain. The striking movement by which the 4 ⅕ per cent. of Negroes living in the cities in 1860 has increased to 12 per

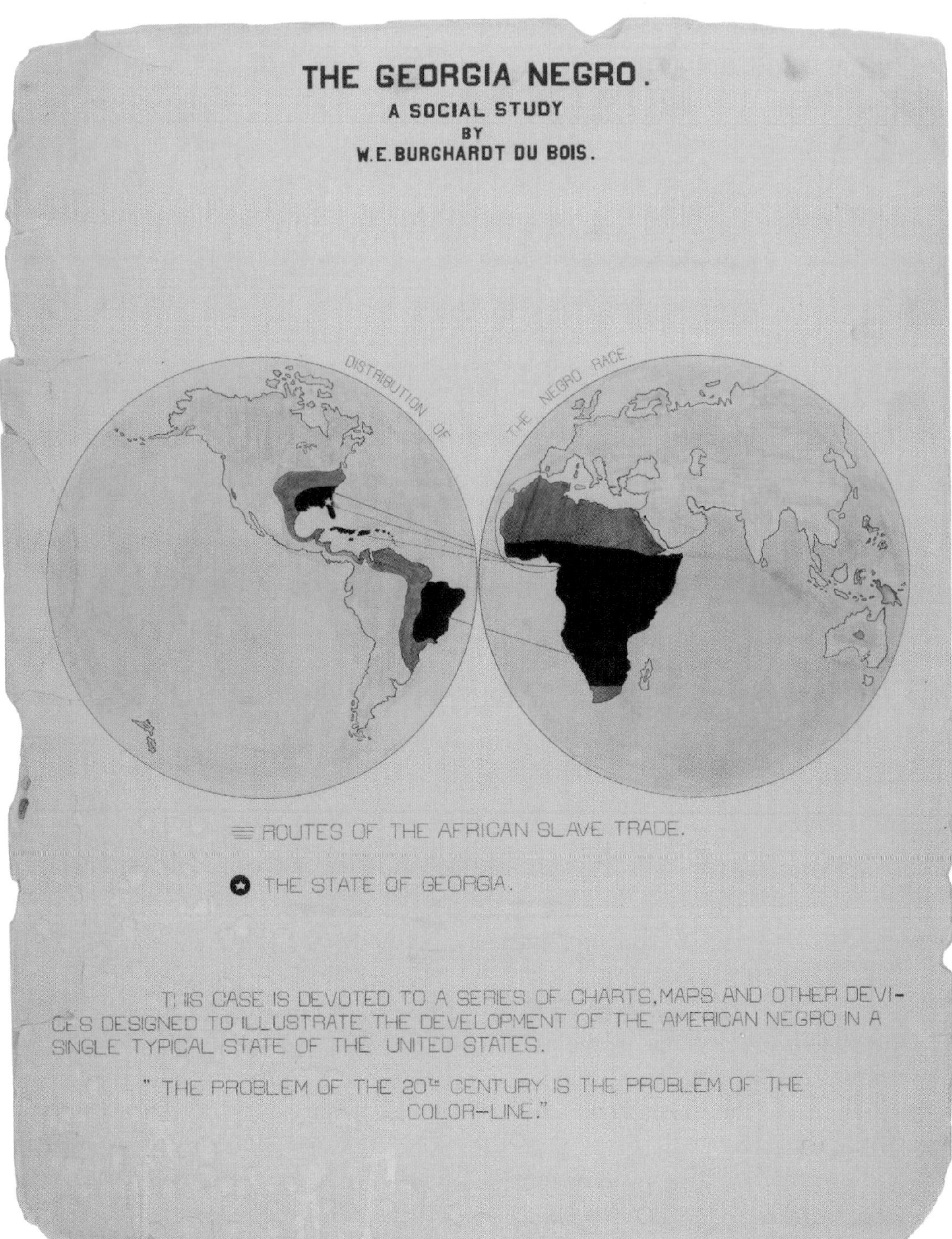

Selection of charts prepared by W.E.B. Du Bois for the Negro Exhibit of the American Section at the *Paris Exposition Universelle* in 1900 to show the economic and social progress of African Americans since emancipation. All chart images from Library of Congress, Prints & Photographs Division.

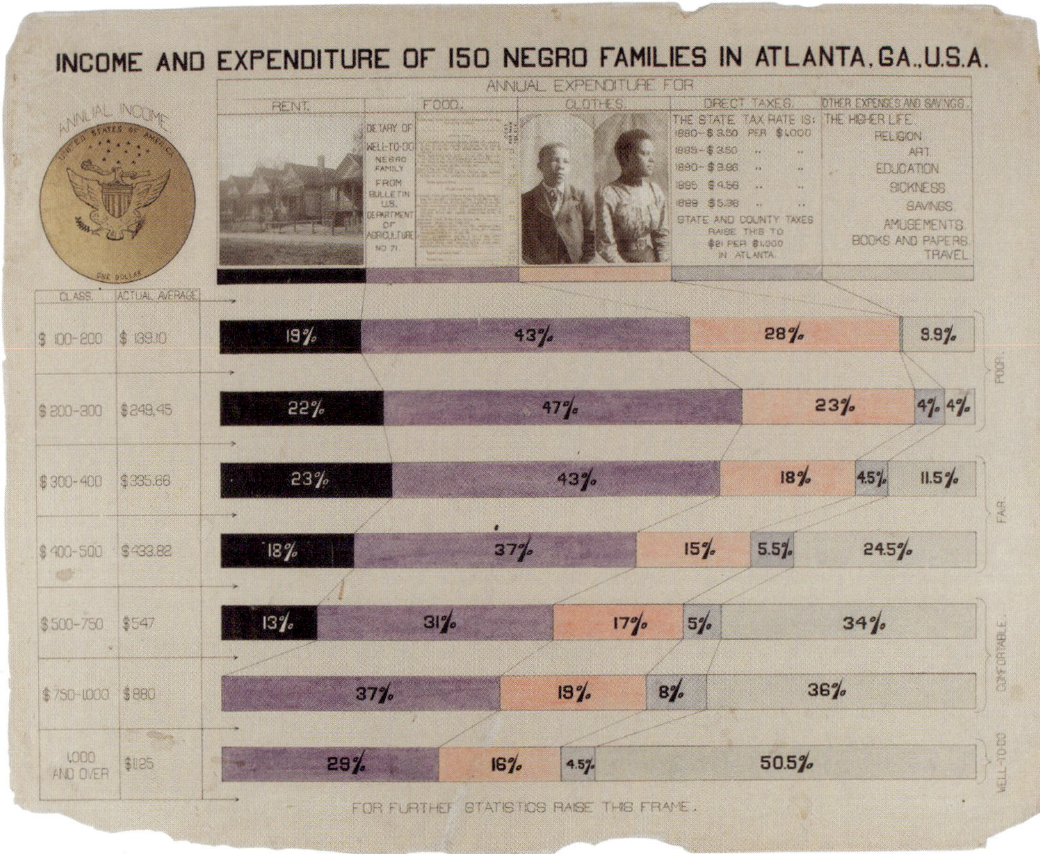

cent. in 1890 is shown, as is also the fact that recognized mulattoes have increased 50 per cent. in 30 years, even in the defective census returns. Twenty per cent. of the Negroes are shown to be home-owners, 60 per cent. of their children are in school, and their illiteracy is less than that of Russia, and only equal to that of Hungary.

It was a good idea to supplement these very general figures with a minute social study in a typical Southern State. It would hardly be suggested, in the light of recent history that conditions in the State of Georgia are such as to give a rose-colored picture of the Negro; and yet Georgia, having the largest Negro population, is an excellent field of study. Here again we have statistics: the increase of the black population in a century from 30,000 to 860,000, the huddling in the Black Belt for self-protection since the war, and a comparison of the age distribution with France showing the wonderful reproductive powers of the blacks. The school enrollment has increased from 10,000 in 1870 to 180,000 in 1897, and the Negroes are distributed among the occupations as follows:

In agriculture, 62 per cent.; in domestic and personal service, 28 per

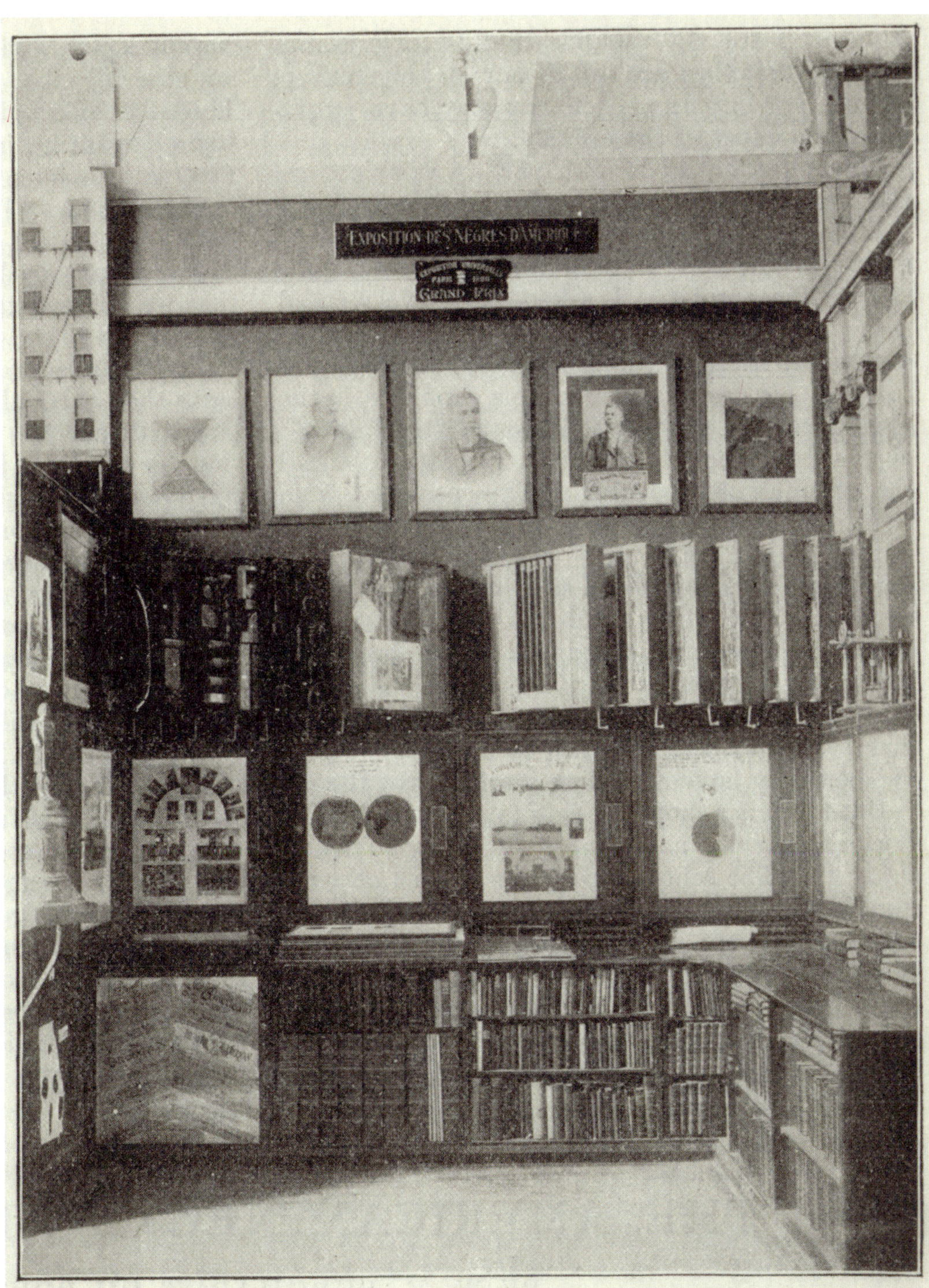

EXHIBIT OF AMERICAN NEGROES AT THE PARIS EXPOSITION.

CITY AND RURAL POPULATION.
1890.

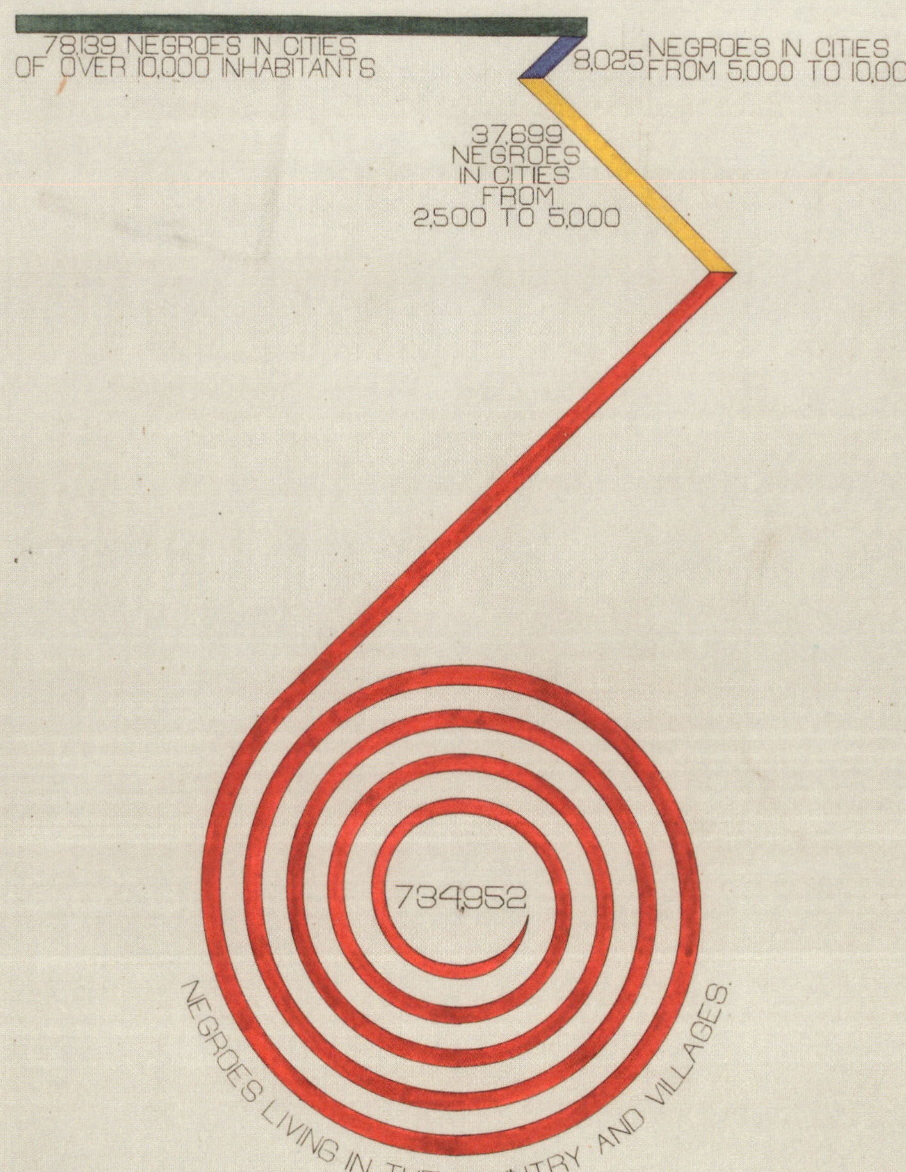
78,139 NEGROES IN CITIES OF OVER 10,000 INHABITANTS
8,025 NEGROES IN CITIES FROM 5,000 TO 10,000
37,699 NEGROES IN CITIES FROM 2,500 TO 5,000
734,952
NEGROES LIVING IN THE COUNTRY AND VILLAGES.

cent.; in manufacturing and mechanical industries, 5 per cent.; in trade and transportation, 4 ½ per cent.; in the professions, ½ per cent.

They own 1,000,000 acres of land and pay taxes on $12,000,000 worth of property–not large, but telling figures; and the charts indicate, from year to year, the struggle they have had to accumulate and hold this property. There are several volumes of photographs of typical Negro faces, which hardly square with conventional American ideas. Several maps show the peculiar distribution of the white and black inhabitants in various towns and counties.

The education of the Negro is illustrated in the work of five great institutions–Fisk, Atlanta, and Howard Universities, and Tuskegee and Hampton Institutes. The exhibit from Fisk illustrates, by photographs and examination papers, the work of secondary and higher education. Atlanta University shows her work in social study and the work of her college and normal graduates; Howard University show the work of her professional schools, especially in medicine, theology, and law. From Hampton there is an especially excellent, series of photographs illustrating the Hampton idea of "teaching by doing," and from Tuskegee there are numerous specimens of work from the manual-training and technical departments.

Perhaps the most unique and striking exhibit is that of American Negro literature. The development of Negro thought–the view of themselves which these millions of freedmen have taken–is of intense psychological and practical interest. There are many who have scarcely heard of a Negro book, much less read one; still here is a bibliography made by the Library of Congress containing 1,400 titles of works written by Negroes; 200 of these

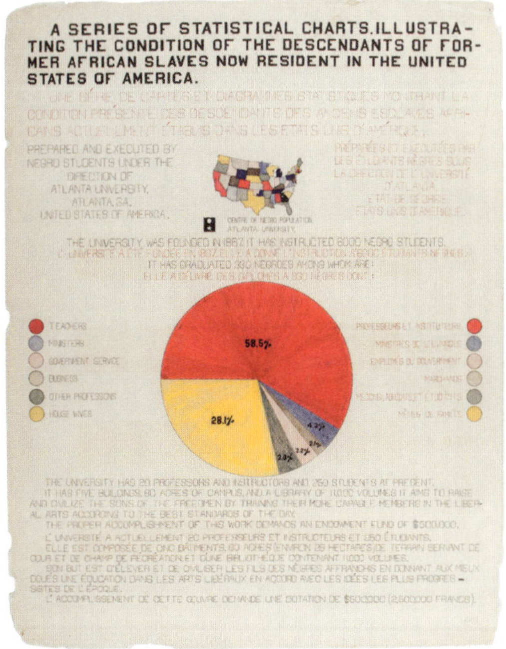

books are exhibited on themselves. The Negroes have 150 periodicals, mostly weekly papers, many of which are exhibited here.

We have thus, it may be seen, an honest, straightforward exhibit of a small nation of people, picturing their life and development without apology or gloss, above all made by themselves. In a way this marks an era in the history of the Negroes of America. It is not a new thing for a group of people to accomplish much under the help and guidance of a stronger group; indeed, the whole Palace of Social Economy at the Paris Exposition shows how

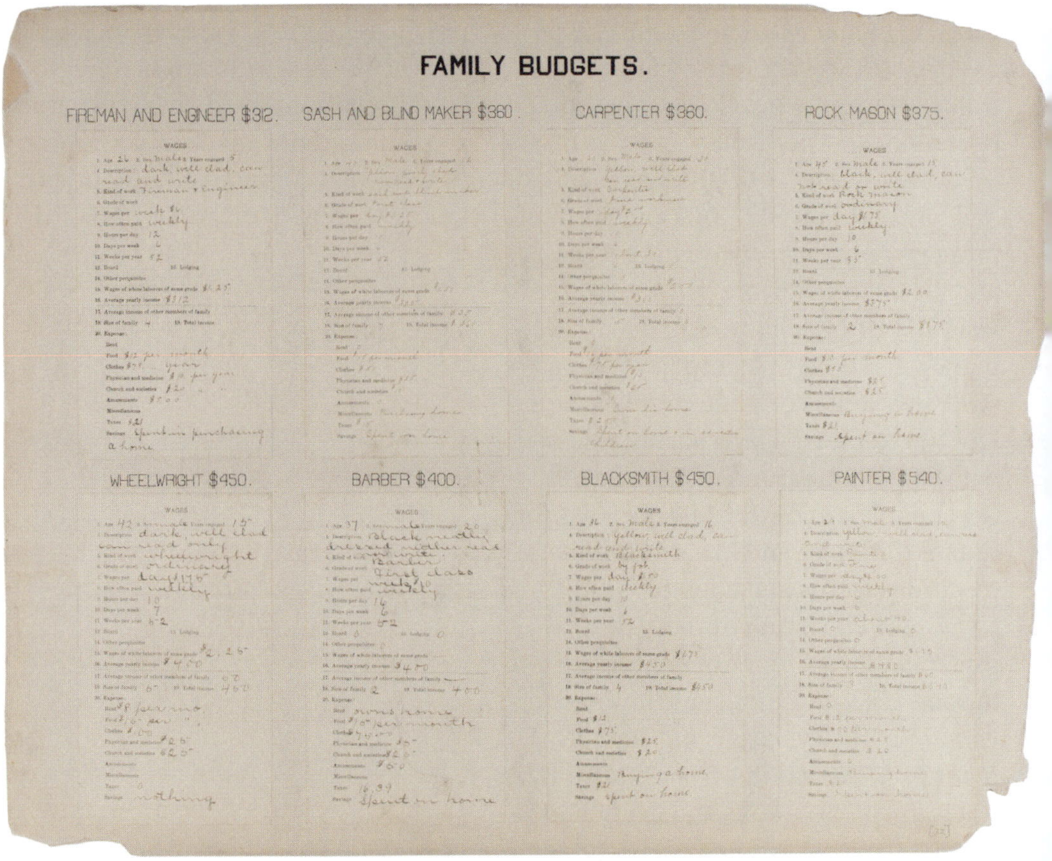

FAMILY BUDGETS.

FIREMAN AND ENGINEER $312.   SASH AND BLIND MAKER $360.   CARPENTER $360.   ROCK MASON $375.

WHEELWRIGHT $450.   BARBER $400.   BLACKSMITH $450.   PAINTER $540.

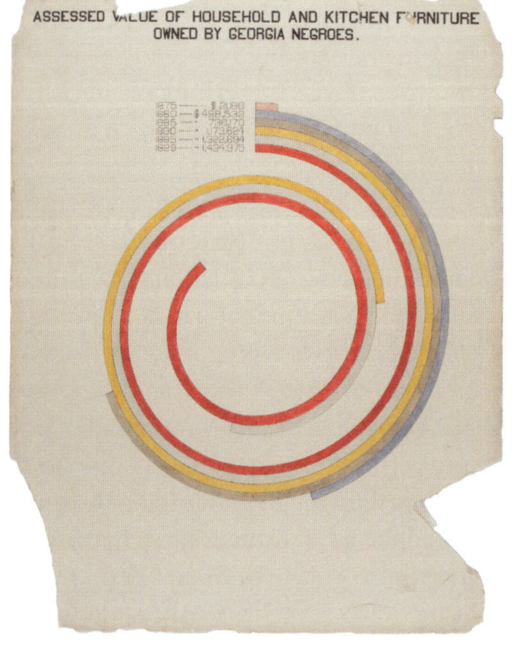

ASSESSED VALUE OF HOUSEHOLD AND KITCHEN FURNITURE OWNED BY GEORGIA NEGROES.

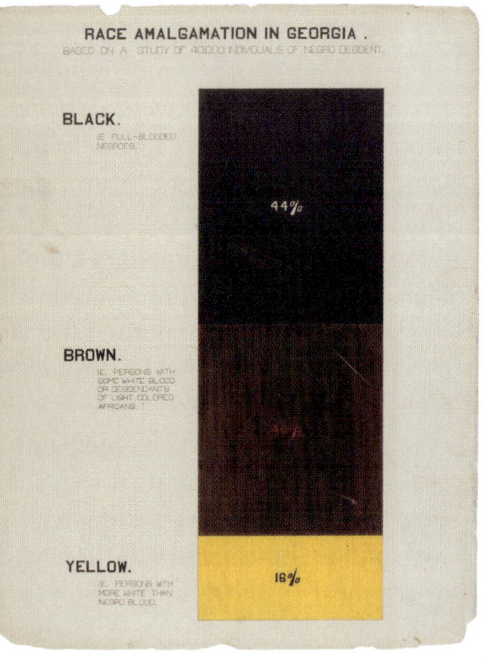

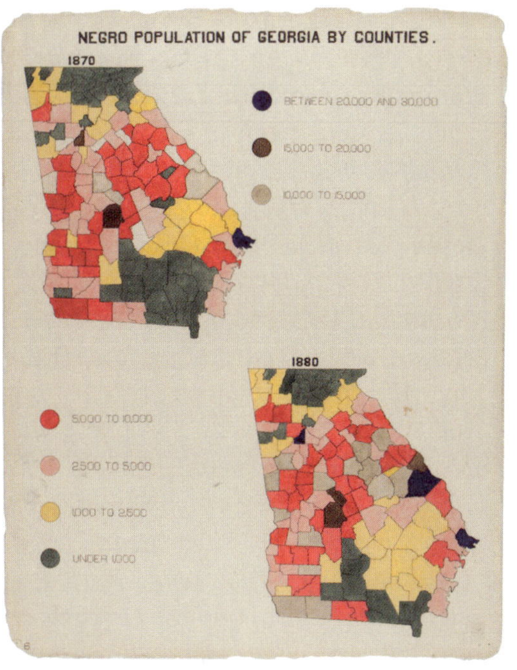

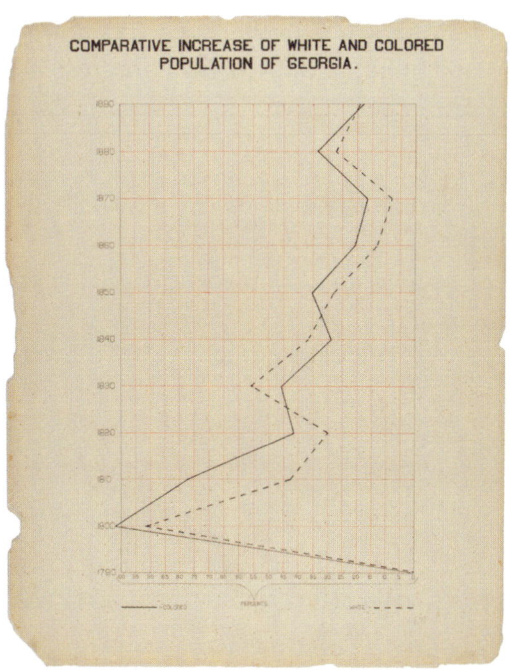

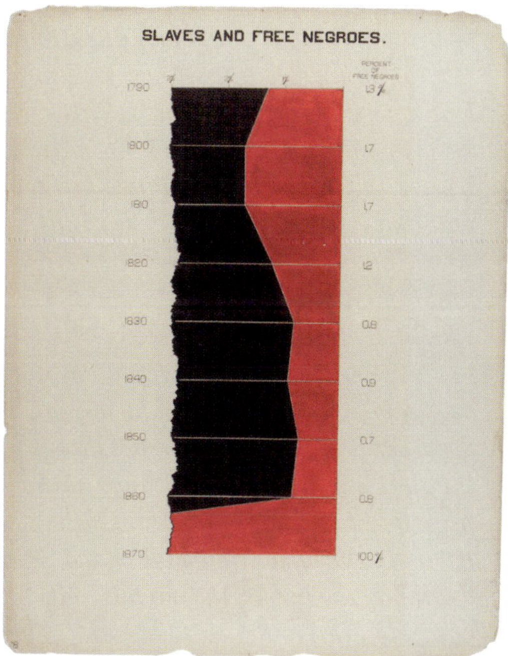

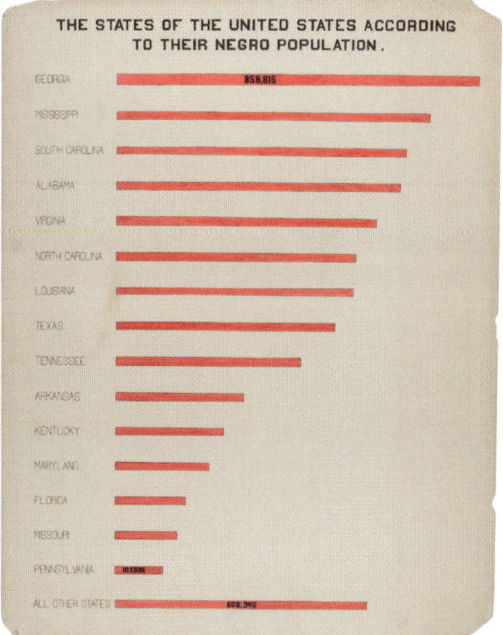

vast a system of help and guidance of this order is being carried on to-day throughout the world. When however, the inevitable question arises, What are these guided groups doing for themselves? there is in the whole building no more encouraging answer than that given by the American negroes, who are here shown to be studying, examining, and thinking of their own progress and prospects.*

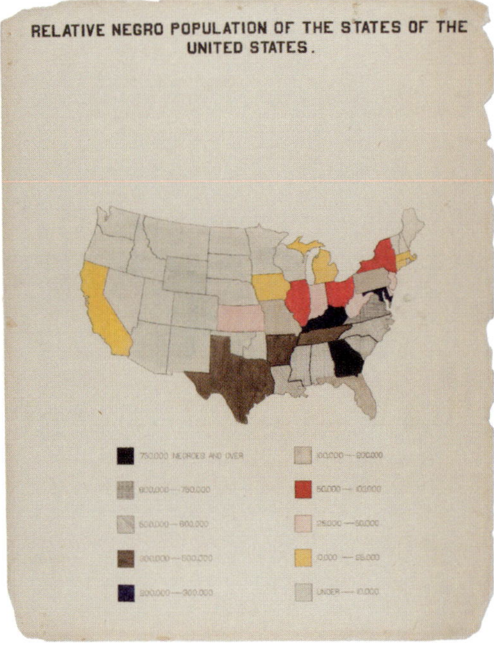

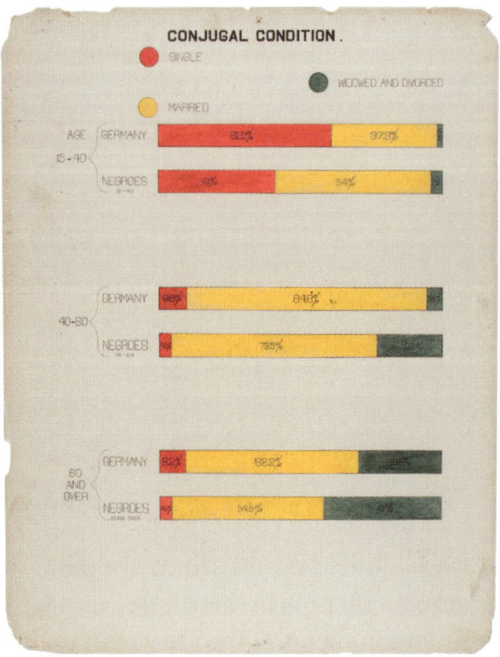

* *Mr. Thomas J. Calloway, the special agent of the Negro exhibit, gives the following list of awards to the exhibit, together with a note of explanation, which we print below:*

Grand Prix—American Negro Exhibit (on the collection as a whole): Hampton Normal and Agricultural Institute, Hampton, Va. Gold Medals—Tuskegee Normal and Industrial Institute, Tuskegee, Ala.; Howard University, Washington D.C.; T. J. Calloway, Special Agent Negro Exhibit (as compiler); W. E. B. Du Bois, Collaborator as Compiler of Georgia. Negro Exhibit. Silver Medals—Fisk University, Nashville, Tenn.; Agricultural and Mechanical College, Greensboro', N. C.; Berea College, Berea, Ky.; Atlanta University, Atlanta, Ga.; Booker T. Wahington, Monograph on Education of Negro. Bronze Medals—Roger Williams University, Nashville, Tenn.; Central Tennessee College, Nashville, Tenn.; Atlanta University, Atlanta, Ga.; Pine Bluff Normal and Industrial School, Pine Bluff, Ark. Honorable Mention—Haines Normal and Industrial Institute, Augusta , Ga.; Claflin University, Orangeburg, S. C.

While these awards represent the appreciation of the several juries, taken together there is not the even balancing that might be wished. Some of the principal features went not installed till after the juries were disbanded. For example, the books, the models, patents, etc., fall under this lists [sic]. The awards, therefore, except in certain cases like Hampton, Tuskegee, Atlanta, etc., do not necessarily represent the strongest features of the exhibit.

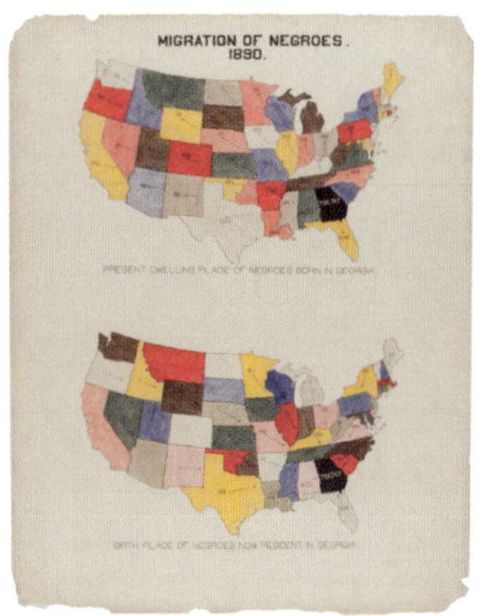
MIGRATION OF NEGROES.
1890.
PRESENT DWELLING PLACE OF NEGROES BORN IN GEORGIA.
BIRTH PLACE OF NEGROES NOW RESIDENT IN GEORGIA.

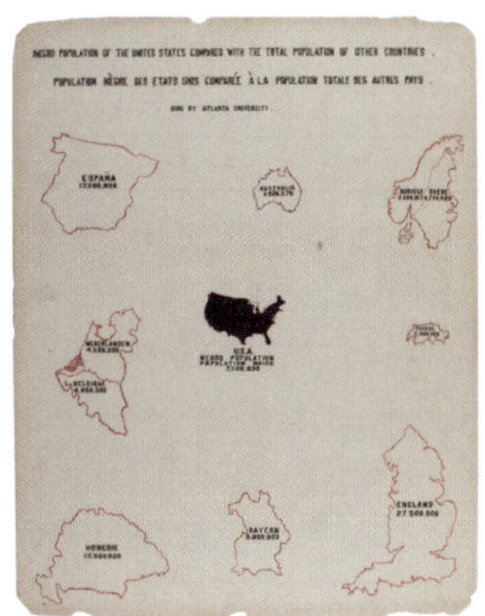
NEGRO POPULATION OF THE UNITED STATES COMPARED WITH THE TOTAL POPULATION OF OTHER COUNTRIES.
POPULATION NÈGRE DES ETATS UNIS COMPARÉ À LA POPULATION TOTALE DES AUTRES PAYS.
DONE BY ATLANTA UNIVERSITY.
ESPAÑA
AUSTRALIA
NORVÈGE SUÈDE
U.S.A.
NEGRO POPULATION
MEXICO
BELGIQUE
JAPON
HONGRIE
BAYERN
ENGLAND

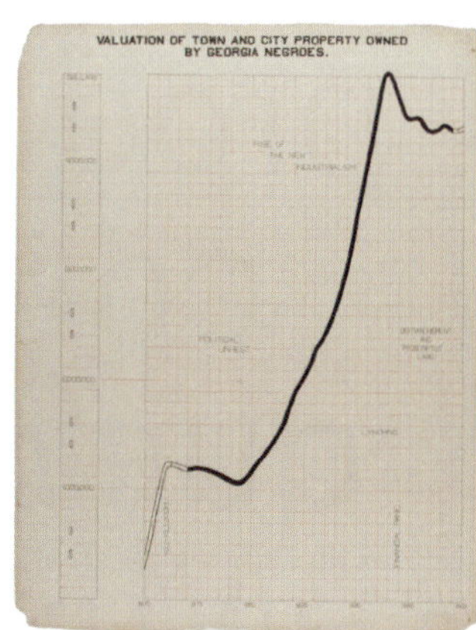
VALUATION OF TOWN AND CITY PROPERTY OWNED
BY GEORGIA NEGROES.

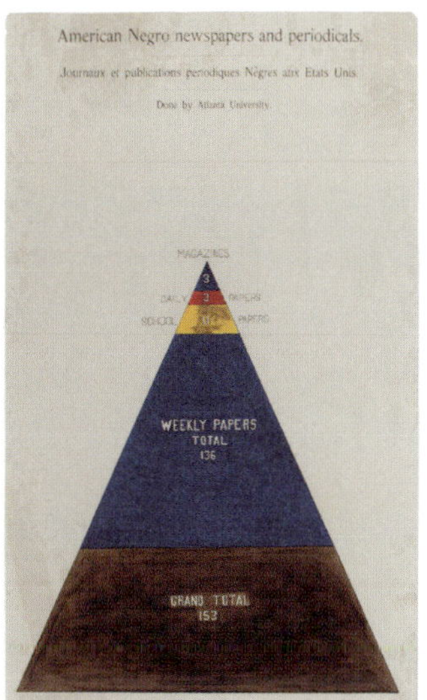
American Negro newspapers and periodicals.
Journaux et publications périodiques Nègres aux Etats Unis.
Done by Atlanta University.
MAGAZINES
DAILY PAPERS
SCHOOL PAPERS
WEEKLY PAPERS
TOTAL
136
GRAND TOTAL
153

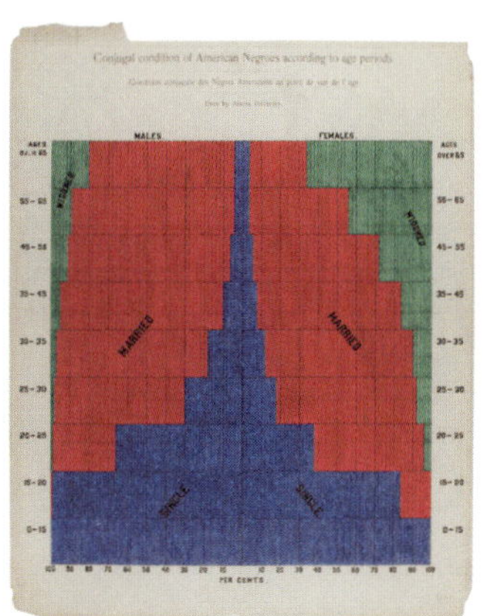
Conjugal condition of American Negroes according to age periods.
MALES
FEMALES
WIDOWED
MARRIED
SINGLE
PER CENTS

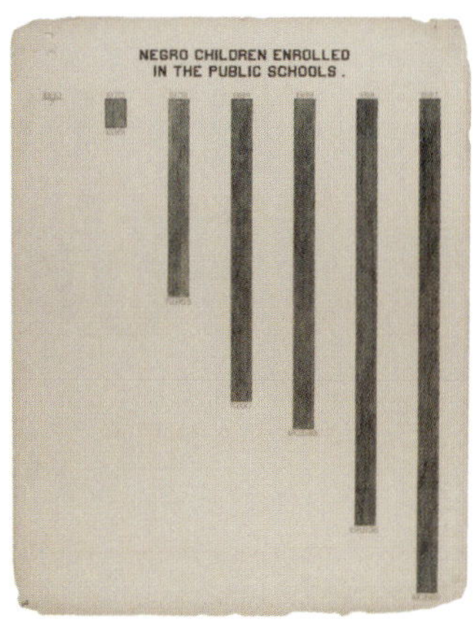
NEGRO CHILDREN ENROLLED
IN THE PUBLIC SCHOOLS.

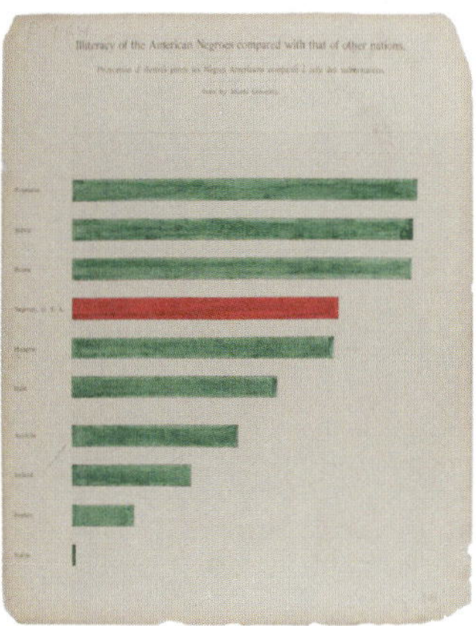
Illiteracy of the American Negroes compared with that of other nations.
Done by Atlanta University.
Negroes, U.S.A.

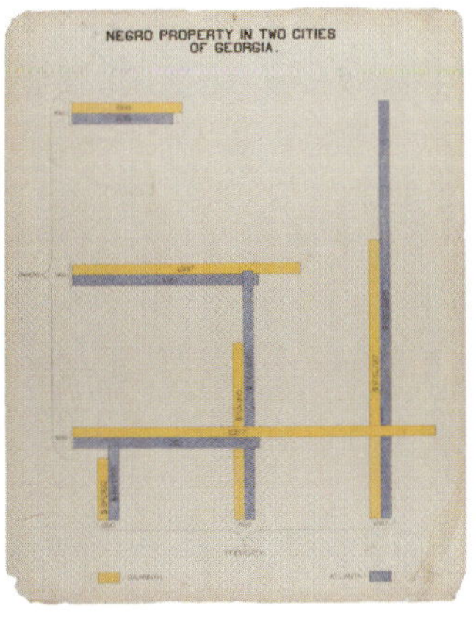
NEGRO PROPERTY IN TWO CITIES
OF GEORGIA.

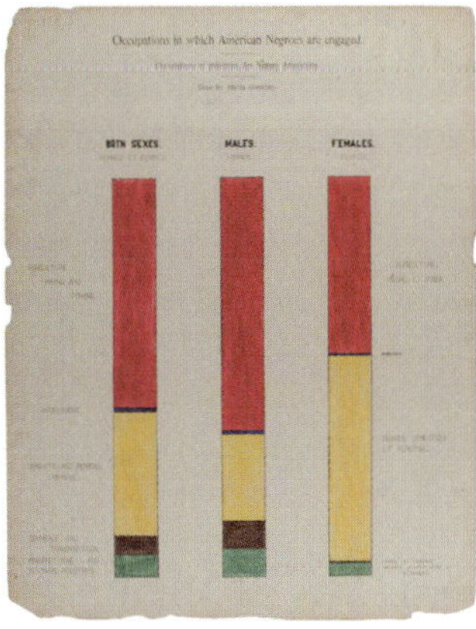
Occupations in which American Negroes are engaged.
BOTH SEXES
MALES
FEMALES

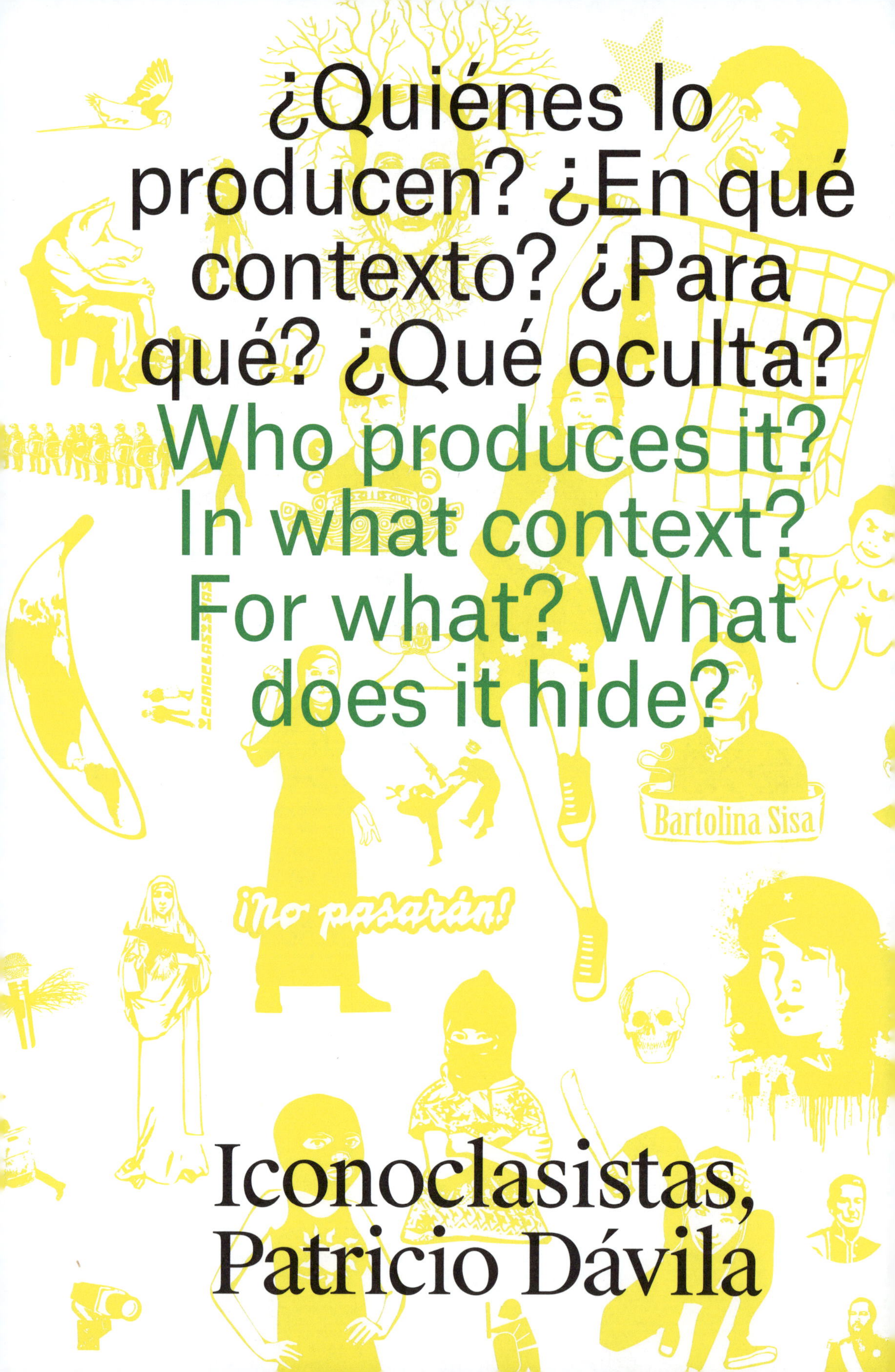¿Quiénes lo producen? ¿En qué contexto? ¿Para qué? ¿Qué oculta?
Who produces it? In what context? For what? What does it hide?
Bartolina Sisa
¡No pasarán!
Iconoclasistas, Patricio Dávila

Iconoclasistas, un dúo formado por Julia Risler y Pable Ares en 2006 y con sede en Buenos Aires, crean proyectos centrados en la comunidad, participativos y pedagógicos. De esta manera, crean recursos y talleres que ayudan a agrupaciones, vecindarios y comunidades a compartir el conocimiento colectivo a través del mapeo y la creación de imágenes.

Patricio Dávila

En la exhibición, *Diagrams of Power*, se presentó el mapamundi "¿A quien pertenece la tierra?" Cerca del mapa se colocó una mesa con su guía sobre el mapeo colectivo y una selección de imagenes que usan para sus talleres. De este modo el visitante puede ver dos ejemplos de sus actividades como colectivo. Me parece que sus actividades tienen dos categorías, la primera es el desarrollo de recursos para el mapeo colectivo y la facilitación de talleres con grupos y comunidades, y la segunda es la creación de proyectos autogestionados como los mapamundis críticos. ¿Cuales son los objetivos de estas diferentes actividades?

Iconoclasistas

Son dos líneas de trabajo complementarias, porque muchos de los mapas críticos que hemos elaborado surgen de talleres de mapeo o de investigación colaborativa con diversas comunidades o agrupaciones. Sí difieren en sus objetivos: si los recursos y metodologías que creamos y liberamos están disponibles para posibilitar (y animar) que todos y todas puedan generar este tipo de

espacio pedagógico-lúdicos, la elaboración de material gráfico, que también es liberado en el sitio web, apunta a producir un material con el eje puesto en lo comunicacional, diseñado a partir de objetivos y públicos específicos (que cuando se hacen en articulación a un taller, se definen con los y las participantes al mismo).

Patricio Dávila

La dimención comunicacional ha sido un tema muy importante para la cartografía moderna. Incluso se desarolló un modelo teórico, llamado el "Map Communication Model", que esta basado en la formula matemática para la comunicación postulada por Shannon y Weaver. Dentro de este marco se trataba de eliminar el ruido y aumentar el señal para producir una comunicación eficiente y eficaz. En muchos casos la decoración o los símbolos ambíguos representaban el ruido que un diseñador necesitaba controlar o eliminar completamente. ¿En sus mapas críticos como funciona lo comunicacional?

Iconoclasistas

Nosotrxs apelamos mucho a lo visual para la comunicación, y utilizamos mucha simbología también, no lo pensamos como algo ambiguo sino como sentidos amplios, abiertos, ya que la idea es interpelar al receptor pero que el sentido no esté dado o cerrado sino que pueda ser completado por otrxs. Es verdad que quizás esto pueda generar "ruido" en términos comunicacionales, pero no es algo que nos preocupe de antemano (por lo menos, y que sepamos, nunca nuestras producciones fueron utilizadas en sentido contrario al cual fueron realizadas). Además a lo gráfico, visual, simbólico, se le suman otros recursos de la comunicación: títulos claros, copetes, pequeños párrafos,

All installation views. Iconoclasistas, *¿A quien pertenece la tierra? (Who Owns the Land?)*, 2017. Courtesy of Onsite Gallery. Photography by Yuula Benivolski.

estadísticas, fuentes consultadas, etc. Recurrimos a ese conjunto de elementos para poder comunicar un mensaje, pero,

como ya dijimos, que a su vez sea abierto a la percepción de los demás.

Patricio Dávila

Con un mapa critico como "¿A quien pertenece la tierra?" se nota que una meta principal es la re-educacion or por lo menos re-orientacion del usuario del mapa—reconociendo el territorio en términos feminista y autóctono. Y en que se comunica visualmente un historia profunda y una realidad rara vez representada en forma de mapa. ¿Como decidieron comenzar el proyecto? ¿Fueron influenciado por un evento específico? ¿Como desarrollaron el diseño y la información?

Iconoclasistas

La génesis de este mapa crítico se remonta al 2015 y se desarrolla a partir de una investigación propia. El mapamundi releva el trabajo de las mujeres rurales y campesinas, unas 1.700 millones en todo el globo, quienes además de producir el 70% de los alimentos que consumimos, resisten y se organizan en sus comunidades. Las prácticas y saberes que sustentan las economías del cuidado de estas mujeres, protegiendo los bienes comunes y la soberanía alimentaria, se encuentran amenaza-

¿Quiénes lo producen? ¿En qué contexto? ¿Para qué? ¿Qué oculta?
Iconoclasistas, Patricio Dávila

das por la destrucción generada por el sistema alimentario agroindustrial y la violencia (genocidios, expulsiones, guerras, etc.) que generan de los proyectos extractivos. El mapa está basado en la proyección Gall-Peters (con con los polos invertidos), descrita por primera vez en 1855 por James Gall y revisitada por Arno Peters en 1974. Esta representación conserva la proporción entre las áreas de las distintas zonas de la tierra, brindando una noción aproximada del tamaño de los países al contrario de la proyección Mercator que agiganta los territorios cuando se aproximan a los polos. Tuvo especial relevancia en los años '70, cuando los movimientos de liberación nacional se enfrentaron al dominio occidental del mundo. La elegimos porque nos ayuda—tanto espacial como simbólicamente—a visibilizar de manera más clara los territorios y países con mayorías campesinas y rurales, la diversidad biocultural, los principales proyectos extractivos y los conflictos armados que se generan a partir de la depredación de la naturaleza y los intentos de normalización occidental.

Patricio Dávila

¿Cómo funciona la estética en el mappa Mundi en comparación con los mapas colectivos? Mientras que uno está muy pulido, el otro es muy informal. ¿Esto fue una decisión hecho antemano o es un resultado del proceso mismo?

Iconoclasistas

Sí, la verdad es que depende de cada trabajo. Para el mapa mundi tuvimos todo el tiempo que quisimos porque era un proyecto nuestro, que no implicó trabajar con otras y otros. Muchas de las cartografías críticas tienen un tiempo de salida gráfica (y maduración) bastante rápida porque intervienen en coyuntura y responden a objetivos concretos y colectivos. El mapa mundi es un gusto estético que hacía rato queríamos darnos :)

Patricio Dávila

El mapa mundi es un tipo de mapa que era popular durante la Edad Media. Representa un deseo de incorporar todo de lo que se sabe sobre los territorios. Siempre hay un emfasis sobre un punto de vista, por ejemplo en algunos casos el mapa esta orientado con Jerusalem como el eje del mundo. Con un mapa mundi crítico me imagino que no se trata solamente de privilegiar un punto de vista subalterno sino avanzar otros objetivos también.

Iconoclasistas

Claro, siempre hay un punto de vista y un interlocutor concreto. En cada mapa producido, tanto desde sectores más institucionales como desde los más subalternos, esto es siempre así. Sin embargo los mapas tienen una ambigüedad con la cual nos gusta jugar, es justamente el criterio de "verdad" que manejan. Pues parecería que todo lo que está incluido en un mapa es así, tal cual se expone, no ofrece muchas dudas al lector. Sin embargo, la lectura de un mapa (sobre todo de los mapas hegemónicos) debería obligarnos a realizar esa segunda, tercera y otras decodificaciones, a fin de develar: quiénes lo producen? en qué contexto? para qué? que es lo que dice?, pero fundamentalmente, qué oculta? Nuestros mapas toman esa ambigüedad como potencia comunicativa, y ofrecen un relato colectivo que se teje desde una mirada transformadora y en

sobre un territorio (espacio o conocimiento). Es obvio que no se puede representar todo en un mapa. Algo que es bastante difícil es representar el paso del tiempo, la historia. Una estrategia es usar una plataforma interactiva (sitio web) como se hizo en el proyecto de

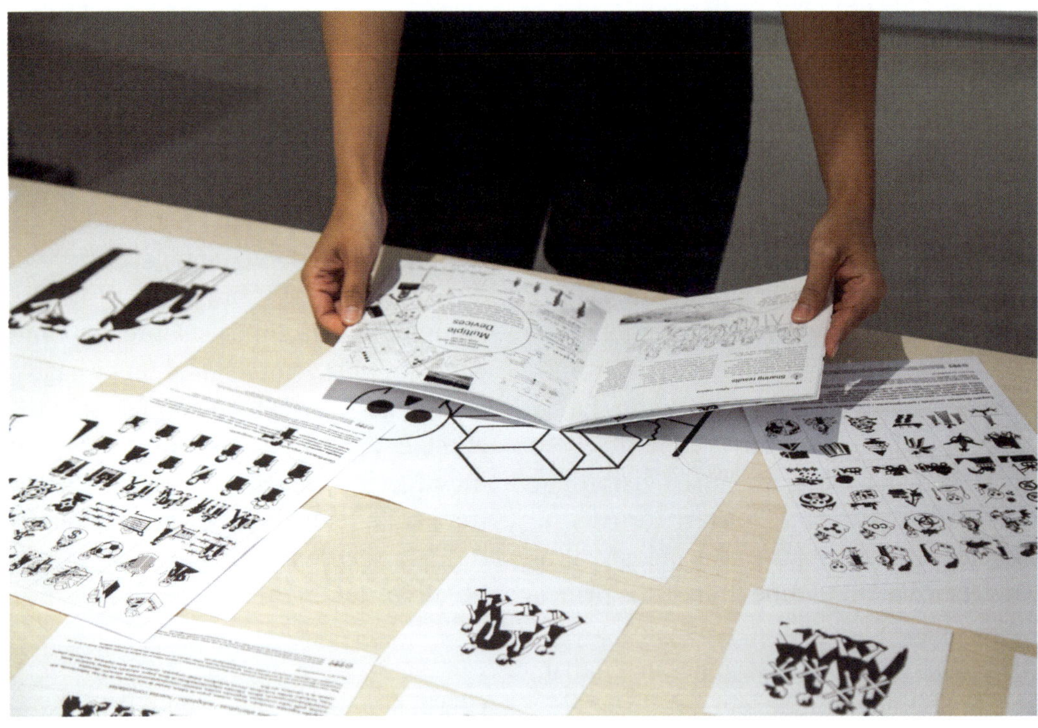

un horizonte de objetivos comunitarios. Su creación es compleja, cada punto significa: el título, los párrafos, los colores, las imagenes, las señalizaciones, etc. Si bien tienen objetivos, a su vez manejan un sentido bastante abierto que se completa en el encuentro con los, las otros y otras.

Patricio Dávila

Para dar la visión que abarca todo, a veces se critica por ser reductivo o, por lo menos, dar una sensación de control

Vincent Brown titulado "Jamaican Slave Revolt" donde se usa un linea de tiempo. Otra estrategia es usar el mapa como herramienta para la educación popular dentro de un evento participativo como los proyectos del Beehive Collective y sus mapas de mésoamerica. ¿Como decidieron que incluir y que excluir? ¿Tienen Uds. estrategias para presentar / animar el mapa mundi crítico?

Iconoclasistas

Tal cual, nosotros no buscamos dar

una visión "que abarque todo". Siempre decimos que un mapa es un foto de un momento que está en continuo cambio y movimiento. Por eso la necesidad de tramarlo las investigaciones colectivas en el marco de procesos más amplios, donde el mapa sólo representa un componente más, que aporta en algo específico, que no se detiene allí sino que funciona como puntapié para otras cosas. Nosotros no trabajamos sólo con mapas, lo hacemos también elaborando colectivamente paisajes, trabajando las tramas temporales, las superficies e intersticios corporales, desde los saberes perceptivos, intuitivos y de la experiencia cotidiana. Nuestros mapas se usan para decorar un espacio, como ilustración de una revista, como material pedagógica en escuelas populares, como soporte para la lucha y comunicación de determinadas problemáticas, entre otros. Para nosotros cada trabajo es diferente y no podemos generalizar la forma de construirlo o difundirlo, porque tiene mucho que ver con quién lo estamos haciendo y en el marco de qué objetivos. Nos manejamos mucho con una planificación pero improvisamos constantemente. Y los materiales que a veces comienzan como mapas, luego mutan a historietas, o textos, o gráficas e iconografías simples.

A partir del mapa mundi hemos comenzado un nuevo proyecto que titulamos "Album Deco", y que apunta a generar un caudal de imágenes que disparen y profundicen el pensamiento crítico, sin la intención de difundir ninguna verdad, sino más bien apostando a

fomentar perspectivas múltiples a partir del desafío presente en las prácticas de decodificar, decolonizar y deconstruir. Nuestro método retoma la antropofagia propuesta por la vanguardia brasilera en los años veinte del siglo pasado, contra "las ideas objetivadas y cadaverizadas", las "élites vegetales", la "verdad de los pueblos misioneros" y las "esclerosis urbanas". Pero apuesta a una práctica creativa que no se limita a devorar y vomitar una nueva forma a la manera de los antropófagos brasileros, sino que introduce una rumiancia: un movimiento constante mediante el cual lo que se incorpora no tiene un carácter estático, sino que es posible de ser regurgitado, mezclado y vuelto a deglutir. El proyecto tendrá un sitio web, publicaciones y talleres donde trabajaremos diversas temáticas a partir de dispositivos gráficos que activen procesos de decodificación, decolonización y deconstrucción.

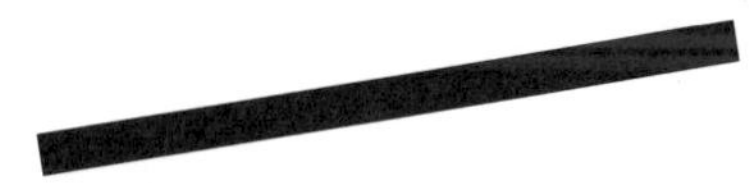

Iconoclasistas, a duo formed by Julia Risler and Pable Ares in 2006 and based in Buenos Aires, create projects that are community-focused, participatory and pedagogical. In this way, they create resources and workshops that help groups, neighbourhoods, and communities share collective knowledge through mapping and the creation of images.

Patricio Dávila

In the exhibition, *Diagrams of Power*, the world map "Who owns the land?" was on display. Near the map a table was placed with your guide on collective mapping and a selection of images that you use for your workshops. In this way the visitor can see two examples of your activities as a collective. It seems to me that your activities have two categories, the first one is the development of resources for collective mapping and the facilitation of workshops with groups and communities, and the second is the creation of self-managed projects like the critical world maps. What are the objectives of these different activities?

Iconoclasistas

These are two complementary lines of work, because many of the critical maps we have drawn up come from mapping workshops or collaborative research with different communities or groups. Yes, they differ in their objectives: if the resources and methodologies that we create and release are available to enable (and encourage) everyone to generate this kind of pedagogical-ludic space, the preparation of graphic material, which is also available on the website, aims to produce a material with an emphasis put on the communicational, designed with a specific public and objectives (that when done in connection to a workshop, are defined with the participants).

Patricio Dávila

The communication dimension has been a very important topic for modern cartography. It even developed a theoretical model, called the "Map Communication Model", which is based on the mathematical formula for communication postulated by Shannon and Weaver. Within this framework it was about eliminating the noise and increasing the signal to produce an efficient and effective communication. In many cases the decoration or the ambiguous symbols represented the noise that a designer needed to control or eliminate completely. In your critical maps, how does communication work?

Iconoclasistas

We make a lot of use of the visual for communication, and we use a lot of symbology too, we do not think of it as ambiguous but as broad, open meanings, since the idea is to interpellate the receiver but the meaning is not given or closed instead it can be completed by others. It is true that perhaps this can generate "noise" in terms of communication, but it is not something that worries us in advance (at least, as far as we know, our productions have never been used in the opposite sense to which they were made). In addition to the graphic, visual, symbolic, other communication resources are added: clear titles, headings, small paragraphs, statistics, consulted sources, etc. We resort to that set of elements to be able to communicate a message, but, as we said, that in turn is open to the perception of others.

Patricio Dávila

With a critical map like "Who owns the

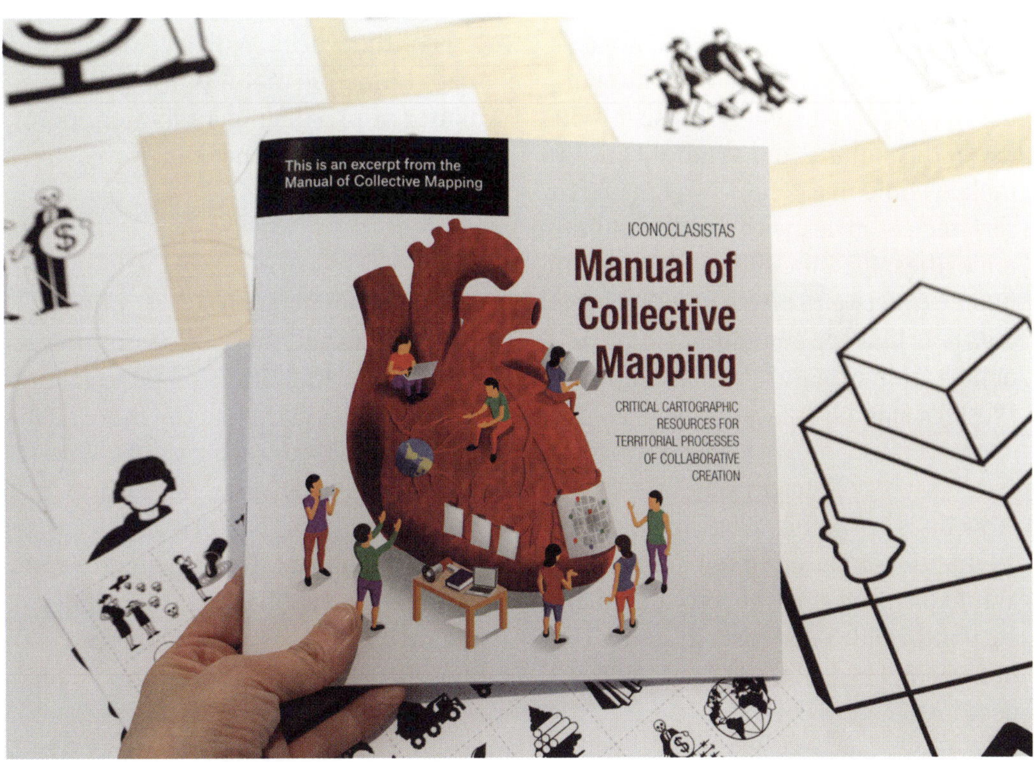

land?" I noted that a primary goal is the re-education or at least re-orientation of the map user–recognizing the territory in feminist and indigenous terms. And in which a profound history and a reality rarely represented in a map is visually communicated. How did you decide to start the project? Were they influenced by a specific event? How did you develop the design and information?

Iconoclasistas

The genesis of this critical map dates back to 2015 and is developed from our own research. The world map reveals the work of rural and peasant women, some 1.7 billion around the globe, who in addition to producing 70% of the food we consume, resist and organize in their communities. The practices and knowledge that sustain the economies of care for these women, protecting common goods and food sovereignty, are threatened by the destruction generated by the agro-industrial food system and violence (genocides, expulsions, wars, etc.) that come from extractive projects. The map is based on the Gall-Peters projection (with the poles reversed), first described in 1855 by James Gall and revisited by Arno Peters in 1974. This representation preserves the proportion between the land area of the different regions of the earth, providing an approximate notion of the size of the countries as opposed to the Mercator projection that enlarges the territories when they approach the poles. It had special relevance in the 70s, when national liberation movements faced the western dominion of the world. We chose it because it helps us—both spatially and symbolically—to make visible in a clearer way the territories and countries with farmer and rural majorities, the biocultural diversity, the main extractive projects and the armed conflicts that are generated from the depredation of nature and attempts at Western standardization.

Patricio Dávila

How does aesthetics work in your mappa mundi compared to collective maps? While one is very polished, the other is very informal. Was this a decision made beforehand or is it a result of the process itself?

Iconoclasistas

Yes, the truth is that it depends on each job. For the world map we had all the time we wanted because it was our project, which did not involve working with others. Many of the critical cartographies have a graphical exit time (and maturation) rather quickly because they intervene in conjuncture and respond to concrete and collective objectives. The world map is an aesthetic treat that we wanted to give ourselves for a while :)

Patricio Dávila

The mappa mundi is a type of map that was popular during the Middle Ages. It represents a desire to incorporate all of what is known about the territories. There is always an emphasis on a point of view, for example in some cases the map is oriented with Jerusalem as the axis of the world. With a critical world map, I imagine that it is not only a matter of privileging a subaltern point of view but to advance other objectives as well.

Iconoclasistas

Of course, there is always a point of view and a specific interlocutor. In each map produced, both from more institutional sectors and from the more subaltern, this is always the case. However, the maps have an ambiguity with which we like to play, it is precisely the criterion of "truth" that they handle. It would seem that everything that is included in a map is as it exists, as it is revealed, does not offer many doubts to the reader. However, the reading of a map (especially of the hegemonic maps) should oblige us to carry out that second, third and other decodings, in order to reveal: who produces it? in what context? for what? what does it say? But fundamentally, what does it hide? Our maps take on that ambiguity as a communicative power, and offer a collective narrative that is woven from a transformative perspective and a horizon of community objectives. Its creation is complex, each point signifies: the title, the paragraphs, the colors, the images, the signs, etc. Although they have objectives, they also manage a quite open sense that is completed in the encounter with the others and others.

Patricio Dávila

To provide a vision that encompasses everything is sometimes criticized for

155

being reductive or, at least, giving a sense of control over a territory (space or knowledge). It is obvious that you can not represent everything on a map. Something that is quite difficult is to represent the passage of time, the story. One strategy is to use an interactive platform (website) as was done in the Vincent Brown project entitled "Jamaican Slave Revolt" where a timeline is used. Another strategy is to use the map as a tool for popular education within a participatory event such as the Beehive Collective projects and its maps of Mesoamerica. How did you decide what to include and what to exclude? Do you have strategies to present / animate the critical world map?

<u>Iconoclasistas</u>
As such, we do not seek to give a "comprehensive" vision. We always say that a map is a picture of a moment that is constantly changing and moving. That is why the need to frame collective research in the context of broader processes, where the map only represents one more component, which contributes to something specific, which does not stop there but works as a jumping off point for other things. We do not only work with maps, we also do it by collectively elaborating landscapes, working the temporal plots, the surfaces and bodily interstices, from perceptive, intuitive knowledge and from daily experience. Our maps are used to decorate a space, as an illustration of a magazine, as pedagogical material in public schools, as support for the struggle and communication of certain

problems, among others. For us, each job is different and we can not generalize the way to build or disseminate it, because it has a lot to do with whom we are working and the framework of objectives. We manage a lot with planning but we constantly improvise. And the materials that sometimes start as maps, then mutate to comics, or texts, or graphics and simple iconographies.

From the world map we have started a new project that we titled "Album Deco", that aims to generate a wealth of images that trigger and deepen critical thinking, without the intention of spreading any truth, but rather betting on fostering multiple perspectives from the challenge present in decoding, decolonizing and deconstructing practices. Our method resumes the anthropophagy proposed by the Brazilian avant-garde in the twenties of the last century, against "the objective and cadaverized ideas", the "vegetal elites", the "truth of the missionary peoples" and the "urban sclerosis". But it bets on a creative practice that is not limited to devouring and vomiting a new form in the manner of Brazilian anthropophagy, but it introduces a ruminance—a constant movement through which what is incorporated does not have a static character, but is possible to be regurgitated, mixed and re-swallowed. The project will have a website, publications and workshops where we will work on various topics from graphic devices that activate decoding, decolonization and deconstruction processes.

¿A quién pertenece la tierra?
Who Owns the Land?

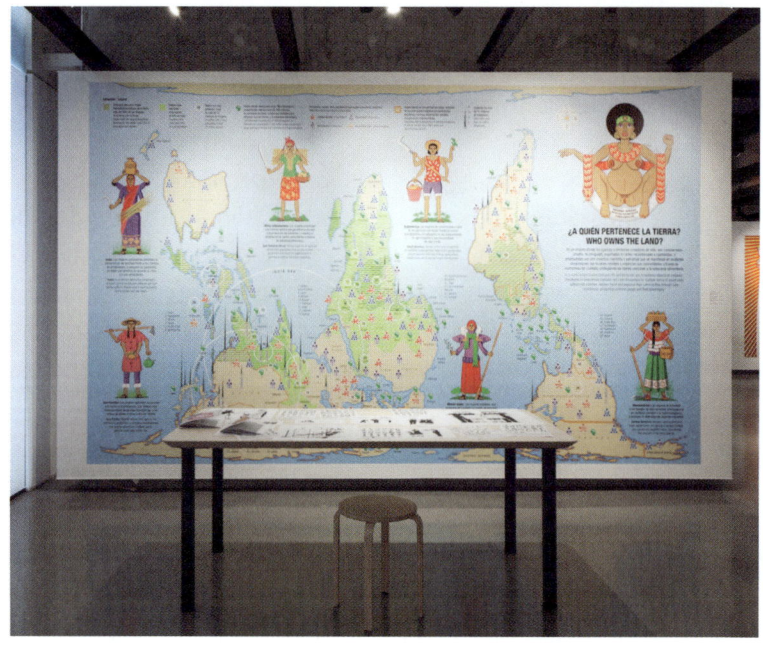

Installation view. Iconoclasistas, *¿A quien pertenece la tierra? (Who Owns the Land?)*, 2017. Courtesy of Onsite Gallery. Photography by Yuula Benivolski.

Iconoclasistas

Este mapamundi releva el trabajo de las mujeres rurales y campesinas, unas 1.700 millones en todo el globo, quienes además de producir el 70% de los alimentos que consumimos, resisten y se organizan en sus comunidades. Las prácticas y saberes que sustentan las economías del cuidado de estas mujeres, protegiendo los bienes comunes y la soberanía alimentaria, se encuentran amenazadas por la destrucción generada por el sistema alimentario agroindustrial y la violencia (genocidios, expulsiones, guerras, etc.) que generan de los proyectos extractivos.

El mapa está basado en la proyección Gall-Peters (con los polos invertidos), descrita por primera vez en 1855 por James Gall y revisitada por Arno Peters en 1974. Esta representación conserva la proporción entre las áreas de las distintas zonas de la tierra, brindando una noción aproximada del tamaño de los países al contrario de la proyección Mercator que agiganta los territorios cuando se aproximan a los polos. Tuvo especial relevancia en los años '70, cuando los movimientos de liberación nacional se enfrentaron al dominio occidental del mundo. La elegimos porque nos ayuda -tanto espacial como simbólicamente- a visibilizar de manera más clara los territorios y países con mayorías campesinas y rurales, la diversidad biocultural, los principales proyectos extractivos y los conflictos armados que se generan a partir de la depredación de la naturaleza y los intentos de normalización occidental.

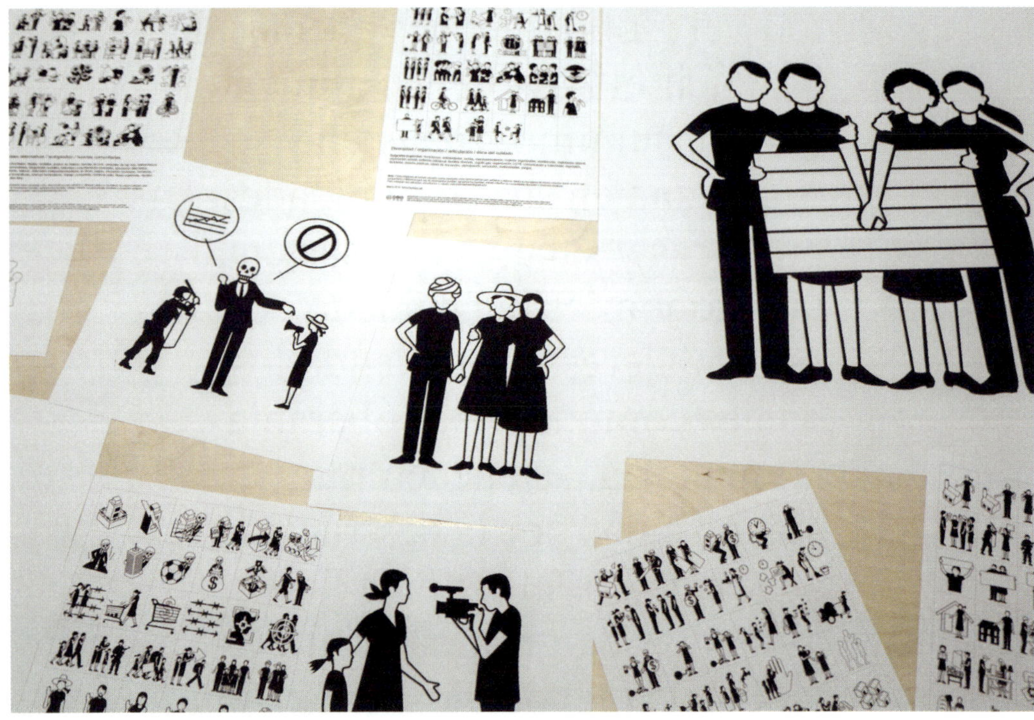

All installation views. Iconoclasistas, *¿A quien pertenece la tierra? (Who Owns the Land?)*, 2017. Courtesy of Onsite Gallery. Photography by Yuula Benivolski.

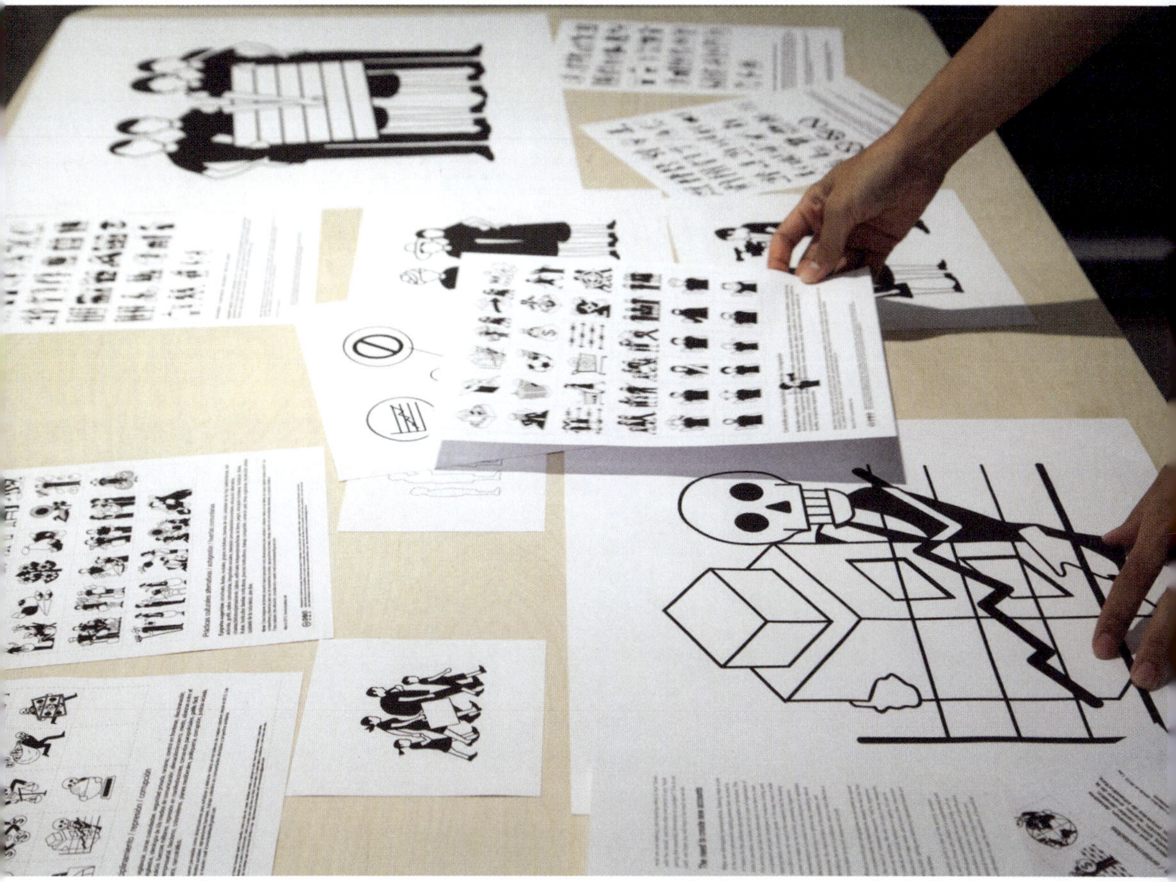

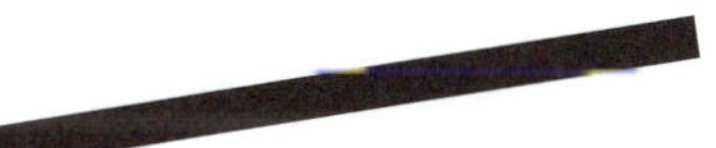

The world map reveals the work of rural and peasant women, some 1.7 billion around the globe, who in addition to producing 70% of the food we consume, resist and organize in their communities. The practices and knowledge that sustain the economies of care for these women, protecting common goods and food sovereignty, are threatened by the destruction generated by the agro-industrial food system and violence (genocides, expulsions, wars, etc.) that come from extractive projects.

The map is based on the Gall-Peters projection (with the poles reversed), first described in 1855 by James Gall and revisited by Arno Peters in 1974. This representation preserves the proportion between the

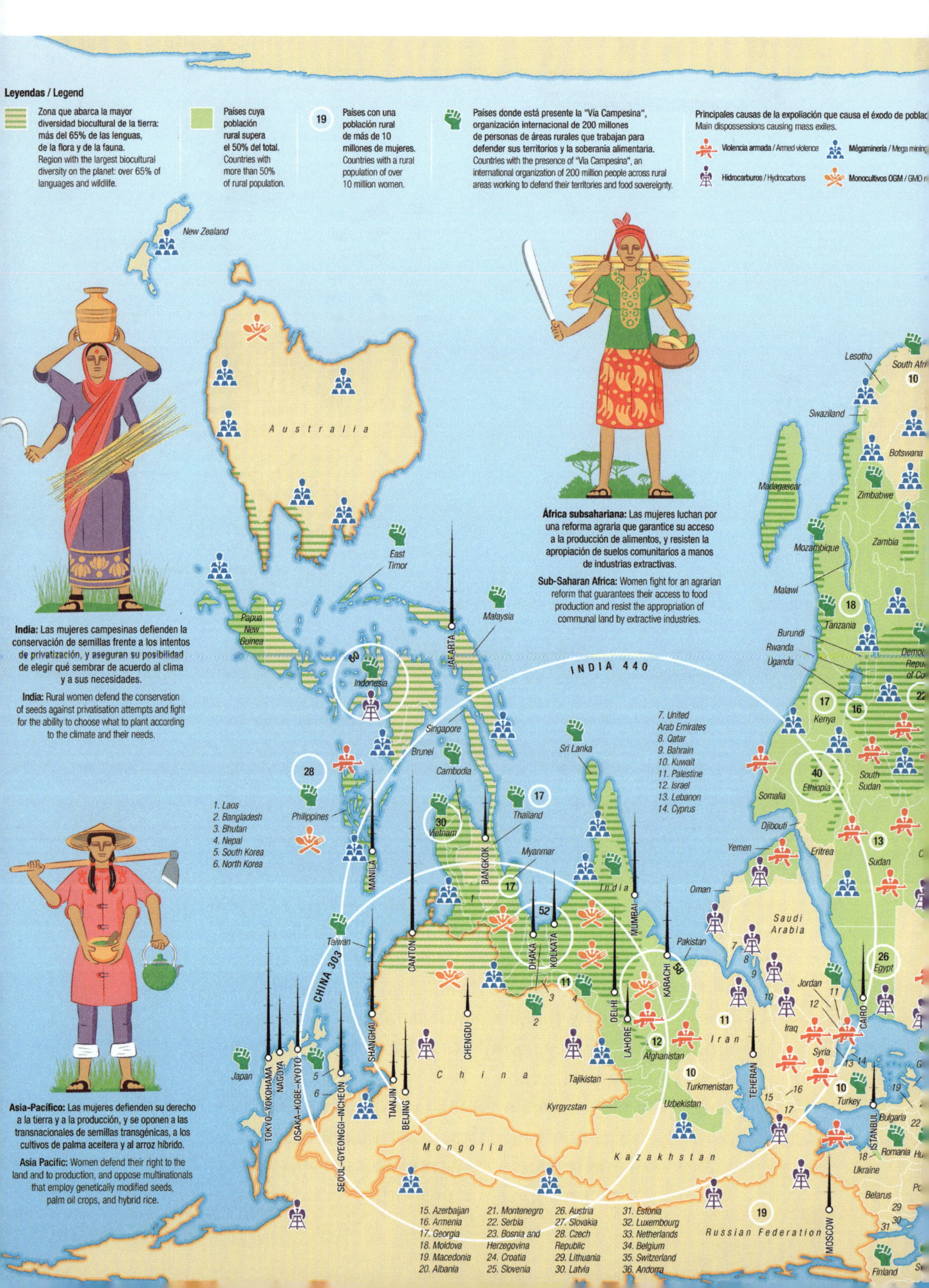

India: Las mujeres campesinas defienden la conservación de semillas frente a los intentos de privatización, y aseguran su posibilidad de elegir qué sembrar de acuerdo al clima y a sus necesidades.

India: Rural women defend the conservation of seeds against privatisation attempts and fight for the ability to choose what to plant according to the climate and their needs.

Asia-Pacífico: Las mujeres defienden su derecho a la tierra y a la producción, y se oponen a las transnacionales de semillas transgénicas, a los cultivos de palma aceitera y al arroz híbrido.

Asia Pacific: Women defend their right to the land and to production, and oppose multinationals that employ genetically modified seeds, palm oil crops, and hybrid rice.

África subsahariana: Las mujeres luchan por una reforma agraria que garantice su acceso a la producción de alimentos, y resisten la apropiación de suelos comunitarios a manos de industrias extractivas.

Sub-Saharan Africa: Women fight for an agrarian reform that guarantees their access to food production and resist the appropriation of communal land by extractive industries.

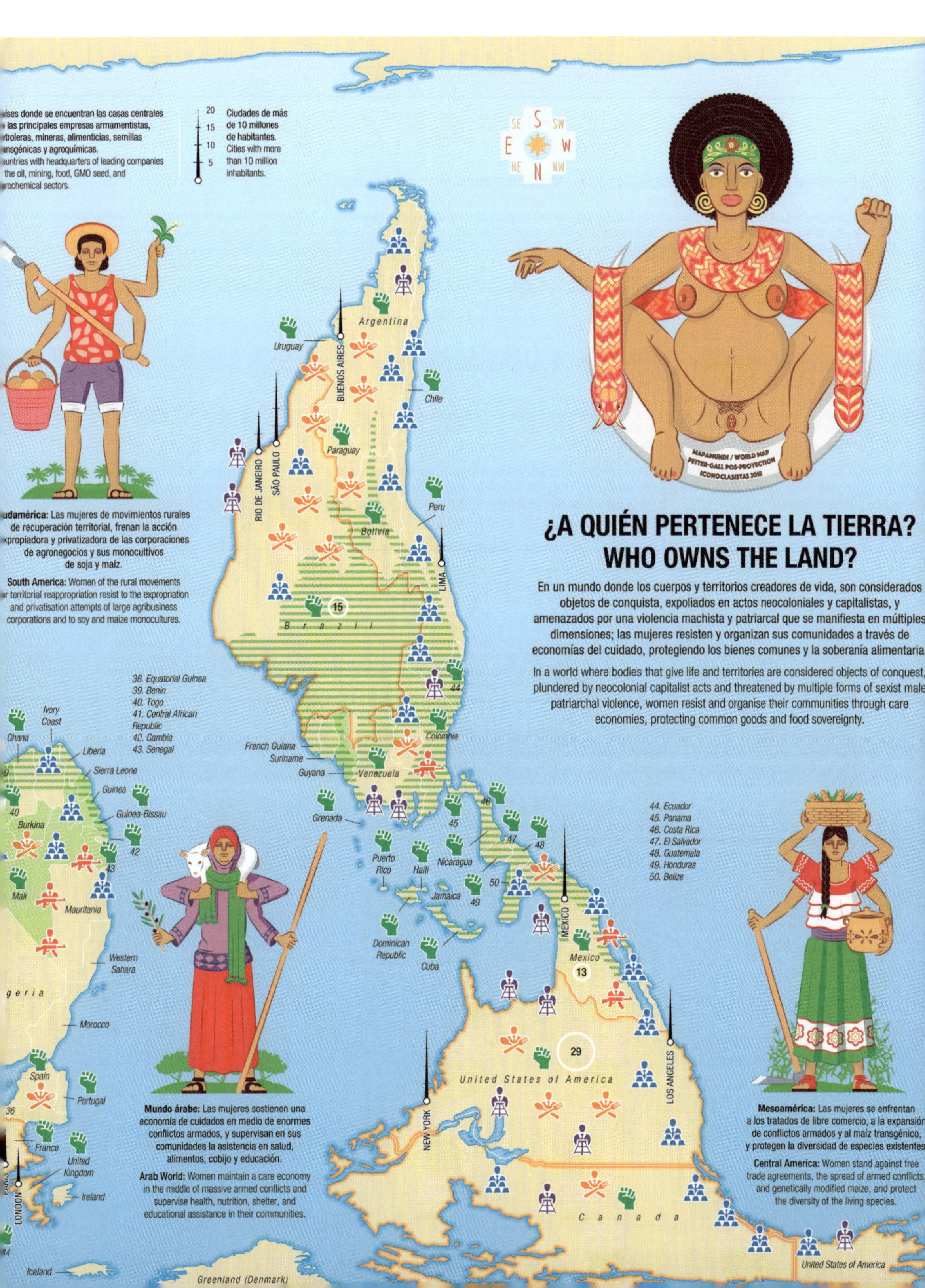

Países donde se encuentran las casas centrales de las principales empresas armamentistas, petroleras, mineras, alimenticias, semillas transgénicas y agroquímicas.
Countries with headquarters of leading companies in the oil, mining, food, GMO seed, and agrochemical sectors.

20
15
10
5
Ciudades de más de 10 millones de habitantes.
Cities with more than 10 million inhabitants.

MAPAMUNDI / WORLD MAP
PETER-GALL POS-PROTECTION
ICONOCLASISTAS 2018

¿A QUIÉN PERTENECE LA TIERRA?
WHO OWNS THE LAND?

En un mundo donde los cuerpos y territorios creadores de vida, son considerados objetos de conquista, explotados en actos neocoloniales y capitalistas, y amenazados por una violencia machista y patriarcal que se manifiesta en múltiples dimensiones; las mujeres resisten y organizan sus comunidades a través de economías del cuidado, protegiendo los bienes comunes y la soberanía alimentaria.

In a world where bodies that give life and territories are considered objects of conquest, plundered by neocolonial capitalist acts and threatened by multiple forms of sexist male patriarchal violence, women resist and organise their communities through care economies, protecting common goods and food sovereignty.

Sudamérica: Las mujeres de movimientos rurales de recuperación territorial, frenan la acción expropiadora y privatizadora de las corporaciones de agronegocios y sus monocultivos de soja y maíz.
South America: Women of the rural movements for territorial reappropriation resist to the expropriation and privatisation attempts of large agribusiness corporations and to soy and maize monocultures.

Mundo árabe: Las mujeres sostienen una economía de cuidados en medio de enormes conflictos armados, y supervisan en sus comunidades la asistencia en salud, alimentos, cobijo y educación.
Arab World: Women maintain a care economy in the middle of massive armed conflicts and supervise health, nutrition, shelter, and educational assistance in their communities.

Mesoamérica: Las mujeres se enfrentan a los tratados de libre comercio, a la expansión de conflictos armados y al maíz transgénico, y protegen la diversidad de especies existentes.
Central America: Women stand against free trade agreements, the spread of armed conflicts and genetically modified maize, and protect the diversity of the living species.

38. Equatorial Guinea
39. Benin
40. Togo
41. Central African Republic
42. Gambia
43. Senegal

44. Ecuador
45. Panama
46. Costa Rica
47. El Salvador
48. Guatemala
49. Honduras
50. Belize

Argentina
Uruguay
Chile
Paraguay
Peru
Bolivia
Brazil
BUENOS AIRES
RIO DE JANEIRO
SÃO PAULO
LIMA
Colombia
French Guiana
Suriname
Guyana
Venezuela
Grenada
Puerto Rico
Haiti
Nicaragua
Jamaica
Dominican Republic
Cuba
Mexico
MEXICO
LOS ANGELES
United States of America
NEW YORK
Canada
Greenland (Denmark)
Iceland
Ivory Coast
Ghana
Liberia
Sierra Leone
Guinea
Guinea-Bissau
Burkina
Mali
Mauritania
Western Sahara
Algeria
Morocco
Spain
Portugal
France
United Kingdom
Ireland
LONDON

S
SE SW
E W
NE SW
N NW

Megaciudades y crisis ambiental

En 2007, por primera vez en la historia, la población residente en ciudades es mayor a la población campesina. Aún así, en las zonas rurales viven unas 3.400 millones de personas que se dedican a producir alimentos y más de la mitad son mujeres. Ellas sostienen prácticas de reciprocidad, preservan las memorias y saberes ancestrales, trabajan y cultivan la tierra en equilibrio con los ciclos de la naturaleza; y aportan una solución a la crisis ecológica y a los desastres climáticos, cada vez más frecuentes en el mundo.

Trabajo rural y doméstico

Estas 1.700 millones de mujeres representan un 25 % de la población mundial, y alimentan a un 70% de los habitantes del planeta. Las mujeres rurales, además del cuidado de sembradíos, la obtención de agua y leña y la cría de animales; realizan un trabajo invisible y no remunerado: el doméstico, el cual incluye el cuidado de los hijos y de personas enfermas, la limpieza del hogar y la elaboración de alimentos, todas labores consideradas como una extensión (obligada) de sus tareas de reproducción biológica.

Éxodo rural y represión

El sistema alimentario agroindustrial, basado en monocultivos y dominado por trasnacionales, alimenta a un 30% de la población mundial, y emplea en condiciones miserables a una ínfima parte de los trabajadores rurales. Destruye el medio ambiente, empobrece y expulsa a los pobladores originarios, mientras se expande a través de la militarización y la represión, generando la pérdida de los derechos colectivos sobre los bienes naturales, y transformando lo común en propiedad privada.

Soberanía alimentaria y cultural

Las mujeres rurales, mediante prácticas de defensa de los bienes comunes, de protección de la cultura popular y solidaria, y de respeto hacia la naturaleza; aseguran la agrodiversidad frente al avance del despojo neocolonial. Custodian, además, las más de 6 mil lenguas vivas en todo el mundo, cada una desarrollada durante siglos de costumbres y portadoras de tradiciones y prácticas riquísimas, mayormente desconocidas, lo que las convierte en guardianas de las memorias de la tierra.

Megacities and environmental crisis

In 2007, for the first time ever, the population living in cities surpassed the one living in the countryside. However, some 3.4 billion people still live in rural areas and work in food production—more than half of them are women. They support reciprocity practices, preserve ancestral memories and know-how, work and cultivate the land in harmony with the cycles of nature, and provide a solution to the environmental crisis and the increasing climate-related disasters worldwide.

Rural and domestic work

These 1.7 billion women represent 25% of the world population and feed 70% of the world population. Aside from tending crops, gathering water and firewood, and raising animals, they perform invisible work. They are not paid for their domestic work, which includes caring for children and the sick, cleaning the home, and preparing food—all activities that are considered an (obligatory) extension of their biological reproductive functions.

Rural exodus and repression

The agro-industrial food system, based on monoculture and dominated by multinational firms, feeds 30% of the world population and employs—in appalling conditions—a minuscule portion of rural workers. It destroys the environment, impoverishes and drives out native populations, and thrives through militarisation and repression—thus causing the loss of collective rights over natural assets and turning public goods into private property.

Food and cultural sovereignty

Through practices that defend public goods, protect shared traditional culture, and respect nature, rural women ensure agricultural diversity in the face of neocolonial dispossession. They are also guardians of the over 6000 languages spoken across the world, which developed over the centuries, bear rich traditions, and are mostly unknown. As a result, these women are the keepers of the memories of the Earth.

Fuentes / Sources: ACNUR, FAO, CEPAL, OXFAM, ONU, PNUD, Worldwatch Institute, Global Witness, Grupo ETC, GRAIN, CLOC-Via Campesina, Mundo Negro, No a la Mina, WoMin, The Internal Displacement Monitoring Centre, Uppsala Conflict Data Program.

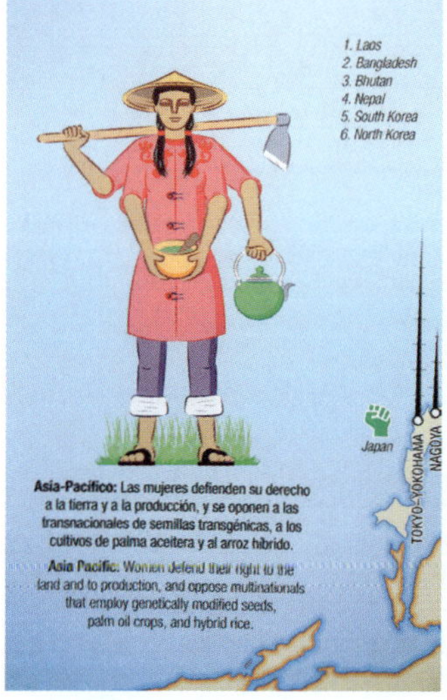

Asia-Pacífico: Las mujeres defienden su derecho a la tierra y a la producción, y se oponen a las transnacionales de semillas transgénicas, a los cultivos de palma aceitera y al arroz híbrido.

Asia Pacific: Women defend their right to the land and to production, and oppose multinationals that employ genetically modified seeds, palm oil crops, and hybrid rice.

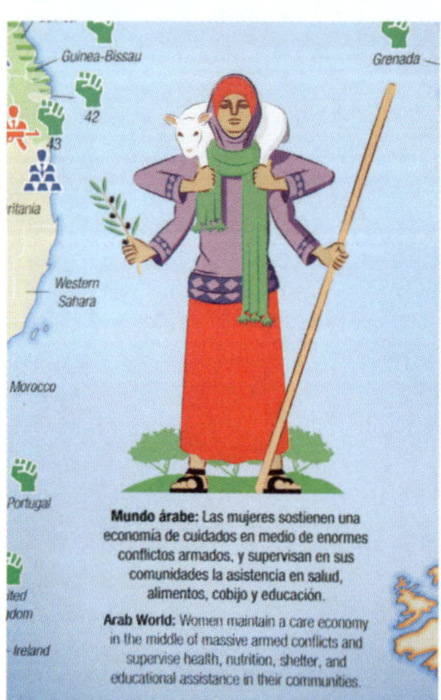

Mundo árabe: Las mujeres sostienen una economía de cuidados en medio de enormes conflictos armados, y supervisan en sus comunidades la asistencia en salud, alimentos, cobijo y educación.

Arab World: Women maintain a care economy in the middle of massive armed conflicts and supervise health, nutrition, shelter, and educational assistance in their communities.

(above and previous page) Iconoclasistas, *¿A quien pertenece la tierra? (Who Owns the Land?)*, 2017. Courtesy of the artists.

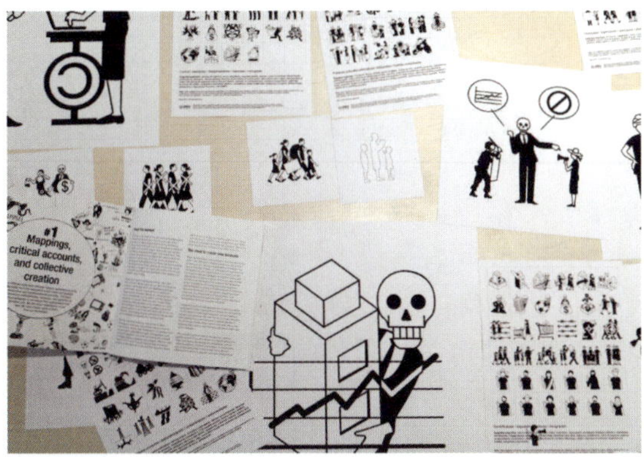

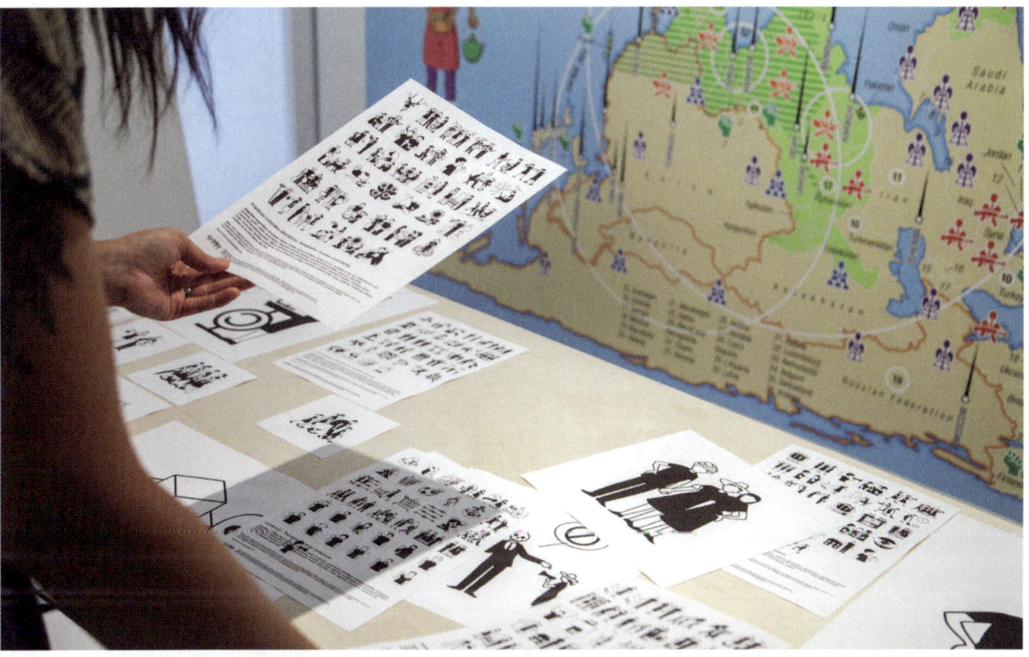

land area of the different regions of the earth, providing an approximate notion of the size of the countries as opposed to the Mercator projection that enlarges the territories when they approach the poles. It had special relevance in the 70s, when national liberation movements faced the western dominion of the world. We chose it because it helps us—both spatially and symbolically—to make visible in a clearer way the territories and countries with farmer and rural majorities, the bio-cultural diversity, the main extractive projects and the armed conflicts that are generated from the depredation of nature and attempts at Western standardization.

Minneapolis and Saint Paul are East African Cities

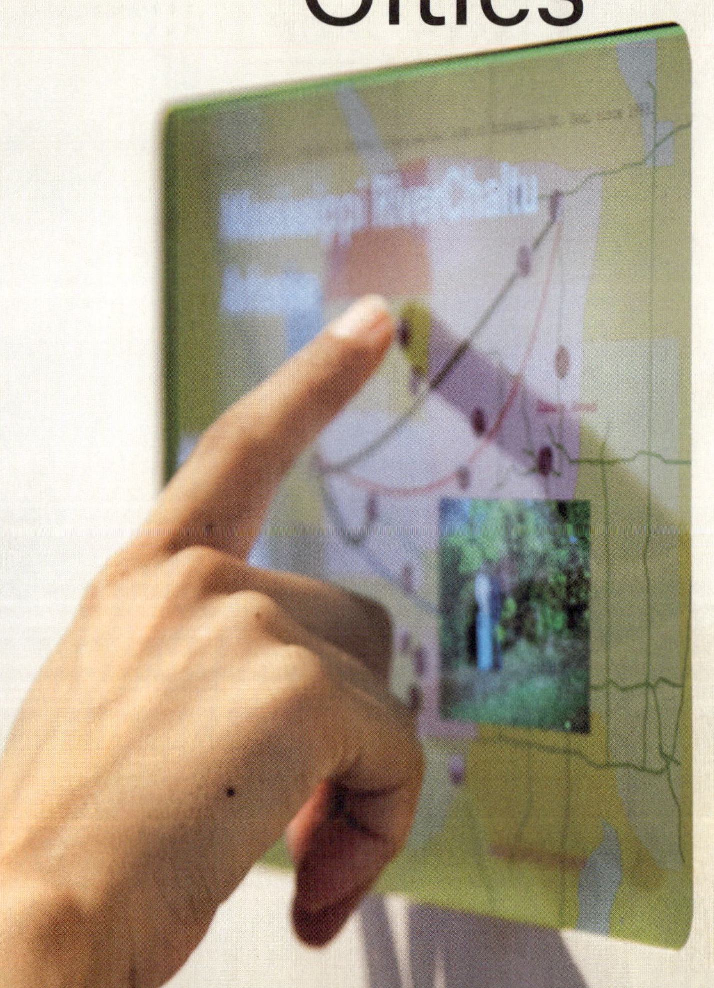

Julie Mehretu + entropy8zuper!

As an immigrant herself, Julie Mehretu has always been fascinated with urban spaces and the ways that city fabrics change as new arrivals are stitched in. The faces of East African immigrants that she found upon initial visits to the Twin Cities reminded her of the Ethiopian-American community where she grew up in Michigan. She knew those faces held fascinating and multi-layered stories of change, movement, community, and growth.

When the Walker subsequently invited Ms. Mehretu to develop a residency project, she immediately decided to encourage the Twin Cities East African community to give "voice" to their own stories. After developing the project concepts closely with her brother David Mehretu, Ms. Mehretu asked 30 young people, most of whom attend Edison and Roosevelt high schools, to spend several weeks recording their own lives through photographs and sound recordings. The images they took range from scenes at the dinner table to choir rehearsal and soccer practice to trips to the mall and local African supermarket. The accompanying recordings of ambient sound animate their narratives in unexpected ways that could not happen through visuals alone.

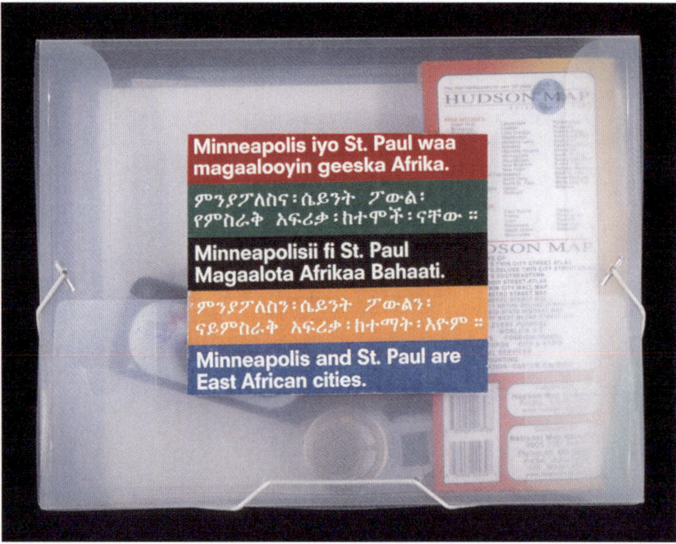

All installation views: Julie Mehretu + entropy8zuper!, *Minneapolis and Saint Paul are East African Cities*, 2003. Courtesy of Onsite Gallery. Photography by Yuula Benivolski.

In an interesting confluence of art and philosophy, Ms. Mehretu's residency project delves into many themes that underlie her painting practice: family history, social and political themes, the individual and community in urban space, and mapping of the self within the larger whole. The self-exploration process initiated by the residency project proved to be a highly organic and creative one that moved several participants to investigate their own family histories and see their own lives in a new and refreshing light. The personal and often moving stories generated by the participants' hard work have been gathered together virtually to create a rich, multi-layered website (www.tceastafrica/walkerart.org) by the award-winning web artists entropy8zuper! (Auriea Harvey and Michael Samyn), which launched in April, 2003. The photographs and sound recording themselves have become part of the permanent collection of the Hennepin History Museum.

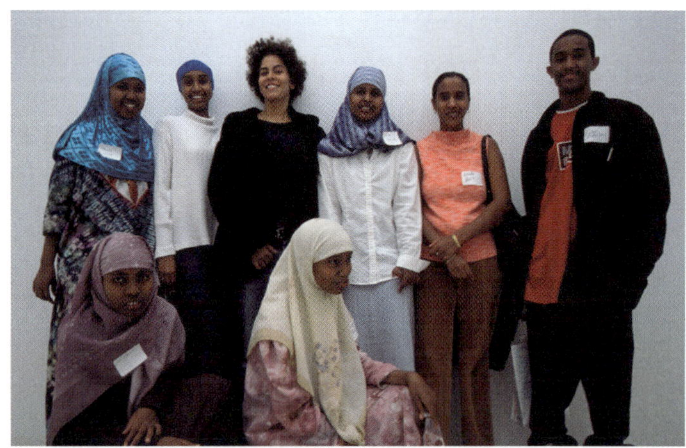

Minneapolis and Saint Paul
are East African Cities
Julie Mehretu + entropy8zuper!

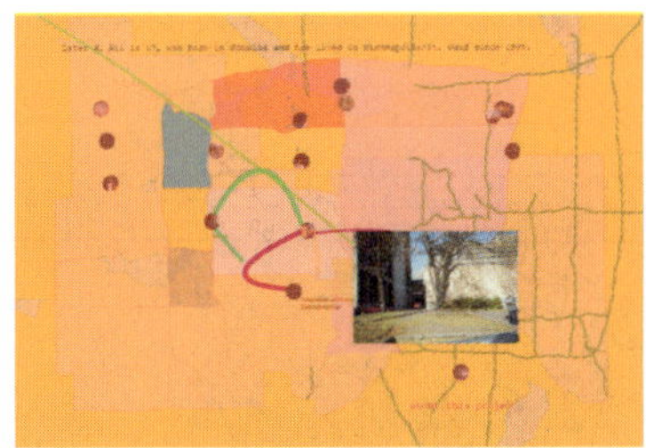

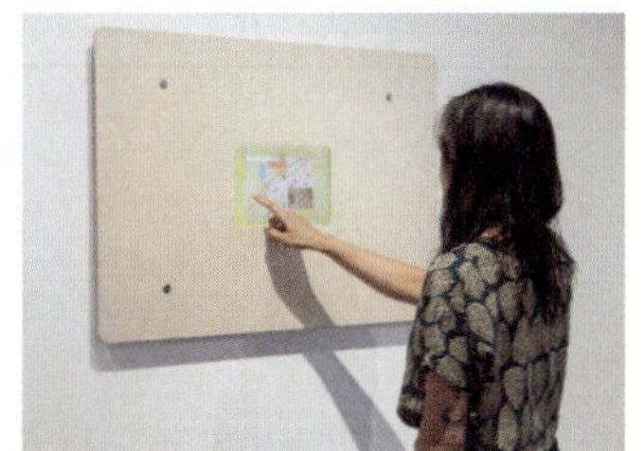

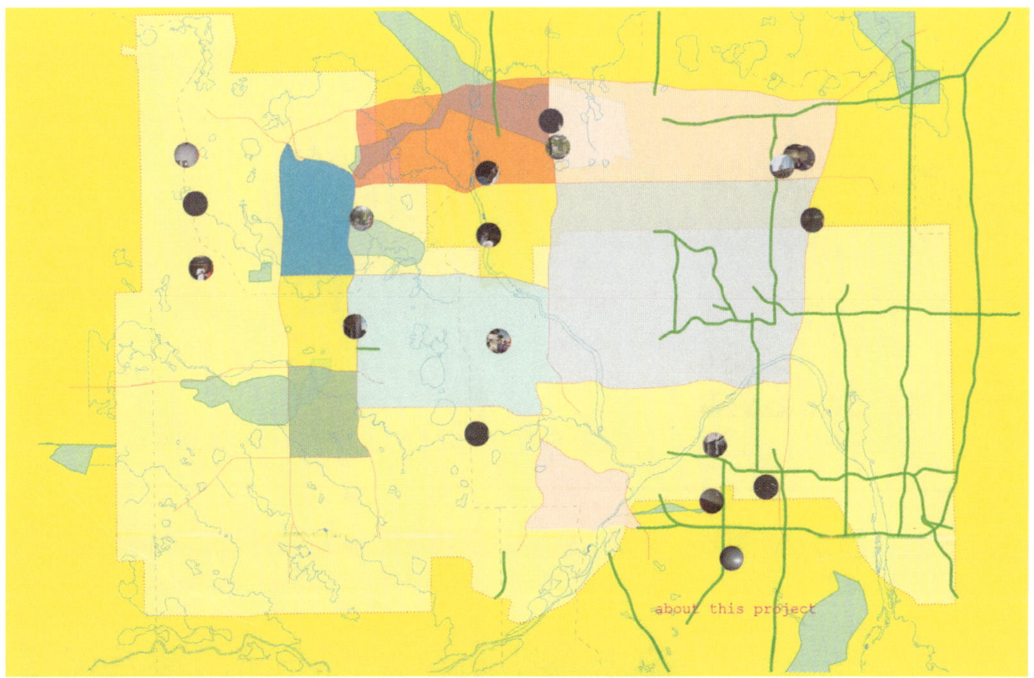

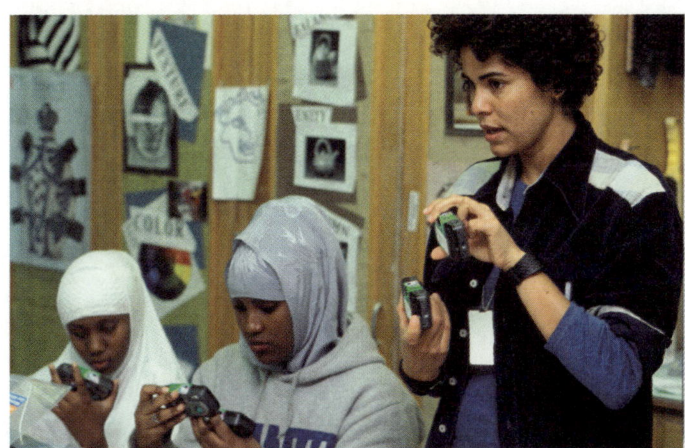

All workshop photographs
courtesy of Walker Art Center,
Minneapolis, USA.

Do the young East African men of Cedar Riverside neighbouhood prefer a game of basketball or soccer? What does a young woman of Somali descent wear to school in snowy Minneapolis? What does the flat of Oromia look like? If you're a recent immigrant from the horn of Africa where do you buy traditional foodstuffs?

This self-ethnographic approach mirrors the artist's own painting process which often examines identity, geography, individual narrative, and personal and cultural history.

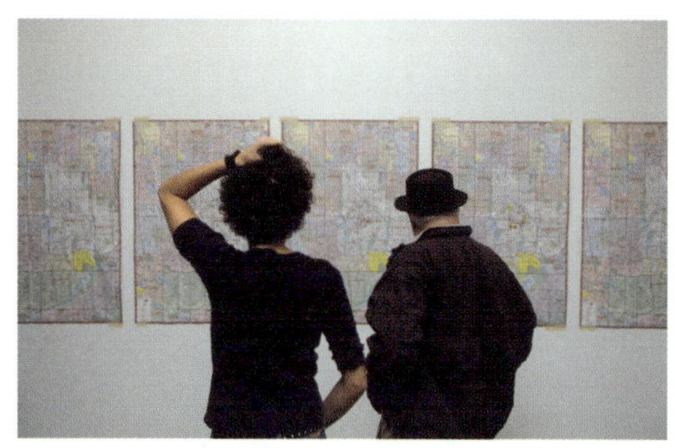

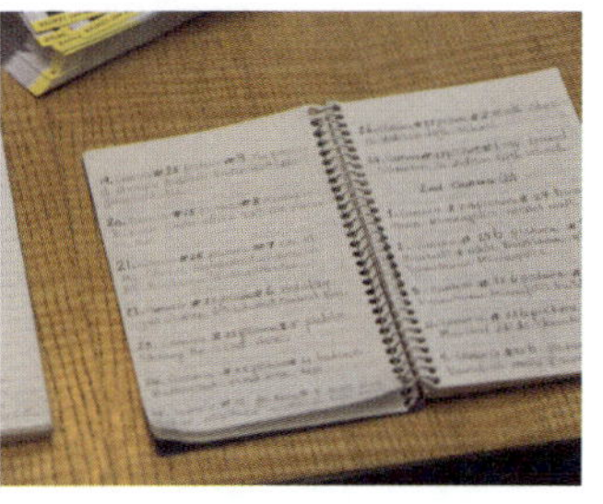

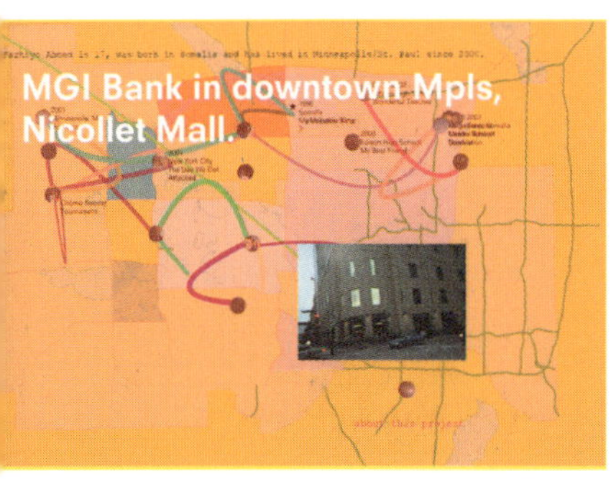

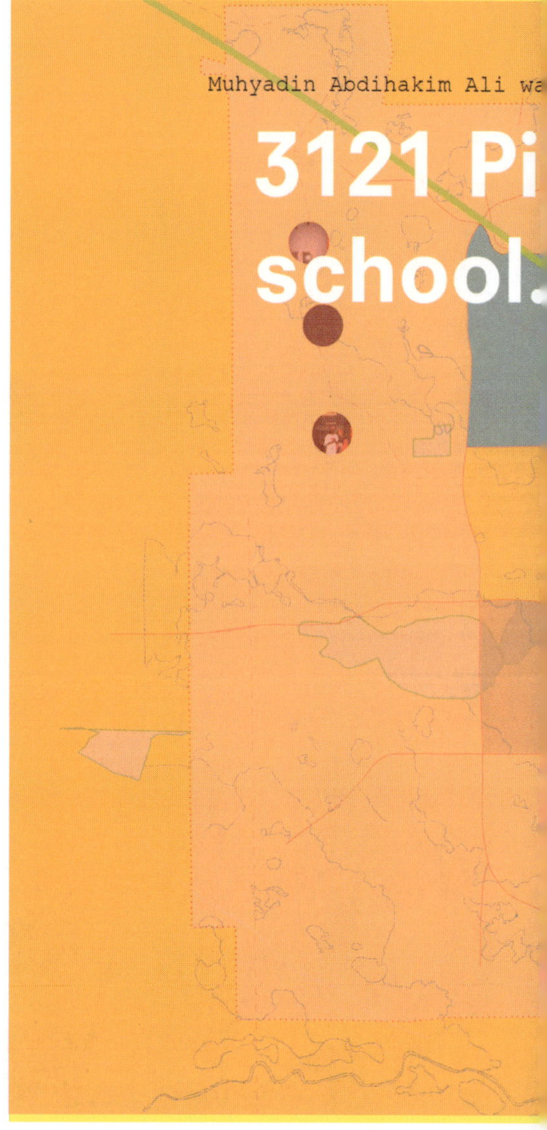

Minneapolis and Saint Paul
are East African Cities
Julie Mehretu + entropy8zuper!

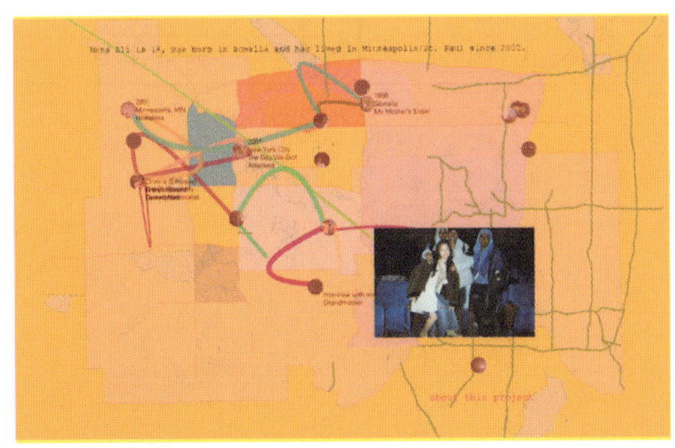

Minneapolis and St. Paul are East African Cities website for Julie Mehretu residency, designed by entropy8zuper!, 2003. Courtesy of www.walkerart.org

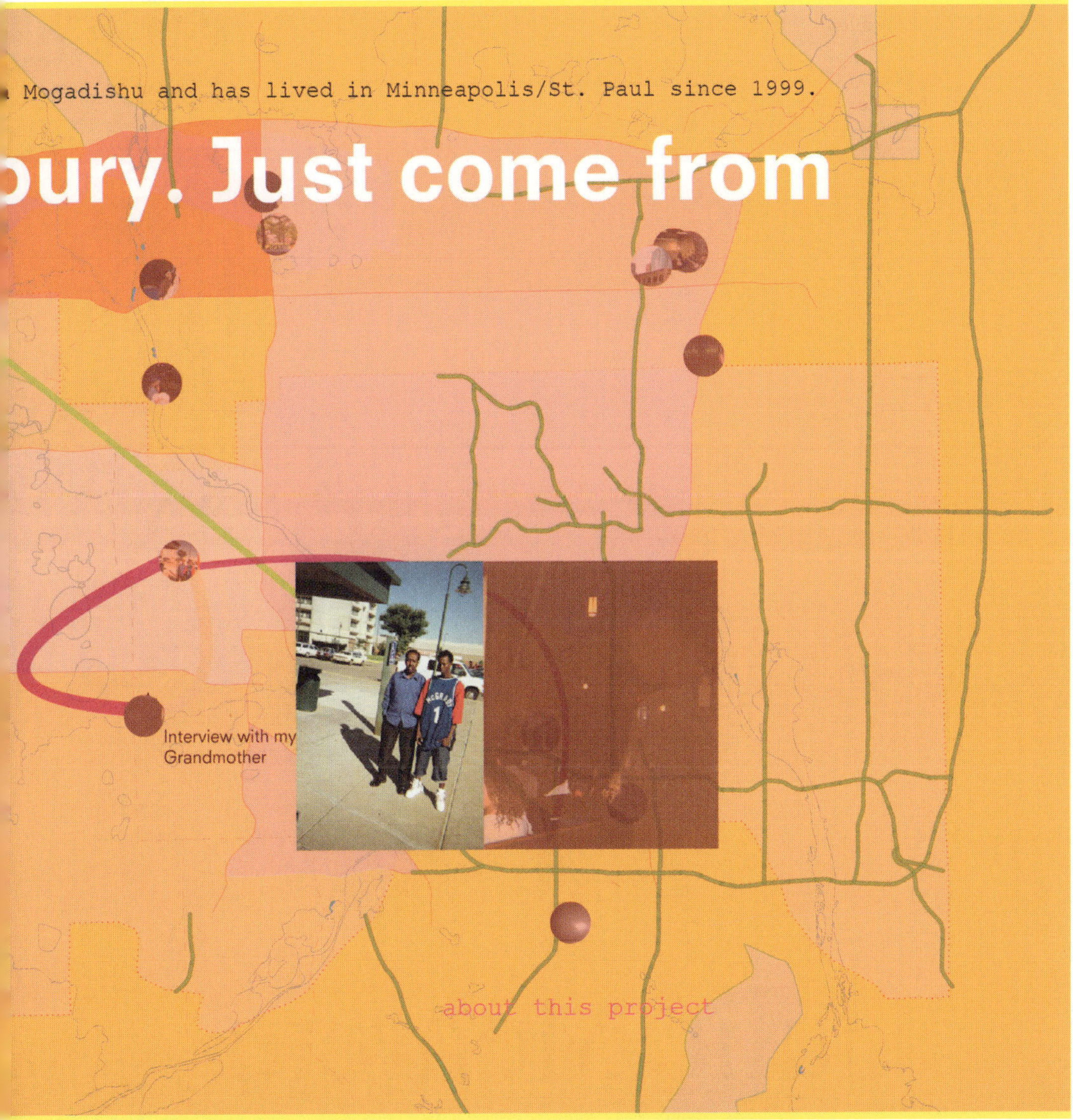

Algorithms, Apparitions and Translations

Series of five etchings with aquatint, drypoint, and engraving (2013). Sheet (each approx.): 31 3/16 x 37 5/16" (79.2 x 94.7 cm)

Publisher: Burnet Editions, New York. Printer: Gregory Burnet. © Julie Mehretu. Image courtesy of Burnet Editions.

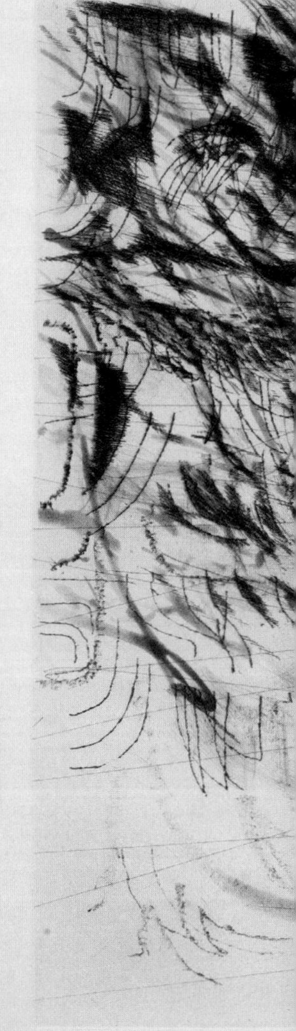

Julie Mehretu

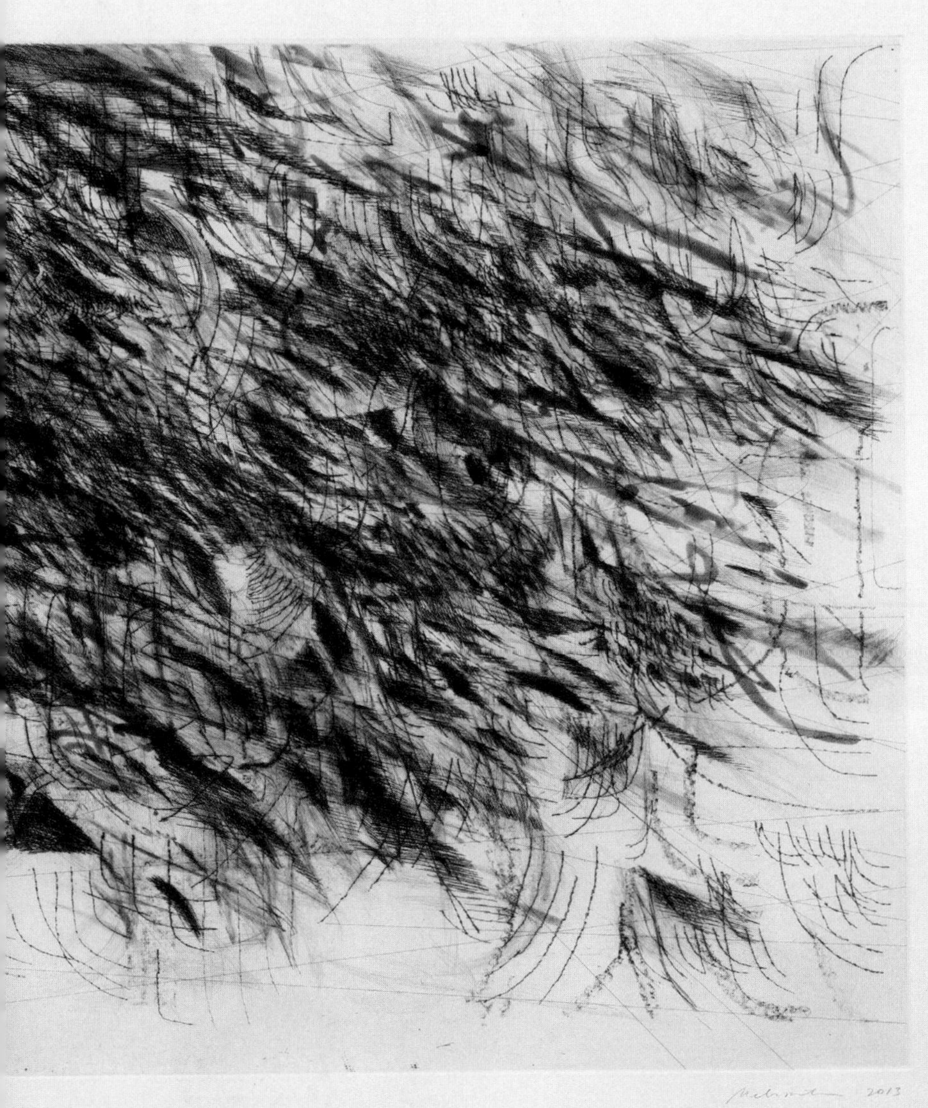

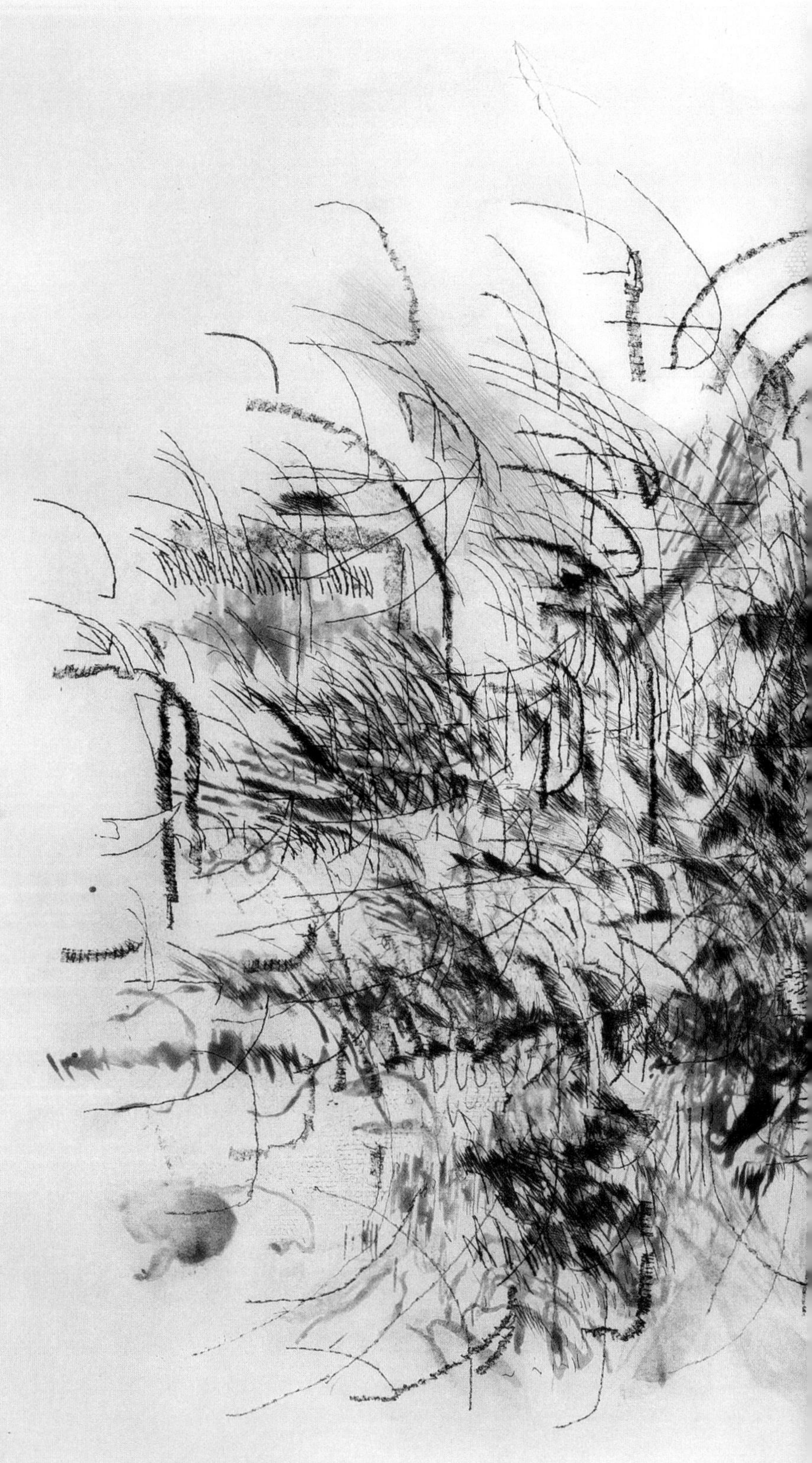

III/VI

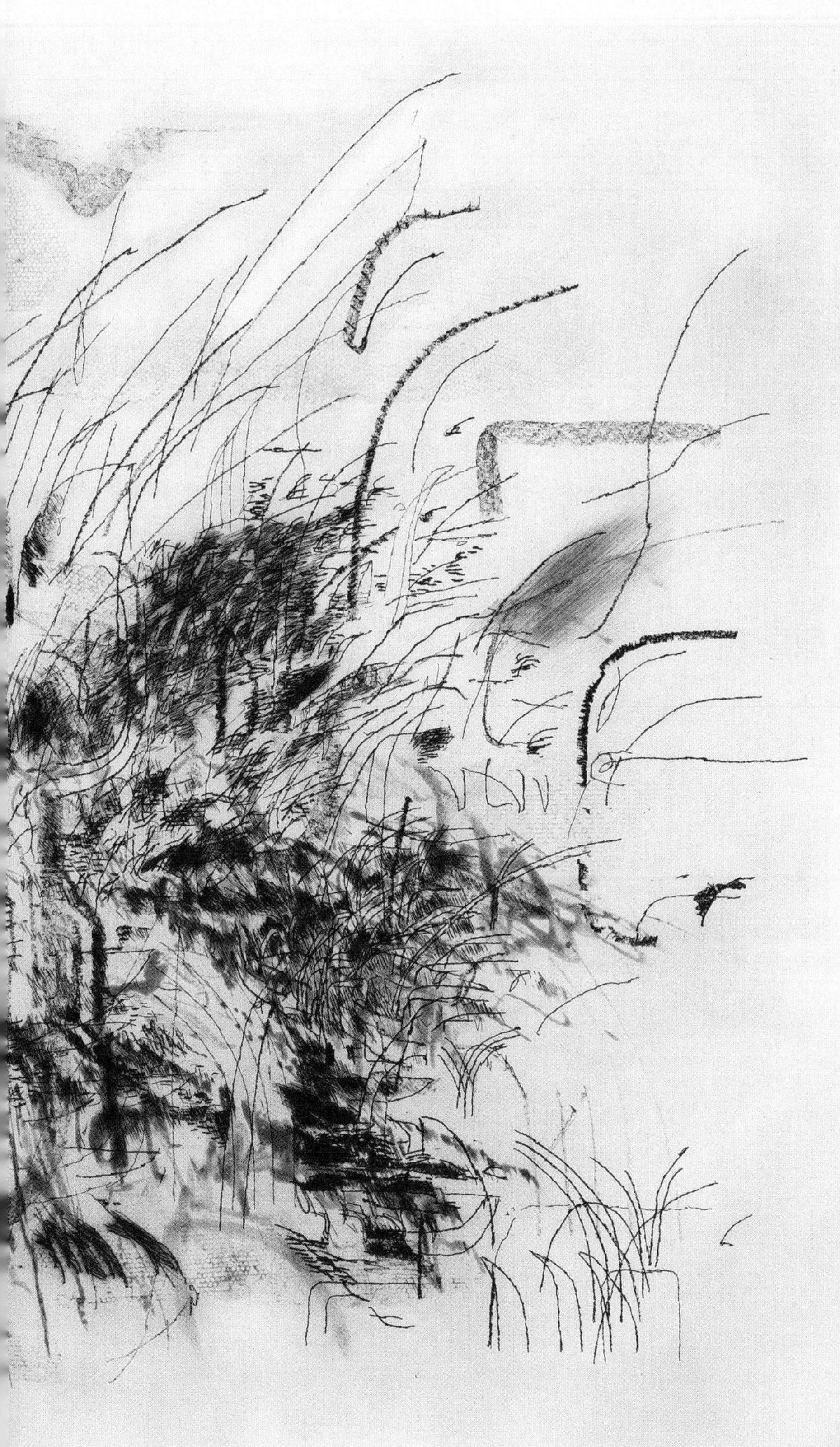

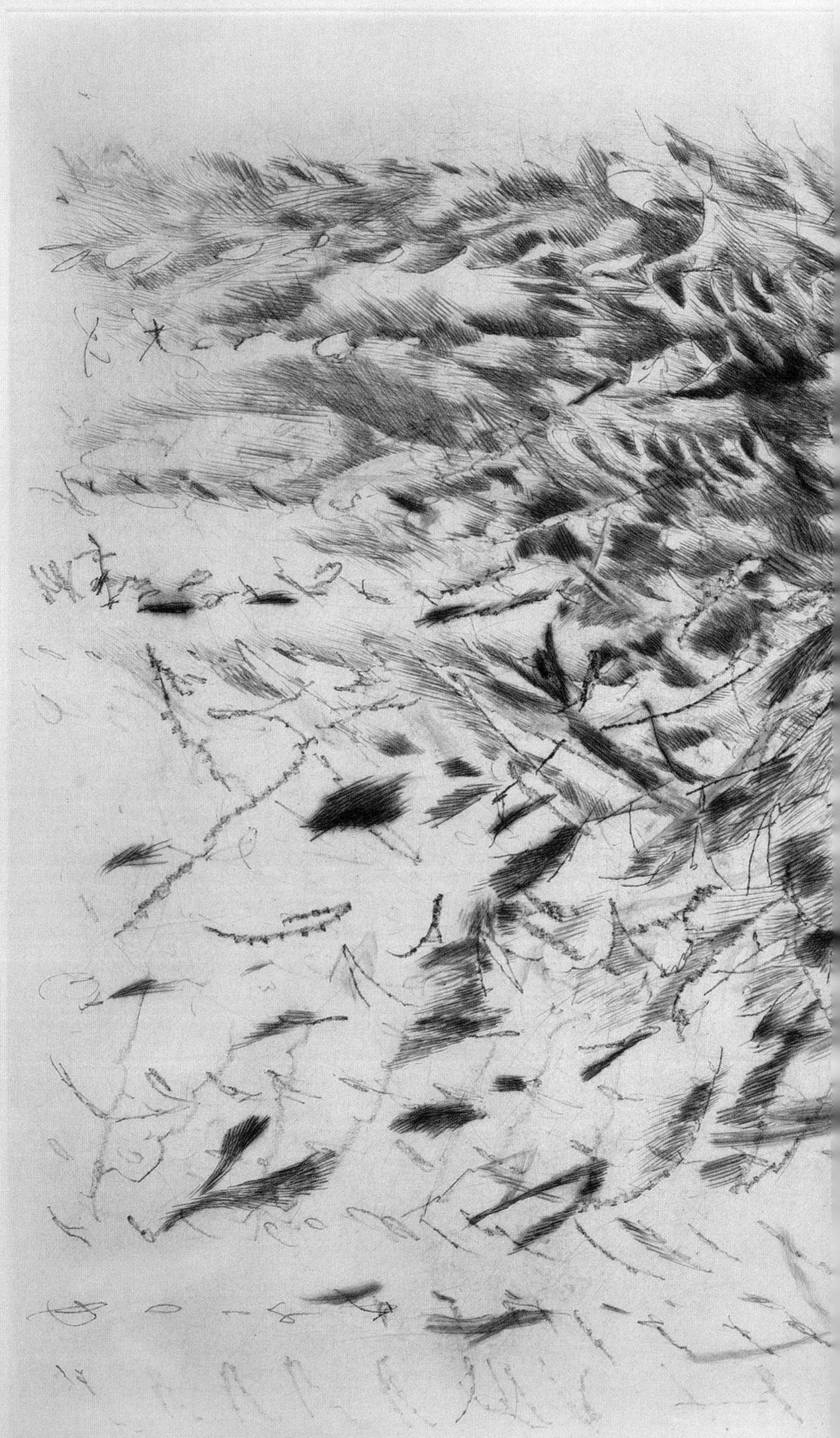

III/VI

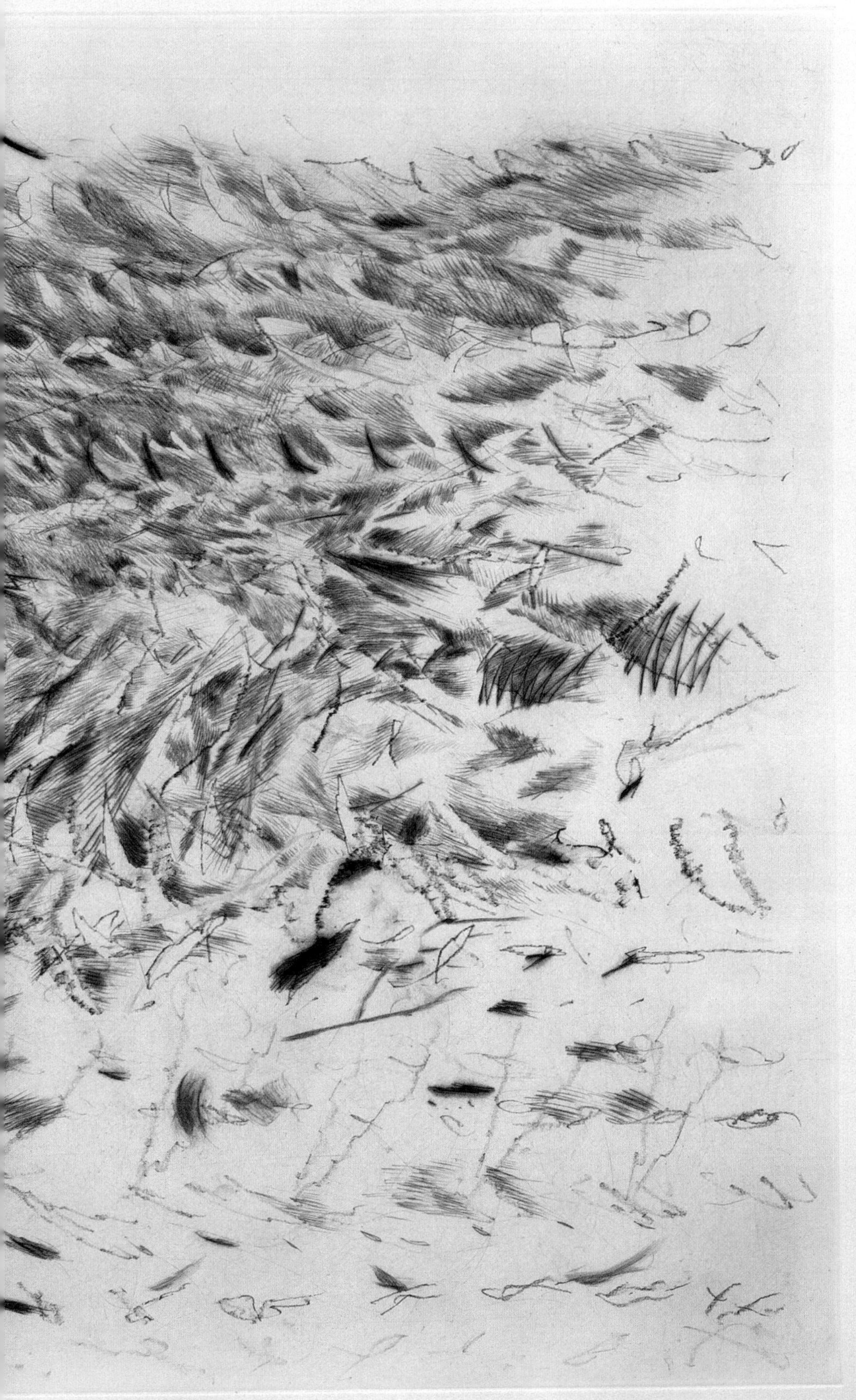
Mel Peter 2013

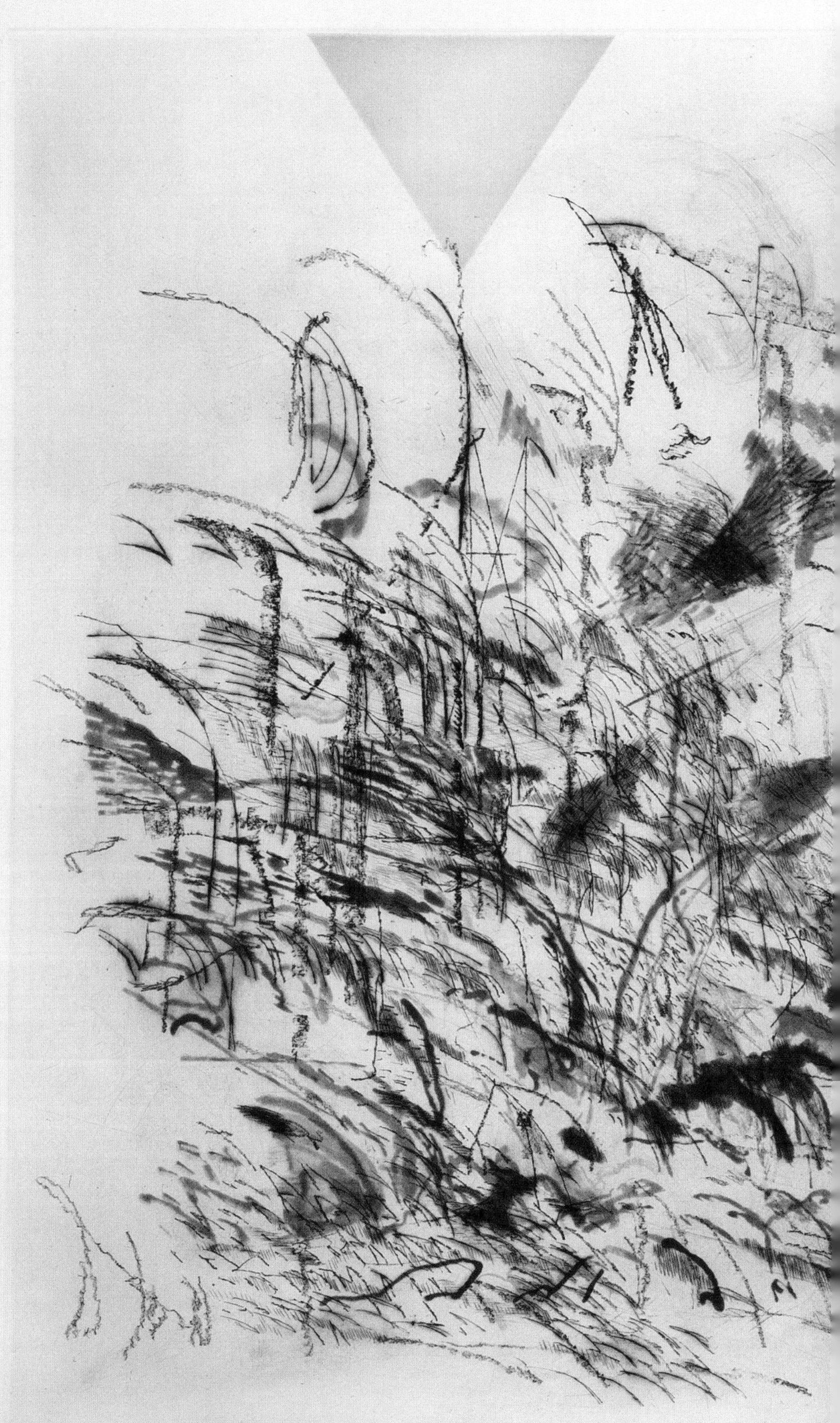

III/VI

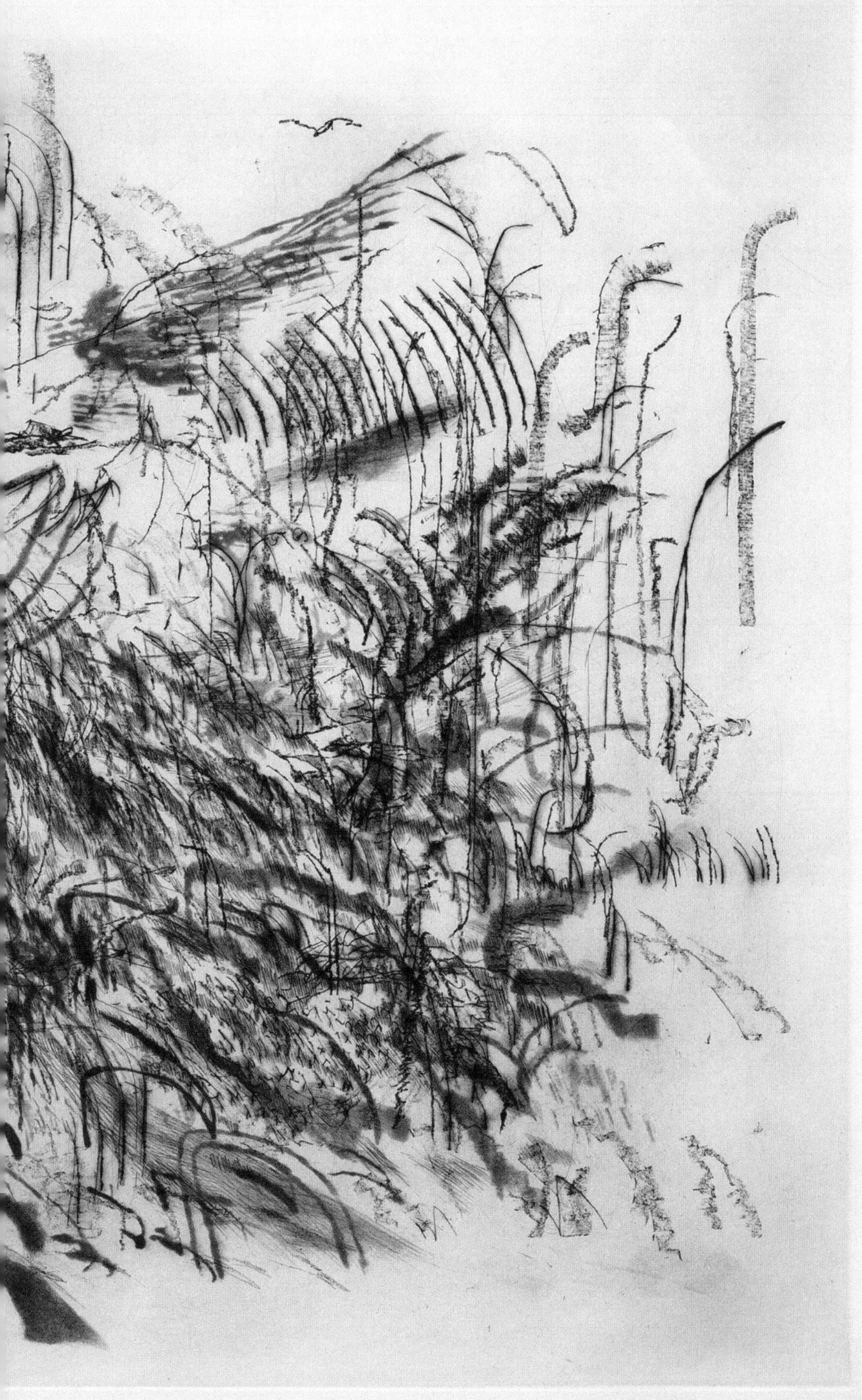

Mehretu   2013

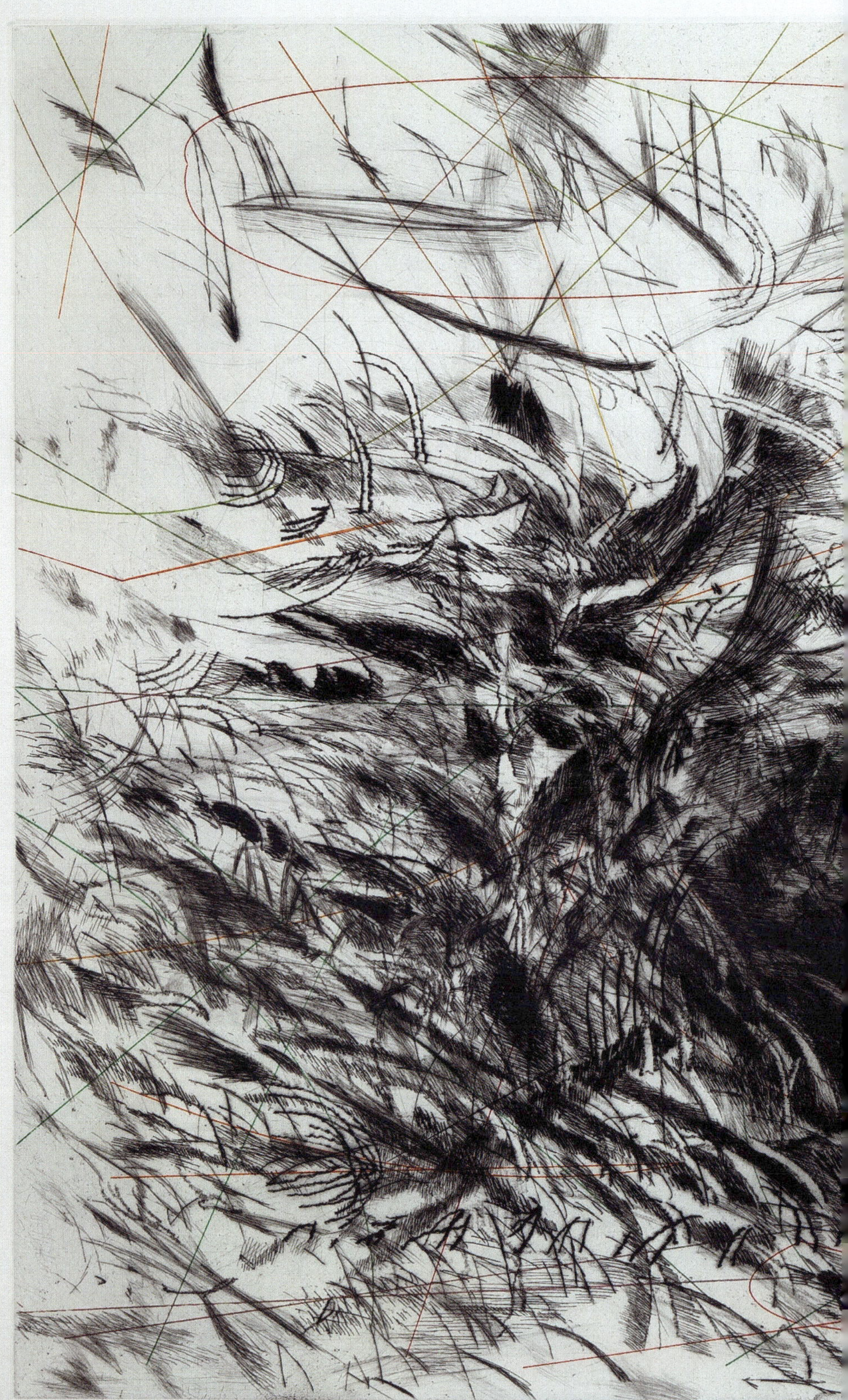

III/VI

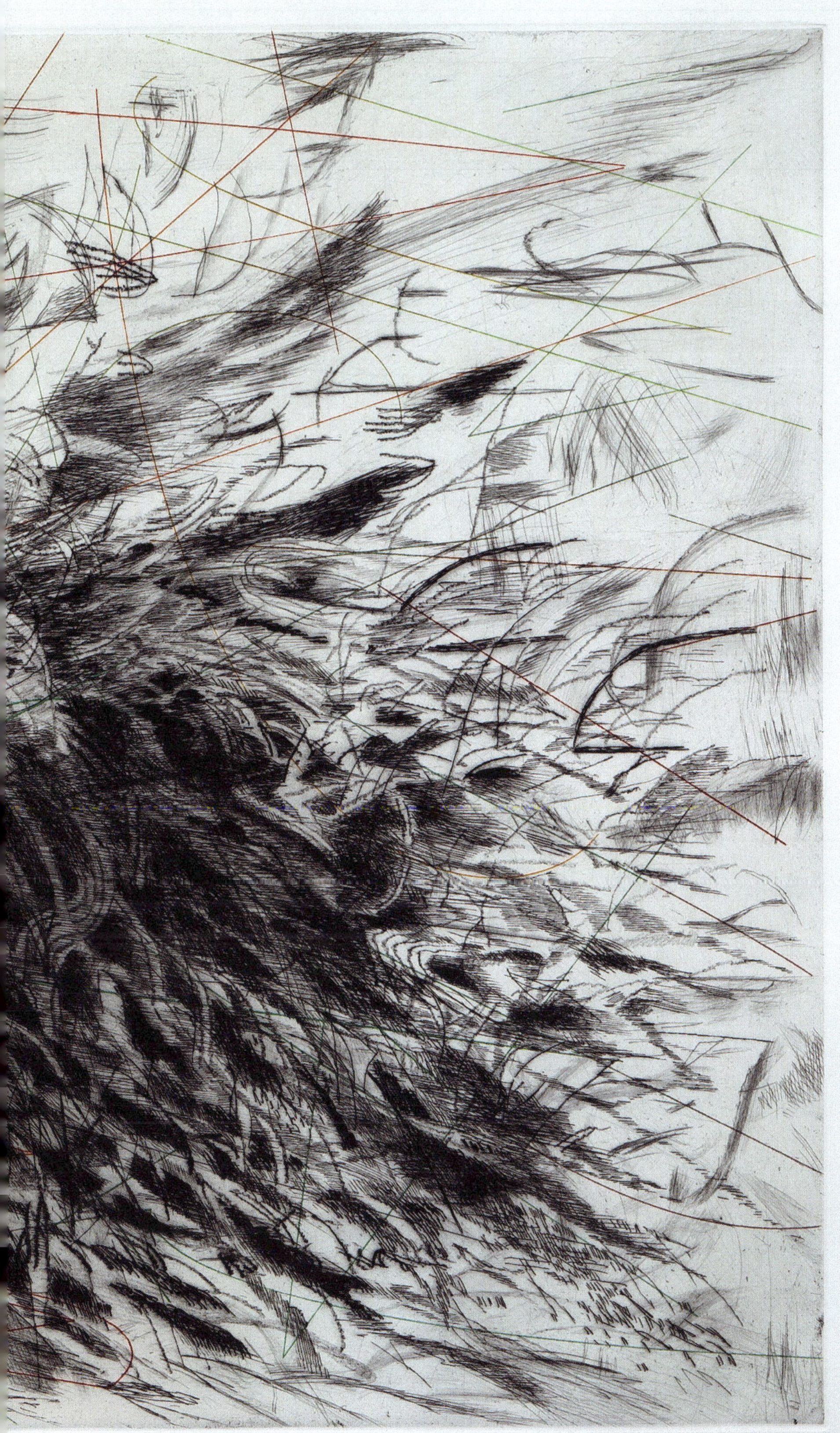

Mehret 2013

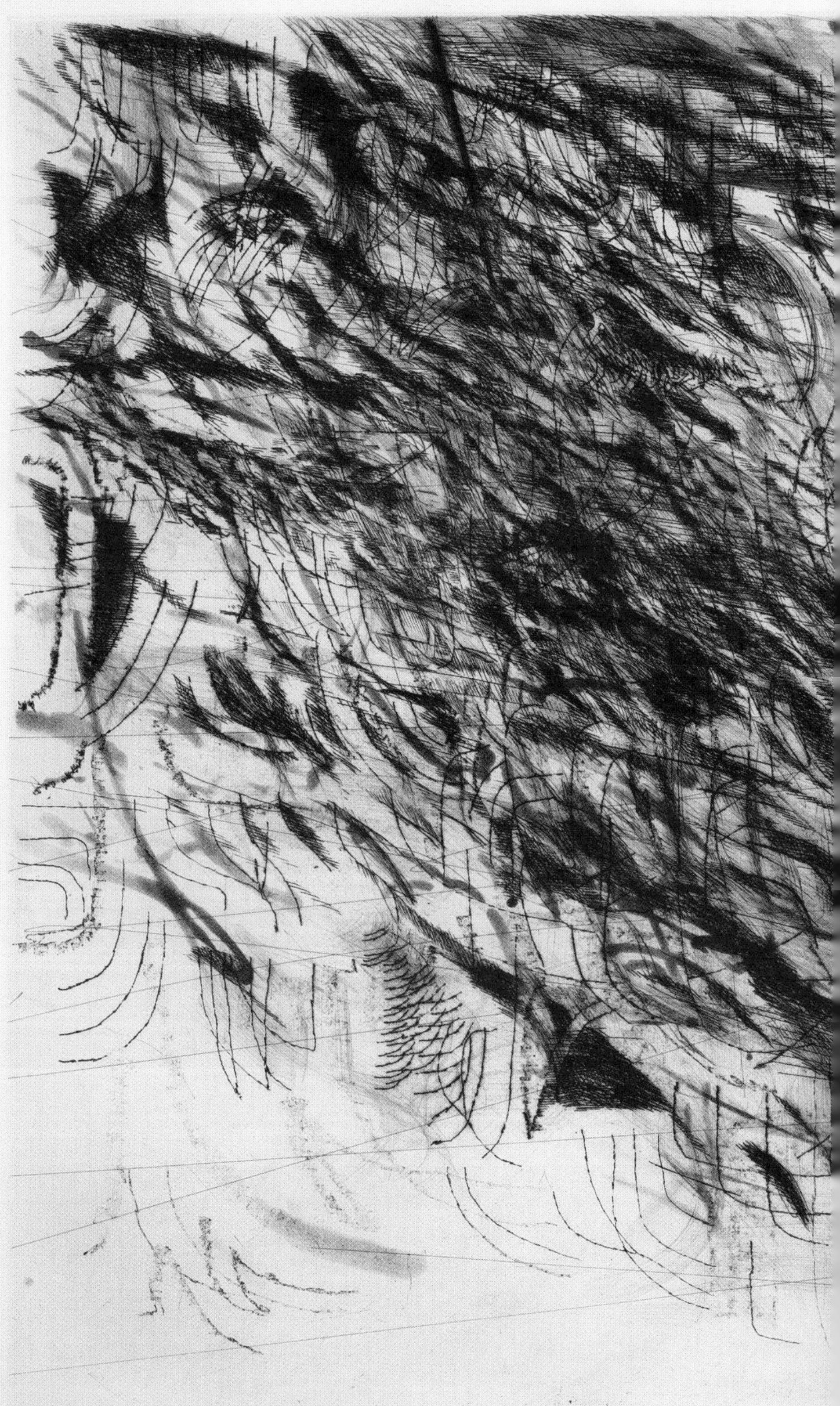

III/VI

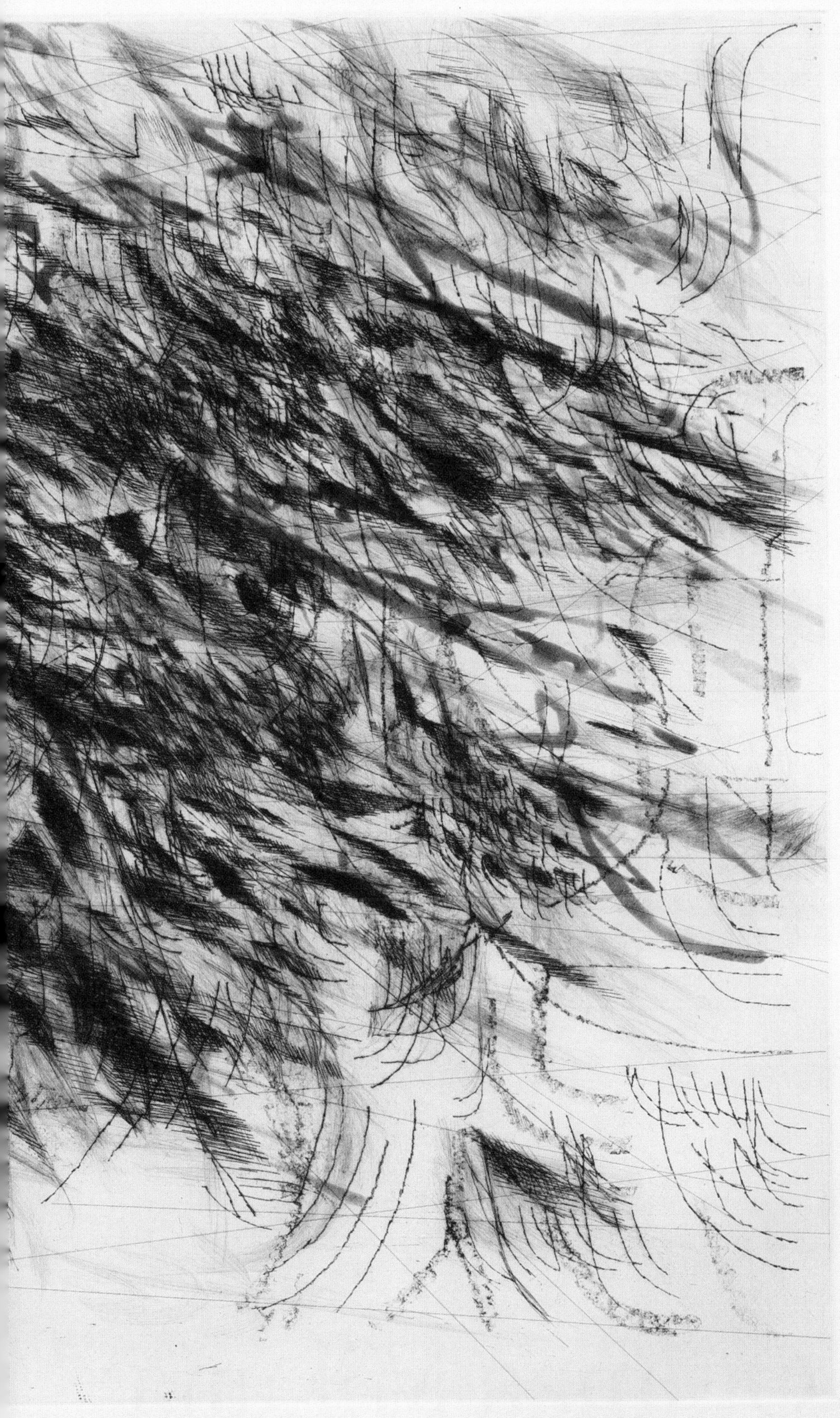
2013

Ogimaa Mikana Community Newsletter

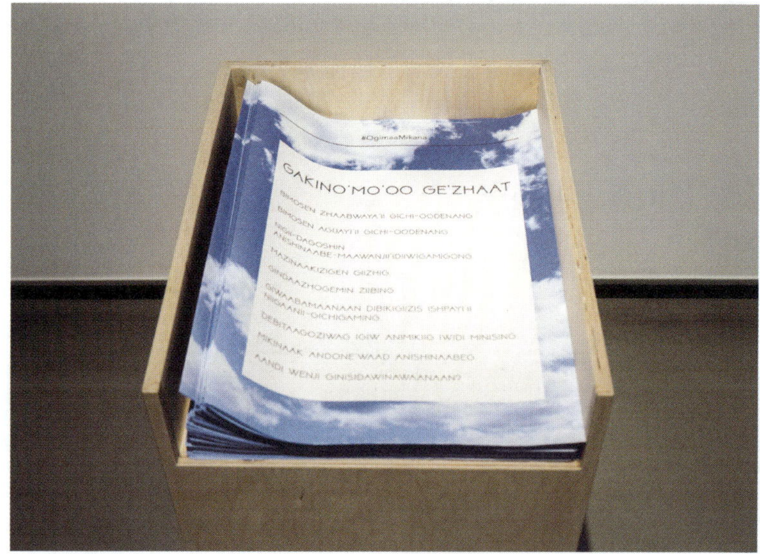

Ogimaa Mikana Community Newsletter,
2018. Printed broadsheet, wood plinth.

Ogimaa Mikana

In the Anishnaabe Turtle Song, our ancestor the great turtle, flies over the earth searching for the Anishinaabeg.

This work, Ogimaa Mikana Community Newsletter, seeks to help mikinaak find us.

For the Anishinaabe, and Indigenous peoples generally, state surveillance is a reality. Whether it's the RCMP monitoring Idle No More activists, federal bureaucrats hacking First Nation leaders social media accounts, police carding, or First Nations daily reporting requirements to the department of Indian Affairs. Simultaneously, this attention also serves to obfuscate and contain. Indigenous peoples have been kept in isolated reserve lands–by law–with little infrastructure to communicate beyond local boundaries. Indeed, so opaque are reserves they don't exist on maps (try to find GPS directions to an address on your nearest First Nation).

Ogimaa Mikana is an artist collective founded by Susan Blight (Anishinaabe, Couchiching) and Hayden King (Anishinaabe, Gchi'mnissing) in January 2013. Through public art, site-specific intervention and social practice, we assert Anishinaabe self-determination on the land and in the public sphere.

Given this restriction on movement, it shouldn't be a surprise that simply walking great distances is a political act. Josephine Mandamin leads walks around the Great Lakes in an effort to protect the water; Theland Kicknosoway and Caribou Legs both walked and ran vast swaths of the country to raise awareness for missing and murdered Indigenous women and girls; the Nishiyuu Walkers travelled from the coast of James Bay to Ottawa to promote unity. At any given time in Canada you can find an Anishinaabe person walking for a cause. While these actions have a political objective, they are also about walking the land, coming to know it, and in some ways, mapping it, just as our ancestors did.

Previous page: installation view. Ogimaa Mikana, *Ogimaa Mikana Community Newsletter*, 2018. Courtesy of Onsite Gallery. Photography by Yuula Benivolski.

In Ogimaa Mikana's contribution to *Diagrams of Power*, we draw on this legacy of walking. We offer new directions to make ourselves recognizable to our relations. This unrepentant mobility and celebration defies the historic restrictions on Indigenous movement while also subverting contemporary state surveillance. We walked, and will continue to walk, an honouring into the urban landscape of Toronto, speaking to each other as Anishinaabeg but also the land.

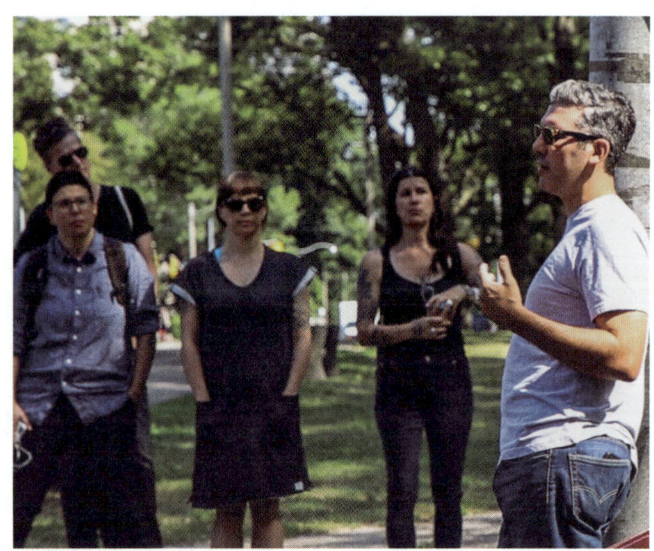

Ogimaa Mikana with assistance from Eliana Macdonald and Margaret Pearce

Capturing our routes digitally, we shared that data with Margaret Pearce and Eliana MacDonald to create counter-maps of the city. Combined with a set of directions, articulated in Anishinaabemowin, the piece is presented in the form of a community newsletter, free for viewers to take.

GAKINO'MO'OO GE'ZHAAT

BIMOSEN ZHAABWAYA'II GICHI-OODENANG.

BIMOSEN AGIJAYI'II GICHI-OODENANG.

NIGII-DAGOSHIN
ANISHINAABE-MAAWANJII'IDIIWIGAMIGONG.

MAZINAAKIZIGEN GIIZHIG.

GINDAAZHOGEMIN ZIIBING.

GIWAABAMAANAAN DIBIKIGIIZIS ISHPAYI'II
NIIGAANII-GICHIGAMING.

DEBITAAGOZIWAG IGIW ANIMIKIIG IWIDI MINISING.

MIKINAAK ANDONE'WAAD ANISHINAABEG.

AANDI WENJI GINISIDAWINAWAANAAN?

#OgimaaMikana

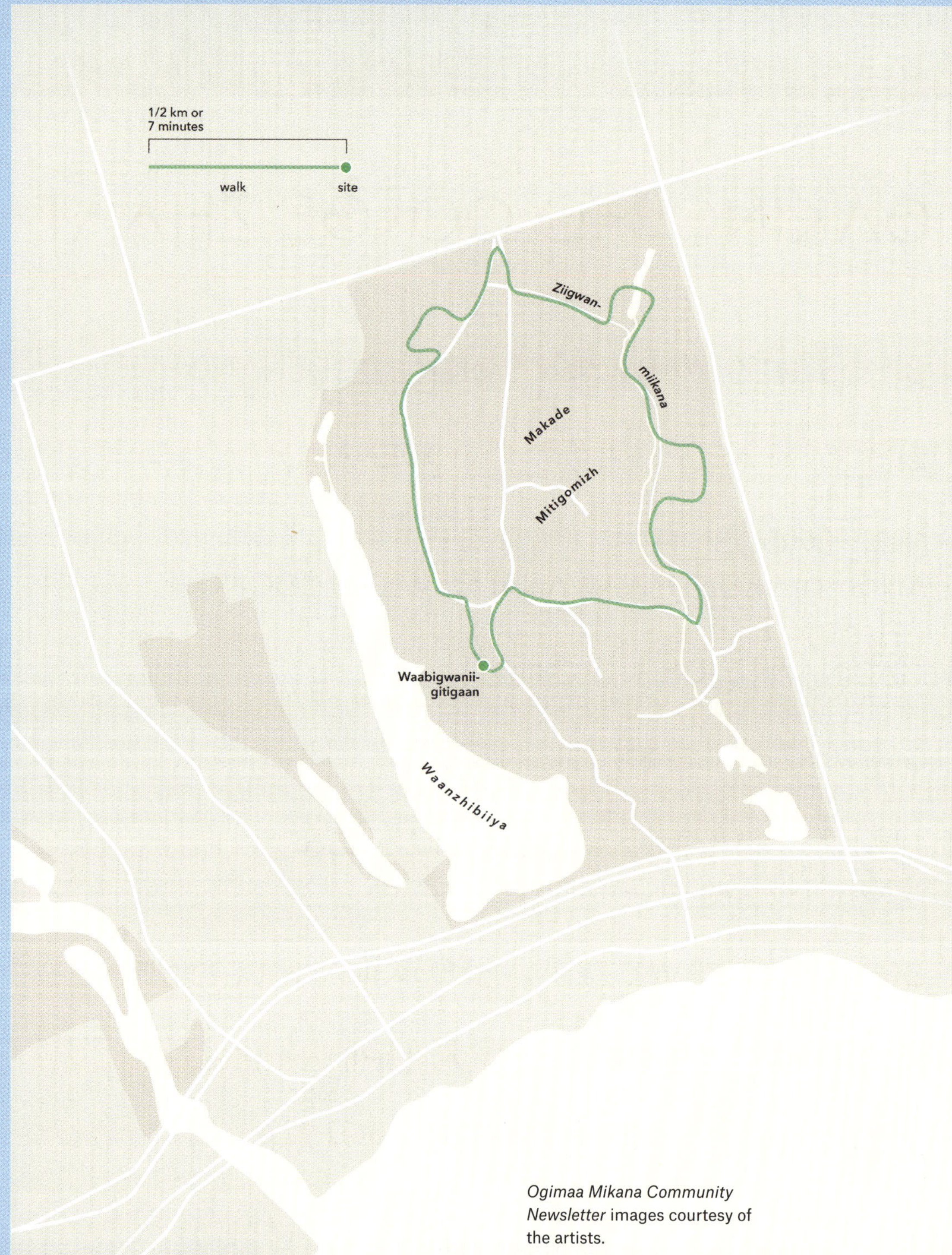

Ogimaa Mikana Community Newsletter images courtesy of the artists.

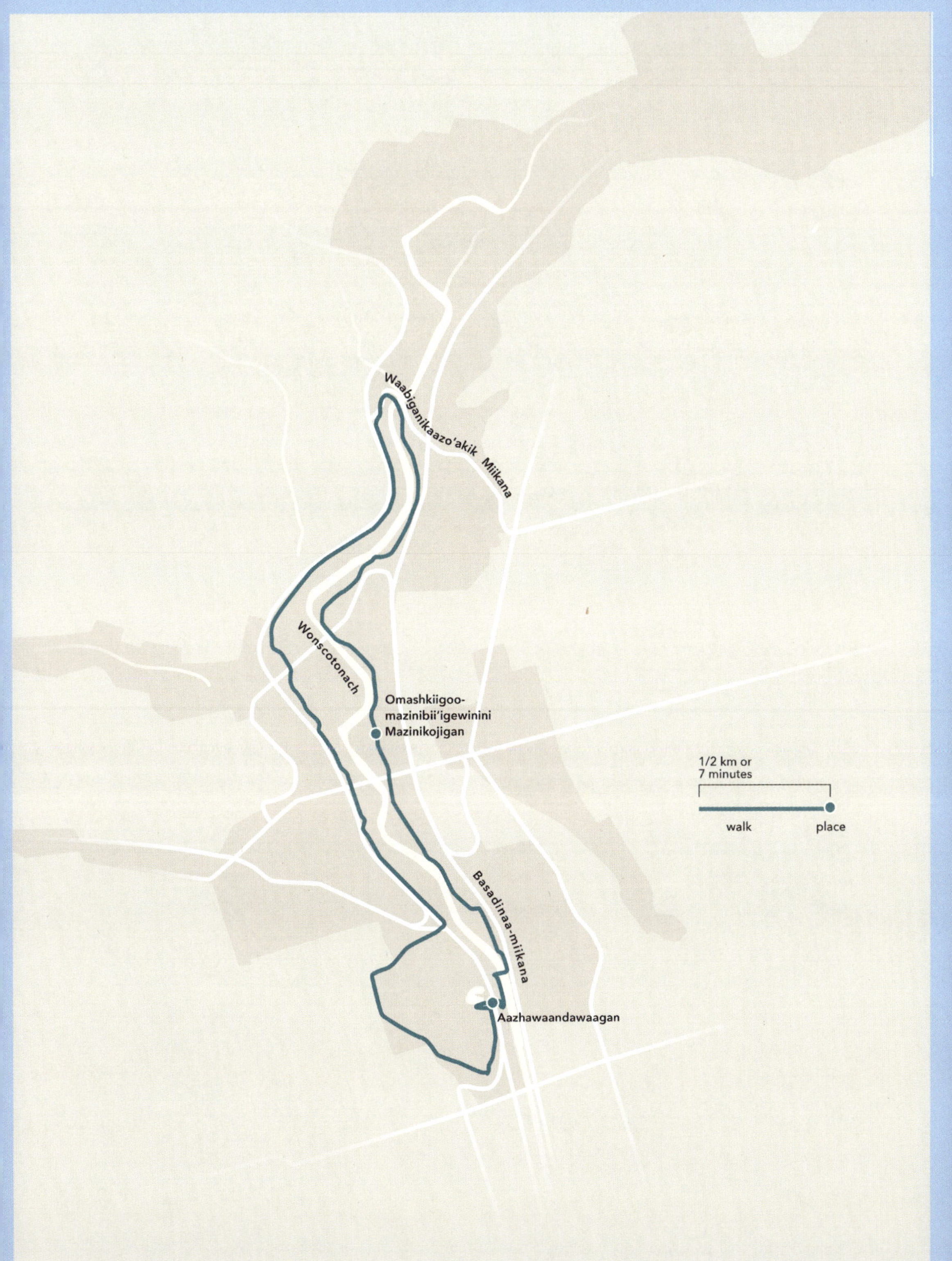
Waabiganikaazo'akik Miikana
Wonscotonach
Omashkiigoo-
mazinibii'igewinini
Mazinikojigan
Basadinaa-miikana
Aazhawaandawaagan
1/2 km or
7 minutes
walk
place

#OgimaaMikana

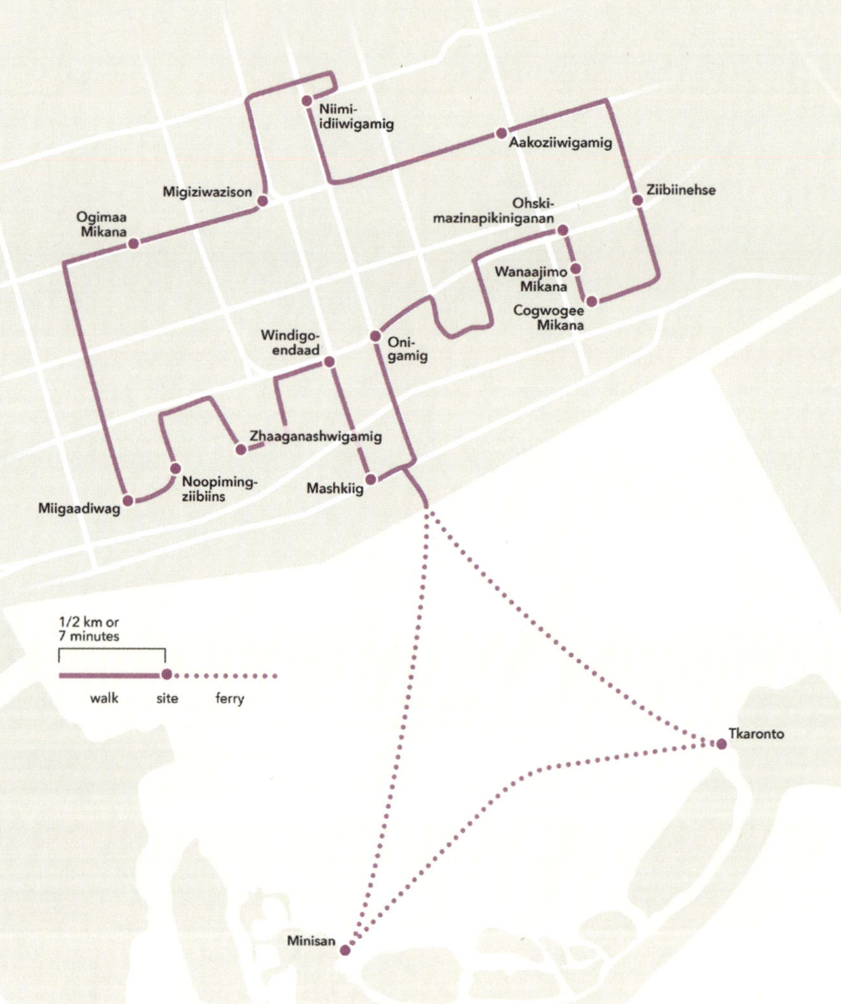

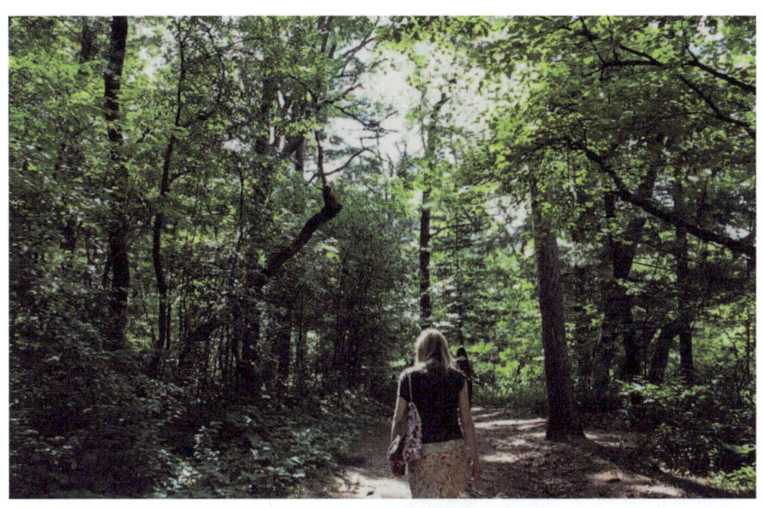

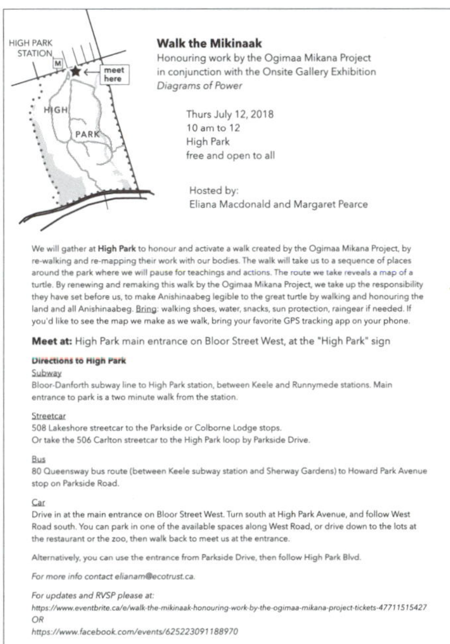

Walk the Mikinaak
Honouring work by the Ogimaa Mikana Project
in conjunction with the Onsite Gallery Exhibition
Diagrams of Power

Thurs July 12, 2018
10 am to 12
High Park
free and open to all

Hosted by:
Eliana Macdonald and Margaret Pearce

We will gather at **High Park** to honour and activate a walk created by the Ogimaa Mikana Project, by re-walking and re-mapping their work with our bodies. The walk will take us to a sequence of places around the park where we will pause for teachings and actions. The route we take reveals a map of a turtle. By renewing and remaking this walk by the Ogimaa Mikana Project, we take up the responsibility they have set before us, to make Anishinaabeg legible to the great turtle by walking and honouring the land and all Anishinaabeg. Bring: walking shoes, water, snacks, sun protection, raingear if needed. If you'd like to see the map we make as we walk, bring your favorite GPS tracking app on your phone.

Meet at: High Park main entrance on Bloor Street West, at the "High Park" sign

Directions to High Park
Subway
Bloor-Danforth subway line to High Park station, between Keele and Runnymede stations. Main entrance to park is a two minute walk from the station.

Streetcar
508 Lakeshore streetcar to the Parkside or Colborne Lodge stops.
Or take the 506 Carlton streetcar to the High Park loop by Parkside Drive.

Bus
80 Queensway bus route (between Keele subway station and Sherway Gardens) to Howard Park Avenue stop on Parkside Road.

Car
Drive in at the main entrance on Bloor Street West. Turn south at High Park Avenue, and follow West Road south. You can park in one of the available spaces along West Road, or drive down to the lots at the restaurant or the zoo, then walk back to meet us at the entrance.

Alternatively, you can use the entrance from Parkside Drive, then follow High Park Blvd.

For more info contact elianam@ecotrust.ca.

For updates and RVSP please at:
https://www.eventbrite.ca/e/walk-the-mikinaak-honouring-work-by-the-ogimaa-mikana-project-tickets-47711515427
OR
https://www.facebook.com/events/625223091188970

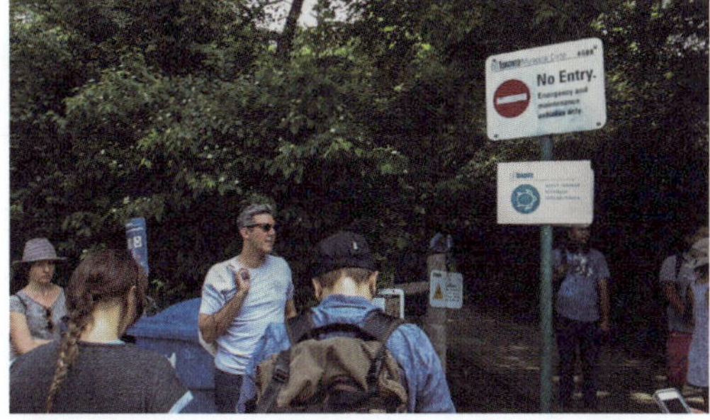

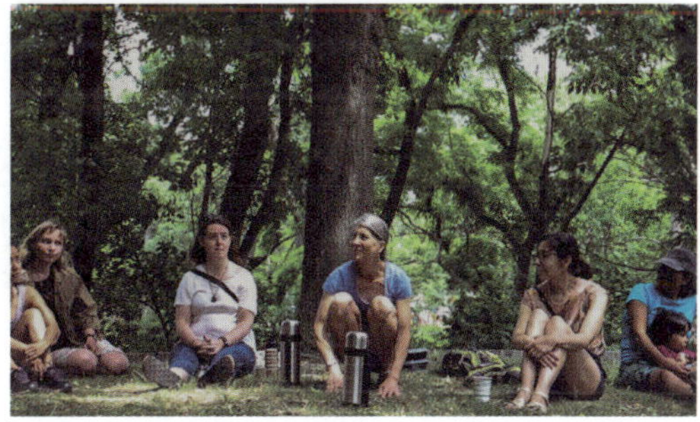

On Thursday July 12, 2018, Eliana Macdonald and Margaret Pearce hosted the Walk the Mikinaak event at High Park in Toronto. Participants walked one of the paths shown in the Ogimaa Mikana Community Newsletter.

An Atlas
of Radical
Cartography
(Revisited)

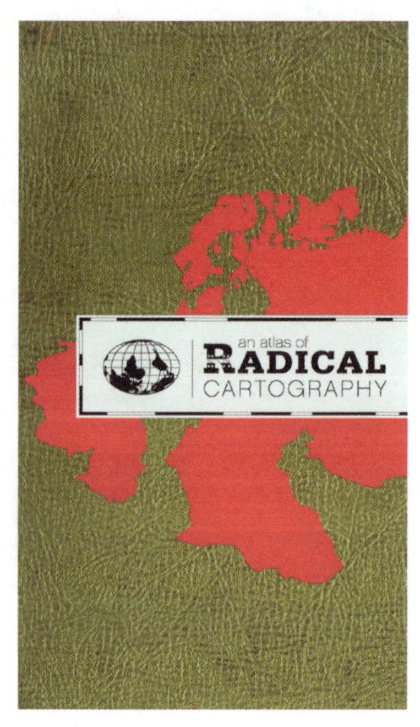

Alexis Bhagat and
Lize Mogel

This Atlas is *an* atlas and *not* the atlas. Rather, it is one of many possible atlases, given the abundance of artists, architects, and others using maps and mapping in their work. While all maps have an inherent politics that often lies hidden beneath an "objective" surface, the contributions to *An Atlas of Radical Cartography* wear their politics on their sleeve. This publication includes ten pairs of politically engaged maps and texts from within the growing movement of cultural producers who have parallel or integrated activist practices.

The simplest of radical cartographies, the "upside-down" world map [is] more than a neat trick, this picture of the world has a historical basis in medieval world maps that were sometimes oriented with East or South at top. The modern north-oriented map continually reproduces the idea of the global North and the global South. The "inverted" map calls into question our ingrained acceptance of this particular "global order." The maps and texts in [*An Atlas of Radical Cartography*] also serve this purpose—to unhinge our beliefs about the world, and to provoke new perceptions of the networks, lineages, associations and representations of places, people and power.

Such new understandings of the world are the prerequisites of change. We define radical

Alexis Bhagat and Lize Mogel, Introduction to *An Atlas of Radical Cartography* (*Journal of Aesthetics and Protest Press*, 2007)

cartography as the practice of mapmaking that subverts conventional notions in order to actively promote social change. The object of critique in *An Atlas of Radical Cartography* is not cartography per se (as is generally meant by the overlapping term *critical cartography*), but rather social relations. Our criteria for selecting these ten maps emphasized radical inquiry and activist engagement.

With that in mind, we intend for *An Atlas of Radical Cartography* to act as a primer on issues which the maps and essays address: identity, land-use, imprisonment, energy, migration.

Radical cartographies are, as Trevor Paglen writes, "a departure point or a tool that can aid in analysis but do not speak for themselves." [They] are part of a fluid movement whose tactics range from art-making to direct action to policy-making. This slow, cumulative, and constant work across many scales of action is what creates social change.

Previous page: Cover. *An Atlas of Radical Cartography*. Courtesy of Lize Mogel and Alexis Bhagat.

Lize

This project began when you invited me to guest edit a special issue of the journal *Perspectives on Anarchist Theory*, about critical cartography and activist maps.

Lex

I was a new member of the editorial board. I had started collecting maps that were being produced at and for anti-capitalist and anti-globalization convergences like "De qué va realmente el Fórum?"[1] by XNET and "Critical Cartography of the Straits of Gibraltar"[2] by Hackitectura, and "A People's Guide to the RNC"[3].

Lize

The trajectory of mapping, politics, and aesthetics that led to our project also included maps coming out of the art and design worlds, like Marc Lombardi and Bureau D'Étude's diagrams of global-political-power connections, cartographers like Philippe Rekacewicz, artists using maps including kanarinka and Ashley Hunt, community cartography projects like the Detroit Geographic Expedition and Institution, and critical cartographers like Denis Wood.

Lex

We wanted to bring together some of these maps that we loved, which were circulating in very different contexts. We wanted to ask writers to respond directly to them, to generate a foundation of critical writing about these kinds of maps.

Lize

Right from the start, we decided that the maps should be more than small illustrations for essays. Especially for me, as an artist who makes maps, it was important that the maps themselves had an equal say, an equal weight.

Lex

We decided to pair one map with one essay. Our open call asked for writers, artists and mappers to submit existing works or ideas, we invited people we knew were doing interesting work into the project, and then we put them together.

Lize

In 2005-2007, digital mapping wasn't very accessible, it mostly existed in the form of GIS applications. Smartphones weren't a thing like they are now. And maps weren't yet fully embedded in our daily, now digital lives.

Lex

Which is why the approaches of artists and designers were so interesting at the time, and much less standardized than you see today.

Lize

After about a year of working on the project, our ambitions outstripped what *Perspectives* could offer in terms of publication format. So we decided to do it independently.

Lex

So we turned it into a book. Our friends at *The Journal of Aesthetics & Protest* said they would take it on. They had just

1 https://xnet-x.net/en/whats-the-forum-really-about/
2 http://www.antiatlas.net/hackitectura-critical-cartography-of-gibraltar-en/
3 http://www.jenniferhayashida.info/the-peoples-guide-to-the-rnc/

started an imprint, and we were the first book that they published.

Lize

It's good that we didn't know at the beginning that it would be so difficult! It was a huge amount of work over more than two years. We were a scrappy, DIY project, self-published. And all of it created by writers, artists, map-makers, designers, and publishers who were also activists.

From the start, we wanted to reach this tripartite visual/spatial/political

Lex

We also decided to make a traveling exhibition of the maps in the book, as very large prints. This was partly to get these kinds of maps out there more broadly in the world, but also to keep interest in the book going. Because it was self-published, we personally took on all of the financial risk, and needed to make sure that we at least covered our printing costs. The exhibition traveled constantly for three years to 15 or so venues, from grassroots/collective media spaces to museums. And we're happy that it's still out there, in the context of *Diagrams of Power*.

Lize

The exhibition had as its base the 10 maps from the book, and we would include maps from local and other artists in each show. This sometimes included video and audio projects in addition to printed maps. This also became a discursive project—we held counter-mapping workshops, and did many, many talks, at least 50 in 5 years. All of this helped make the *Atlas* a key part of an ongoing conversation about mapping and activism that has only multiplied since then.

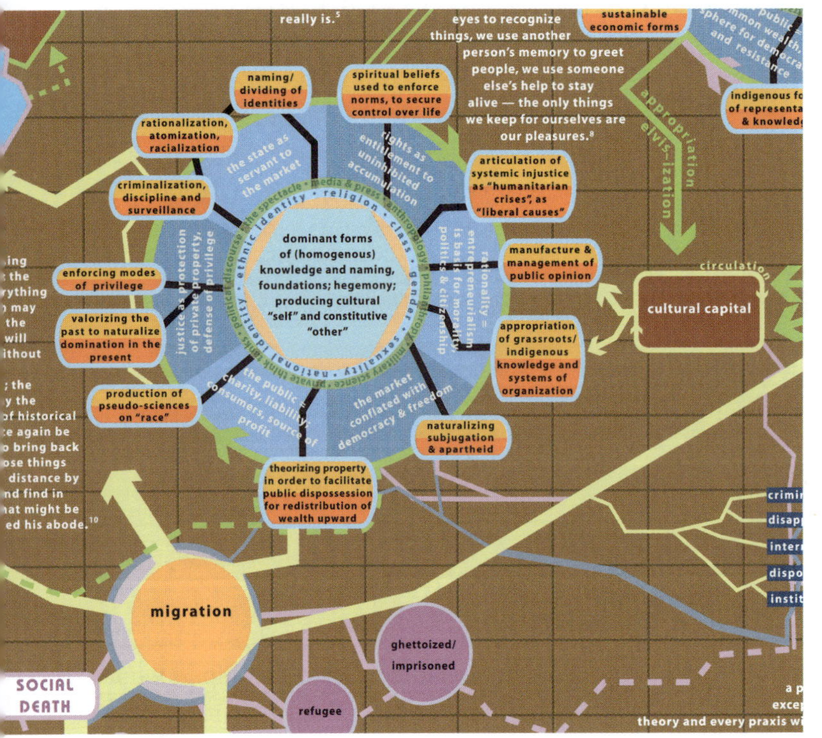

audience: artists and designers; geographers, planners, and architects; and activists who work on social justice issues. And we did just that—the book circulated and was extremely influential in this cross-disciplinary way.

(this page) Ashley Hunt, A World Map: in Which We See..., 2005; (facing page) Jane Tsong, Los Angeles River Ecology, 2007; (next page) An Architektur, Geography of the Fürth Departure Center, 2004.

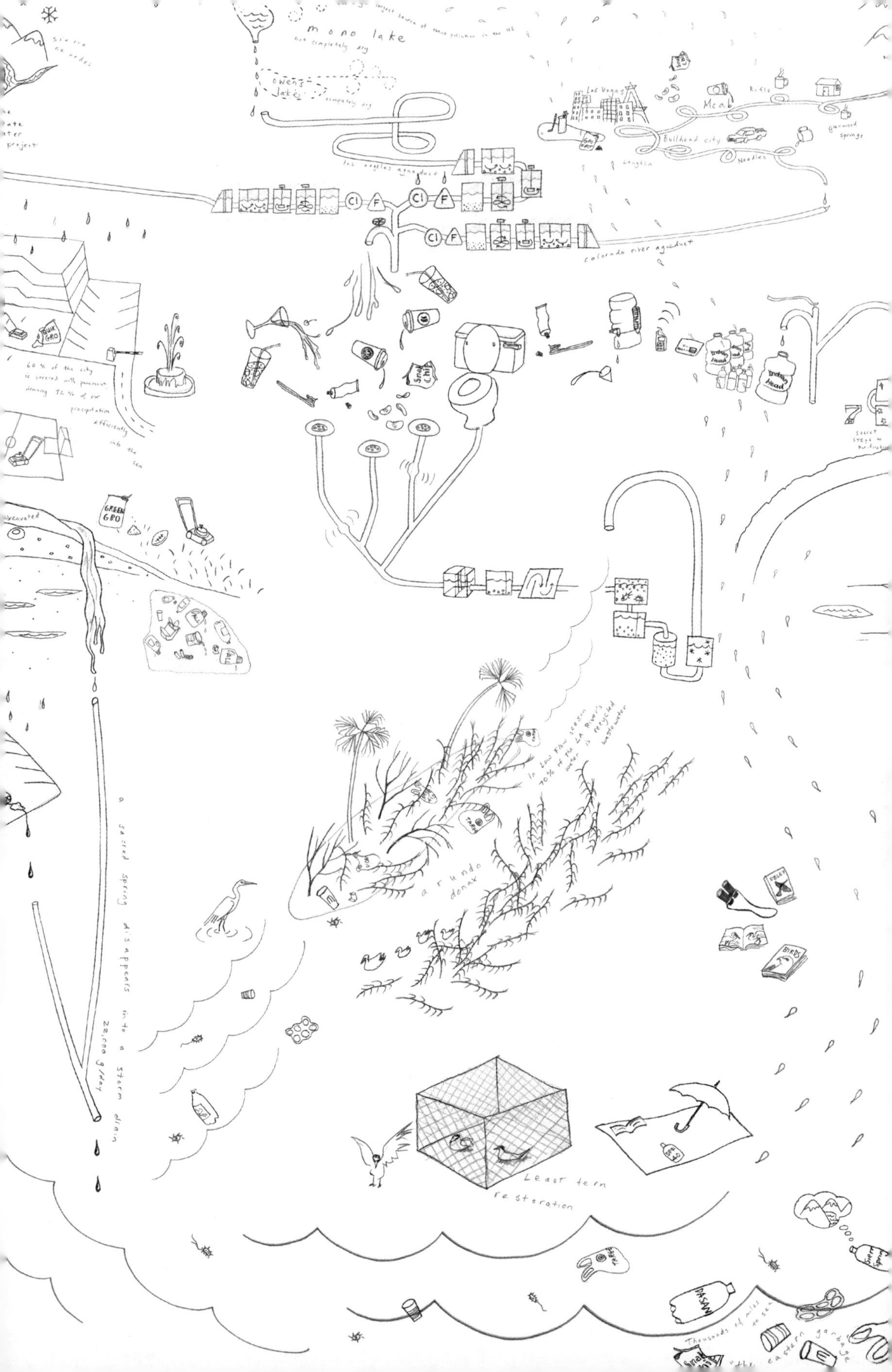

sierra nevada
the state water project
mono lake
not completely dry
owens lake
completely dry
los angeles aqueduct
Cl F
Cl F
Cl F
colorado river aqueduct
Las Vegas
Laughlin
Bullhead city
Needles
Mead
Moab
Rifle
Glenwood springs
QUIK GRO
60% of the city is covered with pavement draining 72% of our precipitation efficiently into the sea
GREEN GRO
excavated
a sacred spring disappears into a storm drain
22,000 g/day
arundo donax
In Low Flow season 70% of the LA River's water is recycled wastewater
secret steps to purification
Least tern restoration
Thousands of miles to sea
eastern garbage

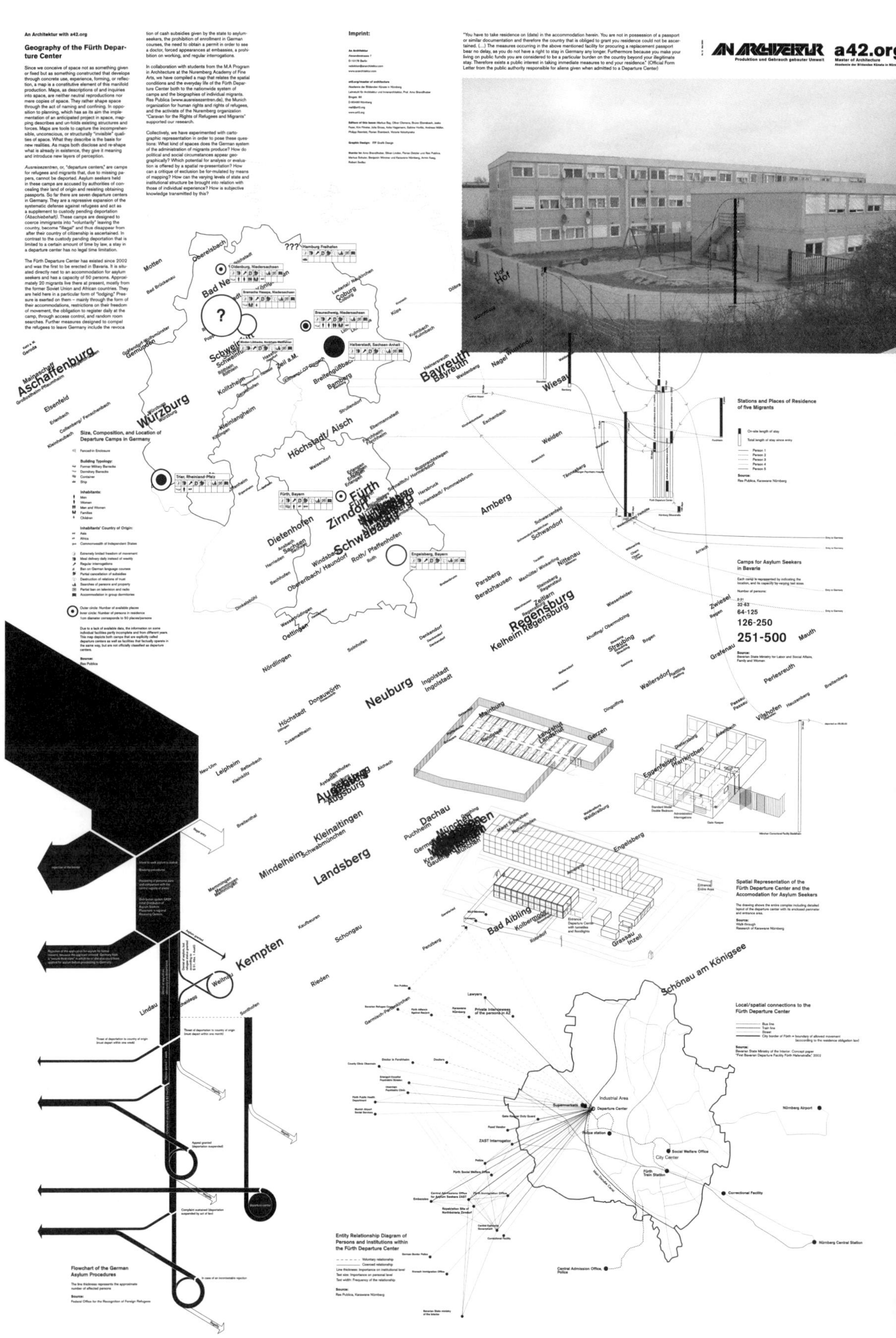

Geography of the Fürth Departure Center

Since we conceive of space not as something given or fixed but as something constructed that develops through concrete use, experience, forming, or reflection, a map is a constitutive element of this manifold production. Maps, as descriptions of and inquiries into space, are neither neutral reproductions nor mere copies of space. They rather shape space through the act of naming and confining. In opposition to planning, which has as its aim the implementation of an anticipated project in space, mapping describes and un-folds existing structures and forces. Maps are tools to capture the incomprehensible, unconscious, or structurally "invisible" qualities of space. What they describe is the basis for new realities. As maps both disclose and re-shape what is already in existence, they give it meaning and introduce new layers of perception.

Ausreisezentren, or, "departure centers," are camps for refugees and migrants that, due to missing papers, cannot be deported. Asylum seekers held in these camps are accused by authorities of concealing their land of origin and resisting obtaining passports. So far there are seven departure centers in Germany. They are a repressive expansion of the systematic defense against refugees and act as a supplement to custody pending deportation (Abschiebehaft). These camps are designed to coerce immigrants into "voluntarily" leaving the country, become "illegal" and thus disappear from after their country of citizenship is ascertained. In contrast to the custody pending deportation that is limited to a certain amount of time by law, a stay in a departure center has no legal time limitation.

The Fürth Departure Center has existed since 2002 and was the first to be erected in Bavaria. It is situated directly next to an accommodation for asylum seekers and has a capacity of 50 persons. Approximately 20 migrants live there at present, mostly from the former Soviet Union and African countries. They are held here in a particular form of "lodging." Pressure is exerted on them – mainly through the form of their accommodations, restrictions on their freedom of movement, the obligation to register daily at the camp, through access control, and random room searches. Further measures designed to compel the refugees to leave Germany include the revoca tion of cash subsidies given by the state to asylum-seekers, the prohibition of enrollment in German courses, the need to obtain a permit in order to see a doctor, forced appearances at embassies, a prohibition on working, and regular interrogations.

In collaboration with students from the M.A Program in Architecture at the Nuremberg Academy of Fine Arts, we have compiled a map that relates the spatial conditions and the everyday life of the Fürth Departure Center both to the nationwide system of camps and the biographies of individual migrants. Res Publica (www.ausreisezentren.de), the Munich organization for human rights and rights of refugees, and the activists of the Nuremberg organization "Caravan for the Rights of Refugees and Migrants" supported our research.

Collectively, we have experimented with cartographic representation in order to pose these questions: What kind of spaces does the German system of the administration of migrants produce? How do political and social circumstances appear geographically? Which potential for analysis or evaluation is offered by a spatial re-presentation? How can a critique of exclusion be for-mulated by means of mapping? How can the varying levels of state and institutional structure be brought into relation with those of individual experience? How is subjective knowledge transmitted by this?

Imprint:

An Architektur
Alexanderstrasse 7
D-10178 Berlin
Lehrstuhl für Architektur und Innenarchitektur, Prof. Arno Brandlhuber

Graphic Design: FP Grafik Design

Lex

Do you think that radical cartography is still a relevant word for this kind of mapping? We decided on using that phrase to define what we saw as a nascent movement.

Lize

I remember our discussion—critical, counter, activist cartography—what do we call it? "Critical cartography" was too firmly established within the realm of academic geography. We were worried that "counter-cartography" wouldn't be legible enough to some of our audience. Radical cartography was the one that stuck. With the knowledge that it was…

Lex

It was catchy! We wanted people to talk about the idea of radical mapping. In activist circles at the time, "radical" implied a concern with systemic change that tackled *root* causes. Etymologically, radical still means "roots", but its everyday meaning has changed. Now you are more likely to hear about "radical Islamists" than "radical environmentalists," and "radical feminist" is more likely to be a smear from a radio host than a self-identification. It's a word that has lost some of its power for activists. What's more useful now?

Lize

When I talk about my own work, I use the term "counter-cartography," and John Emerson's definition of it: "Producing maps that challenge the dominant, mainstream narrative of a site or history, often from an explicitly political or activist perspective, or from the point of view of historically marginalized communities."[4] Another definition, from geographers Leila Harris and Helen Hazen is closer to what we, in 2007, discussed as "radical": "…any effort that fundamentally questions the assumptions or biases of cartographic conventions, that challenges predominant power effects of mapping, or that engages in mapping in ways that upset power relations."[5]

Lex

That sounds good!

Lize

Whatever you want to call it, I'm so pleased that radical, counter, critical mapping continues on, and is more widely understood as a common tool to visualize and work against oppressive and exploitative systems, as well as visualizing and working towards transformative ones. When we started this project, many spatial practitioners—architects, geographers, planners, designers, technologists—didn't always think about how much power they had in representing and producing space and spatial relations. In the discussions around the *Atlas*, we were able to say, "you have a responsibility for the power relations embedded in the spaces you produce" and present some alternatives.

4 Emerson, John. "Cartographies." Social Design Notes, 15 Feb. 2009, backspace.com/notes/2009/02/cartographies.php.

5 Harris, Leila, and Hazen, Helen. 1. "Power of Maps: (Counter) Mapping for Conservation". *ACME: An International Journal for Critical Geographies* 4 (1), 99-130. https://www.acme-journal.org/index.php/acme/article/view/730

All maps from *An Atlas of Radical Cartography*, 2007, Courtesy of Lize Mogel and Alexis Bhagat.

(this page) Brooke Singer, *The U.S. Oil Fix*, 2006/2007; (facing) Installation View. *The Center for Urban Pedagogy (CUP), NYC Garbage Machine*, 2002. Courtesy of Onsite Gallery. Photography by Yuula Benivolski.

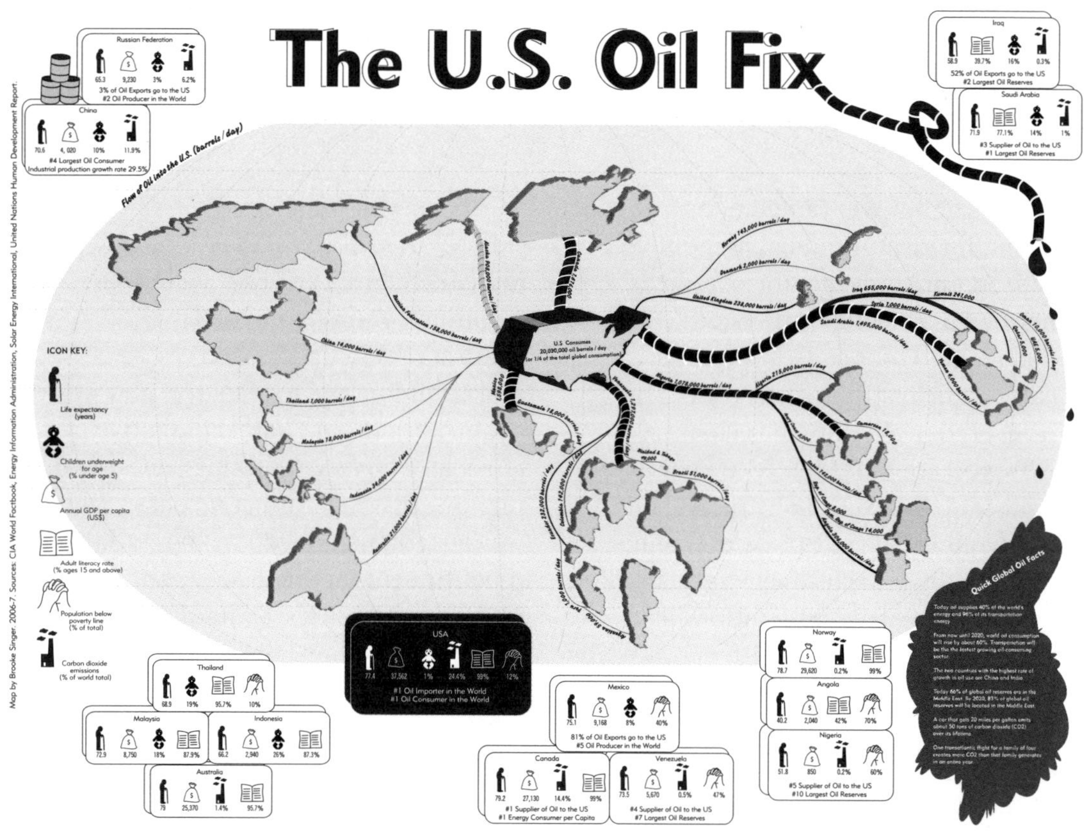

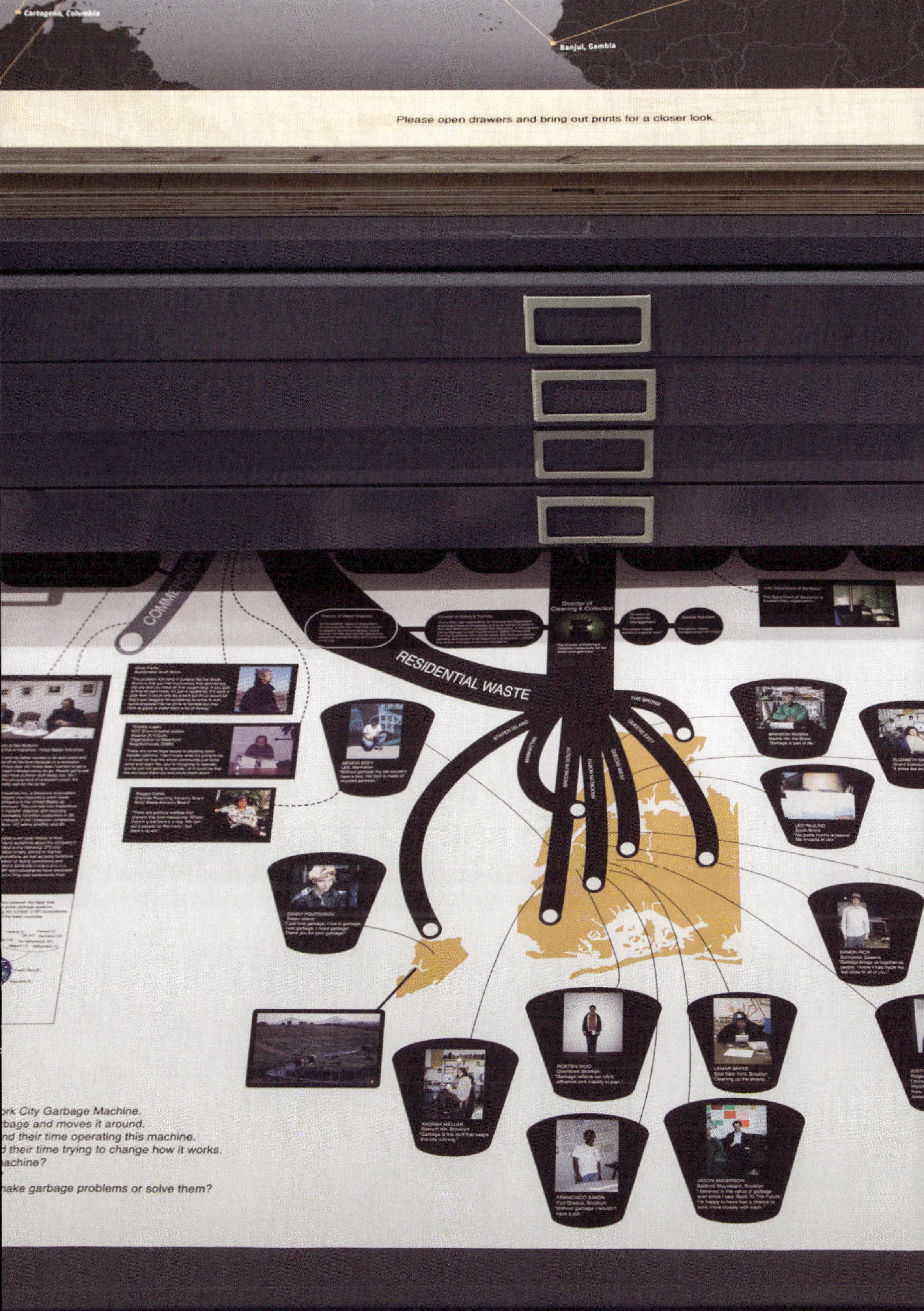

Cartagena, Columbia
Banjul, Gambia
Please open drawers and bring out prints for a closer look.
COMMERCIAL
RESIDENTIAL WASTE
Director of Cleaning & Collection
THE BRONX
STATEN ISLAND
MANHATTAN
QUEENS EAST
QUEENS WEST
BRANDON RIVERA
ELIZABETH
LEO PAULINO
DANNY POUTCHKOV
DAMON RICH
ROSTEN WOO
LEMAR WHITE
ANDREA MELLER
JUSTIN
FRANCISCO SIMON
JASON ANDERSON
ork City Garbage Machine.
rbage and moves it around.
nd their time operating this machine.
d their time trying to change how it works.
achine?
make garbage problems or solve them?

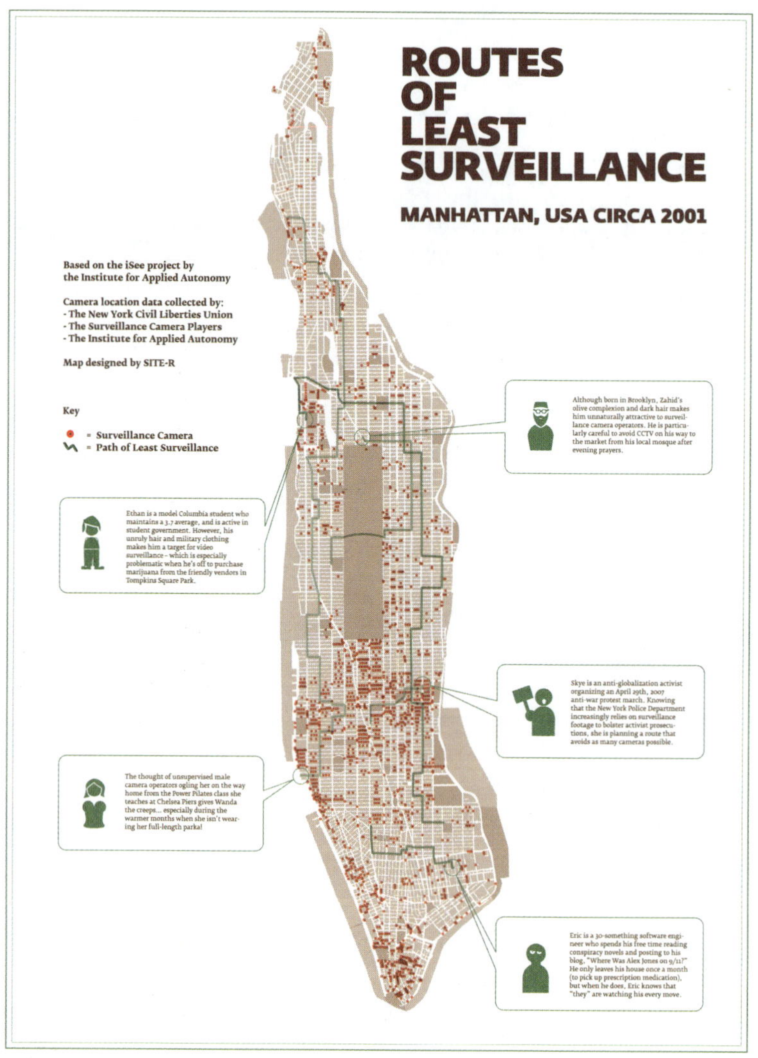

(this page) Institute for Applied Autonomy with Site-R, *Routes of Least Surveillance*, 2001/2007; (facing page, top) *Unnayan, Chetla Lock Gate, Marginal Land Settlement in Calcutta (now Kolkata)*, 1984; (facing page, bottom) Lize Mogel, *From South to North*, 2006.

An Atlas of Radical Cartography (Revisited)
Alexis Bhagat and Lize Mogel

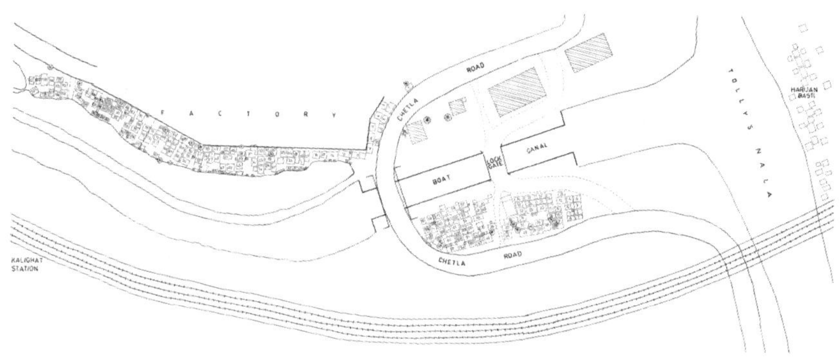

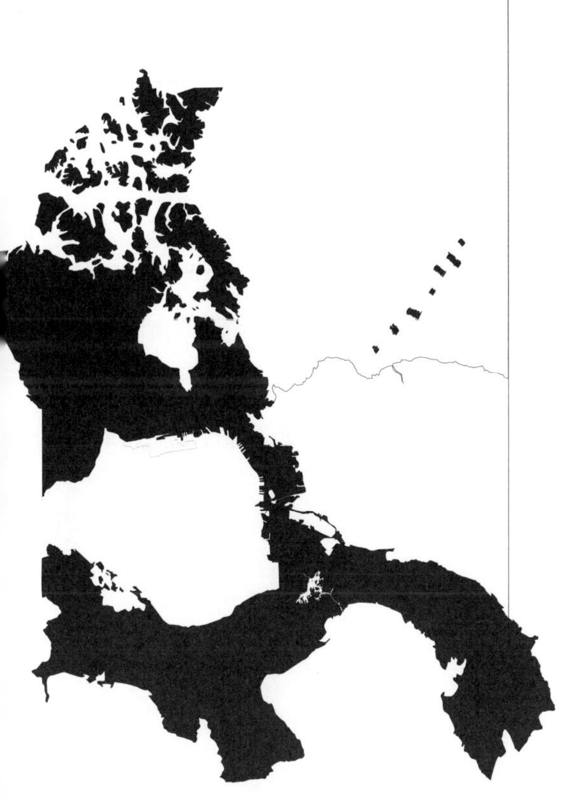

THE MOTHBALL FLEET

The Suisun Bay Reserve Fleet is sometimes known as the "ghost fleet" or the "mothball fleet." Approximately 96 American military ships — tankers, battleships, and aircraft carriers dating from World War II to the Vietnam War are stored in Suisun Bay, near San Francisco. These are part of the National Reserve Defense Fleet, overseen by the U.S. Navy and the Maritime Administration. Other NRDF sites are located in James River, Virginia, and Beaumont, Texas. Some ships are maintained in readiness, to be deployed in civil or military emergencies. Others await the scrapyard in developing countries such as Bangladesh— where contractors take advantage of low-wage labor costs, and less enforcement of environmental, labor, health, and safety regulations. Ships are also donated to individual states to be sunk and turned into artificial fish reefs.

THE NORTHWEST PASSAGE

or Canadian Internal Waters. Because of global warming, the passage is clear of ice for a significant period of time, making it possible for the eventual use of the route for global shipping and military maneuvers. The sovereignity of the passage is in question— Canada claims that it is part of its continental shelf and has taken steps to mark it territory; but other nations, including the United States, claim that it traverses international waters and should not be controlled by Canadian interests. If the Northwest passage was opened, it would provide a faster route from west to east and would be able to accomodate larger vessels than the Panama Canal can currently manage. It would also create potential environmental problems — what would happen if an oil tanker ran aground in these pristine waters?

THE 1915 PANAMA PACIFIC INTERNATIONAL EXPOSITION

San Francisco hosted this World's Fair, which celebrated the opening of the Panama Canal, a strategic, economic, and engineering triumph for the United States. The World's Fair displaced global geography onto a local map- offering pavilions from twenty-two nations as well as five ethnographic side-show displays of Asians and Africans in "native" habitat. The World's fair put San Francisco "on the map" as a viable port city. A 1916 map titled the "Exposition City" focuses not on the Fairgrounds, but on the busy shipping piers along the eastern edge of the city.

CANAL ZONE

The Canal Zone as a sovereign territory of the United States from 1903 until 1999. The area was given to the U.S. after the "bloodless revolution" that secured Panama's independence from Columbia. The Canal Zone surrounded the Panama Canal itself, completing an attempt by French interests. Fredrick Wiseman's 1977 documentary, "Canal Zone," pictures a typical American community —there is little that reveals the location as Central American. Panamanians were excluded from most jobs in the Canal Zone, and Panamanian flags were not permitted to fly (although several were planted in acts of protest in the 1960's). American military bases were constructed, and the School of the Americas operated there for almost forty years. The Canal and the Canal Zone were restored to Panamanian control in 1999. However, improvements must be made to keep pace with the increasing size of ships and the enormous amount of traffic through the Canal.

Vicencio Marquez (México) cruzó 7 veces
...nos escondimos en una como laguna de aguas
negras...llegaron los helicópteros, nos apuntaron
con las armas y nos sentaron bajo la lluvia...el
rico puede ser rico porque se cansó de ser
pobre...

Vicencio Marquez (Mexico) crossed 7 times
...we hid in something like a lagoon of
sewage...the helicopters arrived and they pointed
their weapons at us...the rich can be rich because
they got tired of being poor...

María Vargas (México) cruzó 1 vez
…mi mamá nos trajo a mí, a mi abuela y a una
prima. Una muchacha traía un bebé recién
nacido...caminamos por diez horas en el
desierto...Para mí fue como un día de campo,
pero a mi mamá la agarraron ocho veces...

María Vargas (Mexico) crossed 1 time
...my Mom brought me, my grandmother, and my
cousin. There was a girl with a newborn baby...we
walked for ten hours in the desert...For me it was
like a camping trip, but my Mom was caught eight
times...

Sara Guerrero (Mexico) crossed 315 times
...They want to put you in a little box, to know
how you identify...They don't like the word
'Chicana'...The worst was crossing with my
grandmother and my mother and having to
convince them I was related to both...

Sara Guerrero (México) cruzó 315 veces
...Te quieren encasillar, saber cómo te
identificas...No les gusta la palabra 'chicana'...Lo
peor era cruzar con mi abuela y mi mamá y tener
que convencerlos de que éramos de la misma
familia...

Julián Zugazagoitia (México) cruzó 69 veces
...pues antes de mi greencard fueron muchos
años de humillación y presentar papelitos.
Además no puedes bromear con esta gente...Es
como entrar a un estado policíaco...aunque por
el otro lado ahora significa llegar a casa...

Julián Zugazagoitia (Mexico) crossed 69 times
...well, before my greencard it was years of
humilliation and bureaucracy. Besides, you can't
joke with these people...It's like entering a police
state...on the other hand, now it means I'm
coming home.

(this page and facing page) Pedro Lasch; *Guías de Ruta /
Route Guides, LATINO/A AMERICA series*, 2003/2006.

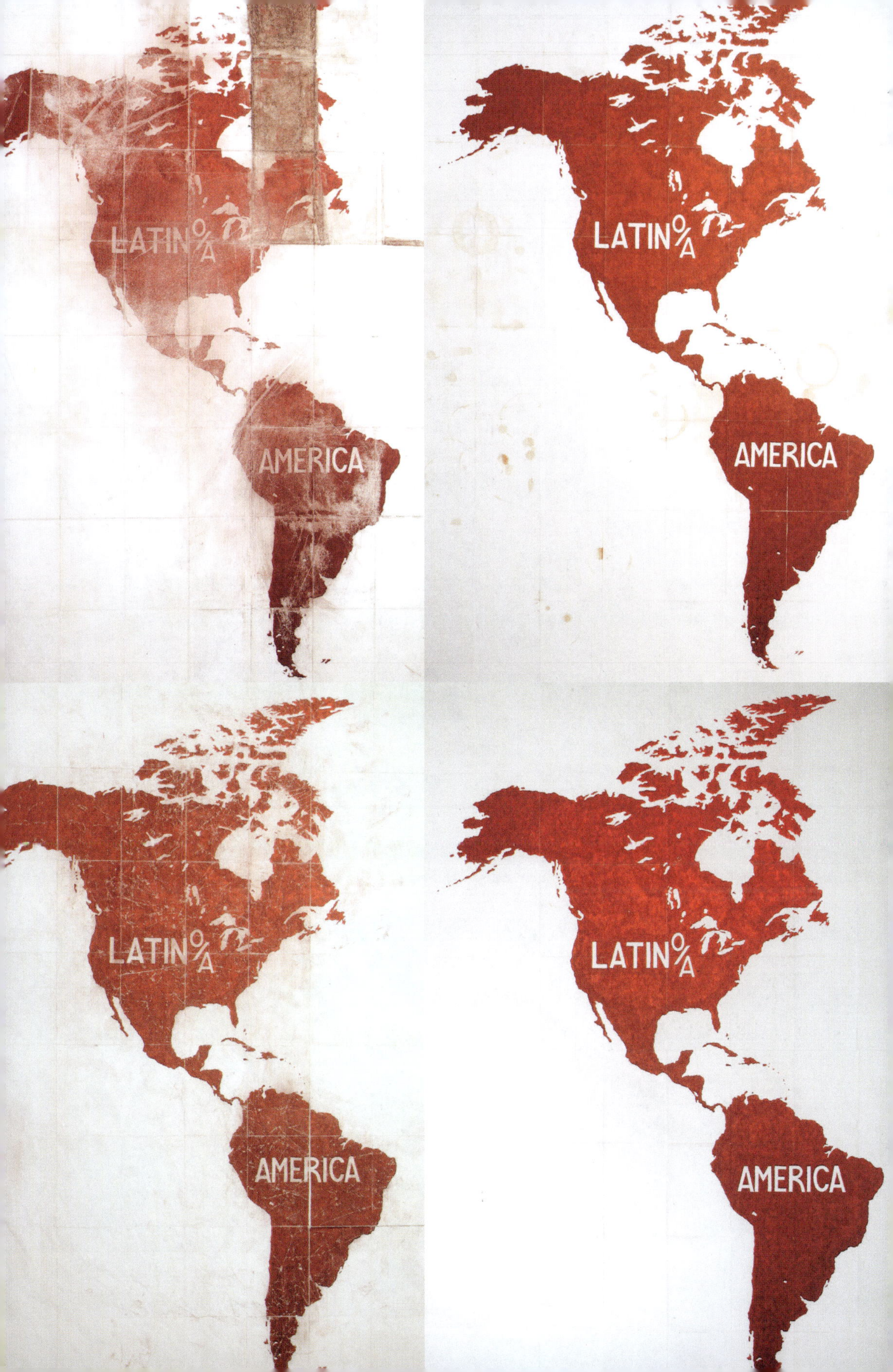

LATIN °/A
AMERICA
LATIN °/A
AMERICA
LATIN °/A
AMERICA
LATIN °/A
AMERICA

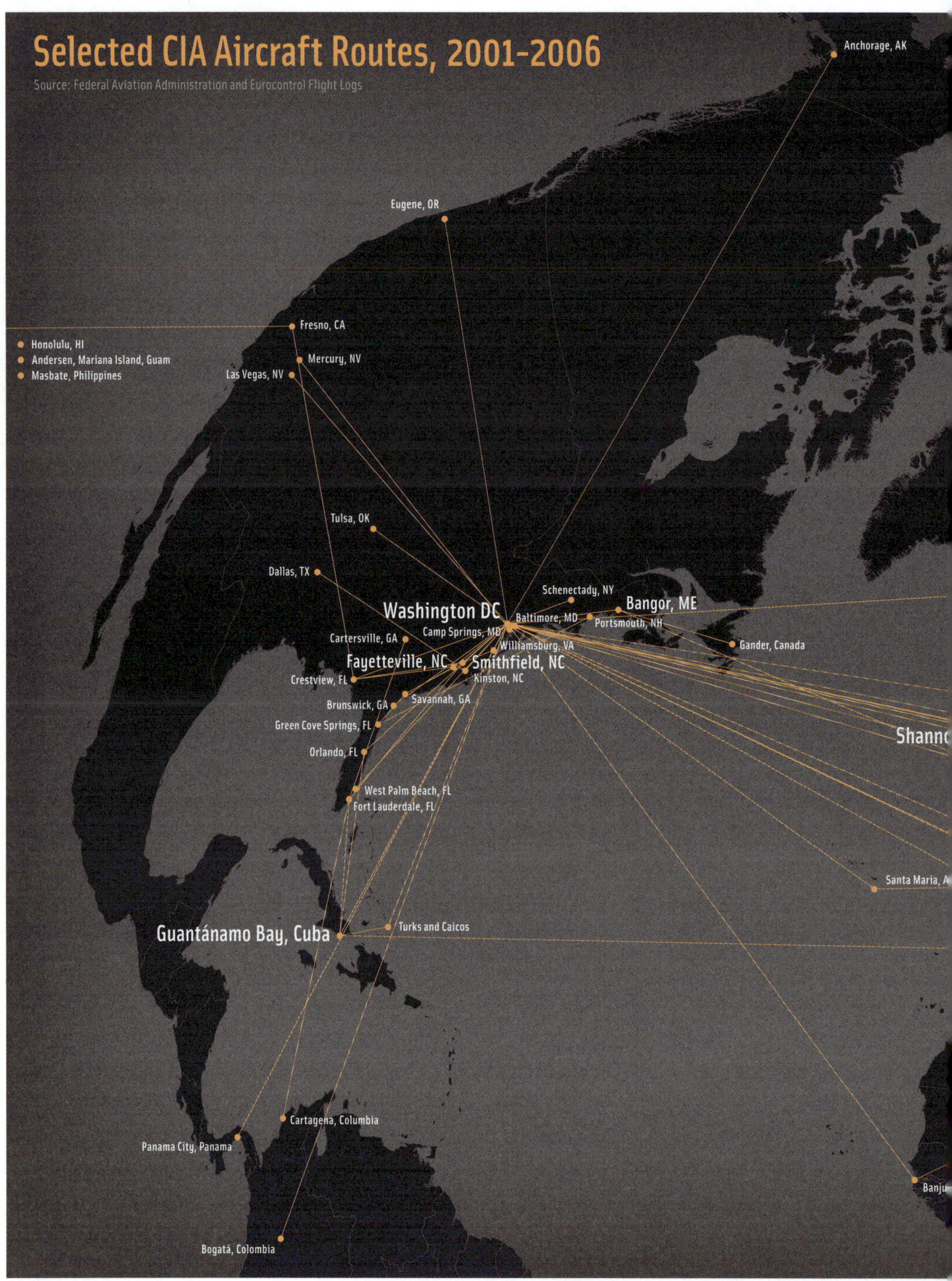

Selected CIA Aircraft Routes, 2001–2006
Source: Federal Aviation Administration and Eurocontrol Flight Logs
Anchorage, AK
Eugene, OR
Fresno, CA
Honolulu, HI
Andersen, Mariana Island, Guam
Masbate, Philippines
Mercury, NV
Las Vegas, NV
Tulsa, OK
Dallas, TX
Schenectady, NY
Washington DC
Baltimore, MD
Bangor, ME
Camp Springs, MD
Portsmouth, NH
Cartersville, GA
Williamsburg, VA
Gander, Canada
Fayetteville, NC
Smithfield, NC
Crestview, FL
Kinston, NC
Shanno
Brunswick, GA
Savannah, GA
Green Cove Springs, FL
Orlando, FL
Santa Maria, A
West Palm Beach, FL
Fort Lauderdale, FL
Guantánamo Bay, Cuba
Turks and Caicos
Banju
Cartagena, Columbia
Panama City, Panama
Bogatá, Colombia

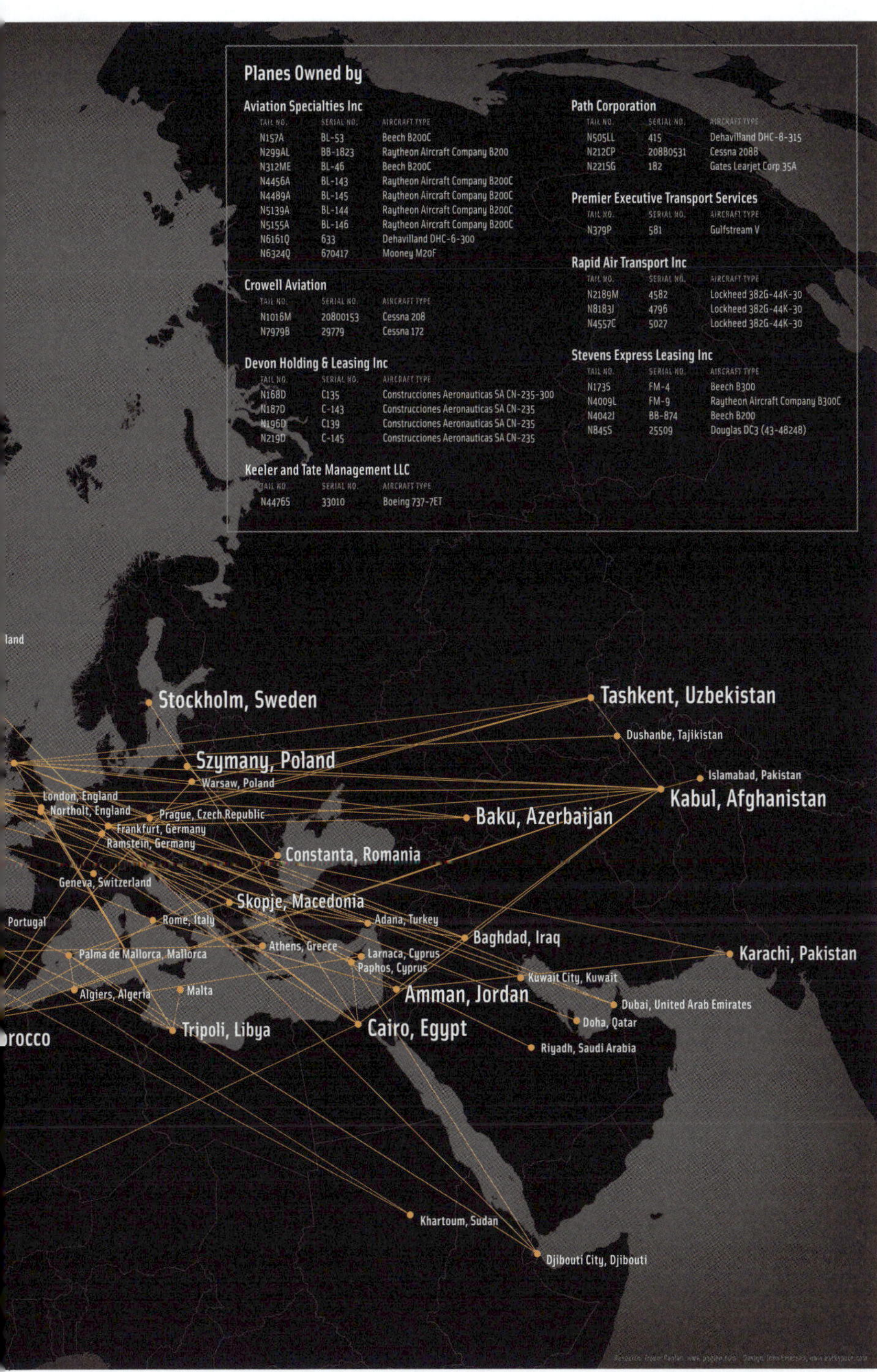

Trevor Paglen and
John Emerson, *CIA
Rendition Flights
2001-2006*, 2006.

El Caso De Ayotzinapa

The Ayotzinapa Case

Forensic Architecture

La noche del 26 y 27 de septiembre de 2014, estudiantes de la Escuela Normal Rural de Ayotzinapa fueron atacados en la ciudad de Iguala, Guerrero, por la policía local en colusión con organizaciones criminales; en los eventos participaron otras ramas del aparato de seguridad mexicano que actuaron o presenciaron los hechos, incluyendo la policía estatal y la policía federal, así como elementos del ejército. Seis personas fueron asesinadas–incluyendo tres estudiantes–, cuarenta resultaron heridas y 43 estudiantes fueron desaparecidos forzadamente.

El paradero de esos estudiantes sigue sin ser aclarado y su estatus de "desaparecidos" persiste hasta hoy. El Estado mexicano, en lugar de resolver este crimen emblemático, le ha fallado a las víctimas y al resto de la sociedad mexicana, al construir una narrativa inconsistente y fraudulenta de los acontecimientos de esa noche.

Forensic Architecture, comisionado y en colaboración con el Equipo Argentino de Antropología Forense (EAAF) y con el Centro de Derechos Humanos Miguel Agustín Pro Juárez (Centro Prodh), concibió una plataforma cartográfica interactiva para mapear y examinar las diferentes narrativas de este evento. El proyecto pretende reconstruir, por primera vez, la totalidad de los acontecimientos conocidos que tuvieron lugar esa noche en Iguala y sus alrededores, con el propósito de proveer de una herramienta forense para seguir investigando el caso.

Los datos sobre los que se basa la plataforma derivan de las investigaciones, videos, historias de los medios de comunicación, fotografías y registros telefónicos disponibles en el domiñio público.

La primera y más importante de las fuentes de FA es el trabajo realizado por un grupo de cinco expertos denominados Grupo Internacional de Expertos Independientes (GIEI), que publicó dos reportes del caso. El GIEI fue nombrado por la Comisión Interamericana de Derechos Humanos para llevar a cabo una investigación exhaustiva del caso, con el consentimiento tanto del Estado mexicano, como de las familias de los estudiantes víctimas y sus representantes. Su trabajo de un año de duración puso de relieve inconsistencias e irregularidades en las investigaciones oficiales del Estado y propuso una serie de recomendaciones sobre la búsqueda de los estudiantes desaparecidos.

Otra fuente importante es el libro del periodista John Gibler, "Una historia oral de la infamia". Desde octubre de 2014, Gibler tuvo entrevistas con los estudiantes supervivientes de los ataques de Iguala. Estos testimonios proporcionan una valiosa historia oral del evento desde el punto de vista de sus víctimas.

Esos documentos de miles de páginas se han transformado en casi cinco mil registros de una base de datos, cada uno registrando un solo suceso; por ejemplo, una comunicación bidireccional, un movimiento, o el mal manejo de la evidencia. Estos registros han sido localizados en tiempo y espacio, y etiquetados de acuerdo con los actores involucrados y el tipo de incidente que describen; además, a cada registro se le asigna una descripción narrativa.

La plataforma permite a las y los usuarios explorar la relación entre miles de eventos y cientos de actores, activando y desactivando diferentes categorías. Además, demuestra gráfica y cartográficamente el nivel de colusión y coordinación entre diversas agencias del Estado y el crimen organizado durante toda la noche.

Así por ejemplo, al comparar los movimientos de diferentes agencias de seguridad–municipales, estatales y federales y del ejército–en relación con los tiempos y la ubicación de los ataque, los investigadores pueden identificar cómo cada uno de los grupos actuaron esa noche y cómo, activamente o por omisión, tienen responsabilidad por lo sucedido.

La plataforma también identifica claramente las contradicciones entre los testimonios de los policías o los miembros de las organizaciones criminales,

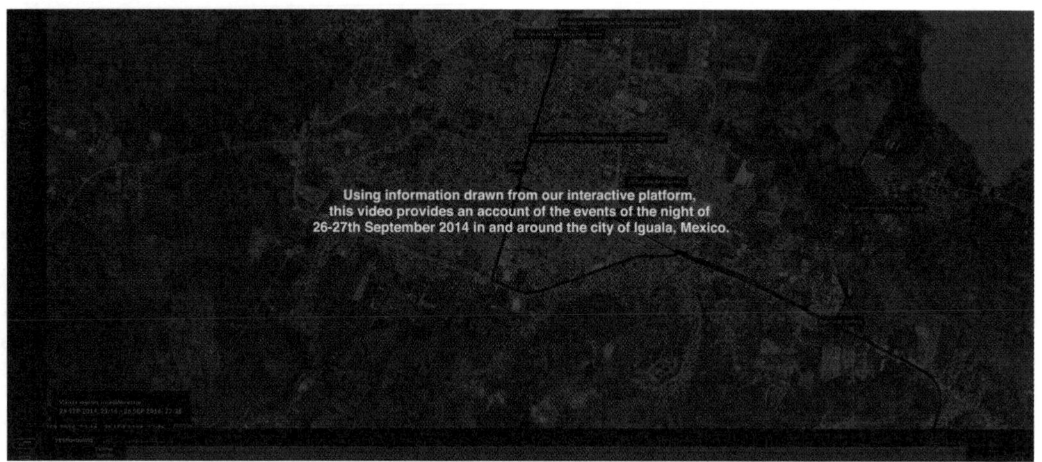

All stills. *El Caso De Ayotzinapa*, 2017. Website and video. Courtesy of Forensic Architecture.

en contraste con los de los estudiantes sobrevivientes o los hallazgos del GIEI. La función "Play" permite observar la forma en la que los eventos se desenvuelven en tiempo y espacio. Esta misma función lleva a las diferentes etapas de los eventos, revelando los movimientos de los cuerpos y de los vehículos durante la noche.

También conduce a modelos interactivos en 3D de tres de las escenas del crimen. Cada escena puede ser navegada y vista desde diferentes perspectivas. Las y los usuarios pueden acercarse a los detalles o experimentar el ataque al nivel de las calles de Iguala, mientras navegan por los diferentes momentos en que se desarrollaron los eventos.

La plataforma también contiene una serie de videos. Cada uno de ellos explica un aspecto de los acontecimientos de esta noche, por ejemplo el escalamiento de los ataques, así como el nivel de colusión y coordinación entre diferentes actores. Algunos videos ofrecen tutoriales que proporcionan una guía de usuario fácilmente accesible para la plataforma.

En suma, este proyecto revela una cartografía de la violencia, que se extiende desde la esquina de una calle en la ciudad de Iguala hasta toda la entidad de Guerrero. Describe, además, un acto de violencia no sólo como un incidente en específico, sino como un acto prolongado que persiste hasta hoy, mientras sigan ausentes los 43 estudiantes.

También busca demostrar las maneras en que iniciativas de la sociedad civil, que llevan a cabo investigaciones independientes con herramientas analíticas novedosas, pueden ayudar a investigar crímenes complejos, así como a confrontar la impunidad criminal y las fallas del sistema de procuración de justicia en México.

Sobre todo, el proyecto reafirma el compromiso de FA por buscar sanar la herida abierta de Ayotzinapa y a trabajar hasta que se esclarezca la verdad y se conozca el paradero de los estudiantes.

NOTA
Si bien esta plataforma busca emplear los datos disponibles de manera objetiva y precisa, la gran cantidad de información relacionada con este caso significa que pueden persistir algunas inexactitudes. FA ha hecho que todos sus datos sean públicos para permitir a los usuarios explorarlo más a fondo y sugerir correcciones o mejoras.

EQUIPO DE FORENSIC ARCHITECTURE
Coordinación, investigación y producción: Eyal Weizman (director de investigación), Stefan Laxness (coordinador del proyecto), Marina Azahua (investigadora), Irving Huerta (CIJ's Gavin MacFadyen Investigative fellow), Nadia Mendez (arquitecta investigadora), Theo Resnikoff (periodista), Belén Rodriguez (arquitecta investigadora), Sarah Nankivell (gestión de programa), Ariel Caine (realización), Nicholas Masterton (realización), Simone Rowat (realización), Nathan Su (realización), Nathalie Tjia (producción y diseño), Bob Trafford (comunicación y producción), Christina Varvia (realización y producción).

Diseño y desarrollo de software: Franc Camps-Febrer (gestión de diseño y desarrollo), Anso Studio (Petros Kataras y Emmanouil Matsis) (diseño e ingeniería 3D), Nestor Camilo Vargas (diseño de interacción).

Gracias especiales a John Gibler, Rosario Güiraldes, Pablo Dominguez, Virginia Vieira, Témoris Grecko, Manuel Ángel Macía, Rosa Rogina, Other Means, Centre for Investigative Journalism (CIJ), Nestor Camilo Vargas, Taller cartográfico "Ariles"- y en especial a las familias de los estudiantes de Ayotzinapa que fueron sujetos a graves violaciones de derechos humanos en la noche de septiembre de 2014, por su incansable lucha por alcanzar la verdad.

Equipo Del Equipo Argentino De Antropología Forense

Equipo Del Centro De Derechos Humanos Miguel Agustín Pro Juárez (Centro Prodh)

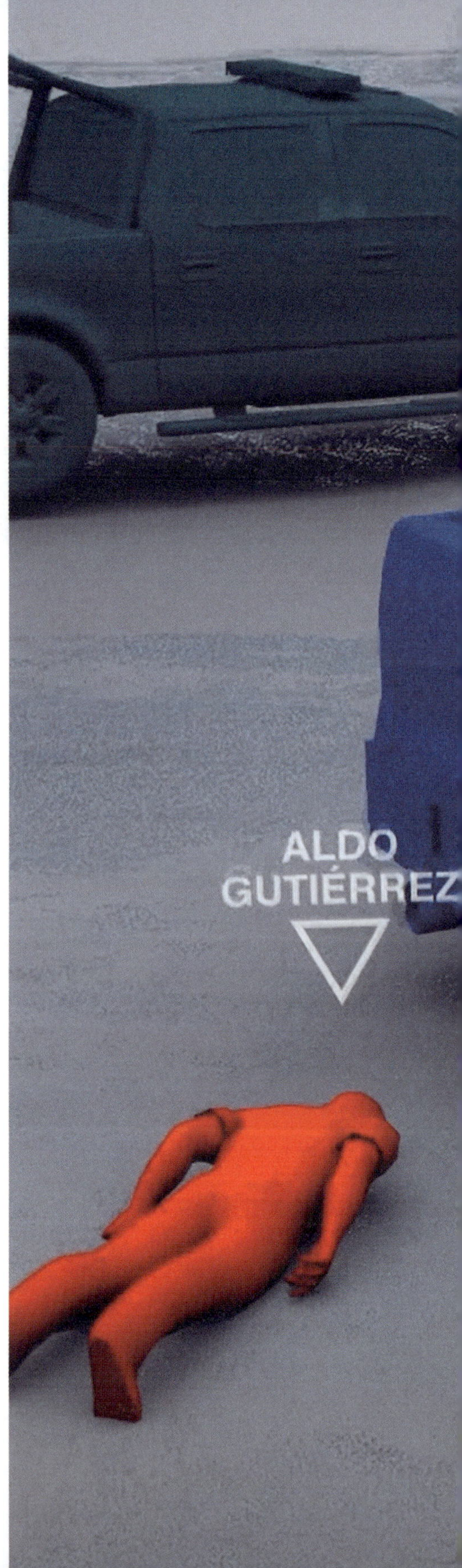

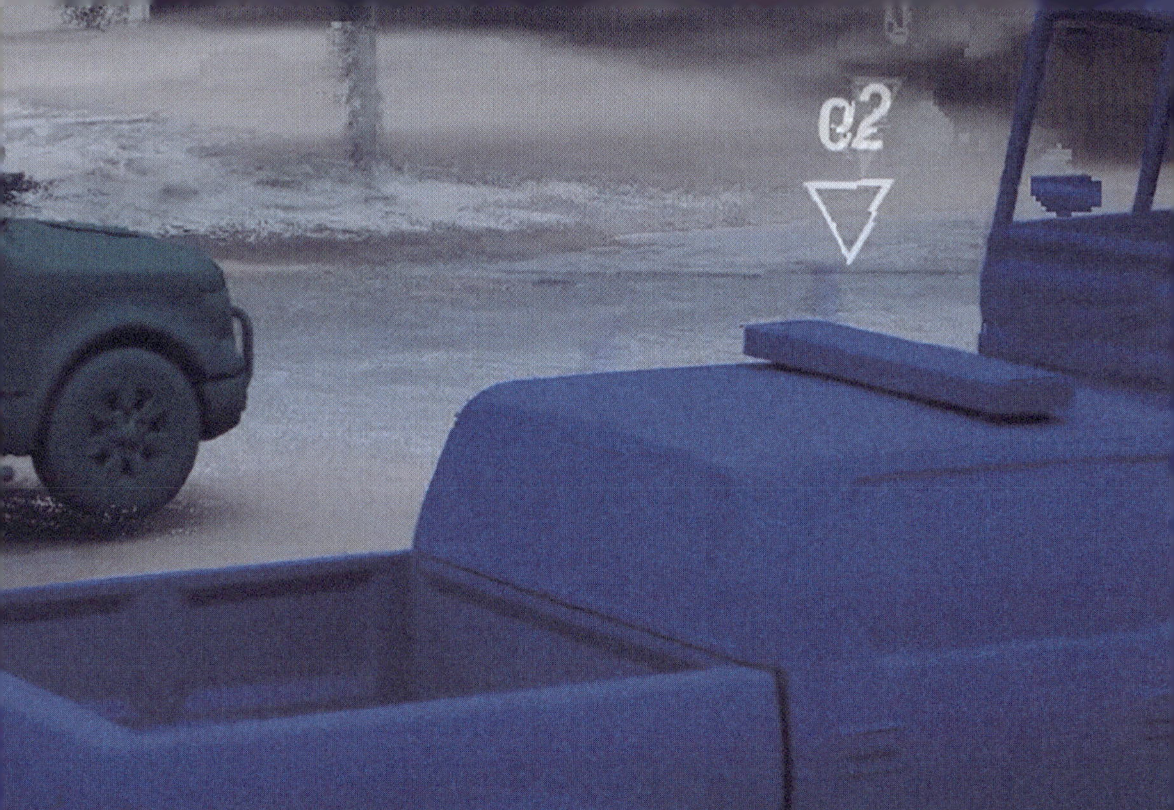

On the night of 26-27 September 2014, students from the Rural Normal School of Ayotzinapa were attacked in the town of Iguala, Guerrero, by local police in collusion with criminal organisations. Numerous other branches of the Mexican security apparatus either participated in or witnessed the events, including state and federal police and the military. Six people were murdered—including three students—forty wounded, and 43 students were forcibly disappeared.

   The whereabouts of the students remains unknown, and their status as 'disappeared' persists to this day. Instead of attempting to solve this historic crime, the Mexican state has failed the victims, and the rest of Mexican society, by constructing a fraudulent and inconsistent narrative of the events of that night.

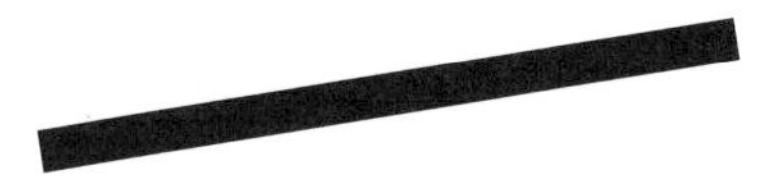

Forensic Architecture was commissioned by and worked in collaboration with the Equipo Argentino de Antropologia Forense (EAAF) and Centro de Derechos Humanos Miguel Agustín Pro Juárez (Centro Prodh) to conceive of an interactive cartographic platform to map out and examine the different narratives of this event. The project aims to reconstruct, for the first time, the entirety of the known events that took place that night in and around Iguala, and provide a forensic tool for researchers to further the investigation.

The data on which the platform is based is drawn from publicly available investigations, videos, media stories, photographs and phone logs.

The first and most important of FA's sources are two reports by a group of five experts referred to as the International Group of Independent Experts (GIEI). The GIEI was appointed by the Inter-American Commission of Human Rights to carry out—with the consent of both the state and the families of the victims—a thorough investigation of the case. Their year-long work highlighted inconsistencies and irregularities in the official state investigations and proposed a series of recommendations regarding the search for the missing students.

Another important source for the work is a book by journalist John Gibler, 'An Oral History of Infamy'. From October 2014, Gibler undertook interviews with the surviving students of the Iguala attacks. These testimonies provide an invaluable oral history of the event from the point of view of its victims.

Thousands of pages of reports have thereafter been broken down into almost five thousand data-points, each recording a single reported incident, such as an instance of two-way communication, movements or the mishandling of evidence. These data-points have been located, timed and tagged according to the actors involved, and the type of incident they describe. Each data-point is also assigned a narrative description.

The platform enables user to explore the relationship between thousands of events and hundreds of actors, by switching different data-tags on and off.

It demonstrates, in a clear graphic and cartographic form, the level of collusion and coordination between state agencies and organised crime, throughout the night.

Comparing, for example, the movement of different security agencies—municipal, state and federal police forces and the military—in relation to the times and location of the attacks, investigators can identify how each of these groups acted that night and how—actively or by omission—they bear responsibility for what transpired.

The platform also clearly identifies contradictions between the testimonies of the police, surviving students or alleged members of criminal organisations and the findings of the GIEI. A 'play' function allows users to observe the way events unfolded in time and space, allowing users to explore the different stages of the events and the movements of people and vehicles throughout the night.

The platform leads to interactive 3D models of three important crime scenes throughout Iguala. Each crime scene can be navigated and viewed from different perspectives. Users can zoom into details or experience the attack from an eye level perspective while the platform takes the user through the different stages of the events.

The platform also contains several videos. Each of these videos explains an aspect of the events of this night— the escalation of attacks, the level of collusion and coordination between different forces. Some videos offer tutorials, providing an accessible user's guide for the platform.

The project thus reveals a cartography of violence spanning from the street corner level to the entire state of Guerrero. It describes an act of violence that is no longer a singular event but a prolonged act, which persists to this day in the continued absence of the 43 students.

It also seeks to demonstrate the ways in which collective civil society initiatives, undertaking independent investigations using innovative analytical tools, could help investigate complex crimes and confront criminal impunity and the failures of Mexican law enforcement.

In particular, it reaffirms FA's commitment to heal the open wound of the Ayotzinapa case, and to work until the truth of the night is clarified, and the students' whereabouts are known.

NOTE

While this platform seeks to employ available data objectively and accurately, the sheer amount of information related to this case means that some inaccuracies might persist. We have made all FA's data public to enable users to further explore it and suggest corrections or refinements.

FORENSIC ARCHITECTURE TEAM

Coordination, research and production: Eyal Weizman (principal investigator), Stefan Laxness (project coordinator), Marina Azahua (researcher), Irving Huerta (CIJ's Gavin MacFadyen Investigative fellow), Nadia Mendez (architectural researcher), Theo Resnikoff (journalist), Belén Rodriguez (architectural researcher), Sarah Nankivell (programme manager), Ariel Caine (film-maker), Nicholas Masterton (film-maker), Simone Rowat (film-maker), Nathan Su (film-maker), Nathalie Tjia (design and production), Bob Trafford (communication production), Christina Varvia (film-making and production).

Design and software development: Franc Camps-Febrer (design and software development lead), Anso Studio (Petros Kataras y Emmanouil Matsis) (design and 3D engineering), Nestor Camilo Vargas (interaction design)

Thanks to: John Gibler, Rosario Güiraldes, Pablo Dominguez, Virginia Vieira, Témoris Grecko, Manuel Ángel Macía, Rosa Rogina, Other Means, Centre for Investigative Journalism (CIJ), Taller cartográfico "Ariles" and the surviving Ayotzinapa students and the families of the 43 disappeared for their tireless struggle for truth.

Equipo Argentino De Antropología Forense (EAAF)

Centro De Derechos Humanos Miguel Agustín Pro Juárez (Centro Prodh)

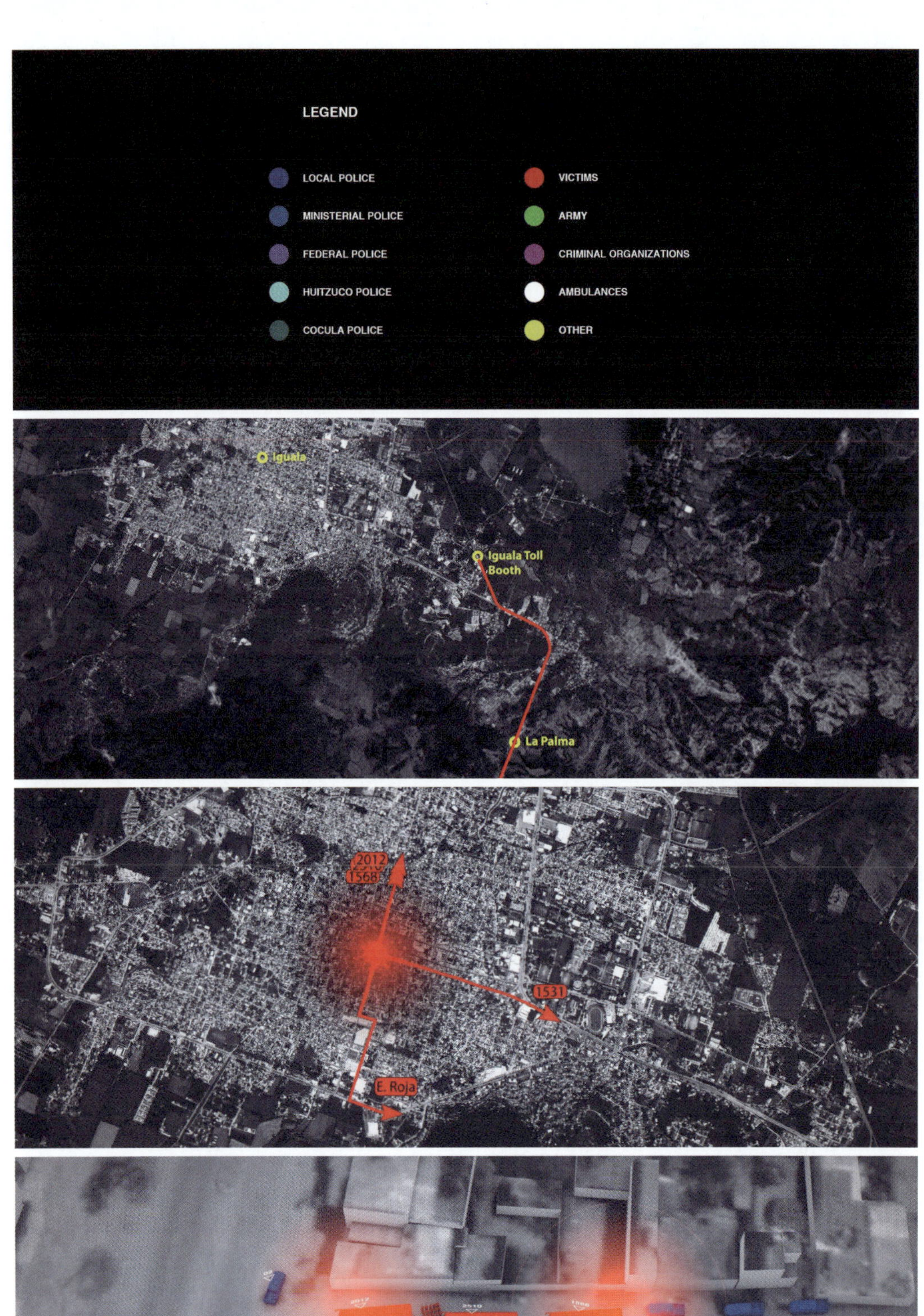

LEGEND
LOCAL POLICE
MINISTERIAL POLICE
FEDERAL POLICE
HUITZUCO POLICE
COCULA POLICE
VICTIMS
ARMY
CRIMINAL ORGANIZATIONS
AMBULANCES
OTHER
Iguala
Iguala Toll Booth
La Palma
2012
1568
1531
E. Roja

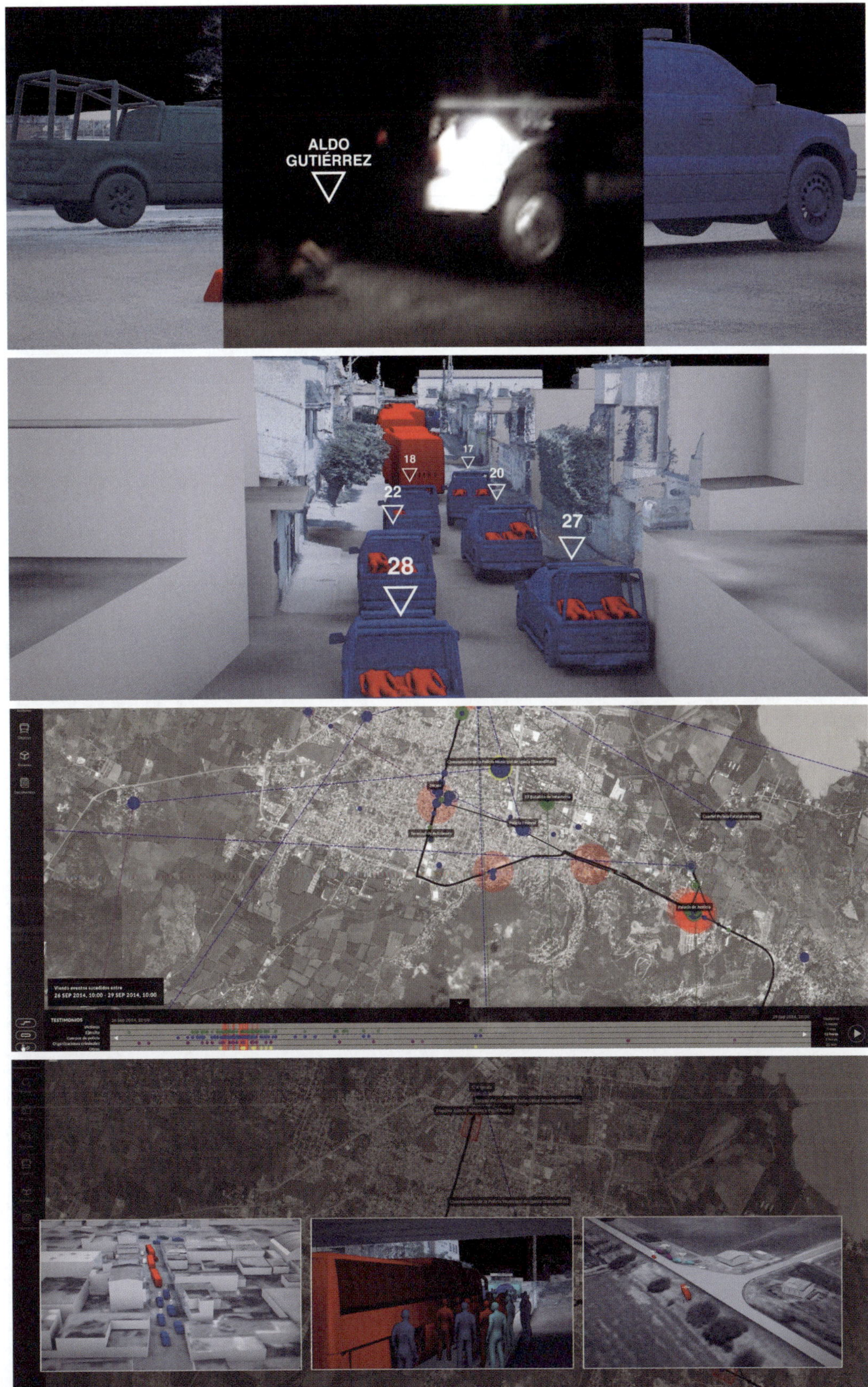

ALDO
GUTIÉRREZ
18
17
20
22
27
28

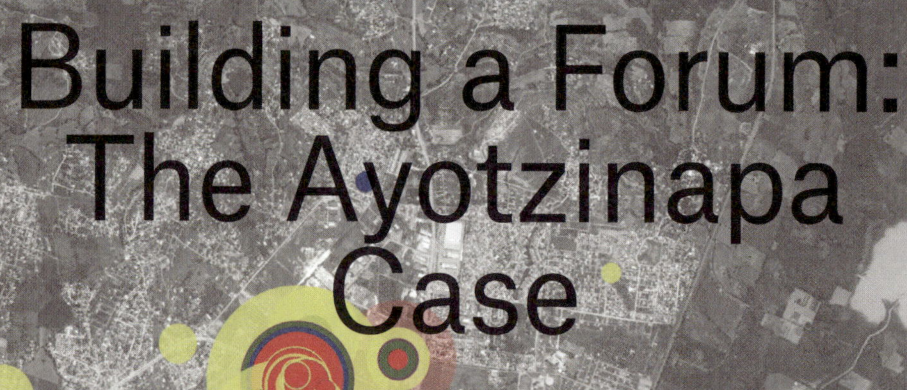

Building a Forum:
The Ayotzinapa Case

Stefan Laxness
with Peter Hall

Founded in 2011, Forensic Architecture is a research agency based at Goldsmiths University in London which has pioneered architectural and media research for human rights organisations, political and environmental justice groups and international prosecutors. Its multi-modal platforms of sites of conflict have furthered a number of cases where forensic methods are used in reverse, to focus on violations of human rights and international humanitarian law, where the claims of the state are under legal scrutiny. In *The Ayotzinapa Case*, Forensic Architecture developed an online platform based on material in the public domain around the forced disappearance of 43 students of the Normal Rural School of Ayotzinapa. On the night of 26-27 September 2014, the students were traveling on buses in Iguala, Guerrero when they were attacked by local police in collusion with criminal organizations. Six people were murdered, including three students, 40 wounded, and 43 students were forcibly disappeared: Their whereabout remains unknown. The Ayotzinapa Case platform reveals in interactive and cartographic form the events before and during the night of 26 September and the subsequent cover-up, implicating state agencies and their apparent collusion with organized crime.

The project was developed in collaboration with the Argentine Forensic Anthropology Team (EAAF) and the Miguel Agustín Pro Juárez Human Rights Center (Centro Prodh). Here, Stefan Laxness, project coordinator for Forensic Architecture, discusses the work of Forensic Archtiecture and the Ayotzinapa Case with Peter Hall.

<u>Peter Hall</u>
Could you explain how the work of Forensic Architecture work is defined in terms of the forum?

<u>Stefan Laxness</u>
The word forensics derives from *forensis*, Latin for 'pertaining to the *forum*'. The Roman forum was a multi-dimensional space of politics, law and economy. This also has something to do with the act of sensing an event, and that act of sensing essentially also happens in those three places: the field, the lab and the forum. The built environment senses the events, as in shrapnel on a wall, for example. It happens when we are analyzing the evidence, capturing that fragment on the wall, and then it happens through the forum where that information is then presented back to an audience.

<u>Peter Hall</u>
That's an inspiring idea that those three parts, the digging, the analyzing and the presenting, all take place within that one word, forensics: unfortunately it's become popularized as the thing that the people with the rubber gloves do after a crime. I also like what's clear about the multi-dimensional approach of your work, that there's a suggestion that it's overcoming the disciplinary silos. So, breaking architecture out of that form-making ghetto. It's also interesting that architecture becomes a witness to events.

<u>Stefan Laxness</u>
It becomes an interface for aggregating information, and the interface for presenting the information. Recently we've been doing a lot of camera calibration and projection mapping, where the image or video is literally projected onto a model, either to reconstruct it or to understand how, where that image or video was taken.

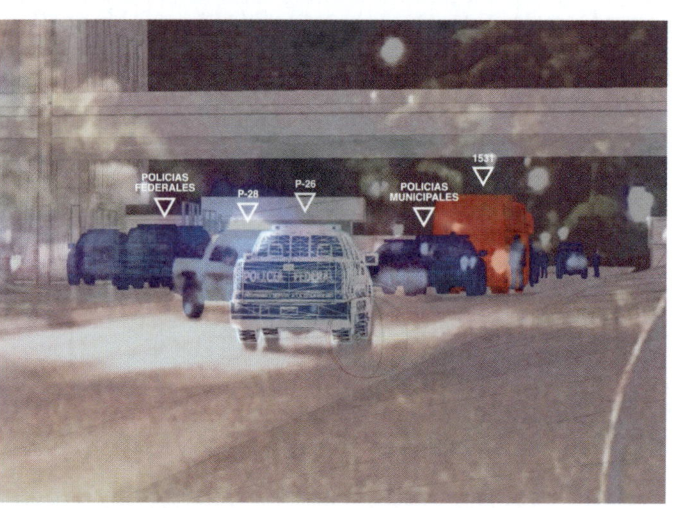

All stills. *El Caso De Ayotzinapa*, 2017. Website and video. Courtesy of Forensic Architecture.

Peter Hall
Is the projection mapping used to gather or to demonstrate, or both?

Stefan Laxness
It's both. We just finished an investigation on the killing of Tahir Elçi who was a prominent Kurdish human rights lawyer in Eastern Turkey. In that incident there were 40 shots fired and he died because of one of them. Every moment of four cameras recording has been calibrated and mapped onto the built environment as a way of just being able to understand the scene better and to reference back to it. It becomes a 3D storage system for this information. A live archive and a live database, but instead of being in a spreadsheet it's actually within the 3D model. It gets used during the research and investigative phase, but then also becomes really crucial for the video investigations which communicate those findings.

Peter Hall
So, jumping to the Mexico project, the Ayotzinapa Case, is there a similar model created for investigation?

Stefan Laxness
Yes. They're both real counter-forensics examples, examples in which we have to use our own methodologies and techniques and tools in order to do an investigation which was not properly done by the state. They both have to do with the fact that there are two incidents in which there was a lack of visibility, and a lack of effective justice. Their lack of visibility means that independent groups like us need to actually start to act.

Peter Hall
So the Ayotzinapa Case began with the EAAF [Equipo Argentino de Antropología Forense] approaching you?

Stefan Laxness
The EAAF and Centro Prodh, which is a human rights organization based in Mexico City, approached us to do something about the case. Following a bit of preliminary research on our end and then a field trip to Mexico, we realized that there seemed to be a real need to hear the versions of the events from the perspective of the victims, and that the state, the prosecutor, had essentially put out their own official version, which was full of gaps, discrepancies and loose ends, but being the state they also had the loudest megaphone to promote their message. Once you start to research it a little bit, you realize that there's a lot of moving parts, people, objects, and places, and it quickly gets very confusing. The thing is, that confusion is what makes it easier to put out one version rather than actually talk about all the intricacies of what actually happened.

A third thing we realized is that if you were to read any sort of news article, whether it's a Mexican one or an international one, the main focus and the main questions were all about the missing bodies. Or, where are the students, the 43 students who disappeared? But there seemed to be less talk about the events that led up to this act of violence.

One of the challenges that we had was the lack of privileged material or primary sources. In Forensic Architecture we are not necessarily experts on Yemen or experts on Syria or experts on mass disappearance, but what we are experts on is looking at material and using that material as a way into a topic. In this case there wasn't any sound, any video and there weren't any images. A lot of that has to do with the fact that it happened at night, and the amount of repression that comes with the cartel violence, but also the state violence. A lot of material wasn't filmed. It also wasn't shared.

So the question became, where do we start? We weren't going to find where the students are, that's for sure. The task that we set ourselves was to create a tool that allows people to explore the case and make new connections from existing material. That's when we agreed that we would start our investigation by analyzing these two reports by the independent group of experts put together by the Inter-American Commission for Human Rights following the incident.

Peter Hall
Why did it get such a lot of coverage?

Stefan Laxness
It was because students were attacked, and the fact that also there were a lot of witnesses. The students' school in Ayotzinapa is traditionally left-wing, and attended by poor, mainly indigenous, farmers. They have a long history of demonstrating and protesting against the state. Educational reform is already up there in the news, and here are seventeen to twenty-year-olds, poor, rural, indigenous farmers who are being attacked by the state.

The Mexican Government agreed to take the help from the Inter-American Commission who sent experts to assist the investigation. The group wrote one report, and finding that the state wasn't being super cooperative, decided to write another report on all the things that they thought were wrong. We chose these two documents because even though they are secondary sources, they were the most cohesive, extensive and to a certain extent trustworthy account of the events that happened that night— and where the discrepancies were. The problem with them is that they're 1,000 pages and nobody's got time to read them. But we saw, just by reading the resumé, that there were people, there were objects, there were locations that kept recurring. Immediately we saw that embedded within the report was a spatial component, that translated differently, could start to reveal certain things.

Peter Hall
The spatial dimension is interesting.

Stefan Laxness
Yes, we thought this is a good opportunity to make the thing more legible and see if we can actually set out new connections between data. That's when we started data mining the two books. We decided that we were going to break down every sentence, every idea, every thought, every concept presented in

these books, and give it a time and space tag, a location and timestamp. We also kept track of the narratives and we started devising a set of tags so we could later filter them on and off. So there's victims, security forces, other governments, suspected members of organized crime. And then there are the vehicles, weapons, and type of incident. That led us to the data mining, or 5,000 points of information. This is all set up in a spreadsheet. So there's always a little bit of negotiation between the spreadsheet and how you data mine, and how that's then meant to be reflected in the platform.

Peter Hall

At this point did you have a user interface or web design team?

Stefan Laxness

We got the user interface actually quite late in the process. The data mining was one of the most important steps for the project. We didn't have a tool to visualize: We had to develop our own, because going into the data mining you know very little about the case. It's like reading a book for the first time. By the time you get to the middle you understand better what happened in the beginning. Same thing here. You start data mining, you know nothing. But the more you read the more you know, and suddenly the more you have to re-evaluate how you've data-mined the first bit.

That led to the problem of how we keep track of all this information, how do we keep track of our mistakes, and how do we keep track of what needs to be improved on? How do we understand the events better, and also in doing so refine that data?

So we started making decisions about how we break down these books

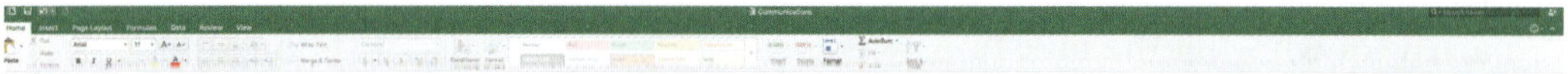

Data Package. *El Caso De Ayotzinapa*, 2017.

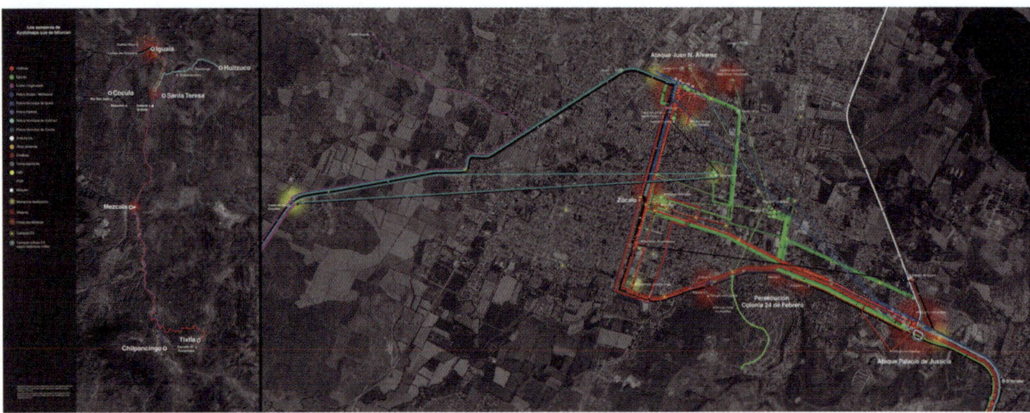

into larger chunks, and in themes.

Those then eventually became working drawings which allowed us to understand things better, but they also allowed us to better present the information and to draw out the main questions, the main problematics that we wanted to communicate to the audience. You can't just overload people with information because that is the same problem that you had in the first place. So the graphics then helped us to narrow down what the questions were and what we wanted to present. For example, the first ones were the most intuitive ones: There are four main events in which people are either killed or kidnapped. Let's break them down, add a timeline. Let's figure out when they start and when they end, and align our data points in time and stack them. Suddenly you can see peaks of activities and understand phases. It is no longer this freak event—as it's described in the official version. You can start to understand it as something that has structure, something that has a form or logic and is describable and quantifiable. So then there's a clarity.

One of the key parts of this project was to understand where and when all the alleged members of criminal organizations were. While the students, the victims, were really good at saying where they were, the alleged members of criminal organization would say, "I wasn't there in this event that you're describing, but so-and-so was there." They would constantly be deflecting their presence and implicating somebody else. But then you also noticed that their testimonies also just don't make much sense and the way they're describing things isn't clear. And that's the first sign that something's a little bit off.

So we couldn't place them because we have to give them a time and a location stamp, but if they're describing one event in one place but saying that they're not there but they're actually saying that they're somewhere else, the question is, how do you actually do this in the data sheet? Are they here or there?

Peter Hall
How do you visualize lies, in some cases?

<u>Stefan Laxness</u>
Exactly. So we came up with the system which was fairly simple, like a space-time matrix where you have time horizontally and you have space vertically. We just started plotting where they say they are at what time. So, if person A says, "I went from A to B to C," but then another person says, "I was here, here, but I saw person A in location E," you start to get the difference between person A's testimony and where other people have placed them. The independent group of experts had identified already that there were three different versions. You map all three of them and then you realize that it's a complete mess. If they had all been telling the truth, their testimonies might all start in different places but they would all end being doing the same thing, which according to them was killing and burning students in the same location. So there would be a convergence. But the lack of convergence suggests that there is confusion, suggests that there are discrepancies, and like you said, suggests that somewhere somebody's not really telling the truth. Essentially that divergence of line, that graphic cloud of narrative lines is the image, or a form of visualization of mass disappearance. It's the clouding of clarity through false positives and false negatives, which is part of the crime, in a sense, or evidence of the crime.

Once you started to overlay the cartel narrative matrix with the narrative matrix of the students and the narrative matrix of law enforcement, and also the narrative matrix of the official version, you see that there is a very quick divergence between the version of the prosecutor from the version of the victims. So that's the first problem. The second problem is that the version of the prosecutor converges very quickly towards the versions of the alleged cartel members.

But there's one version of the events that was the one that had to do with the Cocula dump in which the students were allegedly burned. All the people that gave that testimony, there's strong evidence to suggest that they were tortured in police custody. So the official line aligns with testimony obtained under torture. That, in a sense, is quite a complex thing to explain and visualize, and the video is far more effective at actually just nailing that point and showing the process of how these things are drawn.

So, when Franc [Camps-Febrer] was coding this function, we saw immediately that where the crime scenes happen creates a triangle, which is also where all the government buildings are. If you look at the narratives and where they connect there's only one or two pieces of narrative testimony that link this part of town to the part of town where they were allegedly killed and burned. It's a projection of the narrative of violence from this part of town to a western part of town, which is allegedly based on testimony obtained through torture, and also very weak. This feature was a little bit too complicated to show.

<u>Peter Hall</u>
Right. It's speculative…

<u>Stefan Laxness</u>
For me it was fascinating that in this one small experiment you could suddenly see the projection of violence through narrative being essentially deflected to another place outside of the place where a lot of the violence happened.

<u>Peter Hall</u>
It's interesting how the graphic kind of plotting, tagging, arranging and visualizing of the information revealed the flimsiness of one testimony, just visually.

<u>Stefan Laxness</u>
Yeah. For me it was just glaringly visible. When we held our press conference in Centro Prodh, one of the more mainstream news outlets in Mexico had a journalist there who asked why we made a video of the events that did not mention the dump in Cocula where the students were allegedly burned.

The Centro Prodh member rebuked the journalist and said that the whole point is that the video is an extensive account of the known events of violence that happened that night, leading up to when the students are kidnapped. Because the thing is, once the students have been taken and put into the back of police cars, everything beyond that point is a form of speculation. And the Cocula dump had already been debunked by another expert who was at the table. So the head of Centro Prodh was saying that the dump deliberately

doesn't feature in this video because we wanted to achieve clarity on this event, not speculation.

<u>Peter Hall</u>
So, the motive for this kind of deflection is to draw attention away from the complicity of the state?

<u>Stefan Laxness</u>
I would be speculating if I were to answer that, but what's important, what is certain is that, based on the testimony of police officers, of other witnesses of police officers and the victims, that violence happened along the axis [where the Government buildings are located]. These things say a lot about the level of involvement of police vehicles and CCTV cameras that night; the use of all this infrastructure that's meant to protect citizens being used against them. They say a lot about the level of coordination that existed between security forces, either to act violently against the students or also just not act.

It also showed the coordinated nature of the violence, the fact that the actual moments in which the students are put in the back of the police trucks and taken away and disappeared, happened in two different locations. There's violence against bodies but also violence against evidence, which we're able to show through, for example, explaining how the CCTV cameras disappeared—the ones right in front of one of the crime scenes. The lack of transparency is the continuation of the act of taking the bodies, which is a violence against evidence. So, the mass disappearance is a two-part act, one that is punctual and one that is continuous.

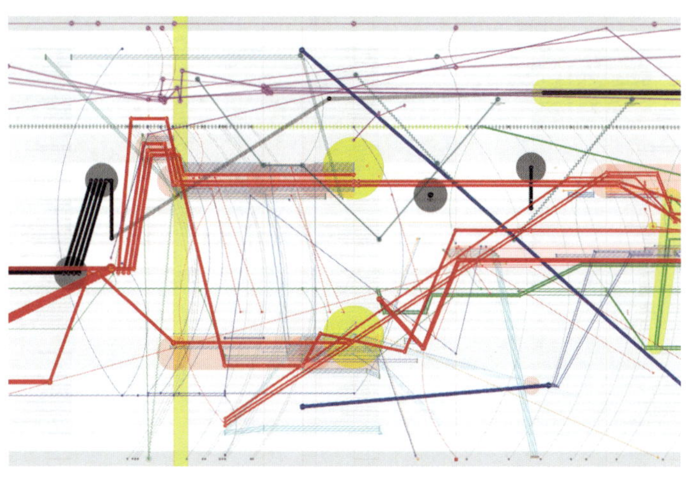

Peter Hall
There's an interesting connection to a chapter in the Forensic Architecture book which describes an inter-relation between satellite resolution and the capabilities of drone bombing, how it's possible to cover up drone bombing by not having a satellite resolution available. It's a similar effect to what you were talking about, violence against evidence.

Stefan Laxness
Yeah. One can argue that the process goes further. One of the people that we worked with, a researcher, she showed me the photocopies that the judiciary will get in cases that they need to prosecute. These are photocopies of the evidence but the photocopies are done on really bad toner printers, and that's what they make judgments on. In a sense, the process of hiding CCTV cameras, omitting evidence, extends all the way up to doing a bad reproduction in which you can't actually see the evidence being presented.

Peter Hall
From the graphic communication perspective there are familiar challenges here, of using a visual language that suggests certainty, which I think pertains to a particular problem of how you show thematic links that are not definite but speculative. Another issue is that you need to simplify to make accessible and understandable, but it is always at the risk of distortion.

Stefan Laxness
But not necessarily, because we did five videos for this project, and two of them are fairly dense information-wise. One of them is the summary of the events that night, which is not at all speculation. That is a list based on corroborated evidence. That's a 20-minute long video, but it is probably one of the most disseminated pieces from this investigation.

Peter Hall
It's interesting that the visualization, the mapping is important for the process of discovering and recognizing patterns, but in the process of communicating, sometimes you need a narrative to lead you through the visualization.

Stefan Laxness
Yeah, accessibility was the point of the videos. The platform in itself is com-

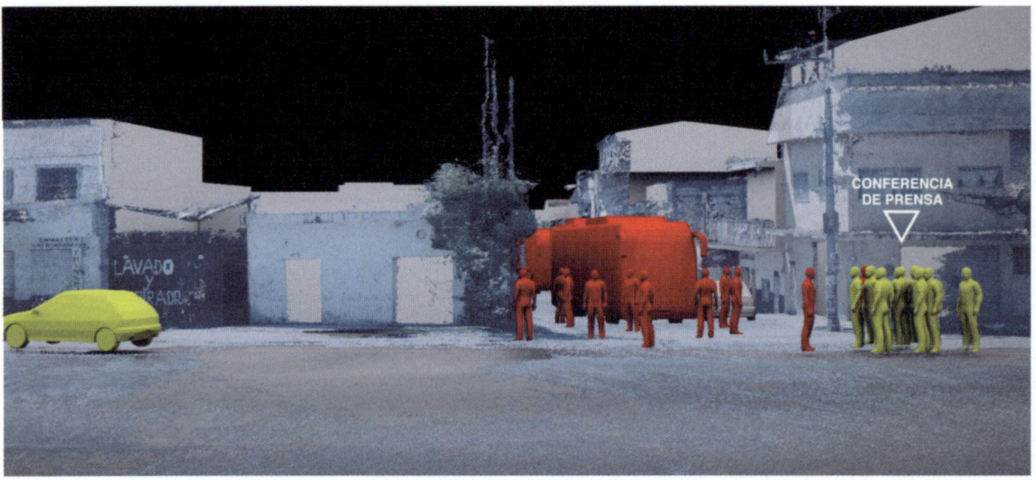

plicated. A lot of people are not used to multi-layer interfaces, and in some extreme cases, there are people who can't read and write who care deeply about this case. So obviously the platform may not be accessible to the people who don't have a powerful computer, don't have an internet connection, things like that. The videos were created because we needed to give people another way in. If you watch the videos, then you can better understand where to direct your energy when you're using the platform. But we had to go through a very long decision-making process, what do we choose to say in these videos?

Peter Hall

Was 3D modeling an important part of this project?

Stefan Laxness

It was important in order to quantify the amount of people and objects present at the scenes. It did, however, become important when it came to presenting. For example, when we were breaking down each of the crime scenes and aligning all these points on the timeline we were also counting where every person is, where every car is, and we needed to lay those out. The 3D models weren't necessarily used in an operative way but for starting to represent the scene, and as a collector for quantifying things. There were 40 police cars in this scene, for example. That's a lot of police cars. The official version once again makes it sound like a rogue police officer and an odd car were involved. No, no. Here, every level of law enforcement has made an appearance. Even from other cities. That's when the scale of the event becomes apparent.

Peter Hall

What do you think the impact of this project has been?

Stefan Laxness

So, how one measures impact I think is difficult. For me the main impact of the project is that now there is a historic document out there that anybody can use in order to start their own research on this, and that can start to spread and present the version of the events from the standpoint of the victims. They would essentially avoid, bypass doing what we did, which was spend nine months breaking everything down. The platform has been used by some journalists in Mexico. So it was a minor victory there. But the main goal of the project was to create documents that brought to the forefront an alternative version to what the state was saying. When I say alternative, it's not one that's made up. It's one that aligns more closely with that of the victims. There was a success in doing that because the documents that we put out were fairly clear and they did get a lot of circulation. And that plays a small role in shifting the debate a little bit.

On the more immediate level, the families of the victims have a document that they can easily share with people they don't know, but also their friends. They were telling me that even talking to their friends about this has been difficult because of the complexity, so these documents were also given to them on USB sticks so that they could share them back in their home states.

It also has to do with how then the project is presented and in what context. When the project was launched, we organized a joint press conference held at Centro Prodh and we invited both people from the human rights world, and some journalists and media outlets from the art and museum worlds because we were having an exhibition as well. That created a collapse of two worlds, which in Mexico, don't normally mingle. Already that is

the creation of a strange forum, right? Then on top of that, then we had our opening two days later at the MUAC, the Museum of Contemporary Art of Mexico City, which was a good demonstration of the role of the art space for disseminating this type of work. The topic of human rights in the art gallery in Mexico is not common, and people that go there are not necessarily people that would engage with this sort of work; it's not what they're looking for. But also the Museum of Contemporary Art is interesting because it's part of UNAM, one of the largest Latin American universities. It's free tuition and it brings in people from all over the continent, a lot of very different socio-economic groups. So, suddenly this art space here is also collapsing another set of worlds. There's the art goer, and this university that actually has reached far beyond the boundaries of the university, and there's a place for discussion about this topic. We trained some of the students to be able to explain the murals to people that were there.

<u>Peter Hall</u>
So you end up with a forum.

<u>Stefan Laxness</u>
Yeah, a forum. The fact that the videos were widely disseminated for me was a little bit of victory. Now, there is something that's more important, which maybe I should have started by mentioning, is that with the new government, because they've elected a new president who's from a different party, there are talks now of reopening the case.

Visualizing Spatial History through the Archives of Slavery

Historians must always contend with questions about the uses of archives and archival sources in the making of history. Even the most conservative practitioners of the craft acknowledge that our sources are artifacts of complex processes rather than transparent reflections of past worlds; archival traces must therefore be interpreted with great care. However, when we shift our emphasis from historical recovery to rigorous and responsible creativity, we recognize that archives are not just the records bequeathed to us by the past; archives also consist of the tools we use to explore it, the vision that allows us to read its signs, and the design decisions that communicate our sense of history's possibilities.

Mapping a Slave Revolt

Vincent Brown

The historical geography of enslavement offers few sure routes to dependable knowledge. Searching archival records and the historiography of slavery for insights into enslaved experience often makes us feel as if we are facing the void: absence, silence, negation, death, perhaps even cultural genocide.

Reprinted with permission from Vincent Brown; *Mapping a Slave Revolt: Visualizing Spatial History through the Archives of Slavery*. Social Text 1 December 2015; 33 (4 (125)): 134–141.

But if, as Saidiya Hartman has recognized, "history is how the secular world attends to the dead," then perhaps the silences, absences, and deaths that make up slavery's history give historians a great opportunity and a special responsibility to reimagine what we do and how we do it.[1] New work in what is often dubbed digital humanities accords special prominence to questions of scholarly ingenuity. Historians are increasingly aware of the challenge and opportunity posed by the digital revolution to customary ways of conducting research and presenting findings. The late dramatic expansion of computing power allows for the evaluation of great amounts of data in which previously obscured patterns may now be observed,

queried, interpreted, and displayed. This enables the production of graphics that can illustrate some of the contours of social life. When animated by time-based media or laid out within temporal diagrams, such graphics can condense analytical storytelling in the form of data visualizations, setting seemingly static images in motion as historical processes are seen to unfold.[2] This has been a particular interest of mine as one who hopes to represent the history of slavery in media beyond the textual. I believe that only by wrestling imaginatively with difficult archival problems can we hope to find new avenues for pondering and representing history's most painful and vexing subjects.

This happens only when historians put in the creative work. I learned as much when I attended the "Humanities + Digital: Visual Interpretations Conference" hosted by the HyperStudio at the Massachusetts Institute of Technology in May 2010. The event fostered a "cross-disciplinary exploration of the aesthetics, methods, and critiques of information visualization in the humanities, arts, and social sciences."[3] And yet among the impressive array of presen-

---

1 Hartman, *Lose Your Mother*, 18; see also Gikandi, "Rethinking the Archive of Enslavement."

2 Burdick et al., *Digital_Humanities*; see esp. Rigney, "When the Monograph Is No Longer the Medium"; Cohen and Rosenzweig, *Digital History*; and Weller, *History in the Digital Age*. Over the last few years, I have been working in Harvard University's History Design Studio (historydesignstudio.com) to join a commitment to the professional practice of history with an experimental approach to form and presentation. Our goal is to embed historians' core values and methods in the innovative products of artisanship and craft. Extensive use of primary sources, attention to processes of change over time, keen historiographical awareness, and an overarching respect for evidence form the basis

of projects in multimedia storytelling and analysis. Thinking creatively about the design and presentation of our research, we attempt to stretch the canvass of historical scholarship. This work draws inspiration from parallel projects such as the Digital Scholarship Lab at the University of Richmond (dsl. richmond.edu), the Roy Rosenzweig Center for History and New Media at George Mason University (chnm.gmu.edu), the Spatial History Project at Stanford University (web.stanford. edu/group/spatialhistory/cgi-bin/site/index.php), and eHistory at the University of Georgia's Center for Virtual History (www.ehistory.org).

3 HyperStudio, "Humanities + Digital: Visual Interpretations Conference 2010"; Bailey, "All the Digital Humanists Are White."

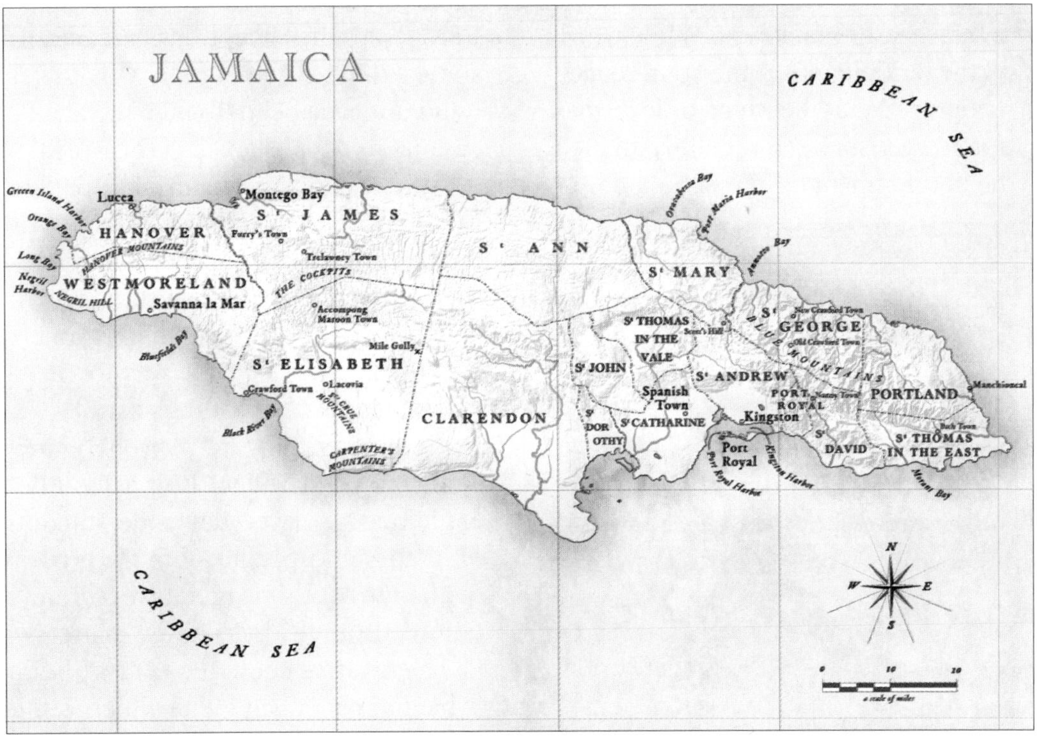

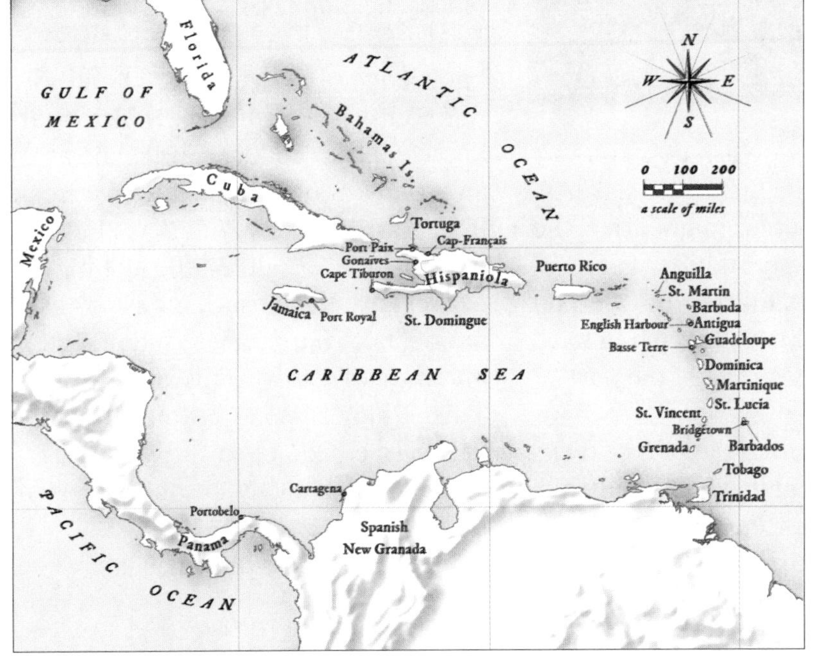

All maps drawn by Molly Roy and appear in Vincent Brown, *Tacky's Revolt: The Story of an Atlantic Slave War* (Cambridge, Mass.: Harvard University Press, 2020).

All installation views. Vincent Brown, *Jamaican Slave Revolt*, 2012. Website. Courtesy of Onsite Gallery. Photography by Yuula Benivolski.

tations at the meeting, there was almost no discussion of Africa and its diaspora, slavery, or blackness. While nearly all the participants at the conference recognized that the kinds of information to be visualized indelibly shaped the development of new scholarship,

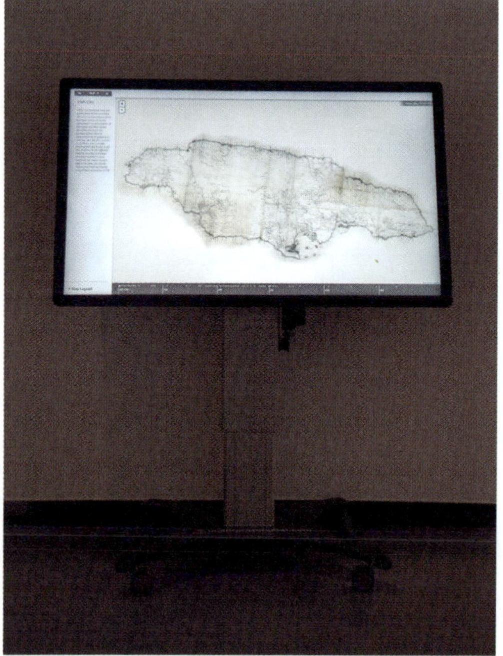

none were prepared to ask how conversations about the history of slavery and its archival sources might affect the future of visual interpretation. Perhaps appropriately, this task was left to scholars of black history prepared to paint more vivid portraits of the past and future.[4]

Europeans often thought of their slave colonies as fundamentally alien places, atavistic spaces of degeneracy and violence comprising a "torrid zone" beyond the boundaries of civilization. Where this imagined geography shaped European self-perceptions and even, to some extent, colonial policy making, it did not even begin to map the actual circuits of consequence in the world of Atlantic slavery. Historians are thus presented with the challenge of charting intelligible patterns in space and time, even while the sources we study inscribe mystifying geographical distinctions, producing silences in the way we discuss the landscapes of the past.

In *Silencing the Past* (1995), the anthropologist Michel-Rolph Trouillot explained how everyday understandings of history encapsulate both the process of change over time and its representation. "Both the facts of the matter and a narrative about those facts, both 'what happened' and 'that which is said to have happened.' The first meaning places the emphasis on the sociohistorical process, the second on our knowledge of that process." Trouillot was concerned to show how historical knowledge is produced over time as an artifact of power and how silences in historical understanding result from the creation of sources, the making of archives, the retrieval of events as moments of importance, and the interpretation of retrospective significance.[5] This argument is most often considered in regard to textual narrative, but it applies just as easily to conceptions of historical space.

Fortunately, there has lately been

---

4 For a promising recent theorization of the challenge, see Harrell, Phantasmal Media. Also see the online work of Jessica Marie Johnson, especially *Diaspora Hypertext, the Blog* at diasporahypertext.com.

5 Trouillot, *Silencing the Past*, 2.

6 White, "What Is Spatial History?"

7 For eighteenth-century histories of the war and its aftermath, see Long, *History of Jamaica*, 447–72; and

a spatial, even a cartographic emphasis in humanistic and social scientific study that encourages scholars to think more explicitly about how we can represent changing spatial linkages without reverting to the traditional geographic divisions. New historical cartographies allow us to visualize the networks and circuits that define spatial history, which the historian Richard White has succinctly characterized as the study of movements (of people, plants, animals, goods, and information) over time. With movement, interaction, and transformation, patterns are made and remade. By tracing these patterns, historical analysts can develop a visual language that may recover and illustrate spatial practices and processes. This is a thematic historical cartography, seen less as a technoscientific form of observation than as a rhetorical practice that can define, clarify, and advocate visions of the world that might otherwise go unarticulated. Cartographic visualization can be, says White, a fundamental part of historians' analytical process: a means of doing research, generating questions, and revealing historical relations.[6] New techniques present novel opportunities, but they also highlight the limitations of the archival material they employ.

My own online map of an African insurrection in the Caribbean offers a telling example. *Slave Revolt in Jamaica, 1760–1761: A Cartographic Narrative* (revolt.axismaps.com) interprets

the spatial history of the greatest slave insurrection in the eighteenth-century British Empire. Taking advantage of Britain's Seven Years' War against France and Spain, more than a thousand enslaved blacks revolted over the entire

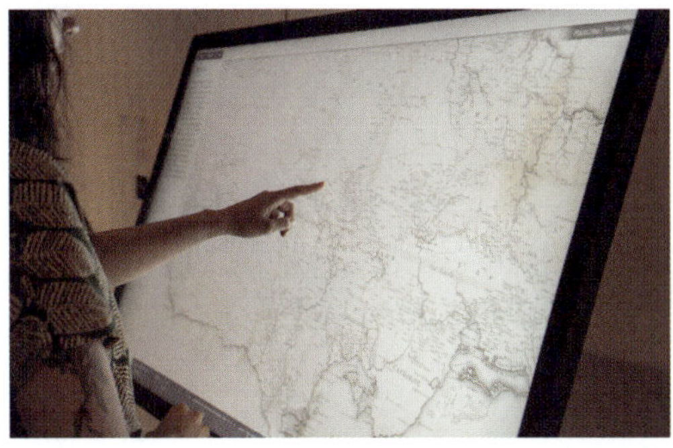

course of the uprising, which began on 7 April 1760, in the parish of St. Mary's, and continued until October of the next year. During eighteen months the rebels managed to kill sixty whites and destroy thousands of pounds worth of property. During the suppression of the revolt and the repression that followed, over five hundred black men and women were killed in battle or executed or committed suicide. Another five hundred were transported from the island for life.[7] To teachers and researchers, the cartographic visualization of the revolt offers a carefully curated archive of key documentary evidence. To all viewers, the map suggests an argument about the strategies of the rebels and the tactics of counterinsurgency and about the importance of the landscape to the course of the uprising, and no less important, the project highlights the

Edwards, *History of the West Indies*, 75–79. Recent accounts include Bollettino, "Slavery, War, and Britain's Atlantic Empire," 191–256; Brown, *Reaper's Garden*, 129–56; Burnard, Mastery, Tyranny, and Desire, 170–74;

Hart, Slaves Who Abolished Slavery, 130–56; Craton, Testing the Chains, 125–39; Reynolds, "Tacky and the Great Slave Revolt of 1760," 5–8; and Schuler, "Ethnic Slave Rebellions," 374–85.

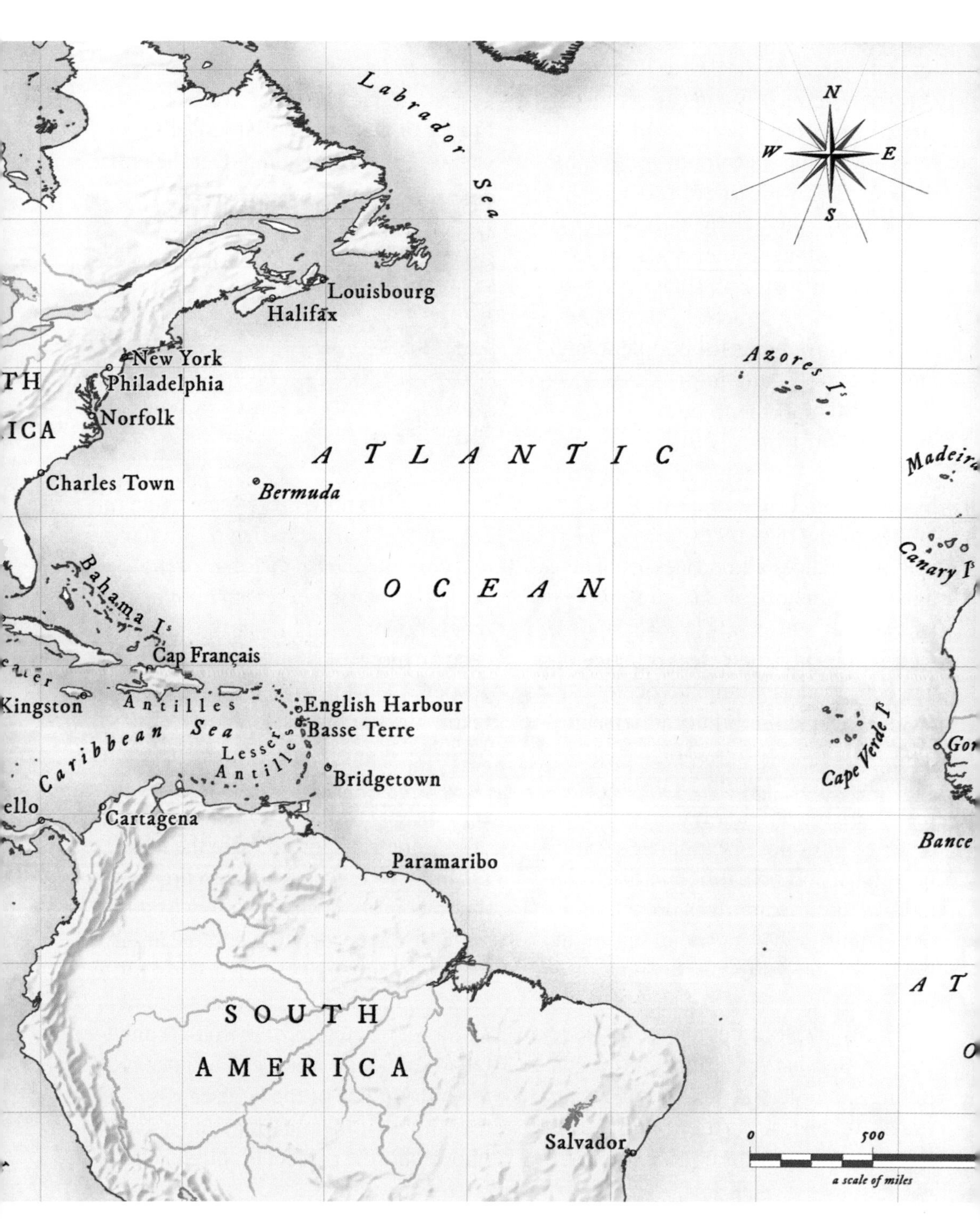
Labrador Sea
N
W E
S
Louisbourg
Halifax
New York
Philadelphia
Norfolk
ATLANTIC
Charles Town
Bermuda
Azores Iˢ
Madeira
Bahama Iˢ
OCEAN
Canary Iˢ
Cap Français
Kingston
Antilles
English Harbour
Basse Terre
Lesser
Antilles
Bridgetown
Caribbean Sea
Cape Verde Iˢ
Gor
ello
Cartagena
Bance
Paramaribo
SOUTH
AMERICA
A T
O
Salvador
0 500
a scale of miles
TH
ICA

difficulty of representing such events cartographically with available sources.

Mapping the revolt and its suppression illustrates something that is difficult to glean from simply reading the textual sources. The colonists and imperial officials who produced the historical record were universally unsympathetic to the rebellion, so their writings skew our understanding toward the perspectives of slaveholders. But we learn something else by plotting the combatants' movements in space. Tracing their locations over time, it is possible to discern some of their strategic aims and to observe the tactical dynamics of slave insurrection and counterrevolt.

The uprising encompassed three major phases of sustained action alongside more dispersed and sporadic skirmishes. The first was the rebellion in St. Mary's, generally named Tacky's Revolt after one of its principal African leaders. This was followed by the much larger Westmoreland parish upheaval, which comprised the largest battles of the conflict. Finally, survivors of the Westmoreland insurrection trekked across two parishes, raiding estates along the way. These campaigns adapted to environmental constraints. On the windward side of the island—the north side—heavy rainfall and dense vegetation limited movement more than on the leeward side, where the drier climate allowed for greater mobility. Still, within each phase of the rebellion, the routes traveled by the rebels through woods, mountains, hills, swamps, and rivers indicated strategic objectives.

Viewed on the map, the insurrection appears to have been the product of genuine strategic intelligence, one that utilized Jamaica's distinctive geography and aimed toward the creation of alternative enduring societies. Recognizing a real threat to the maintenance of the colony, the British mounted a rapid and diversified response, drawing upon the highly coordinated efforts of the regular military, the haphazard and decentralized tactics of the local militia, and the rough-terrain warfare of Maroon allies, each of which traversed the landscape in distinctive ways.

The project's graphic design articulates its historical interpretation. Composed from several eighteenth-century diagrams, a terrain map and an estate map form the base for the narration, which graphically depicts a chronological database of locations. Contemporary accounts of the revolt— culled from diaries, letters, military correspondence, and newspapers— yielded descriptions of the positions, movements, and engagements of rebels and counterinsurgents. These locations were cross-referenced with multiple sources wherever possible; latitudes and longitudes were then reckoned by correlating the base maps with satellite images. The symbol design, in which fading tracer lines track the movement of units, tries to account for the uncertainty of much of the data. Early iterations of the map featured symbols such as pushpins that inappropriately signified too much clarity. But then blurred circles were confusing. Solid lines tracking movement did not reflect

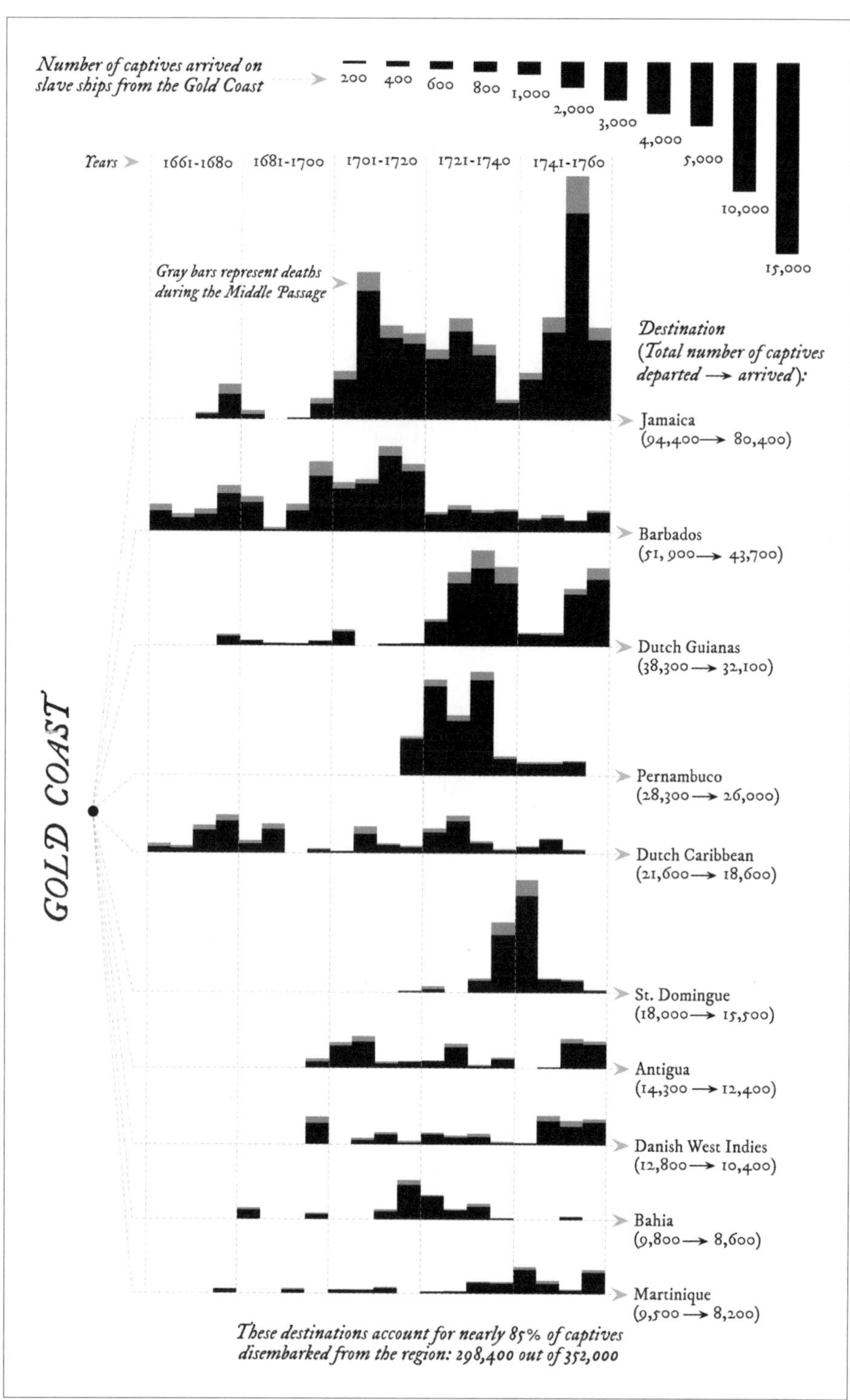
Number of captives arrived on slave ships from the Gold Coast
200 400 600 800 1,000 2,000 3,000 4,000 5,000 10,000 15,000
Years
1661-1680 1681-1700 1701-1720 1721-1740 1741-1760
Gray bars represent deaths during the Middle Passage
Destination (Total number of captives departed → arrived):
GOLD COAST
Jamaica (94,400 → 80,400)
Barbados (51,900 → 43,700)
Dutch Guianas (38,300 → 32,100)
Pernambuco (28,300 → 26,000)
Dutch Caribbean (21,600 → 18,600)
St. Domingue (18,000 → 15,500)
Antigua (14,300 → 12,400)
Danish West Indies (12,800 → 10,400)
Bahia (9,800 → 8,600)
Martinique (9,500 → 8,200)
These destinations account for nearly 85% of captives disembarked from the region: 298,400 out of 352,000

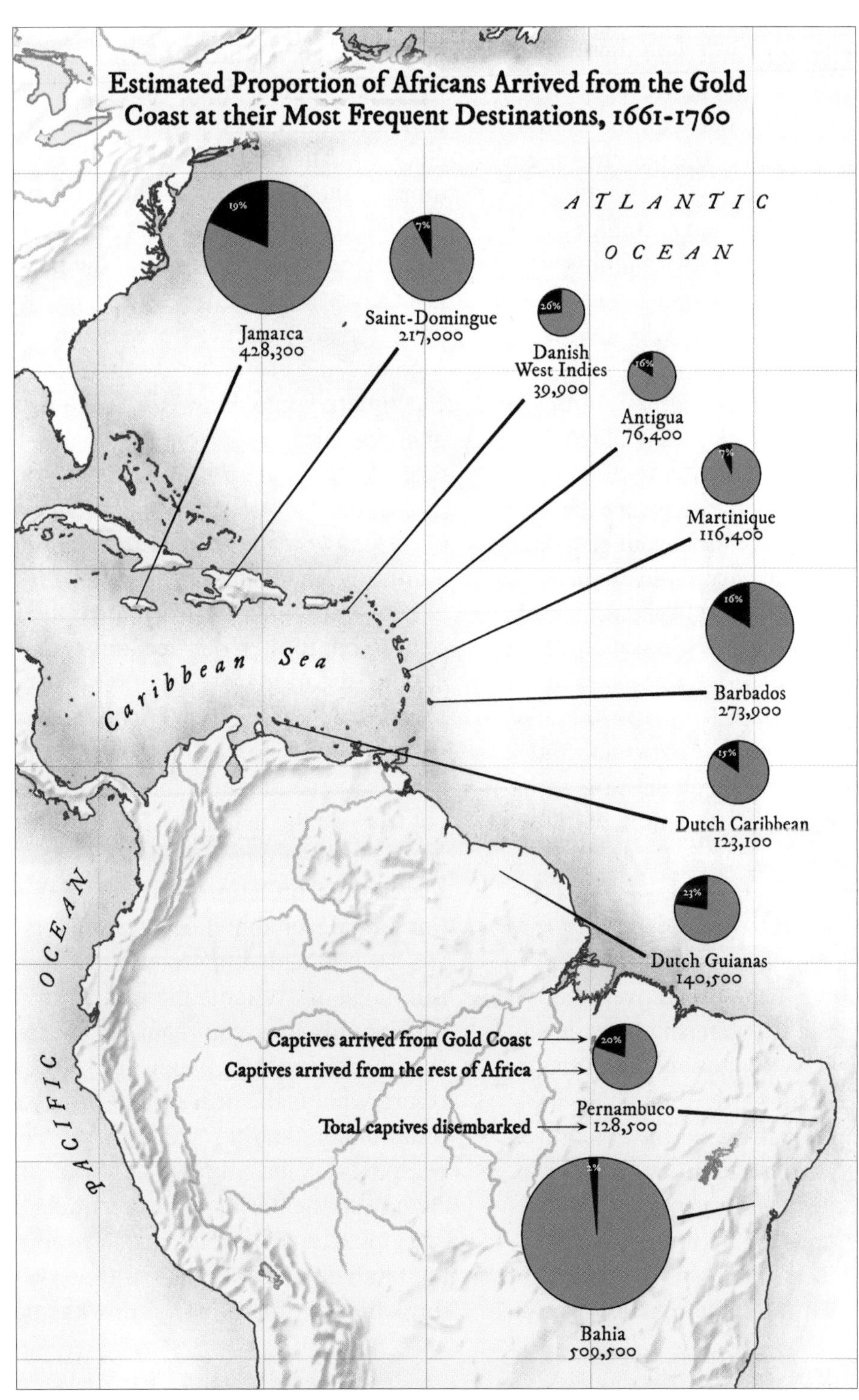

Estimated Proportion of Africans Arrived from the Gold Coast at their Most Frequent Destinations, 1661-1760
ATLANTIC OCEAN
19%
Jamaica
428,300
7%
Saint-Domingue
217,000
26%
Danish West Indies
39,900
16%
Antigua
76,400
7%
Martinique
116,400
16%
Barbados
273,900
15%
Dutch Caribbean
123,100
23%
Dutch Guianas
140,500
Caribbean Sea
PACIFIC OCEAN
Captives arrived from Gold Coast
Captives arrived from the rest of Africa
Total captives disembarked
20%
Pernambuco
128,500
2%
Bahia
509,500

the nature of guerrilla warfare, in which rebels dispersed over the landscape in loose formations and their pursuers hunted rumors and chance sightings. Yet without traces between the points, it became difficult for the map to suggest that the movements were directional. The graphics ultimately attempt to balance intelligibility with ambiguity while maintaining viewers' sense of the interpretive character of the database.

Even as this approach yields new insights, there are significant limitations to plotting a turbulent slave revolt on a map like this. By using British maps that highlight the placement of forts, towns, and estates, our maps tend to reify colonial geography. Even more fundamentally, cartography presumes the natural existence of points on a grid much as history naturalizes the timeline, though these are ultimately folkways for representing space and time that have more in common with slaveholders' epistemes than with those of their slaves. The "rival geographies" of the rebels—their spatial schemas, landmarks and pathways, and sense of temporality—may be irretrievable in cartographic form.[8] Moreover, maps orient viewers by offering an orderly aerial view. But gazing down from above makes it hard to see chaos and confusion, the most essential features of a protracted insurgency. Of course, if this limitation arises from the sources, it also reflects the nature of guerrilla warfare: uncertainty was the rebels' best weapon. For the same reason, quan-

titative reports must also be taken as impressionistic. Like words, numbers produced during the disorienting events were the products of bewilderment, fear, and rumor. If the map draws a clearer picture of the extent and contours of the insurrection, there are entire worlds that it simply cannot convey.

One might protest that the map is a reification of reifications. We have taken the dead artifacts of slaveholders' accounts and given them artificial life as animated data. How can the cameraman purport to represent experience when taking a photograph of a painting of a statue? This is a fair and difficult question, which I can only answer by admitting that I share the tragic compulsion common to historians of the oppressed: though our accounts of slavery are distorted by the mediation of the sources, we persist in trying to explore and explain its past. Knowing that the truth is a receding horizon, we still set out to close the distance. This impulse urges me toward new methods of research, interpretation, and storytelling. For I am never convinced that historians are not neglecting to explore the full range of available material. Have we learned all we can from our sources? If we care to apply new tools to this effort, what is the best way to achieve fuller understanding? Perhaps we can begin by recognizing two major obstacles: first, the unwarranted certitude of empiricist historians, and second, the fatalism and paralysis of those who think that our inability to know the past

8 "Rival geographies" is Stephanie Camp's terminology, taken from *Closer to Freedom*. On alternative ways of knowing and using space in slave societies, see esp.

Camp, *Closer to Freedom*; Kaye, *Joining Places*; and Troutman, "Grapevine in the Slave Market."

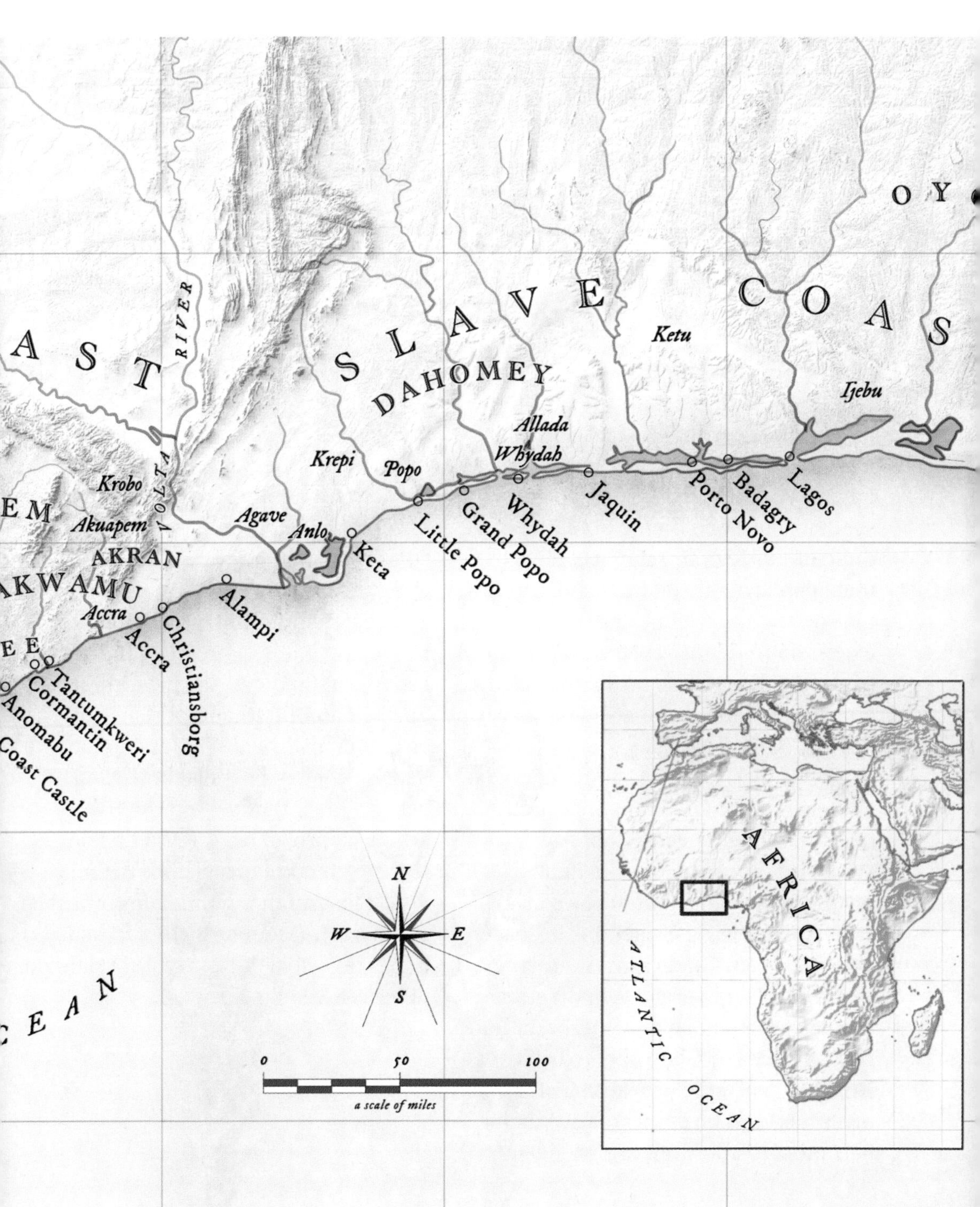
OY
SLAVE COAS
DAHOMEY
Ketu
Ijebu
Allada
Whydah
Krepi
Popo
Whydah
Jaquin
Porto Novo
Badagry
Lagos
Grand Popo
Little Popo
Krobo
Agave
Akuapem
Anlo
Keta
AKRAN
AKWAMU
Accra
Accra
Alampi
Christiansborg
Tantumkweri
Cormantin
Anomabu
Coast Castle
RIVER
VOLTA
AST
EM
EE
E E
N
W
E
S
OCEAN
AFRICA
ATLANTIC
OCEAN
0
50
100
a scale of miles

with certainty means we cannot learn anything new at all.

Historians' engagements with digital techniques may sharpen our approach to the archives of slavery. Scholars working in subaltern history rarely have the kind of big databases that inspire projects in text mining, topic modeling, or network analysis. And our data are debased, compiled from the records of the slavers, the racists, the exploiters, and their bureaucrats. Yet there may be a virtue to this limitation. We can never confuse our sources for the things they describe, and this encourages us to emphasize their qualitative nature. Without big numbers to crunch, scholars must exploit the potential of digital tools to craft scholarly designs that appreciate the interdependency of interpretive knowledge and aesthetic expression.[9] In this way the constraints of the archive compel more careful attention to the form and function—the design—of our scholarly works.[10]

Scholarly design can function as a method for generating research questions about the most appropriate symbols for the phenomena under investigation and about how we see relationships and interactions in space and time. Rather than representing reified artifacts, historical visualizations can narrate a humanistic interpretation. Perhaps, then, the best way to discover what happened in the spatial history of slavery is to be more creative in our narration, to allow our knowledge of

sociohistorical process to be shaped by new modes of historical storytelling. These novel methods may reach even more people. Web-based history offers remarkable possibilities for wide distribution.[11] However, it is too soon to tell how and what users will learn from these new works. In the digital environment we can be more confident in our roles as researchers and producers than in our duty as teachers.

Maintaining historians' traditional emphasis on primary sources, attention to change over time, historiographical awareness, and an overarching respect for evidence-based claims, we may admit more experimental forms of research and presentation without compromising the veracity of historical study. Such a shift will require a deeper exploration of the relation between graphic expression and historical understanding. As I have argued, this will amplify the importance of design in historical scholarship, perhaps softening a persistent tension between quantitative, interpretive, and artistic approaches. Admittedly, this is less a method than a vision. But it is a vision that might, in time, discover the contours of a counterhistory of space, power, and social life—a past that might otherwise remain silenced.

9 Drucker, *Graphesis*.
10 As Elizabeth Maddock Dillon stresses in her contribution to this forum.

11 As Claudio Saunt indicates in his contribution to this forum.

References

Bailey, Moya Z. 2011. "All the Digital Humanists Are White, All the Nerds Are Men, but Some of Us Are Brave." *Journal of Digital Humanities* 1, no. 1. journalofdigital humanities.org/1-1/all-the-digital-humanists-are-white-all-the-nerds-are-men-but-some-of-us-are-brave-by-moya-z-bailey/.

Bollettino, Maria Allessandra. 2009. "Slavery, War, and Britain's Atlantic Empire: Black Soldiers, Sailors, and Rebels in the Seven Years' War." PhD diss., University of Texas at Austin.

Brown, Vincent. 2008. *The Reaper's Garden: Death and Power in the World of Atlantic Slavery*. Cambridge, MA: Harvard University Press.

Brown, Vincent. 2013. *Slave Revolt in Jamaica*, 1760–1761: A Cartographic Narrative. revolt.axismaps.com.

Burdick, Anne, Johanna Drucker, Peter Lunenfeld, Todd Presner, and Jeffrey Schnapp. 2012. Digital_Humanities. Cambridge, MA: MIT Press.

Burnard, Trevor. 2004. *Mastery, Tyranny, and Desire: Thomas Thistlewood and His Slaves in the Anglo-Jamaican World*. Chapel Hill: University of North Carolina Press.

Camp, Stephanie M. H. 2004. *Closer to Freedom: Enslaved Women and Everyday Resistance in the Plantation South*. Chapel Hill: University of North Carolina Press.

Cohen, Daniel J., and Roy Rosenzweig. 2005. *Digital History: A Guide to Gathering, Preserving, and Presenting the Past on the Web*. Philadelphia: University of Pennsylvania Press.

Craton, Michael. 1982. *Testing the Chains: Resistance to Slavery in the British West Indies*. Ithaca, NY: Cornell University Press.

Drucker, Johanna. 2014. *Graphesis: Visual Forms of Knowledge Production*. Cambridge, MA: Harvard University Press.

Edwards, Bryan. 1793. *History of the West Indies*. Vol. 2. London.

Gikandi, Simon. 2015. "Rethinking the Archive of Enslavement." *Early American Literature* 50, no. 1: 81–102.

Harrell, D. Fox. 2014. *Phantasmal Media: An Approach to Imagination, Computation, and Expression*. Cambridge, MA: MIT Press.

Hart, Richard. (1985) 2002. *Slaves Who Abolished Slavery: Blacks in Rebellion*. Kingston, Jamaica: University of West Indies Press.

Hartman, Saidiya. 2007. *Lose Your Mother: A Journey along the Atlantic Slave Route*. New York: Farrar, Straus and Giroux.

HyperStudio. "Humanities + Digital: Visual Interpretations Conference 2010: Aesthetics, Methods, and Critiques of Information Visualization in the Humanities, Arts, and Social Sciences." Massachusetts Institute of Technology. hyperstudio .mit.edu/events/about/.

Kaye, Anthony. 2009. *Joining Places: Slave Neighborhoods in the Old South*. Chapel Hill: University of North Carolina Press.

Long, Edward. 1774. *History of Jamaica*. Vol. 2. London.

Reynolds, C. Roy. 1972. "Tacky and the Great Slave Revolt of 1760." *Jamaica Journal* 6, no. 2: 5–8.

Rigney, Ann. 2010. "When the Monograph Is No Longer the Medium: Historical Narrative in the Online Age." *History and Theory* 49, no. 4: 100–117.

Schuler, Monica. 1970. "Ethnic Slave Rebellions in the Caribbean and the Guianas." *Journal of Social History* 3, no. 4: 374–85.

Trouillot, Michel-Rolph. 1995. Silencing the Past: Power and the Production of History. Boston: Beacon Press.

Troutman, Phillip. 2004. "Grapevine in the Slave Market: African American Geopolitical Literacy and the 1841 Creole Revolt." *In The Chattel Principle: Internal Slave Trades in the Americas*, edited by Walter Johnson, 203–33. New Haven, CT: Yale University Press.

Weller, Toni. 2012. *History in the Digital Age*. New York: Routledge.

White, Richard. 2010. "What Is Spatial History?" Working Paper, Spatial History Lab. web.stanford.edu/group/spatialhistory/cgi-bin/site/pub.php?id=29.

April 10, 1760

Moore has sent "Express's to the Commanding Officers of Crawford Town, Nanny town and Scotts Hall with Orders to March immediately with a Company from such places to their Relief."
—Minutes of the Jamaica Council, 10 April 1760

Map Legend

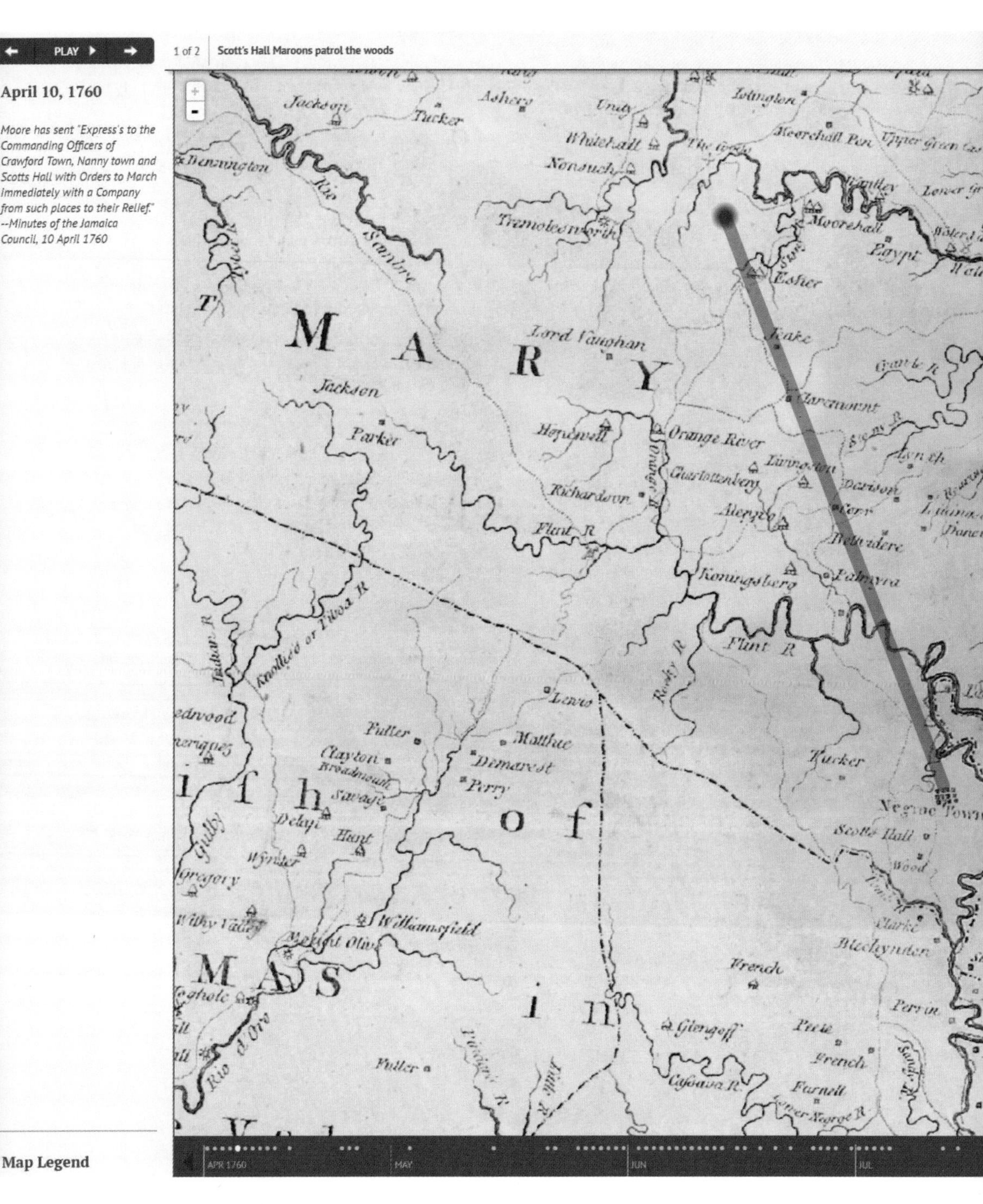

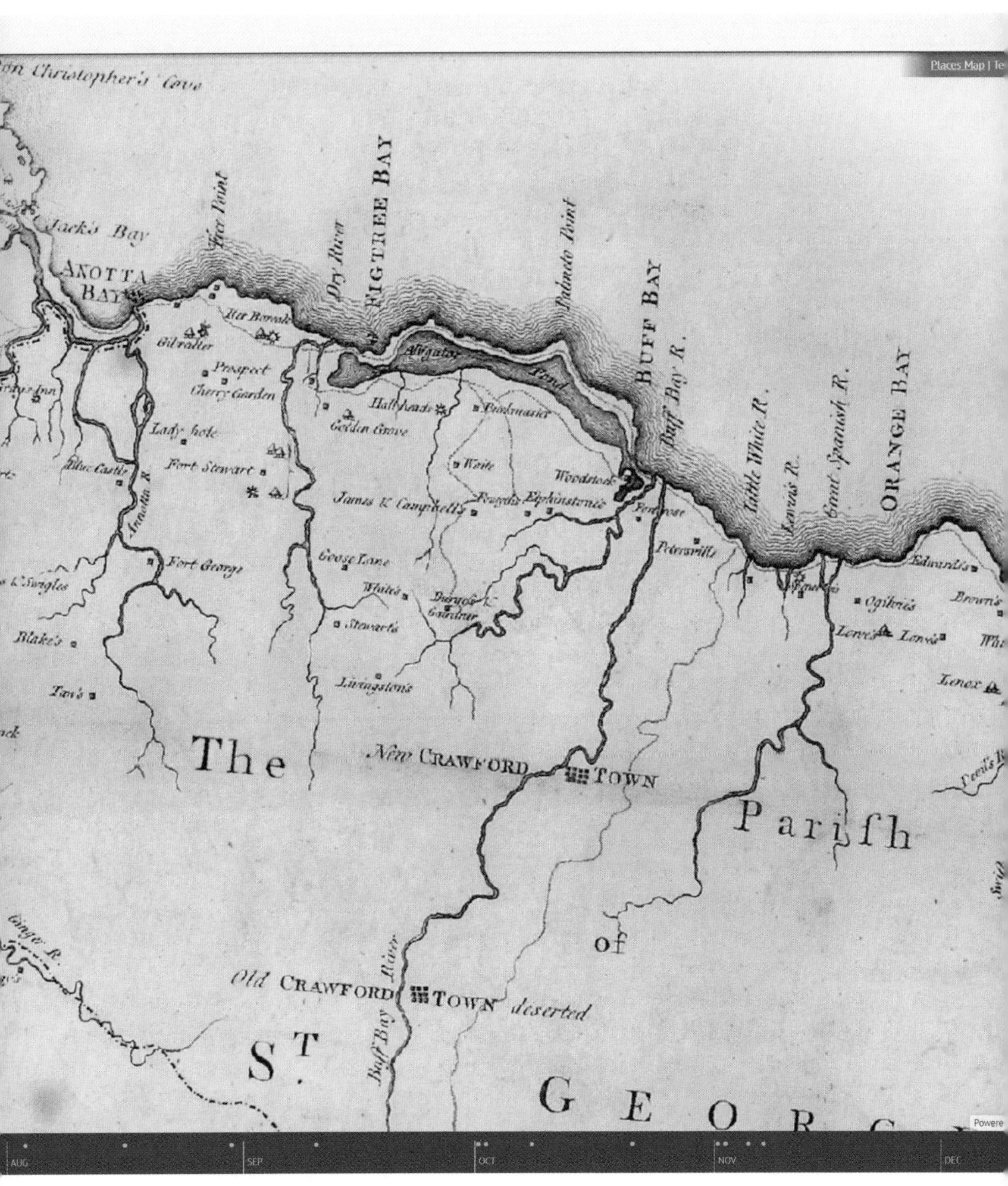

All stills. Vincent Brown, *Jamaican Slave Revolt*, 2012. Website.
Courtesy of the artist.

May 30, 1760

I went to visit the Negroes in their Houses [where] I found also 7 of the wild Negroes, whereof one of the chiefs, is nam'd Acompong, who is a Captain of one of the 5 Towns, wch is call'd after him. His Br. Cudjoe is Coll. Of another. I have been told that in the 5 Towns, wch they, are above 1500 free Negroes, who lead an orderly Life, & have cultivated their own Land. Their Officers or Governors who are call'd Captains have a Pension from the Government. Capn Acompong's Dress was an embroidered Waistcoat, gold Lace around his Hat, a silver chain abt. His Neck to wch was hung a silver Medal wherein, on one side was King George ye 2nd's Picture and on the other his Commission with this subscription Captain Acampong. He had Ear Rings & on each of his Fingers 5, 6, or 7 Rings of silver & on his Feet some Iron Rings, he goes barefooted.-- Zacharias George Caries Diary, 27 March 1755

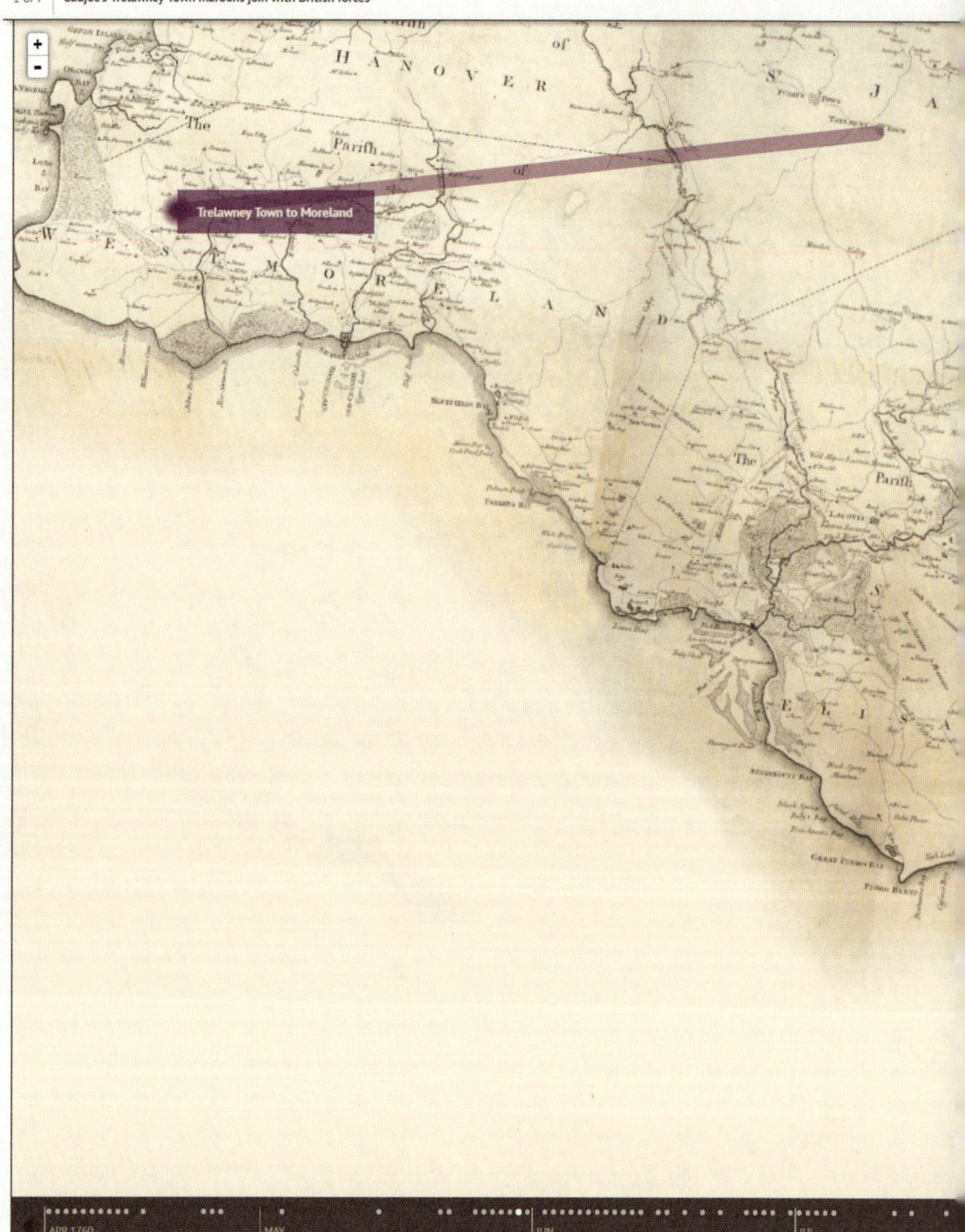

Map Legend

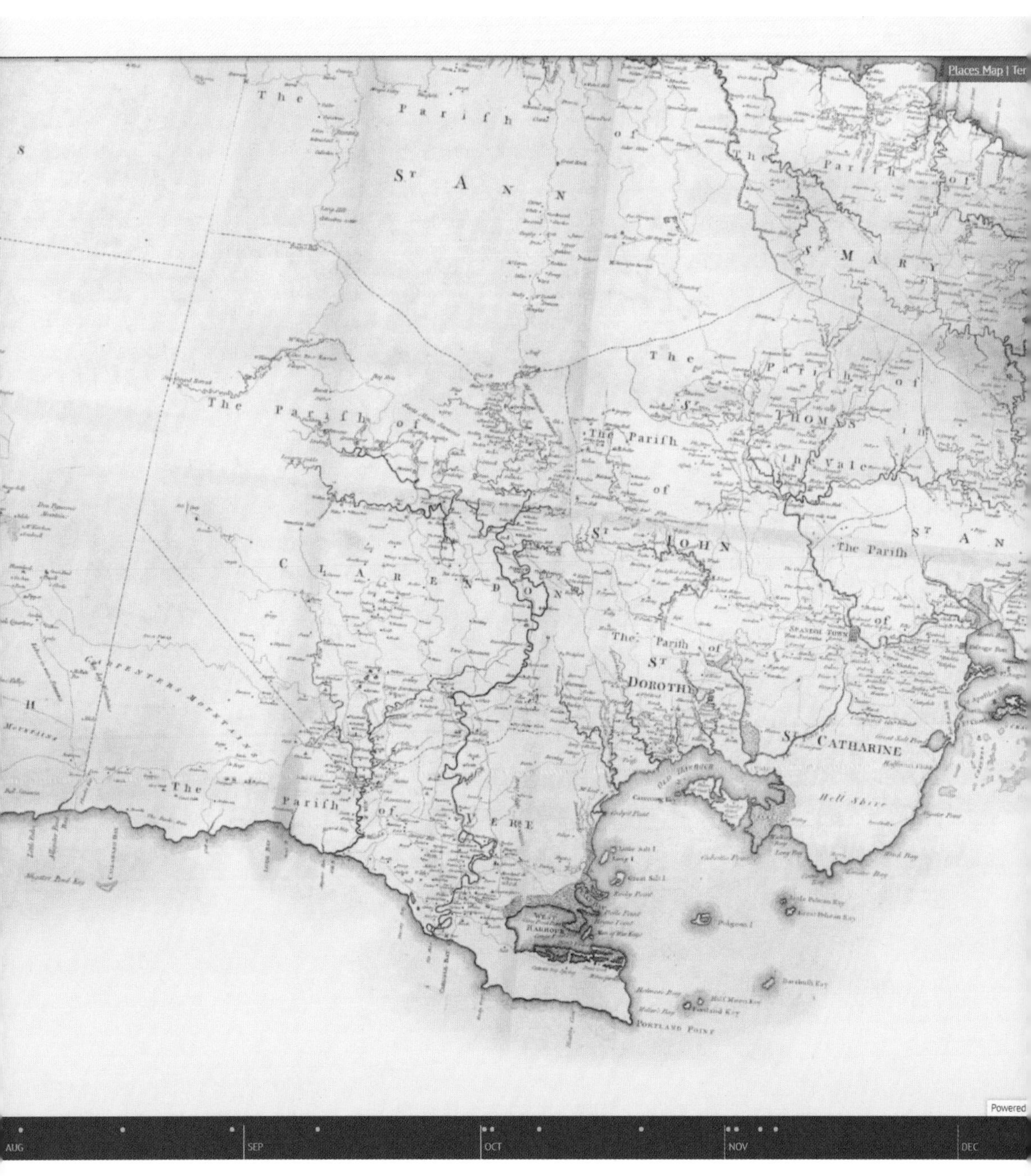
Places Map | Ter
The Parish of St ANN
The Parish of St MARY
The Parish of
The Parish of St THOMAS in the Vale
The Parish of
St JOHN
St ANN
The Parish of
The Parish of CLARENDON
The Parish of St DOROTHY
SPANISH TOWN
St CATHARINE
Hell Shire
The Parish of VERE
OLD HARBOUR
PORTLAND POINT
Powered
AUG   SEP   OCT   NOV   DEC

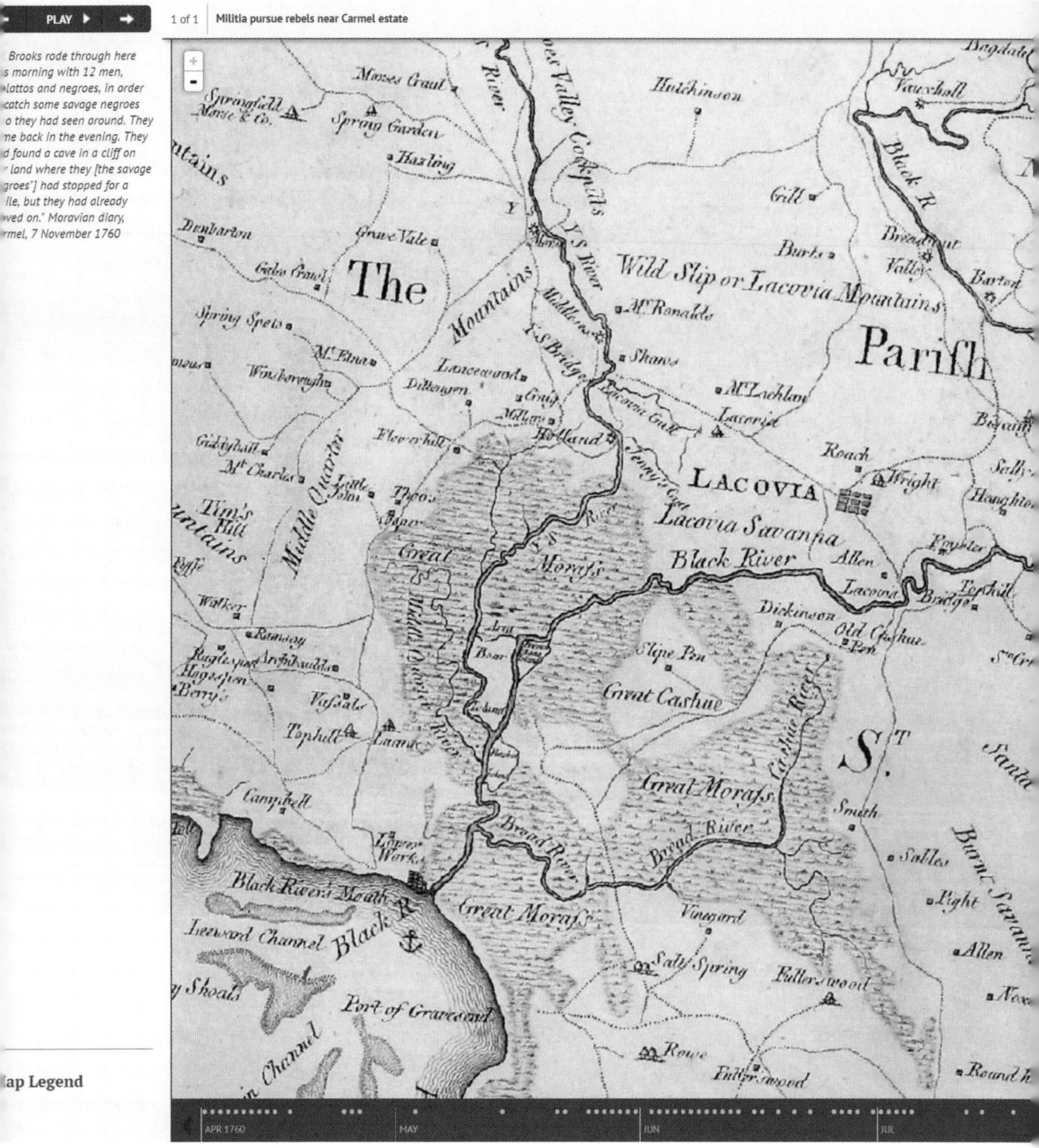

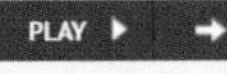

1 of 1 | **Militia pursue rebels near Carmel estate**

… Brooks rode through here [thi]s morning with 12 men, [mu]lattos and negroes, in order [to] catch some savage negroes [wh]o they had seen around. They [ca]me back in the evening. They [ha]d found a cave in a cliff on [our] land where they [the savage [ne]groes"] had stopped for a [whi]le, but they had already [mo]ved on." Moravian diary, [Ca]rmel, 7 November 1760

Map Legend

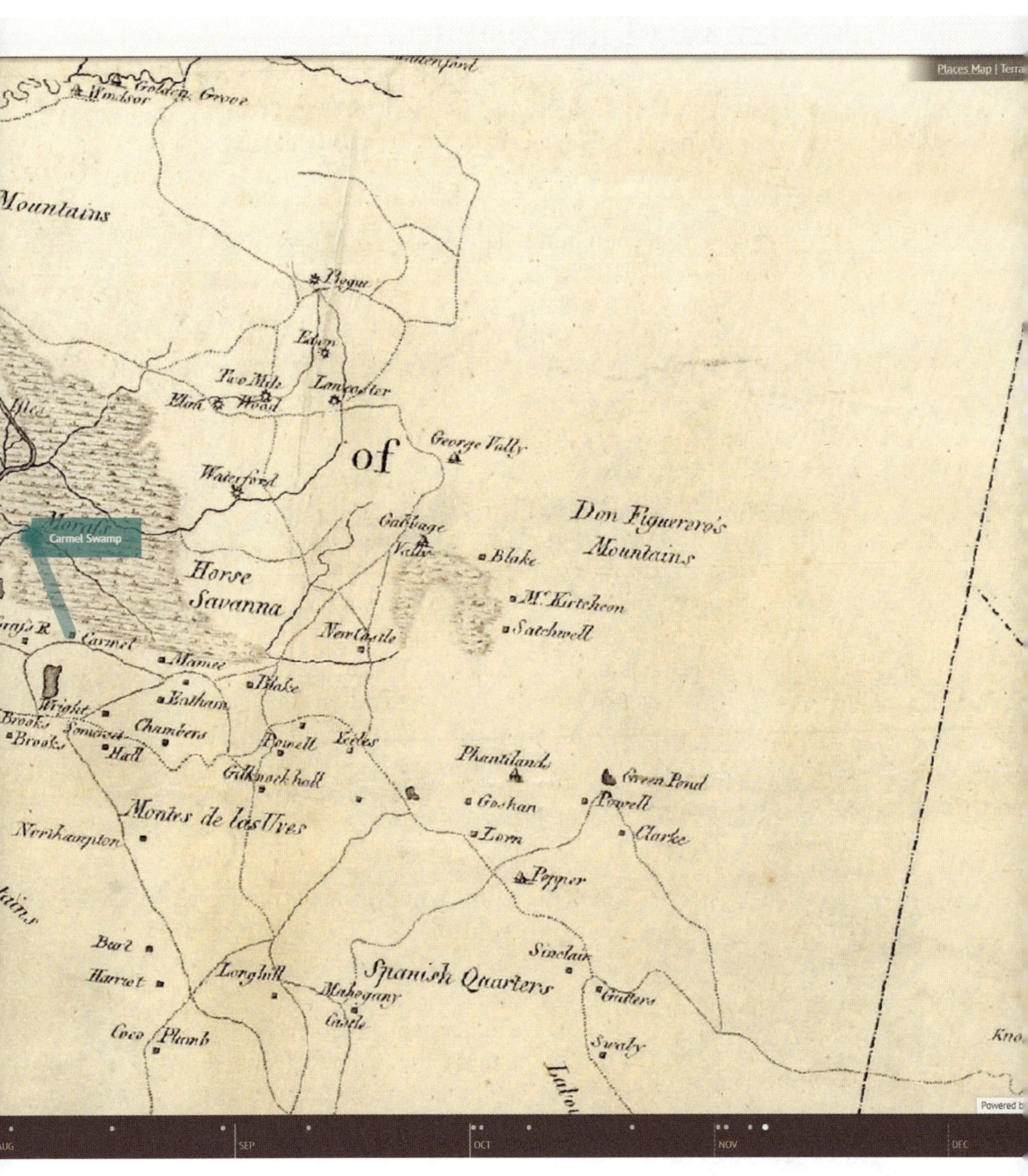
Places Map | Terra
Golden Grove
Windsor
Waterford
Mountains
Bogue
Eden
Two Mile Wood
Elim
Lancaster
George Vally
of
Cabbage Vally
Don Figuerero's Mountains
Blake
Horse Savanna
Morale
Carmel Swamp
Mt. Kitcheon
Satchwell
Grass R.
Carmel
Mamee
New Castle
Wright
Eatham
Blake
Brooks
Chambers
Powell
Veeles
Brooks
Hall
Gilknock hall
Phantilands
Green Pond
Goshan
Powell
Montes de las Vies
Clarke
Norihampton
Lorn
Pepper
Sinclair
Bart
Harriet
Longhill
Spanish Quarters
Gutters
Mahogany
Coco Plumb
Castle
Swaby
Kno
AUG   SEP   OCT   NOV   DEC
Powered b

In 2008, the 21st century became aware of its existence.

Ten years after the detonation of the sub-prime mort-gage market and subsequent domino effect of collaps-ing global financial markets, we must ask ourselves: how have we moved on? Could we possibly have moved past something that hasn't really left us?

We can begin this process with a retrospec-tive of perspective—a post-occupancy of the Crisis.

Department of Un-usual Certainties will mark the 10th anniversary of the Crisis with an exploration into perceived and documented outcomes, as expe-rienced in forms which are not necessarily financial, since the peak of the Crisis in 2008. The goal is to create a series of stories and visualizations that draw comparison with no implication of necessary correla-tion, and illustrate what it means for one figurative century to die so another can live.

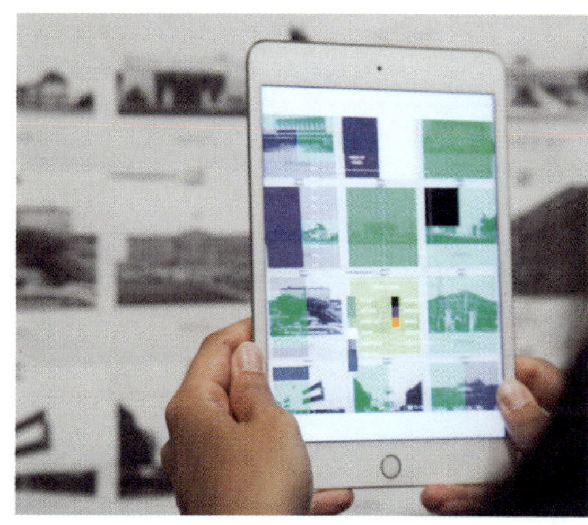

VOL. 1: POLITICS attempts to map the shifts in political leadership and position from January 2007 to June 2018 for all United Nations member and non-member states.

We understand that the Crisis is a milestone that will one day be regarded as ushering in the present and is there-fore worth reflecting on. Retrospective of a Crisis does not attempt to provide answers, only to pose a series of ques-tions through which to create better understanding of the past decade and its impact on our present moment.

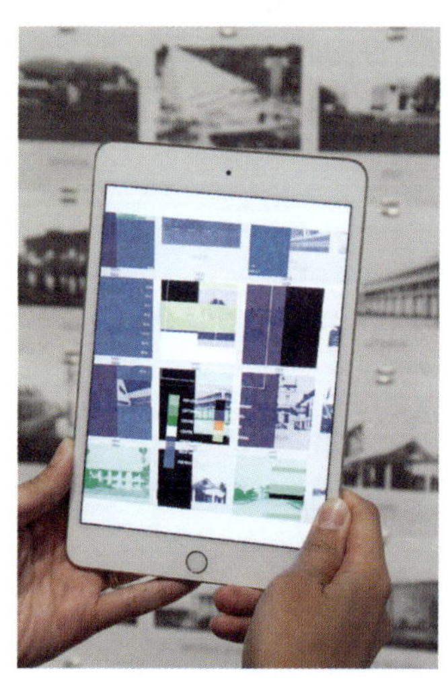

Installation view. Department of Unusual Certainties, *Retrospective of a Crisis, Vol.1 Politics*, 2018. Courtesy of Onsite Gallery. Photography by Yuula Benivolski.

Retrospective of a Crisis

Department of Unusual Certainties

DIAGRAMS OF POWER

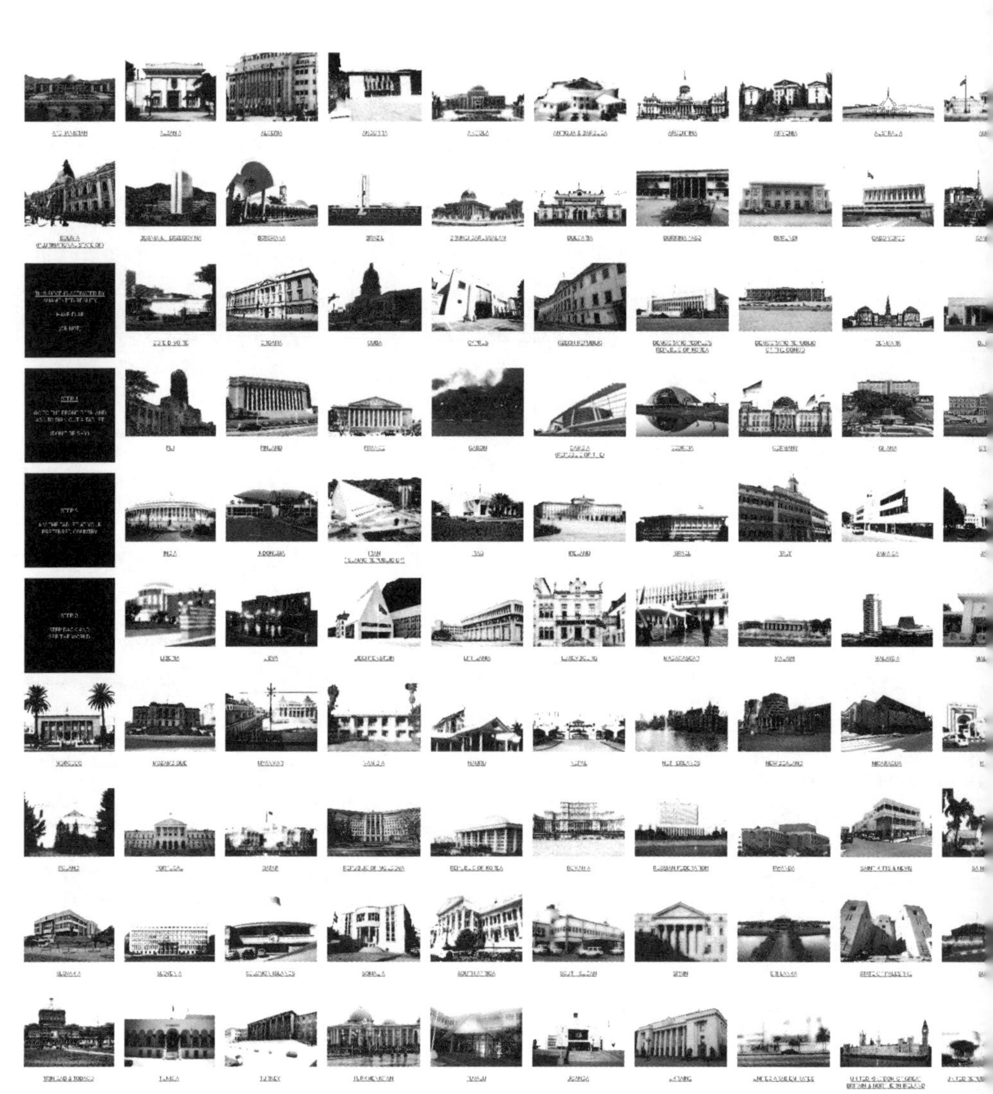

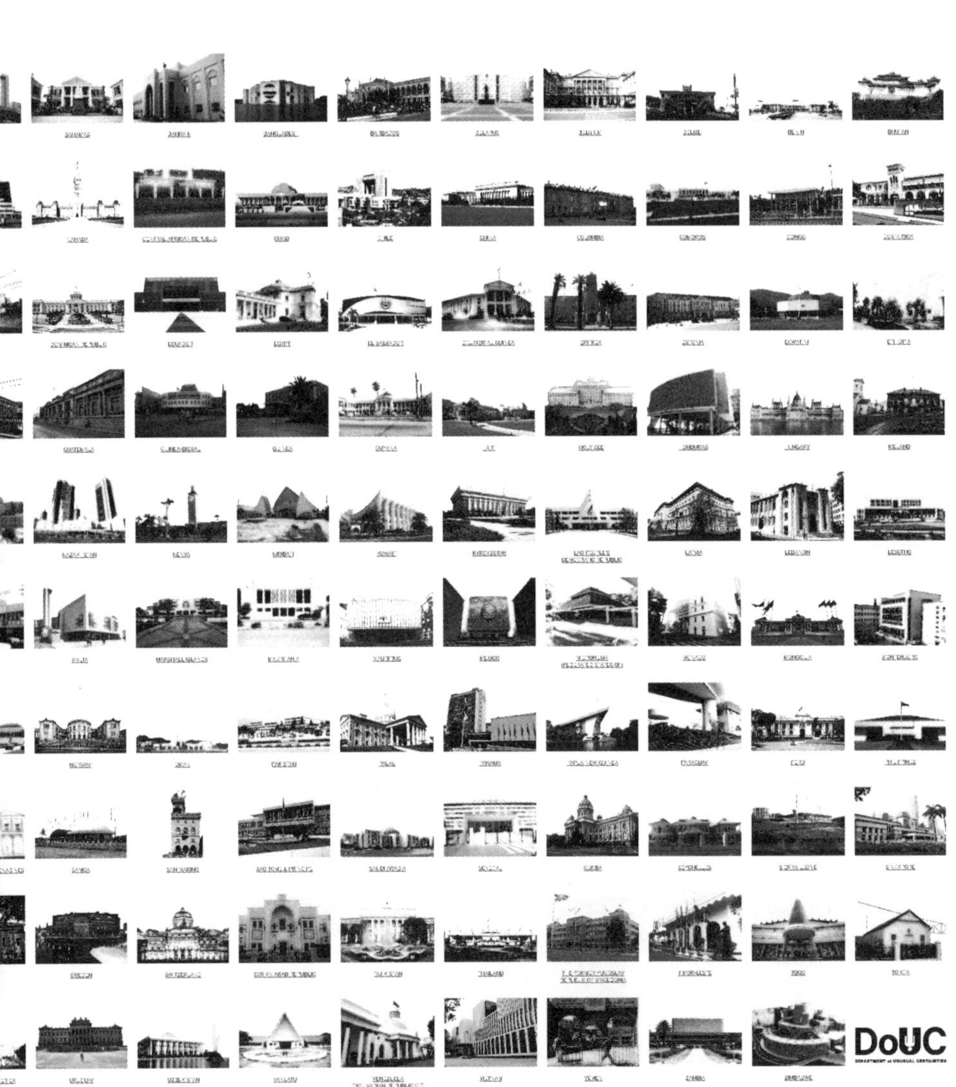

Department of Unusual Certainties, *Retrospective of a Crisis,
Vol.1 Politics*, 2018. Courtesy of the artist.

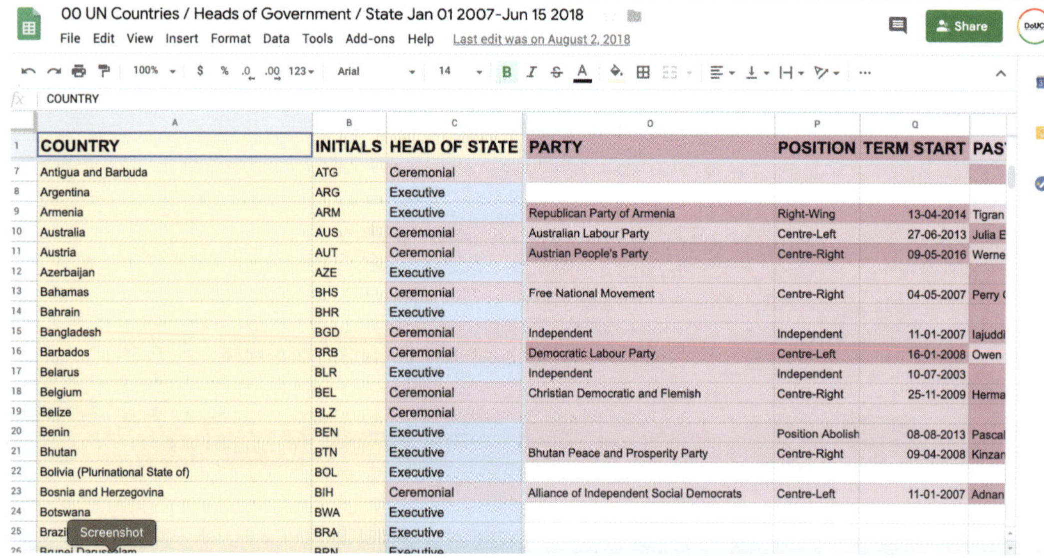

00 UN Countries / Heads of Government / State Jan 01 2007–Jun 15 2018

File Edit View Insert Format Data Tools Add-ons Help   Last edit was on August 2, 2018

100% $ % .0 .00 123▾   Arial   14   B I S A   ▦   ⋯

COUNTRY

	A	B	C	O	P	Q	
1	**COUNTRY**	**INITIALS**	**HEAD OF STATE**	**PARTY**	**POSITION**	**TERM START**	**PAS**
7	Antigua and Barbuda	ATG	Ceremonial				
8	Argentina	ARG	Executive				
9	Armenia	ARM	Executive	Republican Party of Armenia	Right-Wing	13-04-2014	Tigran
10	Australia	AUS	Ceremonial	Australian Labour Party	Centre-Left	27-06-2013	Julia E
11	Austria	AUT	Ceremonial	Austrian People's Party	Centre-Right	09-05-2016	Werne
12	Azerbaijan	AZE	Executive				
13	Bahamas	BHS	Ceremonial	Free National Movement	Centre-Right	04-05-2007	Perry (
14	Bahrain	BHR	Executive				
15	Bangladesh	BGD	Ceremonial	Independent	Independent	11-01-2007	Iajuddi
16	Barbados	BRB	Ceremonial	Democratic Labour Party	Centre-Left	16-01-2008	Owen
17	Belarus	BLR	Executive	Independent	Independent	10-07-2003	
18	Belgium	BEL	Ceremonial	Christian Democratic and Flemish	Centre-Right	25-11-2009	Herma
19	Belize	BLZ	Ceremonial				
20	Benin	BEN	Executive		Position Abolish	08-08-2013	Pascal
21	Bhutan	BTN	Executive	Bhutan Peace and Prosperity Party	Centre-Right	09-04-2008	Kinzan
22	Bolivia (Plurinational State of)	BOL	Executive				
23	Bosnia and Herzegovina	BIH	Ceremonial	Alliance of Independent Social Democrats	Centre-Left	11-01-2007	Adnan
24	Botswana	BWA	Executive				
25	Brazil	BRA	Executive				
26	Brunei Darussalam	BRN	Executive				

Context / Economic History of the Crisis

From a purely economic perspective, detail the events, policies and mechanisms which led to and transpired during the Crisis in order to create a baseline of understanding how and why the Crisis occurred. This summary will give consideration to those details that lay the most appropriate groundwork for the project perspectives.

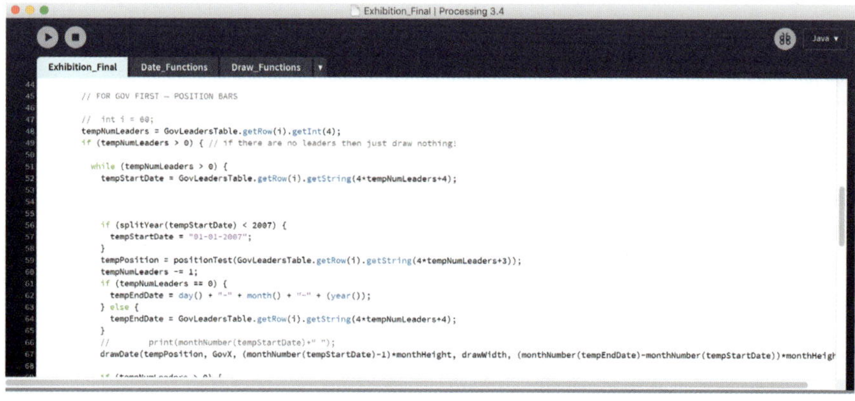

Process work for making
*Retrospective of a Crisis, Vol. 1
Politics*. Courtesy of the artist.

00 UN Countries / Heads of Government / State Jan 01 2007-Jun 15 2018

File   Edit   View   Insert   Format   Data   Tools   Add-ons   Help   Last edit was on August 2, 2018

	A	B	C	D
34	Canada	Ceremonial	Constitutional monarchy	Ministry is subject to parliamentary confidence
35	Central African Republic	Executive	Republic	Presidency is independent of legislature
36	Chad	Executive	Republic	Presidency is independent of legislature
37	Chile	Executive	Republic	Presidency is independent of legislature
38	China	Executive	Republic	Power constitutionally linked to a single political movement
39	Colombia	Executive	Republic	Presidency is independent of legislature
40	Comoros	Executive	Republic	Presidency is independent of legislature
41	Congo	Executive	Republic	Presidency is independent of legislature
42	Costa Rica	Executive	Republic	Presidency is independent of legislature
43	Côte D'Ivoire	Executive	Republic	Presidency is independent of legislature
44	Croatia	Ceremonial	Republic	Ministry is subject to parliamentary confidence
45	Cuba	Executive	Republic	Power constitutionally linked to a single political movement
46	Cyprus	Executive	Republic	Presidency is independent of legislature
47	Czech Republic	Ceremonial	Republic	Ministry is subject to parliamentary confidence
48	Democratic People's Republic (	Executive	Republic	Power constitutionally linked to a single political movement
49	Democratic Republic of the Cor	Executive	Republic	Presidency independent of legislature; ministry subject to parliamentary confidence
50	Denmark	Ceremonial	Constitutional monarchy	Ministry is subject to parliamentary confidence
51	Djibouti	Executive	Republic	Presidency is independent of legislature
52	Dominica	Ceremonial	Republic	Ministry is subject to parliamentary confidence
53	Domi	Executive	Republic	Presidency is independent of legislature

Exploration / Post Crisis Perspectives

Political

Add global context to the Crisis through mapping the shifts in both political leadership and national health metrics since 2008. This component will also highlight major global events (both related and unrelated) and ask how national relationships (trade, migration, etc.) have changed over the last decade.

Personal

Engage the public in a conversation of personal experience since 2008; who was affected by the crisis?; in what tangible and intangible ways?; and how have real people perceived the ongoing effects in their lives?

Digital

In 2007, the iPhone was released. In 2014, Flappy Bird earned $50,000 per day in ad revenue. In 2017, Sidewalk Labs made moves toward land ownership. How can the changing economy of digital products & services be mapped alongside developments in digital access? Can we make predictions or speculate on possible future directions of technology, the economy and the city based on the past digital landscape and trends?

Cultural

The details of the Financial Crisis have been documented and depicted in myriad different media, from Too Big To Fail (Sorkin, 2009) to The Big Short (2015) to Bad Bank (This American Life, 2009), but how has the Crisis been depicted through media not focused on the economic storyline? How have economic realities affected cultural fiction? This component will reflect on how the Crisis has subtly (or overtly) influenced cultural narratives and media through a non-economic lens.

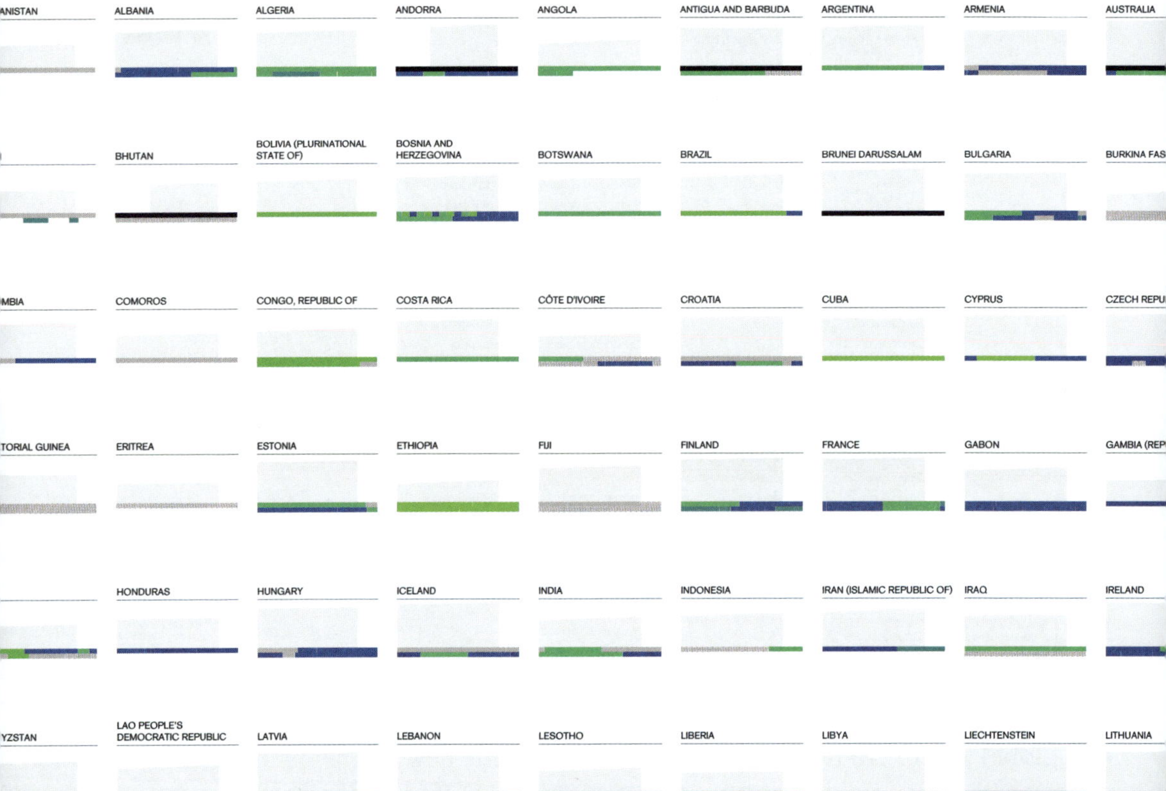

Summary / Retrospective of a Crisis

Document and publish the generated outcomes of and responses to the perspectives and overall project in one publication, providing a retrospective summary and reflection.

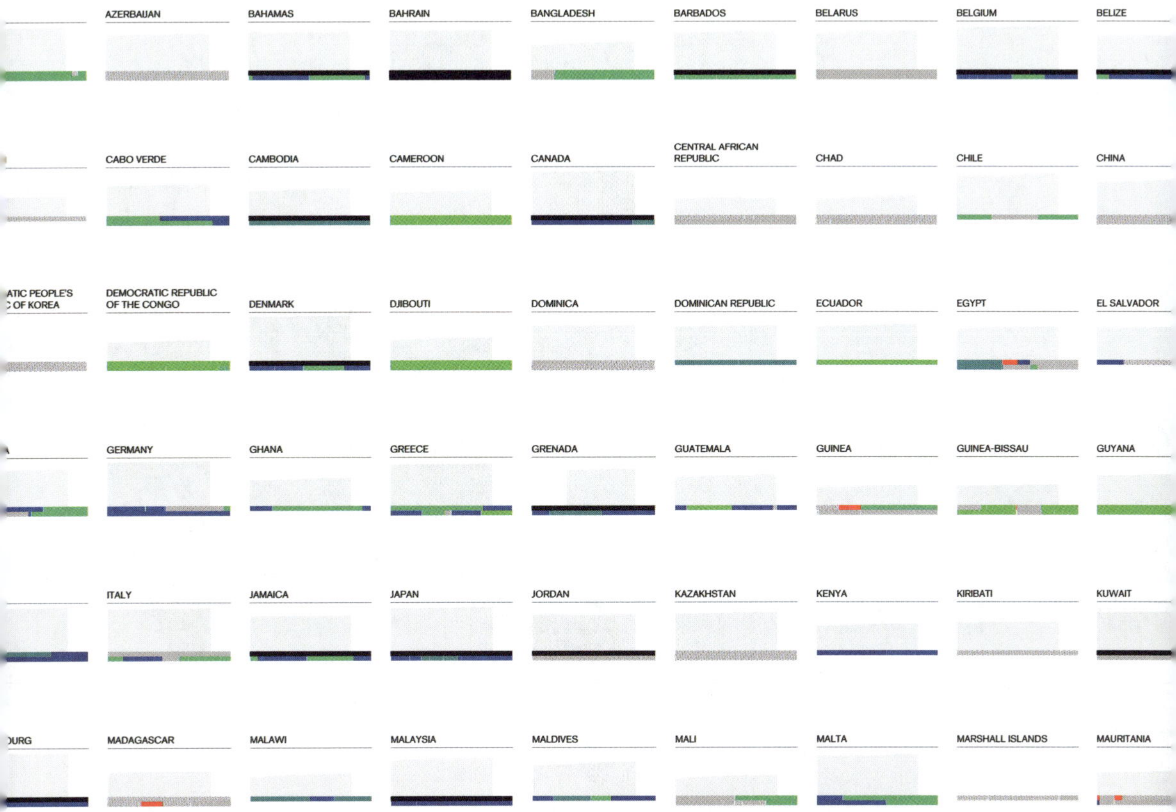

AZERBAIJAN | BAHAMAS | BAHRAIN | BANGLADESH | BARBADOS | BELARUS | BELGIUM | BELIZE

CABO VERDE | CAMBODIA | CAMEROON | CANADA | CENTRAL AFRICAN REPUBLIC | CHAD | CHILE | CHINA

…ATIC PEOPLE'S …C OF KOREA | DEMOCRATIC REPUBLIC OF THE CONGO | DENMARK | DJIBOUTI | DOMINICA | DOMINICAN REPUBLIC | ECUADOR | EGYPT | EL SALVADOR

GERMANY | GHANA | GREECE | GRENADA | GUATEMALA | GUINEA | GUINEA-BISSAU | GUYANA

ITALY | JAMAICA | JAPAN | JORDAN | KAZAKHSTAN | KENYA | KIRIBATI | KUWAIT

…URG | MADAGASCAR | MALAWI | MALAYSIA | MALDIVES | MALI | MALTA | MARSHALL ISLANDS | MAURITANIA

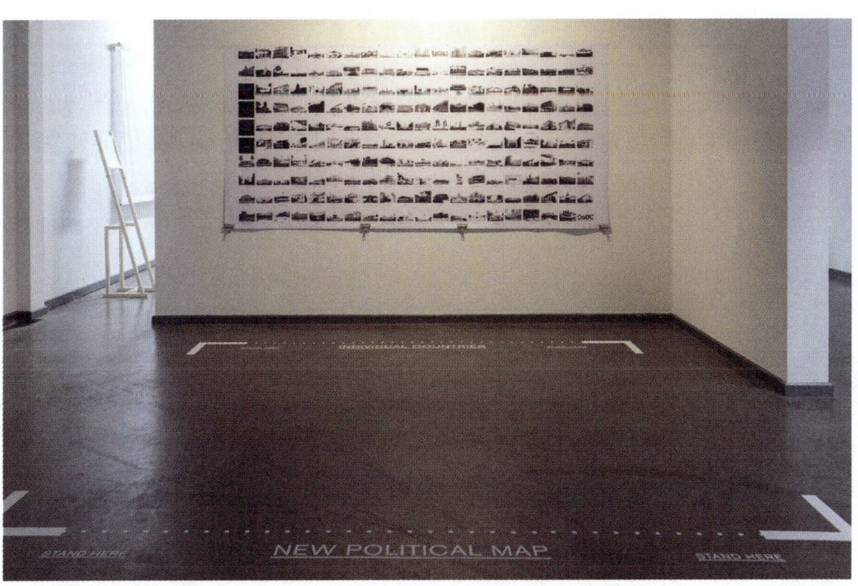

Installation view. Department of Unusual Certainties, *Retrospective of a Crisis*, *Vol.1 Politics*, 2018. Courtesy of Onomatopee Projects. Photography by Blickfanger.

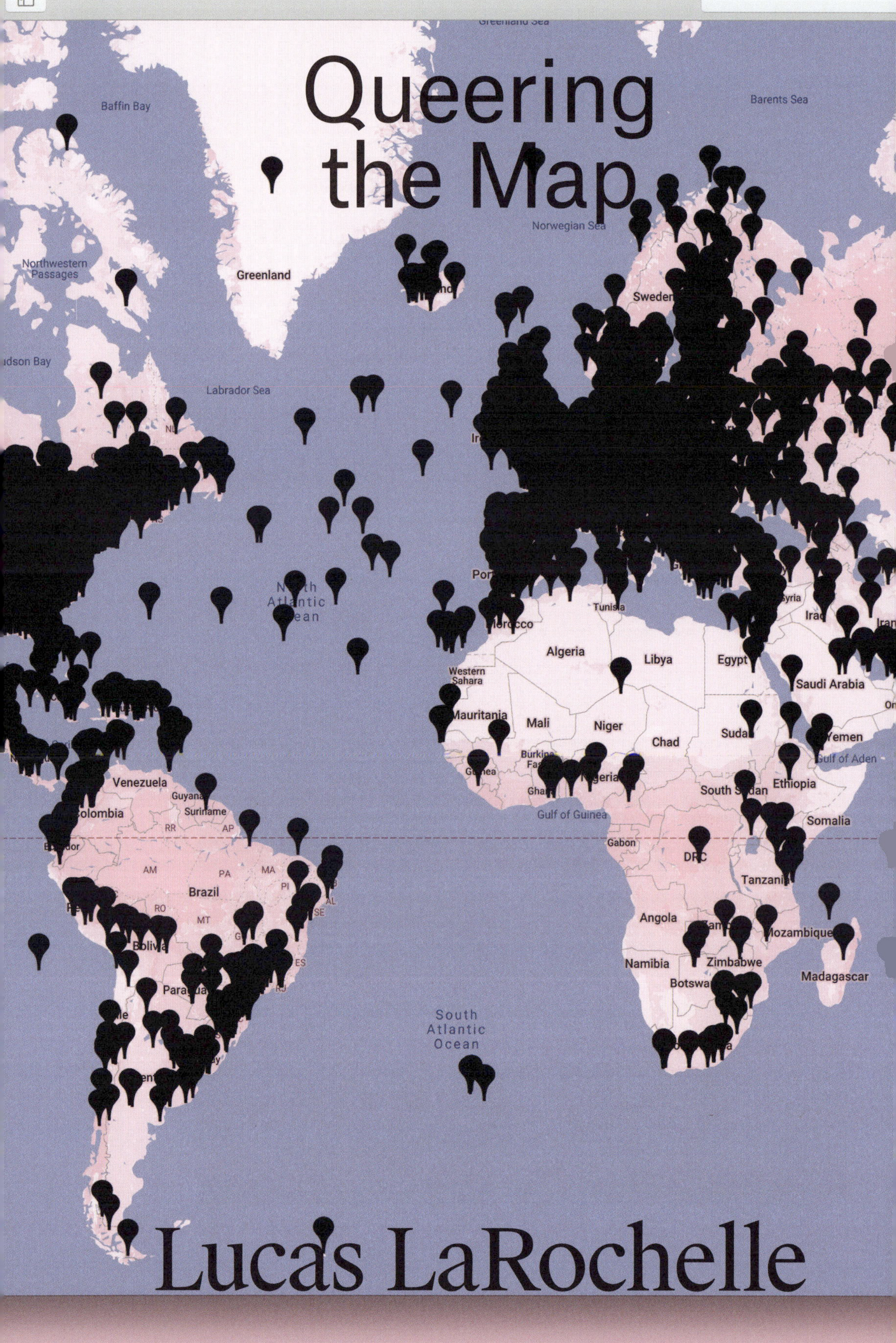

Queering
the Map
Lucas LaRochelle

To queer space is to point to the limits of current realities that do not adequately consider the safety and wellbeing of marginalized bodies, and in doing so, point to other possibilities. These spaces of possibility are often ephemeral, and are produced through the actions of queer bodies resisting or even simply existing in the face of dominant power structures that would rather we not exist. Despite their ephemeral nature, these actions of resistance do not simply disappear into the ether once they have been performed, but rather hold the possibility to act as catalysts for a reimagining of a queerer, more radically open world.

Queering the Map is a community generated digital counter-mapping project that archives queer moments, memories, and histories in relation to place. From direct action activism to conversations expressing gender pronouns, from feelings of isolation to moments of rapturous love, *Queering the Map* functions as a living spatial archive of queer experience. By mapping out queer experience in all of its permutations, *Queering the Map* aims to extend the lingering of these queer potentialities in physical space, by archiving them in virtual space. By merging subjective experience into the collective, *Queering the Map* works to create a sense of queer solidarity across difference and across borders.

Queering the Map was launched in May 2017 to document the diversity and history of queer life. In February 2018, the project went viral, garnering 6,000 new submissions in a period of three days. This level of visibility was inevitably met with resistance, and on February 11, 2018 the site was spammed by Trump supporters who injected malicious code into the database, generating pro-Trump pop-ups across the map. The site was taken down and a call for support was issued, attracting a group of LGBTQ2+ coders who worked collaboratively to ensure the security and sustainability of the site. *Queering The Map* was re-launched on April 3 2018, and now holds over 60 000 stories of queer experience across every continent and in 23 languages. The following are a selection of stories submitted to *Queering The Map* so far:

All stills. Lucas LaRochelle, *Queering the Map*. Website. Courtesy of the artist.

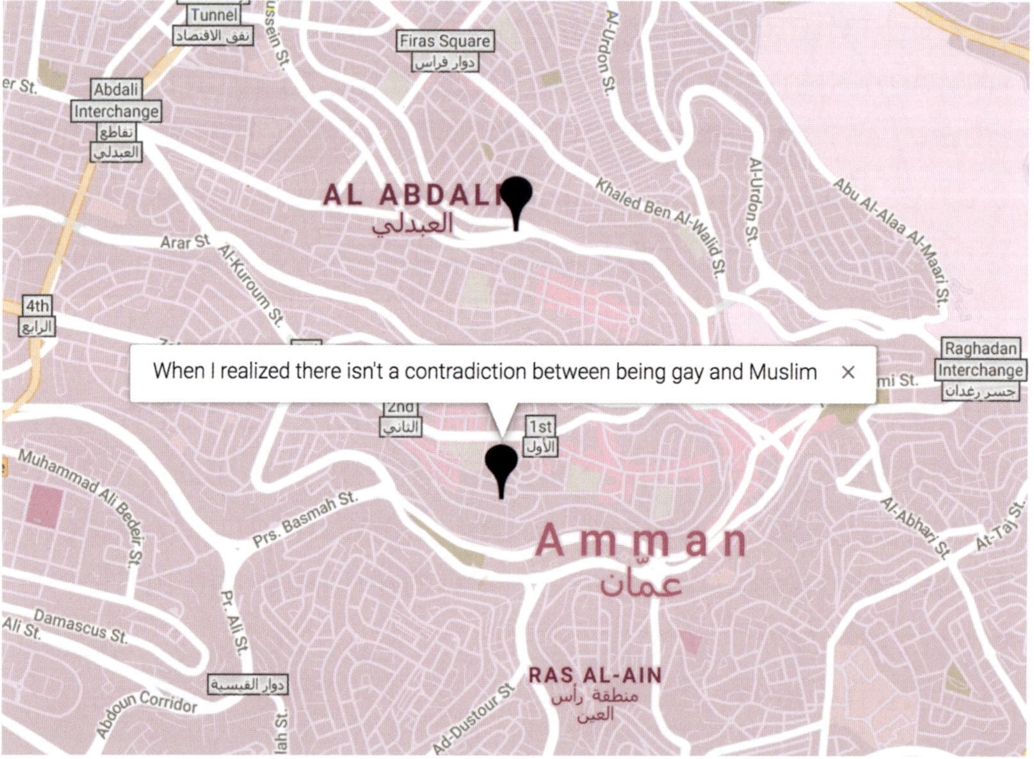

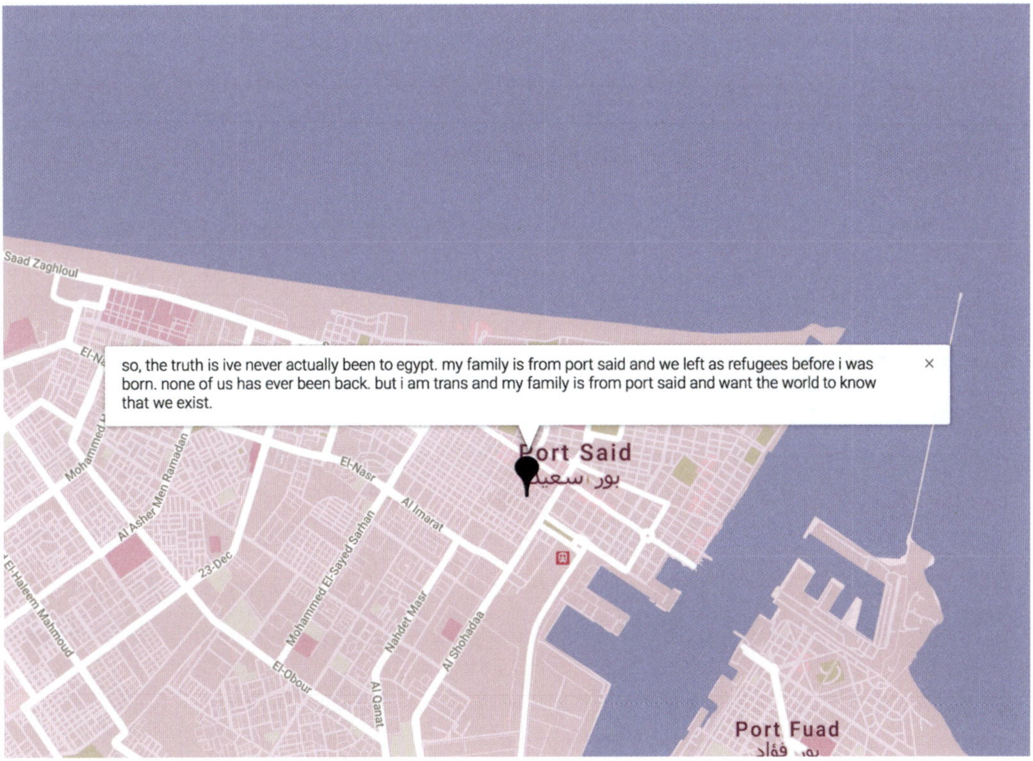

Queering the Map
Lucas LaRochelle

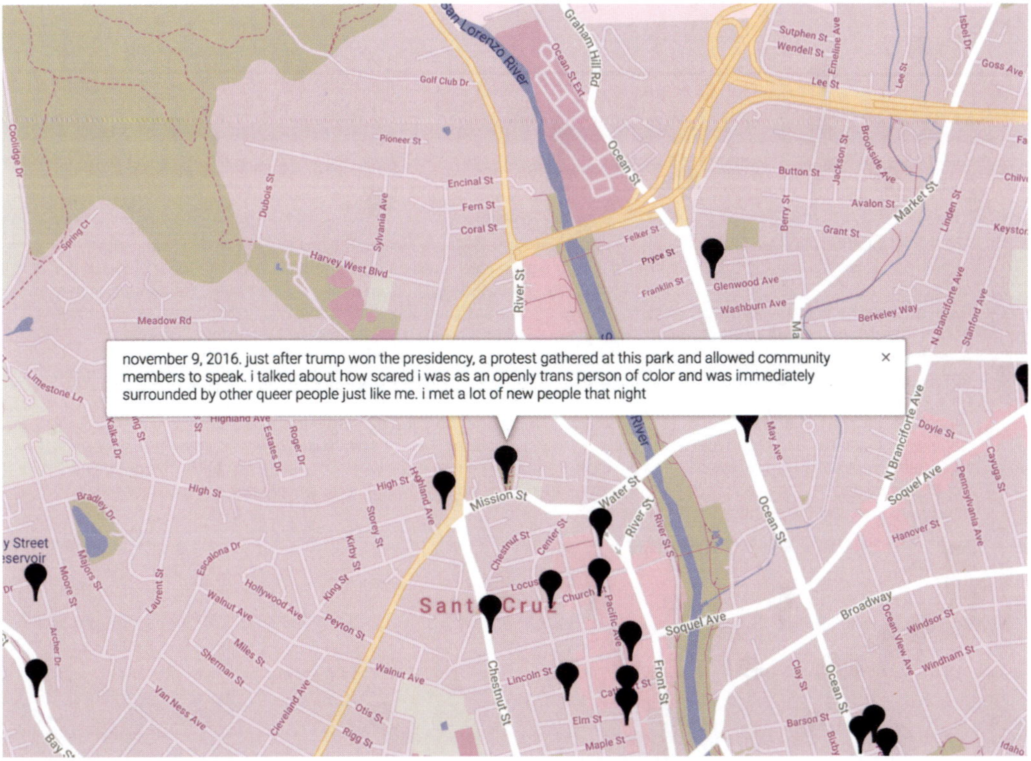

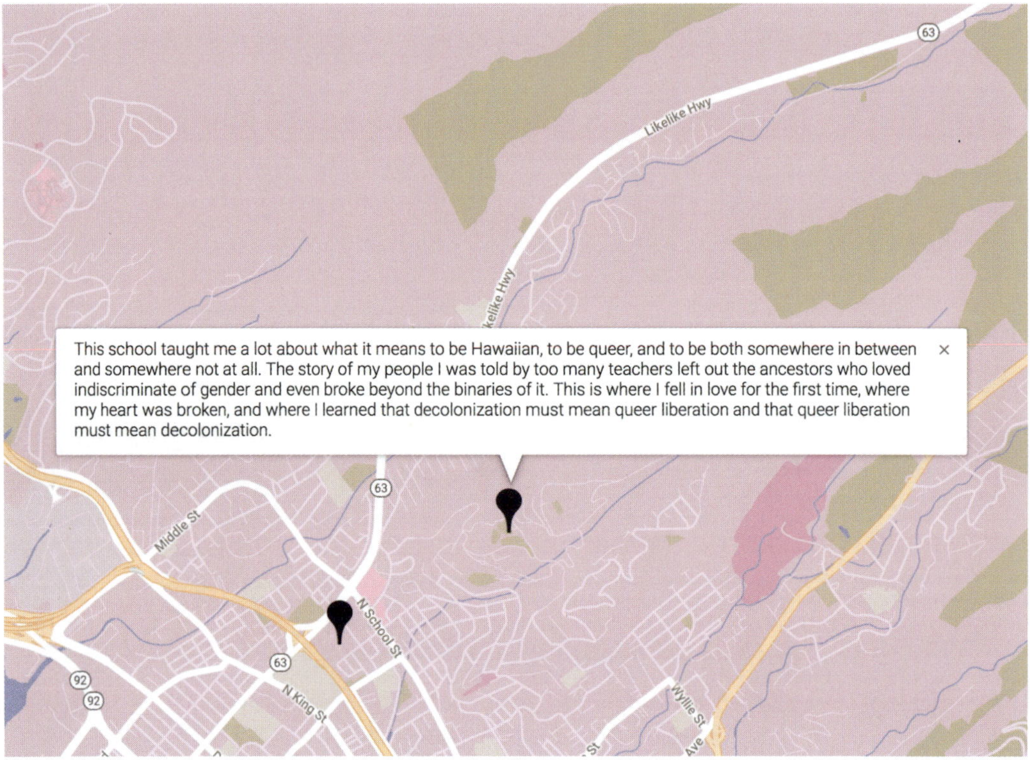

This school taught me a lot about what it means to be Hawaiian, to be queer, and to be both somewhere in between and somewhere not at all. The story of my people I was told by too many teachers left out the ancestors who loved indiscriminate of gender and even broke beyond the binaries of it. This is where I fell in love for the first time, where my heart was broken, and where I learned that decolonization must mean queer liberation and that queer liberation must mean decolonization.

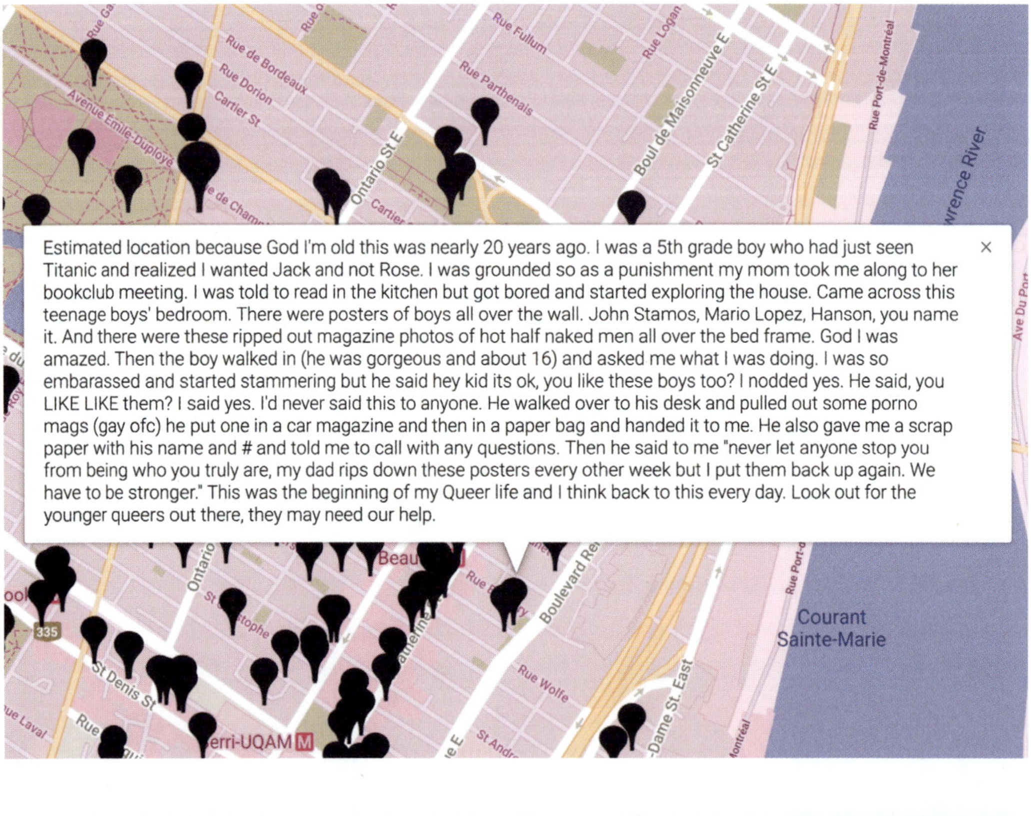

Estimated location because God I'm old this was nearly 20 years ago. I was a 5th grade boy who had just seen Titanic and realized I wanted Jack and not Rose. I was grounded so as a punishment my mom took me along to her bookclub meeting. I was told to read in the kitchen but got bored and started exploring the house. Came across this teenage boys' bedroom. There were posters of boys all over the wall. John Stamos, Mario Lopez, Hanson, you name it. And there were these ripped out magazine photos of hot half naked men all over the bed frame. God I was amazed. Then the boy walked in (he was gorgeous and about 16) and asked me what I was doing. I was so embarassed and started stammering but he said hey kid its ok, you like these boys too? I nodded yes. He said, you LIKE LIKE them? I said yes. I'd never said this to anyone. He walked over to his desk and pulled out some porno mags (gay ofc) he put one in a car magazine and then in a paper bag and handed it to me. He also gave me a scrap paper with his name and # and told me to call with any questions. Then he said to me "never let anyone stop you from being who you truly are, my dad rips down these posters every other week but I put them back up again. We have to be stronger." This was the beginning of my Queer life and I think back to this every day. Look out for the younger queers out there, they may need our help.

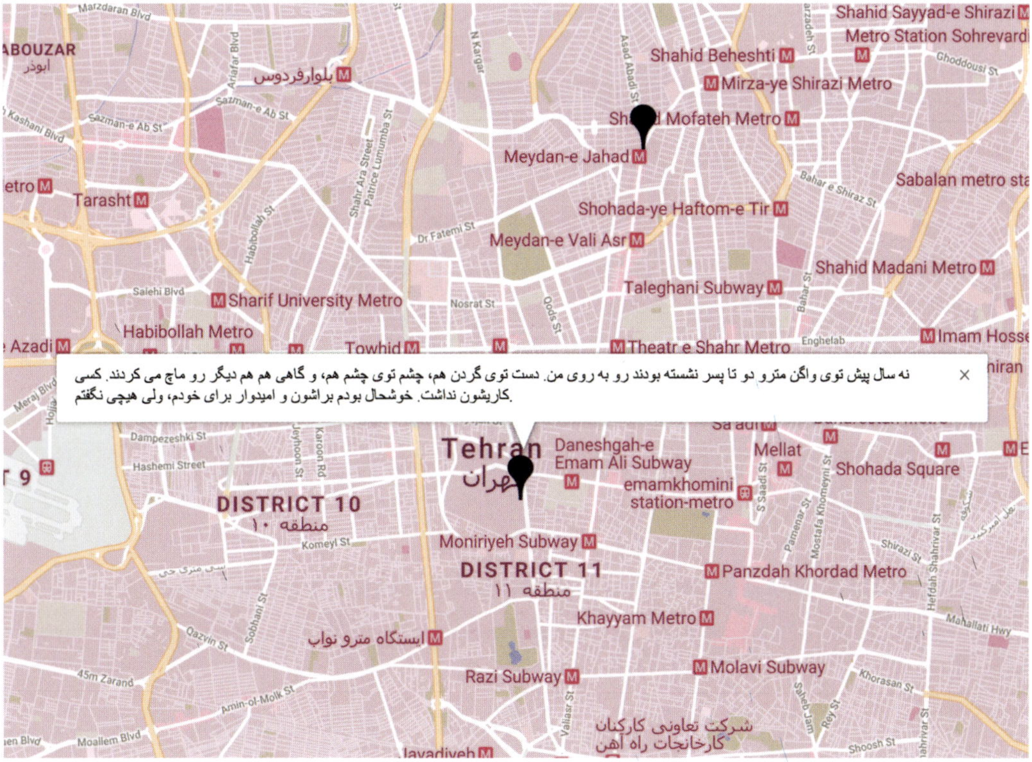

Queering the Map
Lucas LaRochelle

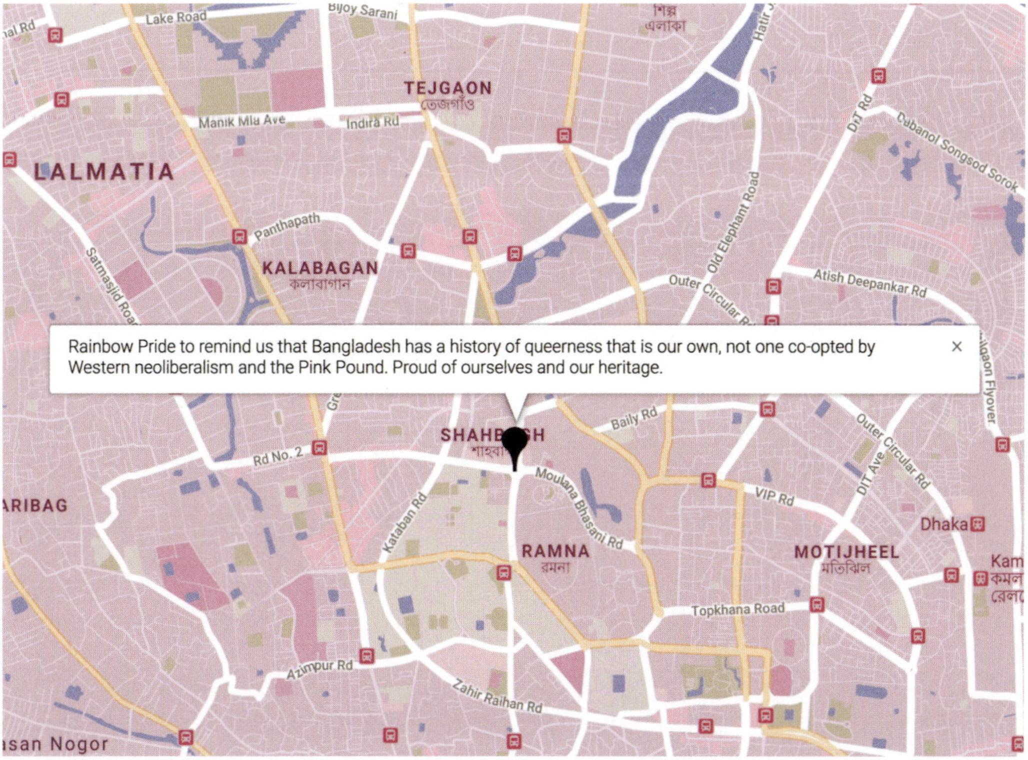

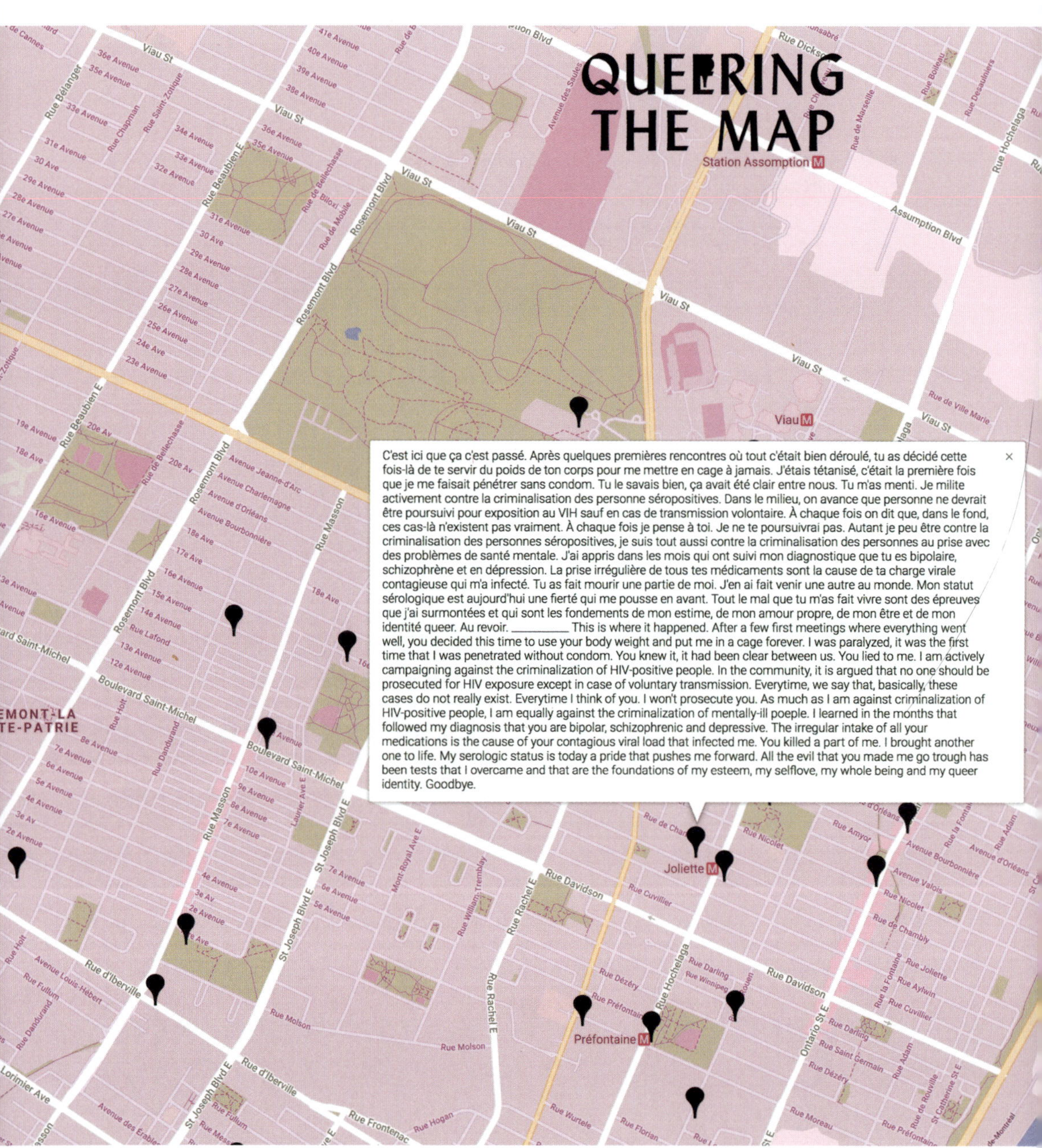

C'est ici que ça c'est passé. Après quelques premières rencontres où tout c'était bien déroulé, tu as décidé cette fois-là de te servir du poids de ton corps pour me mettre en cage à jamais. J'étais tétanisé, c'était la première fois que je me faisait pénétrer sans condom. Tu le savais bien, ça avait été clair entre nous. Tu m'as menti. Je milite activement contre la criminalisation des personne séropositives. Dans le milieu, on avance que personne ne devrait être poursuivi pour exposition au VIH sauf en cas de transmission volontaire. À chaque fois on dit que, dans le fond, ces cas-là n'existent pas vraiment. À chaque fois je pense à toi. Je ne te poursuivrai pas. Autant je peu être contre la criminalisation des personnes séropositives, je suis tout aussi contre la criminalisation des personnes au prise avec des problèmes de santé mentale. J'ai appris dans les mois qui ont suivi mon diagnostique que tu es bipolaire, schizophrène et en dépression. La prise irrégulière de tous tes médicaments sont la cause de ta charge virale contagieuse qui m'a infecté. Tu as fait mourir une partie de moi. J'en ai fait venir une autre au monde. Mon statut sérologique est aujourd'hui une fierté qui me pousse en avant. Tout le mal que tu m'as fait vivre sont des épreuves que j'ai surmontées et qui sont les fondements de mon estime, de mon amour propre, de mon être et de mon identité queer. Au revoir. __________ This is where it happened. After a few first meetings where everything went well, you decided this time to use your body weight and put me in a cage forever. I was paralyzed, it was the first time that I was penetrated without condom. You knew it, it had been clear between us. You lied to me. I am actively campaigning against the criminalization of HIV-positive people. In the community, it is argued that no one should be prosecuted for HIV exposure except in case of voluntary transmission. Everytime, we say that, basically, these cases do not really exist. Everytime I think of you. I won't prosecute you. As much as I am against criminalization of HIV-positive people, I am equally against the criminalization of mentally-ill poeple. I learned in the months that followed my diagnosis that you are bipolar, schizophrenic and depressive. The irregular intake of all your medications is the cause of your contagious viral load that infected me. You killed a part of me. I brought another one to life. My serologic status is today a pride that pushes me forward. All the evil that you made me go trough has been tests that I overcame and that are the foundations of my esteem, my selflove, my whole being and my queer identity. Goodbye.

(English translation, previous page, top right) Tehran, Iran: Nine years ago, there were two boys sitting in the metro wagon facing me. Their hands on each others neck, their eyes on each others eyes, and sometimes also they kissed each other's face. It was nobody's business/no one minded. I was happy about them and hopeful for myself, but I did not say anything.

Territorial Acknowledgment

Queering the Map acknowledges that this project was started on the traditional territory of the Kanien'kehá:ka. The Kanien'kehá:ka are the keepers of the Eastern Door of the Haudenosaunee Confederacy. The island called "Montreal" is known as Tiotia:ke in the language of the Kanien'kehá:ka, and it has historically been a meeting place for other Indigenous nations, including the Algonquin peoples.

To find out on which Indigenous peoples' land you are located, please visit: www.native-land.ca. Beyond simply acknowledging the colonial histories of the land on which you are located, we encourage you to take concrete steps towards decolonization by learning more about the ways in which you can support local Indigenous groups. If you are located in Canada/Turtle Island, a good place to start is www.reconciliationcanada.ca.

The City is not a Laboratory— Property Praxis in the Urban Praxis Workshop

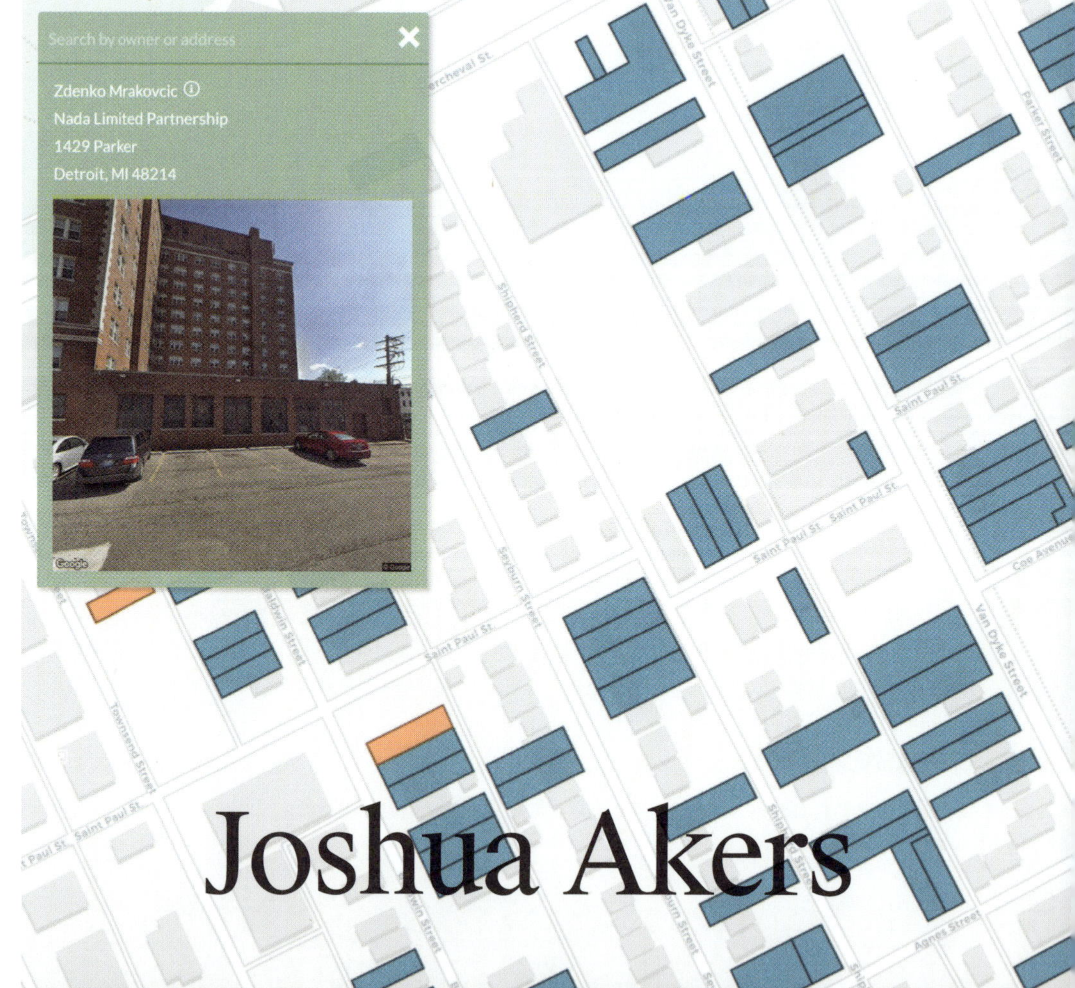

Joshua Akers

Over the past decade, the ubiquity of spatialized data produced a flood of inert and useless maps or, more specifically, maps useful to various accumulation strategies, many reliant on displacement and dispossession. These are displays of information that accept "common sense" explanations of the world, appeal to deductive interpretations of data as fact, or that simply reproduce information "as is" or "toward best use." These practices are not new, but they are dangerous if left unchallenged. Each captures an already existing geographic imagination of economic practice and social division while curtailing alternatives and potential futures.

In Detroit, mapping and data visualization were essential in reestablishing the basic knowledge necessary to operate real estate markets. Much as the physical structures of the city in the decades of chronic decline and intentional neglect, so too did place-based knowledge and all of the attendant attachments that allow for valuation and circulation to operate. The construction of this market knowledge depends on the state and capital and the work of fringe technologists, artists, and designers. The increasing availability of complex mapping tools produced data-derived understandings of the city and new geographic imaginaries serving as a foundation for constructing values and opening potential sites for settlement. It is simultaneously a new process of enclosure and the opening of a neo-colonial investment frontier.

In this context, we situate our projects such as *Property Praxis* and its various outgrowths in the *Urban Praxis Workshop* as counterweights, organizing strategies, and weapons. The projects demonstrate how the social practices and economic processes that produce uneven geographies of "valueless" and "vacant" spaces are neither apolitical nor unintentional. They emphasize the politics of the data, specifically its production and capture, to reveal the systemic and structural practices that result in deeply segregated places and highly concentrated areas of poverty. Projects such as *Property Praxis* forefront these politics not only as revealing these connections, but as a means of strategy in struggle.

These projects work at multiple scales. First, in service to a community and the issues they have identified. A power of cartography is to take the complexity of data, both quantitative and qualitative, and develop a visual tool for strategy. It allows for participants to see the scope of their struggles and, ideally, to organize more effectively by identifying relationship across places and scales. Second, if appropriate, it operates in a public sphere to generate awareness through reframing injustice by illuminating how these practices operate. Third, it challenges the state (big S and small), by demonstrating both its involvement in perpetuating inequality through its actions and inactions. Finally, the development of the information necessary to construct such tools produces new knowledge of the ways in which, in our case, predation and exploitation are operating.

The following are tenets that have arisen from our practice at the *Urban Praxis Workshop* and in the making of *Property Praxis.* This is informed by theory, but it is less about the spatial representation of information and more engaged with conceptions of power and struggle. We often summarize the approach of the *Urban Praxis Workshop* this way: "we come when asked, listen intently, and do what we can with what we are told."

We believe residents facing housing insecurity, concentrated poverty, and the barriers of contemporary racism and segregation are the experts. Those who have self-organized in these conditions are better equipped to identify the challenges they face and the direction they want to go. We are able to provide tools and information that can accelerate their organizing. We can help navigate institutions and bureaucracies. We can generate information that puts their qualitative understanding of these challenges in the form and language of institutional power. We can show how their struggle is relational, systemic, and structural. We can commit public resources (our time and materials) to their struggle.

This is not intended as a prescription, but instead these are lessons from practice. These are drawn from a particular terrain of struggle in Detroit. It is grounded in the immediacy of the moment but also seeking to communicate across space through emphasizing relations of power.

1. It is always an argument
The argument develops from research question(s). This question is developed by the community it serves. In the workshop, our focus is to develop questions that operate in multiple scales—forces, practices, and needs.

One example of this is *Property Praxis*. In late spring 2016, we released an online web map or visualization to the public. This visualization was intended to show both the prevalence of speculation and to serve as a tool for Detroit residents,

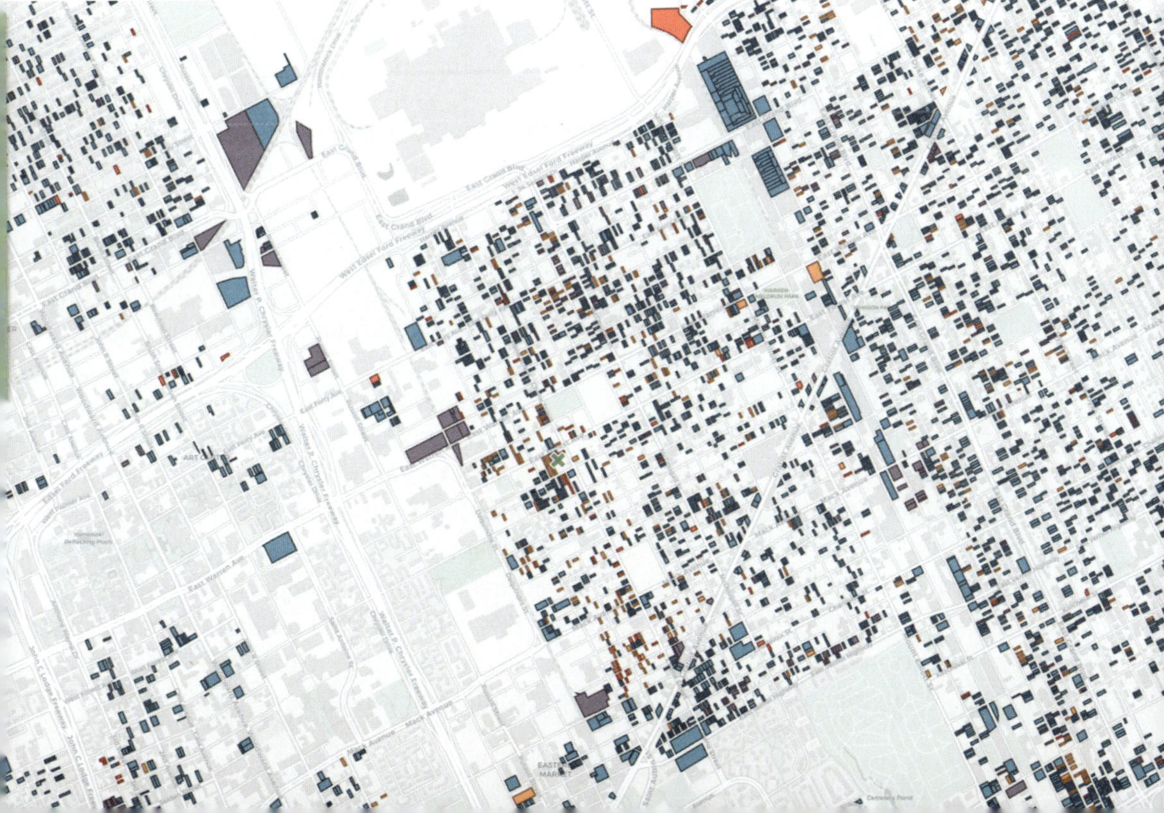

mutual aid organizations, and housing advocates by detailing holdings and the linkages between property holding companies operating in the city.

This project was developed through our work with community groups in Southwest Detroit who were increasingly challenged by the changing nature of speculative activity. Two of the primary issues were understanding the scope of speculation in their neighborhood and across the city and in identifying speculators masking their identity behind Limited Liability Corporations. In this case, the question was how we develop this data for residents and organizations fighting speculation and its incumbent neighborhood instability without further aiding speculation.

The shape of the project was spurred on by more public discussions of speculation. Despite the concerns of residents and community organizations with the changing practices of speculation in the city, Detroit Mayor Mike Duggan, in his first campaign for mayor, said that speculation would not be an issue for his administration because it was not illegal. Then in the spring of 2015, a columnist for one of the local papers published an article praising one of the largest local speculators and his care for his property after being given a personal tour by the speculator. In this case, the question was how we demonstrate the scale of the issue and its actual impacts on both structures and neighborhoods.

The form of the project, came in part due to ongoing debate with local tech start-ups focused on mapping the city, visually cataloging all properties, and deploying econometric models to justify demolition and service withdrawal. For those working on these projects in business and in the city the key tenets were that data was apolitical, mapping merely a representation of fact, and that markets were simply price or value. In this case, the question became was it possible to forefront the politics of property data in a way that challenges these assumptions.

Each of these questions pointed us toward a map, one that illustrated the scope of the issue, provided community organizations and residents with the tool they needed, removed information useful to speculators but leaving enough for them to prey on one another, and finally pushed tech start-ups and others to acknowledge these practices and answer for how these issues affected their models. There are an incredible number of limits in the public facing side of the *Property Praxis* project from its search function to cross referencing and its visual display. In many ways it was a representational tool intentionally handcuffed to make manipulation by speculators more difficult. On the backend, it provided us with an incredibly detailed data set that when placed in conversation with other information, mortgage foreclosures, tax foreclosures, evictions, water shut offs, and other practices of dispossession. This allows us to work directly with residents, activists, housing activists, and attorneys, to build detailed strategy maps and documents. Finally, it produced new knowledge on emerging practices in low income housing markets following the financial crisis.

2. It is about power

Much of what we work with is property data, and we approach this data as a relational and representational. In essence, this information both captures social struggle and is in itself a map of power and practice. This work is situated in direct struggles in neighborhoods and broader struggles around social justice and housing stability in Detroit.

Property data is at the core capturing inequality. The ways in which property is managed, exchanged, practiced, and handled through legal systems offers a means through which to understand systems and structures of inequality. When coupled with experience of residents, activists, and organizers it is a way to build multiple strategies to both intervene in and undermine these exploitative practices. By putting these data sets in conversations and by challenging their framings to develop more comprehensive understanding of the inherent complexities we are able to identify weaknesses and contradictions. This allows for more effective organizing by producing the tools, maps, and information necessary for combatting the political economy of displacement and dispossession.

3. It is a strategy

We produce materials that allow for more systematic approaches to activism and organizing. At times, maps establish a position. Other times, these maps identify relationships or approaches. This is not a static representation of data but instead a platform for action. It can operate in multiple vectors. It relies on an ethics of practice but can also draw on the morality of the reader. The project must make an argument and represent its position.

4. The Message Determines the Medium

Form is determined by whom it is for. Our outputs vary from address lists for organizers to maps detailing transactional relationships and constellations of private ownership. At its best, these projects incorporate quantitative, qualitative, and archival material that can be marshalled in virtual or two-dimensional space or in a form that catalyzes action.

5. The digital as urban form

Not all maps are meant to be seen. The visibility of such projects is determined by its sensitivity. Mapping is a powerful tool, but deep in the drop-down menus and buried in the code these information systems are tethered to a positivist and normative root system predicated on extraction and exploitation. How this information and these practices are deployed is dependent on the user and one should always be mindful that a frame of analysis focused on the mechanisms of displacement, disinvestment, destabilization, and dispossession can also provide the knowledge and strategies in the service of these forces.

A critical culture of permissions and consent that encompass chains of ownership is an essential default in working with marginalized and heavily surveilled communities. Some outputs are not for everyone. The community controls the maps we make and the decision to share is based on shared sensitivity to the power of the map and community control of their information.

All stills. Joshua Akers, *Property Praxis*. Website. Courtesy of the artist.

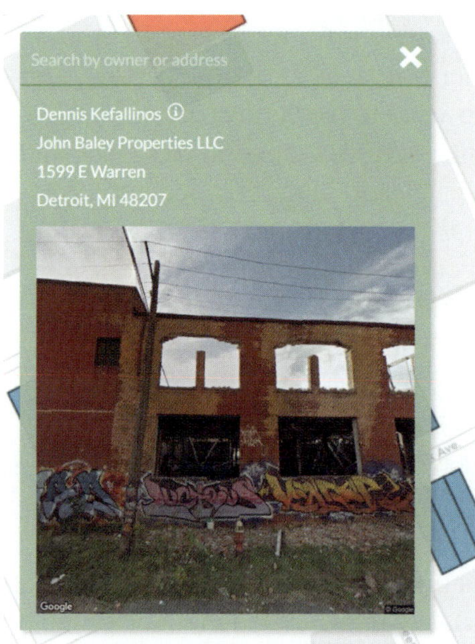

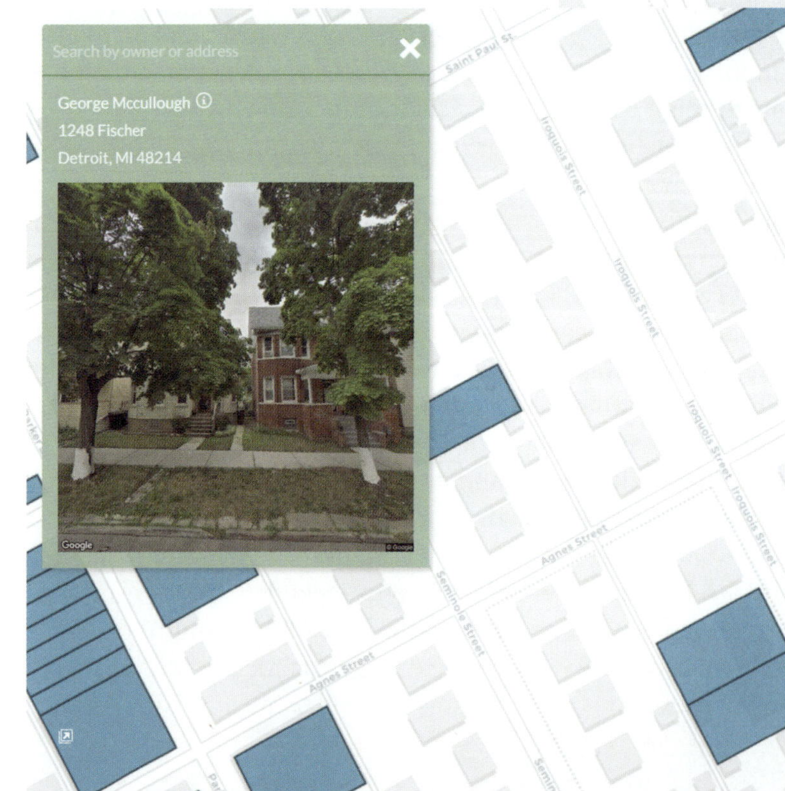

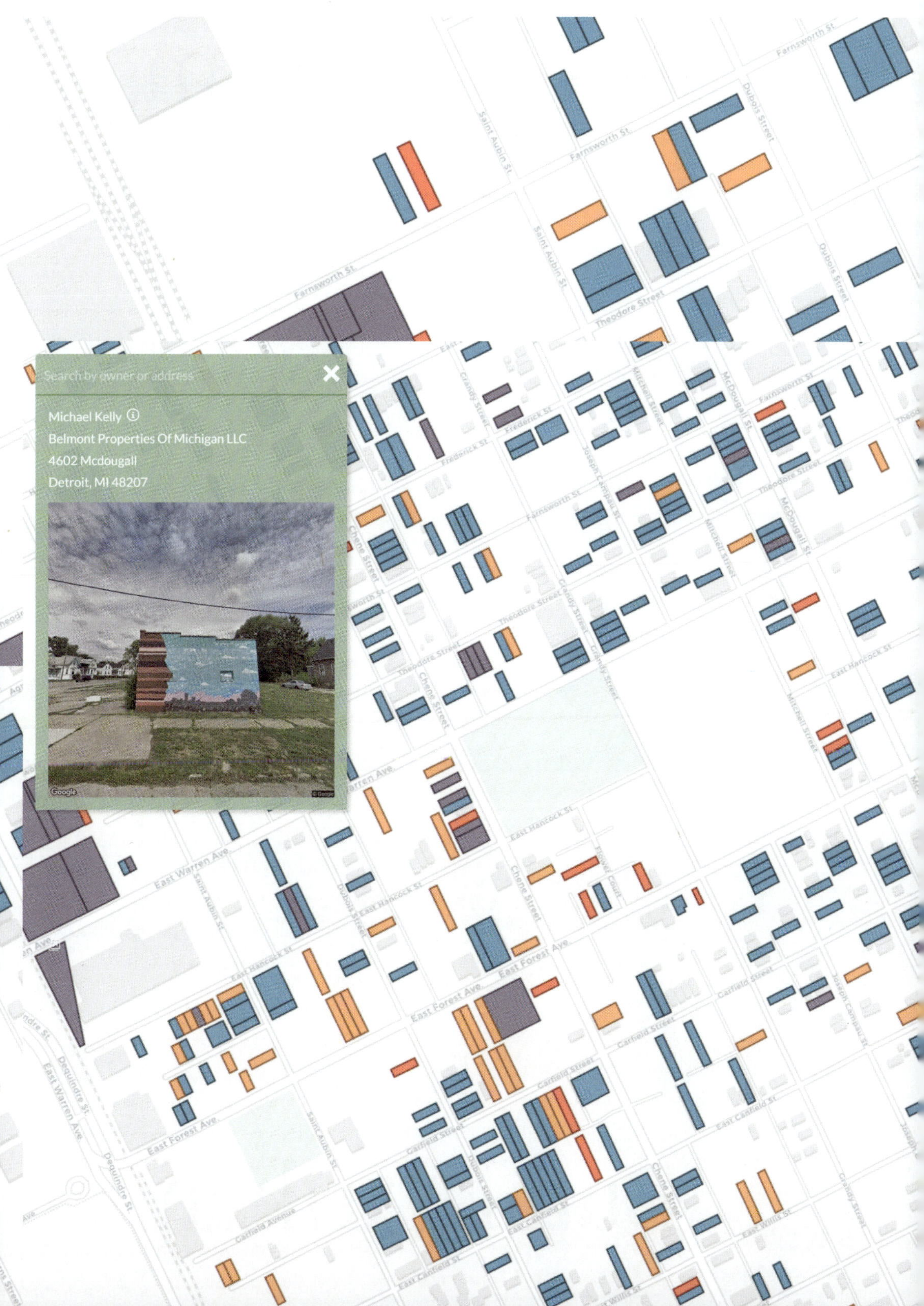
Search by owner or address
Michael Kelly
Belmont Properties Of Michigan LLC
4602 Mcdougall
Detroit, MI 48207
Google

Islam, Republic, Neoliberalism

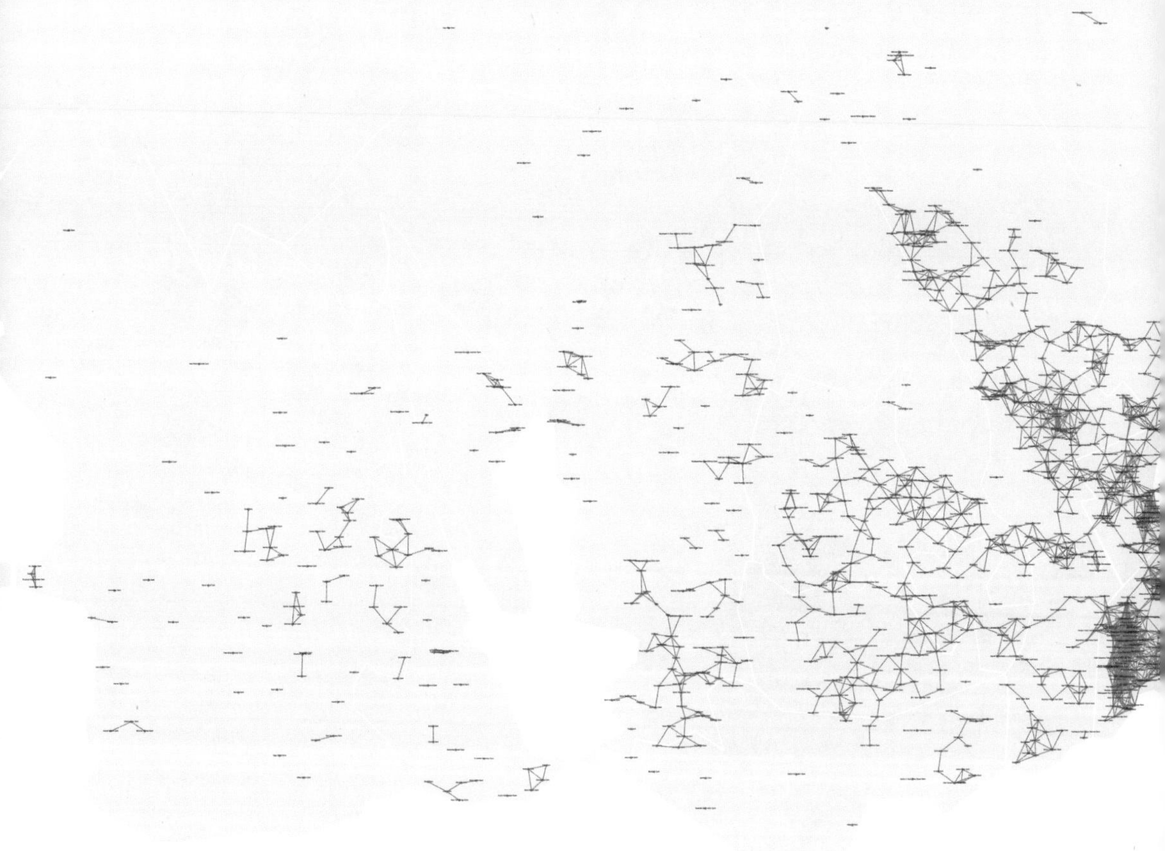

Burak Arikan

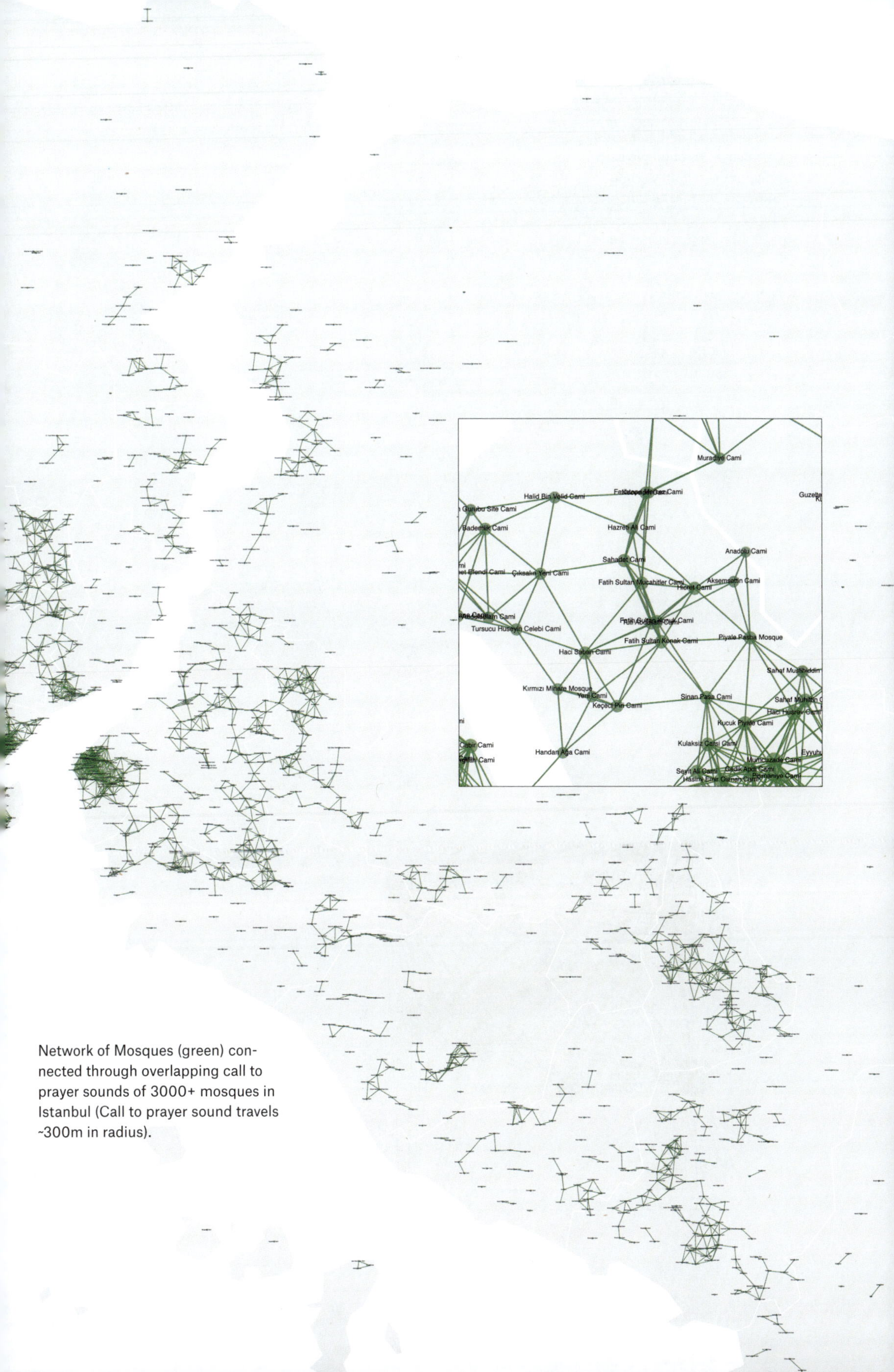

Network of Mosques (green) connected through overlapping call to prayer sounds of 3000+ mosques in Istanbul (Call to prayer sound travels ~300m in radius).

Network of Republic Monuments
(red) connected through physical
proximity of the republic monu-
ments/museums in Istanbul.

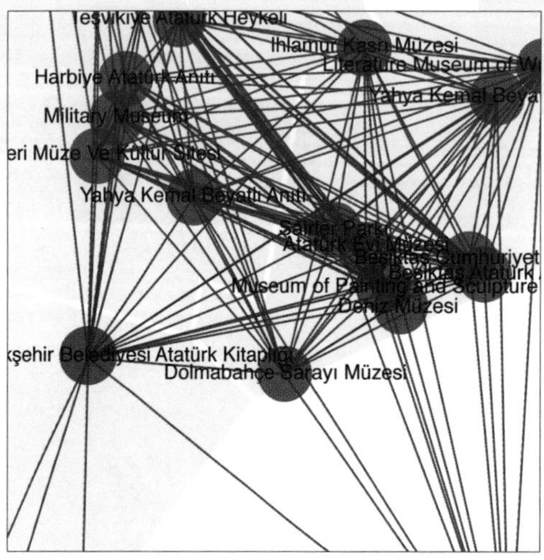

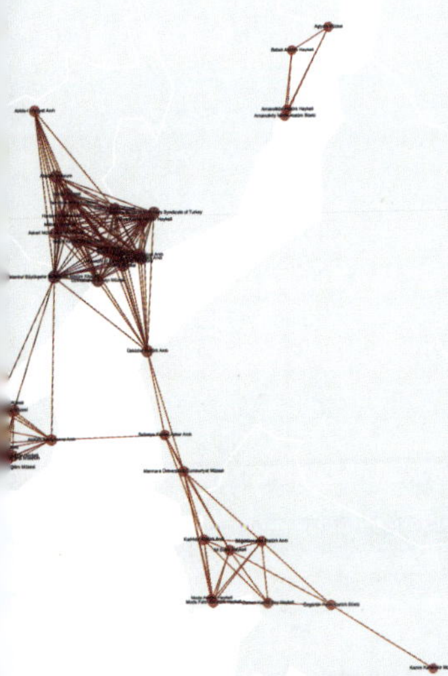

Islam, Republic, Neoliberalism comprises of three network maps where mosques, republican monuments, and shopping centers dispersed throughout Istanbul connect to each other within their areas of influence. These maps present a comparative display of network patterns that are formed through associations linking those architectural structures that represent the three dominant ideologies—Islam, Republic, Neoliberalism—in Turkey.

All maps, Burak Arikan, *Islam, Republic,
Neoliberalism*, 2012. Custom software,
Images courtesy of the artist.

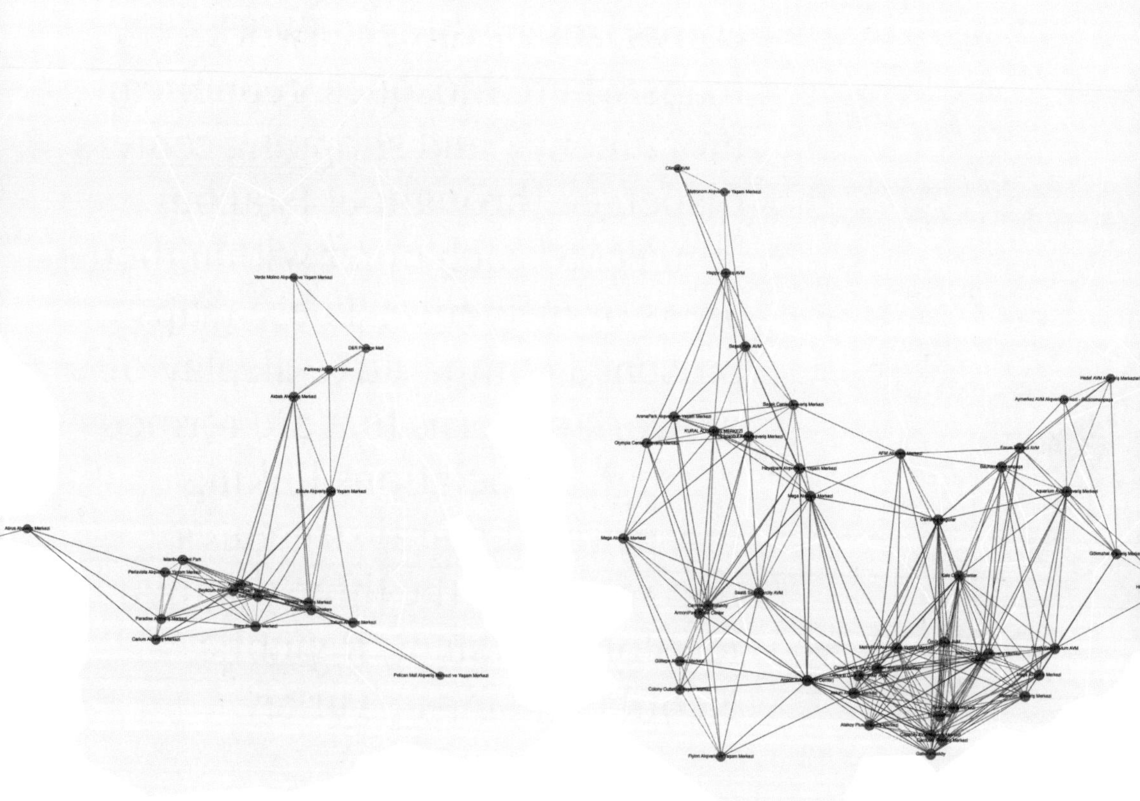

Network of Shopping Malls (blue)
connected through overlapping
range of reach of the shopping malls
in Istanbul.

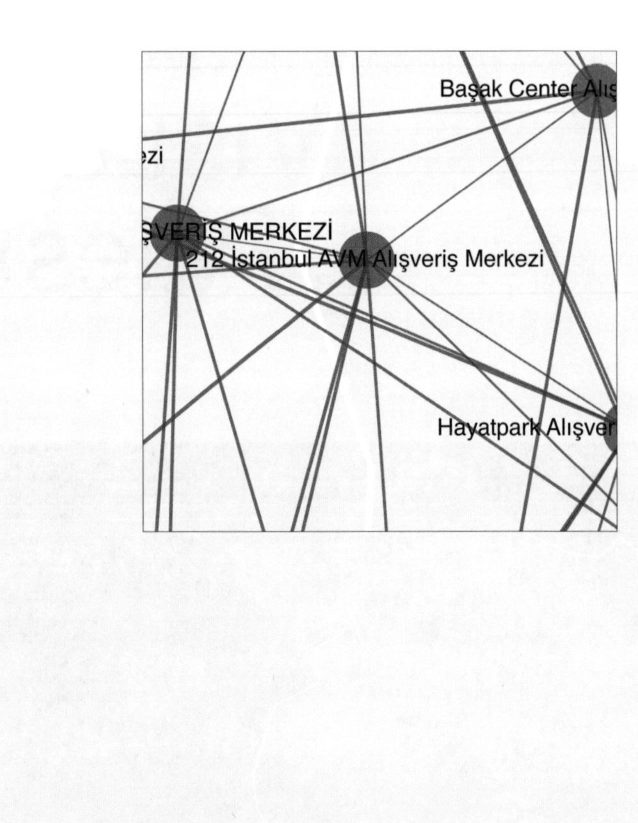
Başak Center Alış
ezi
ŞVERİŞ MERKEZİ
212 İstanbul AVM Alışveriş Merkezi
Hayatpark Alışver

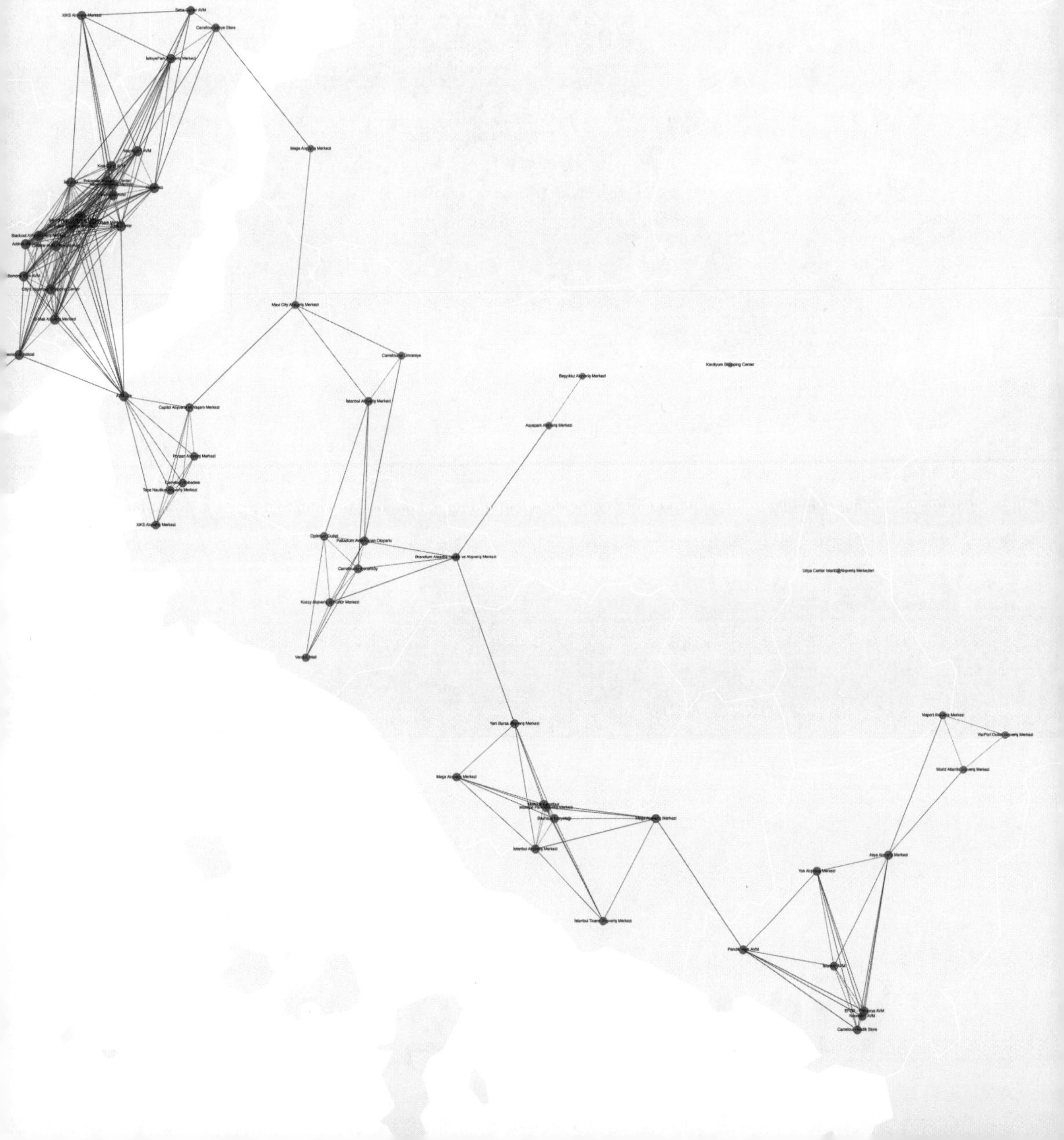

Visualizing
Palestine

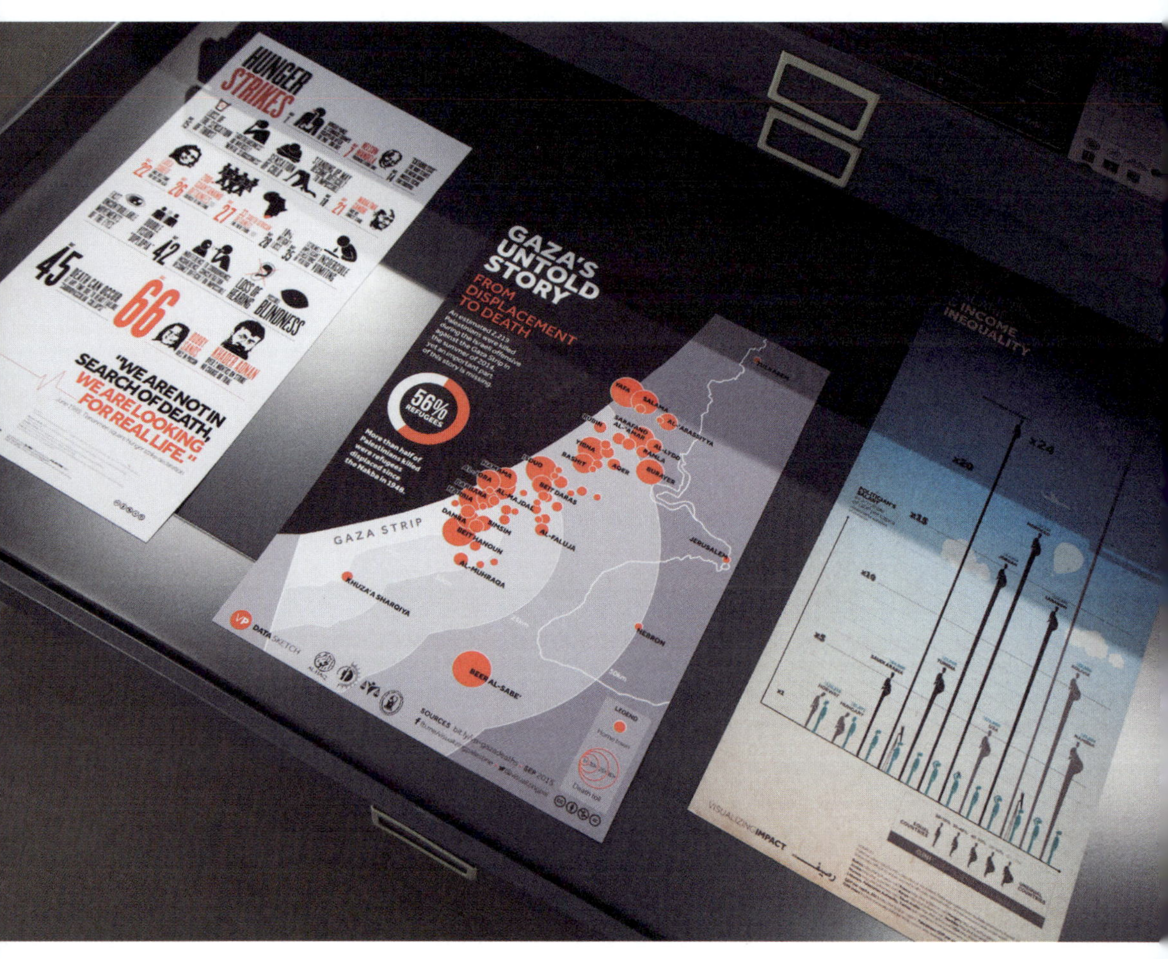

Visualizing Impact

While organising TEDxRamallah in 2011, two of Visualizing Impact's Cofounders, Ramzi Jaber and Joumana al Jabri, were inspired by the wealth of research and documentation being conducted by human rights advocates in Israel and Palestine.

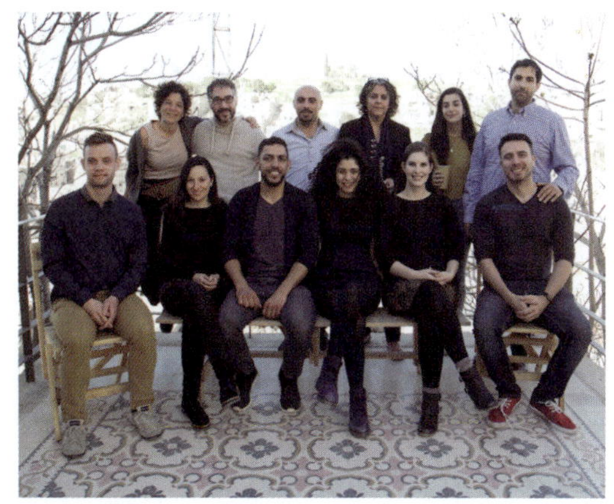

The VP team in Amman, Impact Data Lab Workshop, March 2018. Top row from left: Joumana al Jabri (Co-Director); Ahmad Barclay (Information Architect); Bassam Barham (Web Developer); Iman Annab (Community Manager); Lylla Younes (Data Journalist); Ramzi Jaber (Co-Director). Bottom row from left: Robin Jones (Researcher); Sandy Nassif (Administrator); Morad Taleeb (Web Developer); Yosra Gamal (Information Designer); Jessica Anderson (Operations Manager); Henry Zaccak (Technology Advisor).

They wondered what impact this information might have if more resources and creative energy were channeled toward its mobilization and dissemination. In imagining what that dissemination might look like, Visualizing Impact was born.

Visualizing Impact (VI) is a non-profit collective that uses data, design, and technology for human rights. Our small team has collaborated remotely from multiple countries on a range of issues such as Palestinian human rights, refugee rights in Lebanon, youth unemployment in the MENA region, freedom of expression in Egypt, collective action in the anti-apartheid struggle, the impact of content moderation by social media giants, and online freedom of expression. We have partnered with UN bodies, international and regional human rights organizations, local advocacy groups, and artists to experiment with data-led storytelling for social impact.

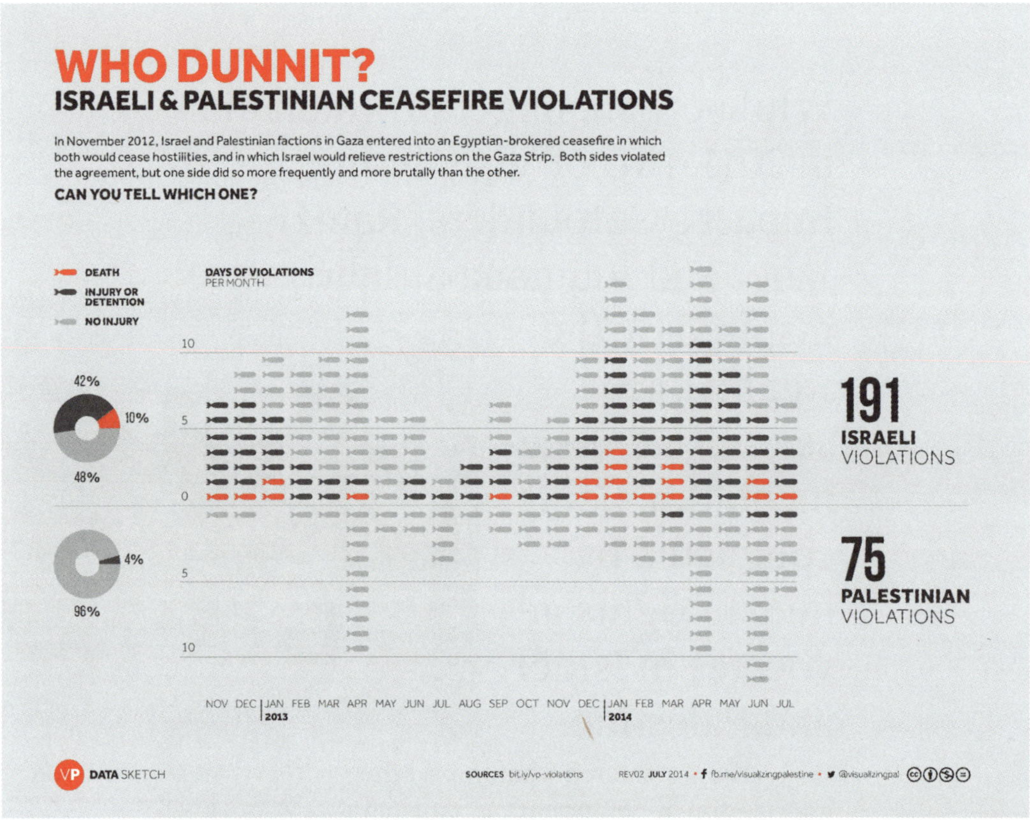

WHO DUNNIT?
ISRAELI & PALESTINIAN CEASEFIRE VIOLATIONS

In November 2012, Israel and Palestinian factions in Gaza entered into an Egyptian-brokered ceasefire in which both would cease hostilities, and in which Israel would relieve restrictions on the Gaza Strip. Both sides violated the agreement, but one side did so more frequently and more brutally than the other.

CAN YOU TELL WHICH ONE?

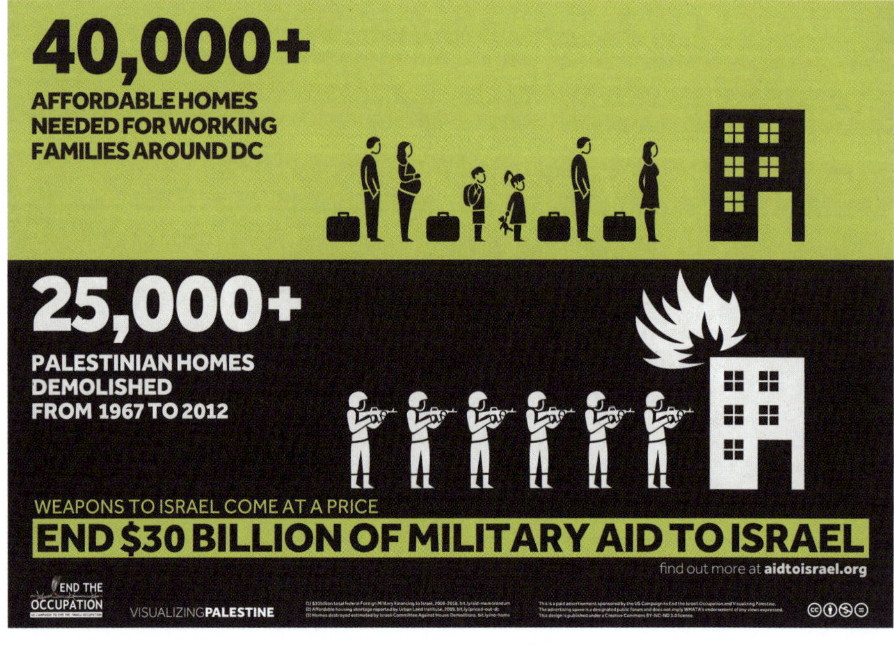

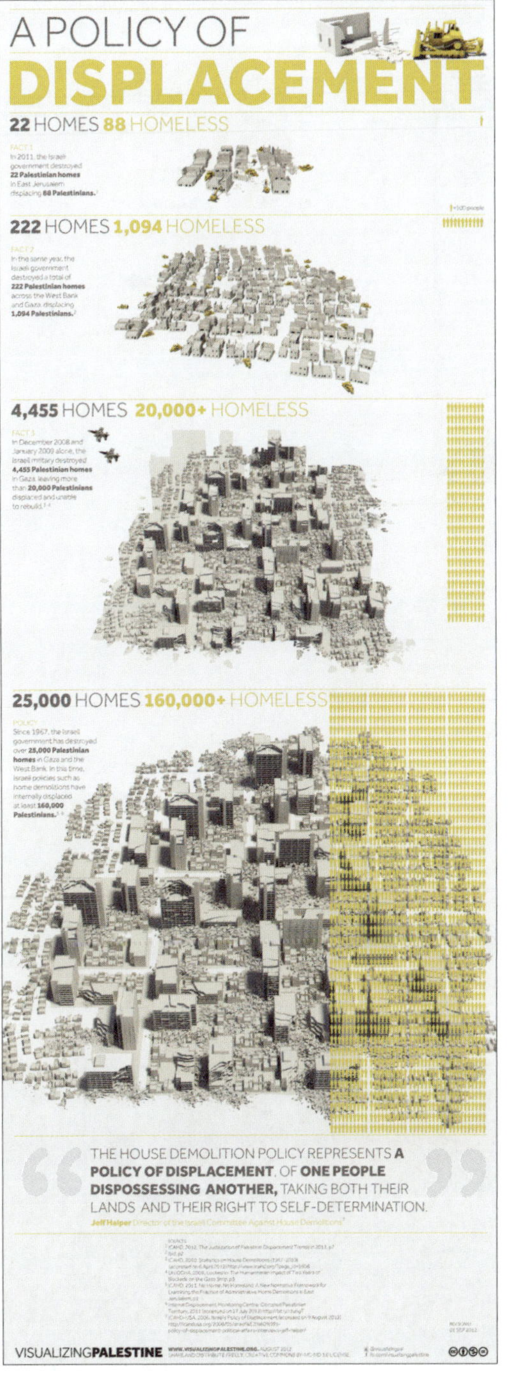

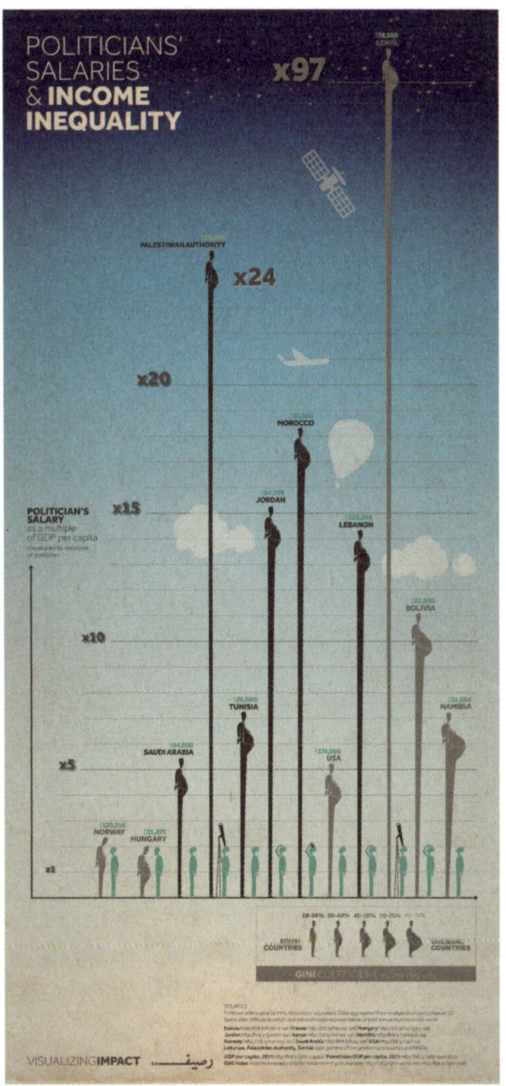

All charts, from the Visualizing Palestine series,
2012-Present. Courtesy of Visualizing Impact.

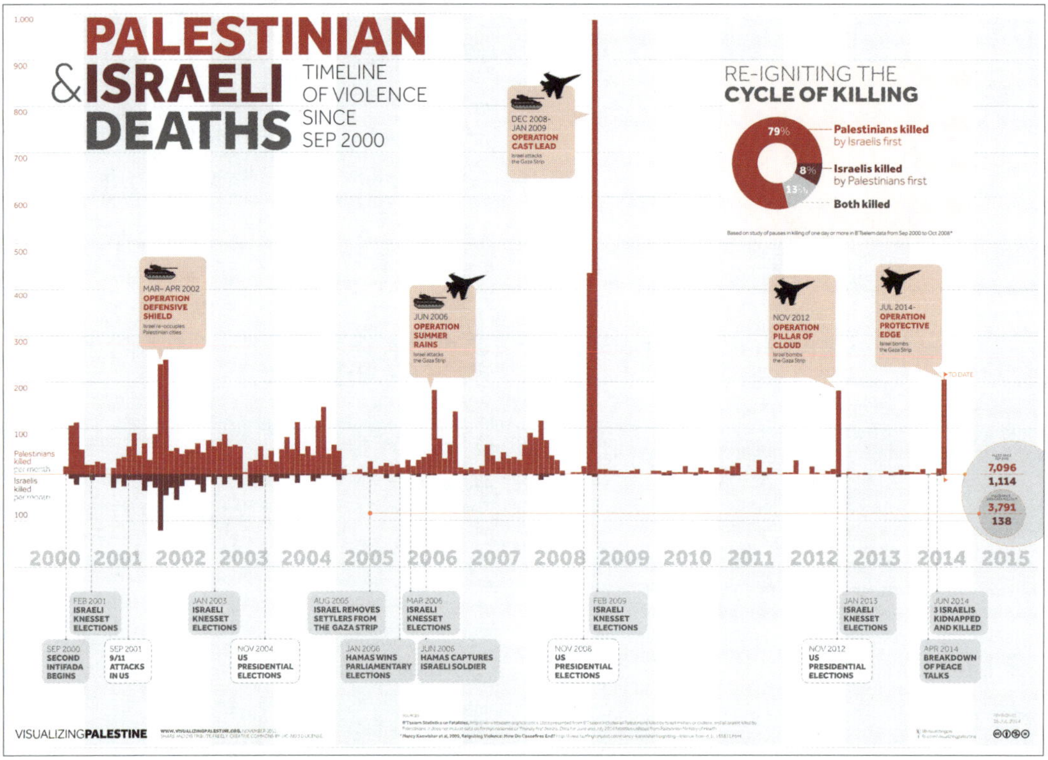

PALESTINIAN & ISRAELI DEATHS
TIMELINE OF VIOLENCE SINCE SEP 2000

RE-IGNITING THE CYCLE OF KILLING
79% Palestinians killed by Israelis first
8% Israelis killed by Palestinians first
13% Both killed
Based on study of pauses in killing of one day or more in B'Tselem data from Sep 2000 to Oct 2008*

DEC 2008–JAN 2009 OPERATION CAST LEAD
Israel attacks the Gaza Strip

MAR–APR 2002 OPERATION DEFENSIVE SHIELD
Israel re-occupies Palestinian cities

JUN 2006 OPERATION SUMMER RAINS
Israel attacks the Gaza Strip

NOV 2012 OPERATION PILLAR OF CLOUD
Israel bombs the Gaza Strip

JUL 2014– OPERATION PROTECTIVE EDGE
Israel bombs the Gaza Strip
TO DATE

Palestinians killed per month
Israelis killed per month

7,096
1,114
3,791
138

2000 2001 2002 2003 2004 2005 2006 2007 2008 2009 2010 2011 2012 2013 2014 2015

FEB 2001 ISRAELI KNESSET ELECTIONS
SEP 2000 SECOND INTIFADA BEGINS
SEP 2001 9/11 ATTACKS IN US
JAN 2003 ISRAELI KNESSET ELECTIONS
NOV 2004 US PRESIDENTIAL ELECTIONS
AUG 2005 ISRAEL REMOVES SETTLERS FROM THE GAZA STRIP
JAN 2006 HAMAS WINS PARLIAMENTARY ELECTIONS
MAR 2006 ISRAELI KNESSET ELECTIONS
JUN 2006 HAMAS CAPTURES ISRAELI SOLDIER
FEB 2009 ISRAELI KNESSET ELECTIONS
NOV 2008 US PRESIDENTIAL ELECTIONS
JAN 2013 ISRAELI KNESSET ELECTIONS
NOV 2012 US PRESIDENTIAL ELECTIONS
JUN 2014 3 ISRAELIS KIDNAPPED AND KILLED
APR 2014 BREAKDOWN OF PEACE TALKS

VISUALIZINGPALESTINE
WWW.VISUALIZINGPALESTINE.ORG, NOVEMBER 2015
SHARE AND DISTRIBUTE FREELY. CREATIVE COMMONS BY-NC-ND 3.0 LICENSE.

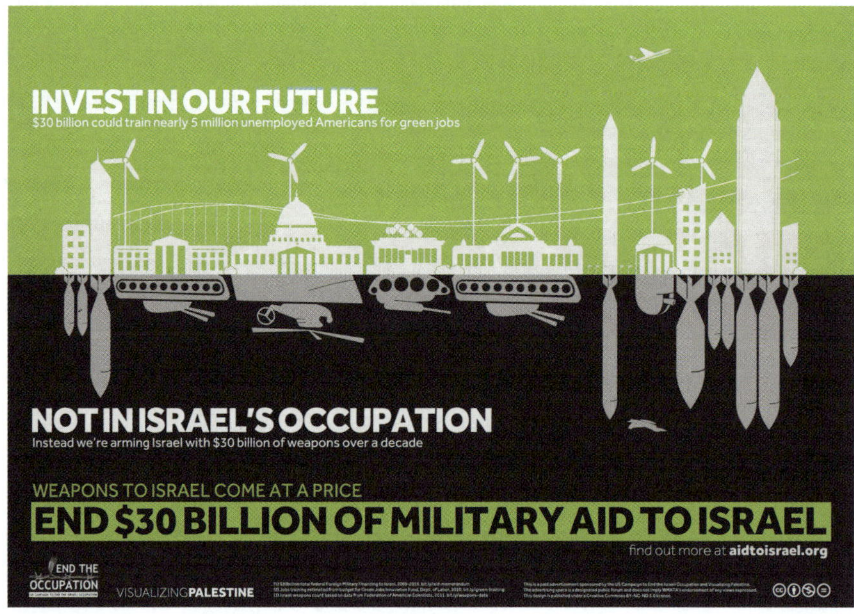

INVEST IN OUR FUTURE
$30 billion could train nearly 5 million unemployed Americans for green jobs

NOT IN ISRAEL'S OCCUPATION
Instead we're arming Israel with $30 billion of weapons over a decade

WEAPONS TO ISRAEL COME AT A PRICE
END $30 BILLION OF MILITARY AID TO ISRAEL
find out more at aidtoisrael.org

END THE OCCUPATION
US CAMPAIGN TO END THE ISRAEL OCCUPATION

VISUALIZINGPALESTINE

<u>On Saturday, August 11, 2018 at 2:30 PM
the workshop Intro to Data Visualization for Social
Justice with Visualizing Impact was held at
OCAD University, Toronto, Ontario</u>

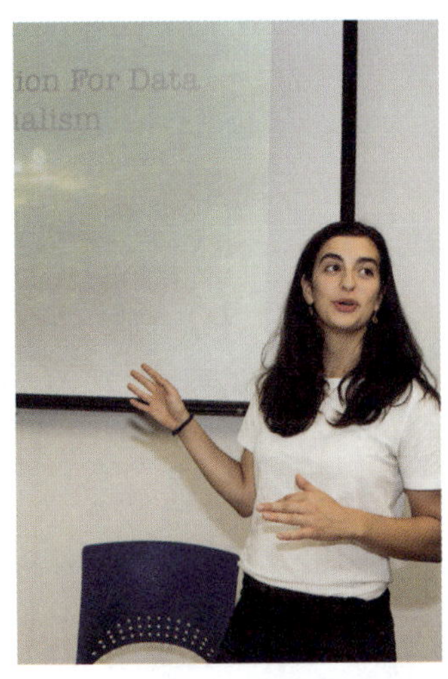

As our name implies, our work is intended to create an impact, and serve as a resource for concrete action. Over the years, we've worked to track and document how our visuals are being used by advocates, educators, and journalists. We have traced them across 65 countries since 2015 and have collected hundreds of testimonials. In 2017, VI visuals were published in the revised edition of *The Design of Dissent: Greed, Nationalism, Alternative Facts, and the Resistance*, by Milton Glaser and Mirko Ilic. Our work has also been recognized by Deutsche Welle's The BOBs Award for Best Social Activism, Prix Ars Electronica's Award of Distinction for Digital Communities, and Information is Beautiful's Community Award.

Reflections on Openness

Sixteen years ago, the Berlin Declaration on Open Access to Knowledge credited the Internet with offering "the chance to constitute a global and interactive representation of human knowledge… and the guarantee of worldwide access." Today, many influential knowledge organizations have embraced the Access to Knowledge (A2K) movement, digitizing their products and information and bringing it out from behind paywalls for anyone to use. Visualizing Impact is one

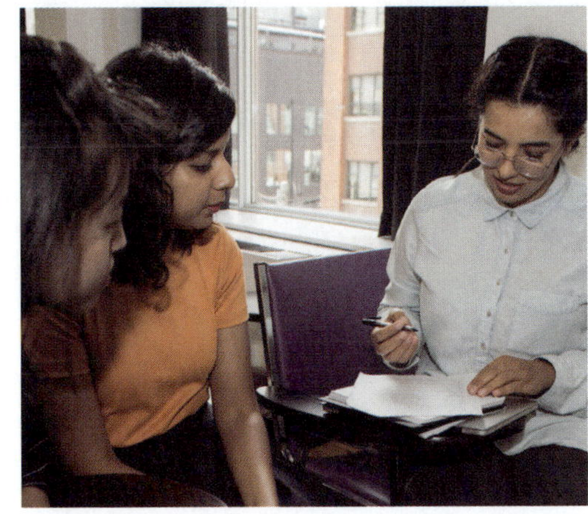

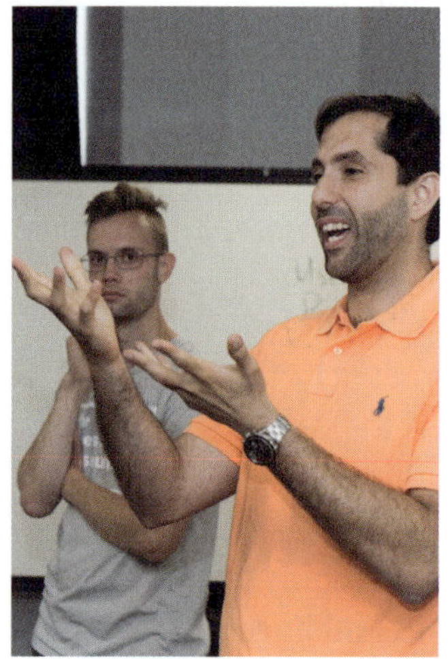

such organization—all VI visuals are published under Creative Commons licensing. But removing the most obvious barriers to access does not mean we are succeeding in making knowledge work for everyone.

Visualizing Impact is participating in *Diagrams of Power* because we share the organizers' interest in the potential of the digital humanities to render power visible. It is critical to ask: whose knowledge is presented to us? Why and how is knowledge produced, captured, stored, communicated? And for whose purposes?

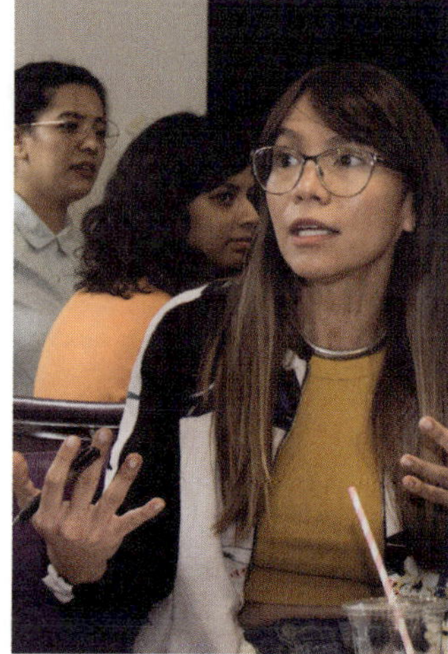

The visuals VI selected for *Diagrams of Power* all come from its *Visualizing Palestine* project, which aims to advance a factual, rights-based narrative of Palestine and Palestinians.

Visualizing Impact's Process

Every visual and project VI undertakes is a team effort that benefits from the diverse skills of researchers, designers, technologists, human rights communicators, organizers, and more.

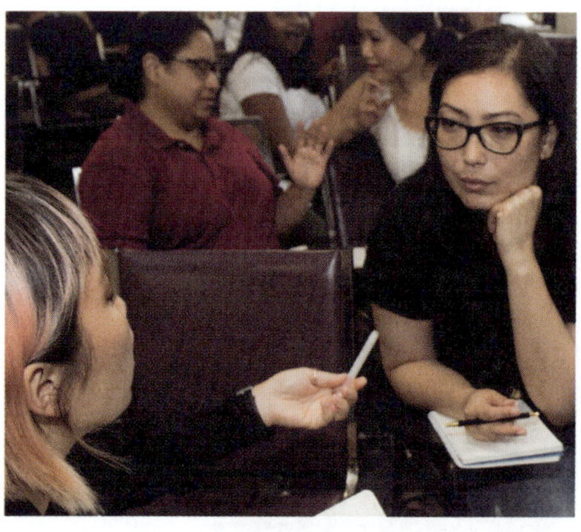

All of VI's work is data-led, so we are constantly exploring what data and information is available on key topics. We work with a variety of data and information produced by outside groups, such as academic research, human rights reports, and geographic data. Sometimes, we also take advantage of digital data via web scraping or API calls. In addition to being able to analyze and understand multiple

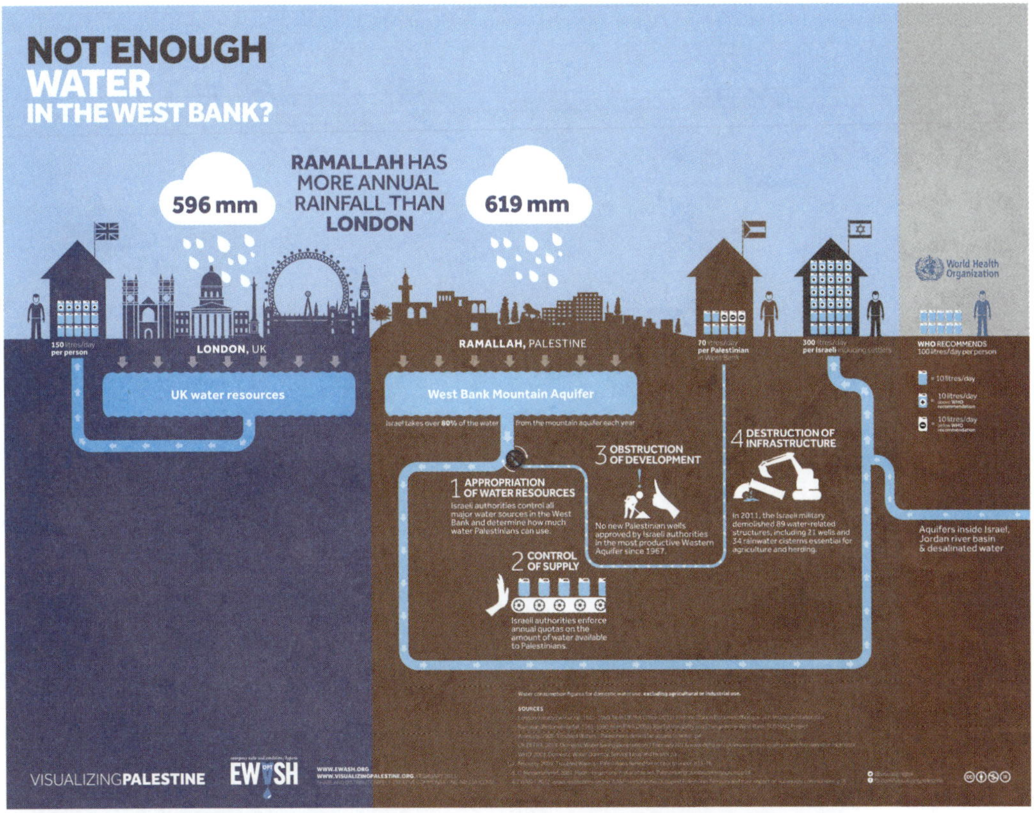

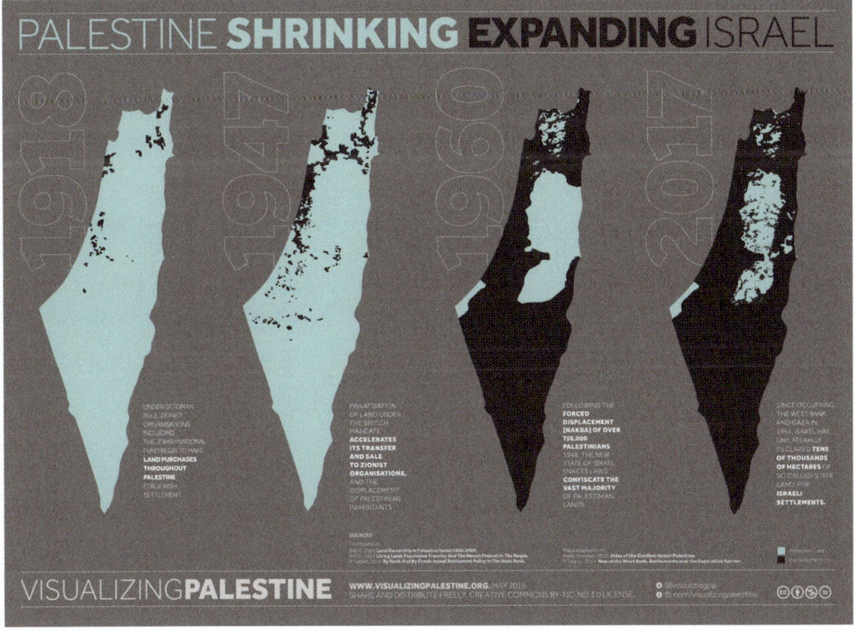

PALESTINE SHRINKING EXPANDING ISRAEL
1918
1947
1960
2017
VISUALIZING PALESTINE

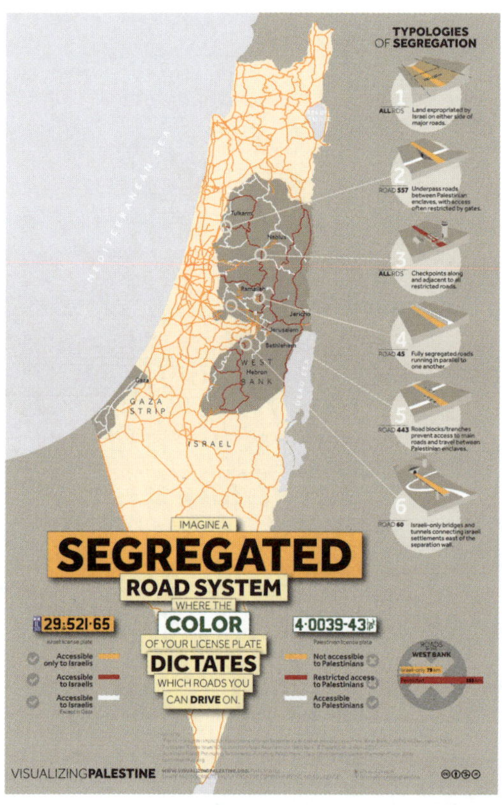

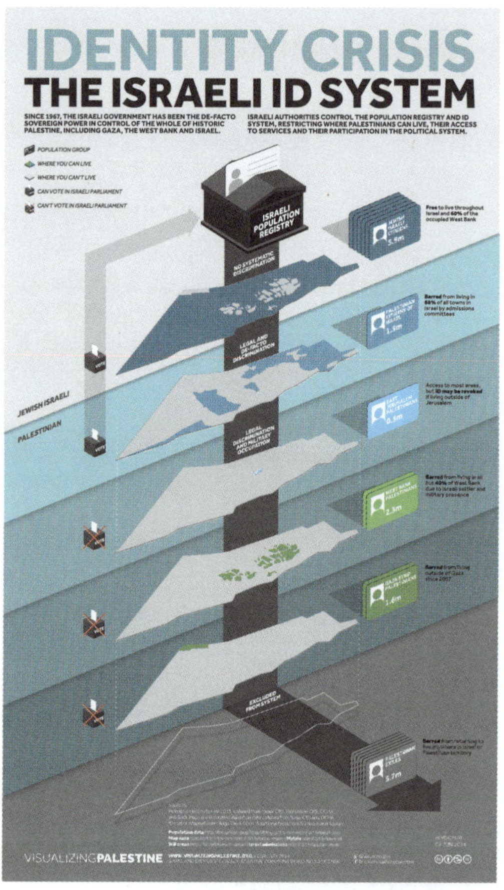

types of information and data, we place significant emphasis on developing creative visual concepts. Brainstorming between researchers, designers, and expert challengers, as well as iterative development of visuals over time, helps us identify stories, complementary datasets, comparisons, or visualization techniques that make information more relevant, concrete, and memorable for different audiences.

One of VI's staple collaboration tools is our design brief. After conducting broad research, we use the brief to drill down into the precise information and main message we want to include in an individual visual. Some

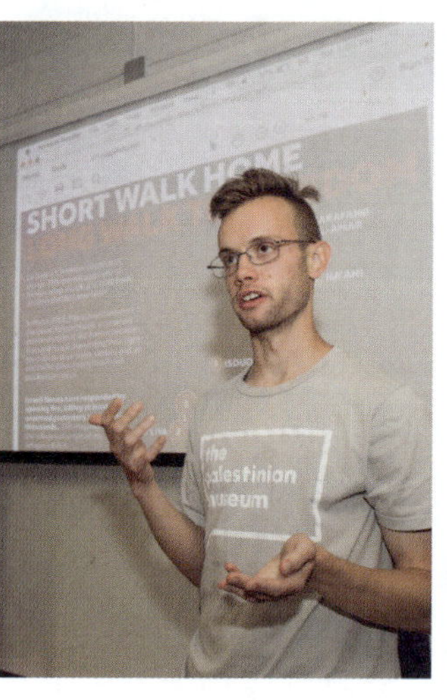

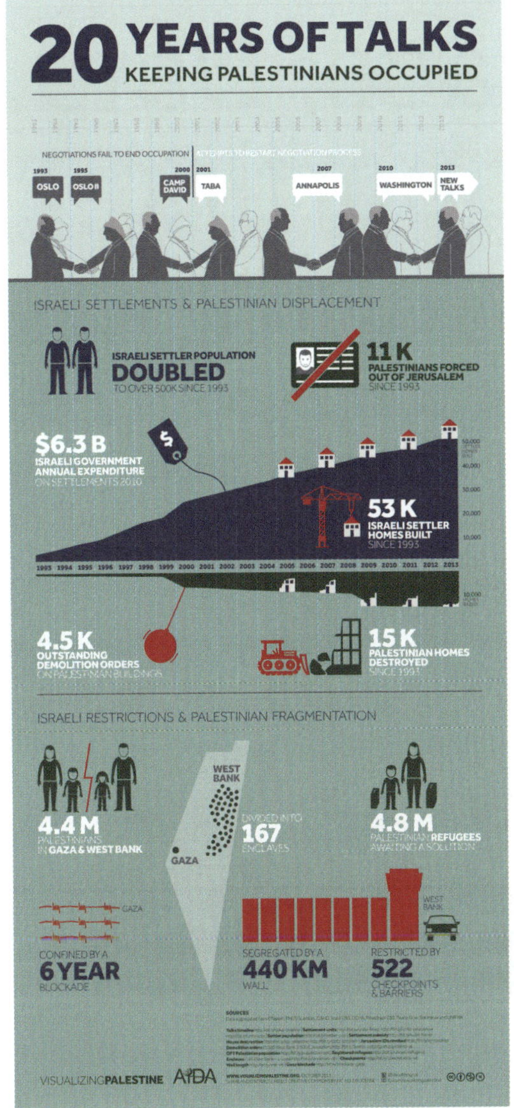

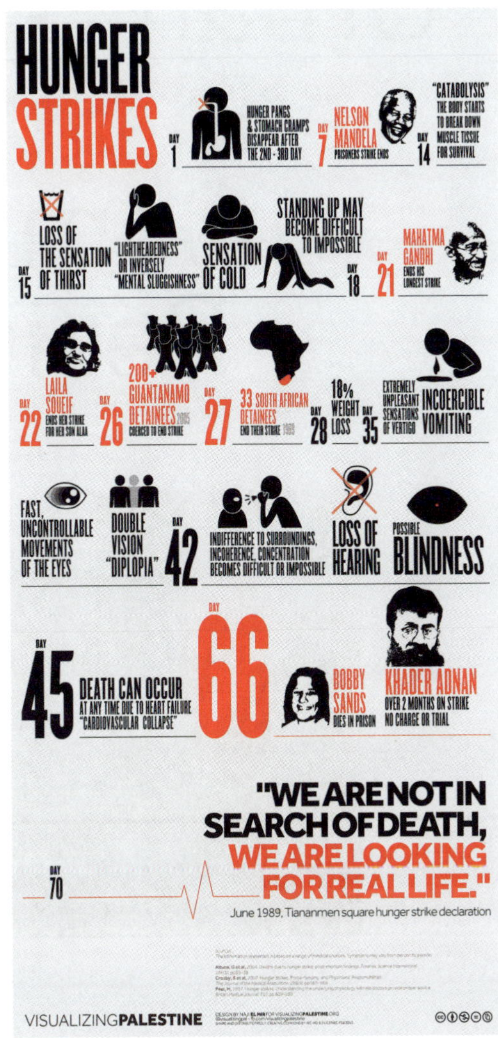

of the other tools we use include ArcGIS, Open Street Map, Illustrator, Tableau, and d3.js.

Once a visual is complete, we use social media, newsletter, and partner networks to disseminate it as widely as possible, and we always track our impact to seek insights on whether our work is effective.

Check out VI's process wheel for a visual interpretation of our process: https://visualizingimpact.org/network#process-wheel

Dialogues Two— Urban Space, Data, and Supporting Community Resistance

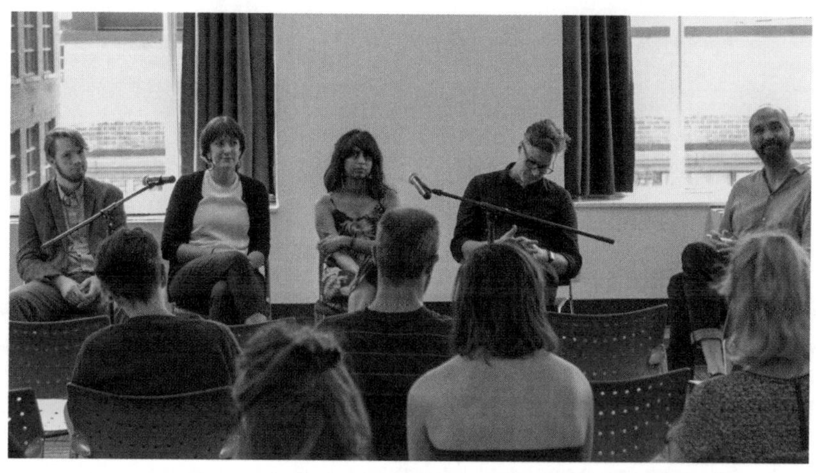

(Left to Right) Alex Hill (Property Praxis), Terra Graziani (The Anti-Eviction Mapping Project), Sheila Sampath (The Public Studio), Joshua Akers (Property Praxis), Patricio Dávila.

Sheila Sampath, Terra Graziani, Josh Akers, Alex Hill

<u>Saturday, September 15, 2018 at 12 PM</u>
<u>OCAD University, Toronto, Canada</u>
<u>205 Richmond St. W. Room 510</u>

Resisting gentrification and displacement needs different kinds of actions including rent strikes, community organizing, sharing information, creative projects, or building support across locations. Data and mapping is one way of supporting these actions by helping analyze patterns, identify bad property owners/managers and share information (e.g. policy, economic, demographic, spatial). We will talk about how designers, activists and researchers, using these tools and others, work in communities to make them more resilient to bad urban policy, real estate speculators and predatory landlords. We will look at how to be accountable to the residents being represented and what tools, processes and methods have been used to make a positive contribution to these movements.

Patricio Dávila

I want to acknowledge the ancestral and traditional territories of the Mississaugas of the New Credit, the Haudenosaunee, the Anishinaabek and the Huron-Wendat. As I make this acknowledgement, it makes me reflect on what the territory has afforded me: a refuge for myself, for my wife and our families, who were also refugees. This discussion is centered around creative practitioners, geographers, researchers, and artists who work with issues around urban space, specifically gentrification, and how they can support efforts to resist the effects of resident displacement.

Sheila, your work at The Public could be described as shifting from servicing to supporting, which aligns well with the *Anti-Eviction Mapping Project*. They not only collect and present data, but they also have a strong, sustainable presence in the community, whether it be to resist eviction or to support someone being displaced. Could you expand on your work, then we'll move to Terra?

Sheila Sampath

I started The Public myself ten years ago in my closet, and now there are five of us, so it's a small group. We come from different backgrounds, from designers to developers, but first and foremost we are activists. I don't think any of us identify as designers before we identify with the communities we are a part of and are accountable to. We are a part of queer, trans, femme POC communities. Myself, I'm part of Tamil communities, and suburban diasporas. Design is simply one tool we use to achieve liberation for these spaces we are a part of. Other tools include childcare, washing dishes, showing up to meetings, organizing. We've recently been doing more facilitation, and opening up programming space, and even just being available to move tables and chairs around. Before I learned how to design things, I was a crisis line counselor, I did court support, and I used to co-organize Take Back the Night, which happened yesterday in Parkdale.

What grounds us is a commitment to a vision for liberation and decolonization for all of us, and accountability to our communities. Because it's necessary. I'm seeing my aunties being kicked out of the community, being violently displaced. We're right across the street from a school. The stuff that I'm seeing there is terrifying to be honest, because it's coming from the playground. There is also the crisis of the current Provincial leadership in Ontario right now.

Going back to your question about our practice at The Public—we just designed a new website, and it was so hard for us to talk about what we do. We also provide emotional support. I did active listening for parents across the street when their kids were being bullied by the people who moved in and bought the $2 million homes in Roncesvalles.

Instead of a practice, it would be better to define ourselves through a commitment to an expansive practice, a commitment to accountability, and a politic.

Terra Graziani

Everything you said resonates with what we do at the *Anti-Eviction Mapping Project* as well. I see mapping as a tool we have learned to help in whatever way that we can, or show up. I'm a student at UCLA, but before going back to school I was in tenant organizing. From that time, I learned all the things that drive me, and I speak for other people in our collective when I say that

we are accountable to the tenant movement. Everything we do is in service to building power first.

I think a few of us in the collective are academics, but we really try to create a space that feels accessible to anyone who wants to show up. Even though we often refer to data and mapping, what we're really is a community space, and all of our work is done in coalition with folks who are fighting eviction on the ground, fighting speculation, fighting police power.

A lot of people use the term 'housing justice', but we show up for tenants' rights. The Los Angeles Tenants Union broadly frames 'tenants' as anyone who doesn't have control over their living situation. This means anyone from a person who doesn't have a home, to someone who is incarcerated, to someone living in a rental unit. We build power using this definition of a tenant, and we center the experience of the tenant in our work rather than a piece of real estate.

Patricio Dávila

This notion of trust is woven into everything you're articulating and I'm wondering how you negotiate that kind of work?

Sheila Sampath

I didn't start the studio with the intention of it being what it is now. It grew organically, and it's a very responsive space, which makes it hard to define. I started designing posters and now we're doing all these weird, different things. The work we're doing tomorrow may not be the work we're doing in a year or two years. I really appreciated what you said Terra, about showing up when you're asked to show up, and you do what you're asked to do. And that's kind of been how we've been.

It's hard to understand what trust is with your coworkers, what it is with your community. I identify with a lot of communities in Parkdale, but I don't live in the neighborhood, and I was really anxious about that relationship.

We were scared of moving into a community and knowing that people in the neighborhood have no reason to trust us. We're just another group of artists that are going to displace people of color and then yell about gentrification when we get displaced–that's the pattern.

There's an alleyway close to our studio in Parkdale, where another group of artists started a mural project called Women Paint TO. They worked with StreetARToronto and the Toronto Police Services to paint the space white as an intersectional feminist mural project. It felt really wrong to us, as part of these communities. It's not intersectional feminism when you partner with the police. It's a form of colonization when you view a space as blank. When you create these distinctions between graffiti and street art, that's a racist, classist distinction. They had asked to use our space to store their materials. We said

no to that. We got into this big argument with them on the Internet, and it exploded into the CBC and NOW and other media outlets. For us, that was an act of accountability that ended up as a by-product of creating deep trust in the community. For us, there is this piece around building power, like Terra, but to build is also to redistribute power. I have the advantage of a university education. I teach here at OCAD University. I get to call myself a designer, so let me use those things to allow other people to also use those things.

Terra Graziani

Our work isn't so much concerned with the products that we put out or the maps that we make, but the relationships that we build along the way and that we show up in whatever way we can. We establish trust by making clear who our production is for. We've been asked by the tenant movement on what policies we've tried to change, and so we began making maps to change eviction policies.

On the other hand, sometimes the work is just for us, within the movement. Sometimes, its purpose is not to try to be legible to the state or policy-makers. That in itself is a form of building power and self-validation.

This especially applies to our *Oral History Project*. We'll have journalists approach us and say, "Do you know a tenant who I can hit up and talk to about being kicked out of their home of 20 years? Or photograph them moving out of their house?" For us, we only ask folks to tell their personal stories if we've already built a relationship with them. In practice, that means showing up to meetings for six months and getting to know them before you ask for an interview at all. We partner with organizations, we go to their meetings, we are members of those groups like the San Francisco Tenants Union. In L.A. we've been working with a group called the Los Angeles Center For Law and Action and the Los Angeles Tenants Union. If we took a journalist's approach, we wouldn't be able to document the same story.

So, we establish trust and just build a sense of whether they want to share their story. It's an evolving process of consent. Afterwards, we send the interview back to them, because if you're using these tools to help a movement, you need to be representing it in a way that those most affected direct.

Patricio Dávila

These ideas around visibility for the communities we're working for resonates with Josh and Alex's work for *Property Praxis*, where they made a concerted effort to not be visible to speculators in Detroit, to avoid the risk of inadvertently reproducing the violence they're trying to resist. Josh or Alex, can you talk a bit about that?

Josh Akers

I think that was the hardest part of this project, yet also one of the things I'm most proud of. What happens with this speculative property investment and neighbourhood decline in Detroit is that this kind of knowledge deteriorates as well. What we see in 2010 as you're trying to transform the city is this reconstruction of both real estate knowledge and the way that the state understands and sees the city. They'd forgotten a lot of this and hadn't been tracking it at all. But working with groups, working with other people, knowing what these maps do even if they don't say they're real estate, watching how that affects different neighborhoods and people, how do we change the framing so that you can see how these speculators are operating, but also masking the information on how to exploit other people?

So, the only thing you see there on the map are speculator properties. So they can prey on themselves, which they already do. They can see where each other holds particular properties. But it doesn't give them any other information about value, we've stripped that.

It has also been received well by community members. There was a testing session for community members, and an older woman across the room says "Oh, that's what's been going on with that house." She had narrowed in immediately on her neighborhood and had understood this place much longer in a different way. She said, "How do I know more about it?" I said, "You click this and you can see their address." It's not about whether or not you can buy it, it's about who is taking what kinds of action in this neighborhood that affects you as a resident.

Patricio Dávila

Alex, can you talk a little bit about that workshop? Why should community members trust you with this map or this

space in order to analyze, yet again, a
space that has been represented many
times, to their detriment?

Alex Hill
For me, it was a critical self-reflection
that I was starting to become one of
those white men in Detroit making
maps of the city. What you didn't really
see in Detroit was people mapping
their own neighborhoods or their own
conditions. So I really wanted to be able
to give that back. And we try to use a
research justice framework because I
am a researcher and I really enjoy the
common thread in this conversation
around showing up. I spent five years
in Detroit just showing up, talking to
people, answering questions about data
before I put anything online or offered
a class.

Originally, I didn't want to do
data and mapping workshops. I actually
wanted to do a workshop on What Is
Research Justice? And how do you make
a researcher support your community
organization rather than extract from
you? But it turned into being able to give
people those skill-sets. It was important to share knowledge around how to
pull down data and visualize it to help
answer questions. We do a monthly free
workshop at community organizations
around the city, and that form of showing up has really helped with growing
the workshop and continuing that
skill-building across the city.

Patricio Dávila
This is a question for any one of you.
How do you negotiate expertise? Who

is an expert in experience or in your
neighborhood? Sheila, you mentioned
being a designer. Having the privilege
of being able to call yourself that and
then having some sort of currency, in a
certain circle. But also there's a certain
set of skills that happen over time,
right?

Sheila Sampath
Yes and no.

Patricio Dávila
Can you talk about that in terms of
having to negotiate with your expertise? In terms of getting a clear sense of
reciprocity?

Sheila Sampath
I think the core of aspects of design involve re-imagination and problem-solv-
ing. I think these skills already exist
in communities when we're navigating
worlds that weren't built for us, that
actively try to work against our best interests. By that very nature of you being
here, you are a designer.

I happened to go to college for a
few years, so I have this thing that says
that I am a designer. But I didn't actually learn much from it, because I already had design skills as a survivor of
violence, as a racialized person, as all
these identities that I hold. With the way
we look at these exchanges that take on
the form of workshops, they are a space
for us to validate each others' expertise.
To redistribute that currency.

There are different forms of
knowledge that we validate in these
spaces. Intuitive ways of knowing,

storytelling as ways of knowing. While some of this is validated by the academy and by designers, some of it isn't. So, our role is to say that these things are valid and adjust our methods to create conditions for people to either visualize or orate or share that expertise and to own it.

With activism, we need to actively put ourselves out of work. We're working for a world where this isn't necessary. I hope that The Public doesn't exist in ten years. It would suck if we still had these conditions that require this space.

Josh Akers

Yeah, absolutely. There are a couple of ways we're trying to subvert the institution as well in Dearborn. Regarding trust, the approach in our projects also changes a lot. It is about learning with, or learning as. Learning with, as opposed to studying on. The academic work that we've done, the questions and data we pursue are in service of a larger understanding that these groups working on eviction are searching for.

Learning with, and thinking alongside the community regarding where to target resources means learning what works and what does not, which can take us in surprising directions. It is about being flexible and willing to move in that way. We have expertise in tools, and we're trying to transfer this expertise. How do we transfer that? How do we get our students to learn from the community, but at the same time continue to learn?

Sheila Sampath

There's also this really functional aspect in community work. As a designer, I am able to get paid for my expertise, but people in the community are not. It's one thing to say to a community member that they are also an expert, but if they don't get paid, they go back to their home and still face eviction.

So, we think about how we can leverage these workshops into actual, tangible opportunities for people. For example, writing letters of reference for employment and paying people, not in honorarium, but hourly for their labour.

When we talk about redistributing power, we're also talking about it within a capitalist system where we're being rewarded for our work and other people aren't. So, we actively try to redistribute the wealth that also comes from that expertise.

Terra Graziani

When I think about expertise in our work, I think about what's at stake, which is people's lives. People facing eviction. Then on top of that, the narrative and the counter-narrative that we're trying to put together.

If these two things are the most important, then the people who are experts are the people who are fighting eviction, who are fighting for their communities and the places that they've lived in for years. The tools are tools. We've learned them out of necessity and if they help, then they help. But I don't feel passionately about mapping. I feel passionately about fighting evictions.

Alex Hill

As a white male who's benefited from bureaucratic systems, I know how to navigate them and I can help translate. How do you leverage your experience to help influence some policy or change the way some system is structured through data and mapping. I may be dreaming too much that it actually happens, but I think that's a key way to think about it.

Patricio Dávila

That makes me think of this notion of translating capital wealth from the academic industrial complex, a term that Sheila introduced me to. I remember Eve Tuck from the University of Toronto speaking about getting grant funding because she's got certain credentials that make it possible. Once she gets them, she redistributes the research funds to projects that would find it difficult to access this funding. These are not huge amounts of money, but it's enough to keep those going. It's often project-based in many cases.

I'm wondering if any of you have experiences about funding to make some of this work possible. Discussing a model that works or doesn't work.

Sheila Sampath

Our model is different than most folks because we're not a non-profit. I don't identify as an academic and I'm not going to be teaching here after this year. So, we fund ourselves by ourselves through our labor. We agree what a living wage looks like for the five of us, and we all make the same amount of money, by designing things for the non-profit industrial complex. That process is harm reduction, right?

Every extra penny that we make goes back into developing community resources like our zine series, our *People's History* posters. Starting up paid residencies for people of color who don't get to identify as artists but want to. Funding our gallery, trying to redefine who gets to call themselves an artist and who doesn't, and what gets seen as art. Running our own programing. It's a lot of independence, expanding our work and forming these relational practices based on what a community is asking of us and what feels right, having our politics grow and develop, being in this lifelong process of and commitment to a politic.

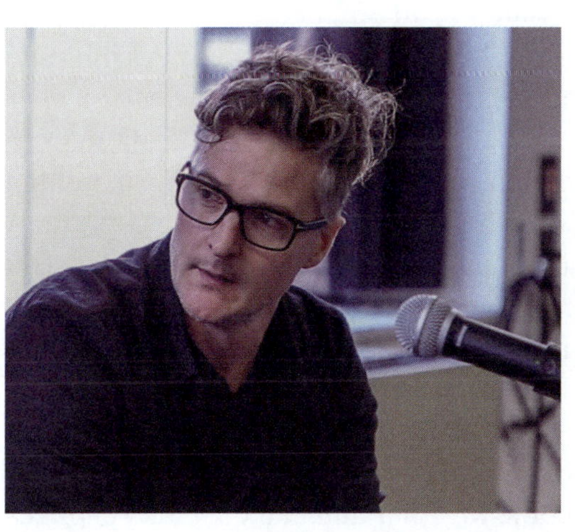

This gives us freedom where we don't have to write a grant. That way, halfway through in a project if the community says, "we don't want to make a map anymore, we actually just want to sit around and talk," we can do that because it's our project.

At times it's been harder. When we moved and our rent increased, we had less revenue to do things, such as our one month residencies for activists and students who are feeling lost in this system. So, we'll reassess and say, "we'll leave the door open and people come in and hang out."

It's a simple model. There is this freedom that comes from running as a business and it allows us to continue to work and evolve and be directly accountable to the needs of our community. If we have a feeling about something, we can just pursue it. It's beautiful.

Terra Graziani

The *Mapping Project* is all volunteer. We have gotten small grants throughout the years but in large part, we fund ourselves through our own labor. And that allows us some freedom. It also creates a lot of problems in that it's a precarious project. People come in and out, people have lives that they have to support with money. And we've put a lot of work together.

I think another piece is that it's worth it. It's worth it to us for the community that it creates, not only with people in the community but us as our own collective in supporting each other. We're all close friends. We're not a business. We're not a non-profit either, we're just a collective. It's just a bunch of people who come together and make things. We all support our lives and then come together to do this work because it fulfills us in various different ways.

It would be great to have some financial support for that, but we've ap-plied for several grants that we don't get because we're too political or we call out property owners. That's kind of how we see the future of it too. I don't really see many opportunities for a magic funding stream.

Josh Akers

I have a similar story with *Property Praxis* project. I don't think I have any favors left with Alex or Erin Pikoff, who is not here, or any of the others. Fortunately, they didn't think about how much work it would take, but we were able to get about $6000 and it took us a year to do it. We had to go through half a million public documents. We had to build this. We tried to build a website from scratch that was also scalable and sustainable or that other people could use and share.

Being in university, I think about what institutional inefficiencies I can capture, to set up and use more space for community meetings and for students. I wish the project was in a storefront in Detroit but instead it's in Dearborn, but that's what we've been able to capture. Also, a lot of our students are first-generation college students, working class, working outside the university trying to make things work. So, we try to pull money from internal grants within the university to create a system that recognizes their labor, yet also engages them in this project and learning from the community.

But yeah, I don't think there's a magic bullet. We've got a strange inquiry from the Ford Foundation last week. We then started this Instagram project that shows speculator companies and the properties that they own, and they never emailed back. It's just one of those things. Oftentimes when you're asked within the institution whether that's NSF or whether that's foundation money, they're asking you to change the project deliverables. And you lose that flexibility you're talking about.

So it's volunteerism and it's labor and it's precarious and at the same time, it has incredible potential.

Terra Graziani
The *Mapping Project*'s work can in large part be characterized as research. Since being back in school, I've recognized this intense disconnect. Foundations want to fund academic research that is validated by being in a university. We want to look at the same issues, but because it's grassroots and coming from people "without expertise", it's not fundable. Despite this, we keep doing the work because we want to center these knowledges and not the ones that come out of the university.

This is a disturbing reality. Funders should think through their funding deliverables. Is community organizing not a deliverable? Maybe for a non-profit, where community organizing then results in a policy change, but what about simply to support people supporting each other, taking care of one another? I think that should be funded. That's one of the most valuable things in my life.

Audience 1
In these projects, are you going out and collecting your own data, or are you working and accessing large sets of data and if so, is that challenging? How does that look for you guys?

Terra Graziani
I can talk about our project. We use so many different data sources. We work with clinic data, and census data for demographics.

In terms of tenant data, it varies depending on what city you're in and whether evictions, displacement, or speculation is tracked. That data is hard to access, even though it's supposed to be public record. It takes a lot of labour to access.

It's also really limited. For example, one of the main sources for evictions information is court data. But it only captures who makes it to court, while many evictions take place through harassment, not fixing a unit, or giving a fake notice. We acknowledge the limitations of the court data when we map it.

In terms of collecting our own data, I think we would think through what the term "data" means.We're doing a narrative map in Boyle Heights in Los Angeles that contextualizes who owns which galleries and where their money is coming from. A few of the galleries are spaces in New York, who have set up satellite locations in Boyle Heights, L.A., which is historically a Latin, and before that, a Jewish neighborhood, and historically low-income. The neighbourhood has been rapidly gentrifying since the galleries. Everyone should follow Defend Boyle Heights on social media—they're resisting this type of gentrification.

We also do oral history work, going out and interviewing people and getting leads for more data sources through these interviews. We do data collection around police presence and calls to police in gentrifying areas.

We also have done community power mapping. In Oakland, we got feedback to map not only we had been lost but also what still remains and what people want to fight for. So, we installed a map of the city of Oakland for three months in a gallery, where people could come in and plot what they found to be valuable in their city. It was things like, "This is where I had my first kiss," or "This is my favorite restaurant."

Alex Hill

It's hard to say there's anything that's raw data. All data is produced. A lot of our projects have run into issues where the bureaucracy has produced the data in a very poor way, so it's difficult for us to use. It's either they're being negligent or they purposely don't want to track certain things. So there's a lot of cleaning up messy data. Academics would have a hard time accepting some of that data.

Josh Akers

What I find fascinating about data is that it's a social process. We try to tell stories about the capillaries of power and how they're affecting people, and that data is either not kept or it's kept in silos that make it really difficult to understand. It's really opaque and difficult to understand what's going on. That's what's really great about *The Anti-Eviction Mapping Project* as well: how do we stitch this information in these disparate places together in a way that allows you to take action on it? It doesn't just allow us to report back on what's going on, but it allows you to understand what it is you're facing. Understanding the absences in that data, as either intentional or a representation of what the state itself, the power of the state can't see. They don't know that it's there or they're not collecting it.

Alex Hill

As part of the research justice framework, I only use free and open-sourced tools, because I want everything I do to be reproducible. If I'm posting a map on the blog, it's linking to the data set and the tools, whether it's QGIS or Inkscape. We use those same free and open-sourced tools for data collection—the database is just a spreadsheet.

Josh Akers

A key is figuring out the question you're

trying to answer with a map or using these tools. What's driving it? What is it that you want that map to do? You can't control exactly how it's received, but you can ask what is it you want it to do, or what could it do. That question will point you to the data you want to find.

Terra Graziani

We use different things based on people's skillsets, but as a collective we all try to learn. We have people who join with absolutely no mapping skills and don't know what the word "data" means, or have their own sense of it. We use ArcGIS Online and CartoDB, which is easy to learn, user-friendly and intuitive. A few of us also know Leaflet. Some people just use Google Maps, and then people draw maps. We paint maps.

Sheila Sampath

We tend to use maps as a way to design programming or co-design programming for the community. One was a map of the resources we have as a group of people, and the resources that we feel that we want. We started to name businesses in the area: "This business has space. This business has a big working kitchen that's not open during the day." We're using that map to form tangible asks and develop a business accountability program, where new businesses who move into the neighborhood are asked to be accountable by sharing their resources with the people who were there before.

We have the advantage of having physical space that people feel a sense of ownership over, so people will come in to add to a map, which allows for a bit of relationship-building through that process. For the resources map, we used a projector to draw it, and had tacks and post-it notes. So it's mapping as a facilitation tool.

Audience 2

Terra, how was it set up in terms of community and power and sharing in that dialogue? I really like what you talked about earlier around tenant rights.

Terra Graziani

Yeah, and the idea that housing is a human right. If you start thinking about it in that way rather than, what is the maximum that I can pay in rent and still survive? We're constantly fighting for certain policy campaigns like rent control. The Los Angeles Tenants Union is fighting for universal rent control and for the overthrow of private property. Affordability is not worrying about where you're going to sleep at night, and if we could all have that, how much would that change our world?

Sheila Sampath

We start from a similar framework. In our community, even though folks are speaking very different languages, they all have a really clear sense of what's right and what's wrong. So, we start off with this basic idea of fairness, which is very intuitive for people, then start to apply more formal language to it so that we begin to bridge the gap.

We had a workshop series where an auntie came in and talked about her awful landlord, saying "It's not right. It's not right." And that resonates with everyone. You can apply anti-capitalist analysis, talk about whether private property should exist, on colonized land. But for our community, the language starts with, "This isn't fair. It's not right to have my landlord drilling all around me, all day and all night, to try to kick me out."

We generally start with these really rad aunties who just know that something isn't right. And starting from this language of fairness, we then move to talk about affordability—imagine not having to fight for fairness all the time, right?

Josh Akers

Regarding tenants, we focus around this idea of mobility. Do people choose to move or are they forced to move? If they're being forced to move, why are they being forced to move, and how is that happening, and people should have a choice in that? It doesn't get you to the question of what is an affordable amount, but people should have a choice. We're in a place like Detroit where some people will make arguments that these people should stay in the neighborhoods that they're in. But that's not the choice everyone wants to make. They need opportunities elsewhere.

The Fair Housing Act of '68 is about desegregating the suburbs as much as it is about keeping people in the city. Detroit is 85% white in the suburbs and 85% black in the city. You want opportunities in the city, but we gotta think more broadly about op-

portunities in the suburbs too. It's a regional issue.

Patricio Dávila

Can you talk a bit more about going across different types of techniques or technologies? We talked about mapping by hand, and that's massively powerful and immediate by representing who's in the room, as opposed to collecting from almost anonymous sources that are more global in nature, in overview, and removed from its context or the imprint of who made it. Can you talk about employing that kind of technique and why you choose one over the other?

Sheila Sampath

It's just been really pragmatic. Part of our money going back to the community means you haven't bought new computers in eight or nine years. There's this technical limitation for us.

Also, we really want people to be able to replicate this project themselves. So when you start to tape together pieces of chart paper and draw a map as you remember, it bridges that gap and people can see directly how their data is being represented and visualized in real time. And they can say, "Well, I want to make a map of all the plants in my neighborhood, or all the yards where I forage food," or whatever that might be.

But also, our presence is physical. We have a physical site, we're connected to the library, to the park and legal services and the health clinic, and so there are folks that feel comfortable coming into our space and we've been doing things to make the space more inviting, even just leaving our door open. Folks can use the washroom when they need to, and we have a sharps container.

We also travel to folks who don't know who we are, who don't know that we're going to be nice to them when they walk in the door, given experiences many people of colour have with other gallery or design spaces. We have set up a table at the library for a day and talked to people and had these artifacts there for them to interact with. For us, our practice is so relational that face-to-face makes sense for us.

When we ran our residency program, at first we made an application on a Google Form. But it only travelled so far. When we started printing it out and setting up a table somewhere instead, offering help like, "I can help you walk through this. What's your idea? What's something you care about? Let's turn that into an idea. Let's write one sentence together." It just bridges those gaps for folks. The people who are most impacted by this system actually don't always have access to computers at all.

Alex Hill

In Detroit, there's a very severe digital divide, where we've mapped out home Internet connections. Very few live in high-income areas, which is a weird thing to say for Detroit. Those higher-income areas have Internet connection, whereas the vast majority of the city does not. So we have to go with paper and pencils as an entry point. Our digital maps have been used as a tool by other organizers, in particular the

one with home Internet access. Because they knew they were missing a whole segment of people if they used only digital platforms, they took the map and canvassed the neighborhoods that had low Internet.

Terra Graziani

Yeah we're always trying to make our work non-digital. Our mural, which is in the exhibition, has people's portraits painted on the wall in an alleyway in San Francisco that has a lot of other murals in it, so they speak to each other.

Using our eviction database, we've also stencil-tagged properties that people have been evicted from. It's a little suitcase that says, "Tenants Were Forced Out Here."

Methods-wise, when we started there were folks in our project who did mapping and then there were folks who did oral history. With every project that we work on, we have a dataset that gets translated to a map, but we're also incorporating narratives and histories, videos, trying to leverage all our skill-sets. Very practically, that's changed what analyses and products we put out into the world.

Josh Akers

Most of the mapping that we do is on physical paper, sitting down with block captains or neighborhood groups and actually having them tell us what's wrong with the map. We build something on their questions, because they live there and they know. And we'll go back and remake those maps and bring them to them for their needs.

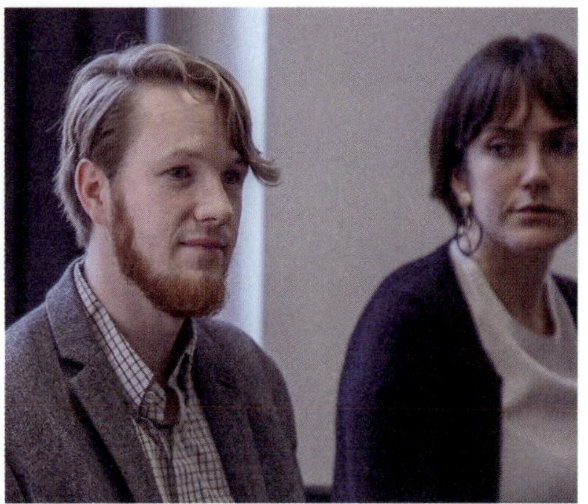

We've started to brand these maps. One, because community members trust the data, but two, we've learned it really frustrates the mayor when they show up with them. It's an act in which community members decided they trust this information because they've been working together on it, and it gives them leverage when they're meeting with city officials about something. They feel like they're armed with better data than what the city has.

Those are their maps. They're not ours. We built them for the community. In some cases, we'll keep some for research purposes, like pictures, but the maps are built with a purpose.They're a tool. They were built around their questions. They know where they want to go, and we're trying to help them get there fast.

Biographies

Joshua Akers

Joshua Akers is an Assistant Professor of Geography and Urban and Regional Studies at the University of Michigan-Dearborn. He is the founder and director of the Urban Praxis Workshop and member of the Property Praxis Research Collective. Akers' research and writing examines the intersection of markets and policy and their material impacts on everyday life. This work has appeared in *Environment and Planning A*, *Geoforum*, *International Journal of Urban and Regional Research*, *Urban Geography*, *Derive*, and *Guernica*.

The Anti-Eviction Mapping Project

The Anti-Eviction Mapping Project is a data-visualization, data analysis, and storytelling collective documenting the dispossession and resistance upon gentrifying landscapes. Primarily working in the San Francisco Bay Area, Los Angeles, and New York City, we are all volunteers producing digital maps, oral history work, film, murals, and community events. Working with a number of community partners and in solidarity with numerous housing movements, we study and visualize new entanglements of global capital, real estate, techno-capitlism, and political economy. Our narrative oral history and video work centers the displacement of people and complex social worlds, but also modes of resistance. Maintaining antiracist and feminist analyses as well as decolonial methodology, the project creates tools and disseminates data contributing to collective resistance and movement building.

Burak Arikan

Burak Arikan is a New York and Istanbul based artist who works with complex networks. He investigates societal issues and develops his findings into abstract machinery, which generates network maps and algorithmic interfaces, results in performances, and procreates predictions to render inherent power relationships visible and discussable. Arikan's software, prints, installations, and performances have been featured in numerous exhibitions internationally. Arikan is the founder of Graph Commons, a collaborative platform for mapping, analyzing, and publishing data-networks.

Josh Begley

Josh Begley is a data artist and app developer based in Brooklyn, New York. Begley is the director of two short films, *Best of Luck with the Wall* (2016) and *Concussion Protocol* (2018). His work has appeared in *The New Yorker*, *The New York Times*, *The Atlantic*, *The Guardian*, *New York Magazine*, the Whitney, the Met Breuer, the Museum of Modern Art, and the New Museum of Contemporary Art.

Joseph Beuys

Joseph Beuys (12 May 1921 – 23 January 1986) was a German Fluxus, happening, and performance artist as well as a sculptor, installation artist, graphic artist, art theorist, and pedagogue. His extensive work is grounded in concepts of humanism, social philosophy and anthroposophy; it culminates in his "extended definition of art" and the idea of social sculpture as a gesamtkunstwerk, for which he claimed a creative, participatory role in shaping society and politics. He is widely regarded as one of the most influential artists of the second half of the 20th century.

Patricio Dávila

Patricio Dávila is a designer, artist, researcher and educator. He is currently Associate Professor in Design at OCAD University. Patricio is co-director of Public Visualization Lab. His research focuses on developing a theoretical framework for examining data visualization as assemblages of subjectivation and power. In his creative practice he has created mobile applications, locative media projects, essay videos, new media installations, and participatory community projects including: *Shadows!*, *Powers of Kin*, *Chthuluscene*, *Tent City Projections*, *The Line*, and *In The Air Tonight*. His research and practice focuses on the politics and aesthetics of participation in the visualization of spatial issues with a specific focus on urban experiences, mobile technologies and large-scale interactive public installations.

Bureau d'Études

Bureau d'Études is an artist collective that lives and works in Saint Menoux, France. For 15 years, the group has developed research on the structures of power and capitalism. The group is currently working on a collective project on agriculture, commons and resymbolizing research: www.fermede-lamhotte.fr.

Department of Unusual Certainties

The Department of Unusual Certainties' objective is to use thoughtful, research-driven design to inspire engagement and dialogue. They practice the tradition of pragmatism, strategically applying design in the physical world to affect the social good. In 2010, Department of Unusual Certainties started as a result of a shared need to ask questions about our everyday existence. This curiosity continues to grow and has manifested over the years through projects that traverse urban design, public art, education, cartography and social engagement.

Catherine D'Ignazio

Catherine D'Ignazio, a.k.a. kanarinka, is an Assistant Professor of Civic Media and Data Visualization Storytelling in the Journalism Department at Emerson College. She is a scholar, artist/designer and software developer who focuses on data literacy and visualization for civic engagement and community empowerment. Her research at the intersection of technology, design & the humanities has been published in the *Journal of Peer Production*, the *Journal of Community Informatics*, and the proceedings of Human Factors in Computing Systems (ACM SIGCHI). She has recently joined the board of directors of Indigenous Women Rising (https://www.iwrising.org).

W.E.B. Du Bois
Scholar and activist W.E.B. Du Bois
was born on February 23, 1868, in Great
Barrington, Massachusetts. In 1895,
he became the first African American
to earn a Ph.D. from Harvard University. Du Bois wrote extensively and
was the best-known spokesperson
for African-American rights during
the first half of the 20th century. He
co-founded the National Association
for the Advancement of Colored People
(N.A.A.C.P.) in 1909. Du Bois died in
Ghana in 1963.

Estudio Teddy Cruz + Fonna Forman
Teddy Cruz is a professor of Public
Culture and Urbanization in the Depart-
ment of Visual Arts at the University of
California, San Diego, and Director of
Urban Research in the UCSD Center on
Global Justice. Fonna Forman is a professor of Political Theory and Found-
ing Director of the Center on Global
Justice at the University of California,
San Diego. Cruz + Forman are princi-
pals in Estudio Teddy Cruz + Fonna
Forman, a research-based political and
architectural practice in San Diego.
Blurring conventional boundaries between theory and practice, and transgressing the fields of architecture and
urbanism, political theory and urban
policy, visual arts and public culture,
Cruz + Forman lead a variety of urban research agendas and civic/public
interventions in the San Diego-Tijuana
border region and beyond. They represented the United States in the 2018
Venice Architectural Biennale.

Forensic Architecture
Forensic Architecture is a research
agency based at Goldsmiths, University
of London, consisting of architects, artists, filmmakers, journalists, software
developers, scientists, lawyers, and an
extended network of collaborators from
a wide variety of fields and disciplines.
Founded in 2010 by Eyal Weizman,
Forensic Architecture is committed to
the development and dissemination of
new evidentiary techniques. It undertakes advanced architectural and media
investigations on behalf of international prosecutors, human rights and civil
society groups, as well as political and
environmental justice organizations,
including Amnesty International, Human Rights Watch, B'tselem, Bureau of
Investigative Journalism, and the UN,
among others.

Terra Graziani
Terra Graziani is a researcher and
tenants' rights activist based in Los
Angeles, CA. She is currently pursu-
ing a Master's in Urban and Regional
Planning at UCLA and works as an
organizer with statewide tenants' rights
advocacy organization, Tenants Together. Terra is also a member of the
Anti-Eviction Mapping Project and has
been involved in documenting the dispossession and resistance of Bay Area
communities through participatory
research, oral history, and data work for
the past two years.

Peter Hall
Peter Hall is Senior Lecturer and Course
Leader, BA (Hons) Graphic Commu-

nication Design at Central Saint Martins, University of the Arts London. His research focuses on mapping and visualization as critical and participatory practices. Dr Hall was previously Programme Director of BA Design and Design Futures at Griffith University Queensland College of Art in Australia (2012-15), Senior Lecturer in Design at the University of Texas at Austin, USA (2007-12), and Lecturer in Graphic Design at Yale School of Art, USA (2000-2007). His recent essays appear in *The Routledge Companion to Criticality in Art, Architecture, and Design* (Routledge 2018), *Encountering Things: Design and Theories of Things* (Bloomsbury Academic 2017) and *Design in the Borderlands* (Routledge 2014). His books include *Else/Where: Mapping—New Cartographies of Networks and Territories* (edited with Janet Abrams, University of Minnesota 2006) and *Sagmeister: Made you Look* (Booth-Clibborn Editions 2001). He is co-founder of DesignInquiry, a non-profit educational organization devoted to researching design issues in intensive team-based gatherings, based in Maine, USA.

Alex Hill

Alex has more than 10 years of experience working with organizations on projects and campaigns that impact policies and communities. As a data nerd and anthropologist, Alex finds meaningful stories to tell whether he's sifting through spreadsheets or interviewing people. Alex is able to combine human experiences with data and analytics to elevate strategies for all types of organizations. Alex's personal research is focused on food access, racial justice, and health disparities.

Iconoclasistas

Formed in 2006, Iconoclasistas is Pablo Ares and Julia Risler. Their projects combine graphic art, creative workshops and community-based research. Their works are offered online through Creative Commons licenses allowing free distribution and encouraging the creation of derivative works. Through the use of graphic devices and the design of several tools, Iconoclasistas fosters critical reflection that supports resistance and transformation.

Lucas LaRochelle

Lucas LaRochelle is a multidisciplinary designer and researcher examining queerness, technology, and architecture. They are the founder of *Queering The Map*, a community generated counter-mapping project that archives queer moments, memories, and histories in relation to physical space.

Queering The Map received an Honorary Mention for the 2018 Prix Ars Electronica, was longlisted for the Lumen Prize for Digital Art and the Kantar Information is Beautiful Awards, and is part of the Library of Congress LGBTQ+ Studies Web Archive. They have given talks, run workshops, and exhibited nationally and internationally, notably at Ars Electronica, Somerset House and SBC Gallery. Their work and writing has appeared in *Accent, Échelles, Perfect Strangers,* and *ROM,* amongst other publications. They are based in Tio:-tia'ke/Montreal.

Stefan Laxness

Stefan Laxness is an architectural researcher and Project Coordinator at Forensic Architecture (FA) where he has led numerous projects, including the Ayotzinapa Case, and developed methodologies for analysing airstrikes in the Middle East and modelling sites from witness testimony. Stefan runs a design studio, Diploma 9, at the Architectural Association in London. He has exhibited work in the Antarctic Pavilion as part of the 2017 Venice Art Biennale and has previously worked at PLP Architecture in London and JAKOB+MACFARLANE in Paris.

Julie Mehretu

In the age of globalization, Julie Mehretu has created a new form of history painting whose themes include identity, cultural history, geography, and personal narrative. Born in Addis Ababa, Ethiopia, raised in East Lansing, Michigan, educated in Rhode Island and Senegal, and she resides in New York City and Berlin. Her life experience is reflected in her visual vocabulary, which is drawn from maps, urban-planning grids, and architectural forms. These are combined to make dynamic, delicate paintings, drawings, and prints that blur the line between abstraction and figuration. Mehretu's art embodies the interconnected and complex character of the world.

Eliana Macdonald

Eliana Macdonald has over 15 years experience working with First Nations, local governments, and communities. An important driver of her work is providing assistance with and information about natural and cultural values that supports informed decision-making: information democracy. She has administered the Aboriginal Mapping Network, published *30 maps in Living Proof*, and authored several useful reports for use by indigenous peoples, including *The Atlas of Cumulative Landscape Disturbance in the Traditional Territory of Blueberry River First Nations* and *Referrals Management Software Tools – An Analysis of the Options*.

Lize Mogel

Lize Mogel is an interdisciplinary artist and counter-cartographer. Her work intersects the fields of popular education, cultural production, public policy, and mapping. She creates maps and mappings that produce new understandings of social and political issues. She has mapped public parks in Los Angeles; future territorial disputes in the Arctic; and wastewater economies in New York City. She is co-editor of the book/map collection *An Atlas of Radical Cartography*, a project that significantly influenced the conversation and production around mapping and activism.

Ogimaa Mikana

Ogimaa Mikana is an artist collective founded by Susan Blight (Anishinaabe, Couchiching) and Hayden King (Anishinaabe, Gchi'mnissing) in January 2013.

Through public art, site-specific intervention, and social practice, Ogimaa Mikana asserts Anishinaabe self-determination on the land and in the public sphere.

Margaret Pearce

Margaret Pearce is a cartographer and writer based in Rockland, Maine. Since 2006, she has dedicated herself to exploring and developing the expressive capacities of cartographic language to represent human experience and dialogues across cultures to decolonize narratives and empower silenced voices. Pearce has eighteen years of experience teaching cartographic design, map history and Indigenous geographies at the university level, most recently as Associate Professor of Geography at University of Kansas. She is an enrolled member of Citizen Potawatomi Nation, and former president of the North American Cartographic Information Society.

Laura Poitras

Laura Poitras is a filmmaker, journalist and artist. *CITIZENFOUR*, the third installment of her post-9/11 Trilogy, won an Academy Award for Best Documentary, along with awards from the British Film Academy, Independent Spirit Awards, Director's Guild of America and others. She recently presented a series of immersive installations and new work for her solo exhibition, *ASTRO NOISE* (2016), at the Whitney Museum of American Art. Her reporting on NSA mass surveillance based on Edward Snowden's disclosures won the George

Polk Award for national security journalism, and shared in the 2014 Pulitzer Prize for Public Service. She is on the board of the Freedom of the Press Foundation, and is co-creator of the visual journalism project *Field of Vision*.

Philippe Rekacewicz

Philippe Rekacewicz is a French geographer, cartographer and information designer and associate researcher at the University of Helsinki. With Philippe Rivière, he developed visionscarto.net, a research website dedicated to "radical and experimental cartography and geography." Rekacewicz follows issues such as demography, refugees and displaced persons, and migration and stateless persons. He has worked on a number of projects bringing together cartography, art and politics, especially studying how communities and political or economic powers produce the cartographic vision of the territories on which they operate, and how they can manipulate those maps.

Sheila Sampath

Sheila Sampath is an artist, educator, and graphic designer crafting creative for social good since 2003. Former chair of the board at the TRCC/MWAR, she has a background in grassroots anti-oppression organizing and activism, which she incorporates into her strategic and participatory approach to graphic design and trauma-informed facilitation. She is the editorial and art director of award-winning feminist magazine, *Shameless*, an assistant professor of alternative and speculative practices at the Ontario College of Art and Design University, a member of the British Council's TN2020 Network, and a fellow of the Royal Society of Artists. Sheila holds a diploma in graphic design from the George Brown School of Design and an Honours BSc. in Sociology and Psychology from the University of Toronto. She has lectured internationally on community-centred creative praxis, alternative media, and anti-oppressive work. Her first book, *Letters Lived*, was published by Three O'Clock Press in the fall of 2013.

Visualizing Impact
Visualizing Impact is a laboratory for innovation at the intersection of data science, technology, and design. Visualizing Impact creates impactful tools highlighting critical social issues around the world.

Set Margins' #33
Diagrams of Power: Visualizing, Mapping,
and Performing Resistance

ISBN 978-90-833501-9-6

Curator / Editor
Patricio Dávila

Assistant Editor
April Xie

Toronto Exhibition
Lisa Smith, Linda Columbus, Francisco Alvarez

Eindhoven Exhibition
Freek Lomme, Josh Plough, Guus van Der Velden

Graphic Design
Ali Qadeer, Patricia Pastén

Printer
Printon AS

Paper
Serixo White 90g/m2, Serixo White 300g/m2

Typefaces
Atlas Grotesk, Suisse Works

www.setmargins.press

Made possible thanks to the support of Public
Visualization Lab/Studio, OCAD University, Onsite
Gallery, Social Science and Humanities Research Council
of Canada (for research engagements), and Canada
Council of the Arts (for Toronto exhbition).

Acknowledgements

Special thanks to Sayeda Akbary, Francisco Alvarez, Greg Burnet, Dave Colangelo, Linda Columbus, Sara Diamond, Yoni Golijov, Renzi Guarin, Jay Irizawa, Ramzi Jaber, David McIntosh, Jana Macalik, Janine Marchessault, Ryan Mason, Immony Men, Ana Rita Morais, Heather Robson, Reza Safaei, Jonathan Silveira, Elke Spitzer, Lisa Deanne Smith, Leila Talei, The Walker Art Center, and all the contributors, artists, designers, workshop and event participants.

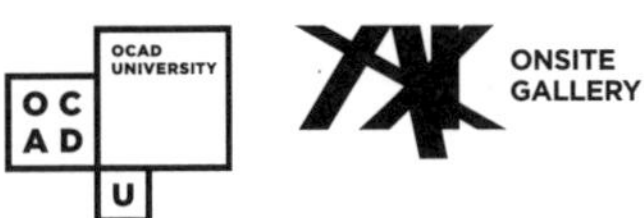

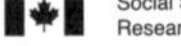

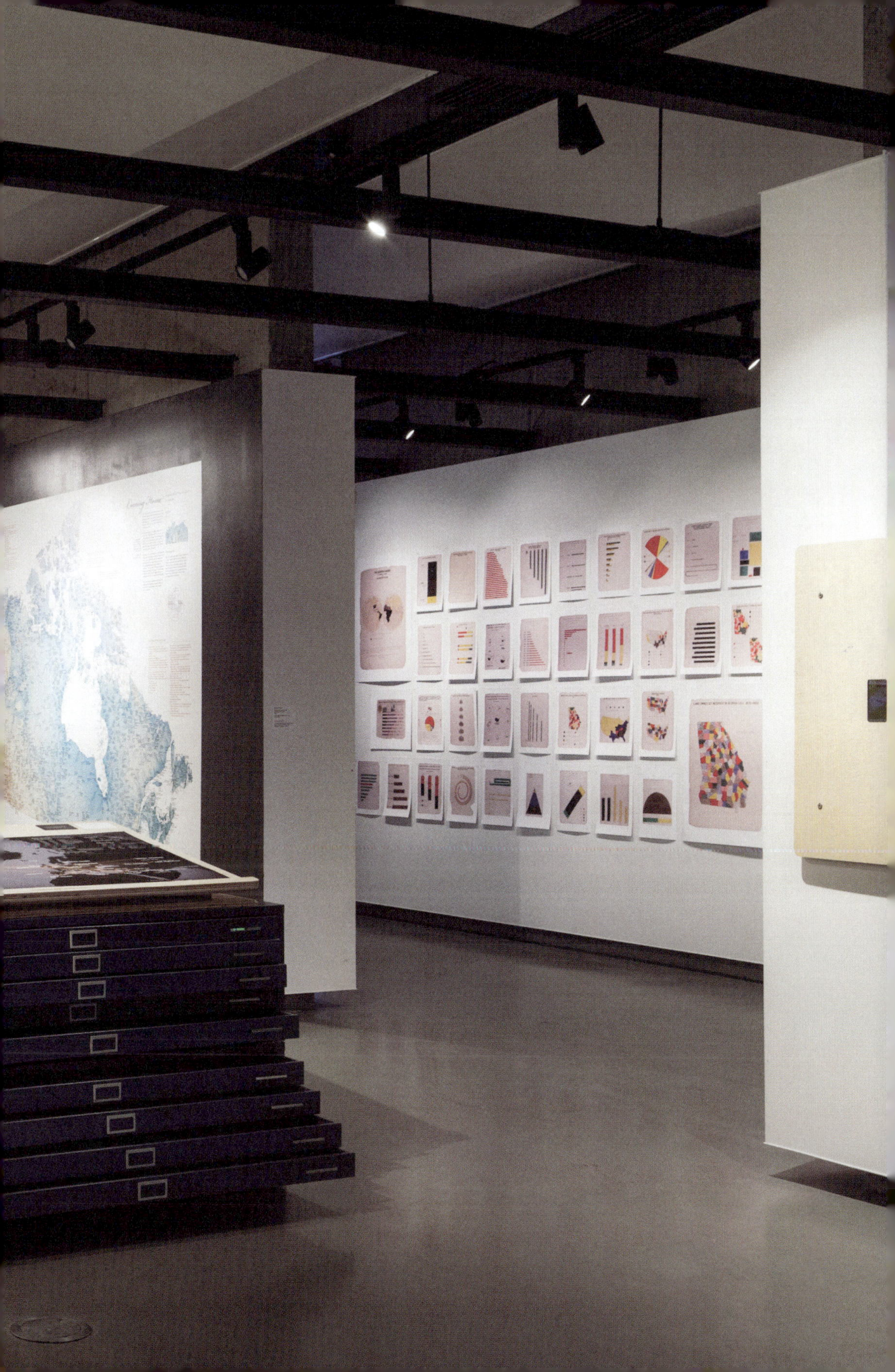